The Routledge Handbook of Hotel Chain Management

Understanding the global hotel business is not possible without paying specific attention to hotel chain management and dynamics. Chains are big business: more than 80 per cent of hotels currently being constructed around the globe are chain affiliated and, in 2014, the five largest brands held over one million rooms. The high economic importance of the hotel chains and their global presence justifies the academic research in the field; however, despite this, there is no uniform coverage in the current body of literature.

This Handbook aids in filling the gap by exploring and critically evaluating the debates, issues and controversies of all aspects of hotel chains from their nature, fundamentals of existence and operation, expansion, strategic and operational aspects of their activities and geographical presence. It brings together leading specialists from a range of disciplinary backgrounds and regions to provide state-of-the-art theoretical reflection and empirical research on current issues and future debates. Each of the 5 inter-related sections explores and evaluates issues that are of extreme importance to hotel chain management, focusing on theoretical issues, the expansion of hotel chains, strategic and operational issues, the view point of the individual affiliated hotel and finally the current and future debates in the theory and practice of hotel chain management arising from globalisation, demographic trends, sustainability and new technology development. This content provides an invaluable resource for all those with an interest in hotel management, hospitality, tourism and business, encouraging dialogue across disciplinary boundaries and areas of study.

This Handbook is essential reading for student, researchers and academics of Hospitality as well as those of Tourism, Marketing, Business and Events Management.

Maya Ivanova is an Assistant Professor in Tourism in Varna University of Management, Bulgaria, and a certified IATA instructor. Her publications have appeared in journals like *Tourism Management Perspectives*, *Anatolia*, *International Journal of Hospitality and Tourism Administration*, *Journal of Hospitality Marketing and Management*, and *Tourismos*. She serves as Editorial Assistant for the *European Journal of Tourism Research*. Dr. Ivanova's research interests include tour operators, airlines and hotel chains.

Stanislav Ivanov is a Professor in Tourism Economics and Vice Rector for Academic Affairs and Research in Varna University of Management, Bulgaria. He is the Editor-in-chief of the *European Journal of Tourism Research* and serves on the editorial boards of 25 other journals. His research interests include hotel chains, destination marketing, tourism and economic growth, political issues in tourism, special interest tourism. His publications have appeared in different academic journals – *Annals of Tourism Research, Tourism Management, Tourism Management Perspectives, Tourism Economics, Journal of Heritage Tourism, Tourism and Hospitality Research, Tourism Today, Tourism, Tourism Planning and Development, Anatolia, International Journal of Hospitality and Tourism Administration, Journal of Hospitality Marketing and Management, Tourismos, Journal of Economic Studies, Journal of Southern Europe and the Balkans* and *South-Eastern Europe Journal of Economics*.

Vincent P. Magnini is a tenured faculty member in Virginia Tech's Pamplin College of Business and he is currently ranked as one of the top 12 most prolific hospitality researchers worldwide. Vince holds Editorial Board appointments on ten of the leading research journals in his field and is a US Fulbright Scholar. Vince's most recent book titled *Performance Enhancers: Twenty Essential Habits for Service Businesses* appeared on the top 1% of Amazon.com's Best Seller Ranking throughout 2014. He has been featured three times on National Public Radio's (NPR's) *With Good Reason*, once on NPR's *All Things Considered* and cited in *The New York Times*.

The Routledge Handbook of Hotel Chain Management

*Edited by Maya Ivanova, Stanislav Ivanov
and Vincent P. Magnini*

Routledge
Taylor & Francis Group

LONDON AND NEW YORK

First published 2016
by Routledge

2 Park Square, Milton Park, Abingdon, Oxfordshire OX14 4RN
52 Vanderbilt Avenue, New York, NY 10017

Routledge is an imprint of the Taylor & Francis Group, an informa business

First issued in paperback 2020

British Library Cataloguing in Publication Data
A catalogue record for this book is available from the British Library

Library of Congress Cataloguing in Publication Data
Names: Ivanova, Maya, editor. | Ivanov, Stanislav, editor. | Magnini, Vincent P.
P., editor. | Routledge (Firm), editor. Title: The Routledge handbook of hotel chain
management / edited by Maya Ivanova, Stanislav Ivanov and Vincent P. Magnini.
Other titles: Handbook of hotel chain management | Description: Abingdon, Oxon ;
New York, NY : Routledge, 2016. | Includes bibliographical references and index.
Identifiers: LCCN 2015042492 | ISBN 9781138805057 (hbk) | ISBN
9781315752532 (ebk) |
Subjects: LCSH: Hotel management—Handbooks, manuals, etc.
Classification: LCC TX911.3.M27 R783 2016 | DDC 647.94068—dc23
LC record available at http://lccn.loc.gov/2015042492

ISBN: 978-1-138-80505-7 (hbk)
ISBN: 978-0-367-66010-9 (pbk)

Typeset in Bembo
by Keystroke, Station Road, Codsall, Wolverhampton

Contents

Contents

Contents

Figures

Tables

Tables

Notes on contributors

Eduardo Anselmo de Castro is Associate Professor of the Department of Social, Political and Territorial Sciences in the University of Aveiro, Portugal. He is the coordinator of the Research Center on Governance, Competitiveness and Public Policies and of the PhD course on Public Policies. He works in the fields of Regional Economics, Strategic Planning and decision Support Systems. He was responsible for Portuguese research teams involved in more than 20 European Union FP and ESPON projects and was responsible for more than 10 projects sponsored by the Portuguese Foundation for Science and Technology.

Walter Fernando Araújo de Moraes is Full Professor of Business Management at the Business Department of the Universidade Federal de Pernambuco (Brazil). He holds a Master's degree in Production Engineering (UFSC), a PhD degree in Management Sciences at the University of Manchester Institute of Science and Technology and a Post-Doctoral degree at the University of Texas at Austin. Currently, he is a member of the Centre for the Study of Business Strategy (CEO/UFPE).

Florian Aubke is an Assistant Professor/Senior Lecturer for Hotel Management at the Department of Tourism and Service Management at MODUL University Vienna. He currently serves as the Dean of the undergraduate school. He has substantial operational experience in the hospitality industry as well as national and international event management experience. Florian received his Bachelor of Business in Marketing and Hospitality Management as well as a Master of Business by Research from Victoria University, Melbourne, Australia. Since his doctoral studies (completed in 2012 with distinction at the Vienna University of Economics and Business), his research focuses on the analysis of social networks, both within and between organizations – with a particular application to the hospitality and tourism industry. Florian is an active member of the International Network for Social Network Analysis (INSNA) as well as the European Chapter of the International Council on Hotel, Restaurant and Institutional Education (EuroCHRIE).

Gökhan Ayazlar received his PhD in tourism from Adnan Menderes University in 2012. Since 2013, he has been an Assistant Professor in the Tourism Faculty at the University of Mugla Sitki Kocman, where he teaches courses on introduction to tourism, international tourism, international hotel management and tourism sociology. He has published articles, book chapters and edited books in the field of his courses. His current research activity is focused on internationalization of tourism enterprises. Gökhan also has over 10 years' experience in hotel management roles which he built up prior to his academic career.

Emily P. Ayscue is a PhD student studying Natural Resources, Recreation and Tourism within the Warnell School of Forestry as well as the Integrative Conservation PhD programme at the University of Georgia. Her research interests include sustainable coastal development and tourism development policy and management.

Melissa A. Baker, PhD, is an Assistant Professor in the Department of Hospitality and Tourism Management at the University of Massachusetts, Amherst. Her teaching focuses on restaurant management, services marketing and human resources management. Her research focuses on service failure recovery, customer complaints and appearance and impression formation.

Cristina Barroco is an Associate Professor at the Polytechnic Institute of Viseu, Portugal – Higher School of Technology and Management, where she coordinates the Bachelor's degree in Tourism. She holds a PhD in Tourism, an MSc in Management and a BSc in Tourism. She is affiliated with the Portuguese Foundation for Science and Technology and is a Member of the research unit of Governance, Competitiveness and Public Policies (GOVCOPP) at the University of Aveiro. Her research focuses on tourism economics, foreign direct investment and new tourism products.

Carlos Pestana Barros is an Associate Professor of Economics at ISEG University of Lisbon. He is a member of the board of many tourism journals, including: *Tourism Management*, *Journal of Travel Research*, *Tourism Economics* and *European Journal of Tourism Research*, for which he is also a reviewer. He has been guest editor of several special issues published in *Tourism Economics* and *Scandinavian Journal of Tourism Research*.

Manuel Becerra (PhD, University of Maryland, USA) is Professor of Strategic Management at the University of Queensland Business School (Brisbane, Australia). He has been published widely in management journals in the areas of corporate strategy and trust.

Cherylynn Becker, PhD, is an associate professor in the Department of Management and International Business at the University of Southern Mississippi, Gulf Coast. She teaches management, human resources management, organisational staffing and cross-cultural management. Her research which focuses primarily on management issues within the field of hospitality and tourism has appeared in journals including the *International Journal of Hospitality Management*, *Journal of Hospitality and Tourism Research*, *Tourism Geographies*, *Tourism Analysis*, *Journal of Hospitality Human Resource* and *Psychology and Marketing*. She serves on the Editorial Review Board for the *Journal of Hospitality and Tourism Research*.

Inès Blal (PhD, Virginia Polytechnic Institute and State University) is an Assistant Professor of Strategic Management at the Ecole hôtelière de Lausanne, HES-SO; University of Applied Sciences, Western Switzerland. Dr. Blal specialises in performance measures of lodging corporations and execution of expansion strategies. Her research has been published in, among other journals, the *International Journal of Hospitality Management* and the *Cornell Hospitality Quarterly*. Her work includes studies of the development department within lodging corporations, the effect of online rating on performance, the impact of the asset light strategy in the industry, methods for scanning the environment, and the financing possibilities for small and medium hotels in Switzerland.

Dr. B. Bynum Boley is an assistant professor of Natural Resources, Recreation and Tourism (NRRT) within the Warnell School of Forestry and Natural Resources at the University of Georgia. His research interest focuses on sustainable tourism with special attention to the congruence of a destination's emphasis on sustainability and its overall competitiveness. This translates into a need for both supply-side and demand-side research to create management and marketing plans that match resident values and destination resources with appropriate tourist segments that will maximize the positive impacts of tourism across the triple-bottom line.

Mariana Bueno de Andrade Matos is a Professor of Tourism and Hospitality Management at the Hotel and Tourism Department of the Universidade Federal de Pernambuco (Brazil). Holds a Masters degree and is a PhD candidate in Business Management at the Universidade Federal de Pernambuco (UFPE), Brazil. Currently, is a member of the Centre for the Study of Hospitality, Tourism and Gastronomy (CHT/UFPE).

Mats Carlbäck has a long practical experience of the hospitality industry, in Sweden and on the international arena, both as entrepreneur and in various management positions. This has led to an extensive network in the industry, on a local, national and international level. His research is mainly focused on performance enhancing methods within the hospitality industry which has led to several articles in renowned publications. Mats's research is based on relevant questions from the practitioners and the aim is primarily to find new applicable solutions/models/methods for an industry in great need of new thinking and increased professionalism. In order to further facilitate the spreading of research, Mats is a contributor to various blogs in Sweden and has columns and editorial work in leading magazines and papers.

Mats is currently dividing his time between developing his own company Fivepointfive AB, and lecturing at the School of Hospitality, Culinary Arts and Meal Science, Örebro University, Sweden.

Prakash K. Chathoth is Professor, Department of Marketing and Information Systems, School of Business Administration, American University of Sharjah, United Arab Emirates. His research interests include topics related to strategic and service management/marketing with a particular emphasis on the service sector, notably the tourism and hospitality industry. Several of his papers have appeared in top-tier journals within the field including *Annals of Tourism Research, Tourism Management, Journal of Sustainable Tourism, Journal of Travel and Tourism Marketing, Journal of Hospitality and Tourism Research, International Journal of Hospitality Management* and *International Journal of Contemporary Hospitality Management*. He serves on the editorial board of nine international research journals and is currently the Regional Editor – Middle East and Africa for the *International Journal of Contemporary Hospitality Management*.

Valentina Della Corte is Associate Professor of Business Management at Federico II University of Naples. She teaches Tourism Business Management, Strategic Management and Marketing Policies, Revenue Management and Management of Cultural Heritage.

She is the author of numerous publications in national and international academic journals such as *Tourism Management, European Journal of Innovation Management, Corporate Ownership and Control, International Journal of Quality and Service Sciences, International Journal of Leisure and Tourism Marketing, International Journal of Marketing Studies, Journal of Management and Sustainability, Mercati e competitività* and *Sinergie*.

Valentina is the author of books published by Elgar, IGI Global, Routledge and McGraw Hill as well as of chapters in books edited by the Italian Egea, CEDAM and Giappichelli.

She has participated in national and international conferences such as Strategic Management Society Annual Meeting, Academy of Management Annual Meeting, Italian Academy of Management Annual Meeting, International Forum of Knowledge Asset Dynamic, International Conference on Tourism (ICOT), International Marketing Trends Conference, Forum on Marketing and Markets, AIDEA Annual Meeting and Sinergie Annual Meeting.

Her research is focused on strategic management and marketing and in particular resource-based theory, business networks and coopetition, dynamic capabilities, value creation and appropriation both intra-firm and inter-firm, innovative marketing in tourism and heritages.

Carlos Costa is Full Professor, Head of the Department of Economics, Management and Industrial Engineering of the University of Aveiro and Editor of the *Journal of Tourism and Development*. He holds a PhD and MSc in Tourism Management (University of Surrey, UK), and a BSc in Urban and Regional Planning (University of Aveiro, Portugal). Carlos is the leader of the Tourism Research Unit and of the PhD Tourism Programme of the University of Aveiro. He is also Scientific Coordinator of the 'idtour-unique solutions' (tourism spin-off company of the University of Aveiro). Carlos is involved in a number of national and international tourism projects.

Irena Erbakanova is a lecturer at Varna University of Management. She is teaching various tourism and hospitality related subjects like Hotel Operations Management, Current Issues in Hospitality and Tourism, Special Interest Tourism, etc. Although her experience in the research field is quite new, from 2004 to 2011, mostly during her studies, Irena Erbakanova focused on working in the hospitality industry. The practical experience she gained was in properties ranging from 3 to 5 stars in departments including front office, housekeeping, food and beverage, marketing and quality.

Dr. Elena García de Soto-Camacho's main research interests are in the Strategic Management field, especially in internationalisation process and in the tourism industry. At present, she is a lecturer at the University of Huelva, where she has served in several positions. In addition she is a member of the Spanish-Portuguese Network of Researchers on Tourism (REINTUR) and the Iberian Circle of Business Economics (CIBECEM). In 2004 she formed the Research Group 'Innovation and Development Strategies in Tourist Firms' (GEIDETUR), included in the Andalusian Government's Plan of R&D&I.

Fernando José Garrigós Simón has a PhD in Management and is Associate Professor in the Department of Business Organization, Universitat Politecnica de Valencia (Spain). He also has an MSc in Tourism Management and Planning from Bournemouth University, and a degree in Economics from the University of Valencia. He has taught or researched in universities in France, Germany, USA, UK, Australia, Singapore and Thailand. His primary areas of research include Tourism Management and Knowledge Management. He has been published in international books and journals such as *Annals of Tourism Research*, *International Journal of Contemporary Hospitality Management*, *International Journal of Technology Management*, *Journal of Knowledge Management*, *Small Business Economics*, *Management Decision*, *The Service Industries Journal*, *Tourism Economics* and *Tourism Management*.

Dr. Sjoerd Gehrels is UAS Professor of Innovation in Hospitality, Stenden Hotel Management School, Netherlands. Sjoerd commenced higher education in 1989 after 10 years in the hospitality industry and is currently course leader for the Masters in International Service Management, and UAS Professor of Innovation in Hospitality at Stenden HMS. Sjoerd holds an MSc from Surrey, an MBA from Oxford Brookes and an EdD from Stirling, and is now Postdoc at UALg, Portugal. His recent, Centre of Expertise in LTH, funded research project examines Employer Branding applications. Sjoerd is co-editor of the Research in Hospitality Management journal and member of the European Journal of Tourism Research editorial board.

Oksana Gerwe is a doctoral candidate at IE Business School, Madrid (Spain), where she is doing her doctoral degree in the field of Strategy. Her research interests are in the areas of value creation and value capture, demand-driven strategy and collaborative consumption.

Anderson Gomes de Souza is Professor of Tourism and Hospitality Management at the Hotel and Tourism Department of the Universidade Federal de Pernambuco (Brazil). He holds a Master's and PhD degree in Business Management from the same institution, having developed part of his dissertation at the NHTV Internationaal Hoger Onderwijs Breda (The Netherlands). Currently, he is a member of the International Academy for the Development of Tourism Research in Brazil (ABRATUR), of the Centre for the Study of Marketing and Personnel (MKP/UFPE), the Centre for the Study of Hospitality, Tourism and Gastronomy (CHT/UFPE) and the Eductur – Education in Tourism: Teaching and Research (UFPE).

Ulrike Gretzel is Professor of Tourism in the UQ Business School, University of Queensland, Australia, and a member of the Smart Tourism Research Centre at Kyung Hee University, South Korea. She received her PhD in Communications from the University of Illinois at Urbana-Champaign. Her research focuses on technology use in tourism, with an emphasis on social media, both from organizational as well as consumer perspectives, and the design of intelligent systems, in particular recommender systems. Her research has been published in major tourism and eCommerce journals. She has also co-authored and co-edited several books related to technology in tourism.

Dr. Michael J. Gross is a Lecturer with the School of Management at the University of South Australia in Adelaide. Michael holds a Bachelor of Science in Business Administration (BSBA) degree with a major in Hotel and Restaurant Management from the University of Denver, USA, Master's degrees in Education (MPET) and Business (MBA) from Deakin University, Australia, and a PhD from the University of South Australia. He has an extensive professional background in international hospitality management with some of the world's leading hotel firms. He currently teaches in hospitality and tourism programmes at the undergraduate and postgraduate levels. His research and publishing focus on hospitality management and tourism management areas, with particular interests in development and internationalisation of hospitality firms, China hospitality industry, international education, destination marketing, destination image, lifestyle tourism, consumer involvement and place attachment.

Demian Hodari (PhD, University of Surrey) is an Associate Professor of Strategic Management at the Ecole hôtelière de Lausanne, HES-SO – University of Applied Sciences Western Switzerland. Dr. Hodari specialises in the strategic partnerships between hotel owners, management companies and general managers, and the ensuing performance implications. His research has been published in, among other journals, the *Cornell Hospitality Quarterly*, the *International Journal of Hospitality Management* and the *Journal of Hospitality Financial Management*. He is a frequent speaker at international hotel investment conferences and his practitioner-oriented research is regularly published in industry trade publications.

Dr. Stanislav Ivanov is a Professor in Tourism Economics and Vice Rector for Academic Affairs and Research in Varna University of Management, Bulgaria. He is the Editor-in-chief of the European Journal of Tourism Research (http://ejtr.vumk.eu) and serves on the editorial boards of 25 other journals. His research interests include hotel chains, destination marketing, tourism and economic growth, political issues in tourism, and special interest tourism. His publications have appeared in different academic journals – *Annals of Tourism Research, Tourism Management, Tourism Management Perspectives, Tourism Economics, Journal of Heritage Tourism, Tourism and Hospitality Research, Tourism Today, Tourism, Tourism Planning and Development, Anatolia, International Journal of Hospitality and Tourism Administration, Journal of Hospitality Marketing and Management, Tourismos, Journal of Economic Studies, Journal of Southern Europe and the Balkans* and *South-Eastern Europe Journal of Economics*.

Dr. Maya Ivanova is an Assistant Professor in Tourism in Varna University of Management, Bulgaria, and a certified IATA instructor. Her publications have appeared in journals like *Tourism Management Perspectives, Anatolia, International Journal of Hospitality and Tourism Administration, Journal of Hospitality Marketing and Management* and *Tourismos*. She serves as Editorial Assistant for the *European Journal of Tourism Research* (http://ejtr.vumk.eu). Dr. Ivanova's research interests include tour operators, airlines and hotel chains.

Magdalena Kachniewska is Associate Professor in Tourism Department, Warsaw School of Economics (WSE). She is a member of the Tourism Research Working Group at the Polish Ministry of Sport and Tourism, an expert of the Hotel Market Institute, and senior consultant of the Polish Tourism Organisation.

She is a member of the Scientific Council of e-TravelForum and 'New technologies in travel sector – Tech.Travel Award' contest. She has been the leading consultant at the opening stage of 26 hotels in Poland and Slovakia. She has been the president of Efekt Hotele Co, General Manager of Best Western Krakow Premier Hotel, and General Manager of Express by Holiday Inn Hotel. Until 2012 she was a member of the Supervisory Board at the European Mortgage Fund (managing four hotels in Poland).

Ákos Kátay is Assistant Professor at the Institute of Tourism and Business Studies at Kodolányi János University of Applied Sciences, Székesfehérvár – Budapest, Hungary, and PhD candidate at the Doctoral School of Earth Sciences of the University of Pécs. He has extensive practical experience in the hotel sector, and represents KJU in the Hungarian Hotel & Restaurant Association. His PhD research focuses on the interrelationship of the Hungarian hotel industry's spatial expansion and market activity and its environment.

Dr. Mahmood A. Khan is Professor in the department of Hospitality and Tourism Management, Pamplin College of Business at Virginia Tech's National Capital Region campus. His area of expertise is hospitality franchising and he is the author of seven books, including the latest edition of *Restaurant Franchising: Concepts, Regulations, and Practices*. He serves on several journal editorial boards, and is an Associate Editor of the Cornell Hospitality Quarterly. He is also Senior Acquisition Editor for Apple Academic Publications. He has been invited by national and international institutions to serve as a speaker, keynote speaker, and seminar presenter on different topics related to franchising and services management. He is a Fellow of the Academy of Nutrition and Dietetics.

Dr. Khan has received the Steven Fletcher Award for his outstanding contribution to hospitality education and research. He is also a recipient of the John Wiley & Sons Award for lifetime contribution to outstanding research and scholarship; Donald K. Tressler Award for scholarship; and Cesar Ritz Award for scholarly contribution. He also received the Outstanding Doctoral faculty award from Pamplin College of Business.

He has served on the Board of Governors of the Educational Foundation of the International Franchise Association, on the Board of Directors of the Virginia Hospitality and Tourism Association, as a Trustee of the International College of Hospitality Management and as a Trustee on the Foundation of the Hospitality Sales and Marketing Association's International Association. He is also a member of several professional associations.

Dr. Dimitris Koutoulas has been pursuing a career both as a business consultant and an academic over a period of more than two decades. He serves as Assistant Professor at the University of Patras teaching Tourism and Hospitality Management and Marketing. Koutoulas also works as a marketing consultant and project manager mainly in the tourism, hospitality, publishing and events industries. His work has covered nearly every aspect of applied marketing and management ranging from market research and hotel concept development to mystery guest inspections and online marketing. Koutoulas has also conducted professional training programmes for hotels and tourism boards. He has implemented projects in 28 countries.

Matthew Krawczyk is a PhD student in the Department of Hospitality and Tourism Management in Pamplin College of Business at Virginia Tech. His research interests include consumer perceptions of market structure in the lodging and restaurant industries, hospitality analytics and exploring methods by which hospitality managers can gain insights from online consumer reviews. His background is centered on over a decade of managerial experience in restaurants, theme parks and hotels.

Kathryn A. LaTour is Associate Professor of Services Marketing, School of Hotel Administration, at Cornell University. Her research focuses on consumer memory processes and hedonic consumer experiences. Her research has appeared in multiple outlets including the *Journal of Marketing, Journal of Consumer Research, Journal of Advertising* and *Journal of Advertising Research*.

Michael S. LaTour was Professor of Marketing, School of Business at Ithaca College. Professor LaTour's research focused on consumer memory processes as well as psycho-physiological response to promotional stimuli. His research appeared in a variety of scholarly outlets including *Journal of Marketing, Journal of Consumer Research, Journal of Advertising* and *Journal of Advertising Research*. Professor LaTour was also former Editor of *Cornell Hospitality Quarterly*.

Dr. Seoki Lee is an associate professor at the School of Hospitality Management of the Pennsylvania State University in the US. His primary research interests focus on corporate social responsibility, mainly in the hospitality context from strategic and financial management perspectives. His research work has been published in various journals such as *International Journal of Hospitality Management, Journal of Hospitality and Tourism Research, Cornell Quarterly* and *Tourism Management*.

Yumi Lim completed her PhD at Virginia Tech and was an adjunct instructor at Virginia Tech and Radford University. Her research interests are branding, brand extension, consumer behaviour and the influence of technology/IT on tourism. Currently, she works as an independent researcher.

Roberto Llorente received an MSc degree in Telecommunication Engineering from the Universidad Politécnica de Valencia (UPV), Spain, in 1998. In 2002 he joined the Nanophotonics Technology Center (NTC) and in 2006 he received his PhD. Currently, he is Associate Professor, lecturing telecommunications subjects in the UPV, and Head of the Optical Systems and Networks Unit in the NTC. He has been leading NTC activities in European research projects FP5-TOPRATE and FP6-UROOF and has coordinated FP7-UCELLS and FP7-FIVER projects. He has authored more than 120 papers in leading international journals and conferences and has authored three patents. His current research focuses on telecommunications infrastructures for social benefit.

Maria de Lourdes Barbosa is a Professor of Tourism and Hospitality Management at the Hotel and Tourism Department, and of Business at the Graduate Program in Business Administration of the Universidade Federal de Pernambuco (Brazil). She holds a Master's degree and PhD in Business Management from the same institution. Currently, she is the research leader of the Centre for the Study of Hospitality, Tourism and Gastronomy (CHT/UFPE), and also a member of the Centre for the Study of Marketing and Personnel (MKP/UFPE).

Vincent P. Magnini, PhD, is a tenured faculty member in Virginia Tech's Pamplin College of Business. He is currently ranked as one of the top 12 most prolific hospitality researchers worldwide. Vince holds Editorial Board appointments on ten of the leading research journals in his field and is a US Fulbright Scholar.

Vince's most recent book, *Performance Enhancers: Twenty Essential Habits for Service Businesses*, appeared on the top 1% of Amazon.com's Best Seller Ranking throughout 2014. He has been featured three times on National Public Radio's (NPR's) *With Good Reason*, once on NPR's *All Things Considered* and cited in the *New York Times*.

Aurelio G. Mauri graduated in Business Administration at Bocconi University (Milan, Italy), and is at present Associate Professor of Tourism and Services Marketing at IULM University, Milan, Italy. He has extensive and varied teaching experiences in various European Universities. His research interests include services marketing, service quality, customer satisfaction, revenue management, word-of-mouth and brand management. He is the author of several articles and books.

Felix T. Mavondo is Professor of Marketing in the Department of Marketing at Monash University, Australia. Felix has published in Marketing and Tourism and his teaching interests are in Quantitative Methods, Research Methods and Strategic Marketing. Felix has served on editorial boards of marketing and communication journals and is an ad hoc reviewer for many top journals. Felix's research interests are in dynamic capabilities, business-to-business marketing, Strategic Marketing and tourism. His passion is supervising doctoral students and helping to realise their potential.

Dirisa Mulindwa's educational background is in tourism development, and his PhD awarded in 2009 by Anglia Ruskin University focused on the relationship between Community-based Ecotourism and Poverty Alleviation in Bigodi Parish near Kibale National Park, Western Uganda. Over the years Dirisa's research interests have expanded into web 2.0 technologies in hospitality, hotel growth strategies and issues of authenticity, ethnicity and the representation of food in ethnic restaurants.

Yeamduan Narangajavana is Researcher and Lecturer at Universitat Jaume I (Spain). She has a PhD in Marketing from Universitat Jaume I, and an MSc in Tourism Management and Marketing from Bournemouth University (UK). She received her Bachelor's degree in Business Administration from Chiang Mai University (Thailand). She has been the coordinator of the tourism department for the faculty of business in Walailak University, and has also been lecturer at Dusit Thani College. Her interests include tourism and marketing, revenue management and price analysis. She has published in international books and journals such as *Annals of Tourism Research, International Journal of Contemporary Hospitality Management, Encontros Bibli, Journal of Air Transport Management* and *Tourism Management.*

Peter O'Connor, PhD, is Professor of Information Systems at Essec Business School, France, where he also serves as Director of the Global MBA and the MBA in Hospitality Management. His research, teaching and consulting interests focus on technology, distribution, e-commerce and electronic marketing particularly applied to the hospitality sector. He has previously held a visiting position at the Cornell Hotel School and worked in a variety of positions within hospitality, in sectors as diverse as luxury hotels and contract food services.

Emmanouil F. Papavasileiou is a Research Fellow in International Labour Mobility, at the University of Portsmouth (UK). Previously he gained commercial experience working overseas (Greece) within the Hospitality and Health Care sectors, developing human resource management practices for both public and private organisations. His main area of research concerns inter-generational differences and their impacts on workplace dynamics and managing people. Emmanouil's research has been published in journals and conference proceedings such as the *International Journal of Human Resource Management.*

Yákara Pereira Leite is Professor of Business Management at the Business Department of the Universidade Federal Rural do Semi-Árido (Brazil). Yákara holds a Master's degree and PhD in Business Management from the Universidade Federal de Pernambuco, and is currently a member of the Centre for the Study of Business Strategy (CEO/UFPE).

Luiz Pinto Machado, born in Lisbon in July 1962, began his labour activity at the age of 16, working in various roles in different fields of commerce and industry. Soon he became interested in tourist activities, beginning in the hospitality sector in 1978. Luiz worked for several international hotels, and was invited in the early 1990s to teach. His long experience in the industry gives him a huge facility in imparting knowledge. Invitations to teach at a higher level arose. At this point, as a professional in the industry, Luiz saw a great need for studies in tourism and investigation of topics of keen interest to the sector. Luiz joined the best researchers in the field, publishing several papers in relevant scientific journals, books and manuals for students and professionals. He developed parallel interests in professional associations and assumed leadership positions in various institutions involved in the tourist industry. He helped to found the Tourism Observatory at the University of Madeira, where he intends to develop a deep research project in the tourism sector, with the goal of improving the performance of tourism on Madeira and in Portugal. Luiz holds degrees in Hotel and Tourism Management, an MSc in Strategic Management and Tourism Development and a PhD in Economics.

Ige Pirnar currently works as a full-time professor at the Department of BA and is an elected member of the University Executive Board of Yasar University. She has produced eight books in Turkish (three edited and two with co-authors) on topics of International Business:

Key Concepts, International Tourism Management, Convention and Meetings Management, TQM in Tourism, Direct Marketing, PR in Tourism, F&B Management and Quality Management in Services. Her areas of expertise are tourism management, international tourism, global marketing, international management, hospitality marketing, quality management and EU tourism policy.

Dr. Roya Rahimi is a lecturer at the University of Wolverhampton Business School where she teaches across tourism, hospitality, leisure and events subject areas. While undertaking her PhD studies, she was a Research Assistant in the Management Department of Izmir University and, in broadening her knowledge and academic experience, she became a PhD visiting Scholar at the University of Wolverhampton (2010–11).

Her research interests are Customer Relationship Management (CRM) in Chain Hotels, Organisational Culture in Hospitality Businesses, Human Resource Management, Gender issues and Equality and Diversity. She has expertise in Quantitative Research Methods and her work has been presented at various international conferences and has been published in a variety of journals and book chapters. Her industry experience includes 7 years working in the hotel industry in a number of international hotels in various countries. Roya is fluent in three languages (English, Turkish and Persian) and has familiarity with European and Asian cultures. Roya is a fan of using technology in her classes and uses simulating hospitality management software for bringing practice into theory and making students familiar with real work experiences. She is acting as the director of the Visiting Scholar Scheme at the University of Wolverhampton Business School.

Haywantee Rumi Ramkissoon is Associate Professor and Director of the Tourism Research Cluster at Curtin Business School, and research fellow at BehaviourWorks Australia, Monash University. She holds two doctoral degrees in Tourism and Applied Environmental Psychology. Her postdoctoral experience relates to place attachment, and societal innovation and behaviour change. Rumi publishes in leading tourism journals such as *Annals of Tourism Research, Tourism Management, Journal of Travel Research, Journal of Sustainable Tourism, Tourism Analysis, Journal of Hospitality* and *Tourism Research*. She is the book review editor for *Current Issues in Tourism* and Research Note Editor for *Journal of Hospitality Marketing and Management*. Rumi serves on 11 editorial boards of high quality journals in her field.

Tamara Rátz is Professor of Tourism, and Director of the Institute of Tourism and Business Studies at Kodolányi János University of Applied Sciences, Székesfehérvár – Budapest, Hungary. She is the author or co-author of more than 180 publications on tourism, including a number of books on the impacts of tourism, attraction and visitor management, and health tourism and quality of life. Her current research interests include cultural and heritage tourism development, and creativity and innovation in niche tourism development.

Yinyoung Rhou is a PhD student in the Department of Hospitality and Tourism Management at Virginia Tech. Her research interests are in the area of strategic management. She seeks to understand how firms' strategic decisions influence their financial performance in the context of hospitality and the tourism industry.

Viviane Santos Salazar is Professor of Tourism and Hospitality Management at the Hotel and Tourism Department and of Business at the Graduate Programme in Business

Administration of the Universidade Federal de Pernambuco (Brazil). She holds a Master's degree and PhD in Business Management from the same institution. Currently, she is a member of the Centre for the Study of Hospitality, Tourism and Gastronomy (CHT/UFPE), and also a member of the Centre for the Study of Business Strategy (CEO/UFPE).

Rosario Silva (PhD Universidad Carlos III, Spain) is Professor of Strategic Management at IE Business School (Madrid, Spain). Her fields of interest include differentiation strategies and geographic agglomeration in the hotel industry.

Claudia Sima finished her PhD in urban tourism studies at the University of Westminster London in 2013 and now works as Associate Lecturer in Tourism Management with the University of Central Lancashire in the UK. Her research interests include: Generations BB, X,Y, Z, α and their impacts on the tourism, hospitality and events industries, event marketing and social-media commerce.

Carol J. Simon, MBA, is a veteran hotel manager with 37 years of experience, the last 28 years with Crestline Hotels and Resorts. Carol has experience in room management, food and beverage, sales and conference planning, as well as revenue management. Carol has been a General Manager at various hotels and resorts. Carol was an instructor of hospitality management at James Madison University School of Hospitality and Sports Management. Carol is currently an independent consultant specializing in hotel operations.

Manisha Singal is an associate professor at the Pamplin College of Business at Virginia Tech. She teaches graduate and undergraduate courses in hospitality strategic management and finance. Her research explores how the ownership and governance of firms influence their strategic decision-making and financial performance. Dr. Singal serves on the editorial boards of several journals and her research articles appear in both management and hospitality-specific journals, including *Journal of International Management*, *Strategic Entrepreneurship Journal*, *Family Business Review*, *Cornell Hospitality Quarterly*, *Journal of Hospitality and Tourism Research* and *International Journal of Hospitality Management*.

Sujin Song is a graduate student at the School of Hospitality Management of the Pennsylvania State University, US. Her primary research interests focus on diversification strategies and corporate social responsibility in the hospitality industry from strategic and financial management perspectives.

Liliya Terzieva holds a PhD in the field of Economic and Organizational sciences of Leisure, Hospitality and Tourism. She is a lecturer and a researcher as well as the Coordinator of the Master's in Imagineering Programme at the NHTV University of Applied Sciences, Breda, Netherlands. Liliya has a lot of experience in international environment, being a member of diverse EU networks for project development and implementation as well as of the Global network of e-coaches and e-auditors certified by the British Chamber of Commerce and Industry. Apart from a leisure and tourism background, Liliya holds a second Master's degree in Management of Adult Education.

Michael J. Turner (PhD, Griffith University) is a Senior Lecturer in Accounting at The University of Queensland, Brisbane, Australia. Dr. Turner specialises in focusing his management accounting research on the hospitality industry and has developed a particular interest in the management and governance challenges arising in hotels mediated by a management contract. He has refereed publications in hospitality journals such as *International Journal of Hospitality Management, Journal of Hospitality and Tourism Research* and *Journal of Hospitality and Tourism Management,* and accounting journals such as *Accounting & Business Research* and *Accounting & Finance.*

Vivien Ulu is a senior lecturer in Law, Business and Hospitality, and a principal advocate and consultant, at DeUlu Legal and Educational Services Consultants. She is a Lawyer by profession with degrees in Law (LLB and LLM) from Nottingham University and a Postgraduate Research Degree from the University of Oxford, Pembroke College. She has several years of experience in commercial legal practice as well as teaching Law and Business. Vivien's research interests include legal issues in Hospitality, particularly the application of the Law of Agency in Hotel Management Contracts, Regulation and deregulation of Hospitality businesses in Developing Countries and Investor Protection.

Alfonso Vargas-Sánchez is the promoter and Editor-in-Chief of Enlightening Tourism: A Pathmaking Journal (Et). Dr. Vargas-Sánchez's main research interests are in Strategic Management discipline and in the tourism industry, both in companies and in destinations. At present, he is a full professor at the University of Huelva, where he has been distinguished with the 2002/2003 Teaching Excellence Diploma, and the 2006/2007 Teaching Excellence & Quality Award as a member of an online teaching group. Since 2004 he has headed the Research Group named Innovation and Development Strategies in Tourist Firms (GEIDETUR), included in the Andalusian Government's Plan of R&D&I. Prof. Vargas-Sánchez has carried out academic activities, both in research and teaching, in different Universities and higher education institutions around the world, across five continents. Nowadays, he serves as Visiting Professor in the UK at the York St John Business School and the School of Business and Entrepreneurship of the RAU (where in addition he is a member of its Advisory Board), and in the University of the Algarve (Portugal), where he is an invited researcher and has been a member of its General Council. Additionally, he collaborates with the Agency for Assessment and Accreditation of Higher Education in Portugal, as external expert. He has served in several positions in the University of Huelva, where he is Full Professor; in addition he leads the Spanish-Portuguese Network of Researchers on Tourism (REINTUR) and EATSA (Europe-Asia Tourism Studies Association), as Vice-President for Europe. More details are available at: http://www.uhu.es/alfonso_vargas/

Christian Walter lives and works in Vienna. Being a graduate of the Munich University of Applied Sciences, Christian complemented his education in the hospitality business at the University of Westminster in London. In pursuit of lifelong learning, Christian has also completed an executive education curriculum at Cornell University's School of Hotel Administration in Ithaca, USA. He gathered, amongst others, practical experience at the Brenners Park-Hotel & Spa in Baden-Baden and at the Hotel Vier Jahreszeiten Kempinski in Munich. Since 2005, Christian Walter has been with the PKF hotelexperts team in Vienna, one of the leading international hospitality consulting firms with over 500 partner offices in the PKF International network around the world (www.pkfhotels.com). He is a Managing Director and in charge of operator search and selection. In this capacity, Christian is negotiating hotel lease, management and franchise agreements on an ongoing basis. Besides his distinctive preference for travelling, both for business and leisure, he devotes himself to his activity as a lecturer at the IMC in Krems (Austria) and at the ADI (Akademie der Immobilienwirtschaft) in Hamburg. He is also present as a guest lecturer at the MODUL University in Vienna and at the International University Bad Honnef/Bonn. Currently, Christian serves as Regional Vice President (EMEA Region) of the Cornell Hotel Society.

Wei Wang is an assistant professor in the Department of Tourism and Economic Development at the University of Southern Mississippi. She received her PhD in Leisure Behavior with a focus on Tourism Management at Indiana University. A native of Beijing, she worked as a host country national (HCN) for Air Canada where she was responsible for marketing development and establishing relationships with partner businesses, including the Canada–China Business Council and American Chamber of China. In addition she served as an international flight attendant for KLM Royal Dutch Airlines. Her research focuses on consumer marketing in hospitality. Dr. Wei Wang earned her PhD and MS in Tourism, Hospitality, and Event Management from Indiana University. She has completed 12 years of research, education, and industry experience in travel, tourism, and hospitality. Dr. Wang's areas of research include tourist experience; customer service management; and hospitality marketing and management. She has been involved in airline and hotel research projects throughout the United States, China, Canada, the Netherlands and Norway. Prior to her academic career, she worked professionally for international airlines as a Home-Country National (HCN) in Beijing for several different positions, including a reservation and customer service agent, sales and marketing, and as a cabin attendant. With these job experiences, she was able to travel internationally and became equipped with the knowledge to work in multicultural environments with customers and co-workers from all over the world. These unique experiences thus add more multicultural attributes and dimensions on this topic.

Craig Webster earned his MA and PhD degrees in Political Science from Binghamton University (USA). He has taught at Binghamton University, Ithaca College, the College of Tourism and Hotel Management and the University of Nicosia. He is the Editor-in-Chief of Tourism Today and is a Co-Editor of the Cyprus Review. He is a co-editor of *Future Tourism: Political, Social and Economic Challenges*, an edited volume published by Routledge and has published in the *Annals of Tourism Research, Tourism Geographies, Tourism Management* and many other journals. He now teaches at Ball State University in Indiana.

Zheng Xiang, PhD, is an Assistant Professor in the Department of Hospitality and Tourism Management in Pamplin College of Business at Virginia Tech. His research interests include travel information search on the Internet, social media marketing, and the impact of information technology on the tourism and hospitality industries. He uses text analytics as a main research tool. He currently serves as board member of the International Federation for IT and Travel & Tourism (IFITT) as well as editorial board member for several international journals including *Journal of Travel Research* and *Journal of Travel and Tourism Marketing*.

Vladimir Zhechev holds a PhD in marketing and currently works as an Assistant Professor at the University of Economics-Varna (UEV), Bulgaria. He has worked as a consultant at GMSE and has successfully completed over seven European projects in the fields of: higher education, hospitality management, branding, marketing and others. The author is currently managing the Rankings Department at UEV and is responsible for collaborative Joint Degree projects. Vladimir Zhechev has completed specialisations in the UK, Germany, Spain, France, Greece and Cyprus. He has authored academic papers, monographs and book chapters in hotel marketing, general marketing, branding, CRM, etc. and is an editorial board member of the *International Journal of Professional Management*, UK.

Introduction

Maya Ivanova, Stanislav Ivanov and Vincent P. Magnini

The global hotel landscape continually evolves. Ever changing political, economic, cultural and technological forces interplay to influence how hotels should best compete in their respective markets. Understanding the global hotel business is not possible without paying specific attention to hotel chain management and dynamics. Hotel chains are big business: only approximately 19 per cent of new hotels currently being constructed around the world are independent/unaffiliated, which means that more than 80 per cent are chain affiliated (Hood, 2015). In 2014, the five largest brands (Holiday Inn Express, Holiday Inn, Hilton, Best Western, and Marriott) had a combined 1,019,000 rooms; furthermore, there were 14 other brands that each had more than 75,000 rooms (ibid.). The high economic importance of the hotel chains and their global presence determines their economic and social importance and justifies the academic research in the field.

Despite their importance, surprisingly, there is no uniform coverage of hotel chains in our current body of literature. Existing research is largely fragmented and focuses on separate aspects of their activities – e.g. choice of entry mode, partner selection, branding, mergers and acquisitions, factors of internationalisation. Therefore, this Handbook aids in filling the gap in the research literature by providing a comprehensive critical analysis of all aspects of hotel chains – their nature, fundamentals of existence and operation, expansion, strategic and operational aspects of their activities, geographical presence. This Handbook provides a balanced and interdisciplinary approach to hotel chain analysis. It considers simultaneously the view point of the chain and the view point of the individual affiliated hotel. The Handbook's theoretical framework is rooted in the fields of international business, global marketing and branding, and theory of the firm, which makes the Handbook appealing to a wide audience. In summary, this book is an attempt to house key writings in a single book. It is intended to be a major bibliographic resource for all academic researchers, students and practitioners interested in issues dealing with hotel chain management. The research orientation of the Handbook makes it suitable for courses for upper undergraduate, master's and PhD students. Due to the interdisciplinary nature of tourism/hospitality, the Handbook may also be of interest to researchers in non-tourism/hospitality fields like strategic management, international/global marketing and international business. Considering the comprehensiveness of the Handbook it may be very useful to practitioners too – development managers, chief marketing officers and regional area managers of hotel chains. The Handbook uses case studies and examples from various chains and destinations, contributing to its global appeal.

While more detail will be provided in the introductions to each of the sections, a brief synopsis is provided here. The aim of Section I is to lay the foundations of the other sections of the Handbook. It deals with the theoretical issues of hotel chains – their nature, the economic and marketing fundamentals for their existence and development, their strategic environment, economic and socio-cultural impacts on the host communities.

Sections II and III adopt the view point of the hotel chain. Section II focuses on the expansion of the hotel chains and all the decisions that have to be made in relation to their expansion – whether to expand (the decision of expand), where to expand (the choice of a destination), how to expand (the choice of an entry mode) and with whom to affiliate (the choice of a partner hotel). Due to their importance, each type of entry mode is discussed in a separate chapter. Section III deals comprehensively with all strategic and operational issues faced by hotel chains. Their marketing activities receive special interest as marketing is one of the major driving forces behind hotel chain development – branding, pricing, distribution channel management, etc. The section furthermore critically evaluates current debates in all functional areas of chains' operations – human resource management, finances, legal issues, quality management, measuring productivity, etc.

Section IV takes the view point of the individual affiliated hotel. It follows a structure similar to Section II and analyses the affiliation process from the perspective of the hotel. More specifically Section IV discusses issues related with a hotel's affiliation to a chain – whether to affiliate (the decision to be part of a chain or stay independent), how to affiliate (the choice of a type of affiliation), with whom to affiliate (the choice of a chain), the process of affiliation and affiliation evaluation.

The final Section V concentrates on current and future debates in the theory and practice of hotel chain management arising from globalisation, demographic trends, sustainability and new technology development. It also investigates the links between hotel chains and hospitality education.

Sixty-eight prominent researchers from 18 countries on 5 continents have contributed their time and talent to this project. The editors of the Handbook invited to be contributors those researchers and practitioners who have the knowledge and expertise to energise further examination and attention to topics surrounding hotel chain management. The passion of the contributors regarding this subject area shines through in the coming chapters. They infuse their passion into their writings when communicating their expertise regarding their respective topics.

To reiterate, a variety of readers can benefit from this book. The editors hope that you will find this book useful and consider it an initial effort to house key hotel chain management topics in a single resource. Each of the chapters herein perhaps provides more questions than answers which will lead to further development of the literature covering this rich and managerially relevant area of inquiry. Consequently, desired outcomes of this project include increasing our current knowledge-base as well as spawning further inquiry. Consistent with the current trend towards methodological pluralism, the writings in this book can trigger both qualitative and quantitative studies with the impetus of advancing the effective and efficient management of hotel chains.

The contribution of this book to our existing knowledge-base was made possible by the contributors who generously offered their time, talent and knowledge. The editors established only one overarching request for the contributors: the chapter had to provide useful insights related to hotel chain management. Being that English is not the native tongue of many of the contributors, their writings mandated significant effort and polishing. To restate from above, however, their passion and levels of expertise are apparent in their contributions. As a final note, we are grateful for the encouragement and collaboration of Routledge and their professional staff for helping to shape this book into this delivered product. Enjoy!

References

Hood, S. (2015) Hospitality and tourism future trends. Presentation at the Paris and Copenhagen Educator Workshops, 9–12 March, 2015 [Note: Steve Hood is the Senior Vice President of Research for STR].

Section I

Theoretical issues of hotel chains

The first section of the Handbook deals with theoretical issues of hotel chains. Chapter 1 by Maya Ivanova and Roya Rahimi discusses the nature and provides a definition of hotel chains as multi-unit enterprises, and outlines their distinctive characteristics. The chapter elaborates on the background, role and importance of hotel chains in the hospitality industry by analysing the existing definitions of hotel chains and their specific features. It further identifies gaps in the related literature, discusses the interchangeable terms used by different authors and develops a definition of hotel chains.

Chapter 2 by Stanislav Ivanov discusses the economic and marketing fundamentals that determine the existence and development of hotel chains, namely: brand recognition and the significant role of the brand in choice of hotel by hotel guests, high sunk costs, service standardisation, economies of scale, economies of scope and financial benefits of chain affiliation for the individual hotel surpassing the affiliation related costs. The author points out that brand recognition, economies of scope and financial benefits surpassing the costs of the affiliation are the most important forces that will continue to support the establishment of new and the expansion of existing hotel chains. Technology advancement erodes the importance of economies of scale, sunk costs and service standardisation. Furthermore, the author proves that online travel agencies may be considered as substitutes of hotel chains in delivering one of the core benefits sought by hoteliers when they affiliate their properties to chains – the greater market visibility of the hotel. The OTAs may be considered as substitutes of the hotel chains by the customers, because the OTAs' brands, secure reservation systems, convenient payment and hotel ratings decrease the perceived risk of the customers when they book hotel accommodation.

Chapter 3 by Prakash Chathoth delves into the evolution of such chain organisations with the objective of identifying the historical factors that led to their growth. Specifically, it delineates between macro and micro environmental factors that impacted the growth of hotel chains while emphasising inter- and intra-organisational factors such as competition and organisational learning. The chapter also sets out key founders of hotel chains who influenced the growth of such organisational forms. It further highlights their role in expanding the scale and scope of the business, leading to the evolution of the hotel chain organisation. Today, hotel chains have evolved to focus on branding while addressing the consumer's idiosyncratic needs with specific emphasis on experiential attributes.

Chapter 4 by Ákos Kátay and Tamara Rátz presents the main characteristics of the global geographical distribution of hotel chains in 2013, based on analysis of the number of properties and the number of rooms in different quality categories (luxury-upscale, midscale, economy). The geographical framework of the study is defined using the regional classification of UNWTO, with a slight modification in order to provide an adequately detailed spatial analysis. The analysis includes a detailed investigation of the market presence and the fair share of the top 10 global hotel corporations at regional (Africa, Middle East, Americas, Asia and the Pacific, Europe) and subregional levels. Although the chapter is predominantly descriptive in nature, the trends observed in the geographical analysis of hotel chains' market presence and fair share values seem to suggest an ongoing consolidation process in the industry mainly influenced by direct market factors.

Chapter 5 by Valentina Della Corte deals with the strategic environment of hotel chains. The market environment is characterised by particular dynamics in which the strong competition forces hotel chains to find innovative ways and tools to keep their market shares. Their strategic strength and marketing position, however, are higher than that of many single-unit hotels, often becoming pivotal actors in the tourist destinations where they invest. The chapter describes the hotel chain environment, analysing the characteristics of global and local strategies and the challenge of responding to both of them. Literature provides some useful models that help when studying the external and internal environment of hotel chains, both of which are described in the next paragraph. Finally, the chapter outlines the current scenario in which hotel chains operate, introducing some of the main factors to consider in order to achieve competitive advantage.

In Chapter 6, Maya Ivanova and Stanislav Ivanov analyse the heterogeneous and multifaceted nature of hotel chains by developing three partial models, where the chain is presented as a bundle of resources, activities and relationships, which are combined into one integrated model of a hotel chain. Each of the three partial models deals with a specific side of the hotel chain. The Resource-based view model reveals the internal foundations for creating and sustaining a competitive advantage by acquiring, using, managing and sharing resources, organisational capabilities, knowledge and learning. Porter's value chain perspective is focused on implementing the proper activities in a proper way, thus achieving superior performance. By interacting with its various stakeholders, the hotel chain establishes certain relationships with them, which, if suitably managed, can also become a ground for obtaining a competitive advantage. In order to gain a holistic impression of a hotel chain, all three perspectives were combined in one integrated model. The Integrated model could be used as an analytical tool to identify the specific sources of competitive advantage of a particular hotel chain and investigate the potential threats to the chain's competitiveness.

Chapter 7 by Ige Pirnar elaborates on the economic impacts of hotel chains on the host destination. Due to the rapid global growth of the hotel chains, they become economically vital to the destinations they operate within. In order to maximise the economic gains associated with the hotel chains' operations, it is important for related bodies to clearly identify the associated positive and negative possible impacts. Therefore, this chapter analyses these positive and negative possible economic impacts of the global hotel chains on the host destination. Some of the positive economic impacts include source of foreign exchange earnings, provision of employment opportunities, economic diversification, multiplier effect for the economy, etc. As negative economic impacts the author identifies leakages of national income, price rises and hiring expatriate workers. The chapter concludes with an in-depth discussion and analysis of trends affecting the economic impacts of hotel chains on host destinations, since for successful results the related trends should be taken into account and followed up closely.

The last chapter in the section, Chapter 8 by Bynum Boley and Emily P. Ayscue, deals with the socio-cultural impacts of hotel chains. Hotel chains, by their very nature and size, have a predisposition towards large positive and negative environmental, economic and socio-cultural impacts. While minimising the hospitality industry's environmental impacts has been a core aspect of the rhetoric behind the recent CSR/Sustainability movement, the discussion of socio-cultural impacts has often been left to the tourism literature. This chapter takes a critical perspective of the many positive and negative socio-cultural impacts hotel chains have within communities. Positive impacts covered include the potential for hotel chains' architectural design features to bring pride and civic confidence to the local community, as well as hotel chains possessing the potential to increase the quality of life of employees through enhanced educational opportunities. Negative impacts covered include hotel chains' history of providing marginal employment opportunities, economic leakage of tourism dollars, and homogenisation of culture for the sake of hotel chains' allegiance to brand standards. It is suggested that emphasising the management of these socio-cultural impacts on already present CSR initiatives can serve as a way for individual hotel chains to become more competitive in a saturated market and to enhance financial performance.

1

Nature and definition of hotel chain

Maya Ivanova (VARNA UNIVERSITY OF MANAGEMENT, BULGARIA) *and*
Roya Rahimi (UNIVERSITY OF WOLVERHAMPTON BUSINESS SCHOOL, UK)

Introduction

Hotels, both local and international, are considered to be the backbone of the hospitality industry providing accommodation and other services to guests. A significant share in the contemporary hotel industry has been occupied by numerous group entities, mostly also known as 'hotel chains'. According to the latest statistics, several hotel corporations from the top 10 are expected to reach the race for 1m rooms each (Big Brand Report, 2015). The chain-affiliated number of rooms reached 7.85m, which is over 40 per cent of the world supply as of 1 January 2014, according to MKG Hospitality Group (Panayotis, 2014). As prominent players in the hospitality industry, hotel chains have noteworthy influence over the rest. They are mostly major companies, with substantial financial backing, and have a huge impact on the whole sector, introducing innovative practices and technological advances.

Hotel chains have received considerable attention from academic researchers, but a comprehensive review would contribute to our current understanding. Usually hotel chains are used as exemplary case studies but only in a few publications are they the focal point of the research (Gee, 1994). Such studies deal mainly with single cases, or explore a limited number of hotel chains that could not serve for general conclusions, or provide a broad overview of the chains. Additionally, in most papers, the term 'hotel chain' is commonly used, but without a precise explanation or definition. Considering the different studies, surprisingly, a clear and widely accepted definition of the hotel chains as organisations appears to be absent.

Therefore, the current chapter will focus on the role and importance of hotel chains in the hospitality industry by analysing the specific features of the hotel chains and giving a unique definition for this type of accommodation provider. The exploration of the nature of hotel chains will begin by addressing a number of issues, followed by review and analysis of the existing definitions. Finally, a full definition will be offered, taking into account all previously discussed conceptualisations.

Considerations regarding the definition of the hotel chains

Considerations connected with the elaboration of a comprehensive definition of the hotel chains begin with the *used term/name*. The emergence and initial growth of the hotel chains have taken miscellaneous paths, resulting in companies with very diverse organisational structures, divergent strategies and goals. They are even named differently, e.g. '[international] hotel groups' (Alexander and Lockwood, 1996; Burges et al., 1995; Chen and Dimou, 2005), 'branded hotels' (O'Neill and Carlbäck, 2010), 'international/multinational hotel companies' (Altinay and Altinay, 2003), 'multinational hotel firms/groups' (Zhang et al., 2012), 'hotel brands' (Bernstein, 1999; O'Neill and Mattila, 2010), 'branded hotel operators' (Beals and Denton, 2005), 'hotel franchise systems' (Brown et al., 2003), '[international] hotel operators' (Cervino and Bonache, 2005) and 'hotel chain operators' (DeRoos, 2010), most of them used interchangeably. Although there are different terms, researchers have failed to identify that these terms represent the same phenomenon (Holverson and Revaz, 2006), hence the difficulty for them to be defined properly. In our endeavour to provide a valid definition, the above stated characteristics will be considered and included as diverse attributes of one and the same phenomenon.

Another necessary clarification before analysing the nature of a hotel chain concerns the *scope of hotel chains*. Many of the major hotel chains began their development by launching their own brand, mostly deriving from the owners' surnames (Hilton, Marriott, etc.). Later, additional brands were often added to enrich the brand portfolio of hotel companies and attract clients from other segments. The companies, however, continued to be addressed as 'hotel chains', and the creation of new brands was perceived as a strategic marketing approach called 'brand portfolio' (Keller, 2013). In order to avoid any misunderstanding and biased analysis, for the purpose of current study, hotel chains will be considered as the *companies or sub-divisions of companies that encompass hotel properties under a **single** brand*. This means that, for instance, Novotel, Sofitel, Mercure, Ibis, Jurys Inn, Premier Inn, etc. will be considered as hotel chains, not as Accor Corporation who own all of these brands. In a similar vein, InterContinental, Crown Plaza, Holiday Inn and Holiday Inn Express should be considered as hotel chains although they all belong to InterContinental Hotel Group. All major companies holding more than one brand in their portfolio will be referred to as '*hotel corporations*'. Within the limits of a hotel corporation, each hotel chain with its own brand sets its own goals and follows its own customer strategy, aligning it with the general strategic direction of the parent corporation.

Very often hotel chains are associated with the *hotel management companies*, which offer expertise in the management and operation of hotels. They might provide assistance with pre-opening marketing and sales, selection and training of staff and preparation of the day-to-day operations. In addition, they often establish a portfolio of key performance measures to assess the health and success of their managed properties. In some circumstances hotel chains also offer management contracts through which they can manage properties for owners. But apart from managing the hotel assets, the chains provide additional value from their brand (and for this reason are called 'brand operators', (Beals and Denton, 2005)), and the connected product standards and rules. In this way the integrated hotels are united not only by the common management team, but mainly by the brand and its requisites, and the latter is actively used for the positioning and promotion of the property. The ordinary management companies though, work with branded hotels (i.e. already members of any chain, usually on a franchise contract), but do not assign their brand to the hotel. Therefore, for the aims of this handbook, these management companies are not considered hotel chains.

Analogically, if a group of hotels belongs to the same owner and possibly the same management, this does not make them automatically a hotel chain. Provided the hotels share a common brand, concept and comparable product, then we can name this group a hotel chain. The difficulties in providing an accurate definition prove that hotel chains can be complex and compound as organisations. From a successful business model they have evolved to multilevel entities, which not only operate on a multinational basis (and therefore share multinational enterprise traits), but also perform an internal transfer and sharing of resources, common administration, management and creation of value. Therefore, it is essential to compile the variety of their characteristics into a comprehensive definition that would be endorsed by the scientific community.

Review of hotel chains' existing definitions and specific features

The elaboration of a comprehensive definition begins with an analysis of the existing definitions. In the process of seeking exemplary definitions, it turned out that very few of the researchers dare to create such a definition. 'Hotel chain' is extensively used as a concept, but still needs certain clarification. The term itself consists of two parts – 'hotel', indicating, that the company belongs to the hotel industry, and 'chain', associated with a string of similar rings, unified into one system (Dabeva, 1998). Following this logic, the hotel chain literally means a network of *multiple* units that share a *common feature* and operate in the *hotel industry*. Most of the provided definitions seem to derive from this simple interpretation (see Table 1.1).

All of the extant definitions emphasise the *multiunit nature* of hotel chains. Even some of the authors pinpoint an exact number of properties, set as a minimum, in order to consider a group of hotels as a chain. Jafari (2000) begins with 'more than one unit', whereas Peng (2004) sets the boundary at 'two or more hotel units'. Bhatia (2006) raises the qualification

Table 1.1 Definitions of 'hotel chain'

Author	Definition	Essentials
Contractor and Kundu (1998a: 327)	A global hotel firm is defined as one that either has an equity stake in a foreign property, or operates the hotel under a management service agreement, or is a franchiser to the foreign hotel property. Thus, a company could be a global firm without any ownership of a foreign property.	• different ways of affiliation; • global coverage; • chain or brand is not mentioned; • focus on geographical coverage; • different ways to expand
Jafari (2000: 76)	Chain hotels are made up of affiliated properties by virtue of the fact that the chain is contracted on a continuing basis to be responsible for putting in place at least one management function in the whole system. A hotel chain is thus an organisation that competes in the tourism industry, either locally, nationally, regionally or internationally, with more than one unit of similar concept or theme.	• multiple properties; • at least one centralized management function; • geographical distribution; • similar concept
Peng (2004: 242, xi)	Organisations which comprise two or more hotel units operating under a system of decision-making permitting coherent policies and a common strategy through one or more decision-making centres and in which the hotel units and corporate functions are linked to add value to each other by ownership or contractual relationships.	• minimum number of hotels; • centralised management; • coherent policy; • added value for both sides; • different ways of affiliation – ownership and contractual

(Continued)

Table 1.1 (Continued)

Author	Definition	Essentials
Bhatia (2006: 193)	A chain consists of three or more properties owned or managed by the same company and operated under the same brand.	• minimum number of properties mentioned; • common brand for all the properties; • way of comprising the portfolio of hotels – only ownership and management contract pointed out
Brookes (2007: 114–15)	The international hotel firm is defined as a discrete organisational entity with responsibility for developing, operating and supporting single or multiple branded portfolios.	• discrete entity; • managing multiple brand portfolio
Andrews (2009: 19)	A hotel chain is a series of hotels under a common brand name spread both nationally and internationally.	• multiple hotel units; • common brand; • national or international coverage/geographical distribution
Ivanova (2013)	A group of hotels, sharing a common brand aiming for a better market position through a combination of resources, activities and relationships, operating on a national and/or international level.	• multiple hotels; • common brand; • marketing aim; • resources, activities and relationships as building blocks of the organisation; • geographic level of coverage
Smith Travel Research	A nationally recognised brand or chain or a closed hotel. Generally STR will create or designate an affiliation once the company has a minimum of eight properties in its portfolio.	• multiple hotels, with a specified minimum number; • common and nationally recognised brand

to 'three or more properties' to reach the highest limit of a minimum of eight hotels needed to form a chain (STR, n.d.). The absolute number of properties is usually employed in classifications and statistical studies, as well as laws and any other legal documentary. Consequently, the different boundaries could be explained with the particular methodology applied by institutions and agencies on local and national levels. Also, they imply the lack of a unified statistical methodology in the hospitality industry in a worldwide context, despite the numerous efforts to establish such.

The multiunit nature of hotel chains comes as a prerequisite for some special management considerations, concerning both *the internal organisation*, and *the operation on multiple markets* (Jones, 1999). The internal organisation of the chains is affected in terms of *coordination, communication and administration of multiunit organisations* (typical for big companies and multinational corporations), as well as *resources, information and knowledge sharing* (connected with the experience of difficulties because of the heterogeneous and intangible nature of services) and *maintaining the same level of quality among the properties* (leading to establishment of standards and rules).

Processes, concerning *coordination, communication and administration* of such a multiunit entity like the hotel chain, have provoked numerous scientists to discuss and match different concepts to explain them. Resource-Based View (RBV) (Brown et al., 2003; Dev et al., 2002), Transaction Costs Approach (TCA) (Contractor and Kundu, 1998b; Chen and Dimou, 2005), Agency Theory (Alon et al., 2012; Contractor and Kundu, 1998a), Stakeholders and Network concepts (Altinay and Miles, 2006), are among the frequently cited frameworks utilised to develop a detailed picture of the versatile nature of the hotel chains. Each of the theories employs a separate perspective of the firm, using specific terminology and assumptions to illustrate the crossing relationships, information and communication flows, contractual links and evolving problems that enable success, competitiveness, and failures of large multi-unit and multinational companies like hotel chains. In the light of the above theories, hotel chains are presented as complex and compound organisations that need deeper exploration and precise conceptualisation.

The *fluent transfer and exchange of these resources* within the chain is considered a significant part of the internal organisation, as well as a key to protect and maintain the competitive advantage of the chains (Brown et al., 2003; Dev et al., 2007). However, this transfer and exchange is impossible for most of the chain hotels because of the geographical distribution of their properties (Cooper, 2006). Additionally, the intangible product, (i.e. providing accommodation service), restrains the distribution and sharing of tacit knowledge and industry know-how (Erramilli et al., 2002). These problems have been addressed by hotel chains through the establishment of sound internal systems both to facilitate communication and information flows, and to apply efficient *quality management*. The quality control concerns management of tangible and intangible assets, and the service process. In the hotel industry, where services prevail, the main focus is on intangible elements, i.e. service and communication, which are considered crucial for quality perceptions (Crick and Spencer, 2011). The problem with quality control becomes essential for organisations like hotel chains that rely on contractual agreements with hotel members to adhere to the common standards implemented by the chain (Carter and Ragsdale, 2009). Maintaining consistent quality is a balance between the management of human resources (Maxwell et al., 2004; Antony et al., 2004) and setting the proper extent of standardisation (Pullman et al., 2001).

All of the above issues have resulted in building specific attributes that are perceived as the intrinsic features of the hotel chains.

Operating in different markets, hotel chains need to address and adapt to different market characteristics, cultures, legal and other regulations. In addition to their internal complexity, hotel chains have to manage their properties, employees and customers in a multicultural environment. Finding the right balance between preserving their own product features and customisation to the local conditions, implies a shift in the strategic operations management of hotel chains (Jones, 1999). Hence, handling versatile issues within a hotel chain requires multi-competent senior managers (Jones, 1999; Jayawardena, 2000) and a holistic approach towards each of the destinations and properties in the chain.

The *common feature*, as an element, is presented either by the *common brand* (Andrews, 2009; Bhatia, 2006; Brookes, 2007; Ivanova, 2013; STR, n.d.), or as a *concept, theme*, or *feature*, that is valid for all properties in the chain (Jafari, 2000; Peng, 2004). The *brand* is the constituent/ ingredient that makes one group of hotels a chain, i.e. the unique feature, differentiating the hotel chain from its competitors and providing a distinctive flavour, typical only for this group of hotels. The strong brand by itself is considered the best competitive advantage for hotel chains (Bailey and Ball, 2006). Specifically for the hotel industry as service sector, branding is important for reducing the risk to clients and making them loyal (Cai and Hobson, 2004), and at the same time taking a certain position in their minds, becoming easily recognisable and associated with certain characteristics of the product (O'Neill and Xiao, 2006). Nowadays hotel branding is directed more at ensuring experience for the customers, rather than focusing on commoditisation of the product (Fung So and King, 2010). The newly introduced 'lifestyle hotel brands' (Canopy by Hilton, Moxy by Marriott, Ritz Reserve, etc.) emphasise contemporary design, innovative technologies and the personal touch (Jones et al., 2013). Still, they remain clear franchise players (Skinner et al., 2015), although one of their main appeals claims to differentiate from the 'old-fashioned' brands, moving towards a new generation of customers. The brand and its essential role for the hotel chains are examined in detail in a separate chapter of this handbook (see Chapter 18).

Apart from the brand, *similar product, service technology* and *theme* also contribute to building the image of the hotel chain and to creating certain associations in the customer's mind. As service industry firms, hotel chains cannot provide a fully identical product in all of their hotels – the nature of services does not allow for perfect duplication and reproduction (Erramilli et al., 2002). The hotel industry is a service industry with a high human component, influencing the final perception of the product. In order to ensure uniform quality in a multi-unit hotel company like the hotel chain, a system of common rules and regulations should be adopted to predict and control output activities (Sandoff, 2005), i.e. standardisation of services. Hotel chains have introduced the concept of standardisation and have become symbols of its application. Elaboration of uniform standards helps to enable the hotel chains to maintain a consistent level of service (Whitla et al., 2007), thus facilitating both the employees and customers. On the one hand, employees are more easily trained and know how to react in certain situations, whereas on the other, the customers are prepared in their expectations. Although standardisation has its negatives – it is perceived as an emanation of mass tourism used for low-budget products, disregarding the personal characteristics of the customer (Thayer, 1994). The utilised standards and operation manuals serve both as know-how and as a tool for differentiation from the rest of the accommodation establishments. Still, the newest trends show the efforts of the chains to provide a more customised and personalised product – lifestyle, boutique and soft branded hotels, as discussed above.

Another constant element in most of the definitions is the *geographical distribution*. Although hotel chains are addressed as a phenomenon with international/global character, only Brookes (2007) and Contractor and Kundu (1998a) sustain this perception. Many researchers (Jafari, 2000; Andrews, 2009; Ivanova, 2013) recognise that hotel chains are organisations with either domestic/national or international presence. Actually, most of the hotel chains have begun their growth within some national boundaries, and only a few of them could be considered 'born global'. The domestic chains, though, deserve the same attention because they are organisations of the same type, only the scales of operation are within one country. Consequently, the processes, problems and issues, concerning the international hotel chains might be comparable with the ones of the national/domestic chains.

A less frequently discussed feature of the hotel chains appears to be the *centralised management* or certain activities, performed by the headquarters of the chain on a central level. The implementation of such collectively valid actions contributes to the stronger relationships among the properties of the network and their arrangements with the headquarters. Otherwise, only the common brand/feature seems insufficient to unite any group of properties and allows them to be perceived as one entity. The centralised function reflects the common goals shared by all involved hotels. In her definition, Brookes (2007) even specifies on the tasks of the central management: 'developing, operating and supporting' the portfolio of properties. Peng (2004), on the other hand, describes the leading role of the headquarters, naming it 'a system of decision-making', but he also emphasises the 'coherent policies and common strategy' as the crucial link among hotel units. An interesting addition of Peng (2004) appears to be the possibility of more than one decision-making centre within one hotel chain, which could be interpreted in the light of the regional governance, adopted by many of the large hotel chains. The regionalism in a hospitality context facilitates both the operational management of multiple properties and also the product adaptation to local conditions.

Hotel chain expansion and the means by which they increase their hotel portfolio have been a focal point in several studies (Cunill, 2006; Dev et al., 2007; Holverson and Revaz, 2006), dealing with the *different types of affiliation* employed.[1] The array of relationships and engagements between companies spreads over numerous types of affiliations (Anderson and Gatignon, 1986). However, hotel chains usually use only a limited number of them, broadly discussed in the literature (Contractor and Kundu, 1998a; Cunnill, 2006; Chen and Dimou, 2005, etc.). According to the capital involvement of the hotel chain, the entry modes are classified as equity, including full and partial ownership (discussed in Chapter 11 of this Handbook), and non-equity or contractual modes, covering management contract, franchise, leasing and consortium agreement (each of them explored in detail in Chapters 12, 13, 14 and 15). Each of the affiliation types produces different relations and links between the hotel chain headquarters and the members, leading to the identification of different chain types, e.g. 'soft' and 'hard' (Holverson and Revaz, 2006), or corporate and voluntary chains (Dahlstrom et al., 2009). Finding the most appropriate governance mechanism has resulted in delving into the debates on the evaluation of the hotel chain expansion strategies and entry modes used, that predetermine the complex nexus of relationships and contracts existing within each hotel chain.

In the context of existing definitions, Contractor and Kundu (1998a) point out a range of entry modes (franchise, management contract, equity stake/ownership), concluding that all of them may be used by a single chain. Bhatia (2006) mentions only ownership and management contract, while Peng (2004) summarises the possible connection to 'ownership or contractual relationships'. In our search for a definition, we will take a slightly different viewpoint and will place the hotel chain as the main subject, deciding itself what kind of expansion to undertake, depending on its resources, activities and relationships (Ivanova, 2013).

To summarise the above discussion, the typical features, inherent in the hotel chains that make them unique entities, include:

- providing intangible products – service, influencing the whole process of production, marketing and expansion;
- multiunit operation, from which derive a number of issues to be addressed – management of internal information and communication flows, resources and knowledge transfer, operation in multicultural markets;
- common feature – brand, product, concept – serving as a prerequisite for standardisation and differentiation;
- geographical distribution on different levels;
- centralised management, implying elaboration of a common strategy and goals;
- different kinds of expansion, with the non-equity modes dominating.

Finally, we could try to create a working definition of a hotel chain that comprises all of the above discussed ingredients and specific features:

> A hotel chain is a group of hotels, or any accommodation establishments, sharing a common brand and similar concept, implementing at least one centralised function, in order to reach a better market position and improve the performance of all properties. The hotel chains utilise equity and/or non-equity modes for their growth and operate on local, regional, national and/or international level.

If we consider most of the hotel groups as potential chains, then more simplified criteria can be used to identify whether a group of hotels is a chain or not.

A hotel chain is a group of hotels that has:

- a recognizable brand, with a specific message to create a certain association in the customer's mind, in combination with at least one centralised function in the company;
- an analogical product or other common feature (location, event, category – valid especially for the marketing consortia) as a reason for uniting under one brand.

In the light of the above definition a group of hotels is NOT a chain, if:

- hotels are managed by the same company, but are not promoted with its brand;
- hotels belong to the same owner, but are different in terms of product, positioning and target clients and are not operated or marketed under the same brand.

Concluding remarks

The current chapter focused on the role and importance of hotel chains in the hospitality industry. The chapter reviewed previous terms used for these types of accommodations and their scope in internal and multiple markets. Considering the gap in the related literature and interchangeable terms used by different authors and researchers, the chapter proposed a unique definition for this type of accommodation. In this definition, the authors reverse many of the previous viewpoints and place the hotel chain as the focal entity, comprising different elements and controlling resources, activities and relationships within its boundary. The elaborated definition can serve as a basis for future research in this area.

Note

1 For the purpose of this book the term 'way of affiliation' and 'entry mode' will be used as synonyms, interchangeably. The only distinction will be the viewpoint – 'entry mode' implies the position of the hotel chain, whereas 'way of affiliation' is connected with the viewpoint of the individual hotel, incorporated within the hotel chain.

References

Alexander, N. and Lockwood, A. (1996) Internationalisation: a comparison of hotel and retail sectors. *The Service Industries Journal*, 16(4), 458–74.

Alon, I., Liqiang, N. and Wang, Y. (2012) Examining the determinants of hotel chain expansion through international franchising. *International Journal of Hospitality Management*, 31(2), 379–86.

Altinay, L. and Altinay, M. (2003) How will growth be financed by international hotel companies? *International Journal of Contemporary Hospitality Management*, 15(5), 274–83.

Altinay, L. and Miles, S. (2006) International franchising decision-making: an application of stakeholder theory. *The Service Industries Journal*, 26(4), 421–36.

Anderson, E. and Gatignon, H. (1986) Modes of foreign entry: a transaction cost analysis and propositions. *Journal of International Business Studies*, 17(3), 1–26.

Andrews, S. (2009) *Front-Office Training Manual*. 2nd edition, New Delhi: Tata McGraw-Hill.

Antony, J., Antony, F.J. and Ghosh, S. (2004) Research in brief: evaluating service quality in a UK hotel chain: a case study. *International Journal of Contemporary Hospitality Management*, 16(6), 380.

Bailey, R. and Ball, S. (2006) An exploration of the meanings of hotel brand equity. *The Service Industries Journal*, 26(1), 15–38.

Beals, P. and Denton, G. (2005) The current balance of power in North American hotel management contracts. *Journal of Retails and Leisure Property*, 4(2), 129–45.

Bernstein, L. (1999) Luxury and hotel brand. *Cornell Hotel and Restaurant Administration Quarterly*, 40(1), 47–53.

Bhatia, A.K. (2006) *The Business of Tourism: Concepts and Strategies*. New Delhi: Sterling Publishers Ltd.

Big Brand Report (2015) *Hotel News Now*. Online. Available HTTP: <http://www.hotelnewsnow.com/Article/15433/The-2015-Big-Brands-Report>, accessed 14 May 2015.

Brookes, M. (2007) *The design and management of diverse affiliations: an exploratory study of international hotel chains*. (Unpublished doctoral dissertation). The Business School, Oxford Brookes University.

Brown, J.R., Dev, C.S. and Zhou, Z. (2003) Broadening the foreign market entry decision: separating ownership and control. *Journal of International Business Studies*, 34(5), 473–88.

Burges, C., Hampton, A., Price, L. and Roper, A. (1995) International hotel groups: what makes them successful? *International Journal of Contemporary Hospitality Management*, 7(2/3), 74–80.

Cai, L.A. and Hobson, J.S. (2004) Making hotel brands work in a competitive environment. *Journal of Vacation Marketing*, 10(3), 197–208.

Carter, A. and Ragsdale, C. (2009) Quality inspection scheduling for multi-unit service enterprises. *European Journal of Operational Research*, 194(3), 114–26.

Cervino, J. and Bonache, J. (2005) Hotel management in Cuba and the transfer of best practices. *International Journal of Contemporary Hospitality Management*, 17(6), 455–68.

Chen, J.J. and Dimou, I. (2005) Expansion strategy of international hotel firms. *Journal of Business Research*, 58(12), 1730–40.

Contractor, F.J. and Kundu, S.K. (1998a) Modal choice in a world of alliances: analyzing organizational forms in the international hotel sector. *Journal of International Business Studies*, 29(2), 325–57.

Contractor, F.J. and Kundu, S.K. (1998b) Franchising versus company-run operations: modal choice in the global hotel sector. *Journal of International Marketing*, 6(2), 28–53.

Cooper, C. (2006) Knowledge management and tourism. *Annals of Tourism Research*, 33(1), 47–64.

Crick, A. and Spencer, A. (2011) Hospitality quality: new directions and new challenges. *International Journal of Contemporary Hospitality Management*, 23(4), 463–78.

Cunill, O.M. (2006) *Growth Strategies of Hotel Chains: Best Business Practices by Leading Companies*. New York: The Haworth Press.

Dabeva, T. (1998) *Хотелиерство* [Hotel Management]. University of Economics, Varna: University Publishing House.

Dahlstrom, R., Haugland, S., Nygaard, A. and Rokkan, A. (2009) Governance structures in the hotel industry. *Journal of Business Research*, 62, 841–47.

DeRoos, J.A. (2010) Hotel management contracts – past and present. *Cornell Hospitality Quarterly*, 51(1), 68–80.

Dev, C., Brown, J. and Zhou, K.Z. (2007) Global brand expansion: how to select a market entry strategy. *Cornell Hospitality Quarterly*, 48(1), 13–28.

Dev, C., Erramilli, K. and Agarwal, S. (2002) Brands across borders. *Cornell Hotel and Restaurant Administration Quarterly*, 43(6), 91–104.

Erramilli, M.K., Agarwal, S. and Dev, C.S. (2002) Choice between non-equity entry modes: an organizational capability perspective. *Journal of International Business Studies*, 33(2), 223–42.

Fung So, K.K and King, C. (2010) 'When experience matters': building and measuring hotel brand equity: the customers' perspective. *International Journal of Contemporary Hospitality Management*, 22(5), 589–608.

Gee, Ch. (1994) *International Hotels: Development and Management*. Orlando, Florida: The Educational Institute of the American Hotel & Motel Association.

Holverson, S. and Revaz, F. (2006) Perceptions of European independent hoteliers: hard and soft branding choices. *International Journal of Contemporary Hospitality Management*, 18(5), 398–413.

Ivanova, M. (2013) Affiliation to hotel chains as a development opportunity for Bulgarian hotels (in Bulgarian). (Unpublished doctoral dissertation). University of Economics, Varna.

Jafari, J. (ed.) (2000) *Encyclopaedia of Tourism*. London: Routledge.

Jayawardena, Ch. (2000) International hotel manager. *International Journal of Contemporary Hospitality Management*, 12(1), 67–69.

Jones, P. (1999) Multi-unit management in the hospitality industry: a late twentieth century phenomenon. *International Journal of Contemporary Hospitality Management*, 11(4), 155–64.

Jones, D., Day, J. and Quadri-Felitti, D. (2013) Emerging definitions of boutique and lifestyle hotels: a Delphi study. *Journal of Travel and Tourism Marketing*, 30(7), 715–31.

Keller, K.L. (2013) *Strategic Brand Management* (4th ed.). Harlow: Pearson Education Ltd.

Maxwell, G., Watson, S. and Quail, S. (2004) Quality service in the international hotel sector: a catalyst for strategic human resource development? *Journal of European Industrial Training*, 28(2/3/4), 159–82.

O'Neill, J. and Carlbäck, M. (2010) Do brands matter? A comparison of branded and independent hotels' performance during a full economic cycle. *International Journal of Hospitality Management*, 30(3), 515–21.

O'Neill, J. and Mattila, A. (2010) Hotel brand strategy. *Cornell Hospitality Quarterly*, 51(1), 27–34.

O'Neill, J. and Xiao, Q. (2006) The role of brand affiliation in hotel market value. *Cornell Hospitality Quarterly*, 47(3), 210–23.

Panayotis, G. (2014) 2014 Global hotel rankings: the leaders grow stronger; IHG retains top spot. Hotel Online. Available HTTP: <http://www.hotel-online.com/press_releases/release/global-hotel-rankings-the-leaders-grow-stronger-ihg-retains-top-spot>, accessed 14 May 2015.

Peng, W. (2004) *Implementing strategy in hotel chains: An analysis of strategy implementation, action process and content*. (Unpublished doctoral thesis). Caledonian University, Glasgow.

Pullman, M., Verma, R. and Goodale, J. (2001) Service design and operations strategy formulation in multicultural market. *Journal of Operations Management*, 19(2), 239–54.

Sandoff, M. (2005) Customization and standardization in hotels – a paradox or not? *International Journal of Contemporary Hospitality Management*, 17(6), 529–35.

Skinner, M., Bardoul, K. and Berg, P. (2015) *Summary report on lifestyle hotels, soft brand collections and boutique hotels*. The Highland Group. Online. Available HTTP: <http://www.shop.highland-group.net/Lifestyle-Hotels-Soft-Brand-Collections-Boutique-Hotels-Report_c5.htm>, accessed 6 July, 2015.

STR (Smith Travel Research, Inc.) (n.d.) Methodological definition of 'hotel affiliation'. STR Internal Documentation.

Thayer, J.D. (1994) Escaping the chain gang. *The Journal of European Business*, 5(4), 54–58.

Whitla, P., Walters, P. and Davies, H. (2007) Global strategies in the international hotel industry. *International Journal of Hospitality Management*, 26(4), 777–92.

Zhang, H.Q., Guillet, B.D. and Gao, W. (2012) What determines multinational hotel groups' locational investment choice in China? *International Journal of Hospitality Management*, 31(2), 350–59.

2

Economic and marketing fundamentals of hotel chains

Stanislav Ivanov

(VARNA UNIVERSITY OF MANAGEMENT, BULGARIA)

Introduction

Hotel chains are major players in the global hotel market. From both business practice and theoretical perspectives, hotel chains exist as enterprises only if they are more competitive than independent hotels and contribute to increased financial performance of the individual properties that constitute them. If hotels chains are less competitive than individual hotels in attracting guests and generating revenues, and membership in a chain does not lead to improved financial performance of its members, then it does not make economic sense for any independent hotel to be affiliated to a hotel chain. In this regard, this chapter builds on the discussion from Chapter 1 and elaborates the economic and marketing fundamentals that determine the existence and development of hotel chains (Ivanov and Zhechev, 2011), namely:

- brand recognition and significant role of the brand in choice of hotel by guests;
- high sunk costs;
- service standardisation;
- economies of scale;
- economies of scope;
- financial benefits of chain affiliation for the individual hotel surpass the affiliation-related costs

Figure 2.1 depicts the six economic and marketing fundamentals (in italic) and their impact on chains' and individual hotels' revenues, costs and financial performance. The financial performance of the chain and the member hotels depends on the difference between their revenue and costs. The *brand recognition* of the chain leads to decreased perceived risk for the affiliated hotel's customers and its greater market visibility which increase the number of guests, overnights and prices, ultimately resulting in higher revenues for the hotel. The chain incurs expenses to develop and promote its brand, which take the form of *sunk costs* and are one of the barriers to entry into the industry. The individual hotel incurs expenses to be part of the chain, some of which are considered revenues for the chain – franchise/management/

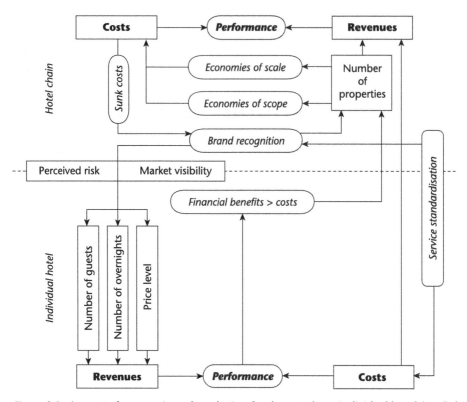

Figure 2.1 Impact of economic and marketing fundamentals on individual hotels' and chains' revenues, costs and financial performance.

membership fees. When *financial benefits from the chain affiliation are greater than the costs associated with it*, the hotel becomes/remains affiliated. When the number of hotels in the chain's network increases, the chain experiences *economies of scale* and *economies of scope* that contribute to cost savings for the chain. Ultimately, the *service standardisation* influences the expenses of the individual member hotel and brand recognition of the chain. Each of these economic and marketing fundamentals is elaborated in detail in the next section of this chapter.

Economic and marketing fundamentals of hotel chains

Brand recognition and significant role of the brand in choice of hotel by guests

The common brand is one of the determining characteristics of hotel chains – hotels in the chain share a common brand which is recognisable by the potential guests (see Chapter 1). Business practice and prior research (Yesawich, 1996) reveal that the brand of the hotel and its popularity play a significant role in customers' choice of a hotel. The chain brand effect on a hotel's financial performance may be evaluated in several directions:

1. *Decreased perceived risk of the choice of a hotel*. Brand familiarity decreases their perceived risk in the decision-making process (Keller, 2013: 436; Lin, 2013), thus when travelling to a new destination many tourists show preferences for the secure choice of chain hotels.

2. *Greater market visibility of the hotel.* The hotel is included in the reservation system of the chain and, through the chain's centralised contracts, in global distribution systems (GDSs) (Amadeus, Sabre, Travelport), online travel agencies (OTAs) (e.g. Booking.com, Travelocity, Expedia), tour operators and travel agents. The hotel is also included in regular marketing communication campaigns of the chain directed towards distributors (push strategy) and direct customers (pull strategy), and in the loyalty programme of the chain. In all cases, these actions lead to greater chances that the hotel is booked by the customers or the distributors.

3. *Increased average daily rate (ADR).* Affiliation to a chain results in a 'brand premium' in the price level of the hotel. Ivanov (2014), in his research about the factors influencing the prices of hotels in Sofia (the capital of Bulgaria), finds that while chain affiliation does not influence weekday prices of the hotels, it has a positive and statistically significant impact on weekend price, i.e. the 'brand premium' has a more tangible effect during periods of low demand.

4. *Increased number of guests.* The chain's brand net impact on the number of guests depends on the balance between the decreased perceived risk and increased market visibility from one side, and the higher price level, from the other. The decreased perceived risk of the guests and increased market visibility of the chain-affiliated hotel improve a hotel's competitiveness and it attracts more guests, while the higher price level makes the hotel less price competitive and dissuades some guests from making a booking at the hotel. Considering that the brand development usually generates more inelastic customer response to price increases and more elastic response to price decreases (Kotler and Keller, 2006: 277), we may say that there is a high probability when a hotel is affiliated to a hotel chain that the effect of the decreased perceived risk and increased market visibility on the number of guests is greater than the effect of the increased price level, and the net impact is increased (although probably only slightly) number of guests.

5. *Increased number of overnights.* This is a result of the larger number of guests staying at the hotel.

The combined effect of the increased number of guests, overnights and price level is the higher level of revenues and improved performance metrics of the chain-affiliated hotel. In recent research, for instance, Enz, Canina and van der Rest (2015) found that chain-affiliated hotels gained higher levels of occupancy and lower RevPAR losses than independent hotels when pricing below competitors. Furthermore, independent hotels were not able to yield as substantial RevPAR gains from pricing at higher levels than their competitors when compared to chain-affiliated hotels. Therefore, affiliation to a chain improves the performance of the hotel compared to its competitors. However, the brand will contribute positively to the financial performance of the hotel if it has a strong, recognisable and positive image among customers and distributors. Therefore, hoteliers have stimuli to affiliate their properties to chains with popular brands and positive image considering their target market segments. When more hotels join the chain, its revenues coming from franchise/management/membership fees increase and the financial performance of the chain improves. As a consequence chains invest heavily in the recognition, image and identity of their brands, which leads us to the second fundamental concept behind hotel chain development – sunk costs.

High sunk costs

Sunk costs are already incurred costs of the firm that are irrecoverable (Carmichael and MacLeod, 2003). Usually they are associated with the marketing and research and development costs (Sutton, 1995: 11). In the field of hotel chains, investments in the development and the improvement of the chain's reservation system and in the brand image are the two most important sunk costs. The image and, less so, the reservation system are unique selling propositions of the chain to its potential members (independent hotels would save costs for designing trustworthy own websites with reliable booking engines and developing a strong image, because the chains have already done so). The more expenses the chains make to strengthen their own image and improve their reservation systems, the higher the financial threshold a new chain needs to overcome to develop a recognisable brand. Therefore, sunk costs may be considered as an entry barrier to the industry because they decrease the potential profits of new entrants (Schmalensee, 2004).

The rise of the OTAs in last two decades partially offsets the importance of the sunk costs for the hotel industry. Until the end of the 1990s, hotel chains were one of the most important pathways to increased market visibility of hotels, alongside GDSs and tour operators, due to their popular brands and online reservation systems. With the exponential growth of the OTAs in recent years, it became easy for the independent hotels to improve their market visibility without the need to join hotel chains. Selling through OTAs also eliminates the necessity for the hotels to adhere to strict chain requirements and service standards that decrease the operational flexibility and independence of the hoteliers. Actually, one might speculate that OTAs serve as substitutes of hotel chains in delivering one of the core benefits sought by hoteliers when they affiliate their properties to chains – the greater market visibility of the hotel. Furthermore, the OTAs' brands, secure reservation systems, convenient payment choices (credit card, PayPal, on-the-spot payment directly to the hotel) and hotel ratings based on customer evaluations, decrease the perceived risk for the customers as well. Therefore, the OTAs may be considered as substitutes of the hotel chains for the customers as well as regarding their decreased perceived risk. However, the OTAs, unlike the hotel chains, do not impose or control the service quality standards of hotels included in their reservation systems, and thus they cannot provide guarantees to their customers regarding the service experience and satisfaction they would receive when staying at the hotels booked via them. On the contrary, some hotel chains, like Hampton Inn, even provide 100 per cent satisfaction guarantees to their guests (http://hamptoninn3.hilton.com/en/about/satisfaction.html) who receive a full refund if not satisfied with the service, which is possible only if the chain has control over the service operations and quality standards applied in the hotel.

Service standardisation

Customers expect to receive the same product quality, regardless of which hotel of the chain they stay at. This is possible only if the chain properties apply the same or similar service procedures, use the same or similar room amenities, etc., i.e. when the hotel service is standardised to a certain degree. Service standardisation means that the chain develops a service operations manual, which stipulates the service delivery procedures to be applied in every member of the chain. Of course, as discussed in Chapter 1, the standardisation aims to provide consistent service among the chain members, but specific service elements and hotel product design might be to a large degree adapted to the local conditions.

In practice, we observe different levels of standardisation – from full description of all service procedures to more general service guidelines depending on the type of affiliation used by the chain. Franchising (Chapter 12), for example, is usually associated with a very high degree of standardisation not only of service delivery process, but the building design as well. At the other extreme, marketing consortia (Chapter 14) are more lax and set mostly general service guidelines which member hotels need to fulfil. The more standardised the service operations, the easier to control the hotel product quality and train new employees, but the more difficult it is to take managerial decisions in situations not elaborated in it. The opposite is also true – less detailed service manuals provide hotel employees with the opportunity to take creative decisions in atypical situations but hinder the training of new employees and service quality control. Therefore, service standardisation should look for an optimal balance between the chain managers' desire for greater control of hotels' operations and service quality and the necessity for flexible managerial decisions by hoteliers depending on the situation. Furthermore, the level of standardisation would depend on the specific market conditions. Hotel chains that operate in one national market could standardise their product and service procedures to a greater extent, compared to chains that operate in markets with diverse economic, social and cultural conditions that need to apply 'glocalisation' strategies and adapt some of their procedures to local situations.

The development of technology has made it possible to standardise and automate the service delivery process to a very high degree. This is especially true for budget hotel chains with limited services. For example, Formula1 hotel chain has standard modular rooms which facilitate the construction of the hotel building, housekeeping and maintenance. Furthermore, the chain transfers the check-in process to the responsibilities of the guest – entry to the hotel room is possible by an access code provided through an 'automatic rooms dispenser' machine (the terminology used by the chain). As an extreme example of standardisation of all physical features and the service processes we may mention the capsule hotels in Japan.

Finally, standardisation of the service process and the hotel product influences the management of human resources in hotel chains. The hotel business is notorious for attempting to cut costs by using a large number of low skilled, part-time and seasonal employees and interns, many of whom have limited knowledge, skills and work experience. In this regard, service standardisation and elaborate service operations manuals facilitate the training of new employees, staff rotation and the implementation of service quality control procedures.

Economies of scale

Economies of scale (the decreased costs per unit as production volume grows) are considered one of the major driving forces behind the development of a hotel chain (Contractor and Kundu, 1998; Holloway, Humphreys and Davidson, 2009: 315). In the field of hotel chains they are a self-nurturing process – the more extensive the chain's network, the more the properties among which it distributes its fixed costs for marketing, administrative personnel, development and maintenance of the reservation system, etc. This decreases the fixed costs of the chain per one member hotel, which are calculated either as an absolute amount of money or as a percentage of the expenses (or revenues) of individual properties in the chain's network. Lower fixed costs per member hotel create conditions for a decrease in the chain affiliation fees leading to its competitive advantage over other chains in attracting individual hotels as members in its network, thus further increasing the number of properties affiliated to the chain. In addition, in the case of contracts for centralised supplies (e.g. linen, toiletries, room furniture, etc.), the greater number of hotels in the chain increases its bargaining power with suppliers due to the higher purchase volume, leading to lower prices for the centralised supplies. Therefore, the chain has economic stimuli to affiliate as many properties to its network as possible.

The economies of scale depend to a great extent on the level of standardisation of the hotel chain's product and the service operations procedures among its members. High level of standardisation implies the use of the same supplies, room amenities, kitchen equipment, hotel facilities, etc., which leads to higher purchase volumes by the chain and lower prices. The necessity to adapt the product to local conditions decreases the purchase volume per item and the opportunities for lower prices.

The importance of the economies of scale has been eroded in recent years by several factors. First, new technologies, like 3D printing for example, allow significant cost savings for many products produced even in extremely small quantities (Petrick and Simpson, 2013), i.e. the chain does not need to purchase very large quantities to receive low prices. Second, in the field of services, customers look for coherent service quality (Clarke, 2000: 27), and not for exactly the same physical features (of the hotel product). Therefore, the chain has to adapt the physical features of its product to local market conditions (e.g. kitchen/restaurant/ room design), which decreases its opportunities to utilise the economies of scale via large volume purchases of the same items. Third, despite the massive introduction of various technologies in hotels (magnet cards for access control, in-room tablets, etc.) that increase the productivity of the hotels, human resources continue to play the major role in the service process, especially in mid- and upscale hotels, and put limits on productivity growth through economies of scale. Moreover, all these technological innovations are available to both independent and chain-affiliated hotels, thus further offsetting any competitive advantages created by the economies of scale for chain-affiliated hotels.

Economies of scope

Economies of scope are cost advantages that stem from the variety of the products that companies produce (Panzar and Willig, 1981). In the context of hotel chains, the economies of scope are derived from the different macro-, micro- and internal environments every hotel in the chain operates in. This provides the chain with the opportunity to 'learn' and develop its operations and service standards in different economic, social and cultural settings. Moreover, the knowledge gained in one market by one hotel could be transferred, under certain conditions, to other hotels in the chain and improve their efficiency, which is not achievable by the independent properties. The knowledge generated by the hotel managers and employees may take two forms – tacit and codified knowledge (Brown et al., 2003; Cooper, 2006). Tacit knowledge is the knowledge gained by hotel managers and employees through their work experience and is not written. Codified knowledge is written and is expressed in the form of service operations manuals, written procedures, internal memos, reports and other documents within the organisation. The codified knowledge is more easily shared among the member hotels than the tacit knowledge as member hotels receive the service operations manuals and various reports from the chain's (regional) headquarters. Tacit knowledge obtained in one hotel is shared with other chain member hotels through various ways: rotation of the managers and other employees among chain members (in the case of affiliation via management contract, full or partial ownership), training sessions on which trainers and trainees share their experience and decisions taken in various situations, formal and informal conversations between managers of member hotels during annual meetings or other special events organised by the chain, etc. Tacit knowledge may be transformed into codified knowledge by including the best practices developed by some member hotels in the chain's service operations manual and making them part of its standard procedures and compulsory for all other chain members. Therefore, by operating in different environments the chain has greater opportunities to learn and improve its services than independent hotels do.

Financial benefits of chain affiliation for the individual hotel surpass the affiliation-related costs

An independent hotel will join a hotel chain only if the financial benefits from the chain affiliation surpass its affiliation-related costs. As already discussed, chain affiliation increases the revenues of the hotel via the chain brand effect (see Figure 2.1). However, affiliation to a chain entails not only higher revenues but expenses as well. For example, hotels need to pay a royalty fee for the use of the brand, management/franchise/membership fee (depending on the type of affiliation contract), use particular types and brands of supplies, that might be more expensive than unbranded ones, have more employees and pay larger insurance premiums to fulfil their chain's requirements, and prepare monthly/quarterly/annual reports, etc., thus leading to higher initial and operational expenses for the affiliated hotel, compared to the independent one. If the financial benefits for the individual hotel from the membership in the chain are higher than the expenses for maintaining the membership, the individual hotel has incentives to be a chain member. This membership will be maintained as long as it is more profitable for the hotel to be affiliated rather than independent. Nevertheless, it is very difficult to measure the role of the chain affiliation in the increase of a hotel's performance metrics (sales, ADR, RevPAR, GOPPAR): Is the higher performance of the hotel a consequence of its sales staff's increased efforts or a result of the greater market visibility and brand recognition of the hotel due to its chain affiliation? When hotels receive bookings from the chain's proprietary reservation system and the distribution channels associated with the chain (i.e. those channels, in which the hotel appears thanks to the affiliation to the chain), their managers and owners see the *direct* contribution of the chain affiliation to the financial performance of the hotel. However, one cannot be definitely sure whether the guest chose the hotel due to the chain's brand and whether they would have selected it if it were independent (Cho, 2005: 132). This uncertainty in the contribution of chain affiliation to the financial performance of the member hotel makes hotel owners and managers quite sensitive towards the fee they have to pay to the chain. Paying franchise/management/membership fees only for the direct contribution of the chain to the financial performance of the hotels, stimulates the chain to improve the financial performance of its members and tangiblises the benefits chain hotels receive from their affiliation to the chain. The marketing consortium Magnuson hotels (http://magnusonworldwide.com/independents/), for example, ties its fees to the actual reservations produced by the chain.

Concluding thoughts

This chapter analysed the economic and marketing fundamentals behind the emergence and development of the hotel chains as business enterprises. We claim that the hotel chains will exist as enterprises if only they are more competitive than independent hotels and contribute to increased financial performance of the individual properties that are part of their network. Our analysis revealed that from managerial perspective, *brand recognition*, *economies of scope* and *financial benefits surpassing the costs of the affiliation* seem to be the most important forces that will continue to support the establishment of new and the expansion of existing hotel chains. Recent technological developments have eroded the importance of *economies of scale* and the *sunk costs* so that we may witness the successful development of small boutique hotel chains with only a few or tens of hotels and with various levels of *service standardisation*. Such chains may be developed either by newly established companies or as new brands of the existing hotel corporations.

References

Brown, J.R., Dev, C.S. and Zhou, Z. (2003) Broadening the foreign market entry mode decisions: separating ownership and control. *Journal of International Business Studies*, 34(5), 473–88.

Carmichael, L. and MacLeod, W.B. (2003) Caring about sunk costs: a behavioural solution to holdup problems with small stakes. *The Journal of Law, Economics & Organization*, 19(1), 106–18.

Cho, M. (2005) Transaction costs influencing international hotel franchise agreements: the case of the Holiday Inn Seoul. *Journal of Vacation Marketing* 11(2), 121–34.

Clarke, G. (2000) *Marketing a Service For Profit. A Practical Guide to Key Service Marketing Concepts*. London and Dover: Kogan Page.

Contractor, F.J. and Kundu, S.K. (1998) Modal choice in a world of alliances: analyzing organizational forms in the international hotel sector. *Journal of International Business Studies*, 29(2), 325–57.

Cooper, C. (2006) Knowledge management and tourism. *Annals of Tourism Research*, 33(1), 47–64.

Enz, C., Canina, L. and van der Rest, J.-P. (2015) Competitive hotel pricing in Europe: an exploration of strategic positioning. *Cornell Hospitality Tools*, 15(2). Online. Available HTTP: <http://scholarship.sha.cornell.edu/cgi/viewcontent.cgi?article=1198&context=chrpubs >, accessed 13 April 2015.

Hampton Inn (2015) 100% satisfaction guarantee. Online. Available HTTP: <http://hamptoninn3.hilton.com/en/about/satisfaction.html>, accessed 7 December 2015.

Holloway, J.C., Humphreys, C. and Davidson, R. (2009) *The Business of Tourism*. Harlow: Pearson Education Ltd.

Ivanov, S. (2014) *Hotel Revenue Management: From Theory to Practice*. Varna: Zangador.

Ivanov, S. and Zhechev, V. (2011) Hotel marketing (in Bulgarian). Varna: Zangador.

Keller, K.L. (2013) *Strategic Brand Management: Building, Measuring, and Managing Brand Equity* (4th ed.). Harlow: Pearson Education.

Kotler, P. and Keller, K.L. (2006) *Marketing Management* (12th ed.). Upper Sadler River, NJ: Pearson Prentice Hall.

Lin, Y.-C. (2013) Evaluation of co-branded hotels in the Taiwanese market: the role of brand familiarity and brand fit. *International Journal of Contemporary Hospitality Management*, 25(3), 346–64.

Panzar, J.C. and Willig, R.D. (1981) Economies of scope. *The American Economic Review*, 71(2), 268–72.

Petrick, I.J. and Simpson, T.W. (2013) 3D printing disrupts manufacturing. How economies of one create new rules of competition. *Research Technology Management*, 56(6), 12–16.

Schmalensee, R. (2004) Sunk costs and antitrust barriers to entry. *The American Economic Review*, 94(2), 471–75.

Sutton, J. (1995) *Sunk Costs and Market Structure: Price Competition, Advertising, and The Evolution of Concentration*. Cambridge: MIT Press.

Yesawich, P.C. (1996) So many brands, so little time. *Lodging Hospitality*, 52(9), 16.

3

Historical evolution
of hotel chains

Prakash K. Chathoth

(AMERICAN UNIVERSITY OF SHARJAH, UAE)

Introduction

Chain organisations have been the mainstay of the international hotel industry over the past several decades while being the benchmark of product and service quality as well as growth and development globally (Nykiel, 2005). Such organisations emerged in the mid-twentieth century with the advent of the airline mode of travel, which led to the emergence of the multiunit hotel organisational form (also known as hotel chains) in the late 1950s and 60s (Kim, 2001). This paved the way for the internationalisation of hotels (Strand, 1996) led by firms such as Holiday Inn, Hilton and the like, who were the leaders in globalising the hotel brand in a post-World War II era.

The growth of multiunit hotel organisations in the international hotel industry led to the standardisation of hotel products and services. Contractual modes such as franchising and management contracts were used by hotel chains as vehicles to grow with standardisation as the basis (Strand, 1996; Chathoth and Olsen, 2003). This was also a result of the operator's ability to manage growth while addressing the consumer's need for consistency in product quality. Hotel chains' growth, primarily based on contractual modes of development, led to agreements or alliances between parties to give rise to a multiunit organisational form with units having similar characteristics (Greve and Baum, 2001).

The evolution of multiunit or chain organisational forms is a topic of relevance and importance especially within the hospitality sector that has historically tracked the emergence and growth of such type of firms. This chapter uncovers the evolution of such organisational forms from a historical perspective including their growth while also focusing on key founders of hotel chains who influenced the scope of development.

The chapter is organised as follows: it first delves into the evolution of hotel chains. This is followed by an in-depth analysis of the history and evolution of such firms, including learning mechanisms and their respective roles in the evolution of such organisational forms. The founders of hotel chains are paid tribute to in a section at the end on the role they played in the growth and development of the industry.

Evolution of hotel chains: an industry perspective

The industry identifies Hilton and Holiday Inn as one of the earliest forms of the hotel chains that came into existence in the 1950s. In the case of Hilton Hotels, the founder Conrad Hilton from Texas, USA, 'decided to build hotels abroad' with a belief that 'Western hoteliers were destined to go wherever jets flew their customers: globalization and the rise of emerging nations have led to a decades-long boom' (Economist, 2013). On the other hand, Holiday Inn focused on the interstate auto traveller (Nykiel, 2005), who was on the lookout for a suitable product during his/her travels. The positioning of the hotel was such that it targeted consumers across multiple consumer market segments. The room rates were reasonable and the amenities and facilities in the rooms were standardised to the extent that they complemented the firm's growth strategy, which enabled it to begin franchising operations in 1954 (IHG, n.d.).

Three phases are integral to the evolution of hotels (Economist, 2013) which in turn have had an impact on the growth and development of hotel chains (see Figure 3.1). The *first phase* was during the time period mid-1900s–1960, described as the '*the age of the grand hotel*' (Economist, 2013). During this period, transportation was mainly through railways and ocean liners with affluent travellers being the primary consumers of hotel products. This led to the development of grand hotels that were primarily independent or a component of a small chain with distinct features and characteristics. Examples ranged from the Waldorf Astoria, New York, the Ritz, Madrid (ibid., 2013), to George V, Paris, and the Savoy Hotel, London.

The *second phase* started in the 1960s (ibid., 2013) which saw the growth of hotels as chains. This started with the rise of multiunit hotels through the internationalisation of hotel chains such as Hilton and Holiday Inn. Later on, chains such as Intercontinental, Marriott, Hyatt and others joined the bandwagon to lead the industry into a phase wherein commodification was the buzzword. Standardisation of hotel amenities and facilities led to the expansion of hotel chains, which meant that employees in different units had to match the brand standards irrespective of consumer tastes. To manage the hotel chain in different geographical regions of the world called for quality standards that were implemented through sets of rules and regulations.

The underlying business model used by hotel chains during the second period was such that the strategic elements of the business were separated from the functional/service elements. The growth of Hilton hotels reflects how the firm was able to centralise the strategic elements of growth and development while dealing with the functional/operating elements at the local level (Strand, 1996). Getting the local owner to take care of the day-to-day operations with supervision from corporate managers meant that the chain could focus on growing the brand globally without having to worry about local connectedness, business practices and cultural norms. Franchising, management contracts, as well as spinoffs (e.g., Marriott) were all products of the growth and development of the industry during this time period (Chathoth and Olsen, 2003; Economist, 2013).

The *third phase* was a product of the gaps that remained unplugged during the *second phase*; primarily, the growing level of detachment between the guest and the hotel. The 1980s saw the inception of the boutique hotel concept leading to the growth of hotels that focused on idiosyncratic needs and wants of customers (Economist, 2013; Aggett, 2007). This started gaining ground in the late 1990s and during the first decade of the new millennium. Hotel chains such as Bvlgari (by Marriott) at the luxury level, 'W' (by Starwood) at the premium/upscale level and Joie de Vivre (a California-based hotel chain) at the mid-market level, to

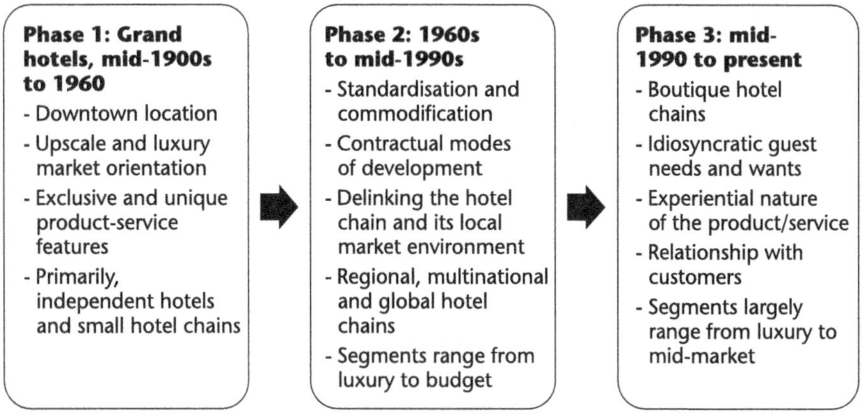

Phase 1: Grand hotels, mid-1900s to 1960	Phase 2: 1960s to mid-1990s	Phase 3: mid-1990 to present
- Downtown location - Upscale and luxury market orientation - Exclusive and unique product-service features - Primarily, independent hotels and small hotel chains	- Standardisation and commodification - Contractual modes of development - Delinking the hotel chain and its local market environment - Regional, multinational and global hotel chains - Segments range from luxury to budget	- Boutique hotel chains - Idiosyncratic guest needs and wants - Experiential nature of the product/service - Relationship with customers - Segments largely range from luxury to mid-market

Figure 3.1 Evolution of hotel chain characteristics.

name a few, emerged that revolutionised hotel chains' orientation towards their markets and individual customers.

No longer were standards maintained to suit the needs of the hotel chain; rather, the focus was on the customer to create unique and memorable experiences (Chathoth et al., 2013). This was also a product of changing times with scholars such as Pine and Gilmore's (1998) 'experience economy' calling for businesses to focus on unique experiences while building relationships with customers.

The growth and evolution of hotel chains detailed above could be attributed to Kim's (2001) view that such firms grew due to the prevalent conditions during the industrial and post-industrial era with the advent of technologies related to transportation and communication. Specialisation led to information asymmetry between the buyer and the seller giving rise to the multiunit firm. Specifically, Kim pointed out that multiunit firms were superior as they were 'better able to solve the problem of asymmetric information than the traditional single-unit firms' (p. 306). He identified a specific characteristic of multiunit organisations that is central to their inception, emergence and growth – these organisational forms used their brand names and size as a 'commitment device, which credibly signalled to buyers that the cost of reneging was significant' (ibid.). This in turn gave them the required economies of scale to benefit from reduced advertising costs. Further, the chain organisational forms arose because they were able to create trust in consumers due to their investments in branding and advertising, which were costs that these firms had to incur to sustain the interests of consumers across various geographic locations (ibid.).

Historical growth of hotel chains

Kim's conceptualisation of the growth of multiunit firms could be extended to the hotel industry. The growth of Holiday Inn and Hilton hotels in the 50s, 60s and 70s could be attributed to the advent of airline travel during the post-Second World War era. The fact that Holiday Inn and Hilton grew at an unprecedented rate during this time period is explained by the quality perception of travellers towards hotels both within and outside the United States. The emergence of chains filled this quality gap that independents could not address. This gap was even more evident in the international hotel industry, as seen in the growth that Hilton witnessed during this period. They were able to grow at an exceptional rate using management-based contractual agreements with no equity participation in the alliance, moving into global locations such as Hungary, Russia and Turkey in a short period of time (Strand, 1996). Through this, they were able to grow their brand, essentially replicating their prototype in various locations. As the chain grew from one to several units, a horizontal relationship between units within the chain was established.

It should be noted that the change in the external environment in terms of technological, socio-cultural and economic factors led to a shift in the strategy of hotel chains (Olsen et al., 1998). In the 60s and 70s, some chains such as Holiday Inn continued with their original strategy by aggressively pursuing growth (USA Today, n.d.), instead of offering multiple products while differentiating and targeting different consumer segments. In the 70s, hotel chains such as the Intercontinental and Hilton targeted the higher end of the market while addressing different needs and wants of consumers. Hotels/motel chains emerged at the lower end such as Days Inn, Ramada Inn, Motel Six and Howard Johnson, which targeted the low-cost consumer. A clear demarcation between hotel market segments in the 70s and 80s (Hill and Jones, 1995) influenced firms such as Intercontinental, Hyatt, Radisson and Howard Johnson to target specific market segments. The demarcations across consumer segments later influenced the hotel product and market characteristics while giving rise to brands. Today, firms such as Marriott International offers 16 hotel brands, all of which are hotel chains themselves. Marriott's strategy lies in the following statement: 'From luxurious resorts to urban retreats, bold boutiques to spacious suites, there's a Marriott® hotel brand as unique as the reasons you travel. The choice is all yours . . . the pleasure is all ours' (Marriott Brands, n.d.).

The literature also provides a basis for understanding the historical evolution of chain affiliations. The success of Holiday Inn through its franchising strategy is well documented. The imperative for growth in the 50s and 60s was largely attributed to the corporate objective of attaining unit growth in terms of numbers (Nykiel, 2005). Location was an essential element of this growth imperative, which complemented the franchising strategy. In this regard, Ingram and Baum (1997) delved into the chain affiliation of hotel units or components in the time period 1890–1980. Using a sample of firms from the Manhattan area, they observed that only 3 per cent of US hotel chains during this time period actually had franchise operations. This was explained by the authors using the rationale from Brickley and Dark (1987) as well as Martin (1988), that franchising was less popular as a vehicle of growth within urban areas 'because of lower costs of monitoring and lower economic risk' (p. 71).

Being part of a chain brings benefits to the incumbents such as survival chances under most circumstances. However, firms such as Holiday Inn, Ramada and other firms at the lower end of the market used the franchising mode of development. Note that management contracts, executed between corporate bodies and their hotel components, grew as a form of contractual arrangement from the 1970s and were made popular by firms such as Hyatt, Hilton, Marriott and the like. The growth of alternative vehicles also resulted because of environmental downturns, which forced corporations to make equity investments in the hotel unit as the unit owners were not willing to take more risk than they needed to. In the franchising mode, the degree of risk exposure tilts in favour of the franchiser, thereby exposing the franchisee to a higher level of risk (Chathoth and Olsen, 2003).

External factors that led to the growth and development of the hotel industry, specifically chain organisations, include population trends, travel, transportation, evolution of people's lifestyle in society, a shift in consumer needs, wants and tastes, technological developments as well as globalisation (Nykiel, 2005). These forces led to evolutionary mechanisms that were strategic initiatives on the part of hotel corporations. As a result, management strategies evolved, which as per Nykiel (2005) ranged from geographic expansion (e.g. Ramada), product branding (e.g. Marriott) and ownership (e.g. Four Seasons), to franchising (e.g. Holiday Inn); brand collection (e.g. Cendant) and management contracts (e.g. Hyatt Hotels).

Today, the leading hotel chains are global firms with units spread across several continents and countries. A list of top ten hotel chains as of 2013/2014 is included in Table 3.1.

Table 3.1 Ranking of hotel chains

Ranking order	Name	No. of hotels	Brands	Description
1	InterContinental Hotels (IHG)	4800	• InterContinental Hotels & Resorts • HUALUXE Hotels and Resorts • Crowne Plaza Hotels & Resorts • Hotel Indigo • EVEN Hotels • Holiday Inn Hotels & Resorts • Holiday Inn Express • Staybridge Suites Hotels • Candlewood Suites Hotels	IHG has 'Great Hotels Guests Love' comprising nine hotel brands and over 710,295 rooms in about 100 countries. It has established itself as one of the largest lodging firms with the acquisition of Holiday Inn Hotels and Resorts and other chains such as Staybridge Suites and Candlewood Suites (IHG, n.d.).
2	Hilton Worldwide	4200	• Waldorf Astoria Hotels & Resorts • Conrad Hotels & Resorts • Canopy • Hilton Hotels & Resorts • Curio • Doubletree • Embassy Suites • Hilton Garden Inn • Hampton • Homewood Suites • Home 2 Suits • Hilton Grand Vacations	The hotel chain has more than 4200 lodging units, resorts and timeshare properties comprising more than 690,000 rooms in 93 countries (hiltonworldwide.com). The hotel chain has been operating for over 100 years with 12 world class brands at present ranging from full service to limited service hotels (Hilton Worldwide, n.d.).
3	Marriott International	3900	• Bvlgari Hotels & Resorts • The Ritz-Carlton • JW Marriott • EDITION • Autograph Collection • Renaissance • AC Hotels by Marriott • MOXY HOTELS • Marriott • Courtyard by Marriott • SpringHill Suites • Fairfield Inn & Suites	Marriott International, Inc. has more than 3900 properties, 16 brands, and over 80 years of company history. From the opening of the Twin Bridges Marriott Motor Hotel in 1957 to the introduction of the company's first Fairfield Inn and Marriott Suite hotel in 1987, the hotel company has grown to a global hotel chain.

(Continued)

Table 3.1 (Continued)

Ranking order	Name	No. of hotels	Brands	Description
			• Residence Inn by Marriott • TownePlace Suites by Marriott • Marriott Executive Apartments • Gaylord Hotels & Resorts	In 1993, Marriott International, Inc. and Host Marriott Corporations were created through a spin off, following which it acquired the Ritz Carlton Hotel in 1995 (fully acquired by 1999). During this time, in 1997, Marriott added the Renaissance Hotel Group, Towne Place Suites, Fairfield Inn & Suites and Marriott Executive Residences brands to its collection. In the following decade, the firm added SpringHill Suites, the ExecuStay corporate lodging, the Bvlgari Hotels & Resorts, the EDITION brand, the Autograph Collection, and AC Hotels (Marriott, n.d.).
4	Wyndham Hotel Group	7410	• Wyndham Hotels and Resorts • Wyndham Grand Hotels and Resorts • Wyndham Garden Hotels • TRYP by Wyndham • Wingate by Wyndham • Hawthom Suites by Wyndham • Microtel Inn & Suites by Wyndham • Ramada Worldwide	As one of the world's biggest hospitality organisations, it offers leisure and business clients a wide array of accommodation through its main portfolio of famous brands. With more than 55 brands, it has established itself in major markets in the United States and other countries worldwide (Wyndham Worldwide, n.d.).
5	Choice Hotels	6300	• Comfort Inn • Comfort Suites • Quality • Sleep Inn • Clarion • Cambria Suites • MainStay Suites • Suburban • Econo Lodge • Rodeway Inn • Member hotel • Ascend Collection	Choice Hotels International is one of the biggest hotel organisations worldwide. Choice at present franchises more than 6300 hotels and has more than 500,000 rooms in more than 35 countries. Ranging from limited to full service hotels in the economy, mid-scale and upscale segments, Choice-marked properties

Ranking order	Name	No. of hotels	Brands	Description
				give business and recreation tourists a range of experiences from high-esteem to limited service accommodation globally (Choice Hotels, n.d.).
6	Accor	3700	• Sofitel Hotels • Pullman Hotels • MGallery collection • Grand Mercure Hotels • Novotel Hotels • Suite Novotel Hotels • Mercure Hotels • Ibis Hotels • Ibis Styles Hotels • Ibis Budget Hotels • See F1 Hotels • Thalassa sea & spa Hotels • Adagio Hotels • Adagio access aparthotels • Orbis Hotels • The Sebel Hotels	Accor is one of the well-established hotel groups with units located across 92 countries globally. It has more than 3700 hotels and 480,000 rooms. It has 170,000 employees and has been in existence over the past 45 years (Accor, n.d.).
7	Starwood Hotels and Resorts	1200	• St. Regis • The Luxury Collection • W Hotels • Le Meridien • Westin • Sheraton • Aloft • Element • Four Points • SPG Starwood Preferred Guest	Starwood Hotels & Resorts Worldwide, Inc. has more than 1200 properties in over 100 countries. Starwood is a completely incorporated holder, administrator and franchiser of lodgings, resorts and residences with globally recognised hotel brands (Starwood Hotels, n.d.).
8	Best Western	4000	• Best Western • Best Western Plus • Best Western Premier	Best Western International, Inc. has more than 4000 hotels in over 100 countries around the world. Each of its lodging units is owned by individuals, which means there's somebody there to take care of the business and create value for it and for its customer (Best Western, n.d.).

(Continued)

Table 3.1 (Continued)

Ranking order	Name	No. of hotels	Brands	Description
9	Home Inns	2496	• Home Inn • Motel 168 • Yitel • Fairyland Hotel	Home Inns Group was established in 2002 with the objective of providing a comfortable hotel experience to its target audience in China. With reasonable prices and quality accommodation for business and leisure travellers, Home Inns' Motto is: 'Wherever you go, you're always at home.' (Home Inns, n.d.).
10	Carlson	1350	• Quorvus Collection • Radisson RED • Country Inn & Suites • Radisson BLU • Park Plaza	Carlson is one of the biggest privately held organisations, with more than 1350 lodging units in more than 105 countries. Carlson Wagonlit Travel, a subsidiary, is a worldwide pioneer in business travel administration, is in more than 150 countries (Carlson, n.d.).

Sources from which information on hotel chains were retrieved include: Hilton Worldwide (n.d.); Marriott International (n.d.); Best Western (n.d.); Choice Hotels (n.d.); Home Inns (n.d.); AccorHotels Group (n.d.); InterContinental Hotels Group (n.d.); Wyndham Worldwide (n.d.); Starwood Hotels & Resorts (n.d.); Holiday Inn (n.d.); Carlson-Rezidor Hotel Group (n.d.).

Note: The ranking of hotels was compiled from a consensus of multiple sources including Top 10 Largest Hotel Chains in the World 2014 – Listovative (2014), Hospitality Net: World Ranking 2013 of Hotel Groups and Brands (2013), and 2014 Global Hotel Rankings: The Leaders Grow Stronger from hotelon-line.com; IHG Retains Top Spot. (2014).

Historical learning mechanisms and the evolution of hotel chains

According to Greve and Baum (2001), learning in multiunit organisations was 'distinctive because the different parts of the organisation have different experiences' (p. 7). In fact, Ingram and Baum (2001) stated that learning is at the crux of the motivation for 'commensals' to enter into a relationship. Whereas affiliated units were able to learn from each other's experiences, Greve and Baum pointed out that the degree to which they were able to share such experiences depended on the organisation–environment interface as well as how effectively management was able to integrate and disseminate such experiences within the organisation as a whole. The authors further pointed out that the issue multiunit firms faced was whether or not to centralise or decentralise the learning process. An optimal solution called for a good balance between the two with flexibility as the basis for the organisation to manoeuvre through various environmental interfaces. Note that this had a major influence in the growth and development of chain organisational forms within and across international markets for hotels such as Hilton, Hyatt, Marriott and the like.

Ingram and Baum (2001) provided the rationale for the creation of chain organisational forms, suggesting that those firms that lacked their own operating experience were the ones that sought a chain affiliation. In fact, they pointed to a 'competency trap' in multiunit firms while explicating that firms with little operating experience and firms with plenty of it both sought chain affiliations. Firms that 'fall into the competency trap' (p. 112), according to Ingram and Baum, were the ones that accumulated so much experience that they no longer saw the value of new procedures and norms brought about through innovation. Rather, they continued to use their past experience in moving forward in a world that was constantly changing around them.

Ingram and Baum (2001) further elaborated on the concept that local experience of a hotel's unit or component was more valuable to the chain than non-local experience. Using historical information on Manhattan hotels, USA, as an example, they posited that components were less likely to dissolve their relationship with a chain given their high level of local experience. Contrarily, components that had a high level of non-local experience were more likely to dissolve their relationship with chains given that 'non-local experience degrades performance' (Audia et al., 2001: 98).

Moreover, there was a considerable level of learning that took place between components in a chain relationship through the transfer of operating experience among them set up by 'the ownership, incentive and control structures of chain relationships' in hotels (Ingram and Baum, 2001: 111). Research in this domain further established the fact that transfer learning took place at higher levels when there was a common ownership structure among firms within chain organisations as compared to independently owned organisations (Banaszak-Holl et al., 2006).

In other words, from an evolutionary perspective, the highest level of transfer learning among hotels took place when an ownership form of structure was used followed by a management contract and franchising-based contractual agreements, respectively. To benefit from scale economies, historically, standardisation was pursued by chain organisations while creating a perception of quality and reliability among customers. Through this, they were able to leverage resources and optimise on costs while at the same time increasing the level of accountability arising from standards set across units (Banaszak-Holl et al., 2003). Citing Baum (1999), the authors pointed out that 'reliability and accountability reduce customer search and monitoring costs' (p. 4), which in turn increased the value of units or components in being a part of the network of hotel organisations.

The level of learning and the impact of multiunit firms are further exemplified in the case of Hilton that was the first hotel company to introduce a multi-hotel reservations system, the Inter-Hilton Hotel Reservation System, on August 15, 1948 (Hilton Global Media, n.d.). This was the beginning of the modern day reservation system, which was a result of learning and exchange that took place between the individual units and the corporate office leading to the development of systems and processes. These learning mechanisms later led to the creation of the central reservation office in 1955 and, subsequently, the centralised reservation system HILTRON through computerised technology in 1973, followed by HILSTAR in 1999 (Hilton Global Media, n.d.).

In 1949, the effect of evolutionary learning was further exemplified by Hilton when it adapted 'business and industrial methods of hotel operations' for developing a pre-costing system. This top-down adaption process was established through a chain-to-component learning and implementation mechanism followed by component-to-component learning interfaces 'when the system was adopted in the Stevens Hotel (now Hilton Chicago) in Chicago and extended to The Palmer House Hilton and other units of the Hilton group, revolutionizing both the hotel and restaurant industries' (Hilton Global Media, n.d.). These systems were subsequently used for the growth of the firm to international locations through the inception of Hilton International in 1949. The evolutionary learning mechanisms exemplified here reflect how multiunit firms or chain organisational forms are able to learn from their units or components using bottom-up mechanisms as well as how the units are able to adopt state-of-art systems through a top-down learning approach from the corporate office. As a result, these firms are able to evolve into superior organisational forms over a period of time. A major underlying factor in the inception, growth and development of hotel chains was the people who founded them; some of them are profiled in the following section.

Prominent founders of hotel chains

The growth and development of hotel chains are attributable to the entrepreneurs who founded them. Some of these founders revolutionised the development of the hotel industry in that they were able to influence the direction of evolution of their chains and the industry as a whole. One such exemplar lies in the establishment of Hilton Hotels Corp. by Conrad Hilton (1887–1979), who became a successful hotelier after the First World War, when he purchased several properties in Texas during its oil boom. In 1919, he bought the Mobley Hotel in Cisco, Texas, following which, in 1925, he built the Hilton Hotel in Dallas, Texas. His acquisitions during and after the Second World War included the 3000-room Stevens Hotel (now the Chicago Hilton) and the Palmer House in Chicago and the Plaza and Waldorf Astoria in New York City. In 1946, he formed the Hilton Hotels Corporation and, in 1948, he formed the Hilton International Company, which came to number more than 125 hotels. With the purchase of the Statler chain in 1954, Hilton created the first major chain of modern American hotels – that is, a group of hotels that follow standard operating procedures in marketing, reservations, quality of service, food and beverage operations, housekeeping and accounting.

Unlike Conrad Hilton, Cesar Ritz was a hotelier who, as an operator of the Grand National Hotel in Lucerne, managed the property. His management skills and vision enabled him to rise from a hotel operator to one of the most celebrated hoteliers from Europe. Two hoteliers, who emerged from the United States with equal prominence were William Waldorf Astor and John Jacob Astor IV. In 1893, William Waldorf launched the 13-story Waldorf Hotel at Fifth Avenue near Thirty-Fourth Street in New York City. Waldorf Astor's vision was to create a unique hotel that combined the qualities of a European mansion with those of a 'homey' private residence. William Waldorf Astor and his cousin, John Jacob Astor IV, who erected their respective hotels on adjacent sites, decided to combine their hotels four years later. This was achieved by connecting The Waldorf hotel to the 17-story Astoria Hotel through a corridor and the hotel became known to the world as the Waldorf-Astoria. After successfully running the hotel for over 30 years, in 1929, the hotel had to close its doors to give way to the Empire State Building. The hotel was rebuilt as a 2200-room, 42-floor Waldorf-Astoria Hotel at Park and Lexington avenues between Forty-ninth and Fiftieth streets where it currently stands. Later, the hotel changed hands when Conrad N. Hilton acquired the hotel in 1949. Renovations followed in 1988 when the hotel underwent a $150 million restoration. It was designated a New York City landmark in January 1993.

During the early 1950s, as chain organisations started to grow across various industries, Kemmons Wilson started Holiday Inn through the inception of its first hotel in Memphis,

Tennessee. His main objective was to build a hotel chain for families who travelled on high-ways in the United States. Later on, he expanded his target audience to include the business traveller (Holiday Inn, n.d.). Wilson combined his skills as an entrepreneur and as a hotel manager while emphasising innovations in building construction and amenities at the same time. He also brought about changes in hotel development through the introduction of the franchising concept supported through innovations in the reservation systems such as the Holidex central reservation system in the mid-1960s (Holiday Inn, n.d.). He left behind a legacy that aimed at making lodging facilities affordable and comfortable for the travelling public, but these units were able to generate profits for the investor at the same time.

While the Holiday Inn was in its early period of growth in the 1950s, J.W. Marriott (1900–1985) founded the Twin Bridges Marriott Motor Hotel in Virginia, near Washington, D.C., in 1957. Marriott Hotels and Resorts developed the Courtyard by Marriott hotel brand that was unique in that it was developed by the business traveller, for the business traveller. The chain also owned the American Resorts Group in the mid-1980s at the time of J.W. Marriott's death. It was at this time when J.W. Marriott Jr. acquired the Howard Johnson Company, which he later sold to Prime Motor Inns while retaining 68 turnpike units. The hotel chain also focused on its operating system, particularly its Worldwide Reservation Center, which was set up in 1987 in Omaha, Nebraska, making it the largest single-site reservations operation in US hotel history. In the same year, Marriott entered the economy segment while acquiring the Residence Inn Company, an all-suite hotel chain targeted at extended-stay travellers, opening the first Fairfield Inn in Atlanta, Georgia, in 1987 (Marriott, n.d.).

The 1900s saw another hotel chain grow into a global company, which was founded by Ernest Henderson and Robert Moore in 1937. The chain known as the Sheraton, came into existence when the owners acquired their first hotel, the Stonehaven, in Springfield, Massachusetts. The chain expanded from Massachusetts (Boston) to Maine and Florida at such a pace that at the end of its first decade, it received the unique status of being the first hotel chain to be listed on the New York Stock Exchange. Sheraton was later acquired by ITT Corporation in 1968 as a wholly owned subsidiary, and in the 1980s, under the leadership of John Kapioltas, Sheraton's Chairman, President and CEO at the time, it went on receive global recognition as an industry leader in offering modern accommodation and facilities. The chain was later acquired by Starwood Hotels & Resorts Worldwide.

Ray Schultz was another prominent hotelier to emerge in the late 1900s who founded the Hampton Inn hotels in the early 1980s. As part of the Hilton Hotels Corporation, these hotels were positioned as limited-service, targeting the needs of the cost-conscious business and leisure traveller. By 1998, the chain had grown to over 800 hotels. The focus on these market segments made Schultz's contribution to the international hotel industry that much more substantial. Even today, Hampton Inn remains as a benchmark for measuring the quality standards for all mid-priced, limited-service hotel brands.

Other hoteliers emerged in the Eastern and Western contexts that led to the growth, development and internationalisation of the hotel industry. Their contributions led to the growth of different types of hotels ranging from luxury to budget hotels as well as from standardised to boutique forms. Even though it is beyond the scope of this chapter to delve into the contribution of each entrepreneur/hotelier, a brief elucidation of a major hotel design that revolutionised the architecture of hotels is warranted. Particularly, the atrium concept by Hyatt hotels came into prominence through the efforts of its owner Thomas Pritzker in the 1960s when the design was showcased in its Atlanta based unit. The hotel architect John Portman introduced the concept and its uniqueness lay in the architectural design that included guest rooms overlooking the lobby from the first floor upwards to the roof. The magnificence of the Atlanta property is in the impressive atrium and the design of the rooms located on 21 stories overlooking the lobby. The advent of such concepts led hotels to become an architectural marvel with the introduction of contemporary design that aimed at balancing excitement, fun, relaxation and entertainment. Upscale hotel design was revolutionised with Hyatt's atrium concept, which was replicated in various locations as the hotel chain grew across various cities within and outside the United States. Today, exemplars of hotel design are seen in upscale hotels and resorts, particularly boutique hotel chains ranging from luxury chains such as Bvlgari (a Marriott managed property) W Hotel (a Starwood hotel brand) to Joie De Vivre, which is largely a mid-priced hotel chain. Such designs cut across various product-market segments seen in the case of hotel chains such as the Formule One (an Accor hotel brand), which introduced a unique motel concept that combined technology, efficiency and quality to target a traveller in suburban (highway) locations. Needless to say, hotel architectural designs will continue to develop given the evolution of technology.

Summary

This chapter identified the evolution of chain organisational forms in the hotel industry. The historical growth of such organisational forms were described as driven by macro and micro environmental factors, which in turn impacted the evolution of such organisational forms. The nature of evolution was also identified and attributed to some of the underlying factors such as competitive factors and organisational learning. Evolutionary dynamics played its part in the historical development of the hotel industry which contributed to the growth of such organisations leading to globalisation. Learning led to transfer of knowledge from the firm's environment to its units through top-down and bottom-up approaches. Learning also resulted from component-to-component transfer mechanisms driven by technology-based systems and processes. The hotel chain founders who were instrumental in changing the landscape of the industry played a pivotal role in expanding its horizons and the scale and scope of the business with the advent of the multiunit hotel. Today, hotel chains have evolved to focus on branding while addressing the consumer's idiosyncratic needs with specific emphasis on experiential attributes.

References

AccorHotels Group (n.d.) Online. Available HTTP: <http://www.accorhotels-group.com/en/group.html>, retrieved 10 March, 2015.

Aggett, M. (2007) What has influenced growth in the UK's boutique hotel sector? *International Journal of Contemporary Hospitality Management*, 19(2), 169–77.

Audia, P.G., Sorenson, O. and Hage, J. (2001) Tradeoffs in the organisation of production: multiunit firms, geographic dispersion and organisational learning. In J.A.C. Baum and H. Greve (eds), *Multiunit Organisations and Multimarket Strategy: Advances in Strategic Management*, 18, 75–105. Oxford, UK: JAI Press.

Banaszak-Holl, J., Mitchell, W., Baum, J.A.C. and Berta. W.B. (2006) Transfer learning in ongoing and newly acquired components of multiunit chains: U.S. nursing homes, 1991–1997. *Industrial and Corporate Change* 15, 41–75.

Baum, J.A.C. (1999) The rise of chain nursing homes in Ontario, 1971–1996. *Social Forces*, 78, 543–84.

Best Western. (n.d.) Online. Available HTTP: <http://www.bestwestern.com/>, retrieved 10 March, 2015.

Brickley, J.A. and Dark, F.H. (1987) The choice of organisational form: the case of franchising. *Journal of Financial Economics*, 18, 401–20.

Carlson-Rezidor Hotel Group (n.d.) Online. Available HTTP: <http://www.carlson-rezidor.com/>, retrieved March 10, 2015.

Chathoth, P.K. and Olsen, M.D. (2003) Strategic alliances: a hospitality industry perspective. *International Journal of Hospitality Management*, 22, 419–34.

Chathoth, P.K., Altinay, L., Harrington, R., Okumus, F. and Chan, E. (2013) Co-production versus co-creation: a process based continuum in the hotel service context. *International Journal of Hospitality Management* 32(1), 11–20.

Choice Hotels (n.d.) Online. Available HTTP: <http://www.choicehotels.com/>, retrieved 10 March, 2015.

Economist, The (2013). Be my guest: a short history of hotels. *The Economist*. Online. Available HTTP: <http://www.economist.com/news/christmas-specials/21591743-be-my-guest>, published 21 December 2013.

Greve, R. and Baum, J. (2001) Introduction to multiunit, multimarket world. In J.A.C. Baum, and H. Greve (eds.), *Multiunit Organisations and Multimarket Strategy: Advances in Strategic Management*, 18, 1–28. Oxford, UK: JAI Press.

Hill, J.W. and Jones, G. (1995), *Strategic Management Theory: An Integrated Approach*, 3rd ed. Boston: Houghton-Mifflin.

Hilton Global Media (n.d.) Hilton history. Online. Available HTTP: <http://hiltonglobalmediacenter.com/index.cfm/page/29>, retrieved 7 October 2014.

Hilton Worldwide (n.d.) About Hilton Worldwide. Online. Available HTTP: <http://www.hiltonworldwide.com/about/>, retrieved 10 March, 2015.

Home Inns (n.d.) Online. Available HTTP: <http://english.homeinns.com/phoenix.zhtml?c=203641&p=irol-IRHome>, retrieved 10 March, 2015.

Hospitality Net (2013) World ranking 2013 of hotel groups and brands (2013, April, 03). Online. Available HTTP: <http://www.hospitalitynet.org/news/4060119.html>, retrieved 10 March, 2015.

Hotel Online (2014) 2014 Global hotel rankings: the leaders grow stronger; IHG retains top spot. Hotel Online, 23 June, 2014. Online. Available HTTP: <http://www.hotel-online.com/press_releases/release/global-hotel-rankings-the-leaders-grow-stronger-ihg-retains-top-spot>, accessed 10 March 2015.

InterContinental Hotels Group (IHG) (n.d.) Online. Available HTTP: <http://www.entrepreneur.com/franchises/ihgintercontinentalhotelsgroup/282428-0.html>, retrieved 8 March 2015.

Ingram, P., and Baum, J. (1997) Chain affiliation and failure of Manhattan hotels, 1898 to 1980. *Administrative Science Quarterly*, 42, 68–102.

Ingram, P. and Baum, J. (2001) Interorganisational learning and dynamics of chain relationships. In J.A.C. Baum, and H. Greve (eds), *Multiunit Organisations and Multimarket Strategy: Advances in Strategic Management*, 18, 109–39. Oxford, UK: JAI Press.

InterContinental Hotels Group. (n.d.) Online. Available HTTP: <http://www.ihgplc.com/>, retrieved 10 March, 2015.

Kim, S. (2001) Markets and multiunit firms from an American historical perspective. In J. Baum and H. Greve (eds), *Multiunit Organisations and Multimarket Strategy: Advances in Strategic Management*, 18, 305–26. Oxford, UK: JAI Press.

Listovative (2014) Top 10 largest hotel chains in the world 2014. Listovative, November 18. Online. Available HTTP: <http://listovative.com/top-10-largest-hotel-chains-in-the-world/>, retrieved 10 March, 2015.

Marriott Brands (n.d.). Online. Available HTTP: <http://www.marriott.com/marriott-brands.mi>, retrieved 31 March, 2015.

Marriott International (n.d.) About Marriott International: find your world. Online. Available HTTP: <https://www.marriott.com/marriott/aboutmarriott.mi>, retrieved 10 March, 2015.

Martin, R.E. (1988). Franchising and risk management. *American Economic Review* 78, 954–68.

Nykiel, R.A. (2005). *Hospitality Management Strategies*. New Jersey: Prentice Hall.

Olsen, M.D., Tse, E.C-Y. and West, J. (1998) *Strategic Management in the Hospitality Industry*, 2nd ed. New York: Wiley.

Wyndham Worldwide (n.d.) Our company. Online. Available HTTP: <http://www.wyndhamworldwide.com/about-wyndham-worldwide/our-company>, retrieved 10 March, 2015.

Pine, J.B. and Gilmore, J.H. (1998) Welcome to the experience economy. *Harvard Business Review*, 76(4), 1–9.

Starwood Hotels & Resorts. (n.d.) Online. Available HTTP: <http://www.starwoodhotels.com/>, retrieved 10 March, 2015.

Strand, C.R. (1996) Lessons of a life time: the development of Hilton International. *Cornell Hotel and Restaurant Quarterly*, 37, 83–95.

USA Today (n.d.) The history of Holiday Inn hotels. Online. Available HTTP: <http://traveltips.usatoday.com/history-holiday-inn-hotels-61884.html>, retrieved 27 March, 2015.

4

Geographical distribution of hotel chains

Ákos Kátay and Tamara Rátz

(KODOLÁNYI JÁNOS UNIVERSITY OF APPLIED SCIENCES, BUDAPEST – SZÉKESFEHÉRVÁR, HUNGARY)

Introduction

This chapter presents the main characteristics of the geographical distribution of hotel chains worldwide. In order to analyse the geographical distribution of international hotel chains, the database of STR Global (2014) was used. Consequently, the overall assessment is based on the state of the hotel industry in 2013, although certain major changes of the year 2014 have been added in order to provide a comprehensive picture. As indicators, the number of properties was used to illustrate the operational presence of a hotel chain and a corporation owning hotel chains in a given area, while the number of rooms was utilised to represent a chain's or corporation's size.

Geographical units were defined on the basis of regions and subregions delineated by UNWTO (2014), but with certain modifications, in order to provide an adequately detailed spatial analysis. Sub-Saharan Africa was divided into four subregions and the Mediterranean-Southern European region into two separate subregions, taking into consideration the complexity of cultural and physical geographical factors. Consequently, the following geographical division was applied in the study:

- Africa (North Africa, West Africa, Central Africa, East Africa, Southern Africa)
- Americas (North America, Caribbean, Central America, South America)
- East Asia and the Pacific (North-East Asia, South-East Asia, Oceania, South Asia)
- Europe (Central/Eastern Europe, Northern Europe, Southern Europe, East Mediterranean Europe, Western Europe)
- Middle East

Since the current state of the global hotel industry is affected by changes over time, it is necessary to take temporal changes into consideration, despite the predominantly geographical nature of this analysis. As the historical evaluation of hotels chains is discussed in Chapter 3 of this book, this study presents an overview of the geographical distribution of hotel chains in 2013, looking back at the major changes shaping this industry over the previous six years (i.e. pre-crisis, mid-crisis and post-crisis).

In order to illustrate the magnitude of hotel chain supply in a given area, both the number of properties and the number of rooms are provided for each region and subregion. The list of the top 10 hotel chains on a global level was created using the number of rooms of hotel corporations in the year 2013 as a quantitative size indicator (STR Global 2014). According to this indicator, the top 10 global hotel corporations are the following, in alphabetical order: Accor Company (Accor), Best Western International (BW), Carlson Rezidor Hotel Group (Carlson), Choice Hotels International (Choice), Hilton Worldwide (Hilton), Home Inns Group,[1] Intercontinental Hotels Group (IHG), Marriott International (Marriott), Starwood Hotels & Resorts (Starwood) and Wyndham Worldwide.

The different hotel chains belonging to hotel corporations use various classification systems and quality categories to define and differentiate their position, based on the value represented by the chain and the expectations of their target customer groups. These quality descriptors were grouped into three major categories, in order to enable the presentation of the chains' geographical distribution in a relatively straightforward manner:

- Luxury-upscale: luxury, upper-upscale, upscale, full service, premiere, premium, elegant, exclusive, boutique, high-personality, 5-star, 4-star, 5-diamond, 4-diamond[2]
- Midscale: upper-midscale, midscale, mid-priced, extended stay, moderate, upper moderate, selected service, comfortable, casual, with F&B, plus, 3-star, 3-diamond
- Economy: economy, budget, basic, without F&B, inn, motel, 2-star, 1-star, 2-diamond, 1-diamond.

While the market presence of hotel chains in the global, regional, subregional and country-level hotel supply was assessed using the number of properties, the significance (weight) of presence was measured on the basis of their fair share (market share based on the number of rooms available) (Ransley and Ingram, 2012).

Global characteristics of the hotel industry

As a result of continuous development, in 2013 the supply of the global hotel industry has reached almost 160,000 hotels (159,969) and 15 million hotel rooms (14,889,073). However, the rate of growth has slowed down in recent years, both in terms of new establishments and new rooms (see Table 4.1). On a global level, due to a 3 per cent growth compared to 2007, currently more than half of the world's hotel rooms belong to a chain, as indicated by a fair share value of 51.9 per cent (concerning the number of hotel establishments, chain hotels represent 37.8 per cent of the global supply). The top 10 hotel corporations account for 58.6 per cent of the international hotel room supply, with an approximately equal share of the luxury-upscale (20.1 per cent), midscale (18.8 per cent) and economy (19.7 per cent) categories. Among the global hotel chains that operate in all the five main geographical

Table 4.1 Rate of growth in the global hotel industry

	2009/2007	*2011/2009*	*2013/2011*
Number of hotels	+4.0%	+2.6%	+2.5%
Number of hotel rooms	+6.0%	+4.0%	+2.5%

Source: STR Global (2014).

regions, the following three offer more than 200,000 rooms in 2013 (in decreasing order): Holiday Inn, Holiday Inn Express and Best Western.

Africa

In 2013, the hotel supply of the Africa region included 3251 hotels with a room capacity of 321,933. Hotel chains operated 22.5 per cent of the hotels and 33.8 per cent of the rooms. Consequently, the average size of the 732 chain hotel establishments (149 rooms) significantly exceeded the average size of independent hotel units (85 rooms). Neither of the major hotel chains are present in the following countries: Angola, Burundi, the Central African Republic, Comoros, the Democratic Republic of the Congo, Eritrea, Liberia, Niger, Somalia and the British Overseas Territory of Saint Helena. Accor has the highest market share in the region: its seven chains offered 75 hotels with 11,393 rooms (42 per cent in economy category, 29.8 per cent in midscale and 28.2 per cent in luxury-upscale). Among the top 10 global hotel corporations, only Choice is not present in the region. Within the total hotel supply of Africa, the luxury-upscale hotel chains of the top 10 global hotel corporations account for 17.5 per cent of the market fair share, midscale chains for 6.9 per cent and economy chains for 7.5 per cent. The highest number of rooms (9388) is offered by the regionally active Protea hotel group.

The development of the African hotel industry is affected by a wide range of factors. An undersupply of quality hotels due to historic reasons, combined with increasing intraregional demand, improved travel infrastructure and strong GDP growth in the Sub-Saharan region all contribute to encouraging investments by international hotel chains that aim to expand their geographical footprint on the continent (Atkins, 2011, W Hospitality Group, 2014), despite the negative influences of political instability, particularly in North Africa. Although global hotel corporations follow different market entry strategies, common denominators include opening new properties in capital cities and emerging business hubs, and offering economy establishments to the developing domestic markets.

North Africa

Hotel chains are present in all the four countries (Algeria, Morocco, Sudan, Tunisia) of the subregion. In 2013, the hotel supply of the area consists of 807 hotels (138,671 rooms). Hotel chains accounted for 17.8 per cent of all the hotel properties, with 23.5 per cent fair share. Among the top 10 global companies, Choice and IHG are not present in the subregion, while the rest of the leading corporations operate 14 chains with 60 hotels and 10,886 rooms in the area. Their supply represents 33.2 per cent of the hotel chains' room capacity, the majority belonging to the luxury-upscale category, thus contributing to a quality improvement in the subregion's overall hotel industry product. Accor has the largest market share with 43 hotels (6588 rooms), 36.8 per cent of which are in the luxury-upscale category and 48.4 per cent in the budget category. Within Accor's portfolio of hotel chains, Ibis is the most active one in the North African market, operating 21 properties with 2827 rooms. Among other hotel chains present in the subregion, Golden Tulip, Iberostar and RIU are dominant: the three chains together offer 10,909 rooms in the luxury-upscale category. The largest chain in the area, in terms of room capacity, is RIU Hotels of Riu Hotels & Resorts Corporation (4765 rooms).

West Africa

Based on the data of STR Global (2014), hotel chains are not present in two countries of the subregion (Niger and Sierra Leone), while no information is available for Liberia and Saint Helena. The hotel supply has been increasing continuously since the base year of 2007, although with a steadily decreasing growth rate, reaching a total capacity of 534 hotels and 36,827 hotel rooms by the end of the evaluated period. An interesting feature of the subregion's hotel industry is that both in Guinea and in Guinea-Bissau one hotel chain operates one single property – Novotel and Azali Hotels, respectively. Within the subregion, hotel chains account for less than 15 per cent of the hotels and one third of the rooms. Significant development has taken place in Nigeria where hotel chains have registered more than 50 per cent growth between 2007 and 2013, increasing their total capacity to 36 units and 2343 rooms. The number of hotel properties is less than 10 in every other country of the area, and only slight changes have occurred. Among the global hotel corporations, Accor has the highest market presence in terms of hotels, with 22 per cent of the hotels and 21 per cent of the room capacity. Among the top 10, Choice and Marriott International are not present in the West African market, while the seven remaining corporations operate 17 chains and 38 hotels, offering 6253 rooms and representing 52 per cent of the room capacity of hotel chains in the subregion. More than half of these rooms belong to the luxury-upscale category, one quarter to midscale, and 19 per cent to economy. The subregion's largest room capacity is offered by RIU, with 1750 rooms in the luxury-upscale segment.

Central Africa

According to the database of STR Global (2014), no hotel chains operate in three countries of the subregion (Angola, Congo and the Democratic Republic of Congo), while no information is available for the Central African Republic. The area's hotel industry is underdeveloped, consisting of only 32 properties and 2012 rooms in 2013. Hotel chains occupy approximately 40 per cent of the market (with a 40.6 per cent market presence and 43.7 per cent fair share). Six hotel corporations operate in the subregion with eight hotel chains, among which the 484 rooms of the Le Meridien's (Starwood) luxury upscale full-service hotels account for the largest fair share. Among the top 10 global corporations, only Accor (three chains and six hotels), Hilton Worldwide (one and two) and Starwood (one and three) are present in Central Africa, predominantly with their flagship luxury-upscale brands (Hilton, Kempinski, Le Meridien, Sofitel), offering 1782 rooms and representing 88.5 per cent of the total hotel chain supply of the subregion.

East Africa

Based on the data of STR Global (2014), hotel chains are not present in three of the subregion's 18 countries (Burundi, Comoros and Eritrea), while no information is available for Somalia. The area's hotel industry has been growing by 2–4 per cent annually between 2007 and 2013, reaching an overall capacity of 945 hotels and 66,610 rooms by the end of the period. The absolute growth of hotel chains (+55 properties) has exceeded that of independent hotels (+33 properties), but the market presence of hotel chains has still remained under 20 per cent, although their fair share has grown to 28.2 per cent, due to the significantly higher than average size of chain establishments (105 rooms/hotel as opposed to 70 rooms/hotel on average in the area's overall hotel supply). The Serena Group, consisting of luxury resorts, safari lodges and hotels, has the largest market presence and fair share, with 23 properties and 1954 rooms. Among the top 10 global corporations, Choice, Marriott International and Wyndham Worldwide are not present in the area, while the rest of the companies operate 16 hotel chains, 33 hotels and 5740 rooms (31 per cent of the total room capacity of hotel chains in East Africa), among which 71 per cent belong to the luxury-upscale category.

Southern Africa

The overall hotel capacity of the continuously growing subregion is 933 hotels and 75,325 rooms in 2013 (STR Global, 2014), with hotel chains present in every country. Hotel chains account for 35 per cent of the total number of establishments and 55.9 per cent of the room

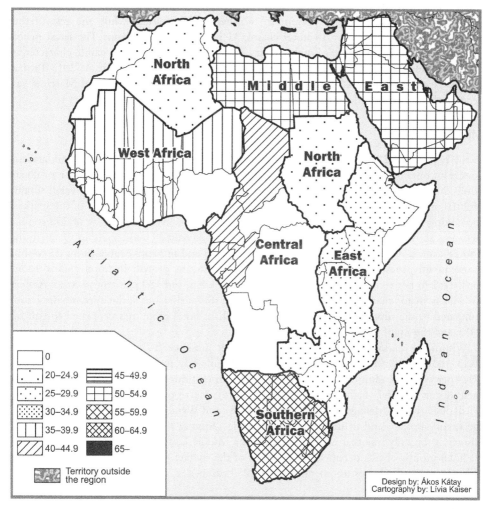

Figure 4.1   Hotel chains' share in the total room capacity of Africa and the Middle East (2013) (per cent).

Source: Authors' calculations based on data provided by STR Global (2014).

capacity of the area, indicating a relatively stable market presence and a slightly decreasing fair share during the assessed period (38 per cent in 2007, 35 per cent in 2013). However, major changes have taken place within the hotel portfolio of the subregion, particularly in South Africa. Accor's Formule1 chain, which operated 23 hotels and 1613 rooms in 2007, was taken over by the Tsogo Sun Hotel Group and rebranded as Sun. This move, together with additional development at the company's other chains (Garden Court, Southern Sun and Stay Easy) resulted in a capacity increase of more than 2700 rooms, predominantly in the economy and midscale categories. Significant expansion was also achieved by the City Lodge Hotels Group, adding 1,400 midscale and economy rooms to their City Lodge, Town Lodge and Road Lodge chains. Further capacity development was realised by IHG, with Holiday Inn opening 400 rooms and Holiday Inn Express 865 rooms, strengthening the corporation's presence in the economy segment. Among the subregion's hotel groups, Tsogo Sun Hotels has the highest market presence in 2013, with 23 per cent of chain hotel properties and 28 per cent of room capacity. Among the top 10 global corporations, Choice and Wyndham Worldwide are not present in Southern Africa either, while the rest of the companies are represented by 14 hotel chains, 31 hotels and 5701 rooms. The latest major development in the subregion's hotel industry, which also illustrates its dynamic character, is the Protea Hospitality Group's takeover by Marriott International: while in 2013 Protea was the largest Southern African chain with 7812 rooms, with the acquisition Marriott has become the largest hotel company in Africa (Marriott International, 2014).

Middle East

In the region, hotel chains are present in every country (although the STR Global database does not contain information on Palestine, further search confirmed the presence of chain hotels there as well). The dynamic growth of the hotel industry has led to an overall supply of 2010 units in 2013, with 394,547 rooms. Hotel chains occupy 40 per cent of the market, accounting for a 51.5 per cent fair share, due to their above average unit size of 252 rooms. Between 2007 and 2013, the number of hotel chains increased considerably in Qatar (from 8 to 28), in the United Arab Emirates (from 59 to 86) and in Saudi Arabia (from 25 to 42). Consequently, these countries also registered a significant growth in hotel chains' room capacity: 296 per cent in Qatar, 212 per cent in the UAE, and 180 per cent in Saudi Arabia. An equally major change took place in Syria during this period, but in the opposite direction: compared to the supply of 2007, the number of chain hotel properties decreased to half by 2013, and the number of rooms to one third.

Within the region, IHG has the largest market presence (9.3 per cent) and fair share (10.3 per cent), with five chains operating predominantly in the luxury-upscale category (71.4 per cent). In addition, the following hotel corporations offer more than 10,000 rooms each: Accor (7 hotel chains), Hilton Worldwide (6), Marriott International (7), Mövenpick (1), Rotana Hotel Management (4), Starwood (8) and Wyndham Worldwide (6), mostly in the luxury-upscale and in the midscale categories. Among the top 10 global corporations, Choice is the only one that is not present in the Middle Eastern region. The remaining top 10 hotel groups' chains occupy 43.7 per cent of the market (fair share 46.8 per cent), with Hilton owning the largest room capacity (12,257 rooms).

Americas

In 2013, 69,945 hotels were present in the region, with a room capacity of 6,331,458. Hotel chains represent 48.9 per cent of the total supply of hotel properties and 63.2 per cent of the hotel rooms. Altogether, the 37,178 chain hotels offer 3,503,145 rooms, which means that similarly to other regions, the average size of chain hotel units (117 rooms) exceeds that of independent hotels (65 rooms on average). Within the region, the following countries and territories have not been conquered by international hotel chains yet: Bonaire, Dominica, Saba, Saint Vincent, Montserrat, Greenland, Saint Pierre and Miquelon, the Falkland Islands and Guyana. Concerning the major corporations' market shares, Hilton Worldwide is the regional market leader, with 11 chains operating 3624 properties and offering 543,514 rooms, predominantly in the luxury-upscale category (58.2 per cent of the corporation's American supply). Due to the Americas region's significance in global tourism, it is not surprising that more than half (53.5 per cent) of the top 10 hotel corporations' room capacity is located in this area. The structural composition of this supply indicates a strong presence of the top 10 companies in the more affordable segment: economy category top 10 chains have a 28.1 per cent fair share in the American market, while the same indicator is 16.6 per cent in the luxury-upscale segment and 8.8 per cent in the midscale category. The hotel chain with the largest room capacity in the region is Holiday Inn Express, with 174,400 rooms.

North America

The continuous development of the subregion's hotel industry during the assessed period led to an overall capacity of 63,875 properties and 5,701,995 rooms in 2013. Concerning the number of establishments, hotel chains occupied 51.5 per cent of the market (with a 65.8 per cent fair share), which seems to indicate a slight increase (1.1 per cent) compared to 2007, although the absolute growth of the sector consisted of 4220 new chain hotels and 450,566 new rooms. Within the subregion, based on the data of STR Global (2014), no hotel chains operate in Greenland, and no data is available for Saint Pierre and Miquelon. The geographical analysis of the hotel chains' room capacity indicates an unequal distribution among the USA (90.6 per cent), Canada (5.7 per cent) and Mexico (3.7 per cent). The top 10 global hotel corporations operate more than 75 per cent of the hotel chains supply, with Hilton Worldwide enjoying the largest share of the chain room capacity (14.4 per cent). More than 100,000 rooms are offered in North America by the following hotel chains: Best Western, Comfort Inn, Days Inn, Courtyard, Holiday Inn, Holiday Inn Express, Hampton Inn, Hilton, Marriott, Motel 6, Quality Inn; their total capacity amounts to 1,341,694 rooms, with 17.7 per cent belonging to the luxury-upscale category, 25.7 per cent to midscale and 56.6 per cent to economy. The single largest chain in the subregion is the Holiday Inn Express of IHG, offering 171,700 rooms.

Caribbean

Due to stable growth within the assessed period, the subregion's hotel supply grew to 1888 properties and 225,891 rooms by 2013. Based on the STR Global (2014) database, no hotel chains are present in Curaçao and in the special municipalities of Bonaire and Saba, while in Grenada, the first hotels chains – the Radisson and the Sandals – opened in 2013. Within the subregion, hotel chains occupy 14.6 per cent of the market, with a significantly higher (41.3 per cent) fair share, due to their considerably higher than average property size (340 rooms/hotel). Two thirds of the total chain hotel capacity of 93,364 rooms are concentrated in the following three areas: the Dominican Republic, Cuba and Puerto Rico. One third of these 61,002 rooms are operated by seven chains of three Spanish corporations, Meliá Hotels International, Iberostar Hotels & Resorts and Riu Hotels & Resorts. The latter group also has a significant share in the Jamaican market (27.5 per cent), while the Meliá chain of Meliá Hotels International represents 18.2 per cent of the chain room capacity of the Bahamas. Their practice illustrates well the traditional objective of Conrad Hilton, according to which a Hilton hotel should be a 'little America' (Boorstin, 1992: 98), and, in the case of these hotels, a 'little Spain'. Among the seven chains, Sol Hotels & Resorts and Meliá Hotels & Resorts offer midscale rooms, while the rest of the chains belong to the luxury-upscale category, with 21,222 rooms. Meliá Hotels International has the largest market presence in the subregion, representing 10.9 per cent of chain hotel properties and 14 per cent of chain rooms. The top 10 global corporations' overall Caribbean capacity includes 102 establishments and 24,413 rooms, predominantly (78.4 per cent) in the luxury-upscale segment. In this subregion, the fair share of the top 10 hotel groups is lower (26.1 per cent) than their market presence (37 per cent), which is explained by their relatively small unit size (239 rooms) in a market where certain other hotel chains, such as the Occidental, the Palladium, the Sandals and the Meliá Hotels International, operate large-scale properties with 400–700 rooms. The largest supply among the Caribbean subregion's hotel chains belongs to RIU Hotels (7104 rooms).

Central America

The subregion's hotel industry developed significantly between 2007 and 2013, due to the expansion of hotel chains, which are present in every country in Central America (the number of properties grew by almost 50 per cent, while room capacity increased by 82 per cent). As a result, in 2013 hotel chains offer 25,737 rooms in 137 hotels, with a 15.2 per cent market presence and 46 per cent fair share. IHG has the largest market share, offering 4292 rooms in 24 hotels, mainly in the luxury-upscale category (66 per cent), but also in the economy segment (33 per cent). Indicating a similar trend, the 113 units (16,295 rooms) operated by the top 10 global hotel corporations also predominantly (76.8 per cent) belong to the luxury-upscale group, complemented by 1689 rooms offered by the originally Spanish Barceló Hotels & Resorts, and 2529 rooms provided by RIU. A unique component of the subregion's hotel industry is the Hard Rock Hotel group's 1200 room property in Panama. Similarly to the Caribbean, the largest supply among the Central American subregion's hotel chains is offered by RIU Hotels (2529 rooms).

South America

According to the STR Global (2014) database, hotel chains are not present in Guyana since 2011, while no data are available concerning the Falkland Islands. The subregion's hotel industry experienced continuous growth in the assessed period, resulting in 3278 properties and 347,574 rooms by 2013. Hotel chains occupy 38.2 per cent of the South American market (fair share 26.8 per cent), with considerable differences among countries concerning the supply's spatial distribution and market trends. The hotel industry of Bolivia, Ecuador, French Guiana, Paraguay, Uruguay and Venezuela is stagnating or decreasing, while Argentina, Colombia and particularly Brazil enjoy significant expansion: more than 80 per cent of hotel chain investments and acquisitions have taken place in these three countries. Accor has the largest market share in the subregion, with 11 chains offering 33,293 rooms in 214 hotels, mainly in the economy (50.6 per cent) and the midscale (43.9 per cent) category. The largest hotel chain of South America is the Ibis of Accor (13,819 rooms), which also has the highest fair share in the hotel chain market (10.1 per cent). The top 10 global corporations account

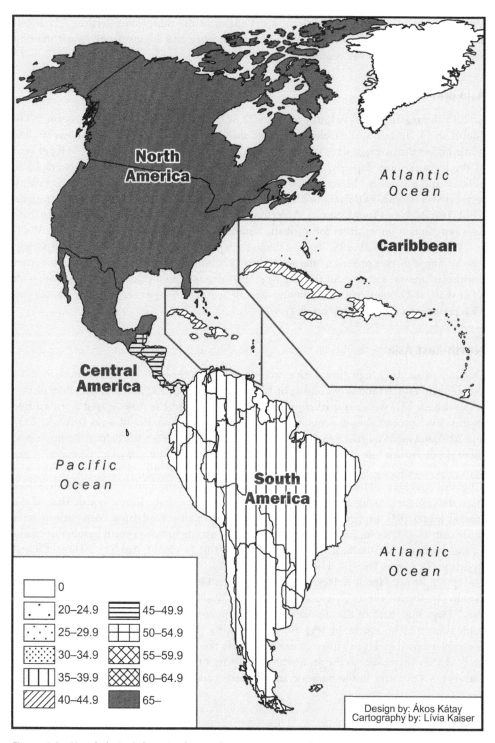

Figure 4.2 Hotel chains' share in the total room capacity of the Americas (2013) (per cent).

Source: Authors' calculations based on data provided by STR Global (2014).

for 61.5 per cent of the total supply of hotel chains in the subregion operating 531 hotels and 81,659 rooms (29 per cent in the midscale category, and approximately equal share of the luxury-upscale and the economy segments).

Asia and the Pacific

In 2013 the region's hotel industry includes 22,527 properties with 3,224,863 rooms (STR Global, 2014). In terms of establishments, the share of chains is 42.4 per cent; however, due to the higher than average size (165 rooms/unit) of chain hotels, they represent 48.8 per cent of the region's room capacity. As a consequence of the area's highly diverse geographical, political and economic characteristics, hotel chains have not appeared yet in the hospitality sector of several states of the region (the DPRK, Solomon Islands, Marshall Islands, Micronesia, Cook Islands, Niue, Tonga, Samoa, American Samoa and Timor-Leste), while the database does not contain information for Kiribati, Nauru, Pitcairn, Tokelau, Tuvalu, as well as Wallis and Futuna Islands. Within the region, despite operating only in China, Home Inns Group has the largest market presence, offering 120,946 economy category rooms in 949 properties distributed among 4 chains. All the top 10 global corporations are active in the region, with a fair share of 17.3 per cent in the luxury-upscale segment, 6.2 per cent in the midscale and 15.8 per cent in the economy category.

North-East Asia

Due to a particularly high growth rate exceeding 30 per cent in the assessed period, by 2013 the subregion's hotel industry consists of 13,252 properties (2,320,329 rooms). Hotel chains, which have a 53.7 per cent market presence and 52 per cent fair share, played a crucial role in this development, almost doubling (+91.5 per cent) the number of units between 2007 and 2013, and increasing their room capacity by 69.7 per cent. However, behind the impressive subregional growth rate there is one dominant and fast developing market, China: 97.4 per cent of the new chain hotels opened in the country. Not surprisingly, among the top 10 global companies, Home Inns Group is the most significant market player in North-East Asia, though the Jinjang Holding's four chains' overall capacity almost equals that of the market leader (845 properties, 108,217 rooms). Although several large corporations offer more than 10,000 rooms in the area, their portfolios mainly include a small number of chains in the economy and midscale categories: 7 Days Inn (1 chain), Apa (1), Beijing Capital Tourism (2), Green Tree (1), Huazhu Hotels Group (3), JAL Hotels Company (2), Jinling Group (2), Prince Hotels & Resorts (3), Shangri-La Hotels (2), Sunroute (1), Tokyu Hotels Group (4), Toyoko Inn (1), Vienna Hotel (1) and Washington Hotel (1). Within this group, the 7 Days Inn chain of the similarly named corporation offers the largest capacity in the subregion: 97,956 rooms in 984 hotels in China. The area's luxury-upscale segment is complemented by Hyatt's three chains with more than 14,000 rooms. All the top 10 global corporations are present in the area, with a fair share of 15.8 per cent in the luxury-upscale category, 4.4 per cent in the midscale and 17.6 per cent in the economy segment.

South-East Asia

As a consequence of a stable and balanced growth, the hotel industry of the subregion comprises 4,120 establishments with 594,979 rooms in 2013 (STR Global, 2014). During the assessed period hotel chains' investments and acquisitions resulted in a 36.8 per cent market presence (4.2 per cent growth compared to 2007) and 24.6 per cent fair share (+5.1 per cent). It should be noted though that the independent hotel sector also grew at a remarkable rate (9.6 per cent growth in the number of properties, 14 per cent in room capacity). Concerning the room supply of chain hotels, Vietnam experienced the highest increase rate (84 per cent), while in nominal terms Indonesia registered the largest growth (+20,034 rooms), although Thailand enjoyed almost similar development (101 new properties with 19,568 rooms). The average size of chain hotels shows a decreasing tendency in the period (from 233 to 216 rooms/hotel), while an opposite trend might be observed at independent hotels (from 116 to 121 rooms/hotel). Accor occupies the largest market share in the subregion: its 10 chains operate 143 properties with 32,642 rooms, predominantly in the midscale (41.6 per cent) and the luxury-upscale (32.6 per cent) categories. The area's luxury-upscale supply is boosted by Shangri-La Hotels' two chains with 10,236 rooms. All the top 10 global corporations are present in the area, with a fair share of 23.7 per cent in the luxury-upscale segment, 10.6 per cent in the midscale and 7.7 per cent in the economy category. The largest room capacity (5555) in the subregion is offered by the Aston International chain of Archipelago International.

Oceania (Australasia, Melanesia, Micronesia, Polynesia)

As a result of a steady development throughout the 2007–2013 period, the subregion's hotel industry includes 5128 properties with 309,555 rooms. However, hotel chains are only present in 10 countries out of 24, and both their market presence (27.6 per cent) and their fair share (48 per cent) decreased slightly during the assessed period. Nevertheless, despite a fall in property numbers (–12 units), the hotel chains' room capacity increased (+7,945 rooms). Due to the geographical and economic diversity of the subregion, three distinct development paths may be identified in the hotel chain sector: moderate (Vanuatu and Guam) and significant decline (Papua New Guinea, Northern Mariana Islands and Palau), stagnation in New Caledonia and French Polynesia, but considerable growth in Australia and New Zealand (+8,675 rooms). Accor has the largest market share in this subregion as well: its 13 chains operate 212 properties with 29,632 rooms, predominantly in the midscale (45.7 per cent) and the luxury-upscale (29.4 per cent) segments. The Mantra Hotel Group's overall capacity, divided among three chains, exceeds 10,000 rooms (106 properties, 11,156). Similarly to the previous Asian subregions, all the top 10 global corporations are present in this area, with a fair share of 19.5 per cent in the luxury-upscale segment, 14.8 per cent in the midscale and 13.8 per cent in the economy category. The largest room capacity (8516) in the subregion belongs to the Quest Serviced Apartments chain of the similarly named company.

South Asia

Within the subregion, Iran is the only destination without hotel chains. Between 2007 and 2013, the number of properties grew by 13.7 per cent to 3552 units, while the room capacity increased by 28.2 per cent to 240,134 rooms. Hotel chains contributed to this development by 293 new establishments and 42,842 rooms, thus achieving a 23.8 per cent market presence (847 hotels) and 41.7 per cent fair share (average hotel size: 118 rooms/unit). The growth was concentrated in two destinations: in the Maldives the number of chains almost doubled (25), while the number of properties (34) and rooms (3341) increased by about 50 per cent, resulting in a 27.2 per cent fair share. India experienced an even more significant change, both in absolute and relative terms: the number of chains grew from 82 to 116, leading to

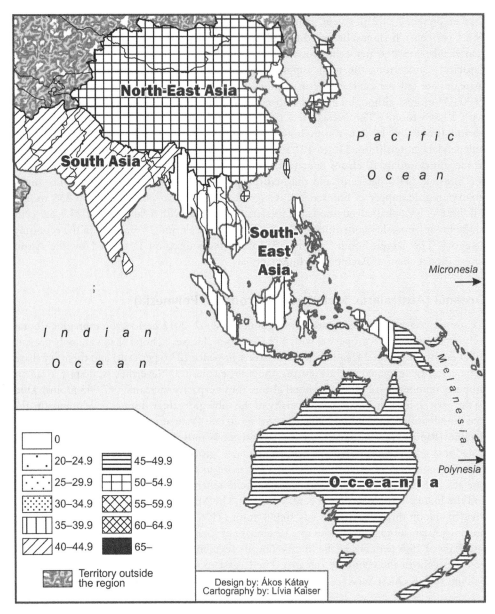

Figure 4.3 Hotel chains' share in the total room capacity of Asia and the Pacific (2013) (per cent).

Source: Authors' calculations based on data provided by STR Global (2014).

759 hotels and 88,260 rooms in 2013 (fair share: 43.9 per cent). The Indian Hotels Company has the largest market share in the subregion: its four chains operate 114 properties with 13,352 rooms, nearly two-thirds belonging to the luxury-upscale category. The global top 10 group is represented by 268 establishments and 39,404 rooms, predominantly in the luxury-upscale (60 per cent), but also in the midscale (27 per cent) segment. Altogether, hotel

chains' fair share amounts to 23.8 per cent at the highest quality level, 10.6 per cent in the midscale and 5 per cent in the economy category. The single largest hotel chain is the Taj Group of The Indian Hotels Company, with 4517 rooms.

Europe

In 2013, the European hotel industry consisted of 58,711 properties and 4,376,138 rooms, with hotel chains being present in almost every country (with the exception of Bosnia and Herzegovina, the Faroe Islands, the Holy See, Liechtenstein and Turkmenistan) (STR Global, 2014). During the assessed period, an opposing trend might be observed between hotel chains and independent hotels: while the growth rate of the latter group seemed to slow down year by year, hotel chains increased their room capacity at a continuously growing rate, adding 60,000 new rooms by 2011 and an additional 72,000 by 2013. Consequently, 60.8 per cent of the region's room capacity increase might be attributed to the development of hotel chains. The average room size of chain hotels (121 rooms/unit) considerably exceeds that of independent hotels (60 rooms), resulting in a 24.5 per cent market share of properties and 39.7 per cent of room capacity. Accor is the market leader on the European continent as well, operating 2460 hotels in 14 chains, with 271,788 rooms. Accor's largest chain is Ibis, offering 77,472 rooms in 23 countries; however, the region's highest room capacity belongs to Best Western (78,538 rooms). All the top 10 global corporations are present in this area, with a fair share of 15.8 per cent in the luxury-upscale segment, 15.8 per cent in the midscale and 13.8 per cent in the economy category.

Central/Eastern Europe

The subregion's hotel supply is relatively underdeveloped, comprising 4967 properties with 439,173 rooms in 2013, although it was growing continuously in the analysed period. Market penetration of hotel chains is relatively low, occupying 16.2 per cent of the market, with a significantly higher 30.3 per cent fair share, due to the larger than average unit size of chain hotels. 77 per cent of the sector's growth was concentrated in three destinations, Poland, Russia and Ukraine, while the majority of the subregion's countries stagnated, with the exception of Estonia where the supply of hotel chains decreased by almost 1,000 rooms, mainly due to independent acquisitions. Accor has the largest market share in the subregion: its 9 chains operate 112 hotels with 20,931 rooms, predominantly in the midscale (65.1 per cent) and the economy (34.4 per cent) segments. Of the area's chain room supply, 59.9 per cent belongs to the global top 10 corporations, mainly in the luxury-upscale (24.7 per cent) and the midscale (25.4 per cent) categories. The single largest hotel chain is the Radisson Blu of Carlson, with 9506 rooms in 14 countries. As the current characteristics of the sector indicate, the subregion has a high potential for expansion, with non-equity entry modes (such as franchise and management contracts) being considered the most suitable ones for international chains (Ivanova and Ivanov, 2014).

East Mediterranean Europe

In 2013, the total hotel capacity of the subregion consists of 2363 properties and 339,748 rooms, with hotel chains registering a 14.3 per cent market presence and a slightly higher (20.6 per cent) fair share. The three countries of the area followed two different paths between 2007 and 2013: Israel and Cyprus experienced a pattern of growth and decline, while Turkey developed significantly, adding 69 hotels (14,027 rooms) to the subregion's overall supply. Hilton Worldwide has the highest market share, offering 27 hotels in 5 chains with 7148 rooms, almost exclusively in the luxury-upscale category. With the exception of Choice, almost all the top 10 corporations are present in the area, accounting for 42.4 per cent of the chains' room capacity, mainly in the luxury-upscale (30.3 per cent) segment, with a small (3.5 per cent) share in the economy category. The largest single hotel chain of the area is Rixos Hotels (4606 rooms) in Turkey.

Southern Europe

As a result of moderate growth rate not exceeding 5 per cent, the area's hotel capacity comprises 15,226 establishments and 1,345,145 rooms in 2013. Since hotel chains only generated 15 per cent of this development (adding 20 new hotels properties to the overall supply), their performance may be considered to be stagnating. None of the countries experienced significant changes during the analysed period: the largest expansion took place in Spain (five new hotels with 4139 rooms), with the smallest in San Marino, where an independent hotel with 91 rooms joined Best Western in 2010, thus forming the total chain hotel capacity of the microstate. In contrast, the Holiday Inn chain of IHG moved out of Bosnia and Herzegovina in 2011; since then, no hotel chains are present in the country. Altogether, hotel chains occupy 16.7 per cent of the Southern European market, with a fair share of 29 per cent. Meliá Hotels International occupies the largest market share in the subregion: its 6 chains operate 113 properties with 32,854 rooms, divided between the midscale (52 per cent) and the luxury-upscale (48 per cent) segments. Three companies' capacity exceeds 10,000 rooms: Iberostar Hotels & Resorts (1 chain), NH Hotel Group (3) and Riu Hotels & Resorts (2). All the top 10 global corporations are present in the area, with a fair share of 26.5 per cent in the luxury-upscale category, 7.1 per cent in the midscale and 5.4 per cent in the economy segment. The largest room capacity (13,956) in the subregion is offered by Sol Hotels & Resorts of Meliá.

Western Europe

As a consequence of continuous and spatially balanced growth, the subregion's hotel sector includes 24,178 hotels offering 1,420,873 rooms in 2013. Hotel chains are present in almost every country (Liechtenstein being the only exception), occupying 26.6 per cent of the market with a significantly higher fair share of 47 per cent, explained by the considerable difference between chain hotels' and independent properties' average size (104 vs. 42 rooms). Hotel chains added more than 500 new establishments (52,003 rooms) during the analysed period, accounting for two thirds of the area's total room capacity increase. Germany proved to be the most dynamically growing destination, followed by the Netherlands and France: the three countries produced 81.7 per cent of the hotel chains' room capacity expansion. Accor is the market leader in Western Europe, operating 1938 hotels in 12 chains, with 198,759 rooms, predominantly in the economy (56 per cent) and the midscale (38 per cent) categories. Similarly large-scale companies – with a capacity exceeding 10,000 rooms – include the Groupe du Louvre (with seven chains among which Campanile, Première Classe and Kyriad offer more than 10,000 rooms each, in the economy segment), B&B Hotels, Maritim, Motel One, NH Hotel Group and Van der Valk Hotels. More than half of the hotel chains' rooms belong to the top 10 global corporations, representing a 12.1 per cent fair share in the luxury-upscale segment, 21.5 per cent in the midscale, and 20.2 per cent in the economy category. The largest supply among the Western European subregion's hotel chains belongs to Ibis (52,797 rooms) of Accor.

Northern Europe

As a result of continuous and stable increase, the subregion's hotel industry includes 4289 properties offering 477,336 rooms in 2013 (STR Global, 2014). The expansion of the industry is mostly due to the performance of hotel chains (which are present throughout the subregion, with the exception of the Faroe Islands). Hotel chains occupy 35.8 per cent of the market, with a 57.4 per cent fair share. The significant difference between the two indicators is explained by the major variance in property size: while the average Northern European independent hotel has 46 rooms, a typical chain hotel's room capacity is 111. Within the subregion, the UK is the fastest developing destination representing about 80 per cent of the area's total growth, Denmark's hotel industry stagnates, Iceland and Ireland lost altogether 2334 rooms between 2007 and 2013, while Sweden's hotel chains experienced a considerable room capacity increase (+7725 rooms) in parallel with a reduction in the independent hotel sector. Among the subregion's hotel chains, the Whitbread Hotel Company and its one and only chain, the Premier Inn, offers the largest supply in Northern Europe (668 properties, 54,015 rooms). The top 10 corporations' fair share in the luxury-upscale segment is 18 per cent, in the midscale category 13.1 per cent and in the economy category 14.3 per cent.

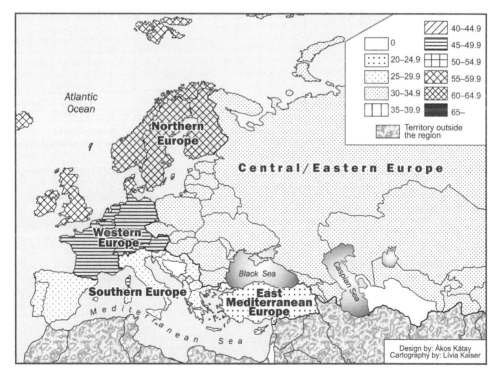

Figure 4.4 Hotel chains' share in the total room capacity of Europe (2013) (per cent).

Source: Authors' calculations based on data provided by STR Global (2014).

Conclusions

Throughout the last decades, most major international hotel companies have developed and implemented extensive international strategies to expand in an increasingly competitive environment and to benefit from business opportunities available in emerging markets. International hotel corporations well established in the mature markets of North America and Europe search for growth potential in the fast-developing Asia-Pacific region (and, to a smaller extent, in Africa and Central and South America), where they need to compete with locally and regionally recognised companies.

The analysis of market penetration and market share data indicates that hotel chains' global strategies are mainly influenced by direct market factors. Globalisation is particularly marked in the efforts to achieve a broad geographical presence in key international markets, through investments and acquisitions, using a wide range of different equity and non-equity entry modes, and aiming to successfully introduce global brands and positioning messages.

The trends observed in the geographical analysis of hotel chains' market presence and fair share values seem to suggest an ongoing consolidation process in the industry, since not all the smaller companies are able to achieve the critical mass necessary to sustain competitive advantages in the global (or even the regional) market.

Notes

1 At the time of completing this manuscript, the operation of Home Inns Group was limited to China; consequently, the corporation and its chains are only mentioned in the analysis of the North-East Asia subregion.
2 Quality symbol used by the American Automobile Association and the Canadian Automobile Association.

References

Atkins, W. (2011) Global hotel chains eye up African expansion. *This is Africa: A Global Perspective*, 15 November. Online. Available HTTP: <http://www.thisisafricaonline.com/Business/Global-hotel-chains-eye-up-African-expansion?ct=true>, retrieved 18 January 2015.

Boorstin, D.J. (1992) *The Image: A Guide to Pseudo-Events in America*. New York: Vintage Books.

Ivanova, M. and Ivanov, S. (2014) Hotel chains' entry mode in Bulgaria. *Anatolia: An International Journal of Tourism and Hospitality Research*, 25(1), 131–35.

Marriott International (2014) Marriott International completes acquisition of Protea Hospitality Group; Becomes the largest hotel company in Africa. Online. Available HTTP: <http://news.marriott.com/2014/04/marriott-international-completes-acquisition-of-protea-hospitality-group-becomes-the-largest-hotel-c.html>, retrieved 13 November 2014.

Ransley, J. and Ingram, H. (2012) *Developing Hospitality Properties and Facilities*. Abingdon: Routledge.

STR Global (2014) *Hotel Census Database*. London: STR Global.

UNWTO (2014) *Tourism Highlights 2014 Edition*. Madrid: UNWTO.

W Hospitality Group (2014) Hotel chain development pipelines in Africa, 2014. W Hospitality Group, Lagos. Online. Available HTTP: <http://w-hospitalitygroup.com/wp-content/uploads/2014/04/HOTEL-CHAIN-DEVELOPMENT-PIPELINES-IN-AFRICA-2014.pdf>, retrieved 13 December 2014.

5

The strategic environment of hotel chains

Valentina Della Corte

(FEDERICO II UNIVERSITY OF NAPLES, ITALY)

Introduction

Hotels chains require a very careful analysis of the external environment, for several reasons. Firstly their context is more complex than other firms, since on one hand they are much involved in globalisation; yet on the other there is growing interest in the demand for experiencing the stay, thus requiring a connection with the territorial identity locally. Secondly, operating in several countries for different market targets, they have to manage complexity and need to apply innovative managerial approaches constantly. The main tools and their use for analysing the environment are therefore examined in this chapter.

Tourism industry involves a huge variety of public and private actors whose primary objective is to reach a competitive advantage in the market. The strategic components of a destination are enclosed in the 6As model whose elements are: access, attractions, accommodation, amenities, assemblage and ancillary services (Della Corte, 2000, 2013); and in the 10As attributes that identify awareness, attractiveness, availability, access, appearance, activities, assurance, appreciation, action and accountability (Morrison, 2013) as the successful destination features.

Stating that a destination is a complex product resulting from the collection of products/ services created by market actors, these overall actors have to manage the relationships they establish in order to achieve common goals and to ensure the destination's success. Hotel firms represent one of the main actors in the tourism industry (the accommodation) without which tourism cannot take place. Within the hotel industry, hotel chains are a specific configuration of accommodation: their environment is characterised by particular dynamics in which the strong competition forces firms to find innovative ways and tools to keep their market shares. Their strategic strength and marketing position, however, is higher than that of many single-unit hotels – they often become a pivotal actor in the tourist destinations where they invest.

The chapter first describes the hotel chain environment, analysing the characteristics of global and local strategies and the challenge of responding to both of them. Literature provides some useful models that help when studying the external and internal environment of hotel chains, both of which are described in a later paragraph. Finally, the chapter outlines the current scenario in which hotel chains operate, introducing some of the main factors to consider in order to reach a competitive advantage.

The hotel chain environment: the match between global and local strategies

In order to understand hotel chain's environment, it is necessary to start from a series of considerations that are strictly linked to the level of competition regarding this subject. As shown in Figure 5.1, the environment is very complex and full of stakeholders with different objectives. It is in fact becoming more and more dynamic and hypercompetitive (D'Aveni, 2010). Hypercompetition is strictly bound to issues like globalisation, abrupt and radical changes in information and communications technology (ICT) and growing variability in demand. Therefore, in the current scenario, the competitive environment is not only defined by geographical boundaries; it has no spatial barriers (Cooper and Wahab, 2005). Even if local competition remains strong, globalisation complicates the competition dynamics, since it favours the presence of megacorporations as well as of other international companies, here including small and medium enterprises, with a wide and varied competitive setting. Besides, there has been the growing role of local factors in shaping specific offers in different countries, leading to the affirmation of 'glocalisation' (Roudometof, 2005). This term has implied a turnaround in tourism markets and has determined the standardisation, homogenisation and integration of marketing activities across markets and, at the same time, the adaptation and customisation of the offers depending on both territory and market peculiarities (Dumitrescu and Vinerean, 2010; Kotler and Caslione, 2009).

Some scholars (Mattila, 1999; Steenkamp and de Jong, 2010) agree with the assumption that globalisation has meant homogenisation of international markets and an increasing similarity of customers' needs and habits, even if demand is far more complex and 'neurotic'

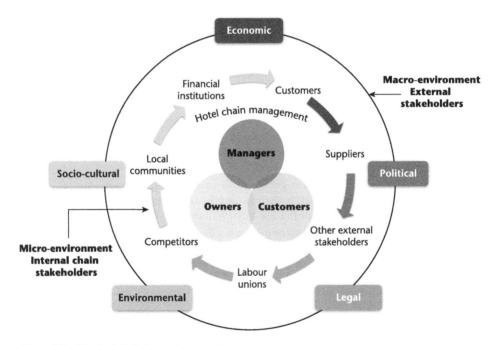

Figure 5.1 The hotel chain environment.

Adapted from: Ivanova and Ivanov (2015).

than in the past. Therefore, hotel chains are called to compete in this by gaining a much wider market and, at the same time, gaining a competitive positioning at a local level: when the issue of globalisation is identified within a specific context, even in the case of hotel chains, the single hotel has to take into account the local dimension. Dealing with its competitive context, for example, a hotel needs to choose which elements to highlight, in order to compete with national and international brands. In these dynamics, territorial characteristics may help by using local peculiarities in order to differentiate the offer, improving the physical plant or hiring local employees. From these reflections, a new issue arises for hotel chains, that is the necessity of finding a balance between standardisation and customisation (Sandoff, 2005). This challenge is even more complicated when hotel chains have to manage the different needs and values of people in culturally diverse countries. The definition of the mix depends on the service peculiarities, on the structure, on the local situational needs, as well as on the personnel management. In order to capture a broader customer base of both domestic and international travellers, hotel companies should satisfy the demands of their guests in a particular market whilst maintaining a homogeneous brand reputation in terms of the level of quality of the services provided (Sandoff, 2005). The evaluation of the environment is then crucial for obtaining a competitive advantage in the market/s where the hotel chain operates as well as in maintaining a high extensive brand reputation.

Recalling the work of Schiffman and Lazar Kanuk (2009), the match between global and local strategies can be related to the product and the communication choices. A global strategy refers to a homogeneous product (a standardised product) and message (standardised communication), while a local strategy considers customised product and message. In the middle, there are the glocal strategies, in which products or messages can be customised in order to better respond to specific customers' needs (Svensson, 2001). Sharing these assumptions, hotel chains have to seek the right balance between local and global strategies and this choice strictly influences the assets of standardisation and customisation implemented in their offer.

Evaluating the environment

In order to successfully compete in the market, a hotel chain has to be able to evaluate the environment in which it operates or wants to operate, and to adopt proactive behaviour in order to face the radical and frequent changes of the environment (Clarkson et al., 2011; Lopez-Gamero et al., 2009) or to anticipate environmental changes and to adapt their products, processes and technologies accordingly. This issue recalls a very relevant topic, both in research and in practice, concerning catching and creating opportunities. This implies, on the one hand, a wider and more intense set of opportunities to catch and/or create through a specific entrepreneurial visionary capability. On the other, the environment and its relative threats are more complex and difficult to manage.

The first step in conducting a useful study of the hotel chain environment is to identify some models of analysis, according to the different dimensions that need to be investigated: the macro- and the micro-environment. The first one can be analysed with the support of the PESTEL model and its extensions. For the micro-environment there are different tools that allow us to obtain significant information from the context: SWOT analysis, which favours firm external and internal analysis, supported by the 'six forces' model of competition related to the external context.

PESTEL factors

The PESTEL model is useful for understanding the strategic environment in which hotel chains operate, including the limits and the possibilities that can hinder or facilitate the firm's performance (Thompson and Martin, 2010). It is important to underline that it is a very subjective analysis, depending on peculiar macro-environmental factors, so it is difficult to extend it to the entire hotel chains category. Nevertheless, for the purpose of this work, some generalisations can be made.

As regards the *political factors*, the major complexities hotel chains have to face are the differences among countries when they develop internationally: globalised environment forces the hotel chains to consider the political peculiarities of all the countries/regions in which they have a branch. The Moscow Aerostar, a joint venture between Aeroflot and an aerospace multinational IMP Group Ltd, was set up in 1988 transforming an old building located in Moscow into a Western-style hotel. In 1991, Russia was just emerging from the communist regime and IMP Limited was the first Western company trying to open a hotel in that situation. Negotiations with political players were an essential requirement for operating successfully (Shea, 1994), trying to transfer some business knowledge.

The *economic factors* include macro-economical factors that can directly affect the hotel companies, such as growth rates, inflation rates, interest rates, exchange rates, labour costs, price fluctuations and monetary policies (McEwen, 2008). These factors have direct implications on tourism demand, cost, prices and profits, not to mention a firm's decision to invest in a new country. They actually influence the hotel chains, for example, in terms of pricing policies, rather than in decisions to enter a certain country. If, on the one hand, these represent a growing pressure for a rapid expansion, on the other, they show how top managers and entrepreneurs adopt the right growth strategies in order to face challenges depending on these economic factors.

The *socio-cultural factors* relate to family structure, buying habits, education level, religion and beliefs, social class and attitudes towards goods and services. The study of these elements may be relevant both for the demand satisfaction and in human resource management (Rothaermel, 2012). The InterContinental group decided to expand into China by the end of 2008, but the management had to adjust its strategy to suit the business culture in China, which differs significantly from those of the US and Europe. For example, the expansion could occur only through managed operations, rather than through direct ownership or franchising. In addition to this, some differences in management style are also necessary. For example, in some Asian cultures eye contact is not sought, as it can make guests feel uncomfortable, while in the Western tradition it is equated with openness and honesty. This has been important in defining how staff members address themselves to certain Asian guests and stimulate the organisation of cross-cultural training programmes (Hardingham, 2012).

As regards the *technological factors*, hotel chains should consider innovations, technological change, legislation regarding technology, investments in R&D, etc. Technology largely influences the product marketing and promotion, with particular relevance to intangible goods and the service industry, whose main example is the tourism sector. More precisely, hotel chains pay particular attention to investments in technology. For example, Best Western introduced a 360 degree virtual tour software for each of its branches, that allows guests to explore the hotels directly from their home and to facilitate the choice of room. The vacation experience is extended and improved: a beautiful interactive panorama is a powerful way to give a true, visual impression of the hotel guest rooms, meeting spaces, leisure facilities and public areas (Best Western, 2013).

Environmental or *ecological factors* include the study of climate change, laws regulating environmental pollution, recycling, waste management and renewable energy, etc. The care for the environment and social responsibility, through the benefits and product preferences perceived, can be a powerful operational tool in attracting and retaining more guests. Incorporating the functional, environmental and emotional benefits into hotel operations is a prerequisite for the creation of a good hotel image (David, 2009). For example, Hilton Hotels have developed and implemented a comprehensive environmental programme, Hilton Environmental Reporting (HER), a computerised reporting tool. It allows water savings, a towel reuse programme, the implementation of lower-wattage light bulbs and benchmarks on environmental performance (Hilton Worldwide, n.d.). Marriott International concentrates on wildlife preservation, waste management and clean-up campaigns (Marriott, n.d.). Aloft brand by Starwood uses environmentally safe cleaning products and provides guests with reserved parking spots for hybrid cars (David, 2009).

Legal factors include certain laws that can affect the business environment, like the anti-trust law, discrimination laws, consumer protection, employment laws, health and safety laws, data protection, etc., which are some of the main determinants of the hotel chain's profit and success. For example, chains have to adjust their practices/standards, according to each country's internal regulations. Some of these legal factors can involve changes in rules and regulation related the outsourced services, consumer protection regulations or the immigration rules for hiring staff.

SWOT analysis

SWOT analysis is the principal marketing tool used by companies in order to analyse the micro-dimension of the operating context (Clark, 1997). It is particularly relevant to hotel chains as their businesses are significantly changing (Helms and Nixon, 2010), due to both the growing world uncertainty surrounding travel, the increasing costs of operating hotel chains (Barros, 2005) and the massive changes in travel booking, transformed by the introduction of web tools, which have modified and reduced the role of the traditional travel agencies. It is important to underline that SWOT analysis is a subjective tool, in the sense that the overall frame changes according to the firm and the perceptions of management. Opportunities and threats from the external environment, in fact, change according to the strengths and weaknesses the single firm has.

The six forces model of competition

As underlined above, one of the main elements a hotel chain has to consider is the competitive scenario: in this perspective, the most acknowledged model that can be applied to hotel chains is Porter's 'five force model' (1985). It is important to specify that since the five forces are the main external threats, they can vary from firm to firm. Moreover, a macro approach would not explain the significant performance differences between firms of the same sector. Singling out the main categories of competitive forces, with reference to hotel chains, it is possible to identify:

- *Current competition*, from other hotel chains located in the same area who offer the same standards and quality. The intensity of this force, in fact, derives from the number and size of direct competitors in the market. The lower the product differentiation and the switching costs, the more intense the rivalry becomes.

• *New entrants*, which refers to hotel chains that decide to enter into the market, and to other independent hotels that adhere to a chain, benefiting from its brand image and/or loyalty. The threat of new entrants is determined by barriers to entry, that include economies of scale, product differentiation, cost advantages not related to the scale, firms' collusion and government policies (Barney, 2006). Hotel chains deal with a high proportion of fixed and total costs, that generate considerable economies of scale (Yu and Huimin, 2005). On the contrary, capital costs are not always contemplated since most hotel chains deal mainly with non-equity expansion forms, hence they are not involved with capital investments. Furthermore, hotel chains adhere to specific standards, such as service quality, so in most cases the differentiation is another strong barrier to entry. Cost advantages can be related to the possibility for single hotels to access some specific resources and competences through the chain. In addition, hotel chains are able to retaliate against other competitors in the market, discouraging the entrance of new firms. Government policies, such as licensing, subsidies or tax incentives do not depend on hotel chains but can represent another barrier of entry for new competitors.

• *Substitute products*, for example other accommodation in the same location that performs the same function, reduces costs, and/or provides higher quality performance with better service due to technological advancement (Porter, 1980), such as independent hotels or vacation ownerships, that can become competitors of the hotel chains in terms of price or quality.

• *Bargaining power of suppliers*, who provide products and services that represent important inputs in the industry's success. For hotel chains, suppliers hardly have a strong bargaining power. One of the key suppliers for hotel chains is trained personnel since they ensure customer satisfaction (Cheng, 2013); hotel chains have solid training programmes that enable them to coach personnel in order to fulfil all the guests' needs.

• *Bargaining power of buyers*, who are the final consumers, in accordance with the B2C perspective, and other actors of the tourism industry, at the B2B level. Nowadays, leisure customers are gaining a greater bargaining power thanks to the new trend of Web 2.0 and the diffusion of the social media communities. Through these and other tools (internet providers like Booking, Expedia, etc.), guests can share information about the experience of their stay, positively or negatively influencing the choices of other potential guests. Leisure customers have a very low bargaining power because their behaviour can't be generalised; although on the other hand, business customers are not as price-sensitive, so they represent less of a threat for hotel chains. Business tourism is normally less sensitive to price and more sensitive to service: the choices of a business tourist are oriented to urban locations and big cities and are influenced by meetings, exhibitions, conferences and commercial activities. Demand is relatively stable throughout the year (Gilbert, 2004). With reference to the business target, tour operators, as well as travel agencies or conference organisers could represent a strong threat for hotel chains since they make bulk purchases of hotel rooms.

Different researchers identify other factors in the overall scheme: *complementors* (Brandenburger and Nalebuff, 1996; Yoffie and Kwak, 2006), can be either some actors of the five forces that nevertheless decide to cooperate, for example, in one specific market or with reference to joint projects, or even companies in other industries with which the firm cooperates, that contribute to reinforcing its market and competitive position (Della Corte and Micera, 2011). The concept of complementors recalls the literature on 'coopetition'. According to the literature on the theme, this describes the situation in which a firm's competitive actions create benefits for other players in the same business (Brandenburger and Nalebuff, 1996) or where a firm simultaneously adopts competition and cooperation behaviours (Tsai, 2002; Eikebrookk and Olsen, 2005), or even cases in which a firm cooperates with some players in some activities whilst competing with the same players in other activities (Bengsston and Kock, 2000; Laine, 2002). For example, Starhotels, an Italian hotel chain, developed partnership networks in order to better utilise revenue management tools (i.e. overbooking) and implement shared strategies of touristic–territorial development which benefit all the local actors (Della Corte, 2013). Indeed, Starhotels group takes into account cancellations and no-shows. In the light of these phenomena, hotels of this chain sometimes sell assets in surplus compared with the actual number of rooms available. This is the reason why they join forces with other local hotels of the same or superior category in order to face a contingent overbooking.

The evaluation of competitive forces is useful for understanding the likely impacts the product/service will have on the market. In any case, product/service creation needs to reflect firstly the needs of the tourist demand in the current scenario. However, it can't be conducted in general, but has to be analysed for each single hotel chain, since the overall set of opportunities and threats depends on the firm's strengths and weaknesses. For example, one of the main strengths of Kimpton Hotels, a chain of boutique hotels, is the strong brand reputation that has led to a high recognition among consumers. Also the entrepreneurial capabilities of the founder, Bill Kimpton, and the executive team's capabilities, allowed the company to always be a prime mover in the sector (Della Corte, 2014). One of the main examples is the firm's network capabilities in activating relations with American and European tour operators. These capabilities, that represent some of the main strengths of the firm, make the exploitation of the opportunity to reach new targets in foreign markets possible (Della Corte, 2014).

Current trends in the strategic environment of hotel chains

Experience-based tourism and the new role of customers

In order to study the strategic environment of hotel chains, it is important to better analyse the crucial role the customers are assuming in the contemporary era. The focus on experience encourages hotel chains to design, intentionally produce, organise, foresee, price and charge for specific and highly differentiated products, creating new value attributes (Pine and Gilmore, 1998). With reference to the role of the customer, this new way of living the holiday derives from 'experiential learning' (people create meaning through direct experience), according to the experience-based approach (Pine and Gilmore, 2011; Stamboulis and Skyannis, 2003; Prahalad and Ramaswamy, 2004). The experiential tourist is more conscious, informed and passionate and asks for highly personalised offers (Andersson, 2007). From the offer side, firms have to leverage on particular atmosphere and unusual surroundings, providing opportunities for 'personal enrichment, enlightenment, stimulation, and engagement as motivators' (Smith, 2006).

From this perspective, some new concepts have been developed over time, such as boutique hotels (Agget, 2007), built on service personalisation in response to customers' needs, the intense relationship between the guest and the hotel personnel and the centrality of the experience, that has to be unique and exclusive (McIntosh and Siggs, 2005). For the hotel chain industry, this also means that the focus on standardisation, which in the past has often been synonymous with quality, needs to shift towards an accurate customisation of the stay, paying specific attention to the variety of the guest's requirements and to the peculiarities of

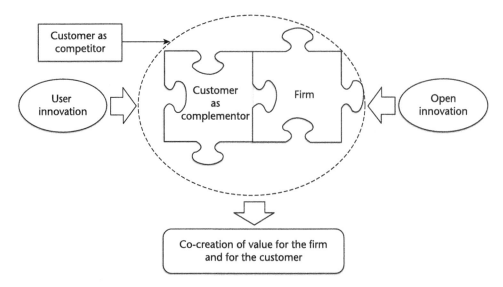

Figure 5.2 Firm–customer process according to an experience-based approach.

the location, in order to satisfy the demanding customer of today (Baum, 2006). In addition to this, perceived value is different all over the world and cultural norms often change according to the geographic area and over time. Hotel chains must have the ability to discern what is valuable and what has to be changed and customised in order to meet the market specificities.

The above reflections allow us to take a step forward in the evaluation of the hotel chains' environment: the experience-based approach radically changes the competitive scenario, analysing hotel chains using a new business model in which the customer is no longer perceived as a competitive force but becomes a complementor. A new, productive relationship between the firm and the customer is created, in which the firm and its customers share ideas, suggestions and needs: in an open and user-innovation approach (Chesbrough, 2003), this allows it to create more personalised, customised offers, matching customers' needs more efficiently. This process is represented in Figure 5.2.

The impact of innovation on hotel chain management

As shown before, the hotel industry has evolved significantly in recent years; this factor complicates a firm's responsiveness to competition, so one of the main strategic aspects firms have to consider is the adaptation of management practices to environmental changes. Innovation in the hospitality industry has received very little attention from scholars (Orfila-Sintes and Mattsson, 2009), but it is a very interesting field of study for hotel firms and particularly for hotel chains, since some authors agree that innovation is related to the firm size (Chung and Kalnins, 2001).

Globalisation trends have modified the stage on which innovations are played out and have intensified the rhythm of change. Therefore, tourism firms need to innovate to survive and to respond to the ever more demanding tourist. At least two major dimensions of change can be identified: new forms of tourism (conventional and mass tourism are in downturn) and the diffusion of information and communication technologies, which have a strong effect on the phases of creation, production and consumption of the tourist product.

Innovation in the service sector can be internally developed or derived from the environment. This view recalls the concepts of open and user innovation, according to which the interactions between external and internal ideas create value (open innovation) (Chesbrough, 2003) and accelerate internal innovation: customers (users) have a key role in leading innovation since firms can use their skills and competences to create or adopt new ideas and solutions (user innovation) (von Hippel, 2005).

The literature on hospitality innovation identifies four clusters (Ottenbacher and Gnoth, 2005):

- innovation in management, which refers to the quality of management processes, to the ICT applications for management and to improvements in the organisational structure;
- innovation in external communications, which considers the high information–intangible content of services products and processes in the hotel industry;
- service scope innovation, which leads to changes in the service output and the incorporation of technological assets to improve the tangible aspects of service delivery;
- innovation in back-office activities, which comprises the incorporation of new technological assets for productivity improvement and for the achievement of a more efficient service delivery.

In our view, this classification needs to be extended, focusing on different aspects of innovation that are not related solely to technological introduction. Looking at innovation in the services sector, we can consider the following different dimensions:

- technological innovation, linked to the adoption of softwares that can improve the human resource management processes, the quality of the service provided, the relationships with the customers, the rates and so on;
- service and marketing innovation, linked to hotels' efforts in getting close to the customers. In this sense, revenue management is gaining even more attention from hotels as a strategic tool for managing demand, competition and costs;
- systemic innovation, which refers to the link between the different hotels in the chain as well as with other chains in the hotel industry or with the other actors of the tourism sector.

With reference to the product/service, technological innovation can have a strong impact on the improvement of the service characteristics that can effectively respond to customers' needs. In this view, hotel chains that introduce technological innovation in their offer improve customer satisfaction by leveraging on the 'delighter' dimension of the product and matching targets with particular needs. For Jewish people, for example, the electronic turn-on and turn-off of the light is a distinctive feature in the choice of their accommodation during the weekend. This kind of innovation, that refers to both radical or incremental changes in technology, can also have an influence on the strategic environment of the hotel chains. The introduction of new technology, for example, requires the interaction between the hotel chain and the suppliers of innovative products and services. In this case, hotel chains must combine their willingness to adopt technological innovation with the right stakeholder of the relevant strategic environment (e.g. the suppliers) that can support these changes with their products and services.

Hotel chains constantly invest in innovation of services and marketing. Global competition, on the one hand, and the conquest of market share, on the other, oblige hotel chains to develop new services and new marketing strategies that have to be aligned with innovative behaviours of these firms. Within the strategic environment, the hotel firms direct this kind of innovation particularly at customers, who acquire an important role for the delivery of service excellence.

Considering the process, the cited dimensions of innovation can significantly improve production or delivery methods for the hotel chain. These involve changes in equipment, human resources and working methods, which are included in organisational innovation, but they may also refer to the even stronger interaction between the firm and the customer, as well as to the creation of relationships with other hotels of the chain. Indeed, systemic innovation requires a collaboration between hotel chains and other actors in the strategic environment. This collaboration allows the leverage of the resources of these actors, in order to achieve strategic goals.

Conclusions

Hotel chains today live in the globalisation era and face its related consequences. They also need to create a customer experience as well as to constantly innovate.

The first challenge refers to the balance between global and local goals. In this scenario, the strategic environment assumes a key role in determining both the direction of innovation and strategies related to the improvement of the customer experience. For this reason, this chapter analysed the strategic environment's interconnections with innovation. Some factors (i.e. PESTEL) and other frameworks or analysis (i.e. the 'six forces' model of competition, SWOT) represent useful tools in order to analyse the strategic environment of a hotel chain. This is shaped by a variety of actors and factors that interplay and influence the strategic choices of this kind of company. Particularly, hotel chains need to implement an experience-based approach that views the customer involved in a process of a co-creation with the firm. Furthermore, hotel chains must apply a high level of innovation that can be of a technological, marketing and service, and systemic nature. Through the adoption of these practices hotel chains improve customer satisfaction.

In conclusion, in the case of hotel chains, multiple and different innovations are required in different countries, trying, at the same time, to create synergies and economies of scope across countries, synthetised into a homogeneous business concept.

References

Agget, M. (2007) What has influenced growth in the UK's boutique hotel sector? *International Journal of Contemporary Hospitality Management*, 19(2), 169–77.

Andersson, T. (2007) The tourist in the experience economy. *Journal of Hospitality and Management*, 7(1), 46–58.

Barney, J. (2006) *Risorse, competenze e vantaggi competitivi*. Roma: Carocci.

Barros, C.P. (2005) Evaluating the efficiency of a small hotel chain with a Malmquist productivity index. *International Journal of Tourism Research*, 7(3), 173–84.

Baum, T. (2006) Reflections on the nature of skills in the Experience Economy: challenging traditional skills models in hospitality. *Journal of Hospitality and Tourism Management*, 13(2), 124–35.

Bengsston, M. and Kock, S. (2000) 'Coopetition' in business networks: to cooperate and compete simultaneously. *Industrial Marketing Management*, 29(5), 411–26.

Best Western (2013, December, 19) BW is changing the way consumers shop for hotels. Online. Available HTTP: <http://www.bestwestern.com/about-us/press-media/press-release-details.asp?NewsID=916>, accessed 10 November 2014.

Brandenburger, A. and Nalebuff, B. (1996) *Coopetition*. New York: Doubleday.

Cheng, D. (2013) Analyze the hotel industry in Porter five competitive forces. *The Journal of Global Business Management*, 9(3), 52–57.

Chesbrough, H. (2003) Open innovation: how companies actually do it. *Harvard Business Review*, 81(7), 12–14.

Chung, W. and Kalnins, A. (2001) Agglomeration effects and performance: A test of the Texas lodging industry. *Strategic Management Journal*, 22(10), 969–88.

Clark, D. (1997) Strategic management tool usage: a comparative study. *Strategic Change*, 6, 417–27.

Clarkson, P., Li, Y., Richardson, G. and Vasvari, F. (2011) Does it really pay to be green? Determinants and consequences of proactive environmental strategies. *Journal of Accounting and Public Policy*, 30(2), 122–44.

Cooper, C. and Wahab, S. (eds) (2005) *Tourism in the Age of Globalisation*. London, UK: Routledge.

D'aveni, R.A. (2010) *Hypercompetition*. New York: Simon and Schuster.

David, F. (2009) *Strategic Management: Concepts and Cases*. New York: Prentice Hall.

Della Corte, V. (2000) *La gestione dei sistemi locali di offerta turistica*. Padova: Cedam.

Della Corte, V. (2013) *Imprese e sistemi turistici. Il management*. Milano: Egea.

Della Corte, V. (2014) Towards a New Model of SMEs' Internationalization. In Todorov, K. and Smallbone, D. (eds) *Handbook of Strategic Management in Small and Medium Enterprises: Theory and Practice*, 204–42. Hershey, Pennsylvania: IGI-Global.

Della Corte, V. and Micera, R. (2011) Resource integration management in networks' value creation. The case of high quality hotels. *Mercati e competitività*, 3, 127–46.

Dumitrescu, L. and Vinerean, S. (2010) The glocal strategy of global brands. *Studies in Business and Economics*, 5(3), 147–55.

Eikebrookk, T. and Olsen, D. (2005) Co-opetition and e-business success in SMEs: an empirical investigation of European SMEs. Proceedings of the 38th Hawaii International Conference on System Sciences (1–10). Hawaii: IEEE.

Gilbert, D.C. (2004) Conceptual issues in the meaning of tourism. In S. Williams (ed.), *Tourism: Critical Concepts in the Social Sciences*. London: Routledge, pp. 45–69.

Hardingham, S. (2012) *Why China? A Study of Why Foreign Hotel Companies are Rushing to Develop New Luxury Hotels in China*. Las Vegas: University of Nevada.

Helms, M. and Nixon, J. (2010) Exploring SWOT analysis – where are we now? A review of academic research from the last decade. *Journal of Strategy and Management*, 3(3), 215–51.

Hilton Worldwide (n.d.) Travel with purpose. 2013–2014 corporate responsibility report. Online. Available HTTP: <http://www.cr.hiltonworldwide.com/sustainability/>, accessed 13 December 2014.

Ivanova, M. and Ivanov, S. (2015) The nature of hotel chains: An integrative framework. *International Journal of Hospitality & Tourism Administration*, 16(2), 122–42.

Kotler, P. and Caslione, J. (2009) How marketers can respond to recession and turbulence. *Journal of Customer Behaviour*, 8(2), 187–91.

Laine, A. (2002) Hand in hand with the enemy – defining a competitor from a new perspective. *Innovative Research in Management*, 1–10. Stockholm: EURAM.

Lopez-Gamero, M., Molina-Azorin, J. and Claver-Cortes, E. (2009) The whole relationship between environmental variables and firm performance: competitive advantage and firm resources as mediator variables. *Journal of Environmental Management*, 90(10), 3110–21.

Marriott (n.d.) Corporate responsibility. Online. Available HTTP: <www.marriott.com/corporate-social-responsibility/corporate-responsibility.mi> accessed 13 December 2014.

Mattila, A. (1999) The role of culture and purchase motivation in service encounter evaluations. *Journal of Services Marketing*, 13(4/5), 376–89.

McEwen, T. (2008) Environmental scanning and organizational learning in entrepreneurial ventures. *Entrepreneurial Executive*, 13, 1–6.

McIntosh, A. and Siggs, A. (2005) An exploration on the experiential nature of boutique. *Journal of Travel Research*, 44(1), 74–81.

Morrison, A.M. (2013) *Marketing and Managing Tourism Destinations*. New York: Routledge.

Orfila-Sintes, F. and Mattsson, J. (2009) Innovation behavior in the hotel industry. *The International Journal of Management Science*, 37(2), 380–94.

Ottenbacher, M. and Gnoth, J. (2005) How to develop successful hospitality innovation. *Cornell Hotel and Restaurant Administration Quarterly*, 46(2), 205–22.

Pine, B. and Gilmore, J. (1998) Welcome to the experience economy. *Harvard Business Review*, 76, 97–105.

Pine, B., and Gilmore, J. (2011) *The Experience Economy*. Boston, MA: Harvard Business Press.

Porter, M. (1980) *Competitive Strategy*. New York: Free Press.

Porter, M. (1985) *Competitive Advantage: Creating and Sustaining Superior Performance*. New York: Free Press.

Prahalad, C. and Ramaswamy, V. (2004) Co-creation experiences: the next practice in value creation. *Journal of Interactive Marketing*, 18(3), 5–14.

Rothaermel, F. (2012) *Strategic Management: Concepts and Cases*. New York: McGraw-Hill.

Roudometof, V. (2005) Transnationalism, cosmopolitanism and glocalization. *Current Sociology*, 53(1), 113–35.

Sandoff, M. (2005) Customization and standardization in hotels: a paradox or not? *International Journal of Contemporary Hospitality Management*, 17(6), 529–35.

Schiffman, L. and Lazar Kanuk, L. (2009) *Consumer Behavior*. New Jersey: Pearson.

Shea, C. (1994) *Moscow Aerostar*, Case 9A92C010, Richard Ivey School of Business. London: The University of Western Ontario.

Smith, W. (2006) Experiential tourism around the world and at home: definitions and standards. *International Journal of Services and Standards*, 2(1), 1–14.

Stamboulis, Y. and Skyannis, P. (2003) Innovation strategies and technology for experienced-based tourism. *Tourism Management*, 24(1), 35–43.

Steenkamp, A. and de Jong, M. (2010) A global investigation into the constellation of consumer attitudes toward global and local products. *Journal of Marketing*, 74(6), 18–40.

Svensson, G. (2001) 'Glocalization' of business activities: a 'glocal strategy' approach. *Management Decision*, 39(1), 6–18.

Thompson, J. and Martin, F. (2010) *Strategic Management: Awareness and Change*. Andover: Cengage Learning.

Tsai, W. (2002) Social structure of 'coopetition' within a multiunit organization: coordination, competition, and intraorganizational knowledge sharing. *Organization Science*, 13(2), 179–90.

von Hippel, E. (2005) *Democratizing Innovation*. Cambridge, MA: The MIT Press.

Yoffie, D. and Kwak, M. (2006) With friends like these: The art of managing complementors. *Harvard Business Review*, 84(9), 88–98.

Yu, L. and Huimin, G. (2005) Hotel reform in China: a SWOT analysis. *Cornell Hotel and Restaurant Administration Quarterly*, 46(2), 153–69.

6

Hotel chains' conceptual models

Maya Ivanova and Stanislav Ivanov

(VARNA UNIVERSITY OF MANAGEMENT, BULGARIA)

Introduction

In their studies of the diverse nature of hotel chains, the researchers have adopted diverse theoretical frameworks to thoroughly present and explain the typical features of these major players in the hospitality world. Each of the applied concepts (transaction cost approach, resource-based view, agency theory, syncretic theory, eclectic framework, stakeholders and network concept, etc.) reveals only part of the hotel chains' characteristics and the reasons behind their establishment and development. When used separately those theoretical concepts describe only a one-sided view of chains' operation. In this regard, in this chapter we propose a comprehensive integrative model of hotel chains, delving deeper in the theory of the firm.

A recognised premise in the theory of the firm (Becerra, 2009) states that each company, including the hotel chain, can be seen from different perspectives – what it possesses and uses (i.e. its resources), what it does (i.e. its activities) and whom it works with (i.e. its stakeholders). The three perspectives, however, need to be perceived as complementary, rather than as alternative to each other, as they view the nature of the firm from different angles. They can be applied simultaneously in the analysis of the hotel chain in order to provide a more holistic perspective of its nature. Moreover, hotel chains themselves appear as multifaceted phenomena that deserve a larger and richer framework. In order to encompass all their inherent attributes, we adopt these three perspectives to develop an integrated model of a hotel chain (Ivanova and Ivanov, 2015). In this chapter we firstly critically evaluate the three perspectives in the context of hotel chains, develop partial hotel chain models based on each of them (namely: resource-based model, value chain model and stakeholder model), and then combine the three partial models into one integrated model of a hotel chain. Figure 6.1 elaborates the steps in the development of the integrated model of a hotel chain from the partial models. The integrated model could serve as an analytical instrument and contribute to the deeper understanding of the entangled resources, activities and stakeholder relationships of and within the hotel chain (Ivanova and Ivanov, 2015).

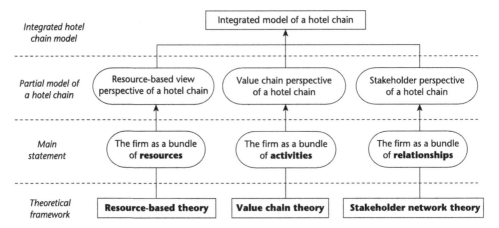

Figure 6.1 Steps in developing the Integrated model of a hotel chain.

Source: Ivanova and Ivanov (2015).

Resource-based perspective of a hotel chain

Resource-based theory of the firm

The resource-based view perspective perceives the firm as a *bundle of resources* from which it derives its competitive advantage (Barney, 1991; Barney and Arikan, 2001; Harrison and Enz, 2005). Once being part of the theory of the firm, and as such explaining the reason for the different performance of similar firms (Madhok, 2002), and the process of firm's growth (Becerra, 2009: 57–59), now, the RBV is already a constant part of the strategic management field, used for providing, formulating and implementing a corporate strategy (Harrison and Enz, 2005; Becerra, 2009; Barney et al., 2001). The main premise of the RBV is that the company is able to achieve superior performance through the effective and efficient use of its internal resources, along with creating and applying unique capabilities and learning (Dev et al., 2002; Foss, 1996). In this process the company continuously expands in order to deploy the maximum number of its resources. Different firms may grow at different rates (Becerra, 2009) due to the heterogeneity of resources and capabilities each firm possesses. In the field of international business and hospitality, RBV is quoted mainly with regard to the international expansion and modal choice (Choi and Parsa, 2012; Contractor and Kundu, 1998; Dev et al., 2002; Peng, 2001) and co-production/co-creation of hotel services (Chathoth et al., 2013).

The basis of the RBV perspective is the firm's *resources*, which could provide a sustainable competitive advantage only if they are valuable, rare, inimitable and non-substitutable (Barney and Arikan, 2001). Resources are usually classified into tangible and intangible (Barney et al., 2001), whereas the intangible resources incorporate not only intangible assets, but also learning capabilities and competences. The academic literature proliferates with different terms such as 'resources', 'assets', 'capital', 'competencies', 'capabilities', 'dynamic capabilities' and 'knowledge', but Barney and Arikan (2001) show that many of these terms convey similar meanings and could be used interchangeably.

For our RBV model of a hotel chain we chose to classify resources into 4 groups, following Barney and Arikan (2001): tangible (physical and financial resources, or 'capital' in the original Barney and Arikan (2001) terminology), and intangible (human and organisational resources). For easier reference under 'intangible resources' we classify assets like trade mark, reputation, service technology, reservation system, etc. which are typical for the hotel chains (as part of the service industry), and the human resources are put in a separate group. In general, physical and financial resources are easy to copy, whereas human and intangible resources are unique, and hence the ones that might form a source of sustainable competitive advantage (Villalonga, 2004; Wright et al., 1994). Additionally, the organisational knowledge, learning and capabilities represent the ability of the firm to learn, innovate and create knowledge (Harrison and Enz, 2005: 93); they play an integrative role for the rest of the resources (Aung, 2000), and influence the choice of non-equity entry mode by the hotel chain (Erramilli et al., 2002). Therefore, the organisational capabilities are identified as a separate group of resources.

Resource-based model of a hotel chain

The RBV model of a hotel chain (Figure 6.2) depicts first, all resources (physical, financial, human, intangible) possessed by the hotel chain's central management and the individual affiliated hotel. Resources are transformed by the individual hotel during the production process (operations) into a product that delivers value to the customer. The specific marketing mix of the hotel is influenced directly or indirectly by the hotel chain's central management requirements and its knowledge, learning and capabilities.

An important point of the model is the dualistic nature of the resources – on the one hand, they belong to the individual hotel or the chain's central management itself, but on the other, they could be used by the other party/the affiliated hotels as well. For example, the central online reservation system belongs legally to the chain, but is used by the individual hotel too; the building as an asset belongs to the hotel (or the owner of the hotel) but it is the physical environment where the chain's product is being produced. This dualism becomes even more important because of the prevalent role of contractual (non-equity) entry modes in the hotel industry, as Cunill and Forteza (2010) and Contractor and Kundu (1998) notice. In non-equity types of affiliation, hotels within the chain keep their judicial independence, yet at the same time utilise some of chain's resources – brand, image, technology. The resources of the individual hotel and the chain's central management are analogous, but different in scale. The main differences stem from the intangible resources and the organisational capabilities – the chain's central management has much stronger brand reputation and image, international experience and knowledge, while the individual hotel works mostly in the local market and has better knowledge of it.

All types of resources are entangled in the production process and transformed into a final product for clients. In this metamorphosis, the organisational capabilities and learning play a *dynamic* role providing unique features for the product and the rest of the marketing mix elements (Madhok, 2002), while the resources themselves are the *static* elements (Hallin and Marnburg, 2008; Madhok, 1997).

The essential role of the RBV model of a hotel chain is threefold: to elaborate a) the types of resources possessed by the chain and the individual property, b) how these resources are transformed into products to create customer value, and c) the resource synergy experienced by both parties in the relationship (the central chain management and the individual hotel). The type of affiliation determines the nature of relations between both sides, and is also a prerequisite for the flow of information, knowledge and resources between them, which enhances their own potential for creating and sustaining a competitive advantage. The closer the relationship, the more effective is the exchange of information, knowledge and resources between the individual hotel and the central chain management.

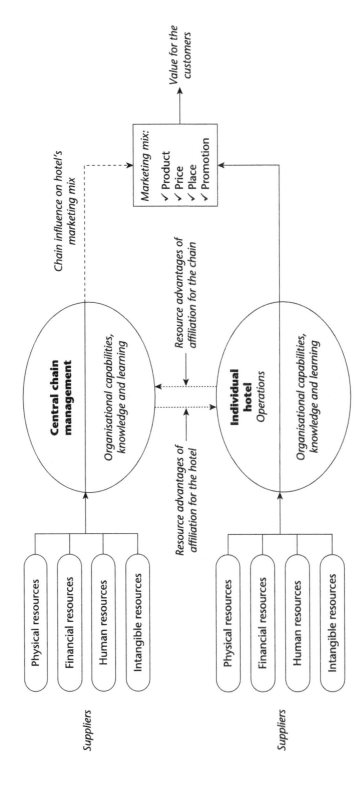

Figure 6.2 Resource-based perspective of a hotel chain.

Source: Ivanova and Ivanov (2015).

The affiliation between the chain and the individual hotel delivers resource benefits to both of them. The hotel, for example, gains advantage from the chain's market knowledge, service experience, brand recognition, service quality standards and operating manuals, while the chain receives increased financial resources (through franchise/management/lease fees), and knowledge about local markets (demand, competition, suppliers, legal system). Hence, both sides win from this resource synergy.

The RBV model depicts the hotel chain as a *bundle of resources*, with special emphasis on the importance of intangible resources, organisational learning, knowledge and capabilities, and on the resource advantages deriving from the hotel's affiliation to the chain and vice versa. However, the RBV perspective of the hotel chain neglects all the process activities that take place within the organisation and lead to the effective and efficient use of resources, and the stakeholders that shape the organisation's decisions – disadvantages that are overcome by the other two partial models to follow.

Value chain perspective of a hotel chain

Developed by Porter (1985), the value chain perspective of the firm holds that competitive advantages of companies stem from the primary (directly connected with the production function of the firm) and the support (forming the basic firm infrastructure) activities companies implement. Furthermore, Porter (1991: 108) argues that resources are only meaningful when allowing performance of certain activities that create advantages in particular markets. The value chain model presents an overview of a company's activities and their contribution to the value created by the company (van Assen et al., 2009). It has also become a useful tool for comparing different performances of firms in the search for competitive advantage, alongside the RBV. Both approaches draw on totally different sources, and just recently they were recognised (Ray et al., 2004), as interconnected and complementary to one another. A set of resources cannot be a guarantee for a sustainable competitive advantage and better performance of a firm – a dynamic element is necessary, in order to 'move' and make use of available resources. In the value chain perspective the role of this dynamic element is performed by the different company activities, while in the RBV it is by the organisational knowledge, learning and capabilities. It is necessary to note that Porter's primary and support activities are different from the organisational learning, knowledge and capabilities in the RBV – the latter stem from the tacit knowledge of the firm, while the former are 'actions that firms engage in to accomplish some business purpose or objective' (Ray et al., 2004: 24).

In Figure 6.3 we develop the value chain model of a hotel chain. It encompasses the value chains of the central chain management (the upper part of the model) and the individual affiliated hotel (the mirror image at the bottom part of the model). The two value chains are integrated predominantly through the primary activities – they can share inbound logistics, distribution, marketing and sales, after sale service, though to different degrees in each case. The only exception is the actual service process (operations), which takes place in the individual property (depicted by the thick line in Figure 6.3) by following the service standards of the chain. The customers consume the product at a particular hotel of the chain, but perceive the combined value, created both by the hotel and the chain's central management. In the case when the hotel is owned by the chain, the boundaries between the hotel and the central chain management blur and sharing activities becomes more intense.

Strategic marketing and branding is usually performed by central chain management, while the individual hotel might invest in a local marketing campaign, but in accordance with

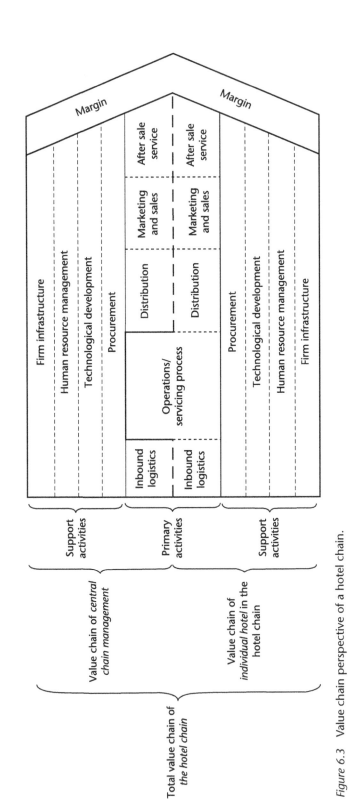

Figure 6.3 Value chain perspective of a hotel chain.

Source: Ivanova and Ivanov (2015).

the general guidelines established by the central chain management. The same applies to the rest of the primary activities, where the individual hotel can adapt to the general standards imposed by the central chain management.

Secondary activities are usually offered as additional optional services by hotel chains' central management to chain members, usually against additional fees (Ivanov and Zhechev, 2011). Each hotel is capable of arranging its own firm infrastructure, human resource management and procurement system, or of using those provided by the central chain management. Among the most commonly used secondary activities are: technological systems (reservation system, accounting system, etc.), special human resources policies (training, education, motivation systems) and administrative services.

The value chain model of a hotel chain reveals both the activities that are shared between the hotel chain and the hotel-member, as well as those that are implemented by each entity separately. The model illustrates how the hotel chain coordinates and distributes the procedures and processes taking place within the central chain management, and within the member hotels. However, this model only partially presents the nature of the hotel chain, neglecting the resources, which are necessary for its operations. Obviously, more ingredients should be added to display the hotel chain features fully.

Stakeholder network perspective of a hotel chain

The last part of the integrated model of a hotel chain comes from stakeholder/network perspective (Coff, 1999; Freeman, 2004, 2010; Ivanova, 2011). The main idea is that in its everyday activities the firm affects directly or indirectly the interests of certain groups, which, on their side, provide the firm with different resources that affect the long-term survival of the firm (Johnson and Vanetti, 2005; Hill and Jones, 1992). According to this perspective, the competitive advantages of a company stem from the proper maintenance of its network of relationships with various stakeholders, i.e. 'any group or individual that can affect or is affected by the achievement of a corporation's purpose' (Freeman, 2004: 229). The stakeholder view changes the notion that the company should have valuable, rare, inimitable and non-substitutable *resources* (RBV perspective), or perform effectively and efficiently its primary and support *activities* (value chain perspective). Through maintenance of a network of reliable *partners* the company will also be able to gain a competitive advantage, although it might not be sustainable in the long run.

The stakeholders often have different and contradictory goals (Ford, 2011), hence the importance of the firm knowing and managing them effectively. Usually stakeholders are divided into internal and external. Harrison and Enz (2005) consider as internal stakeholders the employees, owners and managers, while as external stakeholders – the customers, competitors, suppliers, activist groups, unions, financial intermediaries, the media, government agencies and local communities. The relationships between the hotel chain and its main stakeholders are presented in Figure 6.4 – the stakeholder model of a hotel chain. Upgrading the above classification, the model consists of three levels of stakeholders: a) the *chain* stakeholders – the central chain management/headquarters and the individual affiliated hotels; b) the *internal* stakeholders of the central chain management and the individual affiliated hotels, i.e. the owners, managers and employees; and c) the *external* stakeholders – the customers, suppliers, competitors, local communities, intermediaries, financial institutions, media, labour unions, hotel management companies and other external stakeholders. Although many other participants might be considered external stakeholders, we limited their number to the above mentioned ones as mostly affecting the hotel chains and the hospitality industry.

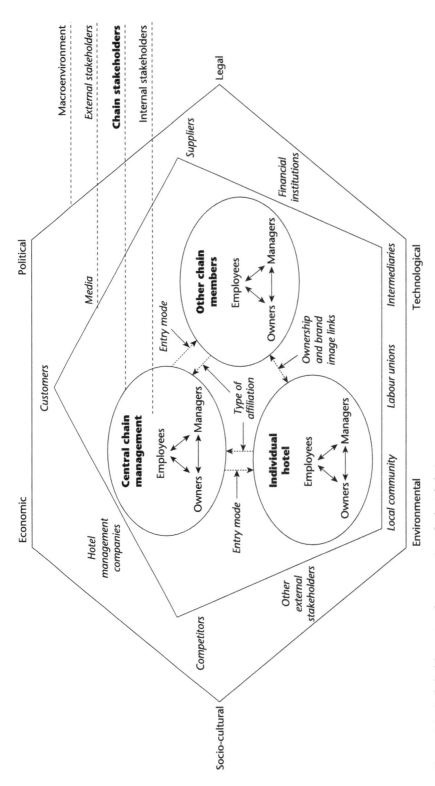

Figure 6.4 Stakeholder network perspective of a hotel chain.

Source: Ivanova and Ivanov (2015).

The model also includes the factors of the *macroenvironment* within which the chain operates – political, economic, socio-cultural, environmental, technological and legislative factors – so that it provides a full vision of a hotel chain's operational and strategic environment. The main focus of the model is on the level of chain stakeholders as they are the building blocks of the hotel chain itself.

Chain stakeholders

The chain headquarters, along with all the affiliated hotels, creates the main circle of stakeholders, named *chain stakeholders* (see Figure 6.4). This is the primary level of a chain's stakeholder network, it is very specific for the hotel chain and is determined by the type of affiliation of hotels to the chain. Most affiliated hotels actually are legally independent organisations, as they are affiliated to the chains by non-equity types of affiliation. The relations between member hotels and the central chain management are highly influenced by the type of contract, the regulations of the respective contracts, but also bear the impact of the cultural differences of the country of origin of the chain and the home country of the individual hotel (Vaishnav and Altinay, 2009). Moreover, the geographical dispersion of the affiliated hotels makes them work in totally different environments, but still, each of the hotels has to consider the marketing activities of the rest, because they share the same brand. Their relations as chain stakeholders are important for the market visibility and image of the brand as a whole.

The other party in the chain stakeholders level – the chain headquarters/central chain management – maintains 'principal-agent' type relationship with the affiliated hotels (according to the agency theory, Eisenhardt, 1989). These relations are typical for the contractual/non-equity forms of entry mode, and they depend on the specific type of affiliation. In a franchising and marketing consortium the individual hotel acts as an agent of the chain, which is the principal, while in management and lease the situation is reversed – the principal is the hotel owner(s), while the role of the agent is played by the chain. The agency relationship between the chain stakeholders may cause certain problems and become even a source of potential conflicts between them (Eisenhardt, 1989; Turner and Guilding, 2010). Such issues are often connected with the contradictory interests and goals of the involved parties (like a higher quality product required by the chain central management, which generates additional costs for the hotels, thus decreasing their bottom line), and information flow asymmetry. The latter happens when the principal has less information about the operational issues taking place in the hotel than the agent itself. In such cases the principal faces a moral hazard situation, because he is never sure that the agent is acting properly. Moreover, additional costs for contractual and operational control are incurred by the principal (Panvisavas and Taylor, 2008).

Internal stakeholders

The internal stakeholders include the owners, managers and the employees in the central chain management and the individual affiliated hotels (see Figure 6.4). Again, many of the relations between them are of a 'principal–agent' type – managers serve as agents of the owners, who are their principals, and employees act as agents of the managers, who are their principals. The last aspect of internal stakeholder relations – between owners and employees – is determined by the size of the company – from a relatively close relationship in small family-run properties, to only marginal connections in large corporations where the managers act as intermediaries between them. Although the interests of the three parties might be divergent, they are united under the assumption of mutual agreement and consensus in reaching the goals of the company (Hill and Jones, 1992). Still, the bargaining power of internal stakeholders is different (Coff, 1999: 125) which may distort the consensus among them closer to the goals of one of the parties.

It should be noted that between the internal stakeholders of different chain stakeholders there also exist connections, not depicted in this model. However, these relations seem quite diverse and generalisation is difficult; most of them are indirect, usually mediated by the chain headquarters. A very appropriate example for care and special maintenance of these relations is the IHG Owners Association comprised of the owners of IHG properties throughout the world (IHG Owners Association, 2012). InterContinental Hotel Group established this association in order to provide a platform for sharing experience, problems and good practices among the owners/managers of the affiliated hotels.

External stakeholders

The third level of the stakeholder network model consists of all those 'friends to grow, foes to know' (Ford, 2011) that form the chain's microenvironment – customers, competitors, suppliers, intermediaries, local community, financial institutions, media, labour unions, hotel management companies and other external stakeholders. Managing relations with each of the external stakeholders is part of chains' strategic management and subject to cultural differences (Jurgens et al., 2010). Each of them affects directly or indirectly the proper development and performance of the chain. *Customers'* needs, wants and preferences determine the specific marketing mix to be used by the chain; the quality of the chain's product depends on the quality of the products provided by the *suppliers*; *competitors* urge the chain to constantly improve and innovate. *Intermediaries* (GDSs, OTAs, tour operators, etc.) influence the hotel chains as they connect them with the customers, while *media* shape the tastes and opinions of the customers. *Hotel management companies* are a specific external stakeholders group. They manage hotels for their owners under a management contract but do not brand the managed hotels under their own flag (if they did they would be considered as hotel chains). Instead, the managed properties could be branded under the flag of a hotel chain or not branded at all. If they are branded under the flag of a chain, then the management company becomes a partner in the relationship between the chain and the individual hotel as an external stakeholder. It is not an internal stakeholder, because the involvement of the management company does not influence the very nature of the hotel chain – the hotel remains affiliated to the chain and branded with its flag.

The stakeholder model acknowledges not only the internal resources or activities as provision for building competitive advantage of the hotel chain, but also adds the impact of external forces. The connections and relations between the company and its stakeholders are the main focus, but still the model is static and does not include input and output elements (like the RBV model) or process elements (like the value chain model). Nevertheless, it provides a useful overview of the hotel chain as a bundle of relationships.

Integrated model of a hotel chain

Each of the above discussed models of a hotel chain (resource-based view model, value chain model and stakeholder model) illustrates the firm from a particular point of view – as a bundle of resources, activities or relationships. However, these perspectives and their respective models of a hotel chain are not alternative, but complementary, and they serve as the basis for the *Integrated model* of a hotel chain (Ivanova, 2013) presented in Figure 6.5.

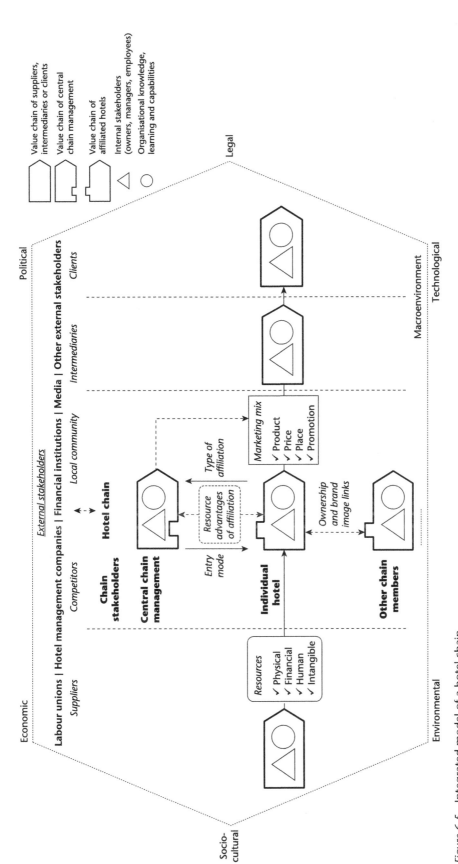

Figure 6.5 Integrated model of a hotel chain.

Source: Ivanova and Ivanov (2015).

The Integrated model depicts the hotel chain in the context of the hospitality supply chain. The hotel chain consists of the chain stakeholders (the central chain management and the individual hotels), each with its own internal stakeholders (owners, managers and employees). Properties get affiliated to the chain through different types of affiliation (franchising, management contract, marketing consortium, full or partial ownership, leasing) which from the point of view of the chain are considered entry modes. The hotels acquire physical, financial, human and intangible resources from their suppliers, and transform them during the service process into a product with the help of the organisational capabilities, knowledge and learning, which is then offered to customers via different intermediaries. Both the hotels and the central chain management experience resource advantages of the affiliation and their respective value chains fit together through the implementation of the primary activities, and especially through the operations (the actual customer servicing process) that take place in the individual hotels. Each hotel's marketing mix is influenced by the chain's central management decisions to a different degree depending on the type of affiliation. Additionally, individual hotels are related to the rest of the properties in the chain through ownership and brand image links. Finally, the hotel chain as a whole is connected with its external stakeholders (suppliers, competitors, intermediaries, clients, local community, financial institutions, media, labour unions, hotel management companies and other external stakeholders) and operates in a specific macroenvironment.

The Integrated model in Figure 6.5 goes beyond the understating of the hotel chain only as a 'bundle of resources' (resource-based view perspective), a 'bundle of activities' (value chain perspective) or a 'bundle of relationships' (stakeholder network perspective). Actually, the hotel chain comprises all these 'bundles' together (Ivanova, 2013). Moreover, the relationships between the hotel chain and all its various internal, chain and external stakeholders (excluding competitors and local communities) are contractually based, which gives the right to consider it as a 'nexus of contracts' or 'bundle of contracts' as well (Jensen and Meckling, 1976; Coff, 1999). The Integrated model demonstrates that sustainable competitive advantage of the hotel chain may come from its resources, activities and good relations with the stakeholders *simultaneously*. If any of these three sources of competitive advantage is not properly managed, the chain could remain competitive in the short run, but in the long run its competitiveness might not be sustainable.

Conclusion

This chapter analyses the heterogeneous and multifaceted nature of hotel chains by developing three partial models, where the chain is presented as a bundle of resources, activities and relationships, which are combined into one integrated model of a hotel chain. Each of the three partial models deals with a specific side of the hotel chain. The resource-based view model reveals the internal foundations for creating and sustaining a competitive advantage by acquiring, using, managing and sharing resources, organisational capabilities, knowledge and learning. Porter's value chain perspective is focused on implementing the proper activities in a proper way, thus achieving superior performance. By interacting with its various stakeholders, the hotel chain establishes certain relationships with them, which, if suitably managed, can also become a ground for obtaining a competitive advantage. In order to gain a holistic impression of a hotel chain, all three perspectives were combined into one Integrated model illustrated in Figure 6.5. The proposed models are applicable for any type of affiliation of a hotel to a hotel chain – equity (full ownership, joint venture) or non-equity based (franchising, management contract, marketing consortium, lease). The Integrated model could be used as an analytical tool to identify the specific sources of competitive advantage of a particular hotel chain and investigate the potential threats to the chain's competitiveness. Moreover, the individual hotels could gain a better picture of their place in the chain and their contribution to its overall performance. Therefore, the Integrated model of a hotel chain could be used by the hotel chains in their strategic analysis process. It is equally suitable for international as well as domestic hotel chains.

References

van Assen, M., van den Berg, G. and Pietersma, P. (2009) *Key Management Models. The 60+ Models Every Manager Needs to Know*. Harlow: Prentice Hall-Financial Times.

Aung, M. (2000) The Accor multinational hotel chain in an emerging market: Through the lens of the core competency concept. *The Service Industries Journal*, 20(3), 43–60.

Barney, J. (1991) Firm resources and sustained competitive advantage. *Journal of Management*, 17(1), 99–120.

Barney, J. and Arikan, A. (2001) The resource-based view: origins and implications. In Hitt, M.A., Freeman, R.E. and Harrison, J.S. (eds), *The Blackwell Handbook of Strategic Management*. Oxford: Blackwell Publishing, 124–88.

Barney, J., Wright, M. and Ketchen, D. Jr (2001) The resource-based view of the firm: ten years after 1991. *Journal of Management*, 27(6), 625–41.

Becerra, M. (2009) *Theory of the Firm for Strategic Management*. New York: Cambridge University Press.

Chathoth, P., Altinay, L., Harrington, R.L., Okumus, F. and Chan, E.S.W. (2013) Co-production versus co-creation: a process based continuum in the hotel service context. *International Journal of Hospitality Management*, 32, 11–20.

Choi, G. and Parsa, H.G. (2012) Role of intangible assets in foreign-market entry-mode decisions: a longitudinal study of American lodging firms. *International Journal of Hospitality and Tourism Administration*, 13(4), 281–312.

Coff, R.W. (1999) When competitive advantage doesn't lead to performance: the resource-based view and stakeholder bargaining power. *Organizational Science*, 10(2), 119–33.

Contractor, F.J. and Kundu, S.K. (1998) Modal choice in a world of alliances: analyzing organizational forms in the international hotel sector. *Journal of International Business Studies*, 29(2), 325–57.

Cunill, O.M. and Forteza, C.M. (2010) The franchise contract in hotel chains: a study of hotel chain growth and market concentrations. *Tourism Economics*, 16(3), 493–515.

Dev, C., Erramilli, K. and Agarwal, S. (2002) Brands across borders. *Cornell Hotel and Restaurant Administration Quarterly*, 43(6), 91–104.

Eisenhardt, K. (1989) Agency theory: an assessment and review. *The Academy of Management Review*, 14(1), 57–74.

Erramilli, M.K., Agarwal, S. and Dev, S.C. (2002) Choice between non-equity entry modes: an organizational capability perspective. *Journal of International Business Studies*, 33(2), 223–53.

Ford, R. (2011) Friends to grow and foes to know: lessons in successful stakeholder management from Orlando. An interview with William C. Peeper, President (retired), Orlando County Convention and Visitors Bureau. *International Journal of Contemporary Hospitality Management*, 23(5), 696–712.

Foss, N. (1996) Capabilities and the theory of the firm. *Revue d'Économie Industrielle*, 77(3), 7–28.

Freeman, R.E. (2004) The stakeholder approach revisited. *Zeitschrift für Wirtschafts- und Unternehmensethik*, 5(3), 220–41.

Freeman, R.E. (2010) *Strategic Management: A Stakeholder Approach*. Cambridge: Cambridge University Press.

Hallin, C.A. and Marnburg, E. (2008) Knowledge management in hospitality industry: a review of empirical research. *Tourism Management*, 29(2), 366–81.

Harrison, J. and Enz, C. (2005) *Hospitality Strategic Management*. New Jersey: John Wiley and Sons, Inc.

Hill, C.W. and Jones, T. (1992) Stakeholder-agency theory. *Journal of Management Studies*, 29(2), 131–54.

IHG Owners Association (2012) Online. Available HTTP: <http://www.owners.org>, accessed 10 June 2012.

Ivanov, S. and Zhechev, V. (2011) Hotel Marketing (in Bulgarian). Varna: Zangador.

Ivanova, M. (2013) Affiliation to hotel chains as a development opportunity for Bulgarian hotels (in Bulgarian). (Unpublished doctoral dissertation). University of Economics, Varna.

Ivanova, M. and Ivanov, S. (2015) The nature of hotel chains: an integrative framework. *International Journal of Hospitality and Tourism Administration*, 16(2), 122–42.

Ivanova, M.G. (2011) Stakeholder model of hotel chains: a conceptual framework. In H.N. Hanbabaeva, T.B. Hristova and A.M. Kurbanova (eds), *Proceedings of the 'Strategic Development of Tourism and Recreation' International Conference*. Mahachkala, Russia, September 2011, pp. 45–49.

Jensen, M.C. and Meckling, W.H. (1976) Theory of the firm: managerial behavior, agency costs and ownership structure. *Journal of Financial Economics*, 3(4) 305–60.

Johnson, C. and Vanetti, M. (2005) Locational strategies of international hotel chains. *Annals of Tourism Research*, 32(4), 1077–99.

Jurgens, M., Berthon, P., Papania, L. and Shabbir, H.A. (2010) Stakeholder theory and practice in Europe and North America: the key to success lies in marketing approach. *Industrial Marketing Management*, 39(5), 769–75.

Madhok, A. (1997) Cost, value and foreign market entry: the transaction and the firm. *Strategic Management Journal*, 18(1), 39–61.

Madhok, A. (2002) Reassessing the fundamentals and beyond: Ronald Coase, the transaction cost and resource-based theories of the firm and the institutional structure of production. *Strategic Management Journal*, 23(6), 535–50.

Panvisavas, V. and Taylor, J.S. (2008) Restraining opportunism in hotel management contracts. *Tourism and Hospitality Research*, 8(4), 324–36.

Peng, M. (2001) The resource-based view and international business. *Journal of Management*, 27(6), 803–29.

Porter, M. (1985) *Competitive Advantage. Creating and Sustaining Superior Performance*. New York: The Free Press. Reprinted in 1998 with a new introduction.

Porter, M. (1991) Towards a dynamic theory of strategy. *Strategic Management Journal*, 12(S2), 95–117.

Ray, G., Barney, J. and Muhanna, W. (2004) Capabilities, business processes and competitive advantage: choosing the dependent variable in empirical tests of the resource-based view. *Strategic Management Journal*, 25(1), 23–37.

Turner, M.J. and Guilding, C. (2010) Hotel management contracts and deficiencies in owner-operator capital expenditure goal congruency. *Journal of Hospitality and Tourism Research*, 34(4), 478–511.

Vaishnav, T. and Altinay, L. (2009) The franchise partner selection process and implications for India. *Worldwide Hospitality and Tourism Themes*, 1(1), 52–65.

Villalonga, B. (2004) Intangible resources, Tobin's *q*, and sustainability of performance differences. *Journal of Economic Behavior and Organization*, 54(2), 205–30.

Wright, P.M., McMahan, G.C. and McWilliams, A. (1994) Human resources and sustained competitive advantage: a resource-based perspective. *The International Journal of Human Resource Management*, 5(2), 301–26.

7

Economic impacts of hotel chains on host destination

Ige Pirnar

(YASAR UNIVERSITY, TURKEY)

Introduction

The tourism industry consists of many sub-industries like transportation companies, hotel and lodging firms, recreation, entertainment, F&B and other related services and infrastructural elements, and destinations' various resources like cultural and heritage resources which are all necessary for the tourism system to run and operate effectively (Tavmergen, 2000; Pirnar, 2011). As it implies, lodging establishments are vital components of tourism systems because they have a very important impact on local and national economies. Since hotel chains usually make up the major part of the whole global accommodation and lodging market, we may conclude that their economic impacts have a very important effect on the economic structure of local economies and the tourism destinations they operate in. Thus, the economic gains of these hotel chains are huge in sum, since their revenues not only come from the tourist (guest) expenses as hotel room spending, but from hotels' various service offerings like F&B, events, MICE, gift shops, health and spa services, etc.

Unfortunately, not all the economic impacts of hotel chains are in favour of the local and national economies and tourist destinations, since there are leakages from these gains in the form of imports and such. Due to the complex nature of the economic impacts of hotel chains, this chapter focuses separately on the positive and negative economic impacts of chains, and attempts to delineate the reasons and group the further impacts for better understanding. The chapter concludes with the trends affecting the economic impacts of hotel chains on host destinations, since it is important to predict the future for better planning and healthy strategies.

Economic impacts of hotel chains on tourism destinations

Hotel chains are formed with the aim of achieving higher profits and a better competitive market position by efficiently coordinating and co-sharing the management functions (Johnson and Vanetti, 2005). They may operate at various levels from local small scale to regional, national or international giant forms where their differential marketing and management advantage comes from sharing a common brand, logo, slogan, popular concept or theme, strategies, innovations and management know-how with exceptionally low operational costs

Table 7.1 Global hotel industry revenue from 2008 to prediction for 2016 (in billion US dollars)

Years	Revenue in billion US dollars
2008	447
2009	395
2010	419
2011	457
2016 (prediction)	550

Source: Statista, statistics and market Data on accommodation, http://www.statista.com/markets/420/topic/1018/accomodation/.

(Weber, 2000; Akyuz, 2008). Due to their advantages over independent hotels, their share in the global hotel market is continuously increasing (Calveras, 2003: 219). In 2012, the 300 best ranked hotel chains owned 54,400 hotels and over 7.2 million rooms, making up around one third of the world's accommodation capacity (IBIS World, 2014). This increase has been constant: the total number of global hotel rooms has reached 19.5 million, with 240,000 additional chain supply rooms added to the market on 1 January, 2014 (Panayotis, 2014).

A comparison of the development processes of hotel chains vs individual hotels indicates that the chain hotel industry concentration is increasing, and there is a trend for both luxury and budget segments resulting from hotel mergers, buyouts and franchise chain operations (Chu, 2014). As the figures in Table 7.1 imply, the global tourism industry's significant increase in arrival and revenue figures had caused a significant increase in the revenues of the major global hotel chains.

This rapid increase in the number of hotels, guest revenues and global hotel market share altogether makes international hotel chains very important economically to the host destinations and countries they operate within. It is important to keep in mind that these vital economic impacts could be negative as well as positive, therefore being aware of them is very important for sound and effective management applications. Due to this importance, the positive and negative economic impacts of hotel chains on the destinations they operate within (as explored by Stynes, 1997; Bulut, 1999; Stynes, 2001; Archer et al., 2005; Ertugral, 2011; Ecer and Gunay, 2014) are summarised in Table 7.2, discussed further in detail below.

Positive economic impacts of hotel chains

The tourism industry generates substantial economic benefits for host destinations. In developing nations especially, one of the primary motives of destinations for investing in tourism is the expected local positive economic impact. Standardised global hotel chains operating at the host destinations are one of the important contributors to this positive economic impact (Brians, 2011). These hotel chains prove to have vital economic effects on local communities by increasing the economic value of the destinations they operate within (Font et al., 2008; Zhang et al., 2009; Rusco et al., 2009).

The general positive economic impacts of chain hotels on any size and position of tourism destination (in the form of a town, a city, a region or a country) may be summarised as follows (Stynes, 1997, 2001; Archer et al., 2005):

• When a region hosts international tourists, hotel chains *bring tourism revenues* which in turn increase overall income level. Therefore, within the same regard, hotel chains are a

Table 7.2 The positive and negative economic impacts of hotel chains on destinations they operate within

Positive economic impacts	Negative economic impacts
• Bring tourism revenues and increase overall income level. • Significant source of foreign exchange earnings. • Provide additional, unqualified and qualified, direct and indirect employment opportunities for local people. • Have an important role in regional and local economic diversification. • Staff salaries lead to economic liveliness and have a multiplier effect on local economy. • Encourage the development of many tourism-related infrastructure and facilities. • Management styles focusing on productivity and efficiency have positive impact on host destination. • Amount of the tourism-related destination investments and the number of the destination-related projects on sustainability and innovation increases. • In mega cities and popular destinations some largest increases as a proportion of existing construction businesses are provided by new hotel chain investments. • Positively impact the quality of local life standards. • Promote the sales of locally produced art objects, handicrafts and creative projects leading to increase in the monetary earnings of local people. • Hotel guests' discretionary spending on local economy, and other payments like additional tax to the government, benefits local economy. • Positively impact entrepreneurship of SME's in the host destinations and related innovation attempts. • Some of the hotel chains overcome the common seasonality problem of the destination's other accommodation businesses. • Successful hotel chains are found to increase the host destination's competitiveness levels. • Establishment of training and learning systems improves coordination among staff, staff qualification and organisational structures. • Hotel chains usually improve the economic welfare of local training professionals by providing extra part-time employment opportunities. • Hotel chains usually have and use their network systems for marketing, reservation and related operations, which consequently help the destination management organisations' promotional efforts. • Hotel chains located at city centres economically aid the related city's/ destination's branding and marketing efforts such that the positive outcomes are very similar to co-branding, co-advertising and co-marketing efforts.	• Leakage of cash flows. • Often built largely with imported raw materials leading to higher import expenditures. • Hiring of foreign expatriates and other foreign staff can lead to a transfer of their salaries to their home countries' economies as savings. • Foreign hotel chains increase the inflation rate (price level of local economy), the land prices, consume the capital of other sectors and sometimes do have oligopolistic negative impacts on the local economies.

significant *source of foreign exchange earnings* for international tourism destinations which are good sources of revenue generators (Bulut, 1999).

- Hotel chains *provide additional, some unqualified, direct and indirect employment opportunities for local people* (Boardman and Barbato, 2008, p. 25). Also, *they create employment opportunities in specialised jobs for qualified staff* like front office and F&B staff, gourmet chefs, social marketing experts for lodging and specialised hotel accountants (Ozdemir and Akpinar, 2002). Some hotel chains are in favour of outsourcing instead of directly hiring their own staff for special job areas like technical services, animation, security, laundry services and housekeeping operations, but outsourcing still has a direct effect on the host destinations' employment numbers (Turksoy and Turksoy, 2007; Tetik and Oren, 2007).

- Since the hotel chains offer various services and offer sustainable and charity programmes, *they play an important part in regional and local economic diversification* (Beyer, 2013). Also, donations, sustainable local PR projects and voluntary support of the chain hotels favour and benefit the local low income population.

- The increased numbers of qualified and non-qualified job opportunities lead to increased incomes for local people (Ecer and Gunay, 2014). This improvement in local peoples' financial situations also leads to *a multiplier effect* when these salaries are spent on purchasing goods and services from the local economy. The phenomenon of currency staying in the local economy and, by changing hands, increasing in value, is known as the *economic liveliness and multiplier effect* (Ertugral, 2011). The size and intensity of the multiplier effect on the destination depends on the following criteria (Archer, 1982: 123):

  o   dimension of the destination area;
  o   proportion of services and goods imported in order to be consumed by guests;
  o   dimension of tourist flows;
  o   guests' expenses/expenditure typology;
  o   availability and reachability of local products and services for supply purchases;
  o   main characteristics of the guest behaviour from a certain region.

- Hotel chains *encourage the development of tourism-related infrastructure and facilities*, such as airports and airstrips, restaurants, museums, attractions, roads and communication facilities, which affects the overall economic structure of the destination (Tavmergen, 1998; Rogerson, 2002).

- Hotel chains place great emphasis on efficiency, and studies show that they are more efficient and productive when compared to non-chain hotels (Brown and Dev, 2000; Oktay and Ozgur, 2008; Petrović et al., 2013). Since there is a direct and positive relationship between the level of productivity and the economic development of the related regions, it may be concluded that *hotel chains have a positive economic impact on host destinations by their management styles focusing on efficiency* (David et al., 1996; Akyuz, 2008).

- When new hotel chains are introduced to a host destination, there is usually an *increase in the amount of the tourism-related destination investments and the number of destination-related projects on sustainability and innovation*, which positively impacts the local economy (Akama and Kieti, 2007; Genc and Pirnar, 2008; McNeill, 2008). Popular global hotel chains usually bring new hotel projects and investments to the destinations they are planning to operate within and these projects are important not only for second tier cities, but also for famous brand mega cities like Istanbul, Dubai and New York, boosting the construction business in these cities. *In mega cities and popular destinations, some of the largest increases as a proportion of existing construction businesses are provided by new hotel chain investments.* Many illustrations of these effects may be found in mega cities like Moscow, Istanbul, Antalya, London, Amsterdam, Berlin, Edinburgh, Zurich, Frankfurt and Vienna (PricewaterhouseCoopers, 2014: 23).

- Chain-affiliated properties such as convention hotels, business hotels, casinos and wellness hotels adopt more IT/new technologies and often focus more on corporate social responsibility projects than budget or independent hotels (Siguaw et al., 2000). As the hotel chains' offerings such as convention and event services, spas and wellness services, sustainable technology applications and social responsibility projects increase, so does their *positive impact on the quality of life standards* of the host destination (Bohdanowicz and Zientara, 2009; Gunlu and Pirnar, 2013). Besides improving the local quality of life, the hotel chains' activities involving events, exhibits, conferences, wellness improvement programmes *promote the sales of locally produced art objects, handicrafts and creative projects leading to an increase in the monetary earnings of local people.*

- Hotel chains also benefit the host destinations through *guests' discretionary spending in the local economy, and other payments to government* related to hotel construction and taxes (ODI, 2012). Hotel chains, with their financial revenues and profit gains, bring additional tax revenue items to host destination's gains (Tavmergen, 1998).

- Hotel chains positively impact *entrepreneurship of SMEs in the host destinations and related innovation attempts.* For example, one of the positive economic impacts of hotel chains on host destinations is through *increasing the innovative measures that these types of hotels bring to the destination.* The research results on the Balearic Islands of Spain showed that chain hotels place a much greater emphasis on technological innovation than independent hotels (Orfila-Sintes et al., 2005: 851). Hotel chains are members of a supplier-driven industry, innovating introduced R&D-embodied technology. It was also found that changing technological and innovative marketing competencies through network relationships in hotel chains leads to *the establishment of training and learning systems improving coordination among staff, staff qualification and organisational structures* (Tremblay, 1998; Jacob and Groizard, 2007: 976).

- Another way in which hotel chains influence their host destinations' economy far more than other accommodation and lodging facilities is that they *overcome the common seasonality problem experienced by other accommodation businesses.* Since most of the chain hotels tend to be open 12 months a year, they provide an economic liveliness for destinations all year round (Rusco et al., 2009; Durna et al., 2013).

- Successful hotel chains are found to increase *the host destinations competitiveness levels* (Claver-Cortés and Pereira-Moliner, 2007). Thus, with the help of sustainable approaches and environmental protection programmes, increased visitor safety and security systems, measures for overcoming seasonality problems, development and implementation of strategic plans and politics, hotel chains often achieve quality and effective results leading to sustainable competitive development of the tourism destinations they operate within (Evans et al., 1995; Flagestad and Hope, 2001; Yoon, 2002). It has also been reported that global chain hotels like Ibis, Hilton, Inter Continental and many others often *implement waste management, energy saving management, environmental protection systems, resource management and similar sustainable hotel systems* (Kirk, 1995; Bohdanowicz et al., 2005; Mensah, 2007). Such sustainability programme applications quite often bring significant *cost benefits at the corporate level* thus positively affecting the destination that the hotel chains operate within (Bohdanowicz, 2006).

- Recently, many hotel chains have been focusing more on providing *continuous learning opportunities* for their staff. Career development and in-house training of hotel chains' staff especially focus on topics such as orientation, improved cooking, serving, servicing, PR and marketing techniques, foreign languages and self-development. These training services are usually purchased from outside sources, mainly from local training professionals already working at language, management and tourism schools. By doing so, hotel chains improve *the economic welfare of local training professionals by providing extra part-time employment opportunities for them* (Yalcin and Iri, 2003).

• Hotel chains usually use their branded network systems for marketing, reservation and related operations, which consequently helps the destination management organisations' *promotional efforts* by *increasing their impact factor, having a synergistic effect on results and even indirectly decreasing destination management organisations' advertising and promotion costs* (Akyuz, 2008). Also, hotel chains located at city centres *economically aid the related cities'/destinations' branding and marketing efforts so that the positive outcomes are very similar to co-branding, co-advertising and co-marketing efforts.* Sometimes, hotel chains that have a unique design, creative architecture and buildings with a themed structure are recognised as important landmarks of the city or the destination (McNeill, 2008).

Negative impacts

It is obvious that hotel chains have many positive economic impacts on the destinations in which they operate, but besides these benefits, they also have some negative impacts. The general negative economic impacts of chain hotels on the destinations were summarised in Table 7.2 and are as follows:

• The main negative economic impact of a hotel chain comes in the form of *leakage*, (monetary assets leaving the host nations' or destinations' economy) in terms of imports for costs of goods and services needed for hotel operations (Tavmergen, 1992). Leakage examples may include: imported raw materials needed for hotel construction, hotel supplies for everyday usage which are purchased from another country, or employing staff from foreign nations (Tavmergen, 1998; Beyer, 2013). Studies indicate that some hotel chains are built largely with imported raw materials, and when built they provide only a limited amount of employment to locals (Supradist, 2004). This leakage becomes very high when hotel chains import everyday food and beverage supplies from other countries and have minimal contact with local economies. Fortunately, this may not be the case for all hotel chains and the leakage related to import supply purchases is in some cases minimal. For example, Telfer and Wall (2000) conducted a study that compared the food supply proce- dures and policies of variously sized hotels (namely 4- and 5-star hotel groups and non-star hotel groups) at two different locations in Indonesia. The results indicated that both chain- affiliated hotels and non–chain-affiliated hotels frequently used local supply networks for their food purchases.

• *Hotel chains often hire foreign expatriates and other foreign staff. Usually these people transfer their salaries to their home countries' economies as savings.* Vaugeois (2000) found that some international hotel chains were more likely to employ foreign expatriates and are not in favour of providing important employment opportunities for local people.

• It has also been suggested that foreign hotel chains *increase the inflation rate* (price level of local economy), the land prices, consume the capital of other sectors and sometimes do have *oligopolistic negative impacts* on local economies (Debbage, 1990; Rahovan, 2013; Suzuki, 2013: 495).

Trends affecting the economic impacts of hotel chains on host destinations

It is important to understand the trends affecting the economic impacts of hotel chains upon their host destinations since by studying and using them it is possible to maximise the provided economic gains. Five factors affect the economic impacts of global hotel chains on their host destinations (Aksu and Tercan, 2002; Prideaux, 2005; Line and Runyan, 2012):

1. Globalisation is altering language structures, culture, beliefs, attitudes and preferences of guests and hotel staff.
2. Improvements in technology: growth of e-tourism, digital technology and innovative systems.
3. Changing economic conditions lead guests to search for better price:quality ratio for hotel services.
4. Changes in the demand profiles of guests: customers are becoming more learning- and experience-oriented, showing an interest in local cultures and sustainability. They also have more affinity with technology and digital devices, are fond of smart mobile technology, and are social media friendly. They show changing preferences for their destinations and length of stay, and are demanding different, unique, tailor-made types of tourism.
5. Guests' increasing need for more security: health and safety have become major concerns for hotel chains.

As a result of the stated factors, changes lead to trends which may be further discussed as follows:

• Hotel chains are becoming more sensitive about supporting local trade and local economies which encourages them to have strong relationships with local producers of food and beverage supplies. Thus, locally produced foods are used for hotel chains' services as a result of the application of slow city and slow food movements, organic farming, sustainable hotel management strategies and stronger policies for farmers-to-hotel supply chain relationships (Gunlu and Pirnar, 2013; Thomas-Francois et al., 2014).

• Hotel chains increasingly emphasise sustainable and innovative operations due to the many benefits associated with them. Economic viability is a part of the sustainable development strategy practised by many hotel chains. The objective is to create superior value for their shareholders and guests through innovative approaches, corporate social responsibility applications and usage of sustainable development principles which lead to an increase in revenues and better productivity while minimising costs (Blake et al., 2006). To summarise, sustainable and innovative operations by hotel chains usually lead to gains in economic benefits in the form of higher competitiveness, better brand image of the hotel and higher levels of customer satisfaction (Khunon and Muangasame, 2013; Kapiki et al., 2014).

• Another economic trend affecting destinations is the increase in strategic partnerships and alliances among the hotel chains (Pirnar, 2015). This collective application leads to a greater integration of hotel chains' 'back-office' functions and optimisation of the positive economic impacts for the host destination's knowledge-based economic structures. With this trend, various parts of the destinations' economic value chain belonging to various hotel chains coordinate and comply with each other, resulting in the formation of synergistic competitor alliances (Contractor and Lorange, 2002; Chathoth and Olsen, 2003; Johnson and Vanetti, 2005; Pirnar, 2015).

- High dependence on information technology (IT) in chain hotels affects host destinations in a way that adapt and become a knowledge-based economy (Aksu and Tercan, 2002).
- Five-star hotel chains operating in the developing countries like Turkey, have an influential emphasis on luxury travel and affluent travellers which in turn positively affects and increases the amount of the foreign tourism earnings and economic gains of the destination (Pirnar et al., 2011).
- International and national hotel chains are becoming more and more specialised in good management practices and economic efficiency which in turn impact the overall economic situation of the host destinations they operate within (Yu and Lee, 2009). Some of these good management practices leading to productivity are: usage of transnational ownership structures and outsourcing, applying cross-border marketing collaborations and co-branding and adapting advanced hotel technology and transferring know-how (Hjalager, 2007: 437).

Conclusion

This rapid growth of national and international hotel chains makes them very important economically to the destinations they operate in. The positive economic impacts of these hotel chains are commonly associated with: increased foreign exchange earnings, increased income and increased employment opportunities (both qualified and non-qualified) in the host destination, increased local salaries leading to a higher multiplier effect and a livelier economy, local economic diversification and voluntary efforts to support local low-income people. More positive impacts occur in the form of investments in infrastructure and construction businesses, an increase in the host destinations' competitiveness levels, and improvements in destinations' economic development which are all stimulated by hotel chain efforts. Therefore, it may be concluded that hotel chains indeed support local destination economies in many ways, especially if the negative impacts like leakages can be minimised.

Further improvements may be achieved if a sustainable supply-chain management between local marketers (of products in the form of food and non-food items and services) and hotel chain purchasing systems can be established.

References

Akama, J.S. and Kieti, D. (2007) Tourism and socio-economic development in developing countries: a case study of Mombasa Resort in Kenya. *Journal of Sustainable Tourism*, 15(6), 735–48.

Aksu, A.A. and Tarcan, E. (2002) The Internet and five-star hotels: a case study from the Antalya region in Turkey. *International Journal of Contemporary Hospitality Management*, 14(2), 94–97.

Akyuz, S. (2008) *Cok uluslu otel isletmelerinde verimlilik anlayisi: Istanbul ornegi* [The productivity concept in MNC hotels. Case of Istanbul] (Unpublished Master's thesis). Balikesir University Social Sciences Institute, Balikesir.

Archer, B.H. (1982) The value of multipliers and their policy implications. *Tourism Management*, 3, 236–41.

Archer, B., Cooper, C. and Ruhanen, L. (2005) The positive and negative impacts of tourism. In W.F. Theobald (ed.), *Global Tourism*, 3rd edition. Burlington, MA: Elsevier, pp. 79–102.

Beyer, M. (2013) Economic impacts of all-inclusive resorts – facts, approaches, constraints and recommendations. *2nd Executive Symposium for Innovators in Coastal Tourism Development*, 15–18 May 2013, Los Cabos.

Blake, A., Sinclair, M.T. and Soria, J.A.C. (2006). Tourism productivity: evidence from the United Kingdom. *Annals of Tourism Research*, 33(4), 1099–1120.

Boardman, J. and Barbato, C. (2008) Review of socially responsible HR and labour relations practice in international hotel chains: working paper. International Labour Office, Geneva, June 2008.

Bohdanowicz, P. (2006) *Responsible resource management in hotels: attitudes, indicators, tools and strategies* (Unpublished doctoral dissertation). KTH Royal Institute of Technology, Sweden.

Bohdanowicz, P. and Zientara, P. (2009) Hotel companies' contribution to improving the quality of life of local communities and the well-being of their employees. *Tourism and Hospitality Research*, 9(2), 147–158.

Bohdanowicz, P., Simanic, B. and Martinac, I. (2005) Sustainable hotels: environmental reporting according to Green Globe 21. Green Globes Canada/GEM UK, IHEI benchmark hotel and Hilton Environmental Reporting. Sustainable Building (SB05) Conference, September 27–29, 2005. Tokyo, Japan, pp. 1642–49.

Brians, A. (2011) *Impact of Globalization on Hospitality*, Munich, GRIN Publishing GmbH, Online. Available HTTP: <http://www.grin.com/en/e-book/211918/impact-of-globalization-on-hospitality>, accessed 10 January 2015.

Brown, J.R. and Dev, C.S. (2000) Improving productivity in a service business: evidence from the hotel industry. *Journal of Service Research*, 2(4), 339–54.

Bulut, E. (1999) *Turizmin Turkiye ekonomisindeki yeri ve ekonomik etkileri* [The place of tourism in Turkish economy and its economic impacts]. Online. Available HTTP: <http://www.ekitapyayin.com/id/025/04.htm>, accessed 1 January 2015.

Calveras, A.L. (2003) Incentives of international and local hotel chains to invest in environmental quality. *Tourism Economics*, 9(3), 297–306.

Chathoth, P.K. and Olsen, M.D. (2003) Strategic alliances: a hospitality industry perspective. *International Journal of Hospitality Management*, 22(4), 419–34.

Chu, Y. (2014) *A review of studies on luxury hotels over the past two decades.* Graduate Theses and Dissertations: Paper 13913. Master of Science Thesis, Iowa State University. Online. Available HTTP: <http://lib.dr.iastate.edu/etd/13913> accessed 10 January 2015

Claver-Cortés, E. and Pereira-Moliner, J. (2007) Competitiveness in mass tourism. *Annals of Tourism Research*, 34(3), 727–45.

Contractor, F. J. and Lorange, P. (2002) The growth of alliances in the knowledge-based economy. *International Business Review*, 11(4), 485–502.

David, J.S., Grabski, S. and Kasavana, M. (1996) The productivity paradox of hotel industry technology. *The Cornell Hotel and Restaurant Administration Quarterly*, 37(2), 64–70.

Debbage, K.G. (1990) Oligopoly and the resort cycle in the Bahamas. *Annals of Tourism Research*, 17(4), 513–27.

Durna, U., Inal, M.E. and Kurar, I. (2013) Ulusal otel zincirinin buyume basarısına iliskin bir degerlendirme: Rixos otel zinciri [An assessment on the national hotel chain growth success: the case of the Rixos hotel group]. In *International Conference on Eurasian Economies*, St Petersburg, Russia, 721–33.

Ecer, F. and Gunay, F. (2014) Measuring the financial performances of tourism firms traded on the Borsa Istanbul through gray relational analysis method. *Anatolia: Turizm Arastirmalari Dergisi*, 25(1), 35–48.

Ertugral, S.M. (2011) Istihdam yapimizin incelenmesi ve Istanbul'daki 5 yildizli otellere yonelik bir çalisma [Analysis of our employment structure and a study on 5 star hotels in Istanbul]. *Istanbul University Faculty of Economics Journal*, 52(2), 1–13.

Evans, M.R., Fox, J.B. and Johnson, R.B. (1995) Identifying competitive strategies for successful tourism destination development. *Journal of Hospitality & Leisure Marketing*, 3(1), 37–45.

Flagestad, A. and Hope, C.A. (2001) Strategic success in winter sports destinations: a sustainable value creation perspective. *Tourism Management*, 22(5), 445–61.

Font, X., Tapper, R., Schwartz, K. and Kornilaki, M. (2008) Sustainable supply chain management in tourism. *Business Strategy and the Environment*, 17(4), 260–71.

Genc, R. and Pirnar, I. (2008) Brand management in DMO's: case study on DMO's role in tourism marketing in Turkey. *Kafkas University Journal of Institute of Social Sciences*, 2, 121–36.

Gunlu, E. and Pirnar I. (2013) Tourism destination's competitiveness factors and their impact on quality of life of the residents: Case of Cıttaslow – Seferihisar. In *6th International Conference on Services Management*, 23–25 June 2013, Northern Cyprus.

Hjalager, A.M. (2007) Stages in the economic globalization of tourism. *Annals of Tourism Research*, 34(2), 437–57.

IBIS World (2014). Global hotels & resorts: market research report. Online. Available HTTP: <http://www.ibisworld.com/industry/global/global-hotels-resorts.html> accessed 5 January, 2015.

Jacob, M. and Groizard, J.L. (2007) Technology transfer and multinationals: the case of Balearic hotel chains' investments in two developing economies. *Tourism Management*, 28(4), 976–92.

Johnson, C. and Vanetti, M. (2005) Locational strategies of international hotel chains. *Annals of Tourism Research*, 32(4), 1077–99.

Kapiki, S.T., Mu, L. and Fu, J. (2014) Assessment of the lodging industry profitability performance: invest in independent or chain ownership? *TURIZAM*, 18(2), 84–94.

Khunon, S. and Muangasame, K. (2013) The differences between local and international chain hotels in CSR management: Empirical findings from a case study in Thailand. *Asian Social Science*, 9(5), 209–25.

Kirk, D. (1995) Environmental management in hotels. *International Journal of Contemporary Hospitality Management*, 7(6), 3–8.

Line, N.D. and Runyan, R.C. (2012) Hospitality marketing research: recent trends and future directions. *International Journal of Hospitality Management*, 31(2), 477–88.

McNeill, D. (2008) The hotel and the city. *Progress in Human Geography*, 32(3), 383–98.

Mensah, I. (2007) Environmental management and sustainable tourism development: the case of hotels in Greater Accra Region (GAR) of Ghana. *Journal of Retail & Leisure Property*, 6(1), 15–22.

Overseas Development Institue (ODI) (2012) *Investing in hotels and demonstrating development impact: Case study of IFC's investment in the Serena Kigali Hotel*, Rwanda (June, 2012). Online. Available HTTP: <http://www.ifc.org/wps/wcm/connect/2e8ac3004b885faebb8ffbbbd578891b/Serena+Kigali+CS.pdf?MOD=AJPERES> 10 January 10, 2015.

Oktay, E. and Ozgur, E. (2008) Influence analysis of accommodation establishments. *Afyon Kocatepe University Journal of Social Sciences Institute*, 10(1), 164.

Orfila-Sintes, F., Crespí-Cladera, R. and Martínez-Ros, E. (2005) Innovation activity in the hotel industry: evidence from Balearic Islands. *Tourism Management*, 26(6), 851–65.

Ozdemir, E. and Akpınar, A.T. (2002) Konaklama İşletmelerinde İnsan Kaynakları Yonetimi, Çerçevesinde Alanya'daki Otel ve Tatil Koylerinde İnsan Kaynakları Profili [The profile of human resources of hotels and resorts Alanya region within the perspective of human resources management in accommodation enrterprises]. *Kocaeli University, Sciences Institute Journal*, 3(2), 85–105, Kocaeli.

Panayotis, G. (2014) 2014 Global hotel rankings: the leaders grow stronger; IHG retains top spot, 23 June, 2014. Online. Available HTTP: <http://www.hotel-online.com/press_releases/release/global-hotel-rankings-the-leaders-grow-stronger-ihg-retains-top-spot> accessed January 12th, 2015

Petrović, M.D., Jovičić, A., Marković, J.J. and Gagić, S. (2013) Territorial expansion of hotel chains in countries of South-eastern Europe. *Journal of the Geographical Institute Jovan Cvijic*, SASA, 63(4), 75–92.

Pirnar, I. (2011) Alternative tourism potential of Aegean region and implications for future. In *9th Asia-Pacific CHRIE (APac-CHRIE) Conference, Hospitality and Tourism Education: From a Vision to an Icon*, The Hong Kong Polytechnic University's School of Hotel and Tourism Management, 2–5 June 2011, Hong Kong.

Pirnar, I. (2015) Partnerships and alliances in tourism: aims & functions. In: D. Gursoy, M. Saayman, and D. Sotiriadis, *Collaboration in Tourism Businesses and Destinations: A Handbook*. Bingley, UK: Emerald Group Publishing Inc., pp. 41–56.

Pirnar I., Icoz O. and Icoz O. (2011) Affluent marketing and implications on hospitality: case from Izmir. In *Advances in Hospitality and Tourism Marketing and Management Conference Proceedings*, 19–24 June 2011, Washington State University & Bogazici University, Istanbul, Turkey, 20–25.

PricewaterhouseCoopers (2014) Room to grow: European cities hotel forecast for 2014 and 2015. Online. Available HTTP: <http://www.pwc.com/en_GX/gx/hospitality-leisure/pdf/pwc-european-cities-hotel-forecast-2014-and-2015.pdf> accessed 2 January, 2015.

Prideaux, B. (2005) Factors affecting bilateral tourism flows. *Annals of Tourism Research*, 32(3), 780–801.

Rahovan, A.L. (2013) Transylvanian hotels and their economic impacts on tourism. *GeoJournal of Tourism and Geosites*, 12(2), 163–74.

Rogerson, C.M. (2002) Tourism and local economic development: the case of the Highlands Meander. *Development Southern Africa*, 19(1), 143–67.

Rusko, R.T., Kylänen, M. and Saari, R. (2009) Supply chain in tourism destinations: the case of Levi Resort in Finnish Lapland. *International Journal of Tourism Research*, 11(1), 71–87.

Siguaw, J.A., Enz, C.A. and Namasivayam, K. (2000) Adoption of information technology in US hotels: strategically driven objectives. *Journal of Travel Research*, 39(2), 192–201.

Statista: The Statistics Portal (2014) Statista, statistics and market data on accommodation. Online. Available HTTP: <http://www.statista.com/markets/420/topic/1018/accomodation/>, accessed 15 March 2015.

Stynes, D.J. (1997) *Economic Impacts of Tourism: A Handbook for Tourism Professionals*. Urbana, IL: University of Illinois, Tourism Research Laboratory, 1–32.

Stynes, D.J. (2001) Estimating economic impacts of tourist spending on local regions: A comparison of satellite and survey/IO approaches. In *Proceedings Censtates TTRA Annual Meeting*, Lisle Illinois, 19–21 Sept, 2001, pp. 209–18.

Supradist, N. (2004) *Economic leakage in tourism sector*, IIIEE Master's Theses 2004:19. The International Institute for Industrial Environmental Economics Lund, Sweden.

Suzuki, J. (2013) Land use regulation as a barrier to entry: evidence from the Texas lodging industry. *International Economic Review*, 54(2), 495–523.

Tavmergen, P.I. (1992) Economic impacts of tourism. *Journal of Treasure and International Trade*, 3(14), 121–26.

Tavmergen, P.I. (1998) Turizmin ekonomiye olumlu etkileri ve Turkiye ornegi [The positive impacts of tourism on economy and the case of Turkey]. *Journal of Treasure*, 12, 53–66.

Tavmergen, P.I. (2000) Uluslararası pazarlama ve ihracatta yönetim organizasyonları [International marketing and export management organizations]. *Journal of Economic Vision (Ekonomik Vizyon Dergisi)*, 71(42), 60–66.

Telfer, D.J. and Wall, G. (2000) Strengthening backward economic linkages: local food purchasing by three Indonesian hotels. *Tourism Geographies*, 2(4), 421–47.

Tetik, N. and Oren, E. (2007) Dis kaynak kullanimi: antalya yoresindeki bes yildizli otellerde bir arastirma [Outsourcing applications: A research on 5 star hotels in Antalya region]. *Journal of Accounting and Finance*, 34, 74–86.

Thomas-Francois, K., von Massow, M., Joppe, M. and Hall, M.S. (2014) Strengthening farmers–hotel supply chain relationships to facilitate agriculture and tourism linkages with local food in Grenada: a service management approach. *TTRA 45th annual international conference: Tourism and the New Global Economy*, 18–20 June 2014, Belgium. Online. Available HTTP: <http://assets.conferencespot.org/fileserver/file/263288/filename/142.pdf> accessed 5 January 2015.

Tremblay, P. (1998) The economic organization of tourism. *Annals of Tourism Research*, 25(4), 837–59.

Turksoy, A. and Turksoy, S.S. (2007) Otel isletmelerinde dis kaynaklardan yararlanma [Optimizing outsourcing in hotel establishments]. *Dokuz Eylul University Faculty of Economics and Administrative Sciences Journal*, 22(1), 83–104.

Vaugeois, N. (2000) Tourism in developing countries: refining a useful tool for economic development. In *6th World Leisure Congress Proceedings*, Bilbao, Spain. Online. Available HTTP: <http://fama2.us.es:8080/turismo/turismonet1/economia%20del%20turismo/economia%20del%20turismo/tourism%20and%20developing%20countries.pdf> accessed 15 January, 2015.

Weber, K. (2000) Meeting planners' perceptions of hotel-chain practices and benefits: an importance-performance analysis. *The Cornell Hotel and Restaurant Administration Quarterly*, 41(4), 32–38.

Yalcin I. and Iri, R. (2003) Hizmetici Egitim, Turkiye'de Bes Yildizli Otellerde Uygulanmayi Bekliyor [Inhouse training, awaiting to be applied at five star hotels in Turkey]. *Gazi University Commerce and Tourism Education Faculty Journal*, 5(1), 91–106, Ankara.

Yoon, S-J. (2002) The antecedents and consequences of trust in online-purchase decisions. *Journal of Interactive Marketing*, 16(2), 47–63.

Yu, M.M. and Lee, B.C. (2009) Efficiency and effectiveness of service business: evidence from international tourist hotels in Taiwan. *Tourism Management*, 30(4), 571–80.

Zhang, X., Song, H. and Huang, G.Q. (2009) Tourism supply chain management: a new research agenda. *Tourism Management*, 30(3), 345–58.

8

Socio-cultural impacts
of hotel chains

B. Bynum Boley and Emily P. Ayscue

(UNIVERSITY OF GEORGIA, USA)

Introduction

Hotel chains, by their very nature and size (around 70 per cent of U.S. hotel rooms – Sadovi, 2013), have a predisposition towards large positive and negative impacts within their host communities. Alongside the economic and environmental impacts commonly associated with hotel chains, there are a host of socio-cultural impacts on the communities in which they operate. These socio-cultural impacts describe the many ways hotel chains can positively or negatively impact the quality of life of community residents and their employees (Sloan et al., 2012). With this emphasis on impact on the community and employee quality of life, there is often some overlap between the socio-cultural impacts of hotel chains and their economic impacts within the community, because both of these factors influence quality of life. These broad socio-cultural impacts range from positive impacts such as increased employment opportunities, spaces for community socialising and urban renewal, to negative impacts such as poorly paid jobs, homogenisation of the host culture and economic leakage of profits.

Despite hotel chains' association with these socio-cultural impacts, the hospitality literature has largely left the discussion of the industry's socio-cultural impacts to the broader tourism literature (Smith, 1979), and has instead tended to focus more on the environmental impacts (Bohdanowicz, 2005; Butler, 2008; Lee et al., 2010; Sloan et al., 2012). This may stem from the fact that there are clearer linkages between environmental sustainability and profitability through the coveted cost savings associated with environmental sustainability and the potential of increased market share gained as a result of increased customer demand for hotels to 'go green'. Socio-cultural impacts of hotels is also a much more nebulous topic that does not easily lend itself to empirical research, unlike environmental impacts (Bohdanowicz and Zientara, 2008). These factors help explain why there has been limited direct discussion of hotel chains' socio-cultural impacts within the hospitality literature as compared to their environmental impacts.

Where socio-cultural impacts are discussed in the context of hotel chains, it is often as a facet of a hotel chain's Corporate Social Responsibility (CSR) programme. Even when discussed within the context of CSR, the socio-cultural impacts of hotel chains are often overshadowed by the hotel chain's environmental initiatives because, as mentioned above, hotel chains' environmental impacts are easier to measure and they also have a more direct relationship with financial performance (Bohdanowicz and Zientara, 2008). The purpose of this chapter is to take a critical perspective on the many socio-cultural impacts hotel chains have within communities. The predominant focus on hotel chains' socio-cultural impacts has been in a positive light and how promoting these positive impacts through CSR programmes relates to financial performance. It is hoped that a more critical discussion will illuminate areas where hotel chains are underperforming and bring awareness to how hotel chains can increase their financial performance through managing their socio-cultural impacts.

TBL sustainability and corporate social responsibility

Within the hospitality literature, there has been a growing emphasis on how hotels perform across the triple bottom line (TBL) instead of solely focusing on the economic bottom line (Boley and Uysal, 2014). This TBL perspective places hotels' environmental and social performance on the same footing as the hotels' economic performance. The concept stems from Elkington's (1997) attempt to broaden businesses' performance metrics to focus

> not just on the economic value they add, but also on the environmental and social value they add – and destroy. At its narrowest, TBL is used as a framework for measuring and reporting corporate performance against economic, social and environmental parameters. At its broadest, the term is used to capture the whole set of values, issues and processes that companies must address in order to minimise any harm resulting from their activities and to create economic, social and environmental values.
>
> (p. 372)

This emphasis on sustainability across the TBL has resulted in many hotel chains adding a corporate social responsibility (CSR) dimension to their business plans. Following the industry's lead, the body of hospitality literature has responded with a variety of recent studies focused on CSR (Bohdanowicz and Zientara, 2008; Font et al., 2012; Kang et al., 2010; Kucukusta et al., 2013). These CSR programmes centre around the premise that 'businesses ought to justify their existence in terms of service to the community rather than mere profit' (Bohdanowicz and Zientara, 2008: 148). Additionally, CSR initiatives place importance on 'dealing fairly with employees, suppliers and customers ... supporting local communities, donating to charitable causes and promoting environmental sustainability' (Bohdanowicz and Zientara, 2008: 148).

While CSR policies have been nearly universally accepted by hotel chains, it should be noted that when talking about socio-cultural impacts of hotel chains, CSR initiatives are mere strategies for dealing with the negative impacts commonly associated with the hospitality industry; they do not constitute positive or negative socio-cultural impacts in and of themselves. These initiatives are used solely to maximise the positive environmental and socio-cultural impacts of hotel chains and to effectively publicise them to their stakeholders. The positive press that comes alongside hotel chains' CSR initiatives is one of the strongest impetuses for the near universal adaptation of CSR across hotel chains; one hotel chain does not want to seem as if they do not care about their impacts when their competitors are promoting their sustainable initiatives. However, adoption of CSR does not always translate into action, resulting in some hotel chains' CSR programmes being criticised as just 'green washing' their impacts (Chan, 2013; Peattie and Crane, 2005).

Despite the critiques of CSR programmes, effectively communicating a hotel chain's positive CSR initiatives has been shown to increase financial performance (Kang et al., 2010; Rodríguez and del Mar Armas Cruz, 2007). This is important to note because it demonstrates that there are real financial incentives associated with caring about how hotel chains impact their communities. While CSR programmes are only strategies for mitigating impacts, these CSR programmes do provide a good avenue for the discussion of the socio-cultural impacts that hotel chains can have within their host communities because they highlight areas where hotel chains are trying to actively benefit communities. They do not, of course, cover the whole gamut of impacts and largely tend to focus on the low hanging fruit which hotel chains can easily fix and publicise. They also generally focus on the operation of the hotel in the post-design and building phases, rather than considering how the hotel chain's positive socio-cultural impacts can be maximised from the beginning: from purchasing the property, through the design of the hotel's exterior and interior, and ultimately to operational aspects of the hotel. While it is difficult for an industry to reflect and examine its positive and negative impacts, a deeper discussion of the socio-cultural impacts of hotel chains promises to improve the chain hotel industry through not only being more respected within the community, but also financially through having more loyal employees, stronger CSR messages, and ultimately a better product to offer guests.

Socio-cultural impacts of hotel chains

As previously mentioned, hotel chains, by their very nature, carry large positive and negative socio-cultural impacts. What distinguishes these socio-cultural impacts from environmental and economic impacts is that these directly affect either the quality of life of the hotel chain's employees, or the quality of life of the host community where the hotel is located. Sloan et al. (2012) summarise the socio-cultural impacts within hotel chains as dealing with 'issues such as: public health, social justice, human rights, labour rights, community issues, equal opportunities, skills and education, workplace safety and working conditions, maintaining and promoting social and cultural diversity, involving communities, consulting stakeholders and the public as well as training staff with regards to sustainable practices' (p. 26).

Positive socio-cultural impacts of hotel chains

Probably the most important and most cited positive socio-cultural impact of hotel chains is their large economic impact within communities; through providing employment to local people and through bringing in tourists who spend their money at the hotel and within the community at various businesses. The US Bureau of Labor Statistics 'National Employment Matrix' shows the hotel industry as providing 1,759,000 jobs in 2010 with the number of total jobs expected to rise to 1,900,900 in 2020. Not all of these jobs are associated with hotel chains, but since hotel chains represent the lion's share of the hotel market (around 70 per cent), it can be gathered that many of these jobs are directly tied to hotel chains and not independent operators. In addition to being a source of employment for communities, the economic impact of the lodging industry in 2013 was estimated at $163 billion in sales, not including the induced economic impact of hotel employee wages, hotel guest spending at local businesses within economy, and the tax revenue raised by hotel stays (AHLA, 2014). These statistics coalesce to demonstrate that the positive socio-economic impacts hotel chains have within communities highly correlate with the positive socio-cultural impacts they have on resident and employee quality of life.

Positive impacts of hotel chain design

In addition to the benefits of employment and economic development associated with hotel chains, properties have the ability to serve as landmarks within cities that residents are proud of, serve as statements of civic confidence within central business districts and be components of urban renewal projects. McNeil (2008) illuminates some of these positive impacts through a description of the importance of the Plaza Hotel managed by Fairmont in New York City. Brown (1967: 230, cited in McNeil, 2008) writes:

> For three generations of New Yorkers, the majestic Plaza, overlooking their own Manhattan oasis of the trees and lakes of Central Park, offered reassurance that a way of life would survive wars, depressions, even death. She was an elegant, yet sturdy, bulwark against all that was brash and mediocre, removed in spirit from the frenzied modern pace, indifferent to encroaching high-rise steel and chrome, serenely secure in her fine heritage.

Hotel chains' benefits to urban renewal initiatives can be seen 'through the refurbishment of historic buildings (including ex-factories and warehouses)' (McNeil, 2008: 387). A prime example of a hotel chain refurbishing a historic building is the InterContinental Hotel Group's Marseille Hotel Dieu. Miguel Ruano, vice president of design and engineering for Europe-IHG, in an interview with the *New York Times*, mentioned that one of the benefits of using old buildings is that 'Banks are much more comfortable providing financing for buildings that are already there' (Zipkin, 2014). Additionally, Zipkin's article notes that 'the architectural features and details can convey more of a homey feel, a sense of individuality'. This is only one example, but there are many more examples of hotel chains using old buildings as ways to save money and increase their competitiveness. Lee (2011) and Strannegård and Strannegård (2012) both note the rising importance of hotels being able to differentiate themselves by their exterior and interior designs. Not only does fitting in with the local character of a location minimise the hotel chains' negative socio-cultural impacts, but it also has competitive implications when guests are trying to pick a hotel that offers more than a bed in a convenient location. Urry (1990) writes that 'The challenge for hotels is meeting certain global brand standards whilst adding local variation to satisfy "new" tourists' (cited in Lee, 2011).

Positive educational initiatives of CSR programmes

Hotel chains also exhibit positive socio-cultural impacts through the educational opportunities they provide to their employees and to the communities where they operate (also discussed in Chapter 38). Two examples of educational initiatives from large hotel chains are Intercontinental Hotel Group's (IHG) IHG Academy and Hyatt's *Pause* Program. IHG Academy operates in partnership with local community organisations to provide work place experience for local community members with the goal of improving their chances for employment within the hospitality industry (IHG Academy, 2014). IHG sees this as a win-win for themselves because they are helping build sustainable communities while also creating a 'talent pipeline for hotels, with ready access to motivated and skilled potential employees' (IHG Academy, 2014). Hyatt's *Pause* programme is summarised by Bohdanowicz and Zientara (2008: 150) as providing the 173 employees of the Hotel Villa Magna-Park in Madrid, Spain, with full employment and 'human capital-enhancing activities (such as English and computer class)' while the hotel was going through a 14-month redecoration process. It is believed that these types of positive socio-cultural impacts focused on education and improving the quality of life of employees will result in more loyal employees and better customer service, which are both very important in an industry that is plagued by high employee turnover and stiff competition (Bohdanowicz and Zientra, 2008; IHG Academy, 2014).

Other positive socio-cultural impacts worth noting from hotel chains are their *philanthropic activities within communities, their unique designs that bring in local art, and their use of local food on their menus*. These philanthropic activities include charitable donations from hotel chains and programmes, such as IHG's 'Shelter in a Storm Program', that support local communities after natural disasters. An example of a hotel chain using local art to enhance its visual appeal to guests and residents is the new Westin Hotel in Cleveland, Ohio (Chilcote, 2014). The Westin uses over 1,500 works by local artists to transform the 'formerly dreary concrete monolith into a showcase of modern design and local artwork' (Chilcote, 2014). The hotel's emphasis on art even includes a 30-foot tall mural of the Cuyahoga River Valley on the exterior of the hotel. Greg Peckham, executive director of the LAND Studio in Cleveland, mentions that 'The owners wanted to create a real streetscape: they wanted people to come in, for it to be a living room for the city' (Chilcote, 2014). It is believed that this type of emphasis on local art has synergistic effects on the community and on hotel competitiveness (Boley and Uysal, 2014). Examples of hotel chains using local food on their menus are numerous. One example of a firm encouraging its chefs to use local products whenever possible is Fairmont Hotels and Resorts (Mohn, 2010). Fairmont has even started growing their own food on hotel roofs such as at the Fairmont Vancouver Airport. One traveller acknowledged that seeing a menu with items from the hotel's garden 'caught their eye' (Mohn, 2010). Hotel chains increasingly using local food within their restaurants not only benefits the local economy and reduces the number of 'food miles' between production and consumption, but also provides one more variable for customers to distinguish the quality of the hotel from its competitors. As seen in the next section, these positive socio-cultural impacts can be easily turned into negative impacts depending on the management and philosophy of the hotel chain.

Negative socio-cultural impacts of hotel chains

While hotel chains do have many positive socio-cultural impacts as mentioned above, these 'best practices' are not employed by all. Additionally, hotel chains by their very nature (outside entities coming into communities with universal standards of service) can have far-reaching negative impacts. Like most businesses, hotel chains are first and foremost focused on profit and most likely choose to operate within the community, because the community provides some type of commodity that can be exploited for a profit. This becomes a primer for most of the negative socio-cultural impacts mentioned below, because hotel chains are not tied to the local community by ownership or values as locally owned businesses may be. This is not to critique hotel chains, but a statement of their nature to help explain why they have these negative socio-cultural impacts within communities.

Negative impacts of hotel employment

Despite the job creation capacity of hotel chains mentioned earlier, the quality of hotel chain employment is often criticised as marginal. This criticism stems from hotel jobs being poorly paid, involving long hours, being part-time and seasonal, resulting in physical injuries and separating minorities from higher paying front-line service positions. For example, the average hotel housekeeper in the USA in 2013 made $10.48/hour for a mean annual wage of $21,800/year (US Bureau of Labor Statistics). Research has also shown that hotel housekeepers' occupational injury rates are higher than the national average from the nature of cleaning multiple hotel rooms day after day (Krause et al., 2005). Another aspect of hotel work often criticised is the predominance of minorities in the labour intensive, low paying jobs of hotel chains. Thomas (1980) reviews a study from Koziara and Koziara (1968) that found 6.2 per cent of front desk personnel were African-American, while 61.1 per cent of the housekeepers were African-American (Koziara and Koziara, 1968). While these numbers are quite out of date, they speak to social justice issues and the tendency for hotel jobs to benefit some in the community over others. Thomas (1980) quotes Paul Good as saying 'A chambermaid-caddy economy never made anyone except motel owners solvent' (Good, 1968). These negative aspects of employment in hotel chains provide managers with a challenge to increase the quality of life of their employees beyond initially providing them with a job. It also indicates why there is high turnover within the industry. The marginality of employment and high turnover rates provide an avenue for managers to increase hotel performance by findings ways to increase the quality of life of employees, so that they will become more loyal employees that provide better customer service.

Marginal benefits to host communities

In addition to the marginality of employment benefits featured in some hotel chains are the marginal benefits hotel chains have within the community. By being chains, they are often owned by outside entities that take the profits outside the community. This leaves the economic impact that hotel chains often mention as a positive impact on only the wages of employees and other operating expenses that the hotel incurs within the community. The standardisation of design also limits the hotel chain's positive impacts within the community, because it does not bring in local art to the design of the hotel or emphasise local building materials (exceptions mentioned earlier). A concept that hotel chains can embrace to increase their benefits within the community is endogeneity. Endogeneity refers to bottom-up development that is structured to retain maximum benefits in a locality by using local resources (natural, cultural and human) in every step of a hotel's design and operation (Ilbery et al., 2007). Examples of ways in which hotel chains can embrace this concept is through the use of local art in lobbies and guest rooms, local raw materials where possible, hiring local people when there are qualified local employees available and serving locally sourced food within hotel restaurants. While there are certainly costs associated with embracing local-based concepts like endogeneity, there are also potential benefits from having a product that is unique and embedded within the local destination's character (Ayala, 1991; Lee, 2011).

Homogenisation of product

While hotel chains can serve as sources of pride and pillars of civic confidence as mentioned earlier, they can also be sources of contention and embarrassment from their design and footprint not fitting in with the character of the community. Gunn (1997) writes: 'Tourism tends to make the world look the same. There is homogeneity in the chains and franchises proliferated by the business sector.' Nowhere is this homogeneity of product more visible within hotel chains than with Holiday Inn's old slogan, 'The best surprise is no surprise' whose 'slogan was formulated to convey the message that the guest should recognise him/herself no matter if the city was London, Shanghai or Buenos Aires' (Strannegård and Strannegård, 2012). This homogenisation of hotel product is often overlooked in CSR programmes that tend to focus on hotel operations after the hotel is built. Two examples of how the homogeneous nature of hotel chains negatively impacts the local sense of place are provided below. Heat-Moon (1999) writes the following about a hotel chain on the Outer Banks of North Carolina:

> Across the sound at Nags Head, a new highrise broke the flat horizon of the banks where once only small, low buildings stood. 'I hope you're not going to put highrises here too,' I said. 'That's a Ramada Inn.' 'Overwhelms everything out there – no harmony at all between it and the land. Architecture without regard for place or history. They have been Jersey Shored, if you ask me.'
>
> (p. 56)

In another example, Bryson (1989) writes:

> The old cotton warehouses overlooking the river on the Savannah side were splendid. They had been restored without being overgentrified. They contained boutiques and oyster bars on the ground floor, but the upper floors were left a tad shabby, giving them that requisite raffish air I had been looking for since Hannibal ... Towards the end of the street stood a big new Hyatt Regency hotel, an instantly depressing sight. Massive and made of shaped concrete, it was from the F—You school of architecture so favored by the Big American hotel chains. There was nothing about it in scale or appearance even remotely sympathetic to the old buildings around it. It just said, 'F—you, Savannah.' Every few blocks you come up against some discordant slab – the De Soto Hilton, the Ramada Inn, the Best Western Riverfront, all about as appealing as spittle on a johnny cake, as they say in Georgia.
>
> (pp. 80–81)

These graphic examples are mentioned not to belittle hotel chains, but to provide critical reflection on how the standard building design typically associated with hotel chains conflicts with the character of the destination tourists are travelling to see. Building hotel chains that fit within the sense of place can actually provide a competitive advantage from being unique and different, as well as having residents being more supportive of the business. This logic coincides with Pine and Gilmore's (1998) 'Experience Economy' that states that consumers are looking more and more for memorable and unique experiences rather than standardised services.

Linking socio-cultural impacts to financial performance

With some of the most common positive and negative socio-cultural impacts presented, the chapter will conclude with some financial implications for those hotel chains who are able to effectively manage their socio-cultural impacts within the communities where they operate. While there are certainly many intrinsic reasons for hotel chains to manage their socio-cultural impacts within the destination, one has to remember that they are ultimately businesses that have to make a profit. If they are not able to make a profit, they go out of business, and any positive impacts they had within the community will be lost. With this in mind, there are a few strategies hotel chains can embrace to maximise their positive socio-cultural impacts within their communities while increasing their financial profitability.

The first step is for hotel chains to simply acknowledge that their operations have negative impacts within the community. This line of thinking provides hotel chains with specific areas that they can focus on improving. The second important step is for hotel chains to take a broad perspective towards how their socio-cultural impacts influence financial performance. This has already occurred with regards to environmental impacts, but needs to be further embraced for socio-cultural impacts. A third step is for hotel chains to view employees as assets rather than costs on an expense statement. One of the industry's biggest expenses is the high costs associated with employee turnover. If hotel chains are able to increase the job satisfaction of their employees, there could be real gains in employee retention. This would help save money on the costs associated with frequently having to hire and train new employees. It also has implications for guest satisfaction, because employees that are happy, well trained and tenured are likely to provide better customer service than ones that are frustrated and new to the position. A fourth strategy is to embrace Pine and Gilmore's (1998) 'Experience Economy' perspective that states that there has been a paradigm shift amongst consumers away from the focus on standardisation to a focus on what is unique, different and can't be found anywhere else in the world. If hotel chains want to keep their percentage of market share and compete with independent hotels, they need to be increasingly thinking of ways to make their hotel properties unique and special rather than bland and universal. Hotel chains stand to benefit from strategically bringing more aspects of the local character into the hotel's design, atmospherics and restaurants to play on the notion of consumers wanting things that are unique and different, while still providing the same quality associated with certain brands. These unique features of hotel chains could also spur guests to post more on social media sites such as Twitter and Facebook, leading to positive word of mouth for the hotel chain.

While hotel chains stand to financially benefit from maximising their positive impacts and minimising their negative impacts in these ways, the road forward is not without its difficulties. Hotel chains have thrived on providing standardised services across many settings to many guests. This focus on standardisation does not often result in positive impacts on the employees of the hotel or on the community where the hotel operates. Even though the nature of hotel chains poses a significant challenge, this chapter suggests that those hotel chains who are able to effectively maximise these positive socio-cultural impacts will be more competitive than those who do not, because they will have lower costs through happier employees who are less likely to quit and higher returns through guests wanting to pay a premium for the experiences they offer.

References

American Hotel & Lodging Association (AHLA) (2014) Lodging industry profile. Online. Available HTTP: <http://www.ahla.com/content.aspx?id=36332>, accessed 22 August, 2014.

Ayala, H. (1991) Resort landscape systems: a design management solution. *Tourism Management*, 12(4), 280–90.

Bohdanowicz, P. (2005) European hoteliers' environmental attitudes greening the business. *Cornell Hotel and Restaurant Administration Quarterly*, 46(2), 188–204.

Bohdanowicz, P. and Zientara, P. (2008) Hotel companies' contribution to improving the quality of life of local communities and the well-being of their employees. *Tourism and Hospitality Research*, 9(2), 147–58.

Boley, B.B. and Uysal, M. (2014) Competitive synergy through practicing triple bottom line sustainability: evidence from three hospitality case studies. *Tourism and Hospitality Research*, 13(4), 226–38.

Brown, E. (1967) *The Plaza 1907–1967: its life and times.* New York: Meredith Press

Bryson, B. (1989) *The Lost Continent: Travels in Small Town America; And, Neither Here Nor There: Travels in Europe*. New York: Harper Row.

Butler, J. (2008) The compelling 'hard case' for 'green' hotel development. *Cornell Hospitality Quarterly*, 49(3), 234–44.

Chan, E.S. (2013) Managing green marketing: Hong Kong hotel managers' perspective. *International Journal of Hospitality Management*, 34, 442–61.

Chilcote, L. (2014, June 5). Downtown Westin hotel opens with dazzling display of local artwork. *Fresh Water Cleveland*. Online. Available HTTP: <http://www.freshwatercleveland.com/devnews/westinhotel060414.aspx>, accessed 22 August 2014.

Elkington, J. (1997) *Cannibals with Forks: The Triple Bottom Line of 21st Century Business*. Oxford, UK: Capstone Publishing.

Font, X., Walmsley, A., Cogotti, S., McCombes, L. and Häusler, N. (2012) Corporate social responsibility: the disclosure–performance gap. *Tourism Management*, 33(6), 1544–53.

Good, P. (1968) *American Serfs*. New York: Ballantine Books.

Gunn, C.A. (1997) *Vacationscape: Developing Tourist Areas*. Washington, DC: Taylor & Francis.

Heat-Moon, W.L. (1999) *Blue Highways: A Journey into America*. New York: Back Bay Books

IHG Academy (2014) What is IHG Academy? InterContinental Hotel Group. Online. Available HTTP: <http://www.ihgacademy.com/what-is-ihg-academy.aspx>, accessed 22 August, 2014.

Ilbery, B., Saxena, G. and Kneafsey, M. (2007) Exploring tourists and gatekeepers' attitudes towards integrated rural tourism in the England–Wales border region. *Tourism Geographies*, 9(4), 441–68.

Kang, K.H., Lee, S. and Huh, C. (2010) Impacts of positive and negative corporate social responsibility activities on company performance in the hospitality industry. *International Journal of Hospitality Management*, 29(1), 72–82.

Koziara, E.C. and Koziara, K.S. (1968) *The Negro in the Hotel Industry* (No. 4) Industrial Research Unit, Wharton School of Finance and Commerce, University of Pennsylvania.

Krause, N., Scherzer, T. and Rugulies, R. (2005) Physical workload, work intensification, and prevalence of pain in low wage workers: results from a participatory research project with hotel room cleaners in Las Vegas. *American Journal of Industrial Medicine*, 48(5), 326–37.

Kucukusta, D., Mak, A. and Chan, X. (2013) Corporate social responsibility practices in four and five-star hotels: perspectives from Hong Kong visitors. *International Journal of Hospitality Management*, 34, 19–30.

Lee, T.J. (2011) Role of hotel design in enhancing destination branding. *Annals of Tourism Research*, 38(2), 708–11.

Lee J.S., Hsu L.T., Han H. and Kim, Y. (2010) Understanding how consumers view green hotels: how a hotel's green image can influence behavioural intentions. *Journal of Sustainable Tourism* 18(7), 901–14.

McNeil, D. (2008) The hotel and the city. *Progress in Human Geography*, 32(3), 383–98.

Mohn, T. (2010, October 18). Hotels take 'locally grown' a logical step beyond. *New York Times*. Online. Available HTTP: <http://www.nytimes.com/2010/10/19/business/19garden.html?_r=0>, accessed 12 August, 2014.

Peattie, K. and Crane, A. (2005) Green marketing: legend, myth, farce or prophesy? *Qualitative Market Research: An International Journal*, 8(4), 357–70.

Pine, B.J. and Gilmore, J.H. (1998) Welcome to the experience economy. *Harvard Business Review*, 76, 97–105.

Rodríguez, F.J.G. and del Mar Armas Cruz, Y. (2007) Relation between social-environmental responsibility and performance in hotel firms. *International Journal of Hospitality Management*, 26(4), 824–39.

Sloan P., Legrand, W. and Chen, J.S. (2012) *Sustainability in the Hospitality Industry: Principles of Sustainable Operations*, 2nd edn. London: Routledge.

Smith V. (ed.) (1979) *Host and Guests: The Anthropology of Tourism*. University of Pennsylvania Press: Philadelphia.

Strannegård, L. and Strannegård, M. (2012) Works of art: aesthetic ambitions in design hotels. *Annals of Tourism Research*, 39(4), 1995–2012.

Sadovi, M. (2013) This sale isn't for the birds. *Wall Street Journal*. 11 September, 2013.

Thomas, J.M. (1980) The impact of corporate tourism on gullah blacks: notes on issues of employment. *Phylon (1960)*, 1–11.

U.S. Bureau of Labor Statistics (2014) Occupational employment statistics: 37-2012 maids and housekeeping cleaners. Online. Available HTTP: <http://www.bls.gov/oes/current/oes372012. htm>, accessed 22 August, 2014

Urry, J. (1990) *The Tourist Gaze*. Newbury Park, CA: Sage.

Zipkin, A. (2014, March 10). Hotels moving into old buildings. *New York Times*. Online. Available HTTP: <http://www.nytimes.com/2014/03/11/business/hotels-moving-into-old-buildings.html>, accessed 11 August, 2014

Section II

Expansion of hotel chains

In Chapter 9 Michael Gross discusses hotel chains' decisions to internationalise. The issue of growth is ever-present in a hotel chain's strategic planning, and having operated domestically for a period, it is possible or even likely that internationalisation will offer an attractive growth option. The question of whether to internationalise takes foremost place in the internationalisation decision process. The purpose of this chapter is to examine the salient motivational factors involved in the internationalisation decision process for hotel chains. The factors are drawn and synthesised from the generic business and hotel industry-specific internationalisation literature and are analysed using the 4-category typology framework of (1) natural resource seeking, (2) market seeking, (3) efficiency seeking and (4) strategic asset or capability seeking. The aggregate analysis of these factors determines, on balance, the extent of desirability of a firm's preliminary prospects for internationalisation, and its subsequent decision about whether to internationalise.

Chapter 10 by Cristina Barroco, Eduardo Anselmo de Castro and Carlos Costa deals with hotel chains' choice of a destination to enter. The chapter's thorough literature review has shown that although there are many theories to explain international trade, researchers are unanimous in affirming that hotel chains' internationalisation is influenced by pull factors, related to specific characteristics of the host country (contextual and transactional environment), and by push factors, related to specific characteristics of the companies and of their home country. This chapter identifies which factors influence hotel chains' decision when choosing a destination to invest over another. With this purpose, a theoretical model is developed, that includes six pull factors related to the contextual environment and five factors linked to the tourism industry. The model is validated through the survey of foreign investors running accommodation units in mainland Portugal.

In Chapter 11 Yinyoung Rhou and Manisha Singal discuss equity modes of entry of hotel chains. The authors stipulate that selecting the right entry mode by a hotel chain can impact the success or failure of operations in an international market and is therefore an important decision for hotel chain owners and managers. In this chapter Rhou and Singal examine and focus on the entry mode via equity participation that can take the form of greenfield investments, acquisitions and joint ventures. They review the existing literature on this topic, outline the benefits and limitations of each equity entry mode for hotel chains, and outline some gaps for future research in this area.

Chapter 12 by Mahmood Khan deals with one of the most popular entry modes of hotel chains – the franchise agreement. Considering the importance of growth of the hotel sector, expansion strategy should be formulated considering economic, social, cultural and environmental aspects. Hotel chains follow a wide variety of different growth strategies ranging from franchise agreements, management contracts, hotel ownership, leaseholds, mergers and takeovers and joint ventures. This chapter provides a basic understanding as well as serving as a guide to fully comprehending factors involved in expansion through international franchising. The author highlights the major points to be considered when choosing franchise as an entry mode as well as potential pitfalls and common mistakes.

Chapter 13 by Michael J. Turner, Demian Hodari and Ines Blal examines the management contract and the key components that shape its success as an entry mode. Management contracts are increasingly popular among owners because they can gain ready access to the operational expertise required to operate a hotel without any need for operational responsibility. Alternatively, hotel chains find management contracts desirable because they enable rapid expansion at relatively low cost by virtue of there being little to no equity investment. Only when there is an equal balance of power in the relationship between an owner and a hotel chain, however, will both parties be able to best achieve their business goals over time. A one-sided hotel management contract can create conflicts that can result in lengthy and costly legal disputes or early termination of the management contract. The balance of power between hotel owners and hotel chains, however, is constantly shifting. An owner's choice of hotel chain and management contract terms is therefore perhaps the most critical factor which will determine the long-term success of their hotel. In addition to the relationship between hotel owners and hotel chains, this chapter also examines the implications of hotel management contracting on the hotel's general manager, financial controller and bankers and lenders.

In Chapter 14 Gökhan Ayazlar elaborates on the marketing consortium as an entry mode for hotel chains. The raison d'être of hotel consortia is basically the congregation of hotels in order to fulfil achievements that they cannot do alone. In comparison to other entry modes, hotel consortia have relatively lower costs and they have more adaptable standards, which increases their attractiveness. Hotel consortia particularly support their members in the marketing area. Apart from that, they provide services such as purchasing, human resources and sharing experiences in management to their members. In practice there are different types of consortium and membership standards. There are consortia that only provide reservation support, while some consortia inspect their members using secret customers to check their standards. Some consortia provide all advantages of high brand values. Despite many advantages, hotel consortia have some disadvantages, elaborated in the chapter.

Chapter 15 by Anderson Gomes de Souza, Viviane Santos Salazar, Walter Araújo de Moraes, Yákara Pereira Leite and Maya Ivanova explores the nature of the lease contract as an expansion option, used by hotel chains. The lease contract clauses are examined and the advantages and disadvantages for both parties are outlined. Finally, the authors discuss the current application of lease among the top hotel corporations and illustrate their theoretical findings with some interesting cases from Brazil.

In Chapter 16 Elena García de Soto-Camacho and Alfonso Vargas-Sanchez elaborate on the choice of entry mode. The chapter studies the economic rationality of the multiplicity of governance mechanisms used by hotel chains and analyses the factors that determine the choice of entry mode into an external market and its implications on the performance of the strategy in hotel chains. The chapter provides alternatives to the entry in a market under the dynamic approach of real option theory, by analysing several variables such as: the managers' perception of business uncertainty (exogenous and endogenous), structural variables of the company, strategic and control factors, international strategic flexibility and the performance of the international strategy, as a result of the possession and execution of real options. Results show that high levels of perceived uncertainty and the interaction between the size and international experience of the company are negatively related to levels of international investment property, which allow the company to own and implement real options conferring sufficient strategic flexibility to adapt its strategy in response to changes in order to improve organisational performance.

In the last chapter in the section (Chapter 17) Inès Blal, Demian Hodari and Michael J. Turner discuss the selection of a partner hotel by the hotel chain. With the implemention of the asset light strategy and the development of chains, most of the properties that a hotel corporation manages are, today, owned by other entities. In this setting, the partnership that hotel corporations establish with hotel owners becomes an essential element of their successful expansion. For that purpose, hotel chains put in place several mechanisms to manage such assessments, which include reliance on brand standards, use of contractual clauses that secure equilibrium, and ensuring that the fundamentals of tourism and hotel operations are well established in the hotel project itself. Each of these fundamental aspects is discussed in this chapter. The first section of this chapter is an overview of operating models in which partner selection is critical, the focus being on franchise and management contracts. It explains why the selection of hotel partner is a complex process for hotel chain executives as each property pertains to a different context with unique challenges. The second section presents the selection process, looking at the extent of partners' alignment with brand, alignment with actions and general negotiation. It details the evaluation of a set of task-related criteria and partner-related criteria.

9

The decision to internationalise

Michael J. Gross

(SCHOOL OF MANAGEMENT, UNIVERSITY OF SOUTH AUSTRALIA, AUSTRALIA)

Introduction

In the process of contemplating the issue of internationalisation, there are three essential questions that firms must consider (Hollensen, 2001). The first question is *whether* to internationalise. The issue of growth is ever-present in a firm's strategic planning, and having operated domestically for a period, it is possible or even likely that internationalisation will offer an attractive growth option. The second question is *where* to internationalise. Choice of destination is critical, as the firm seeks optimum fit between its capabilities and those of a particular location. The third question is *how* to internationalise. The application of the correct entry mode is essential in order to assure that the business model is sound and sustainable (Clarke and Chen, 2007; Root, 1994). If the first question is answered in the negative, the remaining two questions are inconsequential. Therefore, the question of whether to internationalise takes foremost place in the decision process. Subsequent chapters in this section of the book will address where (choice of destination) and how (entry modes) to internationalise. This chapter will address the primary question of *whether* to internationalise.

Four types of foreign production can be identified for Multinational Enterprises (MNEs) (Dunning and Lundan, 2008: 67):

1. Natural resource seeking
2. Market seeking
3. Efficiency seeking
4. Strategic asset or capability seeking

To appraise possible paths toward internationalisation for such different types of strategic orientation, Dunning (1981) developed a framework named the 'eclectic paradigm theory of international production' as an analysis tool for MNE activity. This framework is also referred to as the 'OLI' paradigm, an acronym representing the three advantages in considerations of ownership, location and internalisation.

The *eclectic paradigm* provides a framework for determining the extent and pattern of both foreign-owned production undertaken by a country's own firms, and that of domestic production owned or controlled by foreign firms (Dunning and Lundan, 2008: 95). It is an analytical tool used to determine the likelihood that foreign direct investment (FDI) should proceed. In addition to wide application in industry generally (Cantwell and Narula, 2003), the eclectic paradigm has also been applied effectively to analysis of the international hotel industry (Dunning and Kundu, 1995; Dunning and McQueen, 1981, 1982a, 1982b; Jones et al., 2004).

The key propositions of the eclectic paradigm are that production financed by FDI and undertaken by MNEs will be determined by the configuration of three factors:

1. The (net) competitive advantages which firms of one nationality possess over those of another nationality in supplying any particular market or set of markets. These advantages may arise either from the firm's privileged *ownership* of, or access to, a set of income-generating assets, or from their ability to co-ordinate these assets with other assets across national boundaries in a way that benefits them relative to their competitors, or potential competitors.

2. The extent to which firms perceive it to be in their best interests to *internalise* the markets for the generation and/or the use of these assets; and by so doing add value to them.

3. The extent to which firms choose to *locate* these value-adding activities outside their national boundaries.

(Dunning, 2001)

In order to consider the question of whether to internationalise, we must think through the motivational factors that guide firms' strategic thinking. Such factors constitute the ingredients within systematic patterns that firms use to synthesise and evaluate a complex mix of motivations (Bartlett et al., 2008). The enquiry is conducted within the context of the firm's alignment of its strategy and structure with the environment (Langton et al., 1992). The aggregate analysis of these factors will determine, on balance, the extent of desirability of a firm's preliminary prospects for internationalisation. If the initial analysis suggests a positive inclination, i.e. there is enough evidence from the motivational factors to advocate that internationalisation may be a desirable path for the firm, then further research consistent with a typical analytical framework such as OLI is indicated.

In the case of hotel chains, the service nature of the business model introduces elements that distinguish it from the export of physical products. Such elements include intangibility, simultaneous production and consumption, heterogeneity and perishability, which must be recognised as embedded in international strategy (Olsen et al., 1998). The decision-making process is in essence a dynamic exercise of environmental scanning and analysis of interrelated factors, whereby the firm assesses an often contradictory body of research knowledge (Olsen et al., 2008). The purpose of this chapter is therefore to examine the salient motivational factors involved in the internationalisation decision process for hotel chains.

Motivational factors for internationalisation

The following section presents factors drawn and synthesised from the generic business and hotel industry-specific internationalisation literature, and are arranged using the 4-category Dunning and Lundan (2008) typology framework presented above.

1. Natural resource seeking

Securing key supplies

The hotel industry relies on people to provide services, thereby making the availability of labour a primary requirement for internationalisation. Labour can often be the highest overall proportional component of a hotel operations cost structure. Depending on a firm's origin and destination perspectives, the prospect of employing people in a foreign country may represent an opportunity for cheaper labour and/or higher levels of skills and knowledge. The most typical historical pattern has been firms from developed countries expanding to developing countries and seeking access to a lower wage population than that of the home country. Outsourcing of some functions can produce savings, such as evidenced in the Asia-Pacific region with countries such as the Philippines and India becoming hubs for reservations and customer services due to low labour costs and the English-speaking capabilities of the populations. Chains willing to make equity commitments perhaps in pursuit of long-term real estate investment returns may consider the acquisition of land and buildings, necessary assets for hotels. The rationale for this is similar to that for labour, that capital will often migrate to those countries that have natural resources such as land that is available in abundance and at an attractive price (Yu, 1999). Supply chain issues are also important, for example food and beverage operations require supplies to be available to meet the quality requirements of recipes and menus. The availability of supplies in a particular location versus the need to import those supplies can have a significant effect on the viability prospects of the food and beverage operations (Kalnins and Chung, 2004).

Acquisition of managerial skills and knowledge

Operating internationally requires the acquisition in the first instance of the skills and knowledge for exactly how to do that. Experience gained through domestic operations may apply to some extent, but a firm contemplating a long-term programme of internationalisation may consider its first foreign hotel an investment opportunity in organisational learning for how to operate internationally. For example, the issue of standardisation versus adaptation needs to be negotiated within a different national context. The conduct of business functions across marketing, human resources, finance, lodging, and food and beverage services must be reviewed, and decisions made about their provision in the light of a new cultural setting (Bayraktaroglu and Kutanis, 2003; Sandoff, 2005). Prospects of international exposure to new sources of information can have an energising effect on the innovation capabilities of the firm, and on its scanning and learning capabilities. Technology also features in conjunction with this, as the pull of access to advanced information and processing tools serves as an incentive to explore international expansion (Jacob and Groizard, 2007). For example, a hotel chain operating exclusively in developed countries may routinely use technological tools associated with its brand such as reservations through locally available toll-free telephone numbers, remote check-in, or a growing suite of internet applications. The prospect of exporting these tools to a developing country that lacks the local managerial capabilities and/or infrastructure to support implementation of such technologies may require the hotel chain to adapt to local environmental conditions.

2. Market seeking

Domestic market saturation

Stable performance in the home market is a prerequisite for internationalisation. A firm with an unstable home base greatly increases the risks of attempting to operate beyond home borders because of the increased level of complexity and additional calls on resources. However, firms, particularly ones from smaller markets (e.g. Singapore), may reach a point of domestic market saturation. Once that occurs, growth options become limited to product extensions (e.g. sub-brands), increase in market share, rise of market size, or foreign expansion. Firms from larger markets (e.g. China) may have more options, as the size of their domestic market may allow them to continue to expand without having the imperative to inter-nationalise thrust upon them (Gross and Huang, 2013). Indeed, Chinese hotel chains provide evidence for this effect, as up to the year 2009, nine of the largest hotel chains in the world were located in mainland China, with all of them achieving that high ranking solely on the basis of domestic development (Gale, 2009).

Increase sales and profits

In pursuit of the maximisation of wealth, the appeal of foreign markets as additional prospective sales populations can be a strong one. The profit and loss dynamics can also provide compelling benefits, as due to shifts in the revenue/cost mix forces, operating in some foreign markets may be more lucrative than in the home market. This is a common growth path choice for hotel chains (Rushmore et al., 2012), and is one that will enable the firm to achieve and exploit economies of scale and scope, positioning it advantageously, particularly over domestic compe-titors (Bartlett et al., 2008). Increasing international visitor flows, access to markets and global-isation of consumer awareness, tastes and communication channels all allow firms to consider a wider range of foreign countries for expansion. The opening of central Europe and the former Soviet Union were examples of such access in the 1990s (Go and Pine, 1995).

Enter emerging markets

International markets grow at different rates. Windows of opportunity are presented during certain historical periods that offer chances for competitive advantage (Van Agtmael, 2007). An example of this has been the opening of the China market through the reforms begun in the 1970s that have generated a proliferation of hotel development (Gross et al., 2013; Zhang et al., 2005).

Expand alliances

Internationalisation can provide opportunities for affiliation with a country that is a member of a major international economic bloc. A presence in a European Union (EU) or North American Free Trade Agreement (NAFTA) country can offer a firm entrée to a group within which barriers to trade are reduced or eliminated.

Defence of domestic markets

First mover status into a foreign market may have a pre-emptive effect on competitors' desire to enter that market. This would be particularly effective in markets where addition of supply carries a high risk. This type of behaviour is defensive in response to actual or perceived threats from competitors or governments which require the firm to protect its market position. The execution associated with this factor may involve a heightened calculus of risk/reward dynamics by the hotel chain. When Sheraton entered the China market in 1985 with the Great Wall Sheraton Hotel Beijing, the firm became the first international hotel brand to openly operate in that country. It exchanged the glitter of the marketing coup accompanying first mover status for a lengthy period of years required to operationally align the brand promise with actual product and service delivery in the hotel (Mwaura et al., 1998; Stross, 1990).

Brand recognition

One of the biggest assets possessed by a domestic chain is the brand associated with its identity. Brand awareness is used as a primary customer retention tool through guest loyalty programmes such as Le Club Accorhotels, HHonors (Hilton), Hyatt Gold Passport, or Starwood Preferred Guest. The recognition and loyalty accrued during domestic operations constitute resources that can be leveraged should the firm decide to go international. The brand promise brings with it expectations of quality and standards that promote familiarity and comfort for home country visitors to the host country hotel. This can also help to familiarise residents and certainly patrons of the host country hotel with the brand, setting up a virtuous commercial cycle that serves to increase the likelihood of becoming customers on visits to the home country and other countries to which the brand expands (Chen and Dimou, 2005; Peters and Frehse, 2005).

Following customers

The opportunity to provide lodging services to outbound tourists may be a significant driver for hotel chains wishing to exploit their guest relationship assets. International visitor flows indicate volume and demographic patterns of travel between countries. A hotel firm may obtain a competitive advantage through strategic attention to the spread of their national outbound travellers. A significant flow of the firm's country's tourists to a foreign country may indicate a potential ready-made market of customers who are familiar with the brand and ready to patronise the brand outside the home country (Majkgard and Sharma, 1998). This may also be seen as a defensive measure, whereby the firm seeks a presence in a market served by its competitors. For example, customer retention pressure may be placed on a firm if a significant competitor expands its presence to a market where the firm does not have a presence. Additionally, the motivations for following leisure tourists can be seen as discrete from following business clients, as the tourist sector is guided more by tourist receipts in the host country, and the business sector more by relations of the hotel firm with domestic and foreign clients (Kundu and Contractor, 1999).

Psychological proximity

The concept of psychological proximity (sometimes referred to as distance) is about the cultural closeness shared by countries. Countries may be culturally close but geographically distant, or vice versa. For example, Australia and Indonesia are geographically close but are culturally distant. However, Australia and England are geographically distant but, owing to colonial history, are culturally close. The relevance of this concept to the decision to go international is compelling, as the risk factors escalate further with psychological distance.

The experiential operating knowledge that a firm gains from its domestic operations is grounded in the cultural setting of the home country. Thus contemplation of going to a host country with psychological proximity is a very different prospect from going to one with significant psychological distance. Aside from practical issues such as language, communication styles, social structure and interpretation of information, the degree of difficulty is also increased by deeply embedded cultural traits of values, attitudes, standards, customs, assumptions and shared common experience. The fit between the home and host country cultures can be expected to have a significant impact on the effectiveness and productivity of a foreign unit (Tihanyi et al., 2005).

Export market drivers

The agendas of governments and trade organisations include promotion of exports primarily to further national economic interests. This factor can apply to both outbound push drivers encouraged by the home country's government and inbound pull drivers encouraged by host country governments (Endo, 2006). Countries compete with each other to attract FDI, and drivers can take the form of either incentives (e.g. subsidies, tax holidays, regulatory relief) or disincentives (e.g. trade barriers such as tariffs, license restriction, currency conditions). Additionally, countries regulate their outbound and inbound FDI flows through bodies such as foreign investment review boards that control the nationality, owner identity, type, volume and timing of investments allowed in or out of the country. In the hospitality industry, demand is affected by tourist flows, which are regulated by governmental travel policies implemented through instruments such as immigration, border control and travel reciprocity practices. China is an example of a country whose government has a clearly articulated policy in place to provide backing for its export industries, as well as an official system of support during the internationalisation process (Kang and Liu, 2007; Luo et al., 2010).

This issue may also be linked with global travel patterns, whereby international visitor flows are often determinants of hospitality industry supply, as firms will be attracted to markets with visitor demand sufficient to sustain viable hotel occupancy. For example, the regulation of global aviation networks that controls international air service operations may facilitate or hinder access by a hotel chain to its existing or prospective customer populations. Such availability may affect the viability of a hotel in a particular destination or in a whole country or region (Duval, 2008).

3. Efficiency seeking

Cost reduction

It is sometimes possible to operate at lower cost levels abroad than at home. The most notable example of this in a hospitality industry context is labour (as discussed above in the 'Natural resource seeking' section), however there are significant other cost factors that may be obtainable more economically outside the home country. The availability and cost of capital has served as a strong driver of internationalisation for hotel chains in the USA, Europe and Asia. The chains that adapt to varying patterns over time are positioned to derive the greatest benefits from this factor (Slattery, 1996). The cost of land is another significant determinant of return on investment. Decisions about a potential type of international hotel and its market positioning will be informed by the overall cost structure, of which land is a major component.

Economies of scale and scope

Scale allows a firm to become more efficient as it integrates experiential knowledge in its progress along an organisational learning path, while scope provides efficiency as increased units of operation allow more economical spread of resources and costs. In a well-managed hotel chain, economies of scale and scope increase as the firm grows (Littlejohn, 2003). These economies are apparent in key product-specific hospitality functions such as accommodation and food and beverage, as well as other business functions and support services. Understanding of these dynamics may inform internationalisation motivations as a firm seeks the best organisational fit for its strategic objectives (Weng and Wang, 2006).

Risk diversification

This factor is akin to the financial investment strategy of not trusting all of one's eggs to be placed in the same basket. Cycles, especially economic ones, tend to affect different parts of the world at different times. The fortunes of a hotel chain whose portfolio is contained solely within the home country are subject to the ups and downs of the cycles of that single country. Internationalisation spreads the risk, and, given sufficient scale and diversity, potentially allows an evening of overall firm earnings across a spectrum of operating unit hotels over time (Capar and Kotabe, 2003). Typical types of hotel firm diversification include adopting products to appeal to new customers (concentric), adopting products to appeal to current customers (horizontal), or undertaking new ventures different to and perhaps complementary with existing products (conglomerate) (Kotler et al., 2006).

4. Strategic asset or capability seeking

Managerial initiative

As internationalisation involves initiation of an organisational change process, a deep sense of commitment from the management is essential. Managerial initiative that is typically manifested as response either to push factors from the home country or pull factors from the host country is required. Such initiative is often linked to individual managers' ambitions and commitment to growth (Lommelen and Matthyssens, 2005).

Competitive pressures

Asset and capability seeking are motivated by a firm's efforts to strengthen its own competitive advantage or weaken that of its competitors. Competitive considerations can provide compelling motivations to go international. This may occur in a proactive sense when an attractive first mover advantage is available in a particular foreign market, or in a reactive sense when domestic market share is under threat by pre-emptive rivals (Littlejohn et al., 2007).

Investment value

The value proposition of hotel properties around the world is variable. While a hotel chain may have a thorough appreciation of the value dynamics in the home market, it is important to understand how values may be different for a given internationalisation opportunity (Lee, 2008). Calculations of investment stakeholder groups (owners, lending institutions and hotel management companies/operators), investment timeframe, and expectations for return on investment take on a different character when assessed in an international context. Firms take diverse approaches to this assessment based on their desire for balance between the resources they are willing to commit and the control they desire over the venture. Those firms that are willing to carry fixed real estate assets on the balance sheet will incur higher levels of investment risk and return/loss. Current strategic trends are towards an 'asset light' approach, whereby firms seek to retain operating capital while committing equity to ventures only to the levels required to obtain a given investment (Verginis, 2013).

Conclusion

As hotel firms have evolved, each has had to consider issues of internationalisation. Some have remained in solely domestic markets, while others have expanded beyond their home market. The global development of the hotel industry has been and will continue to be closely linked with environmental elements, perhaps most notably economic structure (Slattery, 2012). Indeed, even if a hotel chain chooses to remain exclusively a domestic operator, it will face international issues due to linkages of stakeholder relations including but not limited to guests, staff, suppliers and owners (Gross and Huang, 2011).

It is difficult if not impossible to identify a sole reason for making the decision to seek opportunities outside the home country. The outcomes of the analysis of complementary and competing factors will always be mixed and subject to a range of interpretations. There is no such thing as a risk-free embarkation on the path to internationalisation (Aharoni, 1999). For a given firm, there will be opposing factors that argue simultaneously for and against proceeding towards internationalisation. The decision of whether to internationalise is deliberated in an environment of uncertainty, requiring the firm to apply analytical judgment in terms of the alignment of its strategy and structure with the environment (Langton et al., 1992). The rationale will invariably be characterised by a combination of motivating factors that point to a preponderance of evidence, the weight of which will make a sufficiently persuasive case to the hotel chain's ownership and management, and successively to other stakeholders. Presuming that analysis of whether to internationalise yields a green light, it is following the establishment of the foundation of a sound initial decision process that subsequent exploration will be undertaken to examine further internationalisation factors of locations and entry modes.

References

Aharoni, Y. (1999) The foreign investment decision process. In P.J. Buckley and P.N. Ghauri (eds), *The Internationalization of the Firm: A Reader*. London: Thomson Learning, Chapter 1, pp. 3–13.

Bartlett, C.A., Ghoshal, S. and Beamish, P. (2008) *Transnational Management: Text, Cases, and Readings in Cross-Border Management* (5th edn). Boston: McGraw-Hill.

Bayraktaroglu, S. and Kutanis, R.O. (2003) Transforming hotels into learning organisations: a new strategy for going global. *Tourism Management*, 24(2), 149–54.

Cantwell, J. and Narula, R. (eds) (2003) *International Business and the Eclectic Paradigm: Developing the OLI Framework*. London: Routledge.

Capar, N. and Kotabe, M. (2003) The relationship between international diversification and performance in service firms. *Journal of International Business Studies*, 34(4), 345–55.

Chen, J.J. and Dimou, I. (2005) Expansion strategy of international hotel firms. *Journal of Business Research*, 58(12), 1730–40.

Clarke, A. and Chen, W. (2007) *International Hospitality Management: Concepts and Cases*. Burlington, Massachusetts: Butterworth-Heinemann.

Dunning, J.H. (1981) *International Production and The Multinational Enterprise*. London: George Allen and Unwin.

Dunning, J.H. (2001) The eclectic (OLI) paradigm of international production: past, present and future. *International Journal of the Economics of Business*, 8(2), 173–90.

Dunning, J.H. and Kundu, S.K. (1995) The internationalization of the hotel industry: some new findings from a field study. *Management International Review*, 35(2), 101–33.

Dunning, J.H. and Lundan, S.M. (2008) *Multinational Enterprises and the Global Economy* (2nd edn). Cheltenham, UK: Edward Elgar Publishing.

Dunning, J.H. and McQueen, M. (1981) The eclectic theory of international production: a case study of the international hotel industry. *Managerial and Decision Economics*, 2(4), 197–210.

Dunning, J.H. and McQueen, M. (1982a) The eclectic theory of the multinational enterprise and the international hotel industry. In A.M. Rugman (ed.), *New Theories of the Multinational Enterprise*, London: Croom Helm Ltd., Chapter 5, pp. 79–106.

Dunning, J.H. and McQueen, M. (1982b) Multinational corporations in the international hotel industry. *Annals of Tourism Research*, 9(1), 69–90.

Duval, D.T. (2008) Aeropolitics, global aviation networks and the regulation of international visitor flows. In T. Coles and C.M. Hall (eds), *International Business and Tourism: Global Issues, Contemporary Interactions*. Abingdon, Oxon, UK: Routledge, pp. 91–105.

Endo, K. (2006) Foreign direct investment in tourism: flows and volumes. *Tourism Management*, 27(4), 600–14.

Gale, D. (2009) Hotels' 325-Corporate 300 Ranking. *Hotels Magazine*, 43(7), 28–33.

Go, F.M. and Pine, R. (1995) *Globalization Strategy in the Hotel Industry*. London: Routledge.

Gross, M.J., Gao, H. and Huang, S. (2013) China hotel research: a systematic review of the English language academic literature. *Tourism Management Perspectives* (6), 68–78.

Gross, M.J. and Huang, S. (2011) Exploring the internationalisation prospects of a Chinese domestic hotel firm. *International Journal of Contemporary Hospitality Management*, 23(2), 261–74.

Gross, M.J. and Huang, S. (2013) The domestic development experience of a hotel firm with Chinese characteristics: the case of Jin Jiang. *Cornell Hospitality Quarterly*, 54(2), 211–24.

Hollensen, S. (2001) *Global Marketing: A Market-Responsive Approach* (2nd edn). Harlow, England: Prentice Hall.

Jacob, M. and Groizard, J.L. (2007) Technology transfer and multinationals: the case of the Balearic hotel chains' investments in two developing economies. *Tourism Management*, 28(4), 976–92.

Jones, P., Song, H. and Hong, J.H. (2004) The relationship between generic theory and hospitality applied research: the case of international hotel development. *Journal of Hospitality and Tourism Management*, 11(2), 128–38.

Kalnins, A. and Chung, W. (2004) Resource-seeking agglomeration: a study of market entry in the lodging industry. *Strategic Management Journal*, 25(7), 689–99.

Kang, Y. and Liu, W. (2007) Internationalisation patterns of Chinese firms: entry mode, location, and government influence. *International Journal of Business Strategy*, 7(3), 13–31.

Kotler, P., Bowen, J.T. and Makens, J.C. (2006) *Marketing for Hospitality and Tourism* (4th edn). Upper Saddle River, New Jersey: Prentice Hall.

Kundu, S.K. and Contractor, F.J. (1999) Country location choices of service multinationals: an empirical study of the international hotel sector. *Journal of International Management*, 5(4), 299–317.

Langton, B., Bottorff, C. and Olsen, M. (1992) The strategy, structure, environment co-alignment. In R. Teare and M. Olsen (eds), *International Hospitality Management: Corporate Strategy in Practice*. London: Addison Wesley Longman, Chapter 2, pp. 31–35.

Lee, S. (2008) Internationalization of US multinational hotel companies: expansion to Asia versus Europe. *International Journal of Hospitality Management*, 27(4), 657–64.

Littlejohn, D. (2003) Hotels. In B. Brotherton (ed.), *The International Hospitality Industry*. Oxford: Elsevier Butterworth-Heinemann, Chapter 1, pp. 5–29.

Littlejohn, D., Roper, A. and Altinay, L. (2007) Territories still to find: the business of hotel internationalisation. *International Journal of Service Industry Management*, 18(2), 167–83.

Lommelen, T. and Matthyssens, P. (2005) The internationalization process of service providers: a literature review. In P. Pauwels and K. De Ruyter (eds), *Research on International Service Marketing: A State of The Art*. Greenwich, Connecticut: Elsevier JAI Press, pp. 95–117.

Luo, Y., Xue, Q. and Han, B. (2010) How emerging market governments promote outward FDI: experience from China. *Journal of World Business*, 45(1), 68–79.

Majkgard, A. and Sharma, D.D. (1998) Client-following and market-seeking strategies in the internationalization of service firms. *Journal of Business-to-Business Marketing*, 4(3), 1–41.

Mwaura, G., Sutton, J. and Roberts, D. (1998) Corporate and national culture: an irreconcilable dilemma for the hospitality manager? *International Journal of Contemporary Hospitality Management*, 10(6), 212–20.

Olsen, M.D., Sharma, A., Echeveste, I. and Tse, E.C.Y. (2008) Strategy for hospitality businesses in the developing world. *FIU Review*, 26(1), 32–46.

Olsen, M.D., West, J.J. and Tse, E.C.Y. (1998) *Strategic Management in the Hospitality Industry* (2nd edn). New York: John Wiley.

Peters, M. and Frehse, J. (2005) The internationalization of the European hotel industry in the light of competition theories. *Tourism*, 53(1), 55–65.

Root, F.R. (1994) *Entry Strategies for International Markets*. San Francisco: Jossey-Bass.

Rushmore, S., O'Neill, J.W. and Rushmore Jr, S. (2012) *Hotel Market Analysis and Valuation: International Issues and Software Applications*. Chicago: Appraisal Institute.

Sandoff, M. (2005) Customization and standardization in hotels: a paradox or not? *International Journal of Contemporary Hospitality Management*, 17(6), 529–35.

Slattery, P. (1996) International development of hotel chains. In R. Kotas, R. Teare, J. Logie, C. Jayawardena and J. Bowen (eds), *The International Hospitality Business*. London: Cassell, Chapter 4, pp. 30–35.

Slattery, P. (2012) *The Economic Ascent of the Hotel Business* (2nd edn). Oxford, UK: Goodfellow Publishers.

Stross, R.E. (1990) *Bulls in the China Shop: And Other Sino-American Business Encounters*. Honolulu: University of Hawaii Press.

Tihanyi, L., Griffith, D.A. and Russell, C.J. (2005) The effect of cultural distance on entry mode choice, international diversification, and MNE performance: a meta-analysis. *Journal of International Business Studies*, 36(3), 270–83.

Van Agtmael, A. (2007) *The Emerging Markets Century: How a New Breed of World-Class Companies is Overtaking The World*. New York: Free Press.

Verginis, C. (2013) Investing in hotels. In R.C. Wood (ed.), *Key Concepts in Hospitality Management*. London: Sage Publications, pp. 109–13.

Weng, C.C., and Wang, K.L. (2006) Scale and scope economies of international tourist hotels in Taiwan. *Tourism Management*, 27(1), 25–33.

Yu, L. (1999) *The International Hospitality Business: Management and Operations*. Binghamton, New York: Haworth Hospitality Press.

Zhang, H.Q., Pine, R. and Lam, T. (2005) *Tourism and Hotel Development in China*. Binghamton, New York: Haworth Hospitality Press.

10

The choice of a destination to enter

Cristina Barroco (POLYTECHNIC INSTITUTE OF VISEU, PORTUGAL),
Eduardo Anselmo de Castro (UNIVERSITY OF AVEIRO, PORTUGAL) *and*
Carlos Costa (UNIVERSITY OF AVEIRO, PORTUGAL)

Introduction

Many theories have been used to explain international trade and why certain countries attract hotel chains more than others. A thorough literature review has shown that although there are many theories, researchers are unanimous in affirming that hotel chains' internationalisation is influenced by *pull factors*, related to specific characteristics of the host country (contextual and transactional environment), and by *push factors*, related to specific characteristics of the companies and of their home country.

This chapter aims to identify which factors influence the choice by hotel chains of one destination in which to invest, over another. With this purpose, a theoretical model, that includes six pull factors related to the contextual environment and five factors linked to the tourism industry, was developed. This model was validated through questionnaire surveys applied to foreign investors running accommodation units in mainland Portugal. Fifty-three questionnaires were considered valid, representing 64 per cent of the population of foreign investors in Portugal (accommodation sector).

Literature review

Throughout the centuries, literature has witnessed a number of attempts to explain international trade. Successive research in this area has led to a group of theories proposed by various authors who have been crucial in the understanding of the choice of a destination to enter.

The choice of a destination to enter: from classical theories to the present day

Adam Smith's theory of absolute advantage (1776/1977) and David Ricardo's theory of comparative advantage (1817/2004) are the two most noteworthy classical trade theories. Contributions from the neoclassical theories include Heckscher (1919), Ohlin (1933) and Samuelson (1948) with the factor proportions theory and Hymer (1960) and Kindleberger

(1969) with the industrial organisation theory. These theories allow us to conclude that the existence of market imperfections helps feed international trade.

The most important new theories of international trade include the product life cycle theory from Vernon (1966) and Wells (1968), Michael Porter's competitive advantage theory (1990) and the internationalisation theory based on Coase's transaction cost theory (1937) and expanded on by Horst, McManus (1972), Buckley and Casson (1976) and Rugman (1980). Dunning's eclectic or OLI paradigm theory (2001) merges the existing theories, explaining that in order for internationalisation to occur, three sets of factors have to be combined: *Ownership advantages, Locational advantages* and *Internationalisation advantages*.

With the Uppsala internationalisation model (Johanson and Wiedersheim-Paul, 1975), international trade studies crossed the boundaries of economic theory to further include the organisational behaviour theory. Psychic distance, environmental factors, cultural affinities and social ties are considered internationalisation determinants. Schumpeter (1911/2008) was the first to emphasise the importance of innovation, and was then followed by the contributions of Simmonds and Smith (1968), Bilkey and Tesar (1977) and Cavusgil (1980) that corroborated the internationalisation model based on innovation. In 1999, Mintzberg, Ahlstrand and Lampel's resource-based view theory focuses more on intrinsic company aspects. Johanson and Mattsson (1988) and Johanson and Vahlne (1990) identify the importance of network relationships in foreign markets (network theory). According to this theory, human capital as entrepreneurship is the driving force of the internationalisation process. The current theory of international new ventures or born global emerged with Oviatt and McDougall (1994).

The previously mentioned theories provide some insight into the complexity of internationalisation flows; however, an integrated theory that combines these elements in an analytical manner has yet to be developed. Although these theories appear in an isolated manner, they should be understood as complementary and not dissociated or regarded as alternatives.

Key factors influencing the choice of a destination to enter

A review of the literature shows that the choice of a destination to enter is influenced by:

1) Push Factors: characteristics of the company and of their home country;
2) Pull Factors: characteristics of the host country – contextual environment (common to all companies) and the transactional environment (specific to each sector).

Though both factors are important, this chapter will give special emphasis to the pull factors.

According to León-Darder, Villar-García and Pla-Barber (2011: 107), 'some arguments used in manufacturing firms cannot be directly transferred to the hotel industry because unique characteristics of these special services condition the entry mode choice into international markets'. However, for Endo (2006), the determinants for choosing a location to enter into the tourism sector are not very different from other sectors: geographical, cultural and historical proximity, political, economic and social stability of the host country, level of economic development, incentives, availability and quality of infrastructures and specific characteristics of the company (size of the company, ability to obtain economies of scale, international experience).

Regarding the incentives proposed by the government, several authors have highlighted its importance for attracting foreign investors (e.g. Buckley and Geyikdagi, 1996; Sadi and

Henderson, 2001). Some authors have also explored the link between foreign investment in tourism and the existence of GATS – the General Agreement on Trade and Services (e.g. Lee et al., 2002; Te Velde and Nair, 2006).

The size, growth, state and development of the tourism market, the extent of the tourism demand for a specific destination, tourist facilities, the number and type of attractions, availability of skilled workers, labour costs, natural and cultural resources are considered important reasons for choosing a location and attracting hotel chains.

For Snyman and Saayman (2009) there is a correlation between the countries that invest more and the origin of tourists that visit South Africa more. Buckley and Geyikdagi (1996) and Tang et al. (2007) reached the same conclusions in their studies in Turkey and China. The work of Snyman and Saayman (2009) also shows that investors from different home countries were willing to invest in different tourism products.

Table 10.1 summarises the determinants considered by many authors as vital in attracting hotel chains. Despite the importance of all determinants, it is obvious that these are not all relevant at the same time. The research also clearly states that the relevance of each determinant depends on the home and host countries, the characteristics of the companies and the type of sector that is being analysed.

Table 10.1 Summary of pull and push factors influencing hotel chain internationalisation and main authors

PULL FACTORS	MAIN AUTHORS
Geographical and cultural proximity between the host country and home country.	Altinay (2005); Buckley and Geyikdagi (1996); Dunning and Kundu (1995); Dunning and McQueen (1981, 1982); Endo (2006); Go et al.(1990); Gross and Huang (2011); Johnson and Vanetti (2005); Kantarci (2007); Littlejohn et al. (2007); Rodríguez (2002); UNCTAD (2007); Zhang et al. (2012).
Characteristics of the host country	
Political, economic and social stability of the host country.	Alon et al.(2012); Altinay (2005); Buckley and Geyikdagi (1996); Chen and Dimou (2005); Dunning and Kundu (1995); Dunning and McQueen (1981); Endo (2006); Go et al. (1990); Littlejohn, et al. (2007); Rodríguez (2002); Snyman and Saayman (2009); Te Velde and Nair (2006); UNCTAD (2007); Zhang et al. (2012); Zhao and Olsen (1997).
Incentives in the host country: governmental policies, government support, tax incentives.	Buckley and Geyikdagi (1996); Dunning and Kundu (1995); Dunning and McQueen (1981, 1982); Endo (2006); Go et al. (1990); Jarvis and Kallas (2008); Johnson and Vanetti (2005); Kantarci (2007); Karhunen, (n.d.); Sadi and Henderson (2001); Snyman and Saayman (2009); Subbarao (2008); Tang et al. (2007); Te Velde and Nair (2006); UNCTAD (2007).
Existence of the General Agreement on Trade in Services (GATS) in the host country.	Lee et al. (2002); Peric and Radic (2010); Te Velde and Nair (2006).
Accession of the host country to international organisations (European Union, World Trade Organization, etc.).	Aw and Tang (2010); Jarvis and Kallas (2008).

(Continued)

Table 10.1 (Continued)

PULL FACTORS	MAIN AUTHORS
The size, growth, state and development of the tourism market.	Alon et al. (2012); Buckley and Geyikdagi (1996); Dunning and Kundu (1995); Dunning and McQueen (1981, 1982); Go et al. (1990); Johnson and Vanetti (2005); Kantarci (2007); Karhunen (n.d.); Rodríguez (2002); Snyman and Saayman (2009); UNCTAD (2007); Zhang et al. (2012); Zhao and Olsen (1997).
Tourism resources (natural and cultural); tourism facilities, number and type of attractions.	Alon et al. (2012); Buckley and Geyikdagi (1996); Dunning and Kundu (1995); Dunning and McQueen (1981, 1982); Johnson and Vanetti (2005); Karhunen (n.d.); Littlejohn et al. (2007); Snyman and Saayman (2009); UNCTAD (2007); Zhao and Olsen (1997).
Growth of tourism demand	Buckley and Geyikdagi (1996); Dunning and McQueen (1981); Go et al. (1990); Karhunen (n.d.); UNCTAD (2007).
Human capital of the host country: educational level, availability, skilled workers, labour costs.	Buckley and Geyikdagi (1996); Dunning and Kundu (1995); Dunning and McQueen (1981, 1982); Go et al. (1990); Johnson and Vanetti (2005); Karhunen (n.d.); Snyman and Saayman (2009); UNCTAD (2007).

PUSH FACTORS	MAIN AUTHORS
Characteristics of the company	
International experience, size, ability to obtain economies of scale, preference of potential competitors, availability of skilled labour, presence of a subsidiary, transfer of know-how and technology and strategic brand development.	Alon et al. (2012); Altinay (2005); Buckley and Geyikdagi (1996); Chen and Dimou (2005); Dunning and Kundu (1995); Dunning and McQueen (1981, 1982); Endo (2006); Gross and Huang (2011); Johnson and Vanetti (2005); Littlejohn et al. (2007); Rodríguez (2002); Zhao and Olsen (1997).
Characteristics of the home country	
Market size and growth, incentives for internationalisation.	Buckley and Geyikdagi (1996); Dunning and Kundu (1995); Dunning and McQueen (1981, 1982); Gannon and Johnson (1995); Johnson and Vanetti (2005); Kundu and Contractor (1999); Rodríguez (2002).

Endo (2006), Go et al. (1990) and Rodriguez (2002) consider the historical affinities as an influencer in attracting hotel chains, as well as the quality and availability of infrastructures (e.g. Buckley and Geyikdagi, 1996; Dunning and McQueen, 1981; Endo, 2006; Go et al., 1990; Karhunen, n.d.; Snyman and Saayman, 2009; Zhao and Olsen, 1997) and state that hotel occupancy rate, hotel legislation, hospitality level of competitiveness, the activity of tour operators, additional attractions and the supplier costs may also influence the entry of hotel chains into a country. Additional attractions are also mentioned by Buckley and Geyikdagi (1996) and Zhao and Olsen (1997), as well as the attitude of locals toward tourists (Dunning and McQueen, 1981), and the repatriation of capital facilities and profits (Go et al., 1990; Te Velde and Nair, 2006).

On the other hand, there are several factors that can deter hotel chains from investing in a particular destination. Factors that can deter potential investors from investing are the following: inadequate government support; insufficient investment incentives; a lack of supporting infrastructure; difficulties in tackling complex land tenure systems; a multiplicity of agencies, many with overlapping functions; excessive time required to obtain decisions; a lack of adequate local expertise; and inadequate training schemes (Snyman and Saayman, 2009: 50).

According to Forsyth and Dwyer (2003) the tax system may naturally discourage investors from making investments in tourism. In the study carried out by Breda et al. (2008), on the internationalisation of Portuguese companies in Brazil, the following aspects were identified as the main difficulties: tax burden, bureaucracy and the socio-political situation of the host country. Sometimes the internal conditions of the company can also be an obstacle, such as the lack of qualified human resources, firm size, the lack of international experience and its organisational structure.

Conceptual model

The conceptual model built in this study (Figure 10.1) aims to identify which factors influence a hotel chain's willingness to enter a destination. Based on the theoretical framework described, 11 pull factors (characteristics of host country) were selected to integrate the model:

- *6 Specific Factors of the Contextual Environment (SFCE)*: country risk; level of development; regulation; integration in international organisations; cultural and historical affinities; geographical location.
- *5 Specific Factors of the Tourism Sector (SFTS)*: competitiveness of the sector; government policies for the sector; image/brand of the sector; tourism offer; tourism demand.

This model seeks to discover whether the main barriers to foreign investment are related to the SFCE or the SFTS. All factors were explored in the construction of logical relations that underpin the enunciation of the hypothesis. This model was validated through questionnaire surveys applied to foreign investors running accommodation units in mainland Portugal.

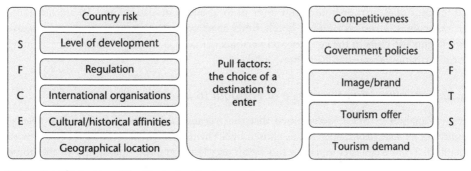

SFCE = Specific Factors of the Contextual Environment
SFTS = Specific Factors of the Tourism Sector

Figure 10.1 Conceptual model.

Empirical research: the case of the Portuguese accommodation sector

With reference to the Portuguese accommodation sector there are some studies (e.g. Breda, 2010; Breda et al., 2008; Gomes and Silva, 2012) that evaluated Portuguese investment abroad, but there are no empirical studies about foreign investment in the Portuguese Tourism sector. However, the presence of hotel chains in the country is evident. This internationalisation happens through equity forms (foreign direct investment: greenfield investment, mergers, acquisitions, joint venture or sole venture) or through non-equity forms (franchise, management contracts, lease and marketing consortium). In their study, Cunill and Forteza (2010), found that the franchise system has become the growth strategy most widely used by hotel chains.

An analysis of the 300 hotel companies ranking (Hotels Magazine, 2012), makes it possible to conclude that 22 are present in Portugal, running a total of 91 hotels, two hotel apartments and two resorts (26,157 beds in total). Moreover, 20 hotel chains of foreign capital can be added, which are not present in the rank 300. These operate 29 hotels, three resorts and six hotel apartments (10,467 beds). Owned by foreign investors are also 29 rural tourism and manor houses (464 beds) and 14 units of local accommodation (215 beds). The hotels operated by foreign groups represent 22 per cent of total existing beds in Portugal (31,579 from 143,552). There are 27 five-star hotels operated by hotel chains (10,802 beds), representing 53 per cent of total beds in five-star hotels in Portugal (20,420).

This empirical research investigates the crucial factors for investing in the Portuguese accommodation sector. With this purpose, a questionnaire was sent to the CEOs/owner of all 83 companies with foreign investment in the accommodation sector in Portugal.

Fifty-three questionnaires were considered valid, representing 64 per cent of the population of foreign investors in the Portuguese accommodation sector. Although the sample may seem small, there were no systematic differences between it and the population. It should be noted that previous studies of hotel chains have used lower rates of response (e.g. Barrowclough, 2007; Buckley and Geyikdagi, 1996; Chen and Dimou, 2005; Contractor and Kundu, 2000; Dunning and Kundu, 1995; Rodriguez, 2002).

An analysis of the country of registration of the surveyed companies suggests that 19 are registered in the Netherlands, six in Germany, six in the UK, five in France, four in Belgium, three in Angola, three in Spain, two in the USA, two in Switzerland, one in Ireland, one in Sweden and one in Malta. In terms of geographical dispersion, investors who answered the survey operate a total of 100 projects (20,999 beds), representing 56 per cent of total beds in Portugal managed by foreign investors. From these, 35 are small companies (investors running rural tourism units, manor houses and units of local accommodation) and 18 are medium/large companies (investors running hotels, hotel apartments, tourist apartments and resorts). Respondents use visits to the country and personal contacts as the main sources for obtaining prior information about the Portuguese market.

Key factors influencing the choice of Portugal to invest

Statistical analysis of SFCE determined that the *geographical location of Portugal is a factor of attractiveness for hotel chains*, since it was chosen by 49 investors, with a mean of >1 (2.34) with p <0.0001. The variables comprising this factor are: 1) geographical proximity to the home country; 2) opportunity to explore neighbouring markets; 3) strategic location (access to markets: intersection of sea and air routes linking Africa to Europe and America); 4) platform partnerships with neighbouring countries of North Africa, but also with markets with fast growing economies such as China, India, South Africa or Mexico.

The nonparametric Friedman test and the Multiple comparisons test shows that the opportunity to explore neighbouring markets (mean = 2.94) and the strategic location of Portugal (mean = 2.65) are the most valued variables by foreign investors.

Despite the fact that cultural and historical affinities have been chosen by 31 investors, at first analysis, there was *no statistical evidence to suggest that cultural and historical affinities are a factor of attractiveness for hotel chains.* However, isolating the small-size investors, the mean is > 1 (1.37) with p = 0.025 (one-tailed test), which indicates that they value these affinities more than large and medium-size investors. Variables comprising this factor are: 1) historical affinities; 2) cultural proximity between Portugal and the home country; 3) language; 4) Portuguese history/international prestige. The variable language is valued less than any of the others (mean = 1.65).

Regarding the Portuguese regulation, this is not considered a factor of attractiveness for hotel chains, presenting a mean of <1 (0.09) with p <0.0001. It was chosen by five investors and they all attributed the rating of least important of the three factors considered in the decision to invest in Portugal. The variables comprising this factor are: 1) tax rates (inflation); 2) exchange rates; 3) tax burden; 4) legal system; 5) labour law; 6) favourable terms for repatriation of capital and profits; 7) privatisation policy. Tax burden (mean = 6.40) and bureaucracy (mean = 6.20) were identified as major problems.

Portugal's integration in international organisations was chosen by 14 investors; with a mean of <1 (0.49) and p <0.0001, the results show that this is not a factor of attractiveness for hotel chains. All investors who have chosen this factor considered the variable European Union member more important (mean = 7.00) than any other. The least valued variable was the existence of GATS (mean = 1.79). The other variables comprising this factor are: 1) member of European Free Trade Association; 2) member of the Community of Portuguese Language Countries; 3) member of World Tourism Organisation (UNWTO); 4) member of United Nations Conference on Trade and Development (UNCTAD); 5) member of United Nations (UN).

It can also be concluded that although the factor level of risk has been chosen by 26 investors, there was *no statistical evidence (p> 0.05) to suggest that the risk level of Portugal is a factor of attractiveness to hotel chains.* The variables comprised in this factor are: 1) Political stability; 2) Economic stability; 3) Social stability; 4) Safe country; 5) Security of the foreign direct investment legal system; 6) Government policy towards foreign direct investment. The most valued variable in this factor was safety (mean = 5.12).

Finally, the development level of Portugal was valued as an important factor by 30 investors; however, there was *no statistical evidence (p> 0.05) to suggest that the development level of Portugal is a factor of attractiveness for hotel chains.* The variable Portuguese market size (mean = 1.85) was less valued than growing market (mean = 2.78), competitive operational costs (mean = 3.12) and Portuguese market expected growth (mean = 2.25).

Table 10.2 gives an overview of the SFCE that may affect the choice of Portugal for investment.

Concerning the *SFTS* that may affect the choice of hotel chains, the analysis determined that the factor image/brand of the Portuguese tourism sector was chosen by 38 investors and has a mean of >1 (1.58) and p = 0.001, allowing us to conclude that *the image/brand of Portugal as a tourist destination is a factor in attracting hotel chains.* Through qualitative content analysis of this question, it can be said that cultural tourism, sea and sun, food and wine and nature tourism have been identified by foreign investors as the most valued tourism products.

Regarding the factor tourism offer, it was chosen by 44 investors, with a mean of >1 (2.06) and p <0.0001. This allows us to conclude that *the Portuguese tourism offer is a factor of*

Table 10.2 Summary of specific factors of the contextual environment

Factors	N (a)	Mean	Significance (2-tailed)	Variables	Mean (b)	Conclusions (c)
Geographical location of Portugal	49	2.34	0.000	Geographical proximity to the home country	2.53	Yes
				Opportunity to explore neighbouring markets	2.94	
				Strategic location	2.65	
				Platform partnerships with neighbouring markets	1.88	
Cultural and historical affinities	31	1.11	0.025	Historical affinities	2.68	Only for small investors
				Cultural proximity between Portugal and the home country	2.81	
				Language	1.65	
				International prestige with respect to its history	2.68	
Portuguese regulation	5	0.09	0.000	Tax rates (inflation)	5.00	No
				Exchange rates	2.80	
				Tax burden	6.40	
				Legal system	5.40	
				Labour law	5.40	
				Repatriation of capital facilities and profits	2.00	
				Privatisation policy	2.80	
				Bureaucracy	6.20	
Portugal's integration in international organisations	14	0.49	0.000	Member of the European Union	7.00	No
				Member of European Free Trade Association	3.21	
				Member of the Community of Portuguese Language Countries	3.64	
				Member of World Tourism Organization	3.79	
				Member of United Nations on Trade and Development	2.79	
				Member of United Nations	4.79	
				Existence of General Agreement on Trade in Services	1.79	
Risk level of Portugal	26	0.92	0.616			No statistical evidence
Development level of Portugal	30	0.89	0.381			No statistical evidence

Note:
(a) Number of investors who chose these factors (each respondent only chooses 3 factors and sorts them in order of importance).
(b) Each respondent had to order the variables through a ranking scale of importance: 1 = least importance; 2 = intermediate; 3 = most important).
(c) If it is a factor of attractiveness for investment.

attractiveness for hotel chains. The variables comprising this factor are: 1) diversity of tourist attractions; 2) tourism facilities; 3) additional attractions; 4) original tourism products; 5) traditional tourism products (sea and sun); 6) natural tourism resources; 7) cultural tourism resources; 8) pleasant climate; 9) hospitality of the Portuguese people; 10) safety. The variable pleasant climate had the highest mean (7.59), followed by the hospitality of the Portuguese people (7.14).

Despite the tourism demand factor, which has been chosen by 38 investors, on a first analysis there was no statistical evidence to suggest whether this is an attraction factor. However, isolating large and medium-size investors, the mean is >1 (1.56) and p = 0.028 (one-tailed test). Thus, the Wilcoxon-Mann-Whitney test showed that *tourism demand in Portugal is a factor of attractiveness for hotel chains* for large and medium-size investors. The variables comprising this factor are: 1) growth of tourism demand; 2) growth in tourism revenue; 3) average spending of tourists.

Government policies as a factor for the tourism sector were not considered a factor of attractiveness for investment in the sector. It was valued by 12 investors and had a mean of <1 (0.32) at p <0.0001. Variable maintenance of international sites that promote the country has the lowest value (1.92) and the variable tax incentives the highest (3.58). The other variables are: preferential loans, grants and trade fairs/promotional events.

Finally, although the factor of competitiveness of the Portuguese tourism sector has been chosen by 27 investors, there was *no statistical evidence to suggest that the competitiveness of the Portuguese tourism sector is a factor of attractiveness for hotel chains,* with a p >0.05. The variables comprising this factor are: 1) availability of skilled workers; 2) labour costs; 3) staff quality, responsibility and commitment; 4) multilingual skills of the local population; 5) quality of infra-structures; 6) tourism market with little competition; 7) attractive tourism market; 8) occupancy rate; 9) low construction costs; 10) suppliers cost. The attractive tourist market variable had the highest mean (7.78).

Table 10.3 shows the SFTS that may affect the choice of Portugal for investment.

This empirical research also checks whether the countries that invest most in Portugal are the countries that send more tourists to Portugal. Data analysis of the number of foreign investors in Portugal, number of beds operated by foreign, income revenue, guests and overnight stays, showed that this relationship exists: *the countries that invest most in the Portuguese tourism sector are also the ones that send more tourists to Portugal.* The main countries are: Angola, Canada, France, Germany, Netherlands, Spain, Sweden, Switzerland, UK and USA.

Regarding the origin of foreign investment, investors from the Netherlands show a clear demand for the Centre of Portugal. Investors from Angola, Brazil, Netherlands, Ireland and Malta have no investment in the Algarve, while investors from Germany, Belgium and USA prefer this region. These results suggest that investors from different home countries invest in different regions of Portugal.

Finally, taking into account that the choice of a destination by hotel chains can be affected by specific factors of the company, this study sought to assess the relationship between company size (number of rooms managed across the world) and investment in Portugal (number of rooms managed in Portugal). The hotel chain operating more rooms in Portugal (2,985) is Accor, number 5 in the rank worldwide (531,714 rooms in total), according to Hotels Magazine (2012). The second is Vip Hotels (Angolan capital), with 1,903 rooms, and is considered a small group (only operating 3,110 rooms worldwide). The Intercontinental Hotels Group, which is the largest hotel chain in the world (658,348 rooms), only has 1,692 rooms in Portugal. Marriott International is the second (643,196 rooms in total) and in Portugal operates 1,161 rooms. Lastly, the Hilton is the third world hotel chain

Table 10.3 Summary of specific factors of the tourism sector

Factors	N (a)	Mean	Sig. (2-tailed)	Variables	Mean (b)	Conclusions (c)
Portugal's image/brand as a tourism destination	38	1.58	0.001	(d)	(d)	Yes
Tourism offer	44	2.06	0.000	Diversity of tourist attractions	6.09	Yes
				Tourism facilities	3.75	
				Additional attractions	2.80	
				Original tourism products	5.11	
				Traditional tourism products (sea and sun)	4.52	
				Natural tourism resources	6.50	
				Cultural tourism resources	6.55	
				Pleasant climate	7.59	
				Hospitality of the Portuguese people	7.14	
				Safety	5.39	
Tourism demand	38	1.15	0.028	Growth of tourism demand	2.42	Only for large and medium-size investors
				Growth in tourism revenue	1.63	
				Average spending of tourists	1.97	
Government policies for the tourism sector	12	0.32	0.000	Preferential loans, grants	2.58	No
				Tax incentives	3.58	
				Trade fairs/promotional events	2.08	
				Maintenance of international sites that promote the country	1.92	
Competitiveness of the Portuguese tourism sector	27	0.89	0.444			No statistical evidence

Note:
(a) Number of investors who chose these factors (each respondent was required to choose three factors and sort them in order of importance where 1 = least importance, 2 = intermediate and 3 = most importance).

(b) Each respondent was required to order the variables through a ranking scale of importance.

(c) If it is a factor of attractiveness for investment.

(d) The answers were subjected to a qualitative content analysis.

(633,238 rooms in total) and in Portugal only operates 440 rooms. Data analysis helped to confirm that *larger companies are not those that manage more rooms in Portugal.*

Key factors that hinder the choice of Portugal for investment

Although the aim of this research was to identify the main factors of attractiveness for hotel chains, it was also considered interesting to identify the factors that hinder this investment. Using the paired samples t-test and using the nonparametric Wilcoxon, the conclusions reached are the same ($p<0.0001$): the factors that hinder the attraction of foreign investment to Portugal were related to the country's general characteristics. The bureaucracy was the main constraint identified by 86.8 per cent of respondents, followed by tax burden (49.1 per cent), the economic situation in Portugal (45.3 per cent), difficulties in accessing financing (34.0 per cent) and working restrictive laws (34.0 per cent).

Concerning the characteristics of the Tourism sector, the main factors that hinder the investment attraction are: tourism offer too concentrated in territorial terms (39.6 per cent), poor international image of Portugal as a tourist destination (37.7 per cent) and strong dependence of some tourist source markets (32.1 per cent).

Respondents considered as less important factors for attracting investment were: the unsafe country (94.3 per cent), political and social instability (90.6 per cent) and high competition in the touristic market (84.9 per cent).

Concluding remarks

The results obtained in this empirical research indicate that Portugal's geographical location, its image/brand as a tourism destination and the Portuguese tourism offer are considered the key factors influencing hotel chains. Cultural and historical affinities were found to be factors influencing small foreign investors, while tourism demand attracts medium and large investors. This study clearly identifies that the main barriers to foreign investment are bureaucracy, tax burden and Portugal's current economic situation. Moreover, it concludes that the countries that invest most in the Portuguese accommodation sector are also the main generators of tourism to Portugal and that investors from different countries of origin invest in different regions of Portugal.

References

Alon, I., Liqiang, N. and Wang, Y. (2012) Examining the determinants of hotel chain expansion through international franchising. *International Journal of Hospitality Management*, 31(2), 379–86.

Altinay, L. (2005) Factors influencing entry mode choices: empirical findings from an international hotel organisation. *Journal of Hospitality and Leisure Marketing*, 12(3), 5–28.

Aw, Y.T. and Tang, T.C. (2010) The determinants of inward foreign direct investment: the case of Malaysia. *International Journal of Business and Society*, 11(1), 59–76.

Barrowclough, D. (2007) Foreign Direct Investment in tourism and small island developing states. *Tourism Economics*, 13(4), 615–38.

Bilkey, W.J. and Tesar, G. (1977) The export behaviour of smaller-sized Wisconsin manufacturing firms. *Journal of International Business Studies*, 8(1), 93–98.

Breda, Z.M.J. (2010) *Network Relationships and the Internationalisation of the Tourism Economy: The Case of Portuguese Overseas Investment in the Hotel Sector* (Unpublished doctoral dissertation). University of Aveiro, Aveiro.

Breda, Z., Costa, C. and Varum, C.A. (2008) *A internacionalização das empresas portuguesas no Brasil: O caso do sector hoteleiro*. Paper presented at the 2° Encontro Luso-Brasileiro de Estratégia e 2° Encontro Slade Brasil, ISCTE, Lisboa.

Buckley, P.J. and Casson, M. (1976) *The Future of the Multinational Enterprise*. London: Macmillan.

Buckley, P.J. and Geyikdagi, N.V. (1996) Explaining foreign direct investment in Turkey's tourism industry. *Transnational Corporations*, 5(3), 99–110.

Cavusgil, S.T. (1980) On the internationalization process of firms. *European Research*, 8(6), 273–81.

Chen, J.J. and Dimou, I. (2005) Expansion strategy of international hotel firms. *Journal of Business Research*, 58(12), 1730–40.

Coase, R.H. (1937) The nature of the firm. *Economica*, 4(16), 386–405.

Contractor, F.J. and Kundu, S.K. (2000) Globalization of hotel services: an examination of ownership and alliance patterns in a maturing service sector. In Aharoni, Y. and Nachum, L. (eds), *Globalization of Services: Some Implications for Theory and Practice*. London and New York: Routledge, pp. 296–319.

Cunill, O.M. and Forteza, C.M. (2010) The franchise contract in hotel chains: a study of hotel chain growth and market concentrations. *Tourism Economics*, 16(3), 493–515.

Dunning, J.H. (2001) The eclectic (OLI) paradigm of international production: past, present and future. *International Journal of the Economics of Business*, 8(2), 173–90.

Dunning, J.H. and Kundu, S.K. (1995) The internationalization of the hotel industry: some new findings from a field study. *MIR: Management International Review*, 35(2), 101–33.

Dunning, J.H. and McQueen, M. (1981) The eclectic theory of international production: a case study of the international hotel industry. *Managerial and Decision Economics*, 2(4), 197–210.

Dunning, J.H. and McQueen, M. (1982) Multinational corporations in the international hotel industry. *Annals of Tourism Research*, 9(1), 69–90.

Endo, K. (2006) Foreign direct investment in tourism – flows and volumes. *Tourism Management*, 27(4), 600–14.

Forsyth, P. and Dwyer, L. (2003) Foreign investment in Australian tourism: a framework for analysis. *The Journal of Tourism Studies*, 14(1), 67–77.

Gannon, J. and Johnson, K. (1995) The global hotel industry: the emergence of continental hotel companies. *Progress in Tourism and Hospitality Research*, 1(1), 31–42.

Go, F., Pyo, S.S., Uysal, M. and Mihalik, B.J. (1990) Decision criteria for transnational hotel expansion. *Tourism Management*, 11(4), 297–304.

Gomes, L. and Silva. J.R. (2012) Internationalization of Spanish and Portuguese Hotel Networks in Brazil – the Northern Coast of Bahia. *Proceedings of the Tourism and Management Studies International Conference, Algarve*, 1, 145–55.

Gross, M. and Huang, S. (2011) Exploring the internationalization prospects of a Chinese domestic hotel firm. *International Journal of Contemporary Hospitality Management*, 23(2), 261–74.

Heckscher, E. (1919) The effect of foreign trade on the distribution of income. *Ekonomisk Tidskrift*, 497–512.

Hotels Magazine (2012) Special report: hotels' 325. *Hotels Magazine*, 23–44.

Hymer, S.H. (1960) *The international operations of national firms: a study of direct foreign investment* (Unpublished doctoral dissertation), Massachusetts Institute of Technology, Cambridge.

Jarvis, J. and Kallas, P. (2008) Estonian tourism and the accession effect: the impact of European Union membership on the contemporary development patterns of the Estonian tourism industry. *Tourism Geographies*, 10(4), 474–94.

Johanson, J. and Mattsson, L. (1988) Internationalization in industrial systems: a network. In N. Hood and J.E. Vahlne (eds), *Strategies In Global Competition*, New York: Croom Helm, pp. 287–314.

Johanson, J. and Vahlne, J.E. (1990) The mechanism of internationalization. *International Marketing Review*, 7(4), 11–24.

Johanson, J. and Wiedersheim-Paul, F. (1975) The internationalisation of the firm: four Swedish cases. *Journal of Management Studies*, 12(3), 305–22.

Johnson, C. and Vanetti, M. (2005) Locational strategies of international hotel chains. *Annals of Tourism Research*, 32(4), 1077–99.

Kantarci, K. (2007) Perceptions of foreign investors on the tourism market in central Asia including Kyrgyzstan, Kazakhstan, Uzbekistan, Turkmenistan. *Tourism Management*, 28(3), 820–29.

Karhunen, P. (n.d.) *Entry mode choice in transition economies: operations of international hotel companies in Russia*. Center for Markets in Transition, Helsinki School of Economics and Business Administration, Helsinki. Online. Available HTTP: <http://www.chc-int.ru/reports/karhunen.pdf>, aceeseed May 28, 2015.

Kindleberger, C.P. (1969) American business abroad. *The International Executive*, 11(2), 11–12.

Kundu, S.K. and Contractor, F.J. (1999) Country location choices of service multinationals: an empirical study of the international hotel sector. *Journal of International Management*, 5(4), 299–317.

Lee, M., Fayed, H. and Fletcher, J. (2002) GATS and tourism. *Tourism Analysis*, 7(2), 125–37.

León-Darder, F., Villar-García, C. and Pla-Barber, J. (2011) Entry mode choice in the internationalisation of the hotel industry: a holistic approach. *The Service Industries Journal*, 31(1), 107–22.

Littlejohn, D., Roper, A. and Altinay, L. (2007) Territories still to find: the business of hotel internationalization. *International Journal of Service Industry Management* 18(2), 167–83.

McManus, J.C. (1972) The theory of the international firm. In G. Paquet (ed.), *The Multinational Firm and The Nation State*. Toronto: Collier Macmillan.

Mintzberg, H., Ahlstrand, B. and Lampel, J. (1999) *Strategy Safari: A Guided Tour Through The Wilds of Strategic Management*. New York: The Free Press.

Ohlin, B. (1933) *Interregional and International Trade*. Cambridge: Harvard University Press.

Oviatt, B.M. and McDougall, P.P. (1994) Towards a theory of international new ventures. *Journal of International Business Studies*, 25(1), 45–64.

Peric, J. and Radic, M.N. (2010) *Impact of foreign direct investment in tourism on economic growth in developing countries*. Paper presented at the Tourism and Hospitality Management 2010.

Porter, M. (1990) *The Competitive Advantage of Nations*. New York: The Free Press.

Ricardo, D. (1817/2004) *The Principles of Political Economy and Taxation*. Dover Publications.

Rodríguez, R. (2002) Determining factors in entry choice for international expansion: The case of the Spanish hotel industry. *Tourism Management*, 23(6), 597–607.

Rugman, A.M. (1980) Internalization as a general theory of foreign direct investment: A re-appraisal of the literature. *Review of World Economics*, 116(2), 365–79.

Sadi, M.A. and Henderson, J.C. (2001) Tourism and foreign direct investment in Vietnam. *International Journal of Hospitality and Tourism Administration*, 2(1), 67–90.

Samuelson, P.A. (1948) International trade and the equalisation of factor prices. *Economic Journal*, 58(230), 163–84.

Schumpeter, J.A. (1911/2008) *The Theory of Economic Development: An Inquiry into Profits, Capital, Credit, Interest and the Business Cycle*. Translated from the German by Redvers Opie. New Brunswick, US and London, UK: Transaction Publishers.

Simmonds, K. and Smith, H. (1968) The first export order: a marketing innovation. *British Journal of Marketing*, 2(2), 93–100.

Smith, A. (1776/1977) *An Inquiry Into The Nature and Causes of the Wealth of Nations*. London: Edwin Cannan.

Snyman, J.A. and Saayman, M. (2009) Key factors influencing foreign direct investment in the tourism industry in South Africa. *Tourism Review*, 64(3), 49–58.

Subbarao, S. (2008) *A study on Foreign Direct Investment (FDI) in Indian tourism*. Paper presented at the Conference *Tourism in India: Challenges Ahead*, India.

Tang, S., Selvanathan, E.A. and Selvanathan, S. (2007) The relationship between foreign direct investment and tourism: empirical evidence from China. *Tourism Economics*, 13(1), 25–39.

Te Velde, D.W. and Nair, S. (2006) Foreign direct investment, services trade negotiations and development: the case of tourism in the Caribbean. *Development Policy Review*, 24(4), 437–54.

UNCTAD. (2007) *FDI in Tourism: The Development Dimension*. New York and Geneva: United Nations Conference on Trade and Development.

Vernon, R. (1966) International investment and international trade in the product cycle. *Quarterly Journal of Economics*, 80(2), 190–207.

Wells, L.T. (1968) A product life cycle for international trade? *Journal of Marketing*, 33, 1–6.

Zhang, H.Q., Guillet, B.D. and Gao, W. (2012) What determines multinational hotel groups' locational investment choice in China? *International Journal of Hospitality Management*, 31(2), 350–59.

Zhao, J.L. and Olsen, M.D. (1997) The antecedent factors influencing entry mode choices of multinational lodging firms. *International Journal of Hospitality Management*, 16(1), 79–98.

11

Entry modes: ownership (equity modes)

Yinyoung Rhou and Manisha Singal

(VIRGINIA TECH UNIVERSITY, USA)

Concept and importance of entry mode

Many firms have expanded their businesses worldwide, principally in response to significant economic opportunities arising from expanded markets, increased sales and product diversification. In addition, multinational enterprises (MNEs) are able to take advantage of economies of scope and scale by sharing cost-producing activities across geographic markets. For example, MNEs may transfer their core competences (e.g. know-how, operations and management skills, patents, etc.) to foreign subsidiaries so that they can capitalise on a broader capability base. The various economic benefits of internationalisation are also evidenced in the hotel industry.

Spurred in part by an increase in global business and pleasure travel beginning in the late 1960s (which was later heightened by airline deregulation in 1978), and coupled with domestic market saturation in the 1970s and 1980s, US hotel companies increasingly began to expand to foreign locales during this period. The results of these shifts is that US hotel chains now enjoy a strong presence in international markets and receive sales revenue from all around the world. For example, the current growth strategy of Starwood Hotels relies heavily on global market expansion. As of 2014, 78 per cent of its growth occurred outside North America – principally in the Asia-Pacific region: 54 per cent of the pipeline shows new properties in Asia Pacific and 36 per cent shows new growth in China alone (Starwood Hotels and Resorts Worldwide, 2015). Like many other consumer products, a brand name has proven to be vital to the globalisation of US-based hotel chains. A brand image and reputation that is linked to standardised products or services can provide a distinct competitive advantage, especially in the international markets where consumers may not be familiar with local, independent offerings. For these reasons, hotel companies tend to expand abroad with a chain, as evidenced by the fact that approximately 14 million rooms of 149,000 international hotels (nearly 53 per cent) are affiliated with a brand (Wyndham Hotels and Resorts, 2014).

This significant expansion trend is reflected in the business literature, which increasingly examines issues related to a firm's foreign entry mode – namely, 'an institutional arrangement for organising and conducting international business transactions' (Andersen, 1997: 29). The choice of entry mode is regarded as a critical decision in international strategy since it has the potential to leverage the operations and future decisions of a firm in the new foreign market. As such, it is a decision that requires considerable deliberation as often the course of action is irreversible and impacts success not of a particular market but the company as a whole. A firm's choice of foreign entry mode (e.g., wholly-owned operations, franchise, management contract, consortium, leasing and so on) almost immediately adds a level of uncertainty and complexity to its operations. Each mode has strong implications for the investment risks involved, the required resource commitment and the eventual organisational control over foreign markets (Zhao et al., 2004). Important to this investigation is that the unique characteristics of the hotel industry highlight the criticality of the entry mode issue. This industry is wholly dependent on the presence of an actual bricks-and-mortar property in a targeted market, which means that the production and consumption of lodging services occur simultaneously. Therefore, the concept of least-cost route that minimises distance from location of raw materials to final market is perhaps not as applicable to the entry mode choice for chain hotels as it may be for the manufacturing of products. This chapter describes the equity mode choice (where the focal company has a complete or partial ownership stake in the overseas property) before discussing the antecedents of choices made by firms and chain hotels referencing the distinctiveness of the hotel industry. Our discussion of equity entry modes could apply to domestic growth, however it is mostly centred in the context of international expansion where it has received both more scholarly and practical attention.

Characteristics of equity modes in international markets

Entry modes fall into two broad categories: equity entry modes and non-equity entry modes. Equity modes lead to a foreign entrant's financial investment while non-equity modes do not, and thus the latter is, by nature, a contractual mode (Erramilli et al., 2002). Although the use of non-equity modes, including franchising, licensing and management contracts, is widely prevalent in the hotel industry, several large hotel corporations follow a mixed strategy of using both equity and non-equity entry modes depending upon country and context. For example, Hilton Hotels operate their business through three segments: (1) ownership: in 2006 Hilton invested approximately $5.7 billion to acquire its operating subsidiaries worldwide and also acquired the Conrad hotel brand, which had been operated as a joint venture; (2) management and franchise; and (3) timeshare (Hilton Hotels Corp, 2007). Therefore, their sources of revenue differ according to the mode of ownership and participation. In general, hotel companies earn revenue from sales of rooms, food and beverages, and on-site services such as spa-related offerings.

Equity entry modes include wholly owned subsidiaries and joint venture firms. Wholly owned subsidiaries can be further categorised as either *greenfield investments* or *acquisitions*. The former represent the formation of a completely new subsidiary, while the latter refer to taking ownership of existing (local) firms. Consequently, the entry mode via a *greenfield investment* is fully controlled and monitored by the parent firm, but at the same time, the ownership/start-up process inherently takes more time and effort, which is related to higher risk (Gilroy and Lukas, 2006). These potentially negative attributes contribute to the fact that acquisition tends to be favoured as a strategy for entering foreign markets.

Considering that market share is usually affected by market power, *acquisition* is a good way to achieve greater market share in a relatively shorter time. Moreover, acquiring a well-established firm already in operation means that the entering firm can focus on a core competency and work on becoming more competitive in the market (Hitt et al., 2012). Bloomberg Business reported that low borrowing costs and growing competition resulted in more than doubling the value to US $64.4 billion of global mergers and acquisitions (hotels, travel-service companies and tour operators) in 2014 over any of the previous 6 years (Weiss, 2015).

While the acquisition of an existing firm can deliver certain competitive advantages, it does feature some possible challenges that could hinder an immediate return on investment. In other words, it may be difficult to blend diverse organisations due to their unique organisational cultures, management structures, business models, etc. For example, organisational cultural differences induce 'us versus them' thinking, leaving room for potential social conflicts (Vaara et al., 2012). The findings suggest difficulties of integration between acquiring and acquired firms.

Scholars have delineated the essential differences between a greenfield investment and an acquisition in its impact on global expansion decisions (Andersson and Svensson, 1994; Barkema and Vermeulen, 1998; Harzing, 2002; Hennart and Park, 1993). The differences stem from various factors such as existing competitive advantages, timing horizon of expansion, and degree of R&D intensity and cultural distance. For example, Hennart and Park (1993) found that Japanese companies with weak competitive advantage are more likely to expand through acquisitions, while companies with strong competitive advantage are more likely to expand through greenfield investment as a means of more efficiently transferring their strong competitive advantage. Further, acquisition is more likely to be used by firms that have recently started expanding (Andersson and Svensson, 1994). Another generality is that a higher degree of R&D intensity and a greater cultural distance between the home and host country negatively influence the decision to expand via the acquisition method, i.e. firms with high R&D intensity and/or those that are thinking of expanding in culturally distant countries are more likely to use a greenfield investment (Andersson and Svensson, 1994; Barkema and Vermeulen, 1998). In her theoretical study, Harzing (2002) incorporated international corporate strategy into the entry mode choice of multinational companies. Harzing investigated how a firm's international corporate strategy influences the choice of entry mode (i.e., greenfield investment or acquisition) in the light of whether the expansion was global or multi-domestic. Firms with global strategies are interested in the use of firm-specific advantages and cost efficiency; in contrast, firms with multi-domestic strategies are interested in the accommodation of local demands. Thus, Harzing argued that the former are more likely to pursue a greenfield investment, while the latter are more inclined to invest in an acquisition.

In addition to equity modes that directly invest in businesses in foreign locations, (e.g., greenfields and acquisitions), a joint venture represents another strategy for entering a foreign market. In a joint venture, two or more businesses who share profit-earning goals collaborate by sharing key resources (Geringer and Hebert, 1989). An important facet of a joint venture is that participants in this business arrangement do not need to fully merge their entire business operations. Instead, each of the businesses is only responsible for certain components of the new business. Accordingly, this partial form of equity mode is flexible in that a participant's financial commitment and risk exposure are limited only to what they do, which is particularly beneficial in riding out market fluctuations (Buckley and Casson, 2009). In addition, firms can take advantage of greater resources, such as the specialised knowledge and skills of their local partners (e.g. in interpreting local government regulations). The major drawback of the joint venture is the inherent ambiguity of who is in charge of operations – both from a macro and micro perspective (Geringer and Hebert, 1989; Reuer et al., 2014). Possible conflicts in goals, cultures, management styles, etc. could result in poor integration and cooperation.

Given the partial or full ownership aspect, equity entry modes (e.g. a wholly owned operation) are linked to better control of operations; on the downside, equity modes require more resources, thereby assuming a higher risk. In particular, the hotel industry is considered to have a volatile (and thus risky) market due to consumers' discretionary spending on hotel products/services (Singal, 2012) and a large amount of capital is required to acquire fixed assets (e.g., real estate property, equipment and facilities, etc.).

In sum, although equity modes allow firms to retain relatively high control over operations, that level of control can vary widely. The more control firms have, the higher the level of capital requirements, time, and effort that are needed to generate desired outcomes (Erramilli and Rao, 1993).

Choice of equity entry modes in chain hotels

Equity entry modes, as mentioned above, take the form of greenfield investments, acquisitions, or joint ventures. A prevalent theory for explaining a firm's entry mode decision is transaction cost economics (TCE). According to TCE (Williamson, 1975), firms organise transactions in three ways: (a) in full integration mode whereby they internalise the transactions, (b) with only a moderate degree of integration, or (c) with no integration – i.e., transactions are outsourced through market contracts. For certain types of economic activities, a firm can choose either to make the commodity in-house or buy it from an external third party. Such 'make or buy' decisions are related to so-called transaction costs. In formulating an entry mode choice, the main focus of TCE analysis is on one market entry at a time – and minimising transaction costs is an indicator of efficient management of resources (Contractor and Kundu, 1998). Transaction costs generally relate to search costs, contracting costs and monitoring costs. In the context of entering foreign markets, identifying a contractual partner (or not), formulating a contract, conducting actual business practices and enforcing the contract are all part of the transaction costs to be considered. With the inevitable cost increases and the uncertainty associated with doing business on a global scale, transaction costs will increase as well, especially because the costs for controlling a complicated business like a global hotel chain will be very high. Based on TCE, we suggest that, if the costs are low, non-equity modes that are governed by markets are favoured; however, if the costs are high as expected in hotel chains, equity entry modes will be preferred.

Despite the wide use of TCE analysis in entry mode studies (e.g. Brouthers et al., 2003; Erramill and Rao, 1993; Meyer, 2001), other factors can come into play as well – for example, agency theory. In this context, one party (the principal, usually the headquarters of a firm) employs another (the agent, the subsidiary or the franchisee in a host country), who then acts on behalf of the principal. The identification of that agent especially in the case of hotels is usually based on local area knowledge—expertise and the likely demand and cost advantages of doing business in that location. Due to differing risk preferences, coupled with information asymmetry, agents will often act in a manner that may not be in the best interests of the principal (Jensen and Meckling, 1976). Based on the assumption that agents will act in self-interest, a moral hazard problem arises when the principal does not have the expertise or resources required to monitor the actions of the agent. Specifically, a principal bears agency costs when (a) the goals and risk preferences of the agent are not aligned with those of the principal and (b) when it is difficult or expensive for the principal to verify what the agent is actually doing. When agency theory is considered, then, the decision to use an equity mode is related to the problems of monitoring self-interested managers. Indeed, this becomes more likely when the two parties are located on different continents and more pronounced in an international context because, as noted above, it is logistically more difficult to monitor and control a self-interested agent who may be located remotely. For these reasons, agency costs may explain the choice of equity modes for firms expanding overseas. Considering that hotel firms need a physical presence in each location, an equity entry mode serves to reduce agency costs mentioned above as wholly-owned subsidiaries may be easier to monitor than franchised units.

Importantly, determinants of entry mode choice for manufacturing firms cannot be directly applied to service firms (e.g., hotels). Hotel services, unlike goods (that are produced first and then sold), are co-produced with the interaction between the service provider (hotel staff) and customer (guest), an attribute known as simultaneity in production and consumption. In addition, unlike goods, hotel services cannot be stored, i.e., a room not sold for a night cannot be inventoried for future sale, an attribute known as perishability (Erramilli, 1991; Erramill and Rao, 1993). These idiosyncratic attributes highlight the importance of the industry-specific context when considering choice of entry mode (León-Darder et al., 2011). A hotel company's huge capital investment in fixed assets (their properties) also poses a higher business risk in comparison to many manufacturing firms. For example, ongoing owner-invested capital is typically required to retain or upgrade properties (e.g., the installation of a hotel-wide wireless network). There are also real estate market fluctuations to be factored into the choice of entry mode. Consider a hotel company's substantial investment in relatively illiquid real estate holdings (compared to other assets), which limits its ability to adjust easily to fluctuating market conditions. Such burdens will be more obvious during economic downturns when consumer demand and earnings decrease concurrently, and limited discretionary dollars are being directed to more utilitarian needs. In short, wholly owned hotel firms are exposed to far greater risks that may or may not be relevant to franchised or managed properties.

The trend to shift from equity to non-equity modes is therefore gaining ground. Contractor and Kundu (1998) report that in 1998, 65.4 per cent of multinational hotel properties operated under non-equity modes – the two favoured models being franchising and management contracts. At the close of 2013, Marriott Hotels reported that 55 per cent of their entire global inventory was franchised; 42 per cent was under management contract, only 2 per cent was owned or leased, and the remainder fell into the 'unconsolidated joint venture' category, which manages hotels and catering services for franchised properties (Marriott International, 2014). With an even larger percentage of franchised properties (7,425 out of a total of 7,480 hotels), the Wyndham Hotel Group – the world's largest hotel company based on number of properties, earned about 78 per cent of its revenue from its franchising activities in 2013. The remaining earnings came from its 58 managed properties and its two wholly-owned hotels (Wyndham Hotels and Resorts, 2014). Similarly, Hilton ranks among the largest hotel owners in the world based on number of rooms of owned and leased (672,083 hotel rooms in 91 countries and territories), as well as their joint venture hotels. They recently announced that 'our diverse global portfolio of owned and leased properties includes a number of leading hotels in major gateway cities such as New York, London, San Francisco, Chicago, São Paolo, Sydney, and Tokyo' (Hilton Worldwide Holdings Inc.: 9). Hilton's owned properties, however, play a significantly smaller role in their earnings. At the close of the 2013 fiscal year, 610,413 Hilton hotel rooms were operated through non-equity modes (i.e., under management or franchising contracts); in contrast, 61,670 rooms were owned or leased. While this 10 per cent investment in owned properties exceeds that of either Marriott or Wyndham, Hilton has indicated that this share is likely to dwindle in the coming years. In terms of future investments, Hilton has stated that 99 per cent of the 194,572 rooms scheduled to open around the world will be operated via franchises or under management contracts (Hilton Worldwide Holdings Inc., 2014). Similar movement was found even in Shangri-La hotels and resorts that historically avoided non-equity ownership. Although it is still one of the chain hotels with a high level of equity participation, the company has increasingly used non-equity modes like management contract to expand its business in China and other parts of Asia. Recently, Shangri-La Hotels and Resorts announced that the company has signed a management contract with Le Touessrok, Mauritius, to launch the hotel as Shangri-La's Le Touessrok Resort and Spa, Mauritius, in 2015 (Shangri-La Hotels and Resorts, 2014). This type of shift among major hotel chains can be considered as a strategy to reduce capital outlay and risk while still expanding operations in world-wide markets.

As shown in the Table 11.1, the major global hotel chains have substantially expanded through non-equity modes, but equity modes certainly afford some advantages over other modes of entry and expansion. The major advantage relates to the issue of control of operations. Control, defined as the power of a firm to influence organisational systems to improve its competitive position and maximise returns on assets and skills (Agarwal and Ramaswami, 1992), can be the greatest advantage with equity modes of entry. One of the other related advantages with equity modes of operation is that it is relatively easy to maintain service uniformity and adhere to overarching standards across all of the locations – for instance, with respect to maintaining a location's interior and exterior appearance, adhering to safety rules, and establishing a known level of service that employees must follow. As such, maintaining comparably high product and service quality across multiple properties (especially on a global scale) under the equity modes is more effective when a hotel is wholly owned by a parent company.

For these reasons, equity modes are more effective in maintaining the quality of products/ services when the loss of control is detrimental to the brand equity of the chain (Anderson and Gatignon, 1986). This problem is even more critical for reputed chain hotels that are expected to provide certain standard products and services regardless of where they are located. Customers who choose hotel chains over independents do so because they expect a certain level of quality and service standards; second-rate operations may adversely influence the chain's image and reputation, negatively impacting a firm's value over the longer term. The importance of brand standard becomes more salient in the international context. Tourists that travel to foreign countries will be likely to stay in the chain hotels, expecting familiar and standardised quality of service throughout the world. Moreover, considering that risks of knowledge leakage and the possibility of 'know-how spillover' are inevitably increased by international expansion, equity modes that allow full integration of all the resources into one decision-making case afford highly centralised control through hierarchical authority (Gupta and Govindarajan, 1991). In short, foreign entrants who heavily advertise their brands are more likely to use equity modes, in order to protect their brand name (Anderson and Gatignon, 1986).

However, a caution associated with equity mode entry in foreign markets must be noted. Since equity modes tend to feature both high risk and high control, i.e., a trade-off between risk and control (Contractor and Kundu, 1998), direct ownership and other equity mode forms are less likely to be used in countries or markets where there is high political and economic risk and the level of economic development is low (Altinay, 2005). This finding upholds Zhao and Olsen's (1997) earlier study that stresses that political instability becomes a major concern for the equity modes (wholly owned subsidiaries) but are less significant for the non-equity modes (franchising and management contracts). Accordingly, companies tend to shy away from equity-based entry in politically, economically, or financially unstable

Table 11.1 Equity modes in major hotel chains in 2013

Hotel Chain	Home country	Locations	Total number of properties	Number of owned properties	Total number of rooms	Number of owned rooms (percentage)	Sources
InterContinental Hotels Group	US	Worldwide	4,697	9[a]	686,873	3,962 (0.58)	2013 Annual Report
Hilton Hotels and Resorts	US	Worldwide	4,073	155[a]	672,083	61,670 (9.18)	2013 Annual Report
Marriott International	US	Worldwide	3,916	Not available	675,623	13,512 (2.00)	2013 Annual Report
Wyndham Hotels and Resorts	US	Worldwide	7,485	2[b]	645,423	1,175 (0.18)	2013 Annual Report
Accor	France	Worldwide	3,576	1,387[c]	461,719	39,505 (8.56)	2013 Annual Report
Starwood Hotels and Resorts Worldwide	US	Worldwide	1,175	47[d]	346,800	15,900 (4.58)	2013 Annual Report
Carlson Rezidor Hotel Group	US	Worldwide	337	68[e]	75,277	16,732[f] (22.23)	2013 Year-End Report
Home Inns Group	China	China	2,180	872[g]	256,555	92,360[h] (36)	2013 Annual Report
Choice Hotels International	US	Worldwide	6,340	Not available	506,058	Not Available[i]	2013 Annual Report
Hyatt Hotels Corporation	US	Worldwide	548	97[a]	147,388	28,039 (19.02)	2013 Annual Report

Sources: own elaboration, based on: Accor (2014); Carlson Rezidor Hotel Group (2014); Choice Hotels International (2014); Hilton Worldwide Holdings Inc. (2014); Home Inns Group (2014); Hyatt Hotels Corporation (2014); InterContinental Hotels Group (2014); Marriott International (2014); Starwood Hotels and Resorts (2014); Wyndham Hotels and Resorts (2014).

a) including owned/leased hotels; b) including owned hotels; c) including 278 owned and 1109 leased hotels; d) including wholly owned, majority owned, and leased hotels; e) including 68 leased hotels; f) including 16,732 leased hotel rooms; g) including 872 leased hotels; h) including 92,360 leased hotel rooms; i) Choice Hotels is primarily a hotel franchiser with franchise agreements.

locations (Ramon Rodriguez, 2002), instead preferring franchising or other non-equity modes in which royalties and fees provide a stable return.

Hotel chains are also less likely to choose equity entry modes in locations that are culturally different from the country of origin. However, likelihood of firm profitability and availability of internal financial funds are two factors that are conducive to the use of equity based entry modes (Quer et al., 2007). Among other factors, modernisation of facilities, staff training, service innovation and improvements to booking systems seem to encourage hotel firms to use equity modes (Cunill and Forteza, 2010).

In general, although high equity and control modes are not seen as crucial for international hotel expansion, there are nonetheless several factors that influence decisions to choose equity modes. First, hotels with longer international experience and a greater global presence prefer equity modes because they understand that cultural differences can lead to business incongruences that end up negatively impacting income and brand reputation. For example, León-Darder et al. (2011) noted the importance of tight control in the hotel industry to overcome 'cultural distance', which refers to the myriad differences between a firm's home base and its foreign locations. The authors stressed the need for hotel companies to pay close attention to effective communication skills and workforce training based on the preferences and demands of their customers. Thus, hotel chains show a higher propensity to use equity modes when they enter into culturally distant markets in order to provide customised services and maintain the performance of local employees. In short, greater control is desired over foreign subsidiaries from a practical standpoint. Additionally, hotels seem to prefer equity investments in lower-income nations where the potential for return is high (Contractor and Kundu, 1998). Compared to more developed countries, developing countries tend to have a less experienced workforce and weaker managerial capabilities; therefore, equity-mode entry augments for maintaining control resonate in such environments (Graf, 2009).

In contrast, the findings for multinational manufacturing firms (e.g., semiconductor companies) differ somewhat with respect to expansion modes. Anderson and Coughlan (1987), for example, reported that equity ownership in developed countries is the preferred entry mode because (a) the investment risks in the relatively stable environment are assumed to be low, and (b) the return potential is superior to other entry modes. This is also inconsistent with Kim and Hwang's (1992) study of multinational manufacturers. The authors reported that the inherent uncertainty in culturally distant markets leads firms to minimise their capital investments and prefer joint ventures to more expensive wholly-owned subsidiaries.

To put it simply, the manner in which hotel chains organise their transactions in the international context is a major policy decision that has implications for control, quality and, ultimately, the performance of the firm. Considering the distinctive nature of the hotel industry, the use of equity mode in a carefully considered expansion strategy may help hotel firms deal with various markets or obstacles in advantageous ways.

References

Accor (2014) Form 10-K. Online. Available HTTP: <http://www.accor.com/fileadmin/user_upload/Contenus_Accor/Finance/Documentation/2014/UK/2013_registration_document.pdf>, accessed 23 March, 2015.

Agarwal, S. and Ramaswami, S.N. (1992) Choice of foreign market entry mode: impact of ownership, location and internalisation factors. *Journal of International Business Studies*, 23(1), 1–27.

Altinay, L. (2005) Factors influencing entry mode choices: empirical findings from an international hotel organisation. *Journal of Hospitality & Leisure Marketing*, 12(3), 5–28.

Andersen, O. (1997) Internationalisation and market entry mode: a review of theories and conceptual frameworks. *MIR: Management International Review*, 37, 27–42.

Anderson, E. and Coughlan, A.T. (1987) International market entry and expansion via independent or integrated channels of distribution. *The Journal of Marketing*, 51(1), 71–82.

Anderson, E. and Gatignon, H. (1986) Modes of foreign entry: a transaction cost analysis and propositions. *Journal of International Business Studies*, 17(3), 1–26.

Andersson, T. and Svensson, R. (1994) Entry modes for direct investment determined by the composition of firm specific skills. *The Scandinavian Journal of Economics*, 96(4), 551–60.

Barkema, H.G. and Vermeulen, F. (1998) International expansion through start-up or acquisition: a learning perspective. *Academy of Management Journal*, 41(1), 7–26.

Brouthers, K.D., Brouthers, L.E. and Werner, S. (2003) Transaction cost-enhanced entry mode choices and firm performance. *Strategic Management Journal*, 24(12), 1239–48.

Buckley, P.J. and Casson, M.C. (2009) The internalisation theory of the multinational enterprise: a review of the progress of a research agenda after 30 years. *Journal of International Business Studies*, 40(9), 1563–80.

Carlson Rezidor Hotel Group (2014) 2013 year-end report. Online. Available HTTP: <http://media. corporate-ir.net/media_files/irol/20/205430/Reports/2013-Q4.pdf> accessed 23 March, 2015.

Choice Hotels International (2014) Form 10-K. Online. Available HTTP: <http://www.sec.gov/ Archives/edgar/data/1046311/000104631114000004/chh1231201310-k.htm>, accessed 23 March, 2015.

Contractor, F.J. and Kundu, S.K. (1998) Modal choice in a world of alliances: Analyzing organisational forms in the international hotel sector. *Journal of International Business Studies*, 29(2), 325–57.

Cunill, O.M. and Forteza, C.M. (2010) The franchise contract in hotel chains: a study of hotel chain growth and market concentrations. *Tourism Economics*, 16(3), 493–515.

Erramilli, M.K. (1991). The experience factor in foreign market entry behavior of service firms. *Journal of international business studies*, 22(3), 479–501.

Erramilli, M.K. and Rao, C.P. (1993) Service firms' international entry-mode choice: a modified transaction-cost analysis approach. *The Journal of Marketing*, 57(3), 19–38.

Erramilli, M.K., Agarwal, S. and Dev, C.S. (2002) Choice between non-equity entry modes: an organisational capability perspective. *Journal of International Business Studies*, 33(2), 223–42.

Geringer, J.M. and Hebert, L. (1989) Control and performance of international joint ventures. *Journal of International Business Studies*, 20(2), 235–54.

Gilroy, B.M. and Lukas, E. (2006) The choice between greenfield investment and cross-border acquisition: a real option approach. *The Quarterly Review of Economics and Finance*, 46(3), 447–65.

Graf, N.S. (2009) Stock market reactions to entry mode choices of multinational hotel firms. *International Journal of Hospitality Management*, 28(2), 236–44.

Gupta, A.K. and Govindarajan, V. (1991) Knowledge flows and the structure of control within multinational corporations. *Academy of Management Review*, 16(4), 768–92.

Harzing, A.W. (2002) Acquisitions versus greenfield investments: international strategy and management of entry modes. *Strategic Management Journal*, 23(3), 211–27.

Hennart, J.F. and Park, Y.R. (1993) Greenfield vs. acquisition: the strategy of Japanese investors in the United States. *Management Science*, 39(9), 1054–70.

Hilton Hotels Corp. (2007) Form 10-K. Online. Available HTTP: <http://www.sec.gov/Archives/ edgar/data/47580/000110465907014553/a07-941110k.htm>, accessed 21 November, 2014.

Hilton Worldwide Holdings Inc. (2014) Form 10-K. Online. Available HTTP: <http://www.sec.gov/ Archives/edgar/data/1585689/000158568914000006/a2013hwh10k.tm>, accessed 21 November, 2014.

Hitt, M., Ireland, R.D. and Hoskisson, R. (2012) *Strategic Management Cases: Competitiveness and Globalisation*. Cincinnati: Cengage Learning.

Home Inns Group (2014) Form 10-K. Online. Available HTTP: <http://media.corporate-ir.net/ media_files/IROL/20/203641/2013_annual_report_hmin.pdf>, accessed 23 March, 2015.

Hyatt Hotels Corporation (2014). Form 10-K. Online. Available HTTP: <http://investors.hyatt.com/ files/doc_financials/annual%202013/Hyatt-Form-10-K.pdf>, accessed 23 March, 2015.

InterContinental Hotels Group (2014). Form 10-K. Online. Available HTTP: <http://www.ihgplc. com/files/reports/ar2013/docs/IHG_Report_2013.pdf>, accessed 23 March, 2015.

Jensen, M. C., and Meckling, W. H. (1976). Theory of the firm: managerial behavior, agency costs and ownership structure. *Journal of Financial Economics*, 3(4), 305–60.

Kim, W.C., and Hwang, P. (1992) Global strategy and multinationals' entry mode choice. *Journal of International Business Studies*, 23(1), 29–53.

León-Darder, F., Villar-García, C. and Pla-Barber, J. (2011) Entry mode choice in the internationalisation of the hotel industry: a holistic approach. *The Service Industries Journal*, 31(1), 107–22.

Marriott International (2014) Form 10-K. Online. Available HTTP: <http://www.sec.gov/Archives/edgar/data/1048286/000144530514000495/mar-q42013x10k.htm>, accessed 21 November, 2014.

Meyer, K.E. (2001) Institutions, transaction costs, and entry mode choice in Eastern Europe. *Journal of international business studies*, 32(2), 357–67.

Quer, D., Claver, E. and Andreu, R. (2007) Foreign market entry mode in the hotel industry: the impact of country- and firm-specific factors. *International Business Review*, 16(3), 362–76.

Ramón Rodríguez, A. (2002) Determining factors in entry choice for international expansion. The case of the Spanish hotel industry. *Tourism Management*, 23(6), 597–607.

Reuer, J.J., Klijn, E. and Lioukas, C.S. (2014) Board involvement in international joint ventures. *Strategic Management Journal*, 35(11), 1626–44.

Shangri-La Hotels and Resorts (2014, June) Shangri-La hotels and resorts signs management contract for a resort in Mauritius. Online. Available HTTP: <http://www.shangri-la.com/corporate/press-room/press-releases/shangri-la-hotels-and-resorts-signs-management-contract-for-a-resort-in-mauriti/>, accessed 16 March, 2015.

Singal, M. (2012) Effect of consumer sentiment on hospitality expenditures and stock returns. *International Journal of Hospitality Management*, 31(2), 511–21.

Starwood Hotels and Resorts (2014) Form 10-K. Online. Available HTTP: <http://www.sec.gov/Archives/edgar/data/316206/000119312514065122/d645634d10k.htm>, accessed 21 November, 2014.

Starwood Hotels and Resorts (2015) Form 10-K. Online. Available HTTP: <http://www.sec.gov/Archives/edgar/data/316206/000119312515062758/d838837d10k.htm>, accessed 16 March, 2015.

Vaara, E., Sarala, R., Stahl, G.K. and Björkman, I. (2012) The impact of organisational and national cultural differences on social conflict and knowledge transfer in international acquisitions. *Journal of Management Studies*, 49(1), 1–27.

Weiss, R. (2015, January) Global tourism M&A doubles as online agencies squeeze incumbents. Online. Available HTTP: <http://www.bloomberg.com/news/articles/2015-01-23/global-tourism-m-a-doubles-as-online-agencies-squeeze-incumbents>, accessed 15 March, 2015.

Williamson, O.E. (1975) *Markets and Hierarchies. Analysis and Antitrust Implications*. New York, NY: Free Press.

Wyndham Hotels and Resorts (2014) Form 10-K. Online. Available HTTP: <http://www.sec.gov/Archives/edgar/data/1361658/000136165814000005/wyn-20131231x10k.htm>, accessed 21 November, 2014.

Zhao, H., Luo, Y. and Suh, T. (2004) Transaction cost determinants and ownership-based entry mode choice: a meta-analytical review. *Journal of International Business Studies*, 35(6), 524–44.

Zhao, J.L. and Olsen, M.D. (1997) The antecedent factors influencing entry mode choices of multinational lodging firms. *International Journal of Hospitality Management*, 16(1), 79–98.

12

Entry modes: franchise

Mahmood A. Khan

(VIRGINIA TECH UNIVERSITY, USA)

Introduction

Franchising – the most dynamic business arrangement – has become the dominant force in the distribution of goods and services nationally and internationally. National and international experts have predicted that franchising will become the primary method of doing business worldwide, with over 400 US franchise systems operating internationally (International Franchise Association, 2015; Khan, 2014). The term *franchise* has its origin in the French word meaning 'free from servitude'. Roughly translated that would mean that a businessman is free to run his own business. It is used as a noun as well as a verb. Strictly from the business point of view, a franchise is a right or privilege granted to an individual or a group (Khan, 1999). Since there are certain rights which pass from one party to another, there are legal aspects that should also be considered in any definition of franchising. From a legal standpoint, according to a report by the Committee on Small Business, United States Congress (1991), 'franchising is essentially a contractual method for marketing and distributing goods and services of a company (franchisor) through a dedicated or restricted network of distributors (franchisees)'. Under the terms of this legal franchise contract, the franchisor grants the right and licence to franchisees to market a product or service, or both, using the trademark and/ or the business system developed by the franchisor. Therefore, the contract imposes obligation on both parties. The franchisor must provide the product/service, a successful system with a proven marketing support, and training. The franchisee brings financing, management skills, and a determination to own and operate a successful business. The entire system is locked into legal and business boundaries, with several vested ownerships to an extent that it is difficult to manoeuvre. The International Franchise Association (2015), the major franchising trade association, defines franchising as 'a method for expanding a business and distributing goods and services through a licensing relationship. In franchising, franchisors (a person or company that grants the license to a third party for the conducting of a business under their marks) not only specify the products and services that will be offered by the franchisees (a person or company who is granted the license to do business under the trademark and trade name by the franchisor), but also provide them with an operating system, brand and support.'

Services management and franchising

In the area of services management, franchising has two unique features; first, it typically occurs in businesses where there is a notable service component that must be performed near customers, such as in restaurants and hotel chains. The compelling reason for this is that service-providing outlets must be replicated and dispersed geographically. Secondly, franchise contracts typically reflect a unique allocation of responsibilities, decision rights and profits, between a centralised principal (the franchisor) and decentralised agents (franchisees) (Combs et al., 2004). Testing an agency-based organisational model of internationalisation through franchising in the hotel sector, it was found that a hotel franchisor's decision to internationalise through franchising is positively related to the percentage of franchises, the ratio of franchised units to the total number of units. It also highlighted the empirical modelling related to international franchising of hotels, which presents unique characteristics among franchising companies, due to a high investment capital requirement, maturity in the product life cycle, and a high level of standardisation and globalisation of operations (Alon et al., 2012). It was also reported in a study (Moon and Sharma, 2014) that franchised firms create more intangible value than non-franchised firms. In addition, the authors identify optimal proportions of franchised and non-franchised properties that allow lodging firms to maximise profitability and intangible value. The results provide a critical perspective on the discussion of whether or not lodging firms should franchise and, if so, to what extent.

Viewed from the perspective of entrepreneurship, franchising is a vehicle for entering business ownership (Shane and Hoy, 1996). From the marketing point of view, franchising is often considered as a distribution channel (Kaufmann and Rangan, 1990). From the finance point of view it is a capital structure issue (Norton, 1995). Considered from the economics point of view, franchising is a leading venue for understanding the economic structure of contracts (Lafontaine, 1992). Finally from the perspective of strategic management, franchising is an important organisational form (Combs and Ketchen, 1999).

The importance of ongoing franchisor support, and a proven concept in minimising potential risk, has been reported (Baron and Schmidt, 1991; Hunt, 1977; Withane, 1991) as one of the primary reasons for selecting franchising as method of doing business. Other reasons include the role of an established name, lower development costs and operational independence within an individual's decision to elect the franchising channel (Litz and Stewart, 1986; Peterson and Dant, 1990). A franchise system is not only an economic system, but also a social system in which the franchisor and franchisees have a close working relationship (Strutton et al., 1995). Accordingly, the fundamental behavioural dimensions of power/ dependence, communications, and conflict that characterise a social system (Stern and Reve, 1980) are also characteristics of a franchise system.

The basic concepts of franchising have been clearly identified by the US Federal Trade Commission (2015) as follows:

1. The franchisee will obtain the right to operate a business that is identified or associated with the franchisor's trademark, or to offer, sell, or distribute goods, services, or commodities that are identified or associated with the franchisor's trademark;
2. The franchisor will exert or has authority to exert a significant degree of control over the franchisee's method of operation, or provide significant assistance in the franchisee's method of operation; and
3. As a condition of obtaining or commencing operation of the franchise, the franchisee makes a required payment or commits to make a required payment to the franchisor or its affiliate.

Based on an assessment of the above mentioned descriptions and definitions it becomes clear that franchising survives by creating a symbiotic and mutually beneficial relationship between the franchisor and the franchisee. In a study, the franchising advantages were reflected in the attractiveness of the brands, accessibility to international markets, guest satisfaction ratings and flexibility in fees structure (Heung et al., 2008). If properly executed, franchising can result in a win-win-win situation. There are significant advantages to franchisor, franchisee and the consumer. For an entrepreneur, a hotel chain, or a growing company with a potentially successful service process or plan, franchising provides a cost-effective and systematic strategy for marketing and rapid expansion with minimum direct involvement and financial investment. For a prospective franchisee, it represents an opportunity to own and operate a business involving a proven concept or business format with a minimum of financial risk. For potential consumers, franchising provides a way to receive services in a reliable and predictable manner. For the franchisee, the most significant characteristic of a franchise relationship is the minimising of the risk of starting a new business. A franchisee also benefits from consumer recognition of the franchisor's brand name, trademark and service mark. Costly operating and marketing mistakes can be avoided because franchisors provide as a part of agreement, advertising, training, continuous supervision, and assistance.

Franchising as a mode of expansion

Franchising is based on expansion both from the territorial as well as business point of view. The very reason why franchising is used is that it provides easy means of expansion. The franchise agreement clearly states the extent of expansion that is expected by a franchisor from a franchisee. In return, the franchisor provides territorial rights and first right of refusal to the selected franchisee. Therefore, expansion strategy has to be carefully designed based on the needs and situation. Expansion strategy should be based on sound assessment using SWOT (strengths, weaknesses, opportunities, and threats) of a business. Normally, growth strategies fall into four different possible scenarios as identified by the Ansoff's Matrix (Johnson et al., 2011: 232). *Market penetration* involves getting into a market either to obtain a market share, or to establish presence. *Market development* entails developing a market either entering alone, or in partnership with a local business. *Product development* strategy involves developing products for a selected market considering consumer preferences. *Diversification* strategy deals with developing new products for the new market. A successful franchisor is clear as to what strategy needs to be followed and should have a deep understanding of the business environment of the country. Finally, careful implementation of these strategies is essential.

A global hotel firm or hotel chain was defined in a study (Contractor and Kundu, 1998a) as one that either has an equity stake in a foreign property, or operates the hotel under a management service agreement, or is a franchisor to the foreign hotel property. Franchising as an expansion mode has a broad appeal particularly in service organisations such as hotel chains. This was predicted to be due to the low level of risk associated with this mode and the rapid growth opportunity it provides. However, growth through franchising is not a straightforward activity, particularly in European hospitality firms (Altinay, 2007). Several arguments were presented by Cunill and Forteza (2010), relying on several research studies, to support the view that franchise agreements are currently the favourite growth strategy used by hotel chains. These include (a) growth strategies are most popular among consumer-services firms such as hotels; (b) given the characteristics of the hotel industry, such as easy codification of management and control systems, there is a willingness to transfer management know-how; (c) due to the low earning capacity of hotel chains, hotel ownership and the actual running of operations are considered as two separate roles; and (d) the hotel sector belongs to a service industry where it is possible to separate capital investment from management skills.

In a detailed study (Kosová and Sertsios, 2014) using considerable proprietary data on hotel franchising to test for the use of initial conditions/requirements, such as size and/or quality-tier of establishment, in self-enforcing mechanisms it was found that controlling for observable hotel and market characteristics, as well as unobserved differences (i.e. fixed effects) across states, hotel location (e.g. urban vs. rural), brands (or parents) and years, franchised hotels that are far away from their parents' headquarters (and thus are more costly to monitor) tend to have more rooms, are more likely to be a high quality property, and generate higher revenues. However, they also found that such revenue premium of faraway hotels is, in turn, largely explained by the size and quality requirements specified by the franchisor when the hotel starts its operations.

Considering the importance of growth in hotel sector, answers to the following important questions should be considered as an outcome to the expansion strategy:

(a) Will the product/service be marketable in the targeted country or geographical region? For example, does the hotel chain provide services that fulfil the needs of the population?
(b) Can the hotel chain withstand competition from similar concepts or category in the targeted country?
(c) Does the hotel chain have competent and qualified staff, appropriate training materials, operational manuals, and marketing plans for the targeted country?
(d) Is there a good comprehension of the culture, language, and business working conditions in the targeted country?
(e) Are there enough skilled workers available to undertake all operational functions of the hotel chain?

If the answer to all of the above questions is yes, then plans should be made to select the most appropriate mode of entry. Operating hotel chains in foreign countries can create several challenges, therefore careful assessment of all involved factors is necessary.

International franchising

International markets provide new dimensions for the expansion of any business franchise. Increasing population, which is manifold for some countries, and an increase in available disposable income, have created an expanded market. Demographics of countries such as China, Korea, Malaysia, India, and Indonesia are changing rapidly. China and Vietnam are expected to extensively adapt franchising, which is expected to develop very rapidly. The financial status of foreign populations has changed for the better. Because of the increased export of natural products and finished goods, people have more economic resources to hand. In many countries, untapped population growth and industrial expansion are taking place simultaneously. This prosperity has created large numbers of people who want to avail themselves of service outlets such as hotels and restaurants (Khan, 2014).

International franchising is expanding rapidly and notable trends in favour of expansion of hotel chains include (a) increased educational status of the local population, (b) techno-logical advancement facilitating travel, intercultural cooperation, and instant dissemination of information, (c) rapid development of rural areas, construction of highways, improved transportation methods, and overall industrial development, (d) improved economies and increased disposable family income, (e) increased numbers of women in the workforce and of two-income families, (f) ease of using sophisticated management systems, and (g) increased significance of convenience as a result of one or more factors mentioned above.

Reasons for hotel chains to expand internationally by franchising

In his study of international hotel franchise relationships, Connell (1997) reported that while few European hotel companies are large enough to become franchisors, there is evidence of an increasing level of UK franchisee participation. More companies are appraising the advantages and disadvantages of joining franchise systems. In this study, franchisees were motivated by a need to access international reservations systems and to become part of more internationally recognised and technologically advanced chains (Connell, 1997).

Findings in Elango's (2007) study indicate that franchisors seek international markets after they have saturated domestic markets. The counterpoint to this argument is that in the US, there are many states where some brands are still not franchising and are potentially good markets. It was also found that monitoring experience of a franchisor is positively related to the likelihood that a franchisor operates internationally. No differences in franchisee fee were found between franchisors who operate in domestic markets exclusively and those with international operations. In addition, franchisors with international operations have lower royalty rates compared with those that do not (Elango, 2007).

For both short and long term strategies, the global firm has to deal with a multiplicity of partners and organisational forms, each having its own degree of required control. These controls can be classified as 'participatory' controls or 'proscriptive' controls. Participatory controls are related to active participation in the management of an enterprise and may be exercised by 'withholding' or threatening to withhold some asset or capability desired by the other partner. Prospective controls are *de facto* prohibitions. This was further classified into the following categories: (a) daily operational and quality control in each hotel property; (b) control over the physical assets or over the real estate and its attendant risks; (c) control over tacit expertise embedded in the routines of the firm; and (d) control over the codified assets, such as a global reservation system and the firm's internationally recognised brand name (Contractor and Kundu, 1998a).

The primary reasons for hotel chains considering international expansion by franchising are summarised as follows:

1. Franchising is based on expansion. Going international provides an opportunity for developing new markets. Thus in order to increase market share it is highly advisable to enter international markets.
2. Every new outlet will bring in additional revenue for the franchisors. If the franchise model is successful domestically it can add new revenue sources in an international market.
3. With the increase in revenue, the franchisor's corporation will be considered favourably by the investors and stakeholders.
4. If the home market is saturated, international franchising provides a new venue for growth and development. Also, franchisors do not have to depend solely on the home market. Some franchisors have greater income from external markets.

5. If the franchising concept is tried and tested, it will be easier to move it internationally. Existing operations manuals and training programmes can be used with necessary modifications. Existing prototypes can be used to showcase the franchise concept.
6. Entry into foreign markets will provide exposure to the brand as well as help in expansion in nearby areas inciting interest and brand confidence.
7. If the concept of the hotel chain is such that there is no competitor, the franchisor will benefit from the 'first-mover advantage'. The brand recognition as well as the experiential learning will bring long-lasting benefits.
8. Entry into international businesses increases the brand value, thereby increasing the shareholder value. For hotel chains which have proven successful in domestic markets, going international is viewed favourably by the shareholders.
9. Considerable investment is involved in developing a franchise concept. Expanding this to international markets will bring more returns on investment.
10. Hotel chains which have gone international enter into a different category, thus having a competitive advantage in the domestic market.

Points to consider in international franchising

The significance and potential of the success of international franchising are well established. Contractor and Kundu (1998b) proposed that the modal choice is influenced by both the environment, or conditions, in the market in which the hotel property is located as well as the characteristics and strategy of the global hotel firm that decides whether to franchise or to run the property themselves. In any case, careful considerations have to be given before expanding into any country. Points to consider and factors to be evaluated are described below.

Political, environmental and legal considerations

Political stability and legal restrictions are volatile and may change with circumstances. A thorough and careful strategic plan is necessary before entering any foreign market. At times it may be difficult to gauge stability, but past history and the forecasted political environment may be good indicators. Foreign governments may have regulations that make it difficult for any hotel chains to be developed in a particular city or region. For example, the French government has created a historical classification aimed largely at protecting the traditional décor and atmosphere of French buildings. This imposes certain restrictions that may impact the operational aspects of hotel chains. The terms and conditions of contracts of any franchise agreement must therefore be written in a way to allow room for exit or adaptation to unfavourable situations, if necessary.

Associated with the political environment are the monetary restrictions a country may have. If complex bureaucracy is involved or if it is difficult to get money out of the country, franchisers may be at a disadvantage. A fluctuating currency may also have an impact on the profitability of the operation. On the other hand, there are countries, such as India and UAE, that offer incentives for foreign investors and provide special considerations. Local taxes and tariffs should also be taken into consideration. Because hotel chains and real estate are linked, real estate laws and regulations have a significant impact on franchises. In some countries, there is no protection or compensation against real estate losses that result from private or governmental decisions. Also, lease and tenant agreements vary from country to country. Franchise renewals become uncertain under such circumstances. In some countries such as

Vietnam there are no rights of ownership for properties, as all real estate belongs to the government. Such laws are prevalent in many countries. Additional charges may be levied for the processing of legal papers and documents.

Language, culture and traditions

Language plays an important role in the successful operation of a franchise system in foreign countries. A good working knowledge of the language of the country is essential, primarily for three purposes: (1) for effective communication with franchisees and for the complete transfer of the philosophy, strategy, and functioning of the franchise system; (2) for developing and implementing a successful training programme for employees and management personnel; and (3) for providing details of operations and for the development of operation manual(s) for franchisees (Khan, 2014). The language barrier sometimes is a big deterrent to expansion. Sometimes communication effectiveness is lost in translation.

When choosing a possible franchisee, cultural differences between the franchisor and franchisee are taken very much into account because local franchisees must understand the values and strategic policies of the franchisor (Cunill and Forteza, 2010). Cultural differences have an impact on what can be marketed and what type of service is preferred. For example, in many countries of the Middle East and Far East, breakfast is expected as a part of the hotel stay. The type of service and décor preferred are also affected by the cultural norms of a country. As an example, in Saudi Arabia, women do not freely work alongside men in hotels and do not mix freely with men. In many countries, particularly in Middle Eastern countries and also in Switzerland, the concept of queuing or using buffets at banquets is not considered appropriate. In many larger cities, hotels are located in the midst of crowded buildings or have multi-stories or multifunctional properties. In such cases careful site selection is important, and prospective franchisors should research all relevant factors. For example, highway travel may not be as popular in some countries as it is in the United States. On the other hand, train and bus travel may be more popular. Aspects such as the architectural design and colours used in hotels are also very important. Height and lighting restrictions pose considerable problems for franchise hotel chains.

Demographic and economic data

Age, gender, and available disposable income of target customers should be evaluated with special emphasis on the potential for changes in the near future. Generation gaps and preference should be taken into consideration. Some countries, particularly oil rich Middle Eastern countries, have very ambitious plans, possibly due to demands stemming from an increasing population, discovery of natural resources such as oil and gas, or popularity of a travel destination. With a change in the economic conditions, literacy status and working conditions can improve, due to the growing number of educational institutions. Another important factor which is evident in many developing countries is that large segments of the population may migrate or work as expatriates, particularly in the Middle East and some Far Eastern countries. This results in two very important consequences: (a) investment in businesses such as hotel chains; and (b) availability of the workforce, both skilled and non-skilled, which can be utilised in franchise businesses such as hotel chains.

Pine et al. (2000) reported that China's hotel industry was predicted to expand significantly to cope with the forecasted massive future increases in both inbound and domestic tourists. This situation presented a great opportunity for franchising of hotels, especially at the mid-market and budget levels, which is where the great volumes of business lie from both domestic and future inbound tourists. Whether such franchising will be based on foreign brands or newly created indigenous Chinese brands remains a key question that needs answering. Opportunities exist, but a full understanding of China's particular business, social, cultural, economic and political context is essential for foreign companies to succeed, whilst existing and new indigenous companies require greater technical and operating expertise along with the necessary business acumen to operate hotel chains.

Technology transfer

The use of the franchise system of expansion stimulates the economy and the development of infrastructure within a country. The concept of franchising is itself an attraction because it stimulates a chain reaction whereby hotel chains can help build the national economy. A tremendous multiplier effect takes place with each hotel property that is developed. Franchises create job opportunities and help local communities in many different ways. Knowledge gained from experience overseas helps in remodelling or redefining needs, which translates into benefits for franchisors, who can use the modified technology and processes in expanding nationally and internationally. A comparative analysis of international franchises (Connell, 1999) showed different strategies for dealing with two different types of hotel firms. Although these relationships involve companies from the same sector and of similar size and maturity, they illustrate two very different approaches to involvement in international franchising. Marriott and Choice Hotels were comparatively assessed on their strategy related to international expansion. While Marriott and Scotts represented a business format relationship incorporating a broad set of branded service specifications and systems, Choice and Friendly illustrate a lower level of product-system transfer. It was found that international relations were highly dependent on the nature and complexity of products and markets. While Marriott was an intricate and technology-dependent full-service brand which required a high level of standardisation to meet the requirements of the repeat-business travel market, Choice brands offered core service benefits that required less complex operating systems and technologies.

There are other benefits that show how expansion can stimulate the local economy. In another comparative study between the number and the type of technologies transferred among firms located in the original destination (Balearics) and two Latin American destinations (LAC), a positive relationship between hotel innovation rate and hotel size was found, and when the number of innovations per hotel by rooms is standardised, hotels with more experience tend to be more innovative. LAC establishments introduce more process and organisational innovations than Balearic hotels, while this pattern does not seem to be stable across different hotel sizes. It was also found that hotels in LAC countries collaborate with local firms in the introduction of innovations, and for such reason all the establishments ensure staff qualifications are up-to-date with training activities. These two channels suggest the possibility that the local economy may benefit from multinational firms via knowledge spill overs (Jacob and Groizard, 2007).

Points to be considered for hotel chains' expansion by franchising

Hotel chains follow a wide variety of different growth strategies. They can expand through franchise agreements, management contracts, hotel ownership, leaseholds, mergers and takeovers, joint ventures or a combination of any of those (Tse and Olsen, 1990; Okumus,

2004; Cunill and Forteza, 2010). In a study related to the entrepreneurial role of organisational members in implementing franchising decisions in an international hotel group, it was found that human factors play an important role in the franchise expansion process and, in a culturally diverse context, franchising is very much the concern of the development directors who provide the attributes of entrepreneurs externally in the market (Altinay, 2004). A strong link between cultural sensitivity and role performance for both independent and master franchisees was found in a study by Altinay and Brooks (2012). In the case of both individual and master franchise partnerships, it was found that insensitivity to the franchisee's business culture led to the franchisee's negative evaluation of the franchiser's role performance. Also, the franchisor's understanding of the way its franchise partner conducted business in terms of language of business, etiquette and procedures and the adjustments made for local market customs could enable the franchisor to carry out its role more effectively. In a study related to international hotel development in China, Xiao, O'Neill and Wang (2007) discussed the potential of franchising. It was found that the educational background, industry tenure, current hotel's quality level, and preferred hotel type in which to work may influence a potential hotel franchisee's preferences regarding franchising.

Hotel companies in Asia have enjoyed good growth in the last 50 years as a result of several advantages such as the depth of knowledge of the local markets, unique founding vision, strong local identification, and core competencies such as authentic service experience, low cost strategy, and focus strategy. Many hotel companies started and expanded through market penetration to meet the growth of domestic tourism particularly in large domestic markets such as Japan and Mainland China. Key considerations for business expansion should include unique location-specific advantages, and whether the firm has special strategic competencies or competitive advantages in addition to the right organisational capabilities (Lam et al., 2015).

Considering all the different aspects that are related to the expansion of franchised units, several strategic decisions should be considered at the corporate level. Some of the most important points that need consideration are listed below.

1. The decision should be made at the higher level of administration with clear conviction and support. Franchising is a complex long-term commitment and decisions should be made considering the long-term strategy.
2. Franchisees selected in international markets should be intellectually and professionally prepared to learn the procedures and other business methods practised by the franchiser.
3. There should be enough talent, skills, and required technology available in the markets which are indispensable for the functional operation of the hotel chains.
4. The mode of entry and the method of franchising should be clear in the minds of prospective franchisors and franchisees.
5. Local affiliated businesses should be involved in participation, decision making, planning, and other operational aspects of a franchised hotel chain.
6. Franchisors should be sensitive to the needs of the local population and be respectful of their political and religious beliefs and practices.
7. A good business environmental scanning should be conducted and used in all decisions made by concerned parties.
8. Financial aspects including the flexibility of currency exchange should be taken into consideration. Presence or absence of competition needs consideration as well as the potential competition within the foreseeable future.

9. Intellectual property rights and security, which may vary from region to region, should be taken into consideration. Particular emphasis should be given to the protection of trademark, operational procedures, and other legal aspects.
10. Continuous assessment of the franchise system performance, once in operation, should be planned. Other operational needs should be carefully evaluated, since what is taken for granted in the home market may not be available in foreign markets.

Pitfalls and common mistakes

There are many lessons to be learnt and careful planning is needed in order to avoid pitfalls and mistakes. It was reported (Brown and Dev, 1997) that if a franchisor wants to improve the performance of its hotels, it should treat franchisees more like partners than as adversaries to exploit. The benefits of a strong marketing partnership between franchisors and franchisees are manifold and include higher overall performance, higher hotel occupancy rate, higher room rate, higher gross operating profit, higher quality-assurance ratings, and higher guest-satisfaction ratings, all when compared to existing completion. Working in harmony and with judicious use of power are important for developing strong relationships between franchisors and franchisees.

Based on several precautions that can be taken, the following list highlights some pitfalls and common mistakes.

- Making decisions based on information taken from the internet or information provided by unreliable sources. In order to be successful, actual visits and/or first-hand knowledge of the market is essential.
- Lack of a clear plan and strategy for considering changes taking place in the foreseeable future.
- Blindly following competition and making judgments based on the success of a similar concept. What is good for one concept may not be applicable to a similar concept.
- Assuming that a concept will be acceptable based on the information available through the media.
- Failing to register trademarks and other intellectual properties on time, and not considering all legal requirements and implications.
- Not checking the background of prospective franchisees and/or relying on verbal financial commitment. Relying on the franchisee's experiences in other fields that are not related to hospitality can prove to be a liability.
- Not realising the infrastructure and availability of facilities, resources, utilities, and other operational needs of the business.

Types of franchising

Direct franchising

Direct franchising, often referred to as *licensing*, allows a franchisor to set up a franchise in another country using the system trademark, products, and services, and to function as does a franchise in the home country (Khan, 2014). The franchisor sells franchises directly to interested parties situated in the foreign country without the help of a third party. Franchisees are trained by the franchisor and assisted in the start-up and operation of the business. In general, some franchises have foreign subsidiaries that are operated by the franchisor, while others have franchisees who are granted franchises by the company, a subsidiary, or an affiliate which is already present in the foreign country. An affiliate can be a company in which the franchisor has some equity, normally less than 50 per cent, the remaining equity being owned by a resident national. Some countries make it mandatory that a resident national be involved in franchising. Direct franchising can take one of three forms:

(a) **Direct unit franchising.** The franchisor grants a franchise to an individual or a group directly from the country of origin in the same manner as he would grant a franchise in their own country. Thus, there is no difference in granting a franchise domestically or internationally.

(b) **Establishing a branch.** The franchisor establishes a branch office in the host country. This branch acts as the franchisor for the purpose of granting franchises in that country or the region.

(c) **Development agreement.** The franchisor enters into a development agreement directly with a developer who is a resident of the host country. Under the agreement, the developer agrees to develop and own all the franchise outlets in the region.

The advantages of direct franchising to the franchisor include the total control of the franchise system and trademarks, and retaining control over franchise functions such as advertising and promotion. The disadvantages can be attributed to the distance involved in management and controlling. It may be difficult for the franchisor to service the franchise properly as well as provide training to franchising franchisees from the franchisor's home location. Also, decision making on matters that require rapid action may be difficult. This is further complicated when cultural and political issues are involved. From a legal point of view, it may be difficult for a non-resident franchisor to take legal action against a resident franchisee, if necessary, due to jurisdictional restrictions. All of these disadvantages may also prove expensive and cost-prohibitive. In fully owned operations the major advantage is about controls in international operations ranging from operations to the use of brand name and reservation systems.

Master franchising

Master franchisees act like mini-franchisors in other countries. The franchisor enters into a master franchise agreement directly with a sub-franchisor, usually a resident foreign national, pursuant to which the master franchisee may develop franchise outlets and/or is responsible for franchising outlets to others in the foreign country. Master international franchising is a unique mode of entry, sharing some characteristics with other low internalisation modes of entry. Like exporting for manufacturing firms, master international franchising is a mode of entry with the lowest risk and control for service companies. This method is popular in franchising in China, India, and other Asian countries. Franchising is suitable for soft services such as hotels and restaurants for which master franchising is ideal (Alon and Welsh, 2001).

Master franchisees may be individuals, businesses, or conglomerate corporations that assume the rights and obligations to establish franchises throughout the assigned country or region. Potential franchisees deal directly with the master franchisee in all transactions. Master franchisees may open their own hotel chains or grant franchises to others. They also collect fees and royalty payments, which in turn they pay to the franchisor. Master franchisees perform most of the functions that a franchisor normally does, for which they are paid part of the collected fees or royalty fee, as per the agreement. The agreement contract between the franchisor and the master franchisee clearly describes what is expected of each party and sets a specific period within which the master franchisee must meet set objectives. Master franchisees have the responsibility not only to sign up sub-franchisees within specific geographic areas but also to provide them with the training and support that are normally provided directly by the franchisor. Because master franchisees act as representatives of the franchisor, it is imperative to select them carefully based on their potential to perform efficiently on a long-term basis as well as their ability to select sub-franchisees. There is a need for a strong relationship and mutual reliance between franchisor and master franchisees. Situations under which master franchising should be considered are listed as follows:

(a) The flexibility to support the franchise system by master franchising.
(b) The franchisor would like to expand at a relatively rapid pace.
(c) The franchisor does not have or intend to commit a considerable amount of capital.
(d) The country or region being considered has significant and complex differences in language, culture, and legal systems.
(e) There are qualified individuals or corporations present who can run the business at least as well as the franchisors.
(f) Local tax issues and political bureaucracy are complicated.

Master franchising has advantages in that master franchisees have knowledge of the local culture, politics, economics, and market conditions. They are also aware of the qualifications required for the franchisees to be successful. The know-how, motivation, and entrepreneurial skills of sub-franchisees can lower operation costs and help in making faster decisions based on local conditions. The disadvantages of master franchising include the difficulty in enforcing terminations if necessary. Business failure of the master franchisee can affect the entire franchise system and damage done to its reputation may be difficult to repair.

Combining franchise with joint venture

Joint ventures are becoming a popular method for doing business in foreign countries. In a joint venture, the franchisor joins with a local investor thereby forming a joint venture related with the franchise system. In this relationship, the franchisor has more control than in the case of a master franchise. Unlike under master franchise agreements, franchisees do not possess the rights to sub-franchise or establish units within a particular country or region. There is widespread use of recognised business processes in the prospective country or region. The advantages of joint ventures in international markets include reducing business risk, increasing production efficiencies, and overcoming entry barriers as well as better local acceptance of the business. Other advantages include access to resources, flexibility, lower cost of conducting business, and less investment commitment (Khan, 2014).

Combining franchise with management service agreements

A management service contract is a long-term agreement which may range from 10 to 20 years. It has been suggested that management contracts should be viewed as a more hierarchical form of organisation in terms of the degree of control the firm can exercise (Dimou et al., 2003). The legal owners of the property and real estate enter into a contract with a hotel management company (the operator) to run and operate the hotel on a day-to-day basis, but usually not under the latter's name. At the same time, the hotel may have a separate franchise contract with another company (a hotel chain). Quality control, daily management and human resources rests with the hotel management company and not the property owners. Since the property is run under the brand name, the customers do not recognise the difference. However, the quality control standards of the brand (the franchisor) are followed. The international hotel chain (the franchisor) that offers its brand name earns royalties or annual fees for the use of its brand. The hotel management company is paid management fees, often expressed as a percentage of gross revenues (sometimes with annual minimums and lump-sum payments). Also, the management company may earn extra profit margins on any supplies and material it sells to the particular property. For both the franchisor and the hotel management company, such contracts can amount to surer returns without real estate investment risk. Even ordinary business risks are greatly reduced since the hotel operators' take is often a percentage of revenues and not expressed as a percentage of profits as would be the case in equity joint ventures (Contractor and Kundu, 1998a).

A review of the modes of entry by franchisors clearly demonstrates that they vary from country to country and region to region. As an example, in a study related to mode of entry for hotel chains in Bulgaria (Ivanova and Ivanov, 2014) it was revealed that foreign hotel chains prefer to use non-equity entry modes whereas domestic chains have overwhelming preference on ownership. However, both groups of chains agree that franchise and management contracts are the most suitable entry modes into the Bulgarian hotel market. On the other hand, hotels perceive franchise, management contracts, full and partial ownership as nearly equally appropriate.

Pre-assessment of decision-making factors

As an expansion strategy of international hotel firms, the most influential factor for the development decision is the degree of proprietary content and idiosyncratic knowledge embedded in the service provided. The higher the market segment of operation, the higher the specialised skills and managerial expertise required for hotels to operate according to standards; therefore, the more likely a hierarchical mode will be used for their development (Chen and Dimou, 2005).

Cost-benefit analysis of each alternative franchising method and analyses of the environmental data of the selected sites are important considerations. Important factors to consider include (a) availability of human resources, (b) training needs of the franchisees, (c) political stability of the country, (d) level of economic activity and availability/accessibility of financial resources to the franchisees, and (e) cultural differences/barriers within the host country. Based on this evaluation, the method for franchising that best suits the hotel chain's concept should be selected. Studying an international hotel industry in Europe, Altinay and Roper (2005) reported that decisions related to franchisee selection are based on three important contextual variables. These are the strategic context of the organisation, different country markets and the nature of the business itself (franchise partnership). Both partner-related and task-related criteria are employed to select partners. The emphasis placed on these criteria, however, differed in different stages of the decision-making process. As an example, more emphasis was placed on partner-related criteria during the early stages of the decision-making process while the partner-related traits of the franchisees form a context to decide whether the potential franchisees have the ability and the background to meet the task-related criteria.

Conclusion

Considering the rapid use of franchising by hotel firms, further studies are needed to explore different methods that are being used in different countries and regions. Several research opportunities were identified for scholars in the realm of international franchising as a result of an exhaustive literature review (Dant and Grünhagen, 2014). More research into franchising in the developing world is needed. Such investigations may be paired with new paradigms, including the recently advanced consumer perspective, emerging consumer perspectives on American franchise offerings, linking price and performance with satisfaction in franchised outlets, and an increased focus on functional areas such as human resource management.

References

Alon, I. and Welsh, D.H. (eds) (2001) *International Franchising in Emerging Markets: China, India, and Other Asian Countries.* Chicago, IL: CCH Incorporated.

Alon, I., Ni, L. and Wang, Y. (2012) Examining the determinants of hotel chain expansion through international franchising. *International Journal of Hospitality Management*, 31(2), 379–86.

Altinay, L. (2004) Implementing international franchising: the role of intrapreneurship. *International Journal of Service Industry Management*, 15(5), 426–43.

Altinay, L. (2007) The internationalization of hospitality firms: factors influencing a franchise decision-making process. *Journal of Services Marketing*, 21(6), 398–409.

Altinay, L. and Brookes, M. (2012) Factors influencing relationship development in franchise partnerships. *Journal of Services Marketing*, 26(4), 278–92.

Altinay, L. and Roper, A. (2005) The entrepreneurial role of organisational members in the internationalisation of a franchise system. *International Journal of Entrepreneurial Behavior and Research*, 11(3), 222–40.

Baron, S. and Schmidt, R. (1991) Operational aspects of retail franchises. *International Journal of Retail and Distribution Management*, 19(2), 13–19.

Brown, J.R. and Dev, C.S. (1997) The franchisor-franchisee relationship: a key to franchise performance. *The Cornell Hotel and Restaurant Administration Quarterly*, 38(6), 4–38.

Chen, J.J. and Dimou, I. (2005) Expansion strategy of international hotel firms. *Journal of Business Research*, 58(12), 1730–40.

Combs, J.G. and Ketchen, D.J. (1999) Can capital scarcity help agency theory explain franchising? A test of the capital scarcity hypothesis. *Academy of Management Journal*, 42, 196–207.

Combs, J.G., Michael, S.C. and Castrogiovanni, G.J. (2004) Franchising: a review and avenues to greater theoretical diversity. *Journal of Management*, 30(6), 907–31.

Connell, J. (1997) International hotel franchise relationships: UK franchisee perspectives. *International Journal of Contemporary Hospitality Management*, 9(5/6), 215–20.

Connell, J. (1999) Diversity in large firm international franchise strategy. *Journal of Consumer Marketing*, 16(1), 86–95.

Contractor, F.J. and Kundu, S.K. (1998a) Modal choice in a world of alliances: analyzing organizational forms in the international hotel sector. *Journal of International Business Studies*, 29(2), 325–57.

Contractor, F.J. and Kundu, S.K. (1998b) Franchising versus company-run operations: modal choice in the global hotel sector. *Journal of international Marketing*, 6(2), 28–53.

Cunill, O.M. and Forteza, C.M. (2010) The franchise contract in hotel chains: a study of hotel chain growth and market concentrations. *Tourism Economics*, 16(3), 493–515.

Dant, R.P. and Grünhagen, M. (2014) International franchising research: some thoughts on the what, where, when, and how. *Journal of Marketing Channels*, 21(3), 124–32.

Dimou, I., Chen, J. and Archer, S. (2003) The choice between management contracts and franchise agreements in the corporate development of international hotel firms. *Journal of Marketing Channels*, 10(3-4), 33–52.

Elango, B. (2007) Are franchisors with international operations different from those who are domestic market oriented? *Journal of Small Business Management*, 45(2), 179–93.

Heung, V.C., Zhang, H. and Jiang, C. (2008) International franchising: opportunities for China's state-owned hotels? *International Journal of Hospitality Management*, 27(3), 368–80.

Hunt, S.D. (1977) Franchising: promises, problems, prospects. *Journal of Retailing*, 53(3), 71–83.

International Franchise Association. (2015) FAQs about franchising. Online. Available HTTP: <http://www.franchise.org/faqs-about-franchising>, accessed 15 March, 2015.

Ivanova, M. and Ivanov, S. (2014) Hotel chains' entry mode in Bulgaria. *Anatolia*, 25(1), 131–35.

Jacob, M. and Groizard, J.L. (2007) Technology transfer and multinationals: the case of Balearic hotel chains' investments in two developing economies. *Tourism Management*, 28(4), 976–92.

Johnson, G., Whittington, R. and Scholes, K. (2011) *Exploring Strategy: Text and Cases*. 9th edn, Harlow: Financial Times/Prentice Hall.

Kaufmann, P.J. and Rangan, V.K. (1990) A model for managing system conflict during franchise expansion, *Journal of Retailing*, 66, 155–73.

Khan, M.A. (1999) *Restaurant Franchising*, 2nd edn. New York, NY: John Wiley and Sons, Inc.

Khan, M.A. (2014) *Restaurant Franchising: Concepts, Regulations, and Practices*, 3rd edn. New Jersey: Apple Academic Press.

Kosová, R. and Sertsios, G. (2014) *An empirical analysis of self-enforcement mechanisms: evidence from hotel franchising*. Working paper, Universidad de Los Andes.

Lafontaine, F. (1992) Agency theory and franchising: some empirical results. *Rand Journal of Economics*, 23, 263–83.

Lam, C., Ho, G.K. and Law, R. (2015) How can Asian hotel companies remain internationally competitive? *International Journal of Contemporary Hospitality Management*, 27(5), 827–52.

Litz, R.A. and Stewart, A.C. (1986) Franchising for sustainable advantage: comparing the performance of independent retailers and trade-name franchisees. *Journal of Business Venturing*, 13, 131–50.

Moon, J. and Sharma, A. (2014) Franchising effects on the lodging industry: optimal franchising proportion in terms of profitability and intangible value. *Tourism Economics*, 20(5), 1027–45.

Norton, S. (1995) Is franchising a capital structure issue? *Journal of Corporate Finance*, 2, 75–101.

Okumus, F. (2004) Implementation of yield management practices in service organization: empirical findings from a major hotel group. *The Service Industries Journal*, 24(6), 65–89.

Peterson, A. and Dant, R.P. (1990) Perceived advantages of the franchise option from the franchisee perspective: empirical insights from a service franchise. *Journal of Small Business Management*, 28(3), 46–61.

Pine, R., Zhang, H.Q. and Qi, P. (2000) The challenges and opportunities of franchising in China's hotel industry. *International Journal of Contemporary Hospitality Management*, 12(5), 300–07.

Shane, S. and Hoy, F. (1996) Franchising: a gateway to cooperative entrepreneurship. *Journal of Business Venturing*, 11, 325–27.

Stern, L.W. and Reve, T. (1980) Distribution channels as political economies: a framework for comparative analysis, *Journal of Marketing*, 44(3), 52–64.

Strutton, D., Pelton, L.E. and Lumpkin, J.R. (1995) Psychological climate in franchise system channels and franchiser-franchisee solidarity. *Journal of Business Research*, 34(2), 81–91.

Tse, E. and Olsen, M. (1990) Strategies of global hospitality firms. In Teare, R. and Boer, A. (eds), *Strategic Hospitality Management*. London: Cassell Plc.

United States Congress House Committee on Small Business (1991) *Franchises (Retail Trade)*. U.S. Printing Office, p. 210.

United States Federal Trade Commission (2015) Franchise Rule. CFR Parts 436 and 437.

Withane, S. (1991) Franchising and franchisee behavior: an examination of opinions, personal characteristics, and motives of Canadian franchisee entrepreneurs. *Journal of Small Business Management*, 29(1), 22–29.

Xiao, Q., O'Neill, J.W. and Wang, H. (2008) International hotel development: a study of potential franchisees in China. *International Journal of Hospitality Management*, 27(3), 325–36.

13

Entry modes: management contract

Michael J. Turner (THE UNIVERSITY OF QUEENSLAND, AUSTRALIA),
Demian Hodari (ECOLE HÔTELIÈRE DE LAUSANNE, HES-SO //
UNIVERSITY OF APPLIED SCIENCES WESTERN SWITZERLAND) *and*
Inès Blal (ECOLE HÔTELIÈRE DE LAUSANNE, HES-SO //
UNIVERSITY OF APPLIED SCIENCES WESTERN SWITZERLAND)

Introduction

Hotel chains and hotel owners can employ a wide range of international market entry modes such as wholly owned, joint venture, strategic alliance, license or franchise, consortia, or management contract (Clarke and Chen, 2007). Each entry mode differs in its degree of risk, control, commitment of resources required and potential return on investment. This chapter examines the management contract and the key components that shape its success as an entry mode. Sections in turn include: definition; incidence; benefits to owners; benefits to chains; balance of power; potential for acrimony; key management contract negotiation issues; additional stakeholders involved in a hotel management contract; and a conclusion.

Definition

Although there is no standardised management contract (Johnson, 1999), a management contract can be defined as 'a written agreement between the owner of a hotel and an operator (i.e., hotel chain), by which the operator is appointed to operate and manage the hotel in the name, on behalf of and for the account of the owner and the operator is to receive a management fee in return' (Schlup, 2004: 23). Another definition is 'An agreement between a property owner and a management company (i.e., hotel chain), who agrees to take on operational responsibilities. The owner, on the other hand, agrees to finance and build the property, if this is not yet done, and to pay for the management services' (Garcia-Falcon and Medina-Munoz, 1999: 106). A management contract enables a hotel owner to retain legal ownership of a hotel site, building, plant and equipment, furnishings and inventories, while the hotel chain is responsible for the day-to-day business of the hotel (Guilding, 2003). The owner assumes full economic risk associated with ownership of the commercial asset, whereas, the hotel chain is only responsible for operation of the hotel (Schlup, 2004). Hotel chains are agents for the owner and must act in the owner's best interests (Renard and Motley, 2003).

Incidence

Empirical data highlights that during the late 1990s, use of the management contract in North America, Europe and Asia was respectively around 41 per cent, 37 per cent and 42 per cent of hotels (Contractor and Kundu, 1998). Around the same period in time, Slattery (1996) noted 75 per cent of listed Asian hotels operated under a management contract. By early 2000 use of the management contract had increased in the US to 55 per cent (Smith Travel Research, 2003). In Australia and New Zealand more than 50 per cent of hotels currently use a management contract (Turner and Guilding, 2013). Normative commentary points toward the continued increasing popularity of management contracts (e.g., Beals and Denton, 2005; Corgel, 2007; Panvisavas and Taylor, 2006). Table 13.1 ranks the top 20 hotel chains worldwide as at the end of 2013 by number of hotels under management contract. Marriott International, for example, has the highest number of hotels (1,018) managed under a management contract, which accounts for some 26 per cent of all hotels in their system.

According to Rushmore (2002), most first-tier hotel chains have size requirements for hotels they will operate under a management contract. Generally hotels with fewer than 200 rooms are considered too small by these hotel chains because their organisational structure and overheads cannot be sustained. Further, hotel chains typically prefer to manage upscale and luxury hotels, and generally refrain from managing budget or economy hotels as the returns, based on fees, are not sufficient to warrant their investment in managing them. Exceptions are made, however, for factors such as desirable locations or unique property characteristics that would make a particular contract attractive to a hotel chain.

Benefits to owners

Ready access to the operational expertise required to operate a hotel without any need for operational responsibility is increasingly important as hotel ownership continues to shift to entities which seek to invest in the hotel industry but who have little to no interest or ability in daily operations. Bankers and lenders can be more apt to provide financing for hotel projects that rely on the services of hotel chains (Bartl and DiBenedetto, 2003). Economies of scale achieved by large-scale hotel chains can also assist owners to reduce operational expenses through better volume discounts from vendors (Koss-Feder, 1994). Furthermore, access to a larger pool of employees and managers, and proven human resource policies such as training and development, imply that a hotel chain can provide improved service delivery for the owner, which often translates into greater customer satisfaction and thus both occupancy and average daily rate advantages. Hotel chains also have extensive national and international reach and relationships with traditional and online travel agencies as well as other distribution channels and can thus negotiate lower distribution commissions. Hotel owners who engage the services of a hotel chain have been known to double the value of their hotel (Butler and Braun, 2014).

Benefits to chains

Hotel chains are able to rapidly expand at relatively low cost through use of management contracts because they typically invest little to no equity in the hotels they operate under management agreement (DeRoos, 2011). As a result, such arrangements mean that hotel chains usually carry no real-estate risk and little downside risk. They are also able to obtain critical mass by being able to spread head office overhead costs, such as marketing expenses, across multiple hotels (Rushmore, 2002). Hotel chains are therefore able to derive a return

Table 13.1 Top 20 hotel chains (ranked by number of hotels under management contract)

2013 rank	Hotel company	Country	Network breakdown by contract type			Total system hotels	Total system rooms
			Number of hotels under management contract % of total hotels	Number of franchised hotels % of total hotels	Number of owned or leased hotels % of total hotels		
1	Marriott International	USA	1,018 26%	2,672 68%	44 1%	3,916	675,623
2	Accor	FRA	787 22%	1,402 39%	1,387 39%	3,576	461,719
3	InterContinental Hotels Group	GB	711 14%	3,977 85%	9 1%	4,697	686,873
4	Starwood Hotels & Resorts Worldwide	USA	563 46%	551 47%	47 4%	1,175	346,819
5	Hilton Worldwide	USA	498 12%	3,420 83%	197 5%	4,115	678,630
6	Louvre Hotels Group	FRA	299 26%	584 52%	252 22%	1,135	95,271
7	Hyatt Hotels Corp.	USA	239 44%	185 34%	97 18%	548	147,388
8	Carlson Rezidor Hotel Group	USA	235 22%	760 71%	75 7%	1,070	169,000
9	New Century Hotels & Resorts	CHI	148 100%	0	0	148	42,000
10	Meliá Hotels International	SPA	133 44%	28 9%	144 47%	305	78,515
11	FRHI Hotels & Resorts	CAN	107 100%	0	0	109	41,537
12	Shanghai Jin Jiang International Hotel Group Co.	CHI	106 9%	784 66%	300 25%	1,190	165,293

(Continued)

Table 13.1 (Continued)

2013 rank	Hotel company	Country	Network breakdown by contract type			Total system hotels	Total system rooms
			Number of hotels under management contract % of total hotels	Number of franchised hotels % of total hotels	Number of owned or leased hotels % of total hotels		
13	Four Seasons Hotels & Resorts	CAN	92 100%	0 0	0 0	92	20,238
14	Mövenpick Hotels & Resorts	SWI	80 100%	0 0	0 0	80	19,329
15	Grupo Posadas	MEX	79 72%	0 0	31 28%	110	18,795
16	NH Hotels[1]	SPA	77 21%	9 2%	293 77%	379	58,195
17	Kempinski Hotels S.A	GER	73 100%	0 0	0 0	73	19,615
18	Minor Hotel Group	THA	68 66%	0 0	19 18%	103	12,800
19	Barceló Hotels & Resorts	SPA	31 22%	0 0	55 39%	141	37,761
20	Millennium & Copthorne Hotels	GB	28 25%	11 10%	62 54%	114	31,733

Source: Hotels 325 (2014).

1 As of 2014.

from the services they provide through management fees. Thus, they tend to favour management contracts over other entry modes.

Management fees typically comprise a base and incentive component. According to a survey of US and European hotels with a management contract (see Thadani and Mobar, 2014), base fees are typically calculated as a percentage of a hotel's gross operating revenue, which can be either 'constant' across all years or rise over the early years to gradually stabilise. Base fees vary slightly in relation to hotel size but are typically around 3 per cent. In the US, however, base fees display higher variation in terms of hotel size, becoming lower as hotel size increases. Incentive fee structures display greater variation than base fees. Across the entire sample, 28 per cent had a flat fee, 25 per cent were linked to available cash flow, 17 per cent had no incentive fee, 16 per cent were classified as other, 7 per cent were linked to gross operating profit performance and 7 per cent were linked to average gross operating profit performance. Examination of the US sample alone, however, indicated that the incentive fee structure breakdown is quite different, with 56 per cent linked to available cash flow, while 26 per cent had no incentive fee. The remaining categories were 10 per cent flat fee and 8 per cent other.

Hotel chains benefit by being able to use an owner's money to implement a capital expenditure strategy, which can have a profound influence on fees earned and enhancement of their brand's value (Turner and Guilding, 2010a). Hotel chains are able to maintain control over both operations and brand standard compliance as they enter new and existing markets. Together, these help ensure the integrity and value of the brand as well as optimal operational performance since key decisions are under the hotel chain's control. Not to mention that they support entry objectives in a market.

Balance of power

Only when there is an equal balance of power in the relationship between an owner and a hotel chain, will both parties be able to best achieve their business goals over time (Armitstead, 2004; Butler and Braun, 2014). A one-sided hotel management contract can create conflicts that can result in lengthy and costly legal disputes or early termination of the management contract (Dev et al., 2010). These conflicts can, therefore, hinder the entry process for hotel chains. The balance of power is, however, constantly shifting. Normative commentary in the US, for example, suggests that the balance of power in the 1970s favoured hotel chains because of their superior industry knowledge and experience (Beals and Denton, 2005). By the 1990s owners gained the higher-ground in contract negotiations (Eyster, 1993; Hart and Connor, 1994). Throughout the mid-2000s there was a relatively neutral balance between owners and hotel chains (Beals and Denton, 2005). Factors influencing the balance of power include: the degree of competition among hotel chains, where more competition signifies lower power to the hotel chain (Bader and Lababedi, 2007); the relative size of a hotel owner, where larger owners tend to hold more power (Beals and Denton, 2005); and the strength of a hotel chain's brand, where stronger brands tend to give the hotel chain greater power (Forgacs, 2003). Empirical studies on the topic are limited but a relatively recent survey found hotel chains in Australia and New Zealand held around 60 per cent power relative to owners' 40 per cent (Turner and Guilding, 2013).

Potential for acrimony

Much tension can arise between hotel owners and hotel chains due to their differing goals and time horizons (Beals and Denton, 2005). Hotel chains are typically interested in achieving short-term cash flows that have immediate impact on the management fees they collect, while hotel owners prefer the achievement of longer-term goals that sustain the value of their real-estate (Guilding et al., 2001). This situation is known as the 'horizon problem' (Ittner et al., 1997). Hotel chains continually strive to increase their fees earned, the value of their brand and the longevity of management contracts held so that they can secure good opportunities from new contracts and increase the number of rooms under their management (Beals and Denton, 2005). Alternatively, owners typically want to put their limited resources into projects that will maximise bottom-line returns and thus the value of their assets (Beals and Denton, 2005). Often this dichotomy plays out in a particularly aggressive manner surrounding capital expenditures because hotel chains typically recommend how an owner should best invest their money (Turner and Guilding, 2010a).

Key management contract negotiation issues

An owner's choice of hotel chain and management contract terms is perhaps the most critical factor determining the long-term success of their hotel. Management contracts with hotel chains are very difficult or almost impossible to fix once they are in place (Butler and Braun, 2014). Getting the management contract terms right, however, can be a time-consuming and challenging task. Owners need to expend adequate resources on contract negotiation because disputes which have ripened to litigation and arbitration between hotel owners and hotel chains have escalated over the past few years (Butler and Braun, 2014). At the heart of these disputes is the belief that the hotel chain is not running the hotel in a satisfactory manner and is treating the owner unfairly (Butler and Braun, 2014). Owners therefore need to bind hotel chains to contracts which promote goal congruence so that both parties can 'win' (Armitstead and Marusic, 2006). The outcome of the management contract negotiation can have an immediate and lasting effect on the value of a property, the cash flow likely to accrue to the owner, and the performance and manageability of the hotel chain (Goddard and Standish-Wilkinson, 2002). Each one of these consequences has a negative effect on the entry process of the chain. To create a 'win-win' situation, hotel owners and hotel chains need to consider a wide variety of issues in the management contract negotiation (Armitstead and Marusic, 2006). Butler and Braun (2014) provide a comprehensive listing and discussion of the most crucial management contract negotiation points. Table 13.2 outlines each of these points. The terms of a hotel management contract can add – or subtract – a huge amount of value (Butler and Braun, 2014).

According to a survey of US and European hotels, Thadani and Mobar (2014) indicate that the average length of initial management contract term is 18 years. US hotels, however, have a shorter initial term of 16 years and European hotels a longer initial term of 21 years. Renewal terms are typically automatic upon mutual agreement of the owner and the operator and can last anywhere from 1 to 10 years (Detlefsen and Glodz, 2013). The actual number of renewals can be capped or unlimited (Detlefsen and Glodz, 2013).

Management fees in terms of the base and incentive component were discussed earlier in this chapter. Although management fees are intended to promote goal alignment between hotel owners and hotel chains, the degree to which this is the case has been raised as questionable (see e.g., Rivera, 2011; Turner and Guilding, 2010a). Shared investment by hotel chains is becoming less common nowadays due to their pursuit of asset light strategies (Blal and Graf, 2013). Nevertheless hotel chains do sometimes contribute capital, especially in the cases of entry. Owners, however, often find that this can be the 'most expensive' capital they can get (Butler and Braun, 2014: 11).

Table 13.2 Major management contract negotiation points

Subject	Provision
Term	Initial term
	Renewal terms
Fees	Base fee
	Incentive fee
	Fee caps
	Subordination of fees
Alignment of interests, operator incentives	Shared investment
	Credit enhancement
	Key money
	Net operating income or gross operating profit guarantees, guarantees against negative operating cash flow – guarantee, letters of credit or revolvers provided by operator
	Joint venture structure issues
Operator duties	Detailed listing of operator duties
	Limits on operator authority
	Control over reimbursements (such as markups, overhead and travel) and complimentary rooms
Termination	Termination for cause
	Termination on sale
	Termination for failure to satisfy the performance standard
	Termination for convenience
	Termination for failure of brand to maintain: growth trend, critical mass, regional or national marketing
	Termination for bankruptcy or insolvency of brand
	Termination for deterioration in brand or public perception
	Termination for brand's change-in-control or change in key personnel
	Termination by owner for failure or inability to open, get financing, operate profitably, reopen after disaster if expenditure of more than $xx is required
	Transition on termination
Performance tests	RevPAR test
	Budget test
	Owner's Return test
	Two-prong or single prong test
	Measuring period
	Cures
	Provision enabling owner to explore other operators at any time it is uncomfortable with operator, in its sole discretion (no interference or breach)
Operating standard	Fiduciary obligations, maximise net present value to owner, minimise obligation of owner to provide additional investment
Budgets	Content
	Timing
	Operating budget approval
	Capital budget approval
	Budget compliance
Reports and inspection	Periodic reports, annual reports, detail and flash reports
	Audited financial statements
	Right of owner to inspect and audit both financials and operations

(Continued)

Table 13.2 (Continued)

Subject	Provision
Other matters	Who is the employer?
	Union matters
	Licences and permits, including liquor licence
	Subordination, non-disturbance and attornment agreements with lenders now and in the future
	Limitation on owner contributions to working capital
	Right of first refusal
	Non-compete term, area brands
	Indemnification – what exclusions to owner's indemnifications of operator
	Exculpation – limit liability of owner to its interest in the hotel
	Sale of the hotel – operator's transfer of rights under the hotel management agreement – what restrictions or approvals
	Arbitration and expert resolution

Source: Butler and Braun (2014: 18–21).

Operator duties, termination, performance tests and operating standards often go hand-in-hand. Perhaps the most important are termination clauses as they can have a direct and important bearing on hotel value. They can also affect the entry process. Several instances, for example, have been recorded where the ability to terminate a long-term hotel management agreement added significant value. As explained by Butler and Braun (2014), in one case it added $41 million dollars to a luxury hotel. Alternatively there have been cases where the ability to terminate would have added about $50 million in one case, and $65 million in another. The ability to terminate a management contract can sometimes double the value of a hotel (Butler and Braun, 2014). Only around one-third of management contracts enable owners to invoke termination without cause provisions (see Turner and Guilding, 2010a). Enactment of termination without cause clauses is often linked to a penalty fee to be paid by the hotel owner to the hotel chain in relation to management fees (Turner and Guilding, 2010a). Historically, penalties for an owner's early dismissal of a hotel chain ranged from two to four years of management fees due. However, a recent study demonstrates that the present value of penalty fees for early dismissal of a hotel chain can now amount to between 10 and 20 times average annual fees, depending on the years remaining on the contract (DeRoos and Berman, 2014). This empirical evidence supports the argument that termination and performance tests should be considered when assessing management contracts as entry modes. Added to such a substantial financial burden, termination without cause provisions are in some cases also becoming increasingly difficult to invoke because they can contain many qualifications and caveats (Dickson, 2007). Potentially greater difficulty and cost to owners in invoking management contract termination clauses underscore the importance of ensuring that a negotiated management contract is conducive to a high degree of goal alignment. Termination clauses are most often linked to performance tests, which are based on the meeting of minimum accounting metrics such as gross operating profit, net operating profit, cash flow after debt service, occupancy, revenue per available room (RevPAR), owner's priority return, or a negotiated dollar target (see Turner and Guilding, 2010a).

In terms of budgeting, considerable friction between hotel owners and hotel chains is well documented in connection with capital budgeting (see e.g., Turner and Guilding, 2010a; 2010b, 2012, 2013). 'Few, if any organizational decisions carry more profound implications for organizational success than the investment decision' (Guilding, 2006: 400–401). One of the major factors contributing toward the complexity in capital budgeting is the fact that the majority of management contracts require the owner to establish a reserve for the replacement of furniture, fittings and equipment (FF&E) (Haast et al., 2005; Rushmore, 2002). This account pertains to all non-real estate capitalised hotel asset expenditures (Bader and Lababedi, 2007), i.e. the FF&E reserve is designed to fund periodic replacement of FF&E but not the replacement of major building components, such as roofs, elevators and chillers (Mellen et al., 2000). Areas where tension often arises include motives of owners and hotel chains with respect to FF&E reserve accounting, the types of FF&E reserve accounting approaches adopted, how much is assigned to the FF&E reserve, the adequacy of amounts assigned to the FF&E reserve, and the ease with which hotel chains can draw on funds assigned to the FF&E reserve (see Turner and Guilding, 2010b for a comprehensive discussion). Potentially the most favourable clause an owner could negotiate with regard to FF&E reserve accounting would be to have no FF&E reserve whatsoever. Only around 13 per cent of hotels, however, are able to achieve this (Turner and Guilding, 2010b). Failing this, the next best alternative is to negotiate a notional (non-cash) FF&E reserve as opposed to one that is cash funded (Turner and Guilding, 2010b). Finally, owners should seek to retain approval rights concerning release of funds from the FF&E reserve (Turner and Guilding, 2010b).

Operating budgets represent implementation of an owner and hotel chain's vision for the hotel. It too is often the means by which a hotel chain's performance is measured. As a result, owners should always seek to negotiate budgetary approval rights. The problem is that hotel chains are typically in a much stronger position to forecast the potential profitability of a hotel. As a result of its management of the property, hotel chains are even more importantly able to manipulate hotel operations in order to achieve a requisite level of performance. A hotel chain, for example, may push certain expenditure into the following year in order to boost certain income. In the light of these challenges, owners should seek to negotiate clauses which provide them with a significant ability to affect the operations, profitability and success of the hotel.

Additional stakeholders involved in a hotel management contract

In addition to the relationship between hotel owners and hotel chains, implementation of a management contract also has a profound influence on the hotel's general manager (GM), financial controller, as well as bankers and lenders. Figure 13.1 highlights the main relationships arising between these stakeholders involved in a hotel management contract.

Figure 13.1 shows that within a management contract it is usually the hotel chain that engages the hotel's GM and Financial Controller (Guilding, 2003; Rushmore, 2002). In the majority of management contracts, however, the hotel chain's appointment of the GM and Financial Controller requires approval of the owner (Guilding, 2003). There is evidence that hotel owners often pressurise hotel chains to hire GMs of the same nationality as themselves to avoid any mismatches (Gannon and Johnson, 1997). There are, however, variations in the degree of the owners' input to the GM's appointment, based on the terms of the hotel management contract. It is noteworthy that in some situations, the owner pays for the GM's expenses directly (Dickson and Williams, 2006), while in other situations these expenses are initially paid for by the hotel chain but are eventually reimbursed by the hotel owner (Eyster, 1997b). In some management contracts, the owner has the authority to remove the GM for unacceptable performance (Crandell et al., 2004). This arrangement limits the legal obligations of the hotel chain and enables easy transition when one hotel chain is replaced by another

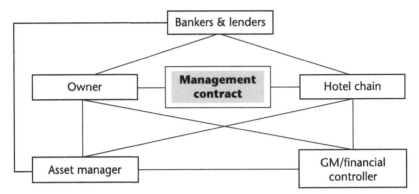

Figure 13.1 Main relationships arising in a hotel management contract.

(Guilding, 2006). It is therefore a critical component for hotel chains willing to enter the market as a replacement for their competitor. This employment arrangement, however, can cause conflicts because although the hotel chain has control over the GM/Financial Controller, the owner also wants to have some influence in this relationship because they ultimately pay their salary. A problem, with particular regard to GMs (as opposed to FCs), is that GMs typically have career patterns that involve a high rate of mobility (Akrivos et al., 2007). GMs are typically transferred either within the same hotel corporation (i.e., to higher levels) (Yeung, 2006) or to other hotel corporations. With this in mind, GMs may be more likely to act in the hotel chain's interests as opposed to the owner's interests because by doing so, this would give the GM a better chance of gaining career promotion with either the same hotel corporation or a different hotel corporation.

Alternatively, owners typically select the GM. For this reason, GMs must be mindful to act in the owner's interests when managing a hotel, or be faced with the prospect of not being selected by owners for GM positions in the future when their current employment contract expires or is terminated. As such, GMs may be more likely to act in an owner's interests as opposed to the hotel chain's interests to ensure future selection by owners for GM positions. These two opposing arguments highlight that GMs are faced with incentives to act in both the owners' and hotel chains' interests. The question therefore becomes, 'In whose interests (i.e., owner or hotel chain) will a general manager act? Guilding (2006: 403) provides some insight into this important question. He notes that GMs are strategically placed 'with respect to mediating the relationship between hotel owner and operator (i.e., hotel chain)'. This suggests GMs must take a relatively balanced approach when acting in the relative interest of owners or hotel chains.

'Asset management is the fiduciary responsibility of optimising the value of ownership's lodging holdings' (Harris and Mongiello, 2006: 302). Figure 13.1 highlights the important role of the asset manager. Nowadays it is relatively commonplace for a hotel owner to engage an asset manager in order to monitor the hotel chain as well as the GM and Financial Controller (Armitstead, 2004). The role of the asset manager generally has four dimensions, which are: (1) to act as a representative for the owner so as to achieve the owner's goals and agendas; (2) to maximise the value of the owner's asset through maximising return on investment; (3) to act as a facilitator for the owner; and (4) to oversee the hotel chain (Feldman, 1995). The level of involvement of the asset manager, however, often differs according to the specific needs of a particular owner (Jacobs, 2005). Owners who use asset managers often realise higher returns than owners who are passive about the monitoring function (Beals, 2004).

Although an owner's engagement of an asset manager is designed to facilitate a more productive alignment of interests between an owner and hotel chain (Feldman, 1995), hotel chains often complain that owner interference can affect their brand and in turn, reduce their fees earned (Schlup, 2004). As a result, several management contracts incorporate a 'non-disturbance' clause whereby owners assure the hotel chain that they will not impede or prevent the hotel chain from doing the job for which they were engaged (Crandell et al., 2004). A further concern of hotel chains is that to enhance the value of their brand to its absolute maximum, they need full control of day-to-day operations (Schlup, 2004). In some instances asset managers may be deprived of information that would enable them to make informed decisions about the hotel chain's work (Schlup, 2004). An owner's engagement of an asset manager can therefore potentially bring with it a more hostile relationship between an owner and hotel chain (Eyster, 1997a). It is therefore important that the asset manager cooperates and collaborates with the hotel chain so that a non-hostile relationship can be developed (Stemerman, 2003). This makes it vitally important that the owner chooses the right asset manager by making sure that they are qualified, capable, creative and cost-effective (Brooke and Denton, 2007).

Bankers and lenders' roles in the management contracting arrangement are provided in Figure 13.1 and they tend to be active in their interactions with hotel owners and hotel chains. This is because bankers and lenders are increasingly resorting to restrictive covenants when extending funds to owners so as to minimise their potential exposure to bankruptcy and late repayment (Wilder, 2004). The majority of hotel management contracts now incorporate a 'lender non-disturbance agreement', which is typically a tripartite agreement between the hotel chain, owner and lender (Dickson et al., 2008). Under this agreement, if the owner declares bankruptcy or defaults on its loan arrangement, the lender has a right to take control of the operation of the hotel (Dickson, 2007). This signifies that a non-disturbance agreement is an important document because it provides the hotel chain with a direct contractual relationship with the hotel owner's bank (Dickson et al., 2008). This relationship can assist the hotel chain to obtain the financier's agreement to give the hotel chain tenure and support its entry strategy (Dickson, 2007). In this way, the management contract survives. It is notable too that hotel owners who engage asset managers can sometimes receive preferential treatment from bankers and lenders because investment risk is seen as lower (Jacobs, 2005). Another element that bankers and lenders assess prior to the provision of debt finance is the appropriateness of a hotel's brand and the effectiveness of the hotel chain (Bartl and DiBenedetto, 2003). In addition, the type of lender attracted to a particular hotel can be associated with a number of hotel specific factors, such as its: (1) pricing category; (2) function; (3) location; and (4) market served (Singh and Schmidgall, 2000).

Conclusion

A popular approach to attracting increased investment into the hotel industry has been the dramatic shift towards the management contract entry mode. The use of management contracts, however, presents a challenge to the industry due to the separation of ownership and management. Its technical specificities should therefore be accounted for when selecting a management contract as an entry mode. Achieving complete goal congruency between a hotel owner and hotel chain is, however, only a theoretical concept because the extent of goal alignment can rest on many major negotiation points. It is the party with the most power that is likely to negotiate the most favourable terms. A one-sided hotel management contract, however, can create conflicts that could result in lengthy and costly legal disputes or early termination of the management contract. Conflicts are only likely to occur because of the long-term nature of management contracts. Despite such challenges, management contracts have allowed many different types of investor to own hotels, such as private equity firms, real estate investment trusts, high net-worth individuals, developers and opportunity funds. Further, the majority of management contracts provide a certain level of protection to owners against an underperforming hotel chain through performance and termination clauses. At the same time, hotel chains have benefited from management contracts as they are able to specialise in hotel operation without as much need to own the underlying real estate while supporting their international strategies. Compared to other entry modes such as owning and operating, franchising or leasing, the activities of the hotel GM, Financial Controller, and bankers and lenders are all influenced by the management contracting arrangement.

References

Akrivos, C., Ladkin, A. and Reklitis, P. (2007) Hotel managers' career strategies for success. *International Journal of Contemporary Hospitality Management*, 19(2), 107–19.

Armitstead, M. (2004) Hotel management and operations options: intellectual capital versus financial capital. *Journal of Retail and Leisure Property*, 3(4), 299–307.

Armitstead, M. and Marusic, M. (2006) Evaluating a deal in the hospitality industry. *Journal of Retail and Leisure Property*, 5(3), 197–203.

Bader, E.E. and Lababedi, A. (2007) Hotel management contracts in Europe. *Journal of Retail and Leisure Property*, 6(2), 171–79.

Bartl, H. and DiBenedetto, R. (2003) Capital for an embattled industry: how hotel investors can tap into the debt market. *Journal of Retail and Leisure Property*, 3(3), 247–59.

Beals, P. (2004) A history of hotel asset management. In P. Beals and G.A. Denton (eds), *Hotel Asset Management: Principles and Practices*. East Lansing, MI: University of Denver and the Educational Institute of the American Hotel and Lodging Association.

Beals, P. and Denton, G.A. (2005) The current balance of power in North American hotel management contracts. *Journal of Retail and Leisure Property*, 4(2), 129–46.

Blal, I. and Graf, N.S. (2013) The discount effect of non-normative physical characteristics on the price of lodging properties. *International Journal of Hospitality Management*, 34, 413–22.

Brooke, J. and Denton, G.A. (2007) CapEx 2007: a study of capital expenditures in the hotel industry. Alexandria, VA: International Society of Hospitality Consultants, pp. 1–98.

Butler, J. and Braun, B. (2014) *The Hotel Management Agreement and Franchise Agreement Handbook*, 3rd edn. Los Angeles, CA: JMBM Global Hospitality Group.

Clarke, A. and Chen, W. (2007) *International Hospitality Management: Concepts and Cases*. Burlington, MA: Elsevier.

Contractor, F.J. and Kundu, S.K. (1998) Modal choice in a world of alliances: analyzing organizational forms in the international hotel sector. *Journal of International Business Studies*, 29(2), 325.

Corgel, J. (2007) Technological change as reflected in hotel property prices. *The Journal of Real Estate Finance and Economics*, 34(2), 257–79.

Crandell, C., Dickinson, K. and Kanter, G.I. (2004) Negotiating the hotel management contract. In P. Beals and G.A. Denton (eds), *Hotel Asset Management: Principles and Practices*. East Lansing, MI: University of Denver and American Hotel and Lodging Educational Institute.

DeRoos, J.A. (2011) Gaining maximum benefit from franchise agreements, management contracts, and leases. Online. Available HTTP: <http://scholarship.sha.cornell.edu/cgi/viewcontent.cgi?article=1294&context=articles>, accessed 8 April 2015.

DeRoos, J.A. and Berman, S. (2014) Calculating damage awards in hotel management agreement terminations. Online. Available HTTP: <https://www.hotelschool.cornell.edu/research/chr/pubs/reports/abstract-18144.html>, accessed 16 April 2015.

Detlefsen, H. and Glodz, M. (2013) *Historical Trends: Hotal Management Contracts*. Chicago, IL: HVS.

Dev, C.S., Thomas, J.H., Buschman, J. and Anderson, E. (2010) Brand rights and hotel management agreements: lessons from Ritz-Carlton Bali's Lawsuit against the Ritz-Carlton Hotel Company. *Cornell Hospitality Quarterly*, 51(2), 215–30.

Dickson, G. (2007) Ten hot management agreement issues in Asia. *Hotels Resorts and Tourism Newsletter*, 1–11 June. Online. Available HTTP: <http://www.bakernet.com/NR/rdonlyres/86BE8EF9-2715-4591-8697-7E25966CFD58/42504/HRTNewsletterJuly2007.pdf>, accessed 2 February 2015.

Dickson, G. and Williams, R. (2006) What's hot and what's not with management agreements? *Hotels, Resorts and Tourism Newsletter*, 1–10 April. Online. Available HTTP: <http://www.bakernet.com/NR/rdonlyres/85BD956A-42E9-40E1-A5BA-93A3F9E72D65/39800/SYDDMS388712v1HRT_Newsletter_April_2005final.pdf>, accessed 13 May 2015.

Dickson, G., Williams, R. and Lee, H. (2008) The 10 seminal issues in contemporary hotel management agreements. *Hotels Resorts and Tourism Newsletter*, 1–14 May. Online. Available HTTP: <http://www.bakernet.com/NR/rdonlyres/8362ADC7-D072-4B9A-985B-307B7C6AEC64/43827/GlobalHRTNewsletter.pdf>, accessed 3 June 2015.

Eyster, J.J. (1993) The revolution in domestic hotel management contracts. *Cornell Hotel and Restaurant Administration Quarterly*, 34(1), 16.

Eyster, J.J. (1997a) Hotel management contracts in the U.S.: the revolution continues. *Cornell Hotel and Restaurant Administration Quarterly*, 38(3), 14–21.

Eyster, J.J. (1997b) Hotel management contracts in the U.S.: twelve areas of concern. *Cornell Hotel and Restaurant Administration Quarterly*, 38(3), 21–34.

Feldman, D.S. (1995) Asset management: here to stay. *Cornell Hotel and Restaurant Administration Quarterly*, 36(5), 36–52.

Forgacs, G. (2003) Brand asset equilibrium in hotel management. *International Journal of Contemporary Hospitality Management*, 15(6), 340.

Gannon, J. and Johnson, K. (1997) Socialization control and market entry modes in the international hotel industry. *International Journal of Contemporary Hospitality Management*, 9(5/6), 193–209.

Garcia-Falcon, J.M., and Medina-Munoz, D. (1999) The relationship between hotel companies and travel agencies: an empirical assessment of the United States market. *The Service Industries Journal*, 19(4), 102–23.

Goddard, P. and Standish-Wilkinson, G. (2002) Hotel management contract trends in the Middle East. *Journal of Retail and Leisure Property*, 2(1), 66–71.

Guilding, C. (2003) Hotel owner/operator structures: implications for capital budgeting process. *Management Accounting Research*, 14(3), 179–99.

Guilding, C. (2006) Investment appraisal issues arising in hotels governed by a management contract. In P.J. Harris and M. Mongiello (eds), *Accounting and Financial Management: Developments in the International Hospitality Industry*. Oxford: Butterworth-Heinemann, pp. 400–22.

Guilding, C., Kennedy, D. and McManus, L. (2001) Extending the boundaries of customer accounting: applications in the hotel industry. *Journal of Hospitality Tourism Research*, 25(2), 173–94.

Haast, A., Dickson, G. and Braham, D. (2005) Global hotel management agreement trends. 1–24 June. Online. Available HTTP: <https://classshares.student.usp.ac.fj/TS108/12009/Course%20Weekly%20Readings/Wk%202%20Global%20hotel%20management%20agreement%20trends.pdf>, accessed 9 April 2015.

Harris, P.J. and Mongiello, M. (2006) *Accounting and Financial Management: Developments in the International Hospitality Industry*. London: Elsevier/Butterworth-Heinemann.

Hart, W. and Connor, F.L. (1994) Owners have power to cancel contracts. *Cornell Hotel and Restaurant Administration Quarterly*, 35(1), 14.

Hotels 325. (2014) *Hotels mag*. Online. Available HTTP:<http:// www.hotelsmag.com>, accessed 13 February, 2015.

Ittner, C., Larker, D.F. and Rajan, R. (1997) The choice of performance measures in annual bonus contracts. *The Accounting Review*, 72, 231–55.

Jacobs, N. (2005) Active asset management: practicalities and realities. Does it really exist? Does it enhance returns? What does it do for risk profiles? *Journal of Retail and Leisure Property*, 4(4), 301–12.

Johnson, K. (1999) Hotel management contract terms: Still in flux. *Cornell Hotel and Restaurant Administration Quarterly*, 40(2), 34–40.

Koss-Feder, L. (1994) Renovations increase as lenders return. *Hotel and Motel Management*, 12(1), 209–24.

Mellen, S., Nylen, K. and Pastorino, R. (2000) CapEx 2000: a study of capital expenditures in the U.S. hotel industry. Alexandria, VA: International Society of Hospitality Consultants, pp. 1–150.

Panvisavas, V. and Taylor, J.S. (2006) The use of management contracts by international hotel firms in Thailand. *International Journal of Contemporary Hospitality Management*, 18(3), 231–45.

Renard, J.S. and Motley, K. (2003) The agency challenge: How Woolley, Woodley, and other cases rearranged the hotel-management landscape. *Cornell Hotel and Restaurant Administration Quarterly*, 44(3), 58.

Rivera, M. (2011) *Hotel Management Fees Miss The Mark*. San Francisco, CA.

Rushmore, S. (2002) Hotel investments handbook. Online. Available HTTP: <http://www.hospitalitynet.org/news/4021216.search?query=chapter+20+hotel anagement+contracts+pdf>, accessed 4 April 2015.

Schlup, R. (2004) Hotel management agreements: balancing the interests of owners and operators. *Journal of Retail and Leisure Property*, 3(4), 331–43.

Singh, A.J. and Schmidgall, R.S. (2000) Financing lodging properties. *Cornell Hotel and Restaurant Administration Quarterly*, 41(4), 39.

Slattery, P. (1996) International development of hotel chains. In R. Kotas, R. Teare, J. Logie, C. Jayawardena and J. Bowen (eds), *The International Hospitality Business*. London: Cassell, pp. 30–35.

Smith Travel Research (2003) Property and portfolio research. *Hotel and Motel Management*, 218(7), 24.

Stemerman, B. (2003) Managing the manager: the owner-management company relationship. In P. Beals and G. Denton, *Hotel Asset Management: Principles and Practices*. Michigan: Educational Institute of the American Hotel Motel Association, pp. 107–16.

Thadani, M. and Mobar, J.S. (2014) HVS Hotel Management Contract Survey. USA. Online. Available HTTP: <http://www.hvs.com/article/7025/excerpts-hvs-hotel-management-contract-survey-%E2%80%93-usa>, accessed 10 April 2015.

Turner, M.J. and Guilding, C. (2010a) Hotel management contracts and deficiencies in owner-operator capital expenditure goal congruency. *Journal of Hospitality and Tourism Research*, 34(4), 478–511.

Turner, M.J. and Guilding, C. (2010b) Accounting for the furniture, fittings and equipment reserve in hotels. *Accounting and Finance*, 50(4), 967–92.

Turner, M.J. and Guilding, C. (2012) Factors affecting biasing of capital budgeting cash flow forecasts: evidence from the hotel industry. *Accounting and Business Research*, 42(5), 519–45.

Turner, M.J. and Guilding, C. (2013) Capital budgeting implications arising from locus of hotel owner/operator power. *International Journal of Hospitality Management*, 35, 261–73.

Wilder, J. (2004) Negotiating replacement reserve helps cash-flow issues. *Hotel and Motel Management*, 219(21), 14.

Yeung, A. (2006) Setting people up for success: how the Portman Ritz-Carlton hotel gets the best from its people. *Human Resource Management*, 45(2), 267–75.

14

Entry modes: marketing consortium

Gökhan Ayazlar

(MUGLA SITKI KOCMAN UNIVERSITY, TURKEY)

Introduction

Rapid changes in market and consumer choices, difficulties stemming from online competition and gradually increasing numbers of rooms are among the problems that contemporary hotels face (Hwang and Chang, 2003; Kim and Oh, 2004). In addition, efforts concerning presentation of products to consumers in wider areas, particularly in international markets, lead hotels to different options. One of these options is to join a brand or a chain. Being a part of a current hotel marketing consortium is considered as one of the most effective ways for self-marketing of independent (Morrison, 1998) and chain hotels (Hwang and Chang, 2003). The marketing consortium alternative provides independence and autonomy for hotels, while enabling hotels to take advantage of the benefits of hotel chains (Holverson and Revaz, 2006). Hotel marketing consortia nowadays have impressive hotel chain examples, like Hotusa Hotels, which have 2,500 member hotels throughout 48 different countries (http://www.hotusa.com/about-us/). Independent hotel establishments, which desire to protect their individual styles or which cannot easily meet product characteristics of other marketing modes, can achieve the benefits of marketing through joining a hotel marketing consortium (Smarandra et al., 2010). In general, the members of hotel marketing consortia are thought to consist primarily of independent hotels. However, in addition to independent hotels, for local (Knowles, 1996) and international (Das and De Groote, 2008) hotel chains, one of the best solutions to marketing problems is to participate in a consortium chain.

The members of a hotel consortium each follow a common style of marketing, which is a significant element of consortium membership, and constitutes a major topic for study in the area of hotel marketing. As regards the financial position of a hotel when belonging to a consortium, however, each hotel is completely independent financially (Holloway and Plant, 1993). Through providing more marketing, the consortium makes the hotels within it become more accessible to travel agencies and international markets. As globalisation continues in business life, it is expected that configurations of hotel marketing consortia are going to be stronger (Carlback, 2012). In this chapter, the consortium configuration, a special marketing mode for independent and chain hotels providing access to wider markets, is analysed. Hotel marketing consortia increase brand values and develop original standards; with these they constitute a remarkable hotel chain structure. In this section we examine the emergence of hotel marketing consortia, their development and classifications. Following this, hotel marketing consortia are analysed in terms of membership, their advantages and disadvantages and their current situation.

The emergence of hotel marketing consortia

A consortium is defined as a congregation of a group of companies that satisfy common needs (Enz, 2010) or fulfil common goals (Knowles, 1996). Companies that ally with others aim to achieve more together than they can alone. The main reason for companies to cooperate is marketing. Go and Pine (1995) draw attention to the significance of branding in the hotel industry and the rapid development of hotel marketing consortia, due to the increasingly difficult conditions for competition in this field. In this respect, hotel marketing consortia help hotel establishments to gather with looser ties and to present their products to the market. This network of distribution brings the strengths of independent establishments into a chain structure, which creates certain advantages. For example, Leading Hotels of The World and Preferred Hotels consortia consist of independent enterprises which target the same market. These enterprises should meet the criteria defined by the hotel marketing consortium, whilst at the same time continuing their activities independently. Besides this, hotel marketing consortium members cooperate with each other in terms of promotion, merchandising, advertising, purchasing and information, and reservation systems (Lazer and Layton, 1999).

Among the research on hotel marketing consortia, a common definition was made by Litteljohn (1982: 79): Hotel marketing consortia are 'organisations of hotels, usually, but not necessarily, owned autonomously, which combine resources in order to establish joint purchasing/trading arrangements and operate marketing services. These aims will often be achieved through the setting up of a centralised office, whose activities will be financed through a levy/subscription on the member hotel units.' In other words, hotel marketing consortia are defined as a management of a common brand, which is founded through the financial contributions of independent hotel enterprises that cannot achieve marketing organisation and success on their own. Knowles (1996) lists the general services provided within this structure as follows:

- Establishment of central reservation offices in major generating regions
- A brand website for all member hotels and reservation links for each member
- A directory list introducing all member hotels
- A sales team that establishes relations between travel agencies, tour and MICE (Meeting, Incentive, Congress, Events) operators and corporate customers
- Participation in travel exhibitions in order to consolidate the brand
- Connection with global distribution systems (GDS), sales opportunities through world-wide travel agencies.

Traditionally, growth attempts of hotel chains have become innovative through franchising, while hotel marketing consortia have developed as an alternative path for the foundation of chain organisations (Litteljohn, 1982). For instance, Western International (now Best Western) was founded in 1948 by various hotels located in the West Coast of USA, mainly to create a mutual referral service. In the succeeding years, Prestige Hotels, the first hotel marketing consortium of England, was established in 1966. Following that, similar organisations have emerged and the number of hotel marketing consortia has increased.

Hotels unite in a marketing consortium to benefit from each other. In order to market their products, hotels use various strategic agreements, such as consortia, reservation networks, affiliations and independent sales representatives. The formats of most of them overlap, therefore it is very hard to differentiate them with clear-cut lines (Lazer and Layton, 1999). Reservation systems such as Keytel Hotels and Roomkey provide hotels with a central reservation system (CRS). This system gives the contact information of the hotels to international visitors, which works in favour of member hotels. Other services of hotel marketing consortia, besides reservation services and determined standards, underline the distinct structure of consortia. However, hotel marketing consortia that are focused mostly on reservation services may challenge this differentiation. Similarly, a difference can be seen between affiliation and consortium. They are both types of hotel chain structure, but there are some differences between them. The most important difference is that hotels with affiliation only partly use the same name, whereas, for example, a Best Western hotel always uses that same brand name. On the other hand, a hotel marketing consortium has fewer rules and its member hotels work for particular goals. The use of the same reservation system is an example of this kind of structure. Some members of hotel chains using the same names can be part of a marketing consortium. Another feature of participating in a hotel marketing consortium is about using a well-known trade mark (Das and De Groote, 2008). In addition, member hotels acquire management services such as purchasing, human resources and education, and marketing through the consortium. Hotel marketing consortia conserve each member's individuality without standardisation of the products and offer benefits similar to franchises (Inkson and Minnaert, 2012).

Development of hotel marketing consortia

Consortia are effective networks of marketing. Uniting of the members' marketing efforts reveals the strengths and reputations of hotel consortia, while it diminishes advertising and reservation costs (Lazer and Layton, 1999). Perhaps not all hotel marketing consortia are as reputable as large hotel chains; however, in the tourism industry there are famous consortia that provide prestige to members. Roper (1995) underlines that hotel marketing consortia determine their field of activity as broad markets or focused markets, and direct their marketing operations accordingly. The general strategies of hotel marketing consortia in these markets are assessed in two dimensions: low cost and differentiation. According to Roper, the majority of hotel marketing consortia, whether they operate in broad or focused markets, prefer low-cost strategies. However, it cannot be said that this approach explains all hotel marketing consortia's growth strategies and success. As in the Best Western case, there are very successful hotel marketing consortia with differentiation strategies.

Roper (1992: 151) summarises the emergence and development of hotel marketing consortia as follows: 'The reduction of hotel operating costs and/or the generation of additional revenue through increased business.' The analysis of hotel marketing consortia reveals that they have structures in which different services are produced. As hotel marketing consortia develop, their services to members increase and simultaneously become more complicated.

According to Roper (1992), the services that hotel marketing consortia provide to members can be examined under three categories:

1. *Market based services.* The main goal of hotel marketing consortia is to provide marketing and promotional services to their members. As in many establishments, marketing efforts are

very important for hotels because the probability of checking products before purchasing is low. Hotel marketing consortia execute two basic strategies for marketing efforts. Firstly, one sort of consortia (e.g. Hospitality Hotels of Cornwall, Wester Ross Hoteliers Association and Southampton Tourism Group) develops specialised marketing expertise through emphasising local features of marketing. These hotel marketing consortia also underline these characteristics by their names. The second type is hotel marketing consortia that specialise in providing promotion and marketing support to the members, such as Leading Hotels of The World, Prestige Hotels and Relais et Châteaux.

2. *Human resources services.* Some hotel marketing consortia provide services concerning human resources education, and particularly management, for their members. Here, the aim is to promote member hotels to a particular level of quality. Accordingly, it is aimed to increase the service quality of employees, who present an abstract dimension of a tourist product. Therefore, with a different point of view, the efficient use of employees is ensured, which is a significant financial issue in hotel establishments.

3. *Services concerning production.* Another service that hotel marketing consortia provide is to support the members with collective purchasing contracts for raw materials that are necessary for produced goods and services. Consequently, costs decrease and the quality of input of raw materials increases. This is the output of hotel marketing consortia services that is provided for their members.

Marketing strategies determined by hotel marketing consortia vary considerably. With regard to these differences, Fyall and Garrod (2005) point out some hotel marketing consortia, such as Small Luxury Hotels of the World, which actively include members in the management styles. In this case, the consortium expects a member to participate in the decisions made by the organisation. Pride Hotels of Britain, however, which operates in the British Isles, founded a marketing committee in order to enlarge its profile, to find new job opportunities and to increase customer demand. In another case, the market of hotel marketing consortia attracts multinational hotel companies as well. Marriott International put its plan, entitled Autograph Collection, into practice for independent hotels in 2009. The membership system has been carried out in six categories: urban edge, boutique arts, exotic retreats, resorts, gaming and iconic/history. The member hotels of the system pay to log into the sales and marketing system and loyalty programme of the company while they still use their own brands (Henderson, 2011). Sigala (2004) indicates that hotel marketing consortia membership can provide the members with access to – and transfers to – technological resources and managerial know-how.

Types of hotel marketing consortia

The rapid development of hotel marketing consortia is accompanied by complexity in consortia activities. The studies concerning classification of hotel marketing consortia generally use the classification suggested by Slattery et al. (1985), who analyse this collective work developed among the hotels in five categories, and determine each category as a different type of consortium.

1. *Pure marketing consortia.* The main argument to include hotels in a consortium is to provide marketing services for them and to reach competitive power that they cannot do on their own. Holloway and Plant (1993) draw attention to the fact that in a marketing consortium, a hotel in a chain can act as an agency in an international hotel reservation

network. This method especially facilitates the competitiveness of smaller hotel chains against larger chains. In particular, the integration of upcoming reservations of consortia members to their own reservation system can be considered as a significant advantage in the hotel chain structure. Dundjeroviç (1999) defines marketing consortia as follows: 'They are the consortia specialised in services such as CRSs, brochure design, and distribution, advertising and sales' (p. 370–71). Marketing consortia have developed two strategic positions. The first type of strategy, such as that used by Best Eastern Hotels LLC, emphasises regional marketing. These consortia generally operate in a particular region and receive the active support of regional tourism councils. The second strategy, as seen in chains like Leading Hotels of The World and Preferred Hotels, specifies the market segment only. According to this point of view, Litteljohn (2011) suggests evaluating marketing consortia under two different headings:

(i)   *Location-based consortia.* For example, Connoisseurs Scotland and Legends of IndoChina cover regions with different sizes and features. Both of them provide original marketing infrastructure support, particularly for developing international tourism.

(ii)   *Market standard niche consortia.* These are consortia specialising in different levels of markets and geographical coverage areas. Kotler et al. (1996) indicate that some consortia support their members in terms of market, conference planners, tour operators' partnerships, corporate meeting planners, travel agents and marketing to wholesalers.

2.   *Marketing and purchasing consortia.* This type emerged following the initial efforts of marketing consortia to increase the number of members. This type of consortium receives discounted prices, with mass purchasing of products used by hotels. New opportunities created through the above-mentioned purchase contracts provide attractive features for hotel managements considering membership. Particularly, these services include discounts in the prices of food items, beverages and consumables, and good rates in credit card commissions (Dundjeroviç, 1999). Interchange and Consort Hotels can be given as an example of such sorts of consortia (http://www.interchangeandconsort.co.uk/).

3.   *Referral consortia.* These are consortia whose activities depend on large-scale airline companies. Hotels connected to airline companies, such as British Airways Associate Hotels and Nikko Hotels, refer to a vertical union achieved by airlines. Consortia member hotels receive their reservations through airline reservation systems. While marketing consortia bring marketing into the forefront, referral consortia with airline companies present growth in the international context, which other big hotels cannot reach on their own.

4.   *Personnel and training consortia.* This type refers to a group of independent hotels operating in the same region. These hotels cooperate on the issues of employee recruitment, selection, training and development. In comparison to the other consortia types, personnel and training consortia consist of smaller hotels which focus on reductions of costs rather than increasing revenue. This type of consortium has a different structure because personnel and training consortia provide training services, which are not income-generating. Hotels gather their resources and unify their operations here too; however, this type focuses only on personnel and training. For example, Concorde Hotels & Resorts supports the member hotels in covering a wide range of solutions in quality, design, purchase, training and IT (http://www.concorde-hotels.com/en/company/our-company.aspx).

5.   *Reservation systems.* These consortia provide only CRSs to their members. Hotel consortia such as Expotel and Supranational Reservations are in this category. Similarly, REZ Solutions and RoomKey.com can be examined in this type of consortium. This type is not

easily perceived as hotel consortia because the reservation system services are limited and corporate identity is blurred. Corporate services provided to the members can be understood as insufficient.

Holloway and Plant (1993) urge that in classification of hotel marketing consortia, common themes developed for member hotels can be taken as a reference. Hotel marketing consortia develop common themes for member hotels as a part of members' marketing policy. For instance, hotels with similar standards, such as common price category or star classification, are classified as 'group marketing consortia'; hotels in the same geographic region that operate on room reservation can be categorised as 'area marketing consortia'.

Membership in hotel marketing consortia

Although hotel marketing consortia have lower costs, they provide similar advantages to other marketing modes. Hotels as members of a marketing consortium share a CRS and have a common image, logo or advertising slogan. In addition to these, hotel marketing consortia present discounts in mass purchasing, management training and continuing education programmes to their members. In comparison to franchises, standards concerning hotel size and appearance are lower; hence, guests may find more variation between the facilities than between franchise members (Walker, 2013).

Independent hotels can be represented by a marketing consortium comprised of their own united resources. By means of a consolidated structure, important opportunities are provided for independent hotels, as the structure of the consortium allows them to enter into competition with multinational companies. Hotel administrations, in return for the benefit from these opportunities, must pay certain amounts for membership. Hotel marketing consortium membership deals vary from country to country. In general, contracts last for at least a year. New members pay a one-time initiation fee and join the hotel marketing consortium. In addition, they make annual payments for using marketing and reservation services (Yu, 1999). Although there is no certain rate, a hotel marketing consortium member's cost per reservation is 1 per cent (Holverson and Revaz, 2006) to 1.2 per cent (Go and Pine, 1995). This ratio can rise to up to 2 per cent in big consortia such as Best Western. Besides fees, members of Best Western Hotels are independent, but they all keep the same standards, depending on brands (http://www.bestwesterndevelopers. com/) (Table 14.1).

Morrison (1994) classifies the costs of hotel marketing consortia membership into three categories: financial costs, operational costs and rules, and sanction mechanism costs. Financial costs refer to the support of the consortia's coordination, management and marketing activities, such as membership fees and commissions. Operational costs may diminish a hotel's capacity for product development and entrepreneurship. New authorities now participate in the decision-making process. Rules and sanction mechanism costs mean the loss of the ability to adapt to market expectation quickly and flexibly. As a consortium's brand value increases, the responsibilities of members and service standards develop. Table 14.2 shows some examples of differences in fee conditions.

Hotel marketing consortia members do not have to follow application standards or an architectural design in the case of a new hotel construction. In this way, members preserve their autonomous structure and manage their establishments while benefitting from global marketing programmes through international reservation systems. In hotel marketing consortia, as in Best Western International, the participant member hotels can end the

Table 14.1 Best Western Hotels' standards

BW Classic Hotel amenities	BW Premier Hotel amenities	BW Plus Hotel amenities
<ul><li>Complimentary breakfast to start the day</li><li>Free high-speed internet service</li><li>Free local calls and long distance access</li><li>Business centre with copy/fax services</li><li>In-room coffee and tea maker</li><li>Guest computer and printer in the lobby</li><li>Fitness centre</li></ul>	<ul><li>Stylish hotel design with detailed finishes</li><li>On-site dining and cocktail bar</li><li>High-end guestrooms and suites</li><li>Modern amenities & features</li><li>Modern and unique exterior design</li><li>Premium linens and towels</li><li>LCD or plasma television with high-definition channels</li><li>In-room safe, refrigerator, microwave and premium clock radio with MP3 connection</li><li>Boardrooms and meeting spaces</li><li>Well-equipped business centre</li><li>Energizing fitness centre</li></ul>	<ul><li>Modern and unique exterior and welcoming lobby</li><li>Upgraded interiors and stylish bath amenities</li><li>Complimentary breakfast in an enhanced dining area</li><li>Convenient in-room mini-refrigerator</li><li>Spacious in-room work desk</li><li>Complimentary high speed internet</li><li>In-room coffee and tea maker</li><li>Fitness centre</li><li>On-site guest laundry and/or same-day dry cleaning services</li></ul>

Source: Best Western (n.d.a,b and c).

agreement when the contract expires, in the case of short-term contracts being made. While franchising contracts generally last more than 10 (Brickley et al., 2006) or 16 (Lafontaine and Blair, 2008) years, the significant difference in hotel marketing consortia contracts can be noticed. Besides this, it is not easy to end franchising or management contracts agreements before they expire. Therefore, international marketing options that are presented in hotel marketing consortia are made through flexible contracts. This attractive feature may explain hotel marketing consortia's rapid development (Table 14.2) in Europe and America (Yu, 1999).

Management of standards was begun with Best Western. This became a model for other hotel marketing consortia. Best Western's system is made up of a 1000-point check list, which was prepared after extensive inspections that were made twice a year (Litteljohn, 1982). In another case, The Design Hotel marketing consortium has 150 unique hotels in 35 countries. The necessary features of these hotels are listed as follows (Page, 2011):

- *Design*: An attractive interior design in line with current fashion. In some facilities it is achieved by cooperation with Armani, Lauren, Bulgari and Versace.
- *Tasteful*: In some areas, cool or minimalist design features are emphasised.
- *Smaller properties*: Generally small hotel establishments that are transformed historical buildings.

In another example, Small Luxury Hotels controls predefined standards through a 'mystery guest' programme and checks whether these standards are fulfilled by member hotels or not. Small Luxury Hotels also tries to make these service standards sustainable. Lastly, an alternative example is World Rainbow Hotels, which is self-described as follows: a global collection of

Table 14.2 Hotel marketing consortia examples

The brands	Headquarters	Brand launched	Scope	Hotels	Website	Fees
Supranational Hotels	London, UK	1974	75 countries	700	http://www.supranationalhotels.com/	Commission based, not disclosed. The brand offers five different membership options: full supranational, colombus, sky hotels, private label and hotlink supranational memberships.
Historic Hotels of Europe	Paris, France	1997	21 countries	500	http://www.historichotelsofeurope.com/	Not disclosed
World Rainbow Hotels	London, UK	2011	120 destinations	1,200	http://www.worldrainbowhotels.com/	*Annual: $379 Marketing: $250–$1,000* Commissions: no charge on GDS* bookings, 15% for reservations coming from the WRH website
Hotusa Hotels	Barcelona, Spain	1977	48 countries	2,500	http://www.hotusa.com/	Commissions: 5% commission guaranteed from the first booking, 7% from 50 bookings per month, 8% from 100 bookings per months. *Membership fee: monthly*
Best Eastern Hotels LLC.	Moscow, Russia	1998	300 cities of Russia	1,600	http://www.besteurasian.com/	*Initial:* equals ten average annual official public prices of a single hotel room (including value added tax), but not less than €1,000. Commissions: not less than 20% price reduction for individual clients.
Preferred Hotel Group	Chicago, USA	1968	85 countries	650	https://preferredhotelgroup.com/	Application: $100–$150 per room *Royalty (annual):* $150–$350 per room *Marketing (annual):* $10,000–$20,000 Percentage of GRR**: 11.5%–2.5%
IBC Hotels	Florida, USA	2008	170 countries	6,300	http://www.ibchotels.com/	10% only for IBC-generated and consumed reservations
Small Luxury Hotels of The World	London, UK	1989	80 countries	520	http://www.slh.com/	Initial: $24,150; First 20 rooms: $22.339; each additional room: $274. *GDS* transactions:* 6% plus $3.54 transaction fee. *Internet transactions via travel agency:* 6% plus $3.54 transaction fee. *All other direct internet transactions:* 10%
Leading Hotels of The World	New York, USA	1928	80 countries	430	http://www.lhw.com/	*Annual:* $1.955 *Percentage of GRR**:* 1.93%
Best Western	Phoenix, USA	1946	100 countries	4,000	http://www.bestwestern.com/	*Affiliation fee:* minimum $42,000 *Percentage of GDS*:* $7.50 per booking

Source: Companies' websites; www.lodgingmagazine.com

*GDS: Global Distribution Systems; **GRR: Gross Room Revenue.

gay and lesbian welcoming hotels. To be approved into Rainbow Hotels, hotels must meet strict selection criteria, which consider the hotels' location, characteristics, category, knowledge of the local gay scene, current involvement with the lesbian, gay, bisexual and transgender (LGBT) community and the hotel's compliance with non-discrimination policies and same-sex benefits for their staff. The consortium operates over 1,200 gay and lesbian welcoming hotels in over 120 destinations (http://www.worldrainbowhotels.com/travel-agents).

Advantages of hotel marketing consortia

The advantages that hotels gain from being in a larger structure and marketing consortia are generally explained through scale economy, which simply refers to a decrease in average unit costs while an increase in production output emerges.

A hotel marketing consortium can be considered as a good alternative for independent hotels in terms of economies of scale. While the hotels included in a hotel marketing consortium keep their independence, they also act cooperatively with other hotels in the areas of purchasing, room reservation, training and marketing. A hotel marketing consortium not only reduces the amount of rivalry between the members but also provides progressively decreasing costs when hotels work cooperatively. However, the overcapacity problem cannot be solved through the growth of a small organisation unit with marketing consortia, but it can still reduce the pressure on the profitability by means of economies of scale (Gu, 2005).

It is clear that when independent hotels join a marketing consortium they acquire similar advantages, like their counterparts in traditional hotel chains. In general, the effects of these advantages can be explained in terms of the hotel marketing consortia type. The advantages provided to independent hotels through the presented services by marketing consortia can be listed as follows: (Holloway and Plant, 1993; Yarcan, 1998; Yu, 1999; Rowley and Purcell, 2001; Holverson and Revaz, 2006; Yeoman and Beattie, 2006; Litteljohn, 2011; Bowie and Buttle, 2013; Niewiadomski, 2014).

- *Increased visibility.* The member hotels of a marketing consortium are listed in a website programme directory and they own special rate access codes through GDS. Hotel marketing consortia aim to provide common benefits without creating destructive competition between the members. Perhaps one of the most important of these benefits is presenting members' hotels to customers' tastes via websites. Through this application, hotels gain a considerable advantage in promotion compared to what they could achieve on their own. Particularly, access to international markets is facilitated and therefore hotels can market their products in a larger area or region.
- *Built travel agency relationship.* Provides specific opportunities by means of previous business relationships between the partners of the consortium and agencies.
- *Increased revenue.* Increase in hotels' room sales through marketing consortia.
- *More marketing opportunities.* Several marketing opportunities for hotels, such as a chance to compete with multinational companies in the international markets and access to global distribution systems.
- *Support.* Hotel marketing consortia support all members in regional and international fairs.
- *Decrease in costs.* For hotel marketing consortia members, output costs can be reduced when they purchase massive amounts from suppliers. Particularly, hotel chains purchase food,

beverages, cleaning and other materials in big amounts from suppliers, so that they can take advantages of the economies of scale.

- *Locational needs.* For example, marketing a specific destination during periods of slack demand/overcapacity.
- *Market niche/branding purposes.* Reaching new customers due to branding, national/international benefits, together with joint services such as central reservations and joint presentation.
- *Brand equity.* Ownership of an internationally known and credible brand value in the short run, which is usually acquired in a very long time.
- *Experience sharing.* This means the participation of the hotel managers in a group to share individual experiences and information on management and marketing.
- *Personnel affairs.* Hotel marketing consortia provide services for their members such as personnel training, sharing training opportunities, job enhancement, career development and promotion opportunities. These services increase the experiences of the employees of member hotels and develop their job-oriented skills.
- *Loose obligations.* One of the financial advantages for preferring consortia is that unlike hotel chain alternatives, consortia have no costly obligations with regard to service standards and physical environment regulations.

There are many advantages of being a part of hotel marketing consortia. These benefits are summarised by Losekoot (2010): 'the personal touch with professional marketing' (p. 101). Nevertheless, it is not realistic to claim that hotel marketing consortia are perfect organisations. As in all similar structures, consortia also have problems.

Problems faced in hotel marketing consortia

Even though hotel marketing consortia clearly provide benefits for their members, it is important to understand that there are problems in practice. For example, each member hotel's autonomy is one of these problems. The challenges that hotel marketing consortia face are sequenced below (Litteljohn, 1982; Holloway and Plant, 1993; Morrison, 1994; Lazer and Layton, 1999; Holverson and Revaz, 2006; Gatsinzi and Donaldson, 2010; Niewiadomski, 2013):

- *Membership implementations.* In the case of offering the opportunity of membership to hotels in different forms and sizes, a hotel marketing consortium may not arrange the correct use of benefits for each member equally. If any subsequent discrepancies appear in the advertisements of members, marketing ways and prices, it means that something is going wrong for the hotel marketing consortium.
- *Customer satisfaction.* For hotels, being members of the same hotel marketing consortium but operating in different markets is the main cause of any customer satisfaction/dissatisfaction problem. Meanwhile, because the travel reasons of customers staying in the member hotels can be different, it is hard to improve the service quality. Clear violations of standards and politics affect customers negatively. Although customers know that consortia members are not the same, they at least expect to get services at a particular level of quality. A negative accommodation experience in a hotel marketing consortium member can affect the other members.
- *Legal implementations.* Common laws are never applied by all countries in the world. This is another matter which is to be taken into account by hotel marketing consortia that

operate at an international level. The use of the implementations of a hotel marketing consortium in all member hotels is restricted by the laws of the countries concerned. Repatriation of fees and visa regulation differences can be mentioned in this structure.

• *Regional differences.* Deficient infrastructure facilities, destination (in)accessibility, deficiencies in the services of meeting the needs of tourists, tourism organisations and the presence or absence of NGOs, (un)availability of qualified labour and shortage of professional hotel schools, can resemble the differences of the member hotels. For a hotel marketing consortium, each is a matter to be studied separately. While being a member of a marketing consortium provides benefits for operating in national and international markets, local small hotels are forced to implement the requirements of a marketing consortium, however onerous.

It is very difficult to control the routine operations of hotel marketing consortia members. A detailed evaluation of the potential members in the beginning may minimise later problems and ensure better preservation of standards. While hotel marketing consortia provide better services, in order to preserve this brand value, they expect higher standards from their members. This development is accompanied by more frequent inspections. Some of these may create financial burdens that the hotels do not budget for (Holverson and Revaz, 2006). The above-mentioned problems can be solved by evaluating hotels with similar infrastructures in a very selective manner in the membership processes (Litteljohn, 1982), preserving the brand value of the hotel marketing consortium. Alternative suggestions, such as members using a hotel marketing consortium's opportunities in turn, can be presented. However, the important thing is that these or similar problems should be discussed beforehand and members should be informed of developments through a general secretariat (Holloway and Plant, 1993).

The current situation in hotel marketing consortia

Clarke and Chen (2007) imply that the hotel marketing consortium option is the most preferred marketing entry mode with franchising and management contract implementations throughout the international hotel industry. Furthermore, it is possible to be a member of a marketing consortium and operate a franchise simultaneously (Confalonieri, 2014). Carlback (2012) emphasizes that the greatest benefit gained from meeting the membership requirements is the advantage over rivals. Besides this, other benefits are sharing the company expenses, the opportunity for more frequent appearances in the market, and reducing agency commissions (Yeoman and Beattie, 2006) without ceding control to the member companies (Niewiadomski, 2014). These benefits can be a great advantage for hotels' planning, growth and improvement. The option of the hotel marketing consortium on behalf of the independent hotel administrator can be explained through four motivational tools, basically (Confalonieri, 2014): (1) organisational needs, (2) production improvements, (3) technological aspects and (4) marketing matters.

Independent hotel managements can use an efficient network acquired with hotel marketing consortium membership in case of unexpected events. Hence, they obtain an organisational benefit in terms of power of rivalry. The most distinctive benefits obtained by means of production are the cost reductions. Common R&D studies, technology and data sharing can be classified as the technological benefits offered for the hotel marketing consortium members. Eventually, the contribution of the hotel marketing consortium to the marketing policies becomes undeniable in reality.

Since the early 1900s when they first emerged, hotel marketing consortia have developed gradually and presented better products. Nowadays, hotel marketing consortia have developed qualitatively and quantitatively. They are among the most preferred entry modes for foreign hotel chains and this was clearly observed in some studies (Yarcan, 1998; Ivanova and Ivanov, 2014). Table 14.2 shows some big brands in the hotel marketing consortia market that developed their marketing strategies from different perspectives.

Conclusion

The concern in looking for new markets in order to survive and handle tough conditions of competition is among the hotel establishments' agenda topics. Therefore, hotel establishments prefer strategic alliances in the projects that they cannot accomplish on their own. In this context, hotel marketing consortia are one of the alternative ways. The share of resources, risks and costs have made hotel consortia an attractive alternative for hotel establishments that plan to expand their markets. The advantages and development of hotel marketing consortia over time show that they will continue to operate in the hospitality industry in the future. Apart from that, the ongoing tendency of globalisation in the tourism and hospitality industry is expected to consolidate consortia structures. In comparison to other entry modes, consortia present more marketing spaces to hotel establishments in a faster and easier way. One of the reasons for this situation is probably the improving standards of hotel marketing consortia. Consortia with higher standards pay attention to brand values and continue to exist in the market as strong hotel chains.

There can be debates about the acceptance of hotel marketing consortia as hotel chains. The main reason for that, as mentioned in the paragraph/section about types of consortia, is related to the service variation provided by consortia for their members. These services imply that it is impossible to talk about a standard consortium structure. There are hotel marketing consortia that provide services at the same level as hotel chains, while some provide only limited services (for example, only reservation transfers). Despite these debates and differentiation of hotel marketing consortia in terms of their structures and services, hotel marketing consortia present advantages and power opportunities that stem from doing business together. In the following years, new destinations in the international tourism industry will be the focus of attention. Hotel establishments will continue to be strong actors on this stage in order to preserve their current shares and hang on to these new competitive markets.

References

Best Western (n.d.a) Best Western brochure for developers. Online. Available HTTP: <http://www.bestwesterndevelopers.com/files/BEST-WESTERN-Brochure.pdf>, accessed 1 August 2015.

Best Western (n.d.b) Best Western Premier Brochure for developers. Online. Available HTTP: <http://www.bestwesterndevelopers.com/files/BEST-WESTERN-PREMIER-Brochure.pdf>, accessed 1 August 2015.

Best Western (n.d.c) Best Western Plus Brochure for developers. Online. Available HTTP: <http://www.bestwesterndevelopers.com/files/BEST-WESTERN-PLUS-Brochure.pdf>, accessed 1 August 2015.

Bowie, D. and Buttle, F. (2013) *Hospitality Marketing Principles and Practice*, 2nd edn. New York: Routledge.

Brickley, J.A., Misra, S. and Horn, L.V. (2006) Contract duration: evidence from franchising. *Journal of Law and Economics*, 49(1), 173–96.

Carlback, M. (2012) Strategic entrepreneurship in the hotel industry: the role of chain affiliation. *Scandinavian Journal of Hospitality and Tourism*, 12(4), 349–72.

Clarke, A. and Chen, W. (2007) *International Hospitality Management: Concepts and Cases*. Oxford: Elsevier.

Confalonieri, M. (2014) An 'atypical' voluntary hotel chain: the Le Mat project. *Tourism Management Perspectives*, 9, 1–4.

Das, V. and De Groote, P. (2008) Globalisation in hotel chains case study: profile of the Bulgarian business traveller. *Bulletin de la Société Géographique de Liége*, 50, 17–26.

Dundjerovic, A. (1999) Consortia: how far can they go towards helping independent hotels compete with chains? *Tourism and Hospitality Research*, 1(4), 370–74.

Enz, C.A. (2010) *Hospitality Strategic Management: Concepts and Cases*. New Jersey: John Wiley & Sons Inc.

Fyall, A. and Garrod, B. (2005) *Tourism Marketing: A Collaborative Approach*. Clevendon, UK: Channel View Publications.

Gatsinzi, J. and Donaldson, R. (2010) Investment challenges in the hotel industry in Kigali, Rwanda: Hotel managers' perspective. *Development Southern Africa*, 27(2), 225–40.

Go, F.M. and Pine, R. (1995) *Globalization Strategy in the Hotel Industry*. New York: Routledge.

Gu, Z. (2005) Economies of scale could be key to profitability. *International Journal of Hospitality and Tourism Administration*, 6(1), 73–85.

Henderson, J.C. (2011) Hip heritage: the boutique hotel business in Singapore. *Tourism and Hospitality Research*, 11(3), 217–23.

Holloway, J.C. and Plant, R.V. (1993) *Marketing for Tourism*, 2nd edn. London: Pitman Publishing.

Holverson, S. and Revaz, F. (2006) Perceptions of European independent hoteliers: hard and soft branding choices. *International Journal of Contemporary Hospitality Management*, 18(5): 398–413.

Hwang, S.N. and Chang, T.Y. (2003) Using data envelopment analysis to measure hotel managerial efficiency change in Taiwan. *Tourism Management*, 24, 357–69.

Inkson, C. and Minnaert, L. (2012) *Tourism Management: An Introduction*. London: Sage Publications.

Ivanova, M. and Ivanov, S. (2014) Hotel chains' entry mode in Bulgaria, *Anatolia: An International Journal of Tourism and Hospitality Research*, 25(1), 131–35.

Kim, B.Y. and Oh, H. (2004) How do hotel firms obtain a competitive advantage? *International Journal of Contemporary Hospitality Management*, 16(1), 65–71.

Knowles, T. (1996) *Corporate Strategy for Hospitality*. Harlow: Addison-Wesley-Longman.

Kotler, P., Bowen, J. and Makens, J. (1996) *Marketing for Hospitality and Tourism*. New Jersey: Prentice Hall.

Lafontaine, F. and Blair, R.D. (2008) The evolution of franchising and franchise contracts: evidence from the United States. *Ohio State Entrepreneurial Business Law Journal*, 3(2), 381–434.

Lazer W. and Layton, R.A. (1999) *Contemporary Hospitality Marketing: A Service Management approach*. Michigan: The Educational Institute of the American Hotel and Motel Association.

Littlejohn, D. (1982) The role of hotel consortia in Great Britain. *Service Industries Review*. 2(1), 79–91.

Littlejohn, D. (2011) Hotels. In B. Brotherton (ed.), *The International Hospitality Industry Structure Characteristic and Issues*. New York: Routledge, pp. 5–30.

Losekoot, E. (2010) Hotel consortia. In A. Pizam (ed.), *International Encyclopedia of Hospitality Management*, 2nd edn. Oxford: Elseiver.

Morrison, A. (1994) Marketing strategic alliances: the small hotel firm, *International Journal of Contemporary Hospitality management*, 6(3), 25–30.

Morrison, A. (1998) Small firm co-operative marketing in a peripheral tourism region. *International Journal of Contemporary Hospitality Management*, 10(5), 191–97.

Niewiadomski, P. (2013) The globalisation of the hotel industry and the variety of emerging capitalisms in Central and Eastern Europe. *European Urban and Regional Studies*, 18,1–22.

Niewiadomski, P. (2014) Towards an economic-geographical approach to the globalisation of the hotel industry. *Journal of Tourism Space, Place and Environment*, 16(1), 48–67.

Page, S.J. (2011) *Tourism Management: An Introduction*, 4th edn. New York: Routledge.

Roper, A.J. (1992) *Hotel consortia: strategies and structure; an analysis of the emergence of hotel consortia as transorganisational forms* (Unpublished doctoral dissertation). University of Huddersfield, West Yorkshire.

Roper, A. (1995) The emergence of hotel consortia as organizational forms, *International Journal of Contemporary Hospitality Management*, 7(1), 4–9.

Rowley G. and Purcell, K. (2001) 'As cooks go, she went': is labour churn inevitable? *International Journal of Hospitality Management*, 20, 163–85.

Sigala, M. (2004) Using data envelopment analysis for measuring and benchmarking productivity in hotel sector. *Journal of Travel and Tourism Marketing*, 16(2–3), 39–60.

Slattery, P., Roper, A. and Boer, A. (1985) Hotel consortia: their activities, structure and growth. *The Service Industries Journal*, 5(2): 192–99.

Smaranda C., Cristina, F., Morgovan, C. and Bota, M. (2010) International Hotel Chain Strategies Used Into The World Compared With Romania. 5th WSEAS International Conference on Economic And Management Transformation, 24–26 October, 2010, West University of Timisoara, Romania.

Walker, J.R. (2013) *Introduction to Hospitality Management*, 4th edn. New Jersey: Prentice Hall.

Yarcan, Ş. (1998) *Türkiye'de Turizm ve Uluslararasılaşma*, 2nd edn. İstanbul: Boğaziçi Üniversitesi Yayınları.

Yeoman, I. and Beattie, U.M. (2006) Tomorrow tourist and the information society. *Journal of Vacation Marketing*, 12(3), 269–91.

Yu, L. (1999) *The International Hospitality Business Management and Operations*. New York: The Howarth Hospitality Press.

15

Entry modes: lease contract

Anderson Gomes de Souza (UNIVERSIDADE FEDERAL DE PERNAMBUCO – UFPE, BRAZIL),
Viviane Santos Salazar (UNIVERSIDADE FEDERAL DE PERNAMBUCO – UFPE, BRAZIL),
Walter Fernando Araújo de Moraes (UNIVERSIDADE FEDERAL
DE PERNAMBUCO – UFPE, BRAZIL),
Yákara Pereira Leite (UNIVERSIDADE FEDERAL RURAL DO SEMI-ÁRIDO, BRAZIL) *and*
Maya Ivanova (VARNA UNIVERSITY OF MANAGEMENT, BULGARIA)

Introduction

An essential part of hotel chain internationalisation is the choice of entry modes. Practice and research prove (Cunill and Forteza, 2010; Contractor and Kundu, 1998) that the most preferred modes of entry are the non-equity modes – management contract, franchise, marketing consortium and lease. However, it is noteworthy that the choice for an entry mode, when it comes to hotel chains, is also influenced by the macro and micro environments. That is, some forces (e.g. economic, political and so forth) must be taken into consideration before a strategy is implemented. Once this first step has been taken, the chain shall establish the most appropriate entry mode: ownership, franchising, management contract or leasing. These, in turn, often end up representing more than just an expansion strategy, but become a management style.

The previous chapters of this book (Chapters 11–14) deal with each of the aforementioned entry modes, and in this chapter we are going to discuss the Lease contract. After analysing the nature of lease, we will explore it as an expansion option used by hotel chains, and will delve into its content. Finally, we will present current usage of lease among the top hotel corporations, with some interesting cases from Brazil.

Lease contract in the hotel industry

According to Ghorbal-Blal (2008), a leasing contract binds a real-estate owner (the lessor) to a tenant (the lessee), where the former can be either a person/s, a corporation, or an institution, stepping into agreement to provide their real-estate property in exchange for a determined payment, and according to the specific terms of the contract. The established relationship is similar to renting, although from a legal point of view there are some distinctions (Ghorbal-Blal, 2008), but further clarification of the terms goes beyond the aims of this chapter.

A lease is usually connected with real-estate investments and management, therefore it is explored in the equity investment literature. The hotel industry is also part of the real-estate market, because of the hotel building, which is a compulsory element, and requires large initial capital investment. Yet, in contrast to the real-estates, the hotel industry is much more a management-intensive business (Gallagher and Mansour, 2000), i.e the cash flow streams are unstable and may depend on external factors, which are beyond the owner's control, like seasonality, for example (Manning et al., 2015). Additionally, a hotel should be run and developed as a successful business for a comparatively long period, which is not valid for most of the rest of the real-estate assets, where the return on investment may begin from the very opening of the building. Another distinction of hotel real-estate market comes from the higher degree of volatility, depending mainly on the changing demand (Gallegher and Mansour, 2000). Therefore, real-estate investments in hotels are considered more risky and require adequate consequent management.

Leasing as an entry mode of the hotel chains

In terms of hotel chains' growth, leasing is considered a non-equity option, because it allows participation without capital investment. The lease is a mode of entry in which a certain building, originally conceived to be a hotel establishment or not, is rented (leased) to a hospitality company so that hotel services can be offered (Sancho, 2001; Vallen and Vallen, 2003). Generally, the financial gains obtained by the owner are earned annually, and may be a steady or semi-steady value (when incorporating a percentage of the enterprise's gains). Thus, the decision to start a new business by leasing a property must be carefully analysed, both qualitatively and quantitatively.

The hotel business itself is three-sided: it includes real-estate investment, together with brand management and hotel operations (DeRoos, 2011). From an owner's perspective the lease contract concerns only the first aspect. In contrast to the other expansion modes (management contract, franchise, joint venture, marketing consortia) where the owner is directly or indirectly involved with the hotel operations, in the lease contract the owner's arrangements are limited to maintenance of the hotel building and the facilities, but he does not interfere in the way the hotel is run. In this way the owner limits risk to the property asset, whereas all the rest of the uncertainty regarding business, marketing and management of the hotel is borne by the operator/the lessee. From the lessee's/hotel chain's point of view, however, lease gives much more freedom for the operations, hence there is a greater control of the product quality and final profits of the venture (Qin et al., 2012; Pages, 2007). Thus, the increased financial risk of the lessee, together with the full operational control, has led the lease contract to be perceived as equal to the ownership, despite its non-equity nature.

Along with the rest of the non-equity entry modes, lease contract could be analysed on the basis of agency theory. Considering that the theory focuses on defining the most efficient contract to conduct the principal–agent relationship (Eisenhardt, 1989), some points must be evaluated. Among these, issues related to people (e.g. self-interest, limited rationality, risk avoidance), to the organisation (e.g. conflicting goals among members) and to the information shall be taken into consideration before entering a new market. Those decisions impact on the type of contract to be sealed, whether behaviour oriented (steady payment system, hierarchy, etc.) or result oriented (commissions, shareholding, property rights, market-place governance, etc.). In the lease contract, in particular, the lessor/owner is the principal and the lessee is the agent (Ghorbal-Blal, 2008). In this agreement, the role of the principal is quite limited, especially in comparison with the other non-equity agency relations (man-agement contract, franchise) – the lessor may control only the proper use and maintenance of the building, but not the business operations. On the other hand, the hotel chain as an agent bears more risk, responsibilities and costs, than in the other entry modes, which increases

Table 15.1 Advantages and disadvantages of leases: owner versus chains

| Owner | | Hotel chain | |
Advantages	Disadvantages	Advantages	Disadvantages
• The owner retains the title to the property and the residual value created at the end of the lease. • The owner incurs minimal financial risk, especially if the hotel chain is reliable. • The owner has no operational responsibilities.	• The chain has little interest in maintaining the property as the lease comes to expiration and might divert the business to other hotels it manages. • The owner is passive and has no control over the hotel's operations. • The owner does not benefit if/when the property is more profitable than expected. • Leases are more difficult to terminate than management contracts because they create a vested interest in the property for the chain.	• The chain retains total control over operations. • The leasehold created by the hotel chain can be realised through a sale (if the lease contract allows it). • The operational upside is retained solely by the chain.	• When the lease term expires the chain loses its rights on the property. • The leasehold loses/ decreases its value as the term comes to an end. • The chain incurs all the operating financial risks. • Leaseholds interests are a liability on the balance sheet that could negatively affect value.

Source: Adapted from HVS (2012).

its investment in the deal and moves the lease contract closer to the ownership on the axe of resource commitment and risk bearing.

Like the other entry modes, the lease contract presents some advantages/disadvantages for both the owner/lessor and the lessee/hotel chain. When it comes to the hospitality sector, for instance, to some extent the greatest risks tend to lie with the hotel chain. That is, external and internal forces may even affect the business's revenue, meanwhile the owner's gain will always be guaranteed by contract. Table 15.1 presents some of the advantages and disadvantages of leases for both the owner and hotel chain operating the business. As it can be observed, the chain assumes all the operating responsibilities together with all the financial risks. Hence, it enjoys the benefits if the business is successful but suffers all the losses if it does not perform adequately.

The lease contract clauses

According to Ghorbal-Blal (2008), rent is the most critical clause in the lease contract negotiation. Regarding this issue, Cunnil (2006) points out that in a leasing agreement, the owner's financial returns generally comprise:

- The payment of a steady fee, which may be adjusted annually, plus
- The payment of a percentage (often around 5 per cent) over the hotel's total gains, or
- The payment of a percentage (often around 15 per cent) over the cash flow, or even
- Any of the two latter, plus a steady extra amount of money

In most cases, the rent/fee structure is determined by the specific market conditions and legal regulations. DeRoos (2011) reports that the three rent options (fixed, fixed+variable, and only variable fee) are almost equally spread.

Apart from the lease fees, duration of the contract is another important issue. Usually, lease contracts are signed for a very long period (from 20 to 50 years) (DeRoos, 2002) – another reason why the lease in many cases is considered closer to ownership, than a non-equity agreement. The compilation of the long term, regular percentage rents and cancellation clauses, however, should be carefully estimated by the future lessee, to balance with the expectations of sales and revenue flows (DeRoos, 2002). Notwithstanding, clauses such as options to renew or terminate, options to purchase, upward-only adjusted rent, FF&E ownership and repair, contingent use of the asset and leasing incentives must be included. Leases of hotels are completely different from the leases of other property assets because hotels form a distinct and very different property asset class. Given these circumstances, the practice of lease has led to the creation of more complex rent clauses in Europe (Ghorbal-Blal, 2008). Contrary to this, however, as pointed out by Huang and Chathoth (2011), some budget hotel chains in China have operated largely by the lease of properties based on a fixed rent. In that sense, most contracts in China tend to be based on an indexed growth, bearing the least risks for the property owner.

What happens on the expiry of a hotel lease? It may not appear to be a priority when negotiating the terms. However, time spent considering this at the outset will certainly be time well spent. Therefore, Romney (2007) observes that, before the lease contract comes to an end, it is important to consider the following issues:

- Who will be responsible for employees in the case of breach of contract?
- What are the effects of the decisions to terminate (or renew) the contract to the brand?
- What will be done with the stocks?
- What will be the impacts of the decisions on future plans?
- To whom belongs the internal information (guests' registration, licences, etc.): to the owner or to the chain?

Thus, the lease contract must necessarily cover issues such these. At the same time, a specific fund for future expenses should be created, which might help in case there is no previous clause in the contract that addresses who should be responsible for those will be for the structural expenses incurred over the leasing period. By indicating what exactly happens when the agreement comes to an end, both owner and chain are more likely to avoid future problems (Romney, 2007).

The adoption of a lease contract by hotel chains in practice

Although the lease mode has demonstrated to be a valuable alternative for chains to explore new and existing markets, Qin et al. (2012) advocate that in the hotel industry, the segmentation strategy adopted may affect a company's decision. Accordingly, luxury segment companies tend to expand mainly through management contracts, whereas economy segment companies prefer expanding through franchising. In a similar vein, Koh and Jang (2009) conclude that less financially distressed hotel firms are more likely to use operating lease.

It is worth noting that, according to an HVS report (2012: 2), leases are the prevailing entry and operating model in the German market. The document highlights, however, that 'even though the future of hotel leases has been questioned by the international investment community, German banks are clearly comfortable with the model'. Nevertheless, in practice contracts have been changing to fit the new market demands. The fixed lease model has slowly been replaced by hybrid structures, which, in turn, mix revenue-based variable rent and fixed-base rent. Similarly, the lease as an entry mode seems to have been successfully adopted in countries like China. As pointed out by Huang and Chathoth (2011), approximately 89 per cent of economic hotels in the country opt for this type of strategy. On the other hand, DeRoos (2002) advocates that owners in Europe and Asia are more risk adverse than their US counterparts. Hence, European and Asian owners are typically comfortable with minimum rents, provided they are stable in the long run, whereas US owners are often focused on return maximisation and prefer management contracts, where they can participate in the profits generated by the property (DeRoos, 2002).

In many cases the lease contract is compared to the management contract, mainly because they have similar relations in agency perspective. In both cases the owner delegates hotel business to the hotel chain, however, the lease provides greater flexibility for the chain in terms of operation and hotel management (Pages, 2007), whereas the management contract distributes control over property assets between the parties. In order to reduce the risks associated with the amount invested, some hotel chains have adopted the management contract to the detriment of the lease. Another alternative to alleviate the greater risk associated with lease, and to bypass the complicated management contract, is the 'sale and lease back' strategy, along with the less popular 'sale and manage back' option (Koh and Jang, 2009; Pages, 2007). Furthermore, especially in the US, specific matters of accounting and legal regulations may affect the preferences of hotel chains for management contract or lease contract (DeRoos, 2011), e.g. hotel firms may have external funds to relieve financial distress (Koh and Jang, 2009). Even so, Romney (2007) advocates that though some chains tend to give preference to management contracts, still a considerable number of investors bets on leases. Thus, the adoption of leasing as an entry mode by hotel chains is likely to remain. Qin et al. (2012) argue that lease can be a better trade-off with regards to profit, control, risk and quality than 'own-and-manage' and franchising modes. Therefore, it is up to the hotel company to analyse the market situation and decide on the proper entry mode. Having said that, the next section will present some cases of chains that have entered new (and existing) markets by adopting the leasing mode.

Table 15.2 represents the current situation (2014–2015) regarding use of lease contracts by the largest hotel corporations. With the exception of Accor, it is evident that most of the hotel corporations in the Western hemisphere rely very little on lease arrangements. The significant drop in owned and leased hotels is especially evident in the previous annual reports of Hyatt (from 45 leased Select-service properties in 2013 there remain only 2 leased in 2014) (Hyatt, 2015). The numbers confirm greater use of lease contract in Europe – Accor hotels are based in France and develop mainly in Europe, most of Carlson Rezidor group's portfolio is located in Europe as well. At the other extreme are the Chinese chains. Most of them were founded 5–10 years ago and operate mainly on the domestic market. Again, dynamics show continuous decrease of lease contracts for hotels in the process of conversion (pipelines) – only 5 per cent of China Lodging group's pipelines in 2015 are going to be under lease contract, in contrast to 2012, when this share was 31 per cent (China Lodging Group, 2015). The same is valid for Home Inns Group, which in 2015 leases only 33 per cent of its hotels, in contrast to 2011 when this share was 89 per cent, as reported by Huang and Chathoth (2011).

Table 15.2 Use of lease contracts by the largest hotel corporations* in 2014

Hotel corporation	Number of owned and leased properties**	Share of owned and leased properties from the total number of hotels	Total number of hotels, belonging to the corporation
InterContinental Hotel Group	8	0.16%	4,942
Hilton Hotels	144	3.33%	4,322
Marriott International	51 (42 leased, 9 owned)	1.22%	4,175
Accor Hotels	1354	36.43%	3,717
Starwood Hotels & Resorts Worldwide	33	2.64%	1,249
Hyatt Hotels Corp.	41 (8 leased, 33 owned)	6.63%	618
Carlson Rezidor Hotel Group	120 leased	11.00%	1,089
Home Inns & Hotels Management, China	914 leased-and-operated	33.23%	2,750
China Lodging Group/ Huazhu Hotel group	616 leased	25.84%	2,384

Source: 2014 Annual reports of the corporations.

* Only hotel corporations using lease contracts are included.
** Most of the corporations provide only one number for owned and leased properties.

Case study: Brazil

In the 1970s, the first hotel chains started to expand their business into attractive new hospitality markets. In Brazil, by that time, public incentives were granted by the State – under special conditions – to encourage the development of certain economic sectors in the country, including tourism (Proserpio, 2007). Thus, the very first chain to enter that unexplored market was the Hilton, established initially in the city of São Paulo, in 1971. Afterwards, still taking advantage of the favourable economic scenario, some other hotel businesses were attracted by the benefits of the Brazilian market. Therefore, international chains such as Holiday Inn, Sheraton (Intercontinental), Meridian, Méditerranée, Novotel and Caesar Park established themselves in the country and competed in order to increase their market share.

It is noteworthy that each of the aforementioned chains defined a particular strategy to enter the market. Notwithstanding, a prominent (and successful) case of the adoption of the leasing mode in Brazil was the Sheraton International. In 1986, the Lebanese entrepreneur Nassib Mofarrej (1915–1988) invested in the launch of a luxury hotel in the city of São Paulo, the Mofarrej Park (Explorador, 2009). However, Mofarrej decided that, instead of taking over the control of his new 32,000m^2 enterprise, the business should be leased to another company. Thus, the Sheraton chain took over the 20-floor business, located at the Paulista Avenue in the centre of São Paulo, in a leasing contract that assured the investor a monthly return of 250,000 dollars (Explorador, 2009). The business, valued at 50 million dollars, was the opportunity found by the Sheraton chain to enter the Brazilian market.

After a 17-year period at the head of the business, in 2003 the Sheraton chain decided to suspend their operations at the Mofarrej. Thereafter, the biggest current Spanish chain, Sol Meliá, saw a great opportunity to explore the Brazilian market. Following its strategy to be among the core hotel operators of the world, the chain has been adopting the so called 'low capital intensity modes' to enter new markets, such as management contracts, franchising and leasing (Exame.com, 2013). The latter was used to explore the Brazilian market when taking over the Mofarrej operations through the Gran Meliá brand.

However, the interest of the chain in the business lasted only for a short period of 7 years. In 2007, when renegotiating the leasing contract with the Sol Meliá, the heirs of the Mofarrej then demanded investments in infrastructure on the part of the chain. Given the circumstances, and the high level of investments involved, the Spanish chain decided not to proceed in the business, opening the opportunity up to other competitors to explore the market (Veja, 2009).

Therefore, willing to take advantage of a potential 11.5 million dollars profit per year, in 2010, the Espírito Santo chain, a Portuguese company owner of the Tivoli brand, leased the business in order to increase their market share in Brazil. The purpose of the deal, according to the marketing director of the chain, was to promote their brand throughout Latin America. As part of the leasing contract, the chain committed to investing approximately 7 million dollars to repair the establishment's structure. Hence, the hotel, which used to have a kind of 'Sultan Palace'-inspired style, gained a whole new modern atmosphere (Veja, 2009).

Considerations and concluding remarks

From this chapter and Chapters 11–14, we can see that each of the entry modes presents advantages and disadvantages for chains, in terms of financial and operational risks, control and investments. Thus, the adoption of an entry mode is often related to factors such as:

- The expansion strategy often adopted by the hotel chain;
- The chain's propensity for risks (lower or higher);
- The specific service to be internationalised;
- The target market.

With regard to the latter two, it has been demonstrated that there is a greater tendency for hotel chains to adopt 'high-involvement' modes, such as ownership, when expanding luxury brands into certain markets. On the other hand, when it comes to the expansion of economic brands, 'low-involvement' modes, such as the lease, seems to be most suitable. Furthermore, it is noteworthy that in more stable markets – the US and Europe – lease contracts are more frequent, in comparison to others, like Brazil. In this sort of market, management contracts have largely been preferred over the others, since it appears to be less risky for the chains.

This chapter presented some of the relevant issues related to the lease of hotel establishments by international chains worldwide. However, since the discussions held herein were not meant to be exhaustive, it is recommended that readers search for new trends in the hospitality sector. Hence, the purpose of this chapter was to provide readers with a set of information that might serve as a starting point to broaden their knowledge on the subject.

References

China Lodging Group/Huazhu Hotels (2015) Investor presentation 2015. Online. Available HTTP: <http://files.shareholder.com/downloads/ABEA-40FHZ9/768184855x0x832216/CA3B6F2E-508C-4C65-8AB9-A427E7656049/HuaZhu_Investor_Presentation_20150528_w_May_28.pdf>, accessed 25 September 2015.

Contractor, F.J. and Kundu, S.K. (1998) Modal choice in a world of alliances: analyzing organizational forms in the international hotel sector. *Journal of International Business Studies*, 29(2), 325–57.

Cunill, O.M. (2006) *The Growth Strategies of Hotel Chains: Best Business Practices by Leading Companies.* New York: Haworth Hospitality Press.

Cunill, O.M. and Forteza, C.M. (2010) The franchise contract in hotel chains: a study of hotel chain growth and market concentrations. *Tourism Economics*, 16(3), 493–515.

deRoos, J. (2002) *Alternative Means of Operating Hotels: A Critical Look at Single Tenant Leases Versus Management Contracts.* Cornell University, School of Hospitality Administration [Electronic version]. Online. Available HTTP: <http://scholarship.sha.cornell.edu/articles/222>, accessed 19 September 2015.

deRoos, J.A. (2011) *Gaining Maximum Benefit from Franchise Agreements, Management Contracts, and Leases.* Cornell University, School of Hospitality Administration [Electronic version]. Online. Available HTTP: <http://scholarship.sha.cornell.edu/articles/309>, accessed 19 September 2015.

Eisenhardt, K. (1989) Agency theory: an assessment and review. *The Academy of management review*, 14(1), 57–74.

Exame.com (2013) Meliá Hotels International anuncia 4 novos hotéis no Brasil e na Itália, além dos resultados do primeiro semestre. Online. Available HTTP: <http://exame.abril.com.br/negocios/releases/meliahotelsinternationalanuncia4novoshoteisnobrasilenaitaliaalemdosresultadosdoprimeirosemester.shtml>, accessed 30 July, 2015.

Explorador (2009) Nassib Mofarrej (1915–1988), empresário libanês radicado no Brasil, austero nos negócios, audacioso. Online. Available HTTP: <http://www.oexplorador.com.br/nassib-mofarrej-1915-1988-empresario-libanes-radicado-no-brasil-austero-nos-negocios-audacioso>, accessed 30 July 2015.

Gallagher, M. and Mansour, A. (2000) An analysis of hotel real estate market dynamics. *Journal of Real Estate Research*, 19(1/2), 133–64.

Ghorbal-Blal, I. (2008) *An exploration of the construct of control in expansion strategies of hotel chains: a multiple case-study.* Unpublished Doctoral thesis, Virginia Polytechnic Institute and State University

Homeinn Hotels Group (2015) Investor Presentation 2014. Online. Available HTTP: <http://media.corporate-ir.net/media_files/IROL/20/203641/Homeinns_Hotel _Group_Investor_Presentation_2Q15.pdf>, accessed 25 September 2015.

Huang, R. and Chathoth, P. (2011) Leasing as a model choice in China's company-run budget hotels: an exploratory study. *Tourism Planning and Development*, 8(1), 37–50.

HVS (2012) Hotel contracts: to lease or not to lease? Online. Available HTTP: <http://www.hvs.com/article/5925/hotel-contracts-to-lease-or-not-to-lease>, accessed 30 July, 2015.

Hyatt (2015) 2014 Annual report. Online. Available HTTP: <http://investors.hyatt.com/files/doc_financials/annual%202014/Hyatt-Hotels-Form-10-K.PDF>, accessed 25 September, 2015.

Koh, J.H. and Jang, S.C. (2009) Determinants of using operational lease in the hotel industry. *International Journal of Hospitality Management*, 28, 638–40.

Manning, C., O'Neill, J., Singh, A.J., Hood, S., Liu, C. and Bloom, B.A.N. (2015) The emergence of hotel/lodging real estate research. *Journal of Real Estate Literature*, 23(1), 1–26.

Pages, T. (2007) 'Asset-Light' – managing or leasing? *Journal of Retail and Leisure Property*, 6, 97–99.

Proserpio, R. (2007) *O avanço das redes hoteleiras internacionais no Brasil.* São Paulo: Aleph.

Qin, Y., Adler, H. and Cai, L. (2012) Successful growth strategies of three Chinese domestic hotel companies. *Journal of Management and Strategy*, 3(1), 40–54.

Romney, C. (2007) What happens on the expiry of a hotel leasing? *Journal of Retail & Leisure Property*, 6(2), 93–95.

Sancho, A. (2001) *Introdução ao Turismo.* São Paulo: Roca.

Vallen, G. and Vallen, J. (2003) *Check-in, check-out: gestão e prestação de serviços em hotelaria.* 6th edn. Porto Alegre: Bookman.

Veja (2009) Hotel Mofarrej passa a ser administrado pelo Grupo Espírito Santo. Online. Available HTTP: <http://vejasp.abril.com.br/materia/hotel-mofarrej-passa-ser-administrado-pelo-grupo-espirito-santo>, accessed 30 July, 2015.

16

The choice of an entry mode by hotel chains

Elena García de Soto-Camacho and Alfonso Vargas-Sánchez

(UNIVERSITY OF HUELVA, SPAIN)

Introduction

In this chapter we shall study the economic rationality of the multiplicity of governance mechanisms used by hotel chains and analyse the factors that determine the choice of entry mode into an external market. Our aim is to propose a model that will serve as a guide to the governance mechanism that is most suitable for hotel chains, distinguishing between equity (full ownership and joint venture) and non-equity modes (franchise, management contract, leasing contract and marketing consortium). The analysis of entry mode choice by hotel chains may be performed from a strictly organisational perspective, seeking the best way to organise the establishments, independently of market characteristics, or from a perspective that includes these characteristics and, as such, incorporates the strategic behaviour of the company. Consequently, the environment, in which a series of substantial changes are undergoing, requires increasingly more attention in line with the emphasis on the strategic direction of these changes. In other words, as hotel chains find themselves increasingly internationalised, it is no longer possible to separate the choice of entry mode from market variables. For this reason the proposed model adopts this dual perspective.

Our proposal is based on the Contractor and Kundu (1998) model, which suggests that the fundamental difference between the various entry modes lies in the assignation of the various proprietary rights regarding the assets required for the production of hotel service, in particular the intangible assets. Each modality requires the chain to exercise different levels of control over the assets, which, from an organisational perspective, presents both advantages and disadvantages.

Hotel sector, asset ownership and organisational typologies

With a view to understanding the advantages and inconveniences which the different entry modes present for hotel chains, it is advisable to distinguish the various roles that, in relation to their contribution to the production of service, exist in the hotel business, namely, the 'manager', the 'operator' and the 'owner' (Fernández and González, 2008). The 'manager' is the physical or legal entity that provides the brand name and the reservations centre, and, in general, oversees the establishment and the strategic organisation of the business. The 'operator' is the entity that provides the accommodation service and reflects the results of this activity in their financial statements. This entity maintains rights of use over all assets and is the beneficiary of the residual income once the owners of the remaining factors of production, that have been used, have been remunerated. Their basic asset is their operating knowledge of how to put the know-how of the manager into practice in a particular establishment. And finally, the 'owner' is the entity that possesses the title deeds of the various facilities pertaining to the hotel.

Regarding the assets that intervene in the hotel industry, the most significant of these are the brand name and the reservation centre (Fernández and González, 2008). Other assets to be taken into consideration are the hotel facilities and the personnel, in particular their training and know-how (Tsaur and Lin, 2004). The means of organising these assets will depend on whether or not the roles of manager, operator and owner are carried out by the same person, or by two, or even three different people, or entities, as the entry mode presents a different organisational model in each case and generates different problems of coordination and control (Contractor and Kundu, 1998).

In the case of direct management of the establishment (self-ownership), therefore, the roles of manager, operator and owner coincide in one company, the chain, which employs all the personnel and owns the brand name, the reservation centre, the intangible assets, the equipment and all fixed and movable assets. In this modality, through ownership, be it full or majority, the chain obtains maximum control and coordination of all assets used in the production of the hotel service. When the chain possesses a minority participation in the company, control over assets will depend on the level of participation and the type(s) of partner(s), and the chain may act as manager, operator and, in part, as owner, in the event they seek a financial or real-estate partner that does not participate in the management of the establishment. On the other hand, if the partner is another hotel company that operates the establishment, the chain will act only as hotel manager and co-owner.

If the chosen entry mode is leasing, either of a premises or of an entire hotel company, the chain then acts as both the operator and manager of the hotel, but is not the owner, either of the building or of the external assets. As a result, the chain has maximum control over all the hotel business assets with one exception, namely, the residual rights of decision concerning the leased assets are possessed by the owner. Similarly, in the case of management contracts, the chain acts as manager and as operator having a degree of control similar to the previous case. In some management contracts, the role of the chain is merely as manager and is the exclusive owner of the reservation centre only, though it maintains control over the brand name, albeit not as completely as in previous cases. The control exercised over other assets, such as fixed assets, equipment and operational know-how, is limited by the contract itself, given that residual control falls to the operator.

In a marketing consortium, independently owned hotels belong to a group of hotels for marketing/branding reasons. They have an international clientele who are familiar with the brand name of the consortium, paying a percentage of their revenue to the company which manages the brand name. Each hotel remains independent from the point of view of ownership and management, taking advantage of being part of a chain with a global reserve system and multi-language website that also features loyalty programmes and participates in fairs and promotional events to promote the brand reputation. The site of the consortium is highly visible, but favours competition between the hotel members.

In a franchise situation, the chain seeks a partner who will start up their own establishment under the directives and brand name of the chain, to the effect that, in contrast to the

Table 16.1 Type of contract and degree of control

Basic assets	Mechanisms of control on assets					
	Equity		Non-equit			
	Full ownership	Joint venture	Leasing contract	Management contract	Marketing consortium	Franchise
Building	Total control	Medium-high control	Without control over the asset	Without control over the asset	Without control over the asset	Without control over the asset
Fixed assets and equipment	Total control	Medium-high control	Medium-high control	Medium control	Without control over the asset	Without control over the asset
Know-how	Total control	Medium-high control	Medium-high control	Medium control	Medium-low control	Medium-low control
Reservation centre	Total control	Total control	Total control	Total control	Total control	Total control
Brand name	Total control	Medium-high control	Total control	Medium-high control	Medium-high control	Medium control

Source: Adapted from Fernandez and Gonzalez (2008) and expanded by the authors.

management contract scenario, the operator also acts as manager of the franchise outlet while the hotel chain acts as a 'distance' manager, with direct control over the reservation centre and indirect control over the brand name. This indirect control is due to the fact that the franchise contract concedes part control of the brand name to the franchisee.

Table 16.1 synthesises the relationship between the type of contract and the degree of control exercised over the basic assets.

Choice of entry mode

As stated previously, our objective is to construct a model that defines the principal determining factors in the choice of entry mode, based on Transaction Cost Theory (TCT), Agency Theory (AT), Resources and Capabilities Theory (RCT) and Real Options Theory (ROT). TCT, in particular the work of Williamson (1979), allows explanation of hybrid organisational forms such as franchising, management contracts and joint ventures. AT, for its part, analyses the means of resolving conflicts of interest in a hotel chain (principal) by delegating the post of hotel director (agent) via a contract between the two parties (Eisenhardt, 1989), as in the case of a franchise and marketing consortium, whereas in the management contract and in the leasing contract the principal appears to be the owner of the hotel, assigning the hotel chain (the agent) to operate the hotel. These two approaches will be complemented by those of RCT (Barney, 1991), which deals with the availability of valuable resources that are costly to transmit. Finally, we will also base our argument on ROT, which focuses explicitly on the role of market uncertainty, both exogenous and endogenous, and its subsequent resolution, in the making of strategic decisions (Tong and Reuer, 2007), affirming that, in order to benefit strategically from uncertainty, companies must create real options as a means of maintaining flexibility in adjustment decisions that arise in response to new opportunities or challenges (Kogut and Kulatilaka, 1994). Consequently, we will complement the traditional analysis of organisational forms with a more dynamic vision where ROT is applied to the choice of entry mode. In order to achieve this, we will group the variables that determine the choice of entry mode into three categories (Contractor and Kundu, 1998; Ramón Rodriguez, 2002; Berbel-Pineda and Ramírez-Hurtado, 2011; Martorell-Cunill et al., 2013): uncertainty, strategic and control variables (focused on contractual risks and growth and differentiation objectives) and the chain's structural variables.

With regard to the effect of uncertainty on the entry mode, our final model responds to ROT logic, which affirms that, faced with high levels of uncertainty, the company will opt for the entry modality that will give it sufficient strategic flexibility to allow it to adapt its strategy in response to changes in the uncertainty (Li, 2007). While studies concerning the entry mode strategy within the hotel sector have included a series of uncertainty variables, these have been limited to one specific type, namely, those of the overall environment, in other words, country risk, cultural distance and the level of economic development (Contractor and Kundu, 1998; Ramón-Rodriguez, 2002; Berbel-Pineda and Ramírez-Hurtado, 2011; Martorell-Cunill et al., 2013). For Miller (1993), however, uncertainty is conceived as a lack of foresight regarding environmental and organisational variables that have an impact on corporate performance.

The reasoning behind transaction costs is that, given a limited rationality, and under conditions of considerable uncertainty, it is difficult to anticipate all the future eventualities in which it may be necessary to adapt partnership contracts. Internalising the activity, therefore, may contribute to the absorption of external uncertainty. However, the reasoning behind transaction costs ignores the advantages of strategic flexibility (Brouthers et al., 2008). From a resource perspective, a high country risk implies a need to protect the company's resources, avoiding outright ownership (Contractor and Kundu, 1998). In high risk countries, on the other hand, companies are required to maintain sufficient flexibility in order to be able to change their revenue method in the event that the initial method becomes inefficient due to unforeseen changes in the environment (Erramilli and Rao, 1993; Altinay and Altinay, 2003; Quer et al., 2007). ROT emphasises that, when uncertainty creates a situation in which the value of an investment opportunity cannot be precisely predicted, companies respond via a limited initial investment, leaving themselves with future investment options (Brouthers et al., 2008). In this case, cooperative entry modes, as franchise, management and leasing contract, are an attractive alternative. Table 16.2 synthesises some of the uncertainties in hotel investment and real options that can control them.

While the majority of attempts when elaborating a model of real options of an international company strategy include uncertainty as an independent variable, they fail to examine in any depth the manner in which the types of uncertainty, both endogenous and exogenous, condition the entry mode into the international market. To this effect, exogenous uncertainty is considered to be that which is not affected by a company's actions, and can only be revealed over time. Examples of this include political and macroeconomic uncertainty. Endogenous uncertainty, on the other hand, may be diminished via the actions of an individual company, a category which includes uncertainty in the microeconomic and sectorial environment and uncertainty on a company level (Miller, 1993; Li, 2007).

Li (2007: 91) puts forward the hypothesis that 'when exogenous and endogenous uncertainty increase, choice of an entry mode that offers a high level of control of international investments with specific assets is less beneficial'. Li and Rugman (2007), however, conclude that the choice of entry mode depends on the magnitude and type of uncertainty and suggest

Table 16.2 Uncertainty and real options

Uncertainty	Risk factors	Real options	Franchise	Marketing consortium	Management contract	Leasing contract	Full ownership	Acquisitions and mergers	Joint venture
Competitive	Competitors can act after (when there are resources)	– Postpone	x		x	x		x	x
		– Abandon or reduce	x		x	x		x	x
	The competitor's response can eliminate the strategic advantage gained	– Postpone	x		x	x		x	x
		– Abandon or reduce	x		x	x		x	x
Environment	The rules are not very satisfactory for this industry	– Postpone	x		x	x			x
		– Abandon or reduce							
	Fail in estimating demand	– Postpone							
		– Abandon or reduce					x		
		– Expand							
	The customers' response can overload the system (overbooking)	– Abandon or reduce		x				x	
		– Expand		x					
	The environment is changing	– Abandon or reduce	x		x	x			x
		– Expand		x					
Technological	The destination is unsuitable to current requirements	– Postpone	x		x	x			
	The destination will be unsuitable in the future	– Abandon or reduce	x		x	x			x

Source: Adapted from Martorell et al., 2008, 2013.

that when uncertainty is both significant and endogenous, multinational companies may prefer entry modes which involve a high level of resource commitment. These hypotheses are in accordance with a number of studies that have shown that market entry that implies a high level of resource commitment contributes to a reduction of uncertainty regarding market competition and offers a higher growth option value when a multinational company is capable of either anticipating new entries by competitors or of forcing existing companies to make room for them (Rivoli and Salorio, 1996; Folta and Miller, 2002; Folta and O'Brien, 2004).

Analysis of the factors that determine the entry mode should focus not only on the market, but also on specific company factors. These may be divided into two groups: on the one hand, structural factors, and, on the other, subjective aspects relating to the control and strategy of the company (Contractor and Kundu, 1998; Ramón-Rodriguez, 2002; Berbel-Pineda and Ramírez-Hurtado, 2011; Martorell-Cunill et al., 2013). In order to analyse the effect of structural factors on the entry mode, we must take into consideration both the size of the chain and its international experience, on the understanding that, within a global hotel environment, this is an industry that requires a high volume of investment that leads to strategic alliances attaining stronger positions, with the result that it is the more experienced, larger companies (those whose volume of activity leads to an increase in international experience) (Contractor and Kundu, 1998; Ramón-Rodriguez, 2002; Berbel-Pineda and Ramírez-Hurtado, 2011) that can more easily obtain the prestige and resources required to forge alliances and find strategic partners.

Concerning the influence of strategic and control factors on the entry mode, we must bear in mind the contractual risks that these factors generate. One of the most important of these is the problem of retention (Williamson, 1979), which has its origin in the specificity of the assets and where the value of the assets diminishes when they are employed in any activity that is not the current one. In the case of the hotel sector, not all assets have the same level of specificity with regard to the chain (Contractor and Kundu, 1998). As occurs with reservation and customer access systems, investment in brand name development is specific to the characteristics of the chain, and reuse of these assets in another hotel chain would mean significant loss of asset value (Bailey and Ball, 2006). The opposite occurs, however, with properties, which are specific to hotel activity but not to a chain, as others may avail themselves of these assets, or function as an independent hotel, thereby notably reducing the specificity problem. Intermediate situations arise in the case of all other assets. So, given that the know-how relating to daily administration, supervision and quality control will, to a great extent, be standardised within the sector, this know-how may be used in other establishments of the same chain, and even in different chains. With regard to other assets and equipment, the most costly of these are not generally personalised and therefore may be reused, as is the case with kitchen equipment and general furnishings. The remaining assets, though they may be personalised, either with logos or because they belong to a particular decorative style, are not high cost, have short repayment terms and, on occasion, may also be reused in other establishments (Fernández and González, 2008).

Another significant contractual risk arises from differing principal and agent interests and the moral risk that these may entail. A number of agent relationships exist within the hotel industry, one of the most significant being that which exists between the person (agent) who oversees the establishment, i.e. the hotel director, or manager, and the head office, or proprietary company of the chain (principal), a situation which appears specifically in cases of franchises and marketing consortia. In this case, a conflict of interests may arise if the objectives of the director, or manager, do not coincide with those of the principal, or owner of the chain. In other words, the principal should verify the work carried out by the director (agent). Consequently, if the hotel chain cannot, or does not wish to, for cost reasons, verify whether or not the behaviour of the agent is in line with that of the company, a problem will arise. It is worth adding that not all establishments are equally easy to control due to the fact that administration of a hotel chain includes activities that are susceptible to being centralised (marketing, treasury and finance administration, control of reservations) while activities relating to the provision of service are by nature geographically dispersed. This necessary dispersion of hotels is what makes direct control by the chain a difficult task, one alternative being the introduction of incentive systems which reconcile the interests of those in charge of the establishments with the interests of those who contract them.

Where coordination costs are concerned, separating the figures of the manager from those of the operator generates a problem regarding the quality of service provided in each establishment (Ramón-Rodriguez, 2002), and this problem may affect the image and brand value of a chain and, consequently, the current and future benefits of the manager. The operator of an establishment is more concerned with the results of his establishment than with the effects of his decisions on brand value and quality of service. This conflict of interests can be resolved by combining the roles of manager and operator in the same person, as is the case when a hotel is privately owned (Chen and Dimou, 2005).

In our model, the gathered primary data have been used to test it — these data relate to questions concerning the importance given to variables traditionally taken into consideration in studies relating to the choice of entry mode into international markets (Contractor and Kundu, 1998; Ramón-Rodriguez, 2002; Berbel-Pineda and Ramírez-Hurtado, 2011; Martorell-Cunill et al., 2013). These variables respond to two fundamental strategic objectives: on the one hand, growth and cost reduction, and on the other, differentiation. The influence, therefore, that economies of scale, reservation systems, or the size of a company may have on the entry mode strategy are variables that we include as part of the growth and cost reduction objectives, while the influence of brand name, investment in training or quality control on the activities would be included as part of the objectives relating to differentiation of the chain.

In relation to the arguments put forward in various previous studies on the objectives that a hotel chain may set with respect to company growth and the reduction of costs, it seems that, within the strategy of the company, more importance is attached to objectives related to possible association with another chain and to reduced investment of resources with the aim of achieving economies of scale, better control over the reservation systems, and increased company size. In contrast, there is another different tendency to avoid developing forms of closer association with other chains and instead to make greater investments of resources with a view to achieving greater control over the staff training, quality and image of the company, in relation to the objectives that the chain may set for improving its image and differentiating itself from competitors (Contractor and Kundu, 1998; Ramón-Rodriguez, 2002; Berbel-Pineda and Ramírez-Hurtado, 2011; Martorell-Cunill et al., 2013).

With regard to the chosen entry mode and the presence of real options in the chain, the theory of real options suggests that, under conditions of high uncertainty, a company will prefer to reduce to the minimum the initial investment while ensuring that it has the option of investing more at a later time, when it will have obtained more information to better re-evaluate the uncertainties actually faced (Rivoli and Salorio, 1996; Brouthers et al., 2008). By doing so, the company obtains access (i.e. ownership) to knowledge about the opportunities for investment and about the related uncertainty. In this way the company can restrict the possibilities open to competitors (by closing distribution channels eliminating possible partners, for example), and gains the opportunity (but not the obligation) to adjust the investment position if the uncertainty is reduced or considered manageable. Therefore, we can state that a company will confront uncertainty by choosing the modes of entry that give it valuable future options (Folta, 1998; Brouthers et al., 2008).

Real options are a clear source of strategic flexibility by capturing the implicit value of the flexibility available to the management. Similarly, these options aid the company management to take advantage of the opportunities for developing the businesses that are presented by a particular strategic investment. Real options allow a company to abandon or sell the investment project before completing it; to change its use or its technology; to prolong its life; to choose one or other capacity of an investment in plant; to make the investment in R&D more flexible; and to postpone, expand, contract, close and even alter a project during its life (Trigeorgies, 1996; Tamayo, 2006; Li, 2007). Thus, real options are presented as a source of strategic flexibility for an organisation, since they allow the decisions taken to be adapted to the real conditions of the business environment (Trigeorgis, 1996; Tamayo, 2006; Li, 2007).

The availability of real options to the company will facilitate the process of organisational change in the face of particular identified contingencies of the business environment. When the directors are aware of these real options, this will give the company valuable strategic flexibility, and should increase the probability that the directors can plan and implement the strategic change necessary for the organisation. Equally, when the company is operating in complex and dynamic settings, strategic flexibility enhances its capacity to respond to the changes in the environment, in the direction required; in other words, it allows the directors to respond when confronted with instability and to develop resources and capabilities to adapt to the changing conditions. If a company is more flexible strategically, its directors will be able to plan beforehand the strategic modifications they consider necessary to adapt to the changes in its environment; this should give the entire organisation greater capacity for adaptation to the requirements of that change that would enable the company to implement successfully the new strategy (Tamayo, 2006).

It is possible to identify two types of result that reflect the international performance of a company: one is the 'image and access results', which show its reputation and degree of access to international markets; and the other factor is the 'financial results', which represent the financial output obtained by the chain and its degree of satisfaction with the existing global strategy. It should be stated, in addition, that the second factor is a consequence of the first, since the image possessed by a company at the international level and its degree of access to major markets condition the international financial performance of the company (Lukas, 2007).

Methodology

We have developed and tested a model that considers the entry mode as a dependent variable that assumes a value of: 1 – if the chain operates as a franchise; 2 – if the chain has a management contract; 3 – for a leasing contract; 4 – for partial ownership (joint venture) and 5 – for full ownership of the establishment. In the proposed explanatory model, marketing consortia have been excluded because these are not so frequently employed by the hotel chains analysed. The population comprises a total of 88 hotel chains, 62 of them Spanish and 26 foreign-owned. The geographic scope of the study covers the whole national territory of Spain. The data collection process was carried out between March 2011 and September 2012, by means of a survey of the directors of the leading Spanish hotel chains with international presence and the directors of the foreign chains operating in Spain. The questionnaire was completed by 35 of the managers of these hotel chains, representing a response rate of 39.8 per cent. Due to the size of the sample, we have applied the Partial Least Squares technique, since the assumed minimum number of observations for it is 30. For the statistical treatment of the data collected, the SPSS Version 19 and Visual-PLS 1.04 bi programs have been used.

Results

In the light of the results obtained, we can conclude that when the exogenous and endogenous uncertainty perceived by the company increases, selecting a mode of entry that offers the company a high degree of control of the international investments is less beneficial, and there is a greater probability that the company would prefer a mode of entry with less commitment of resources as against full ownership.

Looking at the effect that the interaction between company size and its international experience has on the mode of entry to the international market chosen, the high volume of investment that the hotel industry requires means that strategic alliances are a more attractive option. Hotel chains face uncertainty by opting for modes of entry requiring low initial investment which gives them future options, related to both learning and change, as well as growth and of abandonment. With regard to the relationship between real options and strategic flexibility, we conclude that real options are clearly a source of strategic flexibility as they allow for the adaptation of decisions which have been taken with respect to existing conditions in the business environment.

We have also observed that those chains that possess greater strategic flexibility achieve a better fit with the business environment in which they operate, improving their reputation and their degree of access to the market. This allows us to conclude that strategic flexibility is associated positively with this type of international activity. To the contrary, in relation to the hypothesis that the availability of real options in the company is positively associated with access to the markets and the reputation of the company, our results show an influence, but in the opposite direction to that expected. Lastly, we find that the 'financial results' of the international strategy are a consequence of the 'image and access result', since the image of the company on an international scale and the degree of access obtained to the markets condition the international financial results. This must be taken into account when establishing the long term strategic objectives of the company.

Discussion

The theory of real options can be employed to explain the internationalisation strategy of the hotel industry, thereby improving the understanding of this decision and developing a dynamic theory that can be used to analyse the effects that the mode of entry into a foreign market may have in the future and its impact on the company's international performance. The integrated perspective of risk management creates a framework for the identification and evaluation of various types of uncertainties relevant to the formulation of strategies. For the hotel industry, expanding internationally is a fundamental aspect for growth, and as such, is a key element for increased diversification and competitiveness at an international level.

With respect to the factors to take into account when deciding the best mode of entry to the international market, companies are usually faced with a high degree of perceived uncertainty about economic policy. It is therefore recommended that a company should opt for a contractual mode of entry with the object of allowing the company the time and opportunity to learn about the new market, thus reducing the uncertainty and enabling the company to subsequently change the way of operating in the new market, if necessary.

Equally, if there is the perception that the degree of competition in the destination market is intense, or if there is much uncertainty about the future degree of competition, with difficulties in predicting the entry of new competitors, the company should consider entering the market with a mode of entry involving the commitment of minimum resources. Given the large investment required by the hotel industry, and since there is a positive inter-relationship between size and international experience that facilitates the formation of strategic alliances by means of contractual agreements for entering new country markets, those larger hotel companies with more experience should clearly exploit these competitive advantages to form such alliances. This approach would give them valuable strategic options for learning and possibly changing course at less cost, which should translate into an improved international performance for the company. Equally, those chains that do not possess these advantages need to make efforts to acquire them before attempting to expand into other countries. To this end, greater international experience could be gained with a strategy of opening of new establishments in carefully selected foreign countries, thus increasing the number and variety of countries in which the chain has presence and reducing its geographic concentration that would limit the advantages of multinational operations.

Finally, we also confirm that entering a new market by means of contractual forms in the face of large uncertainties creates the option of abandoning it if the conditions are worse than expected, with the object of minimising losses for the chain. However, it is essential for the company to realise that by exercising this option it may harm its reputation, and reduce its prospects of gaining access to that market in the future and obtaining the advantages of the multinational operation. Therefore, before deciding to pull out of the unsuccessful venture, the company will need to weigh up the potential costs and benefits: the reduction of future losses should be set against the impact of the decision on its existing multinational network and the reputation of the chain, particularly when this reputation is considered a strategic asset.

Limitations

It is clear that we have not addressed the full complexity of the variable 'mode of entry'. What we have considered, in effect, is a polytomous ordinal measurement that, when it increases, shows that the multinational possesses a greater degree of shareholder ownership and total control over the hotel in the foreign country. In this measurement, we have not differentiated certain nuances related to some particular situations or formulas, which could enrich the analysis.

The real options have been identified, but they have not been valued. We have not valued the real options open to the chain; we have only considered whether or not the managers have been capable of identifying them, under the assumption that it is their identification that allows them to be executed and exploited. A fundamental reason has been the lack of collaboration by many of the managers of the hotel chains to whom we have addressed our survey, which has reduced the size of the population sampled and has lengthened the time needed to obtain the responses.

Future lines of research

Given that the hotel sector presents peculiarities in respect of the degree of control that the chains can exercise with some of the contractual modes of entry, one line of research could be to test the direction of the hypotheses of uncertainty, for the case of the hotel industry, distinguishing between entry modes that involve control from those that do not, without linking control and ownership.

Another line of research would be centred on the analysis of the conditions in which the multinational companies, integrated into networks, exercise the real options, the modes and the timing of market entry, identifying the variables with most influence in the strategic fit. Equally, more in-depth studies could be made, of the ways in which the generation and exercise of real options impact on the performance of a multinational company.

References

Altinay, L. and Altinay, M. (2003) How will growth be financed by the international hotel companies? *International Journal of Contemporary Hospitality Management*, 15, 274–82.

Bailey, R. and Ball, S. (2006) An exploration of the meanings of hotel brand equity. *The Service Industries Journal*, 26, 15–38.

Barney, J.B. (1991) Firm resources and sustained competitive advantage. *Journal of Management*, 17, 99–120.

Berbel-Pineda, J.M. and Ramírez-Hurtado, J.M. (2011) Does the foreign market entry mode choice affect export performance? The case of the Spanish hotel industry. *Journal of Business Economics and Management*, 12, 301–16.

Brouthers, K.D., Brouthers, L.E. and Werner, S. (2008) Real options, international entry mode choice and performance. *Journal of Management Studies*, 45, 936–60.

Chen, J.J. and Dimou, I. (2005) Expansion strategy of international hotel firms. *Journal of Business Research*, 58, 1730–40.

Contractor, F.J. and Kundu, S.K. (1998) Modal choice in a world of alliances: analyzing organizational forms in the international hotel sector. *Journal of International Business Studies*, 29, 325–56.

Eisendhart, K.M. (1989) Agency theory: an assessment and review. *Academy of Management Review*, 14, 57–74.

Erramilli, M.K. and Rao, C.P. (1993) Service firms international entry mode choice: a modified transaction-cost analysis approach. *Journal of Marketing*, 57, 9–38.

Fernández, M. and González, M. (2008) ¿Cómo organizar una cadena hotelera? La elección de la forma de gobierno. *Cuadernos de Economía y Dirección de Empresas*, 37, 67–96.

Folta, T.B. (1998) Governance and uncertainty: the trade-off between administrative control and commitment. *Strategic Management Journal*, 19, 1007–28.

Folta, T.B. and Miller, K.D. (2002) Real options in equity partnerships. *Strategic Management Journal*, 23, 77–88.

Folta, T.B. and O'Brien, J.P. (2004) Entry in the presence of dueling options. *Strategic Management Journal*, 25, 121–38.

Kogut, B. and Kulatilaka, N. (1994) Operating flexibility, global manufacturing and the option value of a multinational network. *Management Science*, 40, 123–39.

Li, J. (2007) Real options theory and international strategy: a critical review. *Advances in Strategic Management*, 24, 67–101. Online. Available HTTP: <http://ssrn.com/abstract=961265>, accessed 19 April 2009.

Li, J. and Rugman, A.L. (2007) Real options and the theory of foreign direct investment. *International Business Review*, 16, 687–712.

Lukas, E. (2007) Dynamic market entry and the value of flexibility in transitional International Joint ventures. *Review of Financial Economics*, 16, 91–110.

Martorell-Cunill, O., Mulet-Forteza, C. and Otero, L. (2013) Choice of market entry mode by Balearic hotel chains in the Caribbean and Gulf of Mexico. *International Journal of Hospitality Management*, 32, 217–27.

Martorell, O., Mulet-Forteza, C. and Rosselló, M. (2008). Valuing growth strategy management by hotel chains based on the real options approach. *Tourism economics: the business and finance of tourism and recreation*, 14, 511–26. Online. Available HTTP: <http://dialnet.unirioja.es/servlet/articulo?codigo=2740027>, accessed 12 May 2012.

Miller, K.D. (1993) Industry and country effects on managers' perceptions of environmental uncertainties. *Journal of International Business Studies*, 24, 693–714.

Quer, D., Claver, E. and Andreu, R. (2007) Foreign market entry mode in the hotel industry: the impact of country- and firm-specific factors. *International Business Review*, 16, 362–76.

Ramón Rodriguez, A.B. (2002) Determining factors in entry choice for international expansion: the case of the Spanish hotel industry. *Tourism Management*, 23, 597–607.

Rivoli, P. and Salorio, E. (1996) Foreign direct investment and investment under uncertainty. *Journal of International Business Studies*, 27, 335–54.

Tamayo, I. (2006) *Flexibilidad estratégica y opciones reales en los procesos de cambio estratégico* (Unpublished doctoral dissertation). University of Granada, Spain.

Tong, T.W. and Reuer, J.J. (2007) Real options in multinational corporations: organizational challenges and risk implications. *Journal of International Business Studies*, 38, 215–30. doi

Trigeorgies, L. (1996) *Real Options: Managerial Flexibility and Strategy in Resource Allocation*. Cambridge: MIT Press.

Tsaur, S. and Lin, Y. (2004) Promoting service quality in tourist hotels: the role of hrm practices and service behavior. *Tourism Management*, 25, 471–81.

Williamson, O.E. (1979) Transaction-cost economics: the governance of contractual relations. *Journal of Law and Economics*, 22, 233–61. Online. Available HTTP: <http://www.jstor.org/stable/725118>, accessed 5 March 2011.

17

Selecting a partner hotel by the chain

Inès Blal (ECOLE HÔTELIÈRE DE LAUSANNE, HES-SO // UNIVERSITY OF APPLIED SCIENCES WESTERN SWITZERLAND),
Demian Hodari (ECOLE HÔTELIÈRE DE LAUSANNE, HES-SO // UNIVERSITY OF APPLIED SCIENCES WESTERN SWITZERLAND) *and*
Michael J. Turner (THE UNIVERSITY OF QUEENSLAND, AUSTRALIA)

Introduction

Separation of ownership and operating activities constitutes one of the most important changes the hotel industry has seen over the last two decades. A hotel corporation's separation of real-estate ownership from operating activities is referred to as an 'asset light strategy' (Blal and Graf, 2013; Sohn et al., 2013). The implementation of the asset light strategy started to become feasible from the early 1990s onward after the debt market boomed. Conditions became ever more favourable thereafter and into the 2000s as the performance of investment in general equity markets declined amid lower interest rates and lower inflation (Blal and Graf, 2013). As hotel investment became more attractive (Larkin and Lam, 2007), Real Estate Investment Trusts (REITs) soon emerged as one of the predominant vehicles through which new investors could obtain hotel ownership. Marriott, for example, started divesting real-estate assets in October 1993 (Host Marriott 1994 annual report), a move that was soon followed by most of the major international hotel corporations.

The asset light strategy has enabled lodging corporations to grow their portfolios primarily through franchise and management contracts, and in certain regions, leases. In this setting, most of the properties that a hotel corporation manages are owned by other entities. A general absence of real estate ownership signifies that new imperatives drive the performance of hotel corporations. Hotel corporations' successful execution of an asset light strategy hinges to a large extent on their ability to carefully select hotel partners who have specific characteristics and who are willing to sign new franchise and management contracts. In other words, the partnership that hotel corporations (and their relevant chains) establish with hotel owners (i.e., partners) becomes an essential element of their successful expansion and performance.

Selection of a partner that will work hand-in-hand with a hotel corporation to ensure success at the property level is a complex endeavour and entails balancing the interests of both the partner and chain and aligning these to each property's specificities. This fine balance defines the performance and success of hotel chains' pursuit of an asset light strategy. As such, a key driver of success for hotel corporations is the ability to assess the potential of a prospective partner's property and evaluate the likelihood of a successful relationship with the partner. Hotel chains put in place several mechanisms to manage such assessments, which include reliance on brand standards, use of contractual clauses that secure equilibrium, and ensuring that the fundamentals of tourism and hotel operations are well established in the hotel project itself. Each of these fundamental aspects is discussed in this chapter. The remainder of this chapter is structured as follows. There are two main sections. First, there is an overview of operating models in which partner selection is critical, the focus being on franchise and management contracts. The second section presents the selection process, looking at the extent of partners' alignment with brand, alignment with actions and general negotiation.

Operating models

On an international basis, six major foreign market entry methods favoured by hotel corporations include wholly-owned, joint venture, strategic alliance, licensing or franchising, management contracts, or consortia (Athiyaman and Go, 2003). Hotel corporations' adoption of an asset light strategy has seen a growing trend towards the use of non-equity modes, predominantly the franchise and management contract (Clarke and Chen, 2007). Regional differences are apparent regarding the popularity of these two entry modes, which can depend on partner profiles and the state of the tourism industry. Franchise contracts, for example, are more common in mature hotel markets, such as the US. In Europe, management contracts are beginning to replace the more traditional leases, except in specific areas such as Germany and the Nordic countries. In fact, differences in the type of contracts signed vary across partner profiles. The objective and purpose of institutional partners such as insurance companies vary from those of REITs or individual partners and this variability defines the nature of contracts that a hotel chain signs (Turner and Guilding, 2014). Diversity in the profile and aspirations of possible partners creates a complex setting for decision-making, whereby the selection and negotiation process with the partner hotel becomes essential for the success of hotel chains.

Franchise

Hotel franchising is defined as an arrangement where:

> For a fee, an independent hotel adopts the franchiser's name and trademarks and receives services in return, including the preparatory steps of feasibility, site selection, financing, design, and planning.
>
> (Garcia-Falcon and Medina-Munoz, 1999: 106)

Franchising is a popular approach among previously independently owned and operated hotels, because benefits of being part of a chain can be accessed through adoption of a hotel corporation's brand name, trademarks and services, yet partners are able to retain operational control. The median franchise cost in the US is 12 per cent of room revenue (HVS, 2014). Despite this relatively high cost, studies (e.g. Fladmoe-Lindquist and Laurent, 1995; Moon and Sharma, 2014) demonstrate that in both developed and emerging markets, conditions favour hotels that use franchising arrangements as opposed to wholly owned and managed structures due to the expert know-how of hotel chains and their expansive customer base. Hotel franchises are, however, still relatively uncommon in parts of Asia, perhaps due to hotel corporations' perceived fear of handing operational control to their partner amid somewhat uncertain legal environments.

Requirements for selection of a successful franchise hotel partner

A successful franchise contract is one where both the hotel chain and the hotel partner each achieve their expected financial benefits and relevant strategic objectives. For that purpose, the selection process needs to include assessment of the degree of alignment between the interests of the hotel chain and the hotel partner. The extensive use of franchising by hotel chains stems largely from a wide and important range of benefits it provides for them, which include: (1) less capital required for expansion relative to the owner-operator structure (Go and Christensen, 1989); (2) access to the benefits of internationalisation with less risk than direct investment (Aydin and Kacker, 1990); (3) the ability to expand throughout a large geographical area without high parent company costs (Go and Pine, 1995); and (4) the provision of a more stable cash flow compared to the management contract (Madanoglu and Olsen, 2005).

In order to maximise the benefits of franchising, hotel chains need to constantly strive to increase the value of their brand as it is this value that franchisees largely seek access to, along with operational and managerial support. Stemming from this is the main disadvantage of the franchise arrangement, the incidence of agency issues because the day-to-day operations of the hotel are largely delegated to the franchisee partner. As a result, hotel chains must ensure that their partner respects trademarked standard operating procedures and is able to execute the brand's promise. If this does not occur, it can have a detrimental effect on the chain's brand value as it loses coherence and meaning for customers. To overcome such problems, the hotel chain can implement careful governance mechanisms but these can become expensive (Singh et al., 2004). Nevertheless, both the hotel chain and the hotel partner need the brand to develop in order to support their objectives. It is therefore vital that both parties protect the brand and its standards.

Hotel chains' selection of hotel partners for franchising can therefore be reduced to two fundamentals. First, partners (i.e., future franchisees) must present solid financial capabilities that allow them to support the opening and ongoing operation of the hotel property including periodic capital expenditure to maintain brand standards. This entails screening the partner's ability to either raise capital or to have liquid capital on-hand. It is similarly important that maintenance of brand standards is outlined in a legally binding contractual form. Second, the hotel chain needs to ensure that the partner has managerial and operational capabilities suitable for operating the hotel. For that purpose, the hotel chain can either select partners with experience in hotel operations, or propose a supporting network to assist franchisees in their operations. In this case, hotel chains can offer training or headquarter processes to assist management of the unit (e.g. accounting and reporting tools).

Management contracts

The separation of ownership and management which results from use of a hotel management contract is becoming more widespread and is one of the driving mechanisms for the rapid internationalisation of the hotel industry (Slattery, 2012). A management contract is defined as:

> a written agreement between the owner [i.e., partner] of a hotel and an operator [i.e., hotel corporation through their hotel chain], by which the operator is appointed to operate and manage the hotel in the name, on behalf of and for the account of the owner and the operator is to receive a management fee in return.
>
> (Schlup, 2004: 23)

Much of the reason for the popularity of management contracts is that hotels are expensive to build, are highly leveraged, and require an advanced level of knowledge and technology in marketing and professional management to operate effectively. The expertise required to operate a large hotel is more readily available in such an arrangement (deRoos, 2010). Management contracts enable hotel owners to derive the benefits of owning a hotel without the requirement of having to operate it. The proliferation of such contracts has seen the establishment of many global hotel chains pursuing an asset light strategy and the disappearance of some domestic local hotel chains (Cai and Perry-Hobson, 2004).

Requirements for selection of a successful management contract hotel partner

A hotel corporation's objectives when signing a management contract are twofold. First, they continually strive to increase the value of their brand(s) and the longevity of their management contracts so that they can increase their ability to secure new management contracts and increase the number of rooms in their network (Beals and Denton, 2005). With regard to the incentive to maximise their brand's value, it is notable that a large proportion of a typical hotel corporation's assets are comprised of goodwill associated with their hotel chain's brand name(s) (Dev et al., 1995). Second, a hotel corporation's operational remuneration is widely referred to as a 'management fee' and thus hotel chains target a substantial level of cash-flow streams from each property through these management fees.

Three basic management fee structures are found in practice: (1) a base fee only; (2) an incentive fee only; or (3) a base fee combined with an incentive fee (Goddard and Standish-Wilkinson, 2002). The combination of a base and incentive fee is the most common. Hotel chains commonly face a trade-off between supporting the development of their brand versus increasing the management fee collected. For example, within the context of the capital expenditure decision-making process, a proposed expenditure may have a negative impact on profit, thereby potentially reducing the hotel chain's management fee but the chain may still support the expenditure if the benefit to their brand is perceived to outweigh any potential management fee reduction (Turner and Guilding, 2010b).

An important advantage hotel chains derive from use of management contracts relative to franchise contracts is the ability to gain control over the hotel's day-to-day operations. As a result, this eliminates any need for the hotel partner to have managerial and/or operational capability suitable for operating a hotel. A much larger pool of potential hotel partners can therefore be accessed. Nowadays, however, many partners realise that their own interests and those of the hotel chain could diverge. Partners are therefore increasingly employing asset managers to closely monitor the hotel chain's management of their property (Armitstead, 2004). Hotel chains need to be mindful of this and ensure that they select a hotel partner who will not resort to overly restrictive monitoring to the point that they can no longer make the operational and capital expenditure decisions they feel are necessary. At the same time, and as in the franchising arrangement, there is an important need for hotel chains to ensure that hotel partners have solid financial resources so that brand standards can be upheld. Given the predominant importance of ongoing capital expenditure in maintaining brand standards, as a further safeguard the majority of management contracts require hotel partners to establish a reserve for the replacement of furniture, fittings and equipment (FF&E) set at approximately 3 per cent of annual turnover (Turner and Guilding, 2010a). The hotel chain typically administers expenditure from this reserve account. Nevertheless, the FF&E reserve account is about 40 per cent underfunded (Turner and Guilding, 2010a) relative to the true cost of all capital expenditure required to maintain brand standards so it is imperative that hotel chains sign with a partner that understands and supports their brand strategy.

The selection process of hotel chains

A hotel chain's selection of a hotel partner is a complex process that involves an intricate set of tangible and intangible aspects (Altinay, 2006; Ivanova and Ivanov, 2015). It involves an assessment of the property's financial projections as well as the human dynamics that will take place over the length of the contract. In other words, it entails the evaluation of a set of task-related criteria such as the location and the design of the building along with partner-related criteria such as the financial abilities of the partner (Altinay, 2006; Geringer, 1991; Ivanova and Ivanov, 2015). Table 17.1 presents a list of these hotel chain selection criteria.

Three fundamental components shape this multi-dimensional process (Altinay, 2006; Ghorbal-Blal, 2011; Ivanova and Ivanov, 2015), which have a bearing on the extent to which the interests of both parties are aligned. Each, however, addresses these issues from different perspectives. First, the partner's property must align with the hotel chain's strategic imperatives for its brand, which includes the relative fit between location, physical layout, employees, brand standards and objectives. Second, it consists of estimating trade-offs during the contract negotiation phase required to unite the interests of each party. Finally, the selection process needs to consider the mechanisms of alignment of both parties' actions throughout the duration of the contract. Figure 17.1 illustrates this process and the three issues are examined below.

Table 17.1 Hotel chain selection criteria of a hotel partner

Task-related criteria	Partner-related criteria
• Location of the property	• Property's past financial performance
• Accessibility	• Property's track record in the local community
• Characteristics and conditions of building facilities	• Ownership of the property and land
• Possibility of adaptation to chain's brand standards	• Financial stability of the partner
• Experience of employees	• Feasibility study
• Qualification of managers	

Source: Adapted from Altinay (2006); Blal (2013); Ivanova and Ivanov (2015).

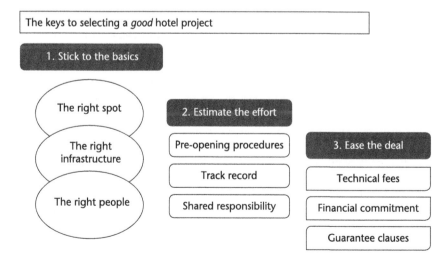

Figure 17.1 Hotel chain selection of a hotel partner.

Source: Blal (2013).

Alignment with the brand

Brand standards

Hotel chains' franchise and management contracts typically include a clause on brand standards. This clause serves two objectives. First, it details the tangible elements that support the implementation and delivery of the hotel chain's brand promise to the hotel property's guests. Every hotel chain has a detailed description of how to execute its brand standards which include specific criteria that the chain requires the partner to implement at the property level. For example, an essential brand standard is the number of rooms the property must have. Some brands revolve around the concept of intimacy or uniqueness and therefore need a smaller number of rooms. New boutique hotel concepts, for instance, usually require less than 200 rooms (Balekjian and Sarheim, 2011). Other brands cater to large tourism destinations and can therefore host more guests such as hotels on the Las Vegas strip or large resorts in popular destinations around the world. Brand standards often also include design and architectural layouts with specific description of space required. They also stipulate the number of restaurants or other outlets, the type of amenities that should be offered and other features that would ensure coherence of the brand for hotel guests across the chain's different properties. This aspect of brand standards is enforced in the case of management contracts to ensure that the owner will invest in these tangible elements, thus securing both the brand and hotel's long-term success. In the case of franchise agreements, the brand standard clause extends to operating standards. These include components that ensure the day-to-day handling of the brand and its operations. Brand standards are essential for hotel chains (franchisers) to ensure consistency and quality of their brand across the network they serve as the control for both task and partner-related criteria.

Selecting the location

The hotel industry's most recognisable quote 'location, location, location' applies because site selection is a primary criterion that a hotel chain considers when deciding upon a hotel partner. It is a fundamental task-related criterion (Ivanova and Ivanov, 2015). Here, it is a matter of selecting a partner with a property in a location that aligns with the needs of the customer base of the brand(s) the hotel corporation is developing. A misfit between the brand and the location of the property is a great risk for both the hotel chain and the partner because it will likely hinder the property's potential to attract the target market(s). The purpose of 'flagging' a property is to attract the brand's customer base. Therefore, alignment between the location and selected brand is a precondition in partner selection. In this step the chain's managers evaluate the hotel's destination attractiveness to the brand's customer base as well as the degree of exposure of the brand(s) to its customer base. This assessment includes a first study of proximity to economic activity, commercial synergies and the overall potential of the tourism destination where the hotel is located. Estimates of the degree of brand competitiveness and potential synergies among the chain's existing brands in the targeted destination are also considered in this first screening. Common practice in the industry when selecting a hotel partner is to conduct feasibility studies for the future property (Hodari and Samson, 2014). Whether conducted externally by an independent consultant, or internally within the chain, these evaluations forecast the main operational drivers (i.e., rates, occupancy, F&B revenues, operating costs) in order to assess the potential fit between the property and a specific brand, the brand and location, as well as to compare the hotel's expected return against the chain's objectives for the brand. It also allows the chain to better define the necessary infrastructure which would best support the brand in this particular property and location.

Selecting the infrastructure

Brand standards stipulate components that comprise the hotel's infrastructure. In particular, they define the total number of rooms in the hotel/project, size of the plot and room size for the business's lodging aspect. For the other part of the operations, the chain's standards also determine the number and size of restaurants and auxiliary service outlets (e.g., SPA, shop, etc.). Once the chain has assessed the property's location and infrastructure, the selection process next consists of assessing the alignment between the partner's view of these points and its disposition to support the hotel chain in implementing them. In the case of a management contract, the hotel chain focuses on ensuring that the physical layout will be financed by the partner and maintained throughout the contract. In the context of a franchise agreement, it will enforce these during the first stages and ensure that they are maintained throughout the duration of the agreement.

Selecting the people

Estimating the costs associated with hiring and training staff in a location with adequate local resources constitutes the third step for ensuring alignment between a partner's property and hotel chain's brand (Fladmoe-Lindquist and Laurent, 1995). At this stage of the selection process, both the hotel chain and its partner have access to local human resources which can implement the brand's standards. In this context, the level of experience in the destination of either the hotel chain or the partner, as well as the knowledge of operations in the destination, are valuable inputs in the contracting process. Any difficulty in recruiting and employing personnel presents a risk for the success of the property in terms of both the hotel chain and its partner. Furthermore, when signing a franchise, the hotel chain needs to select a partner who not only has the required entrepreneurial skills but also the necessary operational competencies (Altinay, 2006). For the latter requirement, the partner (franchisee) can hire a manager who already has the necessary hotel know-how, or who can rely on the hotel chain's (franchiser) support to develop their personal capabilities in this regard. In any case, the hotel chain needs to ensure the partner's commitment to operate the brand as it has been developed. In the case of a management contract, the challenge resides in the capacity of the hotel chain to select, hire, and train employees in the location as they are responsible for executing the brand under their own control.

Alignment of actions

Pre-opening procedures

Just as a hotel chain can sign a management contract or franchise agreement for a new hotel, they often also sign these with existing properties. In mature markets such as the US, 'reflagging' or signing contracts for new brands with an already existing property is in fact the most common practice (Lomanno, 2006). In either case, alignment of interests between the partner and the hotel chain needs to occur during the period before re-flagging or the first opening of the hotel. Any modification to the settled pre-opening procedures of the corporation affects the hotel's likelihood for success. At this stage, it is a matter of assessing the level of effort (or costs) that their company will engage in during the pre-opening stage to align the hotel project with the hotel chain's requirements. In particular, the number of months prior to opening, but most importantly the degree of advancement of the project or works to adapt to the new brand standard is an essential estimate. The earlier a hotel corporation intervenes in the construction of the hotel, the higher the degree of compliance that the hotel project will achieve with one of the chains' brands and thus the lower the control efforts will need to be. Similarly, the closer the compliance of an existing property's brand standards with the new brand's standards, the easier the transition between brands will be for the hotel. Finally, if the pre-opening procedure allows the necessary time to hire the local expertise to operate the hotel, or gain knowledge of the destination, it will increase the likelihood that the collaboration will succeed. In any case, the selection needs to include an assessment of the partner's level of expertise and past experience. Similarly, the willingness of the partner to comply with the brand standards is assessed at this stage. This is a subjective element in the process that requires the ability to assess human potential and manage interpersonal dynamics (Altinay, 2005, 2006; Ghorbal-Blal, 2011). In the case of a management contract, the hotel chain needs to ensure that the owner will provide the sufficient financial and structural support for the hotel chain to operate the property. In franchise agreements, this implies that hotel chains need to focus on selecting partners who will manage and protect their brand standards.

Shared responsibility between the hotel chain and hotel partner

As important as due diligence or estimation of future revenues generated by the property, agreement between the chain and partner regarding roles and responsibilities is essential in a chains' selection of a hotel partner. This choice is intangible and consists of an evaluation of convergence between the chain's expectations and those of the partner. For instance, the discussion about alignment of interests and responsibility in terms of numbers (i.e., expected return, forecasted margins) and time line (i.e., short-term or long-term focus) for each partner are tangible elements that constitute part of the selection process. Intangibles such as estimation of a partner's commitment to the agreement and their willingness to comply with responsibilities stipulated in the contract when needed are associated with interpersonal and human competency. The greater the divergence between the chain and partner's objectives, the more likely it will be that additional efforts will be required to ensure the contract's success. The vast variety of owner types and personalities exacerbate this step's subjective and intangible aspects. Each partner presents a different profile, personality, history and set of objectives (Turner and Guilding, 2014). Any divergence between the interests and the views of the hotel chain and its partner can have an effect on capital spending decisions, which have a profound impact on the performance of the brand and the individual property. This aspect adds a new complexity to the selection process, since the individuality of each partner property and its potential as a hotel need to be taken into consideration along with the individual dynamics.

The negotiation

The signed franchise, lease, or management contract is a reflection of the relative bargaining power between the hotel chain and its partner. A balanced contract, whether management, franchise or lease, reflects an alignment of interests and commitment of both parties to the property's successful management. Uneven clauses favouring one party over the other will affect the relationship and hotel performance. There are nevertheless several contractual elements that a hotel chain needs to negotiate in order to mitigate expansion risk and secure successful implementation of an asset light strategy. Below is a short selection of the contractual elements that help balance a partnership during the negotiation stage of the selection process.

Impact and areas of protection

A clause defining where and when the hotel chain can open a new hotel is usually included in management and franchise contracts. Such a clause covers the impact issue, which occurs when a hotel chain opens a new property that competes with the existing one and takes away its business. Areas of protection can guard the partner from cannibalisation by other units of the hotel chain. But if they are too restrictive, they can prevent the growth of the brand, which in turn can harm both the chain and the partner.

Technical and pre-opening fees

This aspect of the negotiation is specific to management contracts, which typically include a 'technical and pre-opening fees' clause. This pertains to the level of support that the hotel chain will provide to the partner when aligning the property to brand standards. A hotel chain's bargaining power in the deal often determines technical fees attached to the contract. When the power of a hotel chain is low, particularly when chains are in the early stages of development (typically, in the case of a new market), this effort is often assumed by the chain.

Financial commitment

Concession of equity or assets or any form of investment by a hotel corporation in a deal is rare in an industry where companies seek to adopt an asset light strategy. Nevertheless, if the hotel project scores highly in terms of requiring a low level of effort to include it in the network and it conforms to the chain's set of objectives for the particular destination, then the corporation may concede some form of financial commitment. In the case of a franchise agreement, if the contract involves, for instance, a master franchise which sustains expansion goals of the chain, financial commitment can be considered. These special cases require involvement and approval of senior managers at the hotel chain's corporate parent. Financial concession of this kind also implies further effort in terms of control of operations by the hotel chain. This practice is often applied in primary markets which are highly sought-after by most hotel chains due to their strategic importance.

Termination

Management contracts often include performance guarantee clauses to ensure that the hotel chain operates the hotel at the highest possible performance level. Such guarantees can in-crease the alignment of the hotel chain's interests and goals with those of the hotel partner under a management contract. In these cases, the partner's priority clauses or some other sort of earning guarantees are conceded by the hotel chain to the partner to ensure convergence of their efforts and actions. In the case of franchise contracts, termination is attached in connection with the partner's respect of brand standards. But like any other clause within a franchise or a management contract, this tangible element is not the panacea for a successful partnership (Turner and Guilding, 2010b) as unplanned difficulties due to misfit of cultures and personalities must also be managed.

Conclusion

The selection of hotel partner is a complex process for hotel chain executives as each property pertains to a different context with unique challenges. It consists of balancing the operating and strategic imperatives of the hotel chain with the unique profile of the property and partner(s). It thus requires a mix of hotel operating expertise and skills in managing human dynamics. At the heart of this balance are brand standards that ensure execution of expansion strategies of hotel chains through its agreements with its partners.

References

Altinay, L. (2005) The intrapreneur role of the development directors in an international hotel group. *The Service Industries Journal*, 25(3), 403–19.

Altinay, L. (2006) Selecting partners in an international franchise organisation. *International Journal of Hospitality Management*, 25(1), 108–28.

Armitstead, M. (2004) Hotel management and operations options: Intellectual capital versus financial capital. *Journal of Retail & Leisure Property*, 3(4), 299–307.

Athiyaman, A. and Go, F. (2003) Strategic choices in the international hospitality industry. In B. Brotherton (ed.), *The International Hospitality Industry*. Oxford: Butterworth-Heinemann, pp. 142–60.

Aydin, N. and Kacker, M. (1990) International outlook of US-based franchisers. *International Marketing Review*, 7(2), 45–53.

Balekjian, C. and Sarheim, L. (2011) Boutique hotels segment: the challenge of standing out from the crowd. Online. Available HTTP: <http://www.hvs.com/Content/3171.pdf>, accessed 14 October 2014.

Beals, P. and Denton, G.A. (2005) The current balance of power in North American hotel management contracts. *Journal of Retail and Leisure Property*, 4(2), 129–46.

Blal, I. (2013) How hotel developers make expansion strategies happen. *Hospitality Insight*, 5. Online. Available HTTP: <http://www.ehl.edu/eng/Faculty-Research/Research/Publications/Hospitality-Insight>, accessed 20 October 2014.

Blal, I. and Graf, N.S. (2013) The discount effect of non-normative physical characteristics on the price of lodging properties. *International Journal of Hospitality Management*, 34, 413–22.

Cai, L.A. and Perry-Hobson, J.S. (2004) Making hotel brands work in a competitive environment. *Journal of Vacation Marketing*, 10(3), 197–209.

Clarke, A. and Chen, W. (2007) *International Hospitality Management: Concepts and Cases*. Burlington, MA: Elsevier.

deRoos, J.A. (2010) Hotel management contracts: past and present. *Cornell Hospitality Quarterly*, 51(1), 68–80.

Dev, C.S., Morgan, M.S. and Shoemaker, S. (1995) A positioning analysis of hotel brands: based on travel-manager perceptions. *Cornell Hotel and Restaurant Administration Quarterly*, 36(6), 48.

Fladmoe-Lindquist, K. and Laurent, L.J. (1995) Control modes in international service operations: the propensity to franchise. *Management Science*, 41(7), 1238–49.

Garcia-Falcon, J.M. and Medina-Munoz, D. (1999) The relationship between hotel companies and travel agencies: an empirical assessment of the United States market. *The Service Industries Journal*, 19(4), 102–23.

Geringer, J.M. (1991) Strategic determinations of partner selection criteria in international joint venture. *Journal of International Business Studies*, 22(1), 41–61.

Ghorbal-Blal, I. (2011) The role of middle management in the execution of expansion strategies: the case of developers' selection of hotel projects. *International Journal of Hospitality Management*, 30(2), 272–82.

Go, F. and Christensen, J. (1989) Going global. *Cornell Hotel and Restaurant Administration Quarterly*, 30(3), 72–79.

Go, F. and Pine, R. (1995) *Globalization in the Hotel Industry*. London: Routledge.

Goddard, P. and Standish-Wilkinson, G. (2002) Hotel management contract trends in the Middle East. *Journal of Retail and Leisure Property*, 2(1), 66–71.

Hodari, D. and Samson, D. (2014) Settling for less. The institutionalization of the hotel feasibility study. *Journal of Hospitality Financial Management*, 22(2), 97–110.

Host Marriott (1995) 1994 Annual Report. Online. Available HTTP: <https://www.sec.gov/Archives/edgar/data/314733/0000950109-94-000600.txt>, accessed 5 February 2015.

HVS (2014) 2014 United States Hotel Franchise Fee Guide. Online. Available HTTP: <http://www.hvs.com/article/7097/2014-united-states-hotel-franchise-fee-guide/?campaign=email>, accessed 22 October 2014.

Ivanova, M. and Ivanov, S. (2015) Affiliation to hotel chains: requirements towards hotels in Bulgaria. *Journal of Hospitality Marketing & Management*, 24(6), 601–08.

Larkin, D. and Lam, C. (2007) Hotels: the fifth food group? *Journal of Retail & Leisure Property*, 6(1), 23–28.

Lomanno, M.V. (2006) Significant portion of industry involved in conversion activity. *Hotels and Motel Management*, 221(18), 14.

Madanoglu, M. and Olsen, M. (2005) Toward a resolution of the cost of equity conundrum in the lodging industry: a conceptual framework. *International Journal of Hospitality Management*, 24, 493–515.

Moon, J. and Sharma, A. (2014) Franchising effects on the lodging industry: optimal franchising proportion in terms of profitablity and intangible value. *Tourism Economics*, 20, 1027–145.

Schlup, R. (2004) Hotel management agreements: balancing the interests of owners and operators. *Journal of Retail and Leisure Property*, 3(4), 331–43.

Singh, A.J., Schmidgall, R.S. and Beals, P. (2004) A survey of community banker attitudes toward hotel feasibility studies. *The RMA Journal*, 86(7), 54–58.

Slattery, P. (2012) *The Economic Ascent of The Hotel Business*. Oxford: Goodfellow Publishers.

Sohn, J., Tang, C.H.H. and Jang, S.S. (2013) Does the asset-light and fee-oriented strategy create value? *International Journal of Hospitality Management*, 32, 270–77.

Turner, M.J. and Guilding, C. (2010a) Accounting for the furniture, fittings & equipment reserve in hotels. *Accounting and Finance*, 50(4), 967–92.

Turner, M.J. and Guilding, C. (2010b) Hotel management contracts and deficiencies in owner-operator capital expenditure goal congruency. *Journal of Hospitality and Tourism Research*, 34(4), 478–511.

Turner, M.J. and Guilding, C. (2014) An investigation of Australian and New Zealand hotel ownership. *Journal of Hospitality and Tourism Management*, 21, 76–89.

Section III
Strategic and operational management of hotel chains

Section III consists of 14 chapters dealing with strategic and operational management issues of hotel chains. In Chapter 18 Yumi Lim discusses the brand management of hotel chains. The author acknowledges that branding has been a major marketing tool in hotel chain management. Hotel chains have benefited from branding in their product, price, communication and channel-related marketing activities. As growth platforms of brands, brand extensions have been influential areas in marketing. An explosion of brand extensions in hotel chain management occurred in the 1990s. Hotel chains have adapted vertical brand extension strategies by extending their product line to various price and quality level brands. In addition, brand trust and brand loyalty have been important constructs in the marketing literature. The author finds that brand trust has an impact on brand loyalty. In addition, brand loyalty is positively related to brand extensions in hotel chain management.

In Chapter 19 Sjoerd Gehrels analyses the case of a successful well-known international European hotel corporation, starting with the history and development of the company. Next, ongoing changes in brand promise and the further developing of the brand are explored. The internal employer brand is compared with the external brand and improvements are discussed to facilitate a better alignment. Progression into an employment brand is explained as well as the connected diversity strategy for the company. Finally, considerations about how a diversity strategy implementation will impact the viability and business success of the company are shared.

In Chapter 20 Melissa Baker focuses on customer experience management in hotel chains. Managing customer experiences in hotel chains is critical as it relies not only on the individual hotel property, but incorporates all of the experience components at all the hotel properties within the chain. This chapter provides a literature review, current hotel chain examples, and managerial suggestions for managing customer experiences. First, the chapter discusses why it is critical to consider all of the touch points in the stages of experience: pre-arrival, arrival, occupancy, departure, and post-departure. Second, given the high amount of interaction between hotel personnel and customers this chapter discusses the importance of communicating the brand message through interpersonal and non-verbal communication. Third, as service recovery is important in managing customer experiences the chapter discusses service failure, recovery, and managing customer justice perceptions. Lastly, given the increase in online experiences with hotel customers, this chapter discusses how to manage online experiences more effectively.

Distribution channel management is the focal point of Chapter 21 by Peter O'Connor. With electronic distribution becoming an essential part of successfully running a hotel, facilitating this increasingly complex portfolio of routes to the marketplace has become one of the key value-adding activities of a hotel chain with owners and franchisees alike increasingly examining the proportion of business delivered through controlled routes as one of their critical hotel chain selection and evaluation criteria. This chapter traces the growing importance of electronic distribution in the hotel chain–owner relationship, examining many of the challenges currently being faced by chains in managing this increasingly complex environment. In particular the issues of access to world class technology, availability of expertise on distribution issues, superior negotiating power and ability to more fully leverage customer data advantage of working with a hotel chain are debated, with how participation in a chain allows hotels to more effectively play the distribution game highlighted.

Chapter 22 by Aurelio Mauri deals with pricing and revenue management, which are nowadays two crucial subjects for hotel chains. In the current business environment, characterised by increasing digitalisation, globalisation and tougher competition, price has augmented its central role. While traditional approaches are commonly based on costs, in recent years academics and practitioners have highlighted the relevance of value perceptions by customers (value-based pricing). As a result, differential pricing, also known as price discrimination, has been more and more utilised, as it is an effective means that permits sellers to improve corporate profits and to reduce consumer surplus. Revenue management is presented as a collection of coordinated techniques and practices, strictly connected to pricing, utilised for increasing profitability, centrally in service activities. It is analysed as an articulated business process composed by a set of decisions and activities like demand modelling, segmentation, customer profiling, demand forecasting, capacity allocation, and pricing optimisation. Specific revenue management challenges faced by hotel chains are also elaborated.

Chapter 23 by Vladimir Zhechev encompasses the most essential concepts related to integrated marketing communications of hotel chains and delivers contemporary examples of their manifestations. It provides an original conceptual model exhibiting not only the design of integrated marketing communications for hotel chains, but also putting the various communication tools into critical discussion. The chapter also highlights vital metrics for assessing the efficiency and effectiveness of hotel chains' online presence as it is critically important for any promotional undertaking. It also presents the steps for effective marketing communications and addresses fundamental issues related to positioning/repositioning and levels of integrated marketing communications design for hotel chains.

Chapter 24 by Haywantee Ramkissoon and Felix Mavondo is dedicated to customer relationship management in hotel chains. This empirical study bridges the gap in literature by examining the differences between managers' and customers' perceived value across different categories of chain hotels. Findings suggest that managers of different classes of hotels significantly differ in the level of value they perceive they deliver to their customers. Further, a comparison between managers and customers at the same hotels shows that managers across all classes of hotels think they are offering superior customer value but their customers receive much lower value. Findings have implications for alignment, investment and profitability of the organisations. The theoretical and practical relevance are discussed.

Chapter 25 by Vincent Magnini and Carol Simon discusses how hotel chains foster service quality through a focus on employee development and performance. This chapter provides a review of how hotel chains go about fostering cultures in hotels in which high levels of service quality are consistently provided at the frontline. In doing so, this chapter compartmentalises strategies in the following three stages: 1) The pre-training stage entails recruiting and selecting frontline associates who are capable of performing at high levels. 2) The training stage involves arming the frontline associates with the knowledge and skills to deliver top-rate service. 3) The post-training stage encompasses engendering a culture on an ongoing basis in which associates have both the ability and the motivation to deliver high quality experiences for guests.

The purpose of Chapter 26 by Cherylynn Becker and Wei Wang is to introduce the core concepts associated with developing and maintaining a culturally aware workforce in today's global environment. The chapter is organised to address the following concerns: (1) the identification and descriptors associated with the values specific to the major and dominant cultural perspectives: individualism/collectivism, power/distance, uncertainty avoidance, masculinity/femininity, and long-term/short-term orientation; (2) the identification of employment classifications associated with a multi-cultural workforce; (3) the human resource interventions or activities specifically oriented towards effective management of a culturally diverse workforce.

Chapter 27 by Fernando José Garrigós Simón, Yeamduan Narangajavana and Roberto Llorente analyses the management of information systems in hotel chains. In order to do this, the chapter addresses five elements. First, it concentrates on the applications which are useful for the different functions in the organisation. Second, it looks for the connections between the different parts of the organisation, mainly through Enterprise Resource Planning (ERP) systems, focusing on the interchange of data between the functions and the central databases. Third, the chapter emphasises the relevance of the supply chain management and the connections with suppliers. Next, the chapter analyses diverse mechanisms of connections with customers and other stakeholders, through the use of customer relationship management systems or other more evolved systems related to Web 3.0 and the techniques of crowdsourcing. Finally, the chapter highlights the future implementation of new technologies which are being developed at present and may be adopted by hotel chains.

Chapter 28 by Liliya Terzieva elaborates the financial management issues in hotel chains. To survive and thrive in such fast-changing times, hotel chains recognise the necessity to transform their way of thinking and acting, where finance is not an exception. The modern hotel financial management is in the core of hotel management, closely related to all departments, and each link involves capital flow, from purchasing to processing, selling, financial collection, and then back to purchasing.

Chapter 29 by Vivien Ulu and Dirisa Mulindwa provides an analysis of legal issues in chain hotels' relationships with focus on the grievances that arise from hotel management contracts. In the wake of growing legal disputes concerning hotel management contracts, particularly from the USA, and given the global nature of the hotel industry, it is imperative to investigate the legal relationship between hotel chain operators and hotel owners. The chapter examines the nature of terms of hotel management contracts, drawing on the experiences of hospitality legal practitioners and decided cases to provide a needed reality check on the legal issues and to identify the challenges ahead. Rights and liabilities arising from hotel management agreements are explored, in particular from the law of agency and fiduciary duties. The chapter offers an analysis of the current legal position of hotel management agreements based on decided cases and considers the future of hotel management agreements as a viable business model given fears within the industry that recent court decisions will undermine the viability of the model.

Chapter 30 by Carlos Pestana Barros and Luiz Pinto Machado evaluates the productivity in the ENATUR hotel chain (the National Tourism Company in Portugal) from 2000 to 2013 with a DEA-Data Envelopment Analysis model. A comparative analysis is made and policy implications are derived.

In the last chapter in the section (Chapter 31), Manuel Becerra, Rosario Silva and Oksana Gerwe investigate room prices and profits in a large sample of hotels in Spain from 2004 to 2008. The results show that hotels that are part of a hotel company charge higher prices than independent hotels, which is ultimately associated with greater profits per room. Furthermore, this effect is generally greater for chain hotels, i.e., company hotels that actually share the same brand, which charge higher prices than company-managed hotels that do not use a company's brand. The authors argue that these results are due to a combination of internal factors (e.g., economies of scale and knowledge management) as well as external factors (e.g., market power and brand equity) associated with hotel chain management.

18

Brand management of hotel chains

Yumi Lim

(SOUTHWEST MINNESOTA STATE UNIVERSITY, USA)

Introduction

Branding has been a major marketing tool in the last decade, as it has been considered one of the most valuable intangible assets a firm possesses (Keller and Lehmann, 2006). Several definitions exist for a brand. Kotler (2000) defined a brand as 'name, term, sign, or combination of them intended to identify the goods and services of one seller or group of sellers and/or differentiate them from those of the competition' (p. 404). Aaker's definition (1991) of a brand has been accepted widely. He defined the function of a brand as 'to identify the goods or services whether of one seller or a group of sellers and to differentiate those goods or services from those of competitors' (p.7). Further, a brand for a new product is shaped by creating a new name, logo, or symbol and as a result of this it receives 'awareness, reputation, and prominence in the marketplace' (Keller, 2002). As hotel chains, they create their brands and consistently monitor and update their brands. In 2009, Hilton Corporation changed its name and logo from 'Hilton Hotels' to 'Hilton Worldwide' in order to symbolise Hilton's market diversification to the East Coast from the West Coast, and its overseas growth.

Branding research has also been applied to the area of services. De Chernatony and Riley (1998) investigated the definition and principles of services branding with experts' views. They suggested services branding shared common principles with those of products at the conceptual level. However, the method of displaying specific elements of service brands might be different from product brands at the operational level due to the unique characteristics of intangibility, inseparability of production and consumption, heterogeneity, and perishability. In services literature, a brand is interpreted as and considered to be a promise (Ambler and Styles, 1996; Berry, 2000). While the branding concept has been defined in the fields of products and services, there has been a lack of consistent understanding of the concept of brand by hotel industry executives and academics (Olsen et al., 2005). In other words, there is no industry-wide consensus on the definition of a brand. Olsen et al. (2005) concluded that the concept of brand is too complex to be defined by one specific discipline. Topics of branding discussed in the hospitality field include the hotel-restaurant co-branding alliance (Ashton and Scott, 2011; Tasci and Guillet, 2011; Guillet and Tasci, 2010; Boo and Mattila, 2002), hotel brand equity (Tsang et al., 2011), internal branding (Punjaisri et al., 2009;

Hur and Adler, 2011), brand performance (O'Neill and Xiao, 2006), and the concept of brand (Olsen et al., 2005; Hanson et al., 2009).

Topics in branding

Major hotel chains are interested in optimising their brand portfolios to gain synergistic effects (Kwun, 2012). They have developed several brands and tried to maximise profits by utilising their brand portfolios. It is no surprise that giant hotel chains own a number of brands from less than ten brands like Hyatt and Starwood Hotels and Resorts Worldwide, to close to or more than 20 brands like Wyndham Worldwide and Marriott International. The trend of brand portfolios is expected to continue in a global setting. To a greater extent, major hotel chains have gone beyond standardisation for guests who are looking for experiential travel. As a result, the major hotel chains have launched luxury boutique hotels in the last decade (e.g. Aloft, Elements, Indigo, Edition, Andaz) (Kwun, 2012). Recently, Inter-Continental Hotels Group (IHG) completed its acquisition of Kimpton in early 2015. Kimpton is a well-known boutique hotel chain brand (Mangla, 2015). Overall, hotel chains continue to restructure their brand portfolios with their current brands and to develop more high-end and experiential brands (Kwun, 2012).

Topics in the area of branding research that have received attention are brand positioning, brand integration, brand-equity measurement, brand growth, and brand management (Keller and Lehmann, 2006). Brand positioning guides marketing activities and programmes in order to differentiate a brand from others and gain competitive superiority (Keller et al., 2002). It involves establishing key brand associations in the minds of customers. The roles of brand intangibles and corporate images are areas particularly relevant to positioning (Keller and Lehmann, 2006). Specifically, corporate image has been extensively studied (Biehal and Sheinin, 1998). Keller and Aaker (1992) stated corporate credibility is carried out when consumers believe that a company is able to deliver products and services that satisfy customer needs and wants (Erdem and Swait, 2004). Further, they suggested that with successfully introduced brand extensions, perceptions of corporate credibility can be enhanced and evaluations of dissimilar brand extensions can be improved. Research on brand integration suggested that synergistic results in branding and marketing activities could occur when branding and marketing activities work in combination. In other words, the effectiveness of branding marketing activities can be enhanced by integrating brand elements, integrating marketing channels and communications, and combining company-controlled and external events (Keller and Lehmann, 2006).

Benefits and effectiveness of branding

Branding techniques have been applied in the business world according to its benefits: product-related, price-related, communication-related, and channel-related effects (Keller, 2002). The product-related effects of a brand are related to consumer product evaluations, consumer confidence, perceptions of quality, and purchase rate positively related to a brand name. In other words, if consumers are well aware of a brand, their attitude and their purchase intention toward the brand are increased. The effect is considered a price-related effect when the brand leaders have higher priced positions and consumers have a lower level of price sensitivity toward those leaders. Communication-related effects refer to how the evaluation of brand advertising can be positively biased when consumers have positive feelings toward a brand which is well known and well liked. The effect of a well-known brand, which is most likely to have a competitive advantage in marketing activities, is channel-related. Branding tools influencing consumer behaviour include awareness, choice, use, satisfaction, recommendation, trust, and loyalty. They reduce information search costs and risk for consumers and deliver quality, value, promises, and lifestyle enhancement (Kotler and Armstrong, 1996; O'Cass and Grace, 2003). In other words, brands have influence on three primary levels: customer market, product market, and financial market (Keller and Lehmann, 2006).

Research on measuring brand effectiveness (e.g. short-term and long-term effects of advertising and promotion) has been extensively conducted. This research has often considered different outcomes and indicators (e.g. price promotion) of marketing effectiveness (Keller and Lehmann, 2006). Keller and Lehmann (2006) suggested little research on measuring customer mindsets as possible mediating or moderating variables in analysing marketing effectiveness had been examined. While few studies on measuring brand effectiveness have been performed, research on brand extensions as growth platforms of brands is one of the most heavily examined and influential areas in marketing (Czellar, 2003). Identifying key theoretical and managerial issues has been addressed and insights and guidance have been provided in academic studies in marketing (Keller and Lehmann, 2006).

Brand extension

Research on brand extension has investigated how firms should leverage brand equity (Keller, 2002). The definitions of brand extension have been suggested by many researchers (Rangaswamy et al., 1993; Swanminathan et al., 2001). Brand extension usually appears when a company uses its established brand names to introduce new products because brand extension strategies reduce advertising costs, barriers to entry, risks, and leverages brand equity (van Riel et al., 2001).

Brand extensions have two forms: horizontal and vertical. In a horizontal brand extension, an existing brand name is used when launching a new product, the category of which is completely new to a firm. In other words, consumers' judgment of the extension will be developed from the perceived difference between the brand's traditional category and the extension category (Kim and Lavack, 1996; Musante, 2007). On the other hand, a vertical brand extension refers to a brand extension strategy that consists of a new product being introduced in the same product category as the core brand, but at a different price point and quality level (Keller and Aaker, 1992; Sullivan, 1990). In other words, a brand extension product is introduced above (up-market), or below (down-market) traditional price points for the brand (Musante, 2007). Typically, the core brand name follows brand extension name to show the link between brand extension and the core brand name (e.g. Hilton Hotels, Hilton Garden Inn) (Kim and Lavack, 1996).

Studies on brand extension in hotel chain management

Many hotel companies have tried to benefit from their brands' goodwill through brand extension; most major hotels have at least one successful brand extension in their hotel chain strategy (Jiang et al., 2002). Quality Hotels (now Choice Hotels) extended its product line to Comfort Inns and Quality Royale (now Clarion) in 1981 and was one of the first examples of brand extension in the hospitality industry. An explosion of a brand extension in the hotel industry occurred in the 1990s. Holiday Inn introduced Holiday Inn Express and Holiday Inn SunSpree Resort in 1991 and the upscale Holiday Inn Crowne Plaza in 1993. Marriott introduced Courtyard by Marriott in 1983. Hilton announced its brand extension to the

Table 18.1 Brand extensions of major hotel brands

Brand	Brand extensions
Inter-Continental Hotel Group	Candlewood Suites, Crowne Plaza, Holiday Inn, Holiday Inn Express, Holiday Inn Club Vacations, Holiday Inn Resort, Hotel Indigo, Inter Continental, Staybridge Suites, HUALUXE Hotels and Resorts, Even Hotels
Wyndham Worldwide	Wyndham Hotels and Resorts, Wyndham Grand Collection, Wyndham Garden, TRYP by Wyndham, Ramada, Days Inn, Super 8, Wingate by Wyndham, Baymont Inn & Suites, Microtel Inns and Suites, Hawthorn Suites by Wyndham, Howard Johnson, Travelodge, Knights Inn, Wyndham Vacation Resorts, WorldMark by Wyndham, Dream Hotels, Planet Hollywood, Night Hotels, Baymont Inn & Suites
Marriott International, Inc.	Marriott Hotels & Resorts, JW Marriott Hotels & Resorts, Renaissance Hotels & Resorts, EDITION Hotels, Autograph Collection Hotels & Resorts, Courtyard by Marriott, Residence Inn by Marriott, Fairfield Inn & Suites by Marriott, Marriott Conference Centers, TownePlace Suites by Marriott, SpringHill Suites by Marriott, Marriott Vacation Club, The Ritz-Carlton Hotel Company, L.L.C., The Ritz-Carlton Destination Club, Marriott ExecuStay, Marriott Executive Apartments, Grand Residences by Marriott, Grand Residences Marriott, Marriott Executive Apartments, AC Hotels Marriott, Bulgari Hotels & Resorts
Hyatt	Park Hyatt, Andaz, Grand Hyatt, Hyatt Regency, Hyatt Place, Hyatt Summerfield Suites, Hyatt Resorts, Hyatt Residence Club, Hyatt House
Choice Hotels International, Inc.	Comfort Inn, Comfort Suites, Quality, Sleep Inn, Clarion, Cambria Suites, MainStay Suites, Suburban Extended Stay Hotel, Econo Lodge, Rodeway Inn, Ascend Collections
Hilton Worldwide	Conrad, Doubletree by Hilton, Doubletree Club, Embassy Suites, Hampton Inn Suites, Hilton Hotels & Resort, Hilton Garden Inn, Homewood Suites by Hilton, Waldrof Astoria, Home2 Suites by Hilton, Hilton Grand Vacations
Starwood Hotels & Resorts Worldwide	St Regis, The Luxury Collection, W Hotels, Westin Hotels, Sheraton, Four Points, Aloft, Element, Le Meridien, Tribute portfolio

Source: Adapted from Kwun (2010) and updated.

Homewood Suite line in 2000 (Jiang et al., 2002). Currently, Marriott Corporation and Wyndham Worldwide have approximately 15 brands while Intercontinental Hotel Group and Starwood Hotels and Resorts Worldwide have 11 and 10 respectively (see Table 18.1). Even though the lodging companies have leveraged their brand value to the extension brands by adding various sub-brands or extended brands, only studies on brand extension have investigated the hospitality and tourism context (Jiang et al., 2002; Lee, 2007; Kwun, 2010).

Jiang et al. (2002) examined the brand extension phenomenon in the lodging industry. They empirically tested whether brand extensions encourage guests to repeat their stay with a particular chain's brands. They argued that brand extensions could increase customer loyalty because they reduce risk. It was found that a brand extension strategy could be successful for up to three brand extensions. Customers are likely to switch brands when the length of brand extension exceeds approximately three. In addition, they found that customer loyalty and repeat purchase can be boosted by a brand extension strategy. Likewise, Kwun (2010) investigated the effects of brand extensions on the lodging portfolio. He stated that perceived quality and brand effects on attitudes were significantly related to consumer attitude towards brand extensions. The brand effects were measured by brand awareness, brand class and brand reputation. Among the variables of the brand effects, brand reputation was the strongest positive influential factor on brand attitude.

Lee (2007) also investigated the brand extension concept in the lodging industry, by testing the relationships between perceived fit, perceived quality, attitude toward extension, and behavioural intention. He found that consumers evaluated brand extension more favourably if fit or similarity between the parent brand and extension products was good. Also, parent brand quality had an impact on consumers' brand extension evaluation in the lodging industry. In Lee's (2007) study, he applied horizontal brand extension in the lodging industry: the brand extension products consisted of hotels' product brands of beds or pillows.

Brand trust

Trust has been considered a key factor of success in relationship marketing (Morgan and Hunt, 1994). Trust has been described as a relationship quality feature (Dwyer et al., 1987) or determinant of the perceptions of service quality (Parasuraman et al., 1985), loyalty (Berry, 1983), communications between parties (Mohr and Nevin, 1990), and amount of cooperation (Anderson and Narus, 1990). The trust construct has been variously defined as: 'the willingness of the average consumer to reply on the ability of the brand to perform its stated function' (Moorman et al., 1992); 'a generalised expectancy held by an individual that the word of another can be relied on' (Rotter, 1967); 'the extent to which a person is confident in, and willing to act on the basis of the words, actions, decisions of others' (McAllister, 1995); and, 'the willingness of the average consumer to rely on the ability of the brand to perform its stated function' (Chaudhuri and Holbrook, 2001). Brand trust will be the basis on which consumers will decide whether or not to purchase the brand. Therefore, brand trust plays an important role in the buying process (Luk and Yip, 2008).

Chaudhuri and Holbrook (2001) examined the relationship between brand trust along with brand affect and brand loyalty. They found that brand trust and affect had an impact on both purchase and attitudinal loyalty. It was suggested brand trust is associated with brand loyalty because trust is important when exchanging valued relationships, which in turn has an impact on market share and relative price (Chaudhuri and Holbrook, 2001). Luk and Yip (2008) investigated the effect of brand trust on consumers' purchasing behaviour. They found that consumer satisfaction had an impact on brand trust. The brand intentions had a higher effect on purchasing behaviour than brand reliability. Sung and Kim (2010) examined the relationships between brand personality, brand trust, brand affect, and brand loyalty. They also found that brand trust had an impact on brand loyalty. Liao et al. (2010) investigated the impacts of brand trust, customer satisfaction, and brand loyalty on word-of-mouth. They found that brand trust had an impact on brand loyalty, which in turn, influenced word-of-mouth.

Limited studies on brand trust in the hospitality context have been conducted (Lee and Back, 2009; Wilkins et al., 2009). Wilkins et al. (2009) investigated the relationships among service quality, perceived value, customer satisfaction, and behavioural loyalty within the lodging industry, specifically within first class and luxury hotels. They found that brand trust, mediated by brand attitude, is a significant moderator of behavioural loyalty. In addition, service quality was the most influential determinant of loyalty when indirect effects are included.

Brand loyalty

Brand loyalty has been an important construct in the marketing literature for at least three decades (Howard and Sheth, 1969: 232). Aaker (1991) and Dick and Basu (1994) stated that brand loyalty leads to certain marketing advantages: reduced marketing costs, more new customers, greater trade leverage, favourable word of mouth, and greater resistance among loyal consumers to competitive strategies. Moreover, loyalty can be enhanced by brand credibility (Sweeney and Swait, 2008). Brand loyalty has been a main construct of customer-based brand equity, which influences brand extension success (Aaker, 1991). Brand equity can be measured internally by both types of loyalty: behavioural loyalty and attitudinal loyalty. Van Riel et al. (2001) examined the transfer of customer-based brand equity to brand extensions and found that the original brand could be used as a key indication to evaluate extensions.

According to Chaudhuri and Holbrook (2001), brand loyalty, which is related to brand trust and brand affect, has two dimensions: purchase loyalty and attitudinal loyalty. Purchase loyalty and attitudinal loyalty are related to each other. In addition, purchase loyalty has an impact on market share increase, whereas attitudinal loyalty influences a higher relative price for the brand. They suggested brand loyalty is an important construct in the determination of brand performance outcomes.

Several studies of brand loyalty exist in the hospitality field (Jiang et al., 2002; Lee and Back, 2009; Nam et al., 2011; Wilkins et al., 2009). The relationships between brand loyalty and brand extension, and determinants of brand loyalty have been investigated. Specifically, Lee and Back (2009) explored the relationships among brand satisfaction, attitudinal loyalty, brand trust, and brand value in the meetings, incentives, conventions, and exhibitions (MICE) industry. They suggested that brand loyalty is affected by brand satisfaction as the relationship between brand satisfaction and brand loyalty is mediated by brand trust. In addition, attitudinal brand loyalty was significantly associated with brand trust. Furthermore, brand loyalty is influenced by consumer-based brand equity with the mediating effects of consumer satisfaction (Nam et al., 2011). Nam et al. (2011) proposed the five dimensions as key determinants of brand equity: physical quality, staff behaviour, ideal self-congruence, brand identification and lifestyle-congruence. They suggested brand loyalty is positively related with self-congruence, brand identification, and lifestyle-congruence, which means brand loyalty can be developed not only for functional values of brands but also symbolic values generated from self-congruence, brand identification, and lifestyle congruence of the brands. For example, hotel chains should investigate personality characteristics of their brands and create brand image, which is aligned with consumer's ideal self-concept, and use brand personality for their positing strategies in their marketing communications in order to boost their brand loyalty (Nam et al., 2011).

Conclusion

Effectiveness and benefits of brand management has been examined as one of the major marketing tools by researchers and industry practitioners. Hotel chains have mainly utilised brand extension strategy in order to leverage their brands' goodwill. Additionally, research on brand trust, brand loyalty, and brand extension has been highlighted as primary brand management concerns within hotel chain management. Recently, hotel chains have expanded their brands globally because numerous opportunities exist, such as the increasing demand by international travellers. With the global proliferation of hotel chain brands, chain hotel managements should not ignore any potential for cannibalisation of their brands. Thus, studies on the optimisation of hotel chain brands should be further investigated in order to avoid brand cannibalisations. In addition, due to the advances in technology, such as mobile devices, information technology, and online distribution channels, it has been possible for hotel chain brands to engage with guests from the initial search stages through the guests' experience at the hotel and after their experience. Therefore, hotel chains should seek opportunities not only to capitalise on engagement with their guests but also to turn that engagement into revenue. Brand management as a long-term strategic decision of hotel chains is important because brands convey value. Hotel chains ought to make an effort for their brands to remain relevant to the consumer and position top of mind as a preferred choice.

References

Aaker, D. (1991) *Managing Brand Equity: Capitalizing on the Value of a Brand Name*, New York, NY: The Free Press.

Ambler, T. and Styles, C. (1996) Brand development versus new product development: towards a process model of extension decisions. *Marketing Intelligence and Planning*, 14(7), 10–19.

Anderson, J.C. and Narus, J.A. (1990) A model of distributor firm and manufacturer firm working partnerships. *The Journal of Marketing*, 54(1), 42–58.

Ashton, A.S. and Scott, N. (2011) Hotel restaurant co-branding: the relationship of perceived brand fit with intention to purchase. *Journal of Vacation Marketing*, 17(4), 275–85.

Berry, L. (2000) Cultivating service brand equity. *Journal of the Academy of Marketing Science*, 28(1), 128–37.

Berry, L.L. (1983) Relationship marketing. In L.L. Berry, G.L. Shostack, and G. Upah (eds), *Emerging Perspectives on Services Marketing*. Chicago, IL: American Marketing Association, pp. 25–28.

Biehal, G.J. and Sheinin, D.A. (1998) Managing the brand in a corporate advertising environment: a decision-making framework for brand managers. *Journal of Advertising*, 27(2), 99–110.

Boo, H.C. and Mattila, A.S. (2002) A hotel restaurant brand alliance model: antecedents and consequences. *Journal of Foodservice Business Research*, 5(2), 5–23.

Chaudhuri, A. and Holbrook, M.B. (2001) The chain of effects from brand trust and brand affect to brand performance: the role of brand loyalty. *Journal of Marketing*, 65(2), 81–93.

Czellar, S. (2003) Consumer attitude toward brand extensions: an integrative model and research propositions. *International Journal of Research in Marketing*, 20(1), 97–115.

De Chernatony, L. and Riley, F.D.O. (1998) Defining a 'brand': beyond the literature with experts' interpretations. *Journal of Marketing Management*, 14(5), 417–43.

Dick, A.S. and Basu, K. (1994) Customer loyalty: toward an integrated conceptual framework. *Journal of the Academy of Marketing Science*, 22(2), 99–113.

Dwyer, F.R., Schurr, P.H. and Oh, S. (1987) Developing buyer-seller relationships. *The Journal of Marketing*, 51(2), 11–27.

Erdem, T. and Swait, J. (2004) Brand credibility, brand consideration, and choice. *Journal of Consumer Research*, 31(1), 191–98.

Guillet, B.D. and Tasci, A.D.A. (2010) An exploratory study of multi-cultural views on the Disney-McDonald's alliance. *Journal of Travel and Tourism Marketing*, 27(1), 82–95.

Hanson, B., Mattila, A.S., O'Neill, J.W. and Yonghee, K.I.M. (2009) Hotel rebranding and rescaling. *Cornell Hospitality Quarterly*, 50(3), 360–70.

Howard, J.A. and Sheth, J.N. (1969) *The Theory of Buyer Behavior*. New York: John Wiley & Sons, Inc.

Hur, Y. and Adler, H. (2011) Employees' perceptions of restaurant brand image. *Journal of Foodservice Business Research*, 14(4), 334–59.

Jiang, W., Dev, C.S., and Rao, V.R. (2002) Brand extension and customer loyalty: evidence from the lodging industry. *Cornell Hospitality Quarterly*, 43(4), 5–16.

Keller, K.L. (2002) *Branding and Brand Equity*. Cambridge, MA: Marketing Science Institute.

Keller, K.L. and Aaker, D.A. (1992) The effects of sequential introduction of brand extensions. *Journal of Marketing Research*, 29, 35–50.

Keller, K. and Lehmann, D.R. (2006) Brands and branding: research findings and future priorities. *Marketing Science*, 25(6), 740–59.

Keller, K.L., Sternthal, B. and Tybout, A. (2002) Three questions you need to ask about your brand. *Harvard Business Review*, 80(9), 80–89.

Kim, C.K. and Lavack, A.M. (1996) Vertical brand extensions: current research and managerial implications. *Journal of Product and Brand Management*, 5(6), 24–37.

Kotler P. (2000) *Marketing Management: Millennium Edition*. Upper Saddle River, NJ: Prentice Hall.

Kotler, P. and Armstrong, G. (1996) *Principles of Marketing*. Upper Saddle River, NJ: Prentice Hall.

Kwun, D.J. (2010) How extended hotel brands affect the lodging portfolio. *Journal of Retail and Leisure Property*, 9(3), 179–91.

Kwun, D.J. (2012) Brand management in the hospitality industry. *Journal of Tourism and Hospitality*, 1(1). Online. Available HTTP: <http://www.omicsgroup.org/journals/2167-0269/2167-0269-1-e104.pdf>, accessed 3 December, 2015.

Lee, J. (2007) Brand extension in the upscale hotel industry; conceptual model, industry trends and consumer perceptions. (Ph.D Dissertation), Purdue University, West Lafayette.

Lee, J.S. and Back, K.J. (2009) An examination of attendee brand loyalty: Understanding the moderator of behavioral brand loyalty. *Journal of Hospitality and Tourism Research*, 33(1), 30–50.

Liao, S., Chung, Y., Hung, Y. and Widowati, R. (2010) The impacts of brand trust, customer satisfaction, and brand loyalty on word-of-mouth. Paper presented at the Industrial Engineering and Engineering Management (IEEM), *2010 IEEE International Conference on Digital Object Identifier*.

Luk, S.T.K. and Yip, L.S.C. (2008) The moderator effect of monetary sales promotion on the relationship between brand trust and purchase behaviour. *Journal of Brand Management*, 15(6), 452–64.

Mangla, I. (2015, January 23) Major hotel brands compete for space in the boutique hotel trend. *International Business Times*. Online. Available HTTP: <http://www.ibtimes.com/major-hotel-brands-compete-space-boutique-hotel-trend-1793168>, accessed 3 March, 2015.

McAllister, D.J. (1995) Affect-and cognition-based trust as foundations for interpersonal cooperation in organizations. *Academy of Management Journal*, 38(1), 24–59.

Mohr, J. and Nevin, J.R. (1990) Communication strategies in marketing channels: a theoretical perspective. *The Journal of Marketing*, 54(4), 36–51.

Moorman, C., Zaltman, G. and Deshpande, R. (1992) Relationships between providers and users of market research: the dynamics of trust within and between organizations, *Journal of Marketing Research*, 29, 314–28.

Morgan, R.M. and Hunt, S.D. (1994) The commitment: trust theory of relationship marketing, *Journal of Marketing*, 58(3), 20–38.

Musante, M. (2007) Brand portfolio influences on vertical brand extension evaluations. *Innovative Marketing*, 3(4), 59–65.

Nam, J., Ekinci, Y. and Whyatt, G. (2011) Brand equity, brand loyalty and consumer satisfaction. *Annals of Tourism Research*, 38(3), 1009–30.

O'Cass, A. and Grace, D. (2003) An exploratory perspective of service brand associations. *Journal of Services Marketing*, 17(5), 452–75.

Olsen, M.D., Chung, Y., Graf, N., Lee, K. and Madanoglu, M. (2005) Branding: myth and reality in the hotel industry. *Journal of Retail and Leisure Property*, 4(2), 146–62.

O'Neill, J.W. and Xiao, Q. (2006) The role of brand affiliation in hotel market value. *Cornell Hotel and Restaurant Administration Quarterly*, 47(3), 210–23.

Parasuraman, A., Zeithaml, V.A. and Berry, L.L. (1985) A conceptual model of service quality and its implications for future research. *The Journal of Marketing*, 49(4), 41–50.

Punjaisri, K., Wilson, A. and Evanschitzky, H. (2009) Internal branding to influence employees' brand promise delivery: a case study in Thailand. *Journal of Service Management*, 20(5), 561–79.

Rangaswamy, A., Burke, R.R. and Oliva, T.A. (1993) Brand equity and the extendibility of brand names. *International Journal of Research in Marketing*, 10(1), 61–75.

Rotter, J.B. (1967) A new scale for the measurement of interpersonal trust. *Journal of Personality*, 35(4), 651–65.

Sullivan, M.W. (1990) Measuring spillovers in umbrella branded products. *Journal of Business*, 63(3), 309–29.

Sung, Y. and Kim, J. (2010) Effects of brand personality on brand trust and brand affect. *Psychology and Marketing*, 27(7), 639–61.

Swaminathan, V., Fox, R.J. and Reddy, S.K. (2001) The impact of brand extension introduction on choice. *The Journal of Marketing*, 65, 1–15.

Sweeney, J. and Swait, J. (2008) The effects of brand credibility on customer loyalty. *Journal of Retailing and Consumer Services*, 15(3), 179–93.

Tasci, A.D.A. and Guillet, B.D. (2011) It affects, it affects not: a quasi-experiment on the transfer effect of co-branding on consumer-based brand equity of hospitality products. *International Journal of Hospitality Management*, 30(4), 774–82.

Tsang, N.K.F., Lee, L.Y.S. and Li, F.X.H. (2011) An examination of the relationship between employee perception and hotel brand equity. *Journal of Travel & Tourism Marketing*, 28(5), 481–97.

van Riel, A.C., Lemmink, J. and Ouwersloot, H. (2001) Consumer evaluations of service brand extensions. *Journal of Service Research*, 3(3), 220–31.

Wilkins, H., Merrilees, B. and Herington, C. (2009) The determinants of loyalty in hotels. *Journal of Hospitality Marketing and Management,* 19(1), 1–21.

19

An international hotel company's employment brand

Sjoerd Gehrels

(STENDEN HOTEL MANAGEMENT SCHOOL, NETHERLANDS)

Introduction

The hospitality industry is in a constant state of change, which requires management to continuously review and update corporate strategies. Well-established successful international hotel chains with a long history, experience the on-going necessity to monitor their performance and brand promise. Evaluating a company's value proposition is a key process, for which a thorough and objective assessment is needed of how to deliver the guests' desired services (Kwortnik, 2011). The case study presented in this chapter was written based on analysis provided by one of the senior managers in a hotel company and it demonstrates a corporate awareness of making sure the brand is vibrant and ready for the future. After reviewing the material, it was decided to offer the analysis as an anonymous case study to prevent any possible misinterpretations due to the openhearted nature of its content. The company will be referred to as Falcon International Hotels (FIH). Any resemblance with existing hotel chains is left to the imagination of the reader. This chapter outlines how FIH has engaged in the process of analysing its current external brand within a historical and developmental perspective. The ongoing changes in brand promise are explored as well as the major process of developing an employment brand. Internal and external brand are compared in terms of consistency and a set of improvement actions is discussed. The discussion is then taken further to explain how enhancing the company's employment brand and resulting diversity strategy are taken on. This case study was written from an inside-out perspective and although hotels are sometimes referred to as being among the last industries to respond to change (Waldthausen and Oehmichen, 2013), this case study shows how a critical change-driven approach is taken.

Background: history and profile

Falcon International Hotels is a successful international hotel management company of European origin with approximately 100 operating hotel and resorts in the European, South-American, African, Middle Eastern and Asian markets. Sitting in the upscale segment, FIH's competitors include Marriott, Hilton, Sofitel, Mövenpick, Steigenberger and Sheraton. Falcon's first hotel opened in Western Europe in the previous century. From the first hotels in Europe, FIH expanded into other markets. It was under a new CEO's guidance that FIH began to experience rapid growth by switching from a leased model to a management model for all new properties. This change in policy was especially successful in the South American and Asian hospitality market. In comparison to leased hotels (properties owned by FIH with full P&L responsibility), managed properties are owned by private investors or investment groups and FIH is contracted as the managing company. Due to the flexibility FIH gives to the owners, the company is able to present a broad variety of hotels and resorts, each meeting the upscale quality standards while delivering the respective cultural authenticity of the destination. Operating in this manner requires a clearly defined brand recognition value because the hotels themselves look different in every location. It was recognised that the frontline staff who provide the service, and therefore FIH's employees, *are* the brand. Attracting, hiring, developing and retaining of employees, and keeping the engagement level up is crucial for FIH.

Further developing the brand

External brand promise

In order to implement a company culture in line with a renewed brand promise and cascade it down to the hotel level, a co-creation initiative was headed by executive management including the general managers of all hotels. Substantial research went into surveying and interviewing employees, management and customers to assess what they felt represented the brand. A second polling system was created with all of FIH's top 'executive members' from corporate to hotel level. The outcomes presented the following company values: 'Hospitableness, Quality, and Service ... with attention for the Individual'. Additionally, the expected behaviour of employees and management involved was defined. Both values and expected behaviour build the FIH's company culture that characterises the brand internally and externally. From FIH's defined expected behaviour and values, and the vision of the company, the external brand promise was fine-tuned.

Brand analysis

Five years ago, FIH embarked on further defining the external brand promise in order to align it with the company's 2016 strategy. FIH realised that one of their strategic objectives, growth, would require a more international brand perception differentiating FIH clearly from competitors. In order to grow the Falcon brand, the primary focus areas were set as follows:

- Brand assessment
- Public relations
- Customer insights and CRM/loyalty

The brand evaluation was done by an external company and brought back a mixed image of what they thought Falcon represented. This revealed that the concrete positioning in the hospitality market should be strengthened. It became obvious that the strength of the brand actually presented itself in its flexibility to serve business and leisure guests in the same reliable way with high quality everywhere around the globe. Whilst the customers like their FIH hotel experience, the brand itself was perceived as understated and therefore not an immediate first choice. The following issues were identified.

1) *Unclear brand positioning*: customers and employees were confused as to what the FIH brand stands for. The broad variety of different hotels led to mixed signals to customers and confused them by not providing a clear brand recognition value.
2) *Not enough marketing communication*: few customers could recall seeing an FIH property in the media, whilst competitors seemed to be there. This also affects future and current employees in choosing Falcon as a preferred employer.
3) *No loyalty programme and limited follow-up with customers*: customers are not being rewarded enough for staying with FIH. Building customer intimacy is underdeveloped as yet. As a result, customers often identify the company as being in specific countries, not directly seen as an international hotel brand and perceived as a kind of multiple personality brand.

One characteristic remained common among all of the research results. The company stood for high quality upscale service and excellent experiences regardless of location. Due to the variety in the portfolio, it became clear that the company needed to create a strong brand recognition value through its intangible asset of outstanding, reliable and culturally authentic service in all properties.

Brand promise changes

The outcome from research and the common understanding about the need to reposition and redefine the brand led to the concept of 'authentic hospitality'. Customers, both business and leisure, stated that the reason why they decided to stay with FIH was because that unlike other quality brands that want a position in the luxury market segment, FIH allows their customers to feel comfortable and relaxed. FIH adapts to the guest's needs and employees are flexible in accommodating the guest's requests. Quality and service levels were factors that were consistently identified as important and therefore taking the service to the next level seemed the right progression for the external brand promise in order to increase customer intimacy. The customer value label 'authentic hospitality' is best described through:

- Quality of service,
- Value for money
- Consistency and reliability

Furthermore, the advantage of operating 'glocally' (providing a local experience within a globally operating company) was stipulated. In analogy with the guest experience, the idea of being easy to do business with, for the owner/investors, and enjoying one another as colleagues came through as a key driving factor for defining what the brand really is. The marketing concept of increasing customer intimacy gives FIH the ability to become accepted and known as the preferred up-market hotel chain among customers. Customer intimacy creates a virtuous circle: the better FIH knows its customers and their expectations, wishes and difficulties, the better the company will be able to provide excellent service. The more FIH can adapt their service to individual customers, the happier they will be, and the stronger the 'intimacy' between FIH and its customers. Satisfied and happy customers may become loyal customers who stay with FIH not only for business but potentially also for their next private holiday. It is more cost efficient for FIH to provide and deliver service to loyal customers, as employees know from the customer database what these customers expect, and act accordingly, leading to an added value. Customer intimacy increases business profitability and delivers on the expectations of owners/investors as well as other stakeholders.

Internal–external brand alignment

The HR perspective 'employees *are* the brand', in times of 'war for talent', is becoming increasingly important. Employment branding comprises an important factor for competitive advantage. Especially in the hospitality industry, the right employees are crucial for the company's success. HRM and the employee's manager have a variety of available tools and strategies to increase talent flow, development and retention. In order to create an optimised workforce performance, employment branding is still an underutilised tool (Gehrels and De Looij, 2011). Employment branding is a powerful driver of global talent management and an important part of the employment philosophy. As workforce studies show, the reputation of a company as a good employer is an important driver for recruiting the right people, keeping them and securing their engagement (Auger et al., 2013). During the implementation of the brand promise 'authentic hospitality', the company's HRM therefore needed to define what this new external branding meant in terms of attracting, hiring and retaining the right talent. In order to deliver the external brand promise of 'authentic hospitality' there are not only tangible items such as the facilities, cultural authenticity of design and ambience. The determinant to repeat business is the interaction between customers and employees as defined in the 'Servicescape' concept (Bitner, 2000). A logical next question then came up: how can we attract and retain the core talent that is so crucial for the company's success, and how does this materialise in an employment branding strategy? Three components of becoming an employer of choice are (Wickham and O'Donohue, 2009): 1. employee branding strategies; 2. employee brand identity; and 3. employment value proposition. The first, understanding the employee branding strategies, is crucial for determining the strength of the employment brand.

Internal employment branding

FIH explicitly mentions on its career website: career development, mentoring, coaching and a career tailored to one's own abilities and growth for all levels, from graduates to experienced managers, aiming to be acknowledged as the preferred up-market hospitality employer. But does this really differentiate FIH from other hospitality employers, and why do employees choose to work for the company? The hospitality industry has a high turnover (Hemdi and Rahman, 2010) and some employees leave the industry because of limited salary opportunities. FIH as an employer tries to distinguish itself with defined opportunities for career growth, supported by strong learning and development initiatives for its employees, with a hospitality management graduate programme and strong cross-area career planning. Despite all service delivery guidelines, FIH encourages employees to be themselves, service the guest intuitively and foster teamwork in order to deliver the brand promise of 'authentic hospitality' in the best way. In addition, a transparent, market competitive and performance-based compensation strategy provides equal opportunities for each employee ensuring an environment of trustful relationships. Compensation can still be improved as part of the employment branding strategy implementation. Lastly, due to the changing needs of generations, how and what employees' roles and responsibilities are, must be more clearly defined in a broader context and amended to match specific labour supply and demand. Next to developing a compensation strategy, the company's biggest challenge is the recruitment strategy. In a highly competitive labour market, it needs to be clear which attributes are the most important for attracting employees, as defined by Manpower Services (2009):

1) Compensation and job security
2) Development opportunities
3) Quality of management
4) Respect and recognition
5) Teamwork environment

Challenges

It is important for FIH to deal with different generations. Currently, most senior leadership positions are held by 'Baby Boomers' and 'Generation X', while in the future 'Generation Y' will be taking these roles. These generations (Holroyd, 2011) hold different perceptions and expectations of leadership and development. Even if senior management develops strategies to keep up with the employment value proposition, the biggest challenge is the implementation. Communication within the organisation is complex and often strategic initiatives go a long way to reach the end user, the frontline employee. Part of the problem that causes the potential tension between strategic implementation and practical execution is the company's decentralised structure. Each geographical area has its own 'corporate centre' and is responsible for cascading information down to hotels within their area. Therefore, the employment value proposition is not always delivered in the same way, which results in a less aligned workforce and differences in understanding the brand recognition value.

FIH leaves compensation and benefits to each area office (as they have their own P&L responsibility and often legal requirements) to competitively benchmark market salaries. It is the responsibility of the area offices to ensure that their hotels are actually offering a competitive benefits package. The strategy is not to offer the best benefit package in the industry, but to offer more benefits in terms of career growth. In exit interviews, however, people mention: 'my compensation does not reflect my contribution for the company', or: 'company X or Y pays simply more for the same work'.

FIH puts a clear focus on the Employee Value Proposition attribute of 'Opportunity'. There are strict guidelines and definitions connected to values and expected behaviour, and examples of how these are followed in order to align the workforce globally and to create a common understanding of the company culture. The demonstration of company culture is as important as achieving individual goals, both contributing to the company's strategic success. This approach to performance management allows an aligning of the external employee promise to the internal employee branding. HRM audits held by area offices evaluate the quality of the performance reviews in order to ensure that growth is given to those who perform well.

Measuring alignment

The official metric in place to measure whether or not the employment value proposition is met, is through the annual internal employee survey which is structured around expected behaviour, vision and values. The employee survey is broken down in groups of questions in the following categories: Communication and Information, Leadership and Management, Entrepreneurship, Learning and Development and Culture. In the past few years, the company has seen rather steady results, despite the increase in the number of new employees. The annual survey shows that there are areas where certain aspects of the employment value proposition could score higher:

1. Pay and benefits
2. Recognition and praise
3. Employee feedback is welcomed
4. My opinion counts
5. Participation in training over the past 6 months.

The results indicate that there is not yet full alignment between the external employer brand and what is actually delivered with particular regards to pay and benefits, values and the promise of career development. Beyond what current employees say, trying to understand what past employees say is not possible at this time, because there is no tracking system in place that could help to evaluate aspects such as employee turnover rate, time taken to fill vacancies and average duration in position before receiving a promotion. It is clear that the internal employer brand strategy requires development work, particularly with regards to the fundamentals of measuring and benchmarking, in order to know what and how to improve in the areas that have been uncovered by the employee survey. Without the specific measurement systems in place, it is very difficult to expect external recognition for the employment brand.

Strengthening the employment brand

The redevelopment of the brand promise presents a perfect opportunity to re-align and strengthen the vision, values, expected behaviour and strategic objectives properly with the external customer brand promise of 'authentic hospitality'. At the core of the strategy must be the internal brand message. What 'authentic hospitality' means for the employees needs to be defined and be in line with how that affects customer value creation. This core element, that was previously not considered, will bring in line the competencies, needs and requirements for all new hires and current employees to deliver the new 'authentic hospitality' brand promise. A key component will be how to keep the best employees and align them with the requirements of a high quality service culture and a strong focus of being intuitive and authentic. It is key for FIH not to introduce new verbiage for defining company culture but rather to simplify the expected behaviour and values and further define them through brand trainings. Also core to the brand is the uniqueness of each property. Instead of having mandated standard operating procedures, there should be room for each property to develop their own unique personality. The key to stimulating 'entre(intra)preneurship' in the company is to gradually change the culture of how decisions are made. A new more collaborative approach can be taken that starts with the leaders, and is then trickled down to every front line employee. Allowing collaboration between employees gives them room to actually think on their own rather than act as robots.

Measuring effectiveness of the brand strategy

To measure how effective this brand strategy is, and how well aligned the external and internal brand message, some key metrics need to be captured.

- Employee turnover
- Average duration with the company before leaving

- Time to fill vacancies
- Yield ratios for recruitment (applicants, candidates, offers, hires)
- Number of internal candidates promoted
- Average time in roles before promotion
- Number of training days per employee by job category/level and location
- Percentage of completion rate in performance appraisal
- Average change in performance rating by job category related to numbers of training days
- Guest satisfaction index
- Call ups on career pages and sign ups for search agents

In order to capture this data set, it is necessary to have:

- An e-recruitment system and value-based recruiting strategy
- Updated talent management system with career planning, training booking system and succession planning tool used actively

It can be concluded that the implementation of 'authentic hospitality' gives FIH a clear opportunity to re-align the external and internal brand promise. This ensures that the right talents are attracted and hired, and the best employees retained and developed, whereas employees who are not able to embrace the change are shed. Future employees will perceive a variation in the employment value proposition and view FIH more favourably as a prospective employer.

Diversity management and business success

Currently, diversity is addressed as part of a global sustainability programme, which has been developed over the past few years. The company's code of conduct was re-worked and includes statements on FIH's stand on discrimination and harassment, along with definitions of both. The employer sustainability programme encourages the hiring and retention of a diverse workforce, and states that the organisation stands for equal opportunities, and that it works to maintain the highest level of employee engagement and job security. In addition, the company commits itself to a code in order to apply fairness in terms of hiring, promotions and compensation in line with the company's corporate regulations and guidelines. The hospitality industry is typically represented by a very diverse workforce (Forbes, 2012). At the front line, which is FIH's core human capital and of strategic importance, the incorporation of ethnic minorities, religious beliefs, sexual orientations and cultural origins is crucial. The perception of each hotel and therefore its success in the local market and brand value recognition is very much based on high quality and reliable interactions between employees and customers, vendors and local communities. A diverse workforce is an important factor for the success of 'authentic hospitality'. Negative perceptions of stakeholders about the company's ability to manage and respect diversity and inclusion would have a direct impact on results, and potentially trigger a loss of business.

Although the hospitality industry may look diverse, senior management composition in FIH is more homogeneous. Most senior management in the hotels is male, over 40, European and holds a degree in hospitality management. Furthermore, there are many male Europeans managing the corporate office and area offices. This means that a homogeneous senior management team will benefit less from individual perspectives, creativity, innovation, enhanced problem solving and organisational flexibility than a more diverse leadership team. FIH's management may find it challenging to understand and meet the expectations of a variety of customers and hotel owners/investors. It is crucial to recruit a diverse workforce for running the company's business, which will be hindered if there is a perception of limited career development perspectives and non-inclusive company culture and management style. The policies themselves, however, will not transform the organisation into becoming more diverse and changing its management and leadership style. In order to make progress, the senior management team must increase awareness and understanding of diversity, its growing importance in today's highly competitive market and how it supports the business strategy as well as its ultimately positive impact on FIH's performance. Management needs to demonstrate with actions and choices that it truly endorses diversity, and that this is not just because of current trends for promoting diversity. For the company it will be crucial, in order to deliver the brand value and become the leading company in the hospitality upscale market, to embrace diversity, implement it successfully and live it every day.

Putting diversity management into practice

As FIH's diversity and inclusion practices are on a level that can be further developed, the following initiatives should be implemented. First of all, FIH needs to increase the measurement of workforce demographics with the focus on managerial roles and key positions in order to get a current picture of how diverse groups are represented within the organisation's 20 per cent of best paid jobs. The metrics to evaluate the workforce diversity demographics could be included in the monthly key performance indicator reporting. Analogous to the implementation of 'authentic hospitality', FIH's recruiting strategy needs to be aligned with the new requirements for employees delivering the brand promise to the customers. The company culture must increase diversity and demonstrate why a diverse workforce is needed in order to deliver on the brand identity. For example: vacancies should also be advertised through alternative media and a variety of posting possibilities, reaching a more diverse labour pool and ensuring equal opportunities. Another key initiative could be to launch diversity training in the framework of the leadership programme. It is important that senior management and managerial leaders of the organisation thoroughly understand the impact of being an inclusive business and what the company's risks are if it ignores the fact that diversity is going to be a competitive element in the future.

Senior management should promote and sponsor voluntary business network groups set up by the employees with the full backup of management. In addition to being a discussion forum for its members, the organisation should encourage input from these groups on recruitment, leadership, retention, consumer insights and trends which can help the organisation to remain relevant in its product/service offers and in marketing and customer communication. Furthermore, a diversity council should be set up, chaired by a member of senior management and formed by employees with various demographics, from across the organisation (corporate, area offices and hotels), working at various hierarchical levels, of all ages and genders, and of diverse educational and cultural backgrounds. The major task of the diversity council would be to help develop and maintain a relevant diversity strategy and policies. Due to their engagement and impact on the organisation's diversity agenda, members of the diversity council would also function as diversity champions and be liaisons in their area office or hotel. Although diversity should be positioned as an organisational responsibility for implementation, one senior management team member should be given accountability for driving the agenda, strategy and policy, managing diversity metrics, and to be FIH's diversity and inclusion spokesperson. All FIH leaders need to be trained in understanding how people have various cultural and educational backgrounds and therefore may perceive or send information differently in conversations. In order to understand others, the organisation should have its leaders understand how their own national culture is made up in terms of stereotypes, wrong and right, basic laws and manners, power distance and concept of time. In these times of 'Generation Y', discussions and exchange on generational behavioural differences within the 'home culture' are crucial. Hands-on exposure through international transfers within the company and a company philosophy which encourages multicultural teams, will support leaders and employees in understanding team effectiveness through diversity.

Teamwork to enhance diversity

A teamwork culture needs to be further developed and promoted within FIH, and multicultural, diverse, cross-area and cross-departmental teams should be encouraged. Therefore, sourcing staff for global projects has to be done on the principles of the recruiting strategy. Managers should be encouraged also to hire non-conformist individuals who are different from the other team members and the 'average' FIH employee. This will bring drive, energy and a broader background experience within the company's human resources. When dealing with diversity, it is also crucial to enhance the leader's knowledge and skills about conflict management in diverse teams. Dealing with uncertainty and ambiguous situations among diverse teams needs to be incorporated in the leadership development programme. Within FIH, a cultural change is happening with a gradual shift from a homogeneous male-dominated management to a more diverse one that is characterised by creativity, intuition, flexibility and innovation.

Current diversity paradigm

The organisation applies the access and legitimacy paradigm: the idea that diversity should be implemented in order to gain market share in diverse markets. Due to the international nature of FIH's customers, it is important that employees understand the culture, language, wants and specifics of the culture served. Although it may look like FIH is very diverse in its workforce, the matching of internal and external demographics only exists at the level of supporting and frontline employees. Intimate awareness of the cultures served by the company and the cultures in which the organisation operates its hotels can be increased among the group of managers and leaders. This situation is of importance for the company and its strategic goals. Stakeholders will expect the company to pay attention to diversity strategies. The following metrics visualising the degree of diversity will need to be put into place:

1) *Job yield*: needed to understand how attractive the company's employer brand is for various demographic groups and in various jobs and job levels.
2) *Skill inventories*: in order to stay competitive in the hospitality upscale market and current in terms of trends and having the right knowledge, skills, abilities and other attributes that the organisation needs now and in the future, skill inventories need to be available.
3) *Promotion rates*: in order to understand how the diversity policies are being implemented in the organisation, the company needs to capture data on internal promotions (when, who, what).

4) *External market share*: what business and revenue opportunities per population group are not being served as well as they should? Why is this? What can the company do to improve this relationship and to increase market share from these particular groups?

Concluding remarks

In this chapter, an open-hearted analysis is provided of how FIH over previous years has been considering and developing its brand. The notion that changes are triggered by senior management demonstrates that there is a sound mentality driven by the persistent spirit of remaining an important player within the world-wide hospitality industry. For practitioners and future-practitioners in the hotel industry (e.g. students of hospitality management programmes), this case study serves as important 'food-for-thought' about how a company as successful as FIH is consistently seeking further development. This chapter will assist the worlds of practice and (hospitality management) education to engage in discussing the fascinating business of international hotel management.

References

Auger, P., Devinney, T.M., Dowling, G.R., Eckert, C. and Lin, N. (2013) *How Much Does a Company's Reputation Matter in Recruiting?* Online. Available HTTP: <http://sloanreview.mit.edu/article/how-much-does-a-companys-reputation-matter-in-recruiting/>, accessed May 2014.

Bitner, M. (2000) The servicescape. In T.A. Swartz and D. Lacobucci (eds), *Handbook of Services Marketing and Management*. Thousand Oaks: Sage Publications.

Forbes (2012) Top 5 industry sectors in workforce diversity. Online. Available HTTP: <http://www.forbes.com/sites/claraknutson/2012/03/21/top-5-industry-sectors-in-workforce-diversity/>, accessed April 2014.

Gehrels, S.A., and De Looij, J. (2011) Employer branding: a new approach for the hospitality industry. *Research in Hospitality Management*, 1(1), 43–52.

Hemdi, M.A. and Rahman, N.A. (2010) Turnover of hotel managers: addressing the effect of psychological contract and affective commitment. *World Applied Sciences Journal*, 10 (Special Issue: Tourism and Hospitality), 01–13.

Holroyd, J. (2011) Talkin' 'bout my label. Sydney Morning Herald. Online. Available HTTP: <http://www.smh.com.au/>, accessed May 2014.

Kwortnik, R.J. (2011) Building and managing your brand. *Articles and Chapters in The Scholarly Commons*. Ithaca: Cornell University School of Hotel Administration.

Manpower Services (2009) *The power of employment value proposition*. White Paper. Sydney: Manpower Services (Australia) Pty Ltd.

Waldthausen, V. and Oehmichen, A. (2013) *A New Breed of Traveler: How Consumers are Driving Change in the Hotel Industry*. Online. Available HTTP: <http://www.4hoteliers.com/features/article/8022.>, accessed June 2014.

Wickham, M.D. and O'Donohue, W. (2009) Developing 'employer of choice' status: exploring an employment marketing mix. *Organization Development Journal*. 27(3), 77–95.

20

Managing customer experiences in hotel chains

Melissa A. Baker

(UNIVERSITY OF MASSACHUSETTS AMHERST, USA)

Introduction

Creating a customer experience that becomes synonymous with a hotel brand is increasingly recognised as a vital driver of corporate performance (Smith and Wheeler, 2002). Broadly speaking, the customer experience includes both the direct and indirect contact between the customer and the firm (Meyer and Schwager, 2007). Researchers consider different approaches for defining the customer experience: the holistic approach and the co-creation approach. The holistic experience approach refers to the person as a whole, as opposed to simply a customer, in each interaction between the company and the customer (LaSalle and Britton, 2003). The experience co-creation approach implies that companies do not sell experience but, rather, that they provide a platform of experiences that can be employed by consumers to co-create their own experience (Prahalad and Ramaswamy, 2004). More recently, the customer experience is usually conceptualised as holistic in nature and as involving the customer's cognitive, affective, emotional, social, and sensory responses to the firm (Verhoef et al., 2009). In other words, the customer experience is seen as a journey where the service encounters are viewed as interactions embedded in a series of exchanges that may extend over a long period of time, with a variety of providers contributing to the experience (Tax et al., 2013).

In regards to hotel chains, this means that the customer experience relies not only on the individual hotel property, but also incorporates the customer experience at other hotel properties within that chain. Additionally, this can also refer to experiences resulting from online encounters with the hotel chain. Specifically, the internet has had profound effects on service by facilitating customers' ability to become resource integrators (Lusch and Vargo, 2006). This integration increases the ease with which customers can search for hotels. The entire service experience frequently crosses entities to address the customer's needs (Tax et al., 2013) and thus it is important to create value throughout the experience.

Creating value

It is critical to consider the value-creating process which involves the customer as a co-creator of value (Lusch and Vargo, 2006). Co-creation is the constructive customer participation in the service creation and delivery processes requiring meaning and co-operative contributions (Auh et al., 2007). Throughout the customer's experience, competitive advantage is attained through engaging customers in co-production and co-creation. In building and maintaining customers, hotel managers must create positive perceptions of the service consumption experience (So et al., 2013). Co-creation occurs when consumers interact with the organisation (through face-to-face and online mediums) and thereby have an active role in shaping their personal experience (Bolton et al., 2014). The emotional experience and the emotions experienced are major components in the customer experience. Hotel hospitality is not merely about the hotel providing accommodation and the functional needs of the guest, it also involves taking care of the guest's psychological needs. Competitive advantage through innovation can be gained by an understanding of how the customer integrates and experiences the complete hotel experience.

The guest cycle

One important component of managing the customer experience is to identify, from the customer's perspective, all of the touch points that comprise the journey of their experience (Zomerdijk and Voss, 2010). It is generally considered that the stages of the hotel guest cycle are:

1.   Pre-arrival
2.   Arrival
3.   Occupancy
4.   Departure
5.   Post-departure

The first stage involves all experiences before the guest arrives and may include searching websites for information, making reservations, word-of-mouth interactions, and previous interactions with other hotels within the chain. The arrival stage begins once the guest physically reaches the property and involves all the experiences associated with the hotel's entrance, bell persons, front desk, and registration. The occupancy stage involves a myriad of interactions between the guest, the hotel, and all services offered throughout the stay. The departure involves the check-out procedure as well as the guest interactions as they leave the property. However, given the proliferation of online mediators with which the customer can share his or her experience, we posit it is also important to manage post-departure.

Stages of experience

It is important to manage the customer experience as a process, as opposed to an outcome (Yang et al., 2012). The customer experience encompasses every customer experience with the firm over time; from the search process, to purchase, to stay, and post-stay. A strategic emphasis implies that the organisation must assemble and interpret information for each individual customer experience over time (Bolton et al., 2014) and includes every interaction between the customer and the business (Grewal et al., 2009). An emphasis should be placed on the co-production and co-creation that occurs between the employees in the hotel and the customer. Stated differently, the customer experience is all the interactions with the firm, including the servicescape, employees, face-to-face interaction, and electronic channels.

An advantage of mapping out the entire service experience from the customer's perspective is the recognition that the experience frequently involves touch points at multiple parts of the organisation (Sampson, 2012). For example, Canadian Pacific Hotels (CP Hotels) sought to learn what would most satisfy their customers and mapped each step of the guest experience, from check-in, to valet parking, to check-out, and set a standard for each performance of each activity (Day, 2012). Based on that analysis, CP Hotels honed in on what services to offer, the proper levels of staffing, and the service delivery to gain the best customer experience. After implementing the changes, CP Hotels' share of business jumped by 16 per cent (Day, 2012). Two other hotel chains use different methods of engaging the customer at various touch points. Mandarin Oriental hotels has a 'moments of delight' philosophy whereby service representatives are empowered to provide low-cost delights to their customers at key encounter experiences, in order to wow and delight the customer (Mandarin Oriental, 2014). Within their philosophy, Kimpton Hotels seeks to create Kimpton Moments, whereby employees should seek to create heartfelt moments throughout the guest experience with both the guest and with each other (Rohman, 2013).

Individual relevance

Most hotel chains employ significant standardisation across the units which require knowledge transfer from the corporate offices to the individual hotel units (Garcia-Almeida et al.. 2011). From the customer's perspective, strong hotel brands reduce perceived risks and search costs (Kayaman and Arasli, 2007) and simplify the consumer's pre-purchase evaluation of the service (So et al., 2013). While the use of standardisation and scripts have merit, in order to maximise individual customer preferences, hotels should empower employees with the flexibility to modify their approach to fine-tune how to meet individual customers' needs while ensuring an overall consistency with the firm's service strategy (Bolton et al., 2014).

A hotel chain can succeed or fail based on the perceptions of the customer throughout his or her experience. Holiday Inn's brand seeks to deliver consistently high quality, family focused hotel experiences. However, from 2012 to 2013, perceptions of the customer experience slipped 96 places in the Customer Experience Excellence results, dropping from 54th to 150th place. The hotel chain experienced a decline across metrics of personalisation, meeting expectations, integrity, time and effort, resolution, and empathy (Nunwood, 2014). One of the most effective ways is to deliver an experience that is relevant to each hotel guest. This begins the moment they click on a website, through the duration of their stay, to managing post-experience online postings. Relevance may be different for each customer, so it is critical to gather information about each customer and deploy it throughout the organisation. For example, Harrah's hotels, resorts, and casinos have a customer relationship management programme that is distinctive in comparison with general loyalty programmes that simply reward customers for their business, without recognising personal differences and individualistic desires. Specifically, Harrah's monitors how individual customers behave, uncovering what they care about most and then delivering rewards accordingly (Bolton et al., 2014).

Communicating the brand message

Within the hotel experience, the customer looks for specific details within the communication content. A strong service hotel chain brand is essentially a promise of future satisfaction.

It is a blend of what the company says the brand is, what others say it is, and how the company performs the service (Berry, 2000). If customers' service experiences differ from the advertising message, customers will believe their experiences, and not the advertising (Berry, 2000).

Interpersonal communication

The frontline employee plays a vital role in humanising the service brand and helping customers connect emotionally to it by shaping the customers experience across all contact points (Vallaster and de Chernatory, 2005). Frontline employees deal with countless interactions daily and that may sometimes cause them to go on autopilot during their interactions. Additionally, it is not strictly what a service provider says, but how it is said, and how it is acted out through body language (Pease and Pease, 2004). For example, a front desk agent who is on the phone can look a customer in the eye to let them know they will be with them shortly, rather than make no eye contact at all.

Hotel firms should seek to employ those who seek to understand the customer experience, are immersed in the service delivery process, and act as participant observers (Bolton et al., 2014). It is estimated that up to 80 per cent of the meaning of a social encounter is transmitted through nonverbal communication, such as body language, tone, and gestures (Noe et al., 2010). The customer contact employee personifies the firm in the customer's eyes. The frontline employee directly interacts with the customers, providing a link between the external customer, the hotel chain, and the internal operations of the organisation. JW Marriott employees are slated to undergo a new initiative called Poise and Grace whereby they learn the significance of making eye contact and using certain gestures to convey confidence, discipline, and a hospitable presence to guests (Lazare, 2014) which better communicates their brand message.

Nonverbal communication

Nonverbal communication is crucial to service-based businesses because service employees are directly involved in building relationships with customers. Body language is part of the communication and social interaction process that conveys meaning and intentions (Sundaram and Webster, 2000) and gestures and expressions can be used to influence customers (Pease and Pease, 2004). Andaz Hotels (part of Hyatt) conducted training for employees to help them read guests' body language and establish an immediate rapport with guests (Levere, 2010). In Affinia Hotels' body language training, employees are taught to read guests' nonverbal communication. For example, a guest touching his face may mean they are anxious and in need of a speedy check-in (Kelly, 2011).

Genuine smiles can have a large effect on personality attributions as smiling employees are seen as more sincere, competent, and social. Customers believe that genuinely smiling employees will deliver knowledge and courteous service (Magnini et al., 2013). A fake smile can be easily detected as it spreads across the face slower, lasts longer, the eyes are not as narrowed, and the upper lip is exaggerated while the lower lip is less mobile (Pease and Pease, 2004). Specifically, hotel firms should seek to hire individuals who display positive emotions and genuine smiles (Johanson and Woods, 2008). High positive affect individuals tend to experience and display positive emotions such as cheerfulness and enthusiasm (Chu et al., 2012). While some companies conduct smile training, it is better if employees work in an environment where they want to smile (Magnini et al., 2013).

For example, Affinia hotels train employees as early as during orientation to interpret customers' body language. The CEO of Denihan Hospiality Group states that employees are trained to read body language such as feet positioning. If the feet are pointed towards the employee, the guest is actively engaged in the conversation; however, if their feet are pointed away, this indicates the guest is finished with the conversation and would like a speedy check-in or check-out (Denihan, 2011). Furthermore, it is reported that as a result of the body language training initiatives, guest satisfaction scores have increased (Denihan, 2011).

Culture and sub-culture

Many hotel chains exist in a multicultural environment that employs a workforce and serves customers that are culturally diverse. These culturally diversified groups have a strong influence on the way things should be done in a hotel (Chen et al., 2012). It is important that hotels identify service elements that are specific and transferrable to a nation or region. The ways in which customer needs are met should be locally interpreted and contextualised and thus provide meaning to the individual customer (Bolton et al., 2014). The essence of culture is a collective mental programming that conditions, constrains and reinforces the thinking process and results in observable differences in the behaviour patterns of each culture (Hofstede, 1980). It is important to note that country and culture are not synonymous, and that different locales may prefer different customer experiences. That is, the behaviours and preferences perceived positively from one region may not be universally transferred to another region (Baker et al., 2013). Both culture and subculture need to be considered in the management of chain hotels. For example, what is preferable in the Southern section of the USA may not translate into New England (Northern Eastern USA). Unlike some hotel chain operators, Rosewood Hotels and Resorts has 'A Sense of Place Philosophy' where they seek to reflect a destination's unique culture, history and geography in the design and operation of the hotel. (Rosewood Hotels, 2013).

Managing service failure

Broadly speaking, a service failure or recovery encounter is an exchange in which the customer experiences a loss because of the failure and the firm tries to provide a gain, in the form of a recovery effort, to compensate for the customer's loss. Recovery strategies can range from 'do nothing' to 'whatever it takes to fix the problem' (McDougall and Levesque, 1998). Since failures are impossible to prevent for even the best-managed service firms, effective service recovery procedures are a critical component in a company's customer retention strategy (Stauss and Friege, 1999). The way in which a company recovers from service failure should be viewed as a strategic marketing variable, which could be a sustainable competitive advantage in the marketplace (Maxham, 2001). Sometimes those disgruntled customers whom you make the extra effort to gain back become the most loyal customers. An excellent service recovery can potentially increase customer satisfaction and loyalty beyond what they were before a failure (Smith and Bolton, 1998). Effective service recovery is important to retain the goodwill of customers who experience a service failure, and providing fair compensation for perceived damages is essential for recovery (Tax et al., 1998).

Customer justice perceptions

Customer perceptions of justice during a service exchange are largely determined by the customer–employee encounter (Maxham and Netemeyer, 2003) and justice theory is widely accepted as the conceptual foundation for customer assessments during a service experience (Wirtz and McColl-Kennedy, 2010). The three types of justice are distributive, interactional, and procedural.

Distributive justice

Distributive justice involves the perceived fairness of the outcome from a process (Palmer et al., 2000), such as the compensation given to the customer (Tax et al., 1998). The compensation can be monetary compensation or discounts on the hotel stay, or it can take the form of an apology, a future free service, or a replacement. What is important is that customers expect equity in the exchange (Zeithaml et al., 2006). Distributive justice is particularly important in settings where the customers have particularly negative emotional responses (Smith and Bolton, 1998).

Interactional justice

Interactional justice encompasses the manner in which an individual is treated through a process (Sparks and McColl-Kennedy, 2001). Interactional justice deals with how individuals are treated with such qualities as dignity, respect (Spencer and Rupp, 2009), concern, and friendliness (Smith et al., 1999). This form of justice can be the most critical in the hotel industry if customers feel the company and its employees have uncaring attitudes (Zeithaml et al., 2006).

Procedural justice

Procedural justice addresses the perceived fairness of a process (Sparks and McColl-Kennedy, 2001), such as whether the procedures or criteria utilised in making the decision are perceived as being fair. This may include the policies and procedures used, the convenience of the process, and the timeliness and responsiveness of the firm's recovery actions (Tax et al, 1998; Smith et al., 1999). Customers want fair procedures and processes that are characterised by clarity, speed, and the absence of annoyances (Zeithaml et al., 2006).

Managing online experiences

Social network sites, blogs, and third party review sites provide views on hotel experiences and are increasingly important sources of marketing information about the customer experience. The advent of social media sites provides customers with access to, and interest in, posting online reviews, stories, commentaries, and photos of experiences (Sparks and Bradley, 2014). Customers increasingly rely on online search strategies when making product decisions (Sparks and Browning, 2011). Customers are increasingly posting and reading about experiences through Facebook, Twitter, and blogs, as well as reviewing customer experiences through hospitality specific sites such as Yelp and Trip Advisor. The potential reach and impact of the mass communication of online reviews provides hotels with the opportunity to enhance or detract from their brand (Sparks and Bradley, 2014). As such, it is increasingly important to manage the customer experience at every stage, including once they have left the hotel.

Online co-creation and socialisation will continue to affect the experience of the customer who made the post, but also future customers who read the posts. There is a need to highlight and develop new ways to understand the influence of e-conversations in hotels (Shaw et al., 2011). Responding to online reviews is an important part of managing the business's reputation. As such, online reputation management suggests that businesses require a unique skill set to effectively manage online reviews, signifying the importance to hotels of monitoring the online conversation and engaging with customers (Pattison, 2009). Although customers who post online reviews may not expect direct online responses, how the hotel responds (or does not respond) is likely to affect how others perceive the brand and possibly influences their willingness to book a reservation. It is important to note that responses to online reviews are not only an integral part of the customer's experience who posted the review, but is also part of the experience of those individuals who are reading the review.

Customers that use the internet as a channel of communication are increasingly seen as an important information source that is both interpersonal and provides mass communication (Shea et al., 2004). This phenomenon has led to changes in the way firms manage traditional word-of-mouth, and to a greater understanding of electronic word-of-mouth (Libai et al., 2010). Electronic word-of-mouth is information that is communicated via the internet to multiple audiences and remains available over a long period of time (Hennig-Thurau et al., 2010). Many online posts have the potential to be received with similar credibility to that of traditional word-of-mouth (Sparks and Browning, 2011). Positive word-of-mouth is the likelihood of consumers spreading favourable information about a company, including recommending the company (Maxham and Netemeyer, 2003). Negative word-of-mouth refers to the likelihood of consumers spreading unfavourable information, including advising against the company (Blodgett et al., 1997). By sharing bad experiences with others, customers hope to discourage others from purchasing (Gregoire and Fischer, 2008).

Triple A typology

The Triple A typology was developed by Sparks and Bradley (2014) specifically in relation to managing online feedback. The three principles are:

- Acknowledge
- Account
- Action

Acknowledge

The hotel provider should first acknowledge the customer's experience and feedback, which may include thanking them and appreciating the feedback. This may also include an apology or recognition of the experience. In the case of fictitious complaints (Baker et al., 2012), this may involve dismissing the comments.

Account

In many service situations, customers are looking to understand what happened and for the hotel to be held accountable for their actions (McColl-Kennedy and Sparks, 2003). The account equates to the explanation. These could involve providing justifications, such as admitting responsibility or explaining why something occurred; accounts which are similar to sincere apologies or denials. It is important to note that the content of the explanation should be appropriate, with relevant facts and pertinent information to help the customer understand what has occurred.

Action

The action category refers to how hotel providers address the source of the customers' complaints. The response may be to specify actions that have already been taken or ones that are currently under way (Liao, 2007). In addition, it may involve taking specific action with regard to the customer experience, such as providing compensation for a stay.

Conclusion

Managing the customer experience involves all of the touch points throughout the customer interaction with the hotel chain from booking, to occupancy, to post-departure. Throughout the process, an emphasis should be placed on the co-production and co-creation that occurs between the hotel and the customer, both those that are face-to-face and online. Additionally, hotel chain operators need to find the right balance between the standardisation across hotel chain units and meeting individual customer needs. In managing the customer experience, it is important to communicate the right brand message, develop good interpersonal communication, and pay attention to forms of non-verbal communication. Finally, as failures are impossible to prevent, hotel chains need to seek to recover from failures, including online postings, in order to continue managing customer experiences effectively.

There are ample opportunities for future research within these areas. For example, empirical studies are needed that examine the differences of customer experiences within the different stages. There is also a lack of research in the hospitality literature that examines nonverbal forms of interpersonal communication. The most significant area involves researching smiles, but other forms of body language, tone, and appearance are under-researched. Finally, customers are using online mediums during their experiences with hotels. Research should empirically investigate the experiences in online platforms, especially the influence of e-conversations pre-stay and post-stay as electronic word-of-mouth is becoming increasingly common.

References

Auh, S., Bell, S.J., McLeod, C.S. and Shih, E. (2007) Co-production and customer loyalty in financial services. *Journal of Retailing*, 83(3), 359–70.

Baker, M.A., Magnini, V.P. and Perdue, R.R. (2012) Opportunistic customer complaining: causes, consequences, and managerial alternatives. *International Journal of Hospitality Management*, 31(1), 295–303.

Baker, M.A., Murrmann, S.K. and Green, C. (2013) Dining in the city: server behaviors, time preferences, and the effect of urbanization in restaurant. *Journal of Foodservice Business Research*, 16(2), 113–38.

Berry, L.L. (2000) Cultivating service brand equity. *Journal of the Academy of Marketing Science*, 28(1), 128–37.

Blodgett, J.G., Hill, D.J. and Tax, S.S. (1997) The effects of distributive, procedural, and interactional justice on post complaint behavior. *Journal of Retailing*, 73(2), 185–210.

Bolton, R.N., Gustafsson, A., McColl-Kennedy, J., Sirianni, N.J. and Tse, D.K. (2014) Small details that make a big differences: a radical approach to consumption experience as a firm's differentiating strategy. *Journal of Service Management*, 25, 253–74.

Chen, R.X.Y., Cheung, C. and Law, R. (2012) A review of the literature on culture in hotel management research: what is the future? *International Journal of Hospitality Management*, 31(1), 52–65.

Chu, K.H., Baker, M.A. and Murrmann, S.K. (2012) When we are onstage, we smile: the effects of emotional labor on employee work outcomes. *International Journal of Hospitality Management*, 31(3), 906–15.

Day, G.S. (2012) Creating a superior customer–relating capacity. *MIT Sloan Management Review*. 44(3), 77–82. Online. Available HTTP: <http://sloanreview.mit.edu/article/creating-a-superior-customer relating-capability/>, accessed 20 August 2014.

Denihan, P. (2011) Hotels Training Staff to Interpret Body Language. Online. Available HTTP: <http://video.foxbusiness.com/v/1299491120001/hotels-training-staff-to-interpret-body-language/#sp=show-clips>, accessed 20 August 2014.

García-Almeida, D.J., Bernardo-Vilamitjana, M., Hormiga, E., and Valls-Pasola, J. (2011) Cultural compatibility in internal knowledge transfers: an application to hotel chain growth. *The Service Industries Journal*, 31(10), 1645–57.

Grégoire, Y. and Fisher, R.J. (2008) Customer betrayal and retaliation: when your best customers become your worst enemies. *Journal of the Academy of Marketing Science*, 36(2), 247–61.

Grewal, D., Levy, M. and Kumar, V. (2009) Customer experience management in retailing: an organizing framework. *Journal of Retailing*, 85(1), 1–14.

Hennig-Thurau, T., Malthouse, E.C., Friege, C., Gensler, S., Lobschat, L., Rangaswamy, A. and Skiera, B. (2010). The impact of new media on customer relationships. *Journal of Service Research*, 13(3), 311–30.

Hofstede, G. (1980) Motivation, leadership, and organization: do American theories apply abroad? *Organizational Dynamics*, 9(1), 42–63.

Johanson, M.M. and Woods, R.H. (2008) Recognizing the emotional element in service excellence. *Cornell Hospitality Quarterly*, 49(3), 310–16.

Kayaman, R., and Arasli, H. (2007) Customer based brand equity: evidence from the hotel industry. *Managing Service Quality: An International Journal*, 17(1), 92–109.

Kelly, T. (2011, 25 December) Hotel unveils body language training to keep guests happy. *Huffington Post Travel*. Online. Available HTTP: <http://www.huffingtonpost.com/2011/10/25/hotel-body-language-training_n_1030571.html>, accessed 1 August 2014.

LaSalle, D. and Britton, T.A. (2003) *Priceless: Turning Ordinary Products into Extraordinary Experiences*. Boston: Harvard Business School Press.

Lazare, L. (2014, 21 August) JW Marriott turns to Joffrey Ballet to elevate staff service techniques. *Chicago Business Journal*. Online. Available HTTP: <http://www.bizjournals.com/chicago/news/2014/08/20/j-marriott-turns-to-joffrey-ballet-to-elevate.html?r=full>, accessed 1 August 2014.

Levere, J.L. (2010, 6 September) Hotel chains try training with improve and iPods. *The New York Times*. Online. Available HTTP: <http://www.nytimes.com/2010/09/07/business/07hotel.html?_r=0>, accessed 1 August 2014.

Liao, H. (2007) Do it right this time: the role of employee service recovery performance in customer-perceived justice and customer loyalty after service failures. *Journal of Applied Psychology*, 92(2), 475–89.

Libai, B., Bolton, R., Bügel, M.S., De Ruyter, K., Götz, O., Risselada, H. and Stephen, A.T. (2010) Customer-to-customer interactions: broadening the scope of word of mouth research. *Journal of Service Research*, 13(3), 267–82.

Lusch, R.F. and Vargo, S.L. (2006) Service-dominant logic as a foundation for building a general theory. In R.F. Lusch, and S.L. Vargo (eds), *The Service-Dominant Logic of Marketing: Dialog, Debate, and Directions*. New York: Armonk, pp. 406–20.

Magnini, V.P., Baker, M. and Karande, K. (2013) The frontline provider's appearance: a driver of guest perceptions. *Cornell Hospitality Quarterly*, 54(4), 396–405.

Mandarin Oriental (2014) Online. Available HTTP: <http://www.mandarinoriental.com/about-us/mission/>, accessed 1 August 2014.

Maxham III, J.G. (2001) Service recovery's influence on consumer satisfaction, positive word-of-mouth, and purchase intentions. *Journal of Business Research*, 54(1), 11–24.

Maxham III, J.G. and Netemeyer, R.G. (2003) Firms reap what they sow: the effects of shared values and perceived organizational justice on customers' evaluations of complaint handling. *Journal of Marketing*, 67(1), 46–62.

McColl-Kennedy, J.R. and Sparks, B.A. (2003) Application of fairness theory to service failures and service recovery. *Journal of Service Research*, 5(3), 251–66.

McDougall, G. and Levesque, T. (1998) The effectiveness of recovery strategies after service failure: an experiment in the hospitality industry. *Journal of Hospitality and Leisure Marketing*, 5(2-3), 27–49.

Meyer, C. and Schwager, A. (2007) Understanding customer experience. *Harvard Business Review*, 85(2), 116.

Noe, F.P., Uysal, M. and Magnini, V.P. (2010) *Tourist Customer Service Satisfaction: An Encounter Approach*. London: Routledge.

Nunwood (2014, 4 August) A once proud customer experience vision loses sight of the basic: the excellence centre. Online. Available HTTP: <http://www.nunwood.com/holiday-inn-drops-customer-experience-top-100/>, accessed 20 August 2014.

Palmer, A., Beggs, R. and Keown-McMullan, C. (2000) Equity and repurchase intention following service failure. *Journal of Services Marketing*, 14(6), 513–28.

Pattison, K. (2009, 29 July) Managing an online reputation. *New York Times*. Online. Available HTTP: <http://www.nytimes.com/2009/07/30/business/smallbusiness/30reputation.html?pagewanted=all&_r=0>, accessed 1 August 2014.

Pease, B. and Pease, A. (2004) *The Definitive Book of Body Language*. New York: Bantam Books.

Prahalad, C.K. and Ramaswamy, V. (2004) Co-creation experiences: the next practice in value creation. *Journal of Interactive Marketing*, 18(3), 5–14.

Rohman, J. (2013) *The Magic of Kimpton Hotels & Restaurants*. San Francisco: A Great Place to Work Institute.

Rosewood Hotels. (2013) Online. Available HTTP: <http://www.rosewoodhotels.com/en/developers>, accessed 20 August 2014.

Sampson, S.E. (2012) Visualizing service operations. *Journal of Service Research*, 15(2). 1–17.

Shaw, G., Bailey, A. and Williams, A. (2011) Aspects of service-dominant logic and its implications for tourism management: examples from the hotel industry. *Tourism Management*, 32(2), 207–14.

Shea, L., Enghagen, L., and Kholler, A. (2004) Internet diffusion of an e-complaint: a content analysis of unsolicited responses. *Journal of Travel and Tourism Marketing*, 17(2/3), 145–65.

Smith, A.K. and Bolton, R.N. (1998) An experimental investigation of customer reactions to service failure and recovery encounters paradox or peril? *Journal of Service Research*, 1(1), 65–81.

Smith, A. K., Bolton, R. N. and Wagner, J. (1999) A model of customer satisfaction with service encounters involving failure and recovery. *Journal of Marketing Research*, 36, 356–72.

Smith, S. and Wheeler, J. (2002) *Managing the Customer Experience: Turning Customers into Advocates*. New York: Pearson Education.

So, K.K.F., King, C., Sparks, B.A. and Wang, Y. (2013) The influence of customer brand identification on hotel brand evaluation and loyalty development. *International Journal of Hospitality Management*, 34(1), 31–41.

Sparks, B.A. and Bradley, G.L. (2014) A "Triple A" typology of responding to negative consumer-generated online reviews. *Journal of Hospitality and Tourism Research*, (forthcoming).

Sparks, B.A. and Browning, V. (2011) The impact of online reviews on hotel booking intentions and perception of trust. *Tourism Management*, 32(6), 1310–23.

Sparks, B.A. and McColl-Kennedy, J.R. (2001) Justice strategy options for increased customer satisfaction in a services recovery setting. *Journal of Business Research*, 54(3), 209–18.

Spencer, S. and Rupp, D.E. (2009) Angry, guilty, and conflicted: injustice toward coworkers heightens emotional labor through cognitive and emotional mechanisms. *Journal of Applied Psychology*, 94(2), 429–44.

Stauss, B. and Friege, C. (1999) Regaining service customers costs and benefits of regain management. *Journal of Service Research*, 1(4), 347–61.

Sundaram, D.S. and Webster, C. (2000) The role of nonverbal communication in service encounters. *Journal of Services Marketing*, 14(5), 378–91.

Tax, S.S., Brown, S.W. and Chandrashekaran, M. (1998) Customer evaluations of service complaint experiences: implications for relationship marketing. *The Journal of Marketing*, 62(April), 60–76.

Tax, S.S., McCutcheon, D. and Wilkinson, I.F. (2013) The Service Delivery Network (SDN) a customer-centric perspective of the customer journey. *Journal of Service Research*, 16(4), 454–70.

Vallaster, C. and De Chernatony, L. (2005) Internationalisation of services brands: the role of leadership during the internal brand building process. *Journal of Marketing Management*, 21(1-2), 181–203.

Verhoef, P.C., Lemon, K.N., Parasuraman, A., Roggeveen, A., Tsiros, M. and Schlesinger, L.A. (2009) Customer experience creation: determinants, dynamics and management strategies. *Journal of Retailing*, 85(1), 31–41.

Wirtz, J. and McColl-Kennedy, J.R. (2010) Opportunistic customer claiming during service recovery. *Journal of the Academy of Marketing Science*, 38(5), 654–75.

Yang, X., Mao, H. and Peracchio, L.A. (2012) It's not whether you win or lose, it's how you play the game? The role of process and outcome in experience consumption. *Journal of Marketing Research*, 49(6), 954–66.

Zeithaml, V.A., Bitner, M.J. and Gremler, D.D. (2006) *Services Marketing: Integrating Customer Focus Across the Firm*. Boston: McGraw-Hill.

Zomerdijk, L.G. and Voss, C.A. (2010) Service design for experience-centric services. *Journal of Service Research*, 13(1), 67–82

21
Distribution channel management in hotel chains

Peter O'Connor

(ESSEC BUSINESS SCHOOL, FRANCE)

Introduction

Advances in information technology have had a dramatic effect on business over the past three decades (Ham et al., 2005). This is particularly true within the hotel sector, where information technology has fostered a revolution, particularly within distribution, changing forever the nature of the relationship between suppliers, intermediaries and consumers (Law et al, 2012). The perishable nature of the hotel product makes efficient distribution particularly important as an unsold room on a particular night cannot be stored and subsequently resold at a later date. Thus selling each room each night at an optimum price is one of the keys to hotel profitability (Kimes and Wagner, 2001). This requirement has prompted an emphasis on revenue management and, more recently, distribution channel management, as well as driven the development of a large number of information technology-based systems that facilitate and optimise the distribution function.

O'Connor and Frew (2002) define a channel of distribution as one that disseminates relevant, timely and accurate information about a hotel property to prospective customers, as well as provides a mechanism to make, confirm and pay for the booking. As will be discussed, the portfolio of distribution channels available to hotels has exploded in recent years, increasing the complexity of hotel distribution to unprecedented levels. In particular, online travel agents (OTAs) have seized control of the online travel space, dominating the sale of hotel rooms through electronic channels (Murphy and Chen, 2014). Meta-search providers are also vying for consumers' clicks, while hotels themselves would prefer to drive bookings directly through their own brand.com websites – an increasingly difficult prospect given the massive power of intermediaries in the distribution environment. Facilitating this increasingly complex portfolio of routes to the marketplace has become one of the key value-adding activities of a hotel chain, with owners and franchisees increasingly examining the proportion of business delivered through controlled routes as one of their critical hotel chain selection and evaluation criteria.

Before addressing the role of hotel chains in managing distribution, this chapter explores how electronic distribution systems have evolved to help explain where we find ourselves today. The path from manual processes through GDS (Global Distribution Systems) to today's open distribution network enabled by the internet is described. Current challenges being faced by hotel chains, including managing multiple simultaneous distribution channels, working with online intermediaries and reacting to rapidly changing technologies are also discussed to help readers understand the complexity of the current distribution environment. Lastly how hotel chains enable efficient distribution is also highlighted, with the central role that distribution now plays in hotel chain membership underlined.

Information and travel distribution

Information has been described as the lifeblood of travel, as without it the customer's incentive to travel is severely limited (Poon, 1993). The intangible nature of the travel product, which cannot be inspected prior to purchase and is thus completely reliant on information to help customers make a purchase decision, heighten this dependence (Bilgihan and Bujisic, 2014). As Buhalis et al. (1997: 246) point out 'the greater the degree of perceived risk in a pre-purchase context, the greater the consumer propensity to seek information about the product'. To facilitate this search process, the fast, effective and efficient exchange of information between supplier and customer (and/or their agent) is essential.

Consumers traditionally sourced information about travel products in a variety of ways. These included directly from suppliers themselves, or more commonly through intermediaries such as travel agents and tour operators, who essentially acted as information brokers bridging the gap between customers and suppliers (O'Connor and Frew, 2002). Intermediaries typically serviced these information requests either through print-based brochures or personal contact. Both methods are relatively inefficient, with print in particular being static and one-dimensional, with its content quickly becoming outdated (O'Connor, 2008). Personal contact is better, since information can be more closely matched to customers' needs and dynamic information can also be included, but distributing information in such a manner is both time consuming and expensive. These challenges, amongst others, pushed suppliers towards using electronic routes to service customers' information needs. The latter have fewer capacity limitations, offer infinitely more geographical reach, have a lower marginal cost, and also permit the incorporation of dynamic data such as room inventory and rates (O'Connor, 1999). Such benefits have prompted widespread adoption of electronic systems throughout the travel value chain, revolutionising the manner in which travel goods and services are promoted, distributed and sold.

Electronic distribution within travel has its origins in the airline computerised reservation systems of the 1970s. Conceived as internal systems for inventory control, these were subsequently broadened in scope to offer direct access to travel agencies, making the entire information search and booking processes faster, cheaper and more efficient for all concerned (Kärcher, 2006). Deregulation accelerated adoption, with electronic systems becoming to all intents and purposes essential for untangling the complex gamut of airline fares available (Hitchins, 1991). As usage grew airlines began cross-selling complementary products, most notably hotel rooms, to increase service levels and offset high running costs, resulting in today's Global Distribution Systems (GDS) (Beldona et al., 2005). Mergers and acquisitions have resulted in three main players (Amadeus, Travelport and Sabre), used today by approximately 95 per cent of agencies worldwide, making GDS representation essential for hotels wishing to sell through the travel agent community.

Connecting to the GDS requires hotels to have their own computer systems, typically known as central reservations systems (CRS) (O'Connor and Frew, 2002). These manage room inventory, acting as an electronic buffer between the GDS (and, as will be discussed, the growing portfolio of internet-based distribution channels) and the Property Management Systems (PMS) located at each individual hotel. Developing and maintaining such connectivity is expensive, with high upfront capital costs as well as substantial day-to-day operating costs. In addition, the environment is in a constant state of evolution, requiring knowledge, expertise and access to capital for redevelopment purposes. As a result it was the major hotel chains that were first to exploit this opportunity, developing dedicated CRS services to connect to the GDS and distribute their properties. Holiday Inn, now part of InterContinental Hotels and Resorts, claims to be the first hotel chain to sell through the GDS with its Holidex System, with the match between travel agent bookings and its primarily corporate travel focus giving it considerable competitive advantage in the short run. Other major hotel chains followed, using efficient access to the GDS distribution as one of their key arguments for attracting management contracts and franchises.

The web revolution

Until the mid-1990s, electronic distribution was essentially closed, with the GDS limiting access to just retail travel agents. From the hotel's perspective, such channels generated substantial amounts of business, but were expensive to develop and use, had a restricted viewership and offered limited opportunities for differentiation (O'Connor, 1999). Consumer growth in the use of the web as an information and shopping tool in the mid-1990s provided hotels with an opportunity to bypass the powerful GDS, prompting a radical change in distribution by shattering pre-existing relationships in the travel value chain (Kim et al., 2009).

As a medium, the Web was well suited to distribution (Murphy and Chen, 2014). Firstly it allowed full colour, interactive brochures to be placed directly into the hands of customers with a high propensity to travel at relatively low cost (Murphy et al., 1996). It also permits two-way communications, allowing transactions to be carried out directly with the customer and also facilitating Customer Relationship Marketing to better leverage the lifetime value of the customer (Law and Hsu, 2006). And lastly it offered major cost savings as little capital investment was required, and both GDS transaction fees and travel agent commission were eliminated (O'Connor and Frew, 2002). Keen to leverage their existing systems, hotel chains quickly began promoting their properties and distributing over the developing web medium. In general, their efforts have been successful, with (Toh et al., 2011) estimating that approximately 80 per cent of travellers search for hotel information using web tools, with more than half now making their bookings through web channels.

Initially many commentators focused on the web's ability to facilitate direct sales to the consumer, leading to speculative claims about disintermediation and the supposed death of the travel agent (Christou and Sigala, 2006). Suppliers were naturally enthusiastic about this possibility, as fewer (or ideally no) middlemen meant no commissions or transaction charges. Hotel chains were quick to move online, providing both detailed product information and reservation facilities directly to consumers on their own branded websites. And with low barriers to entry, in theory at least the web also offered smaller, independent, properties similar opportunities (Buhalis, 1999). Many took advantage of this potential, with, for example, a variety of studies demonstrating how the usage of the web as a distribution channel had diffused into smaller unbranded hotels into UK (Sigala, 2013), Aragonese (Minghetti 2003), Balearic (Garcés et al., 2004), Scottish (Vich-i-Martorell, 2003), Italian (Buick 2003) and Thai hotels (Sahadev and Islam, 2013). However, although moderately successful at first, independent properties typically quickly hit a barrier, particularly in terms of the budget, resources and technical expertise needed to drive significant amounts of business through their direct web presence.

A key challenge is that most websites limit shoppers to just their own products. For example visitors to Hotel ABC's website typically can only find information about, or reserve that particular hotel. However consumers do not purchase travel in this way. Someone booking a hotel also typically needs an airline ticket or rental car, or to find out something about the destination, or would like to know about visas and health requirements (Guo et al., 2013). To satisfy such diverse information needs, consumers increasingly turned to online travel agency (OTA) websites, whose key differentiators were not only a more complete product range, but also broader choice as they typically simultaneously offered products from multiple suppliers (Lee et al., 2013).

Many OTAs also had their origins outside the travel sector and thus were not blinkered by pre-existing relationships or traditional ways of doing business (Murphy and Chen, 2014). In particular they invested heavily in customer acquisition, both in terms of building powerful travel brands as well as devoting resources to mastering the online search environment to capture customers during the planning stage of their customer journey (Paraskevas et al., 2011). Their combination of powerful brands, high visibility, superior content and in many cases lower pricing has accelerated a trend towards re-intermediation (Buhalis and Licata, 2001), with increasing proportions of business flowing through indirect channels (Law et al., 2013). According to PhoCusWright (2014), OTAs' share of the online hotel market within the United States increased to 48 per cent in 2014, with a further growth to 51 per cent forecast for 2016, giving these online intermediaries unprecedented control over the sale of hotel rooms online.

The growth in importance of the web in the leisure customers' travel search and booking process has also prompted changes in the structure and methods of operation of the major tour operators (Buhalis, 2008). Traditionally vertically integrated, controlling not just supply through their ownership or contracting with hotels, airlines and other travel suppliers but also demand through their networks of owned and franchised retail travel agencies, these mega-travel companies are evolving, increasingly using tactics adopted from their OTA competitors (Bastakis et al., 2004). In an effort to stem the leakage of bookings towards alternative channels, most are disinvesting physical assets and copying the more flexible business practices of the OTAs in an effort to survive in an increasingly electronic marketplace (Guo and He, 2012). Most are attempting to drive increasing amounts of business through online channels, further complicating efforts by suppliers to drive business directly (Berne et al., 2012).

In both cases the big losers tend to be small and independent properties, most of whom lack the awareness, expertise, budget and technical competency to be able to compete effectively in a changed distribution environment (Law and Jogaratnam, 2013). As a result, an increasing number of such properties are being driven to join hotel chains, either by taking a franchise or management agreement, or by joining one of the many soft brands available on the market. Their primary motivations in making such a move is typically to gain access to the superior distribution provided by these players, so as to be able to compete more effectively in today's increasingly competitive electronic marketplace (Green, 2008).

The role of the hotel chain

As Sigala and Buhalis (2002) note, hoteliers that successfully manage their electronic distribution add value, develop their brand, and build customer loyalty; those who fail risk losing increasing numbers of customers to the ever more powerful OTAs. Although the hotel sector remains for the most part highly fragmented, as electronic distribution grows increasingly more complex, leveraging the collective power of a hotel chain has become an increasingly common way of gaining access to the appropriate facilities to be able to play the distribution game effectively (Ling et al., 2011). This section examines four of the key interlinked strengths of hotel chains in terms of electronic distribution identified from the literature, namely: access to technology; distribution expertise; negotiating power; and leveraging customer data, highlighting how membership of a hotel chain has become to a large extent essential for survival in today's highly competitive hotel electronic distribution marketplace (Gazzoli et al., 2013).

Access to technology

As discussed above, gaining access to today's electronic marketplace implies using appropriate information technology-based systems to manage room inventory and rates. In particular the growth in the use of electronic channels by consumers has resulted in an explosion in the variety of channels through which the hotel product can be sold. Working with multiple channels simultaneously implies maintaining and synchronising content, prices and inventory in multiple databases. If done manually, this is cumbersome, labour-intensive and costly, requiring hotels to systematically log into each system, process reservations or cancellations and manually change pricing/availability data to reflect updated market conditions (O'Connor and Frew, 2003).

Having an interface (typically known as a direct connect) between third party systems and the hotel greatly simplifies this process, allowing data to be updated automatically whenever market conditions change, as well as allowing yield management systems to work more effectively based on more complete and accurate data on demand and take-up. This latter point has become increasingly important as the range of distribution channels through which customers can book increases. In general, hotels do a poor job of managing price over multiple distribution channels, with consumers, thanks to highly controversial price parity clauses imposed by the OTAs, more likely to find cheaper prices on indirect channels than on the hotel's own direct website (O'Connor, 2002). Having appropriate systems in place helps to maintain price parity and allow hotels to offer at the very least a 'Best Rate Guarantee' (or alternatively a lower rate to help drive bookings through direct channels) (Chih-Chien and Schwartz, 2006).

However, implementing appropriate technology is both technically difficult and costly. Furthermore, as the number of channels increases, so too does the complexity of the supporting infrastructure and thus the running costs of the system (O'Connor and Picolli, 2003). Typically only hotel chains have the resources, capital and expertise to be able to successfully interface their systems with the majority of options available (Lee and Kim, 2004). This gives chain hotels more coverage, both in terms of number of distribution channels that can be simultaneously used as well as geographically, allowing them to collect demand from a wider variety of places and potentially increase sales. Hotel chains' ability to better leverage technological advances also allows them to more quickly and thoroughly exploit new and developing channels, giving them considerable first mover advantage when compared to independent properties. This ability to more successfully leverage technology-based systems as a competitive weapon is one of the key strengths of hotel chains within the distribution environment, allowing the latter to outperform their independent rivals and deliver superior value to their property owners.

Distribution expertise

Technology continues to develop at a rapid pace, and in fact has been identified as one of the top five most volatile factors affecting the travel sector (Okumus, 2004). Each change presents new challenges and opportunities, making distribution both difficult to understand as well as more challenging to exploit. The adoption of electronic channels by consumers resulted in the addition of a large number of alternative routes to the marketplace that supplemented, but never quite completely replaced, existing intermediaries (Vallespín Arán and Molinillo, 2014). As a result, the variety of both media (web, mobile, social media) and underlying business models (agency, merchant, packaged, opaque, private sale, last minute, group purchase, meta-search) within the distribution environment has become increasingly complex, with a vast set of alternatives now available to distribute the hotel's product to the marketplace (Ert and Fleischer, 2014). In general this development means wider reach, potentially allowing hotels to sell more rooms. However, utilising more channels also implies more knowledge and commitment on the part of the distribution manager, as each tends to have different revenue characteristics, costs and levels of control (O'Connor and Frew, 2002). In effect the decision of which portfolio of channels to use has become increasingly challenging, inflating the amount of expertise needed to successfully navigate this increasingly complex and rapidly evolving environment (Thakran and Verma, 2013). Enz (2003) points out that in reality most suppliers use multiple simultaneous electronic channels without a clear understanding of their impact and the effect this has on their profitability.

This complexity makes it difficult for the generalist managers typically seen in independent hotels to optimise their use of electronic distribution (Hobson and Cai, 2004). Hotel chains, on the other hand, profiting from the economies of scale that size brings, are able to develop specialised teams of personnel dedicated to the distribution and e-commerce functions, allowing them to more professionally manage distribution issues as well as keep up to date on latest developments and trends (Law and Jogaratnam, 2013). Coupled with a hotel chain's more powerful brand and more extensive budget, this greatly increases the chances of their brand.com site being able to compete with the OTA sites and generate direct traffic within today's online marketplace (Chung and Law, 2003). Thus this in-depth understanding of, and expertise in, the rapidly evolving distribution environment is once again a key driver of superior performance in terms of online sales and being able to deliver value to hotel owners and franchisees.

Negotiating power

Scale also has an effect in terms of negotiating power. As already mentioned, with their superior marketing practices and well-adapted product offering, OTAs have in effect taken control of the online travel space. Having incurred considerable costs, many have increased commission levels or introduced new business practices to help recuperate their investments, most notably with the introduction of the merchant model (Murphy and Chen, 2014).

In contrast to the traditional commission-based agent model, where hotels paid a percentage fee each time the intermediary sold a room for an agreed-on price, with the merchant model the OTA negotiates inventory at highly discounted net rates which it subsequently sells at a profit (Toh et al., 2011). Given the dominance that OTAs currently have over online hotel sales, the latter frequently leverage their negotiating power to demand rates significantly lower than what a supplier might freely wish to give (Christodoulidou and Brewer, 2007), as well as insisting on rate parity to insure that cheaper prices are not available through other channels, including the supplier's own brand.com website (Lee et al., 2013). But if hotels wish to be sold through OTA channels, in many cases they have no option but to capitulate and pay the comparatively high commission/mark-up (Green, 2008). And, since their brand.com websites are typically weak, independent hotels are left with few alternatives and are thus particularly vulnerable to such practices (Myung et al., 2009).

In contrast, by virtue of the potential volume that they can bring as a result of their network of properties, hotel chains can in general negotiate better terms and conditions, and in particular less-discounted rates, for their members (Christodoulidou et al., 2013). Several hotel chains, most notably InterContinental Group (Green, 2008) and Choice Hotels International (Lee et al., 2013), have publicly gone to battle over OTA bullying tactics, removing themselves from one or more of the major OTA systems for some time in order to battle for more advantageous agreements. Their actions, as well as strong negotiations by hotel chains in general, mean that average mark-ups/commissions for hotel chains are generally substantially lower than for independent properties (Toh et al., 2011). Given the sheer volume of transactions flowing through the major OTAs for many of the latter, in most cases these distribution cost savings alone more than justify the fees and other costs associated with becoming a member of a hotel chain (Koo et al., 2011).

Hotel chains have also attempted to increase their negotiating power by acting collectively. In 2012 six major hotel brands (Choice Hotels International, Hilton Worldwide, Hyatt Hotels, InterContinental Hotels Group, Marriott International and Wyndham Worldwide) founded Roomkey.com with the objective of offering hotels and their customers an alternative to the major OTAs. The site effectively acts as a demand collection system, targeting exit traffic from its founders' websites in an attempt to redirect this highly qualified traffic to alternative products. As all bookings are made directly, Roomkey.com's cost of distribution is substantially lower than that of an OTA. However, despite its potential, the site has yet to achieve critical mass, leading many to believe that it was introduced solely as a negotiation level rather than as a valid attempt to create an alternative to the global OTAs.

Leveraging customer data

The diversity of electronic distribution channels available today has led to another challenge – ownership of the customer. Travellers now have the ability to search for and book travel products in many different ways, with Google, for example, claiming that a typical leisure customer consults over twenty different websites before committing to a travel purchase. OTA sites are particularly attractive because of their rich feature set, diverse product selection and highly competitive prices (Ling et al., 2014). Such sites almost always provide consumers with a solution as well as, in most cases, several potential alternatives, in contrast to supplier direct sites which may not have a suitable product available or may be booked out for the dates requested (Jeong et al., 2003). In addition several major OTAs have also introduced loyalty programmes that recognise frequent and high value customers and use electronic marketing techniques to develop a closer relationship with them.

Given such utility, how then can suppliers compete? Overdependence on OTA channels is not only costly but also dangerous from a strategic perspective as it gives the online intermediaries increased control of the marketplace. O'Connor and Picolli (2003) highlighted this threat and stressed the need for hotels to drive customers to their direct websites to help regain ownership of the shopping experience. They counsel hoteliers to rethink their approach to distribution and to move away from a shelf space approach – being present on as many channels as possible – towards being more selective in terms of where they sell their products.

O'Connor and Frew (2002) similarly stress the need to drive customers directly, in particular by using sophisticated CRM techniques based on their personal contact with the customer to help build customer loyalty and in this way combat the growing power of the OTAs (Ben Vinod, 2011).

In fact many claim that future success in the hotel sector will depend on this ownership, maintenance and enhancement of customer relationships through direct online channels (Gan et al., 2008). Although independent properties typically have a closer, more personal, connection with their client base, few have the systems and expertise to be able to systematically exploit this knowledge. Scale once again is important here, with hotel chains typically maintaining sophisticated and extensive customer loyalty programmes, often with tens of millions of members, which can be exploited to help generate direct business. In addition, hotel chains frequently have both the expertise and technical resources to be able to exploit this opportunity correctly, leveraging their customer intelligence asset to drive higher proportions of business directly (Toh et al., 2011).

Conclusion

As can be seen from the above discussion, being able to play the distribution game effectively implies having access to the appropriate systems, expertise, budget and increasingly data. By virtue of the scale and business model, hotel chains can leverage these assets to drive superior performance. Independent hotels in contrast are increasingly being exploited by the overly dominant OTAs and, although many maintain direct brand.com websites, most struggle to drive sufficient amounts of business through this channel as a result of their lack of visibility in the hyper-competitive search environment (Herrero and San Martín, 2012). In effect, despite considerable effort, most independent properties are failing to fully exploit the potential of direct online distribution (Díaz and Koutra, 2013), in many cases also displaying an overreliance on indirect web channels with unfavourable commercial conditions.

As a result, a distinct trend towards the adoption of chain membership can be seen, driven to a large extent by hotel chains' superior performance in the distribution arena. Lee et al. (2013) suggest that one of the few ways for hotels to prosper in today's increasingly competitive electronic marketplace is to band together to gain economies of scale, either by forming consortia or by joining a hotel chain. Although doing so typically brings additional costs in the form of management or membership fees, the benefits of doing so are being clearly demonstrated day after day with hotels that are members of chains consistently outperforming independent properties in terms of distribution performance (Enz et al., 2014).

References

Bastakis, C., Buhalis, D. and Butler, R. (2004) The perception of small and medium sized tourism accommodation providers on the impacts of the tour operators' power in Eastern Mediterranean. *Tourism Management*, 25(2), 151–70.

Beldona, S., Morrison, A.M. and O'Leary, J. (2005) Online shopping motivations and pleasure travel products: a correspondence analysis. *Tourism Management*, 26(4), 561–70.

Ben Vinod. (2011) The future of online travel. *Journal of Revenue and Pricing Management*, 10(1), 56–61.

Berne, C., Garcia-Gonzalez, M. and Mugica, J. (2012) How ICT shifts the power balance of tourism distribution channels. *Tourism Management*, 33(1), 205–14.

Bilgihan, A. and Bujisic, M. (2014) The effect of website features in online relationship marketing: a case of online hotel booking. *Electronic Commerce Research and Applications*. 14(4), 222–32.

Buhalis, D. (1999) Information technology for small and medium sized tourism enterprises: adaptation and benefits. *Information Technology & Tourism*, 2(2), 79–95.

Buhalis, D. (2008) Relationships in the distribution channel of tourism: conflicts between hoteliers and tour operators in the Mediterranean region. *International Journal of Hospitality & Tourism Administration*. 1(1), 113–39.

Buhalis, D. and Licata, M.C. (2001) The future of eTourism intermediaries. *Tourism Management*, 23(3), 207–20

Buhalis, D., Jafari, J. and Werthner, H. (1997) Information technology and the reengineering of tourism. *Annals of Tourism Research,* 24, 245–7.

Buick, I. (2003) Information technology in small Scottish hotels: is it working? *International Journal of Contemporary Hospitality Management,* 15(4), 243–7.

Chih-Chien, C. and Schwartz, Z. (2006) The importance of information asymmetry in customers' booking decisions: a cautionary tale from the internet. *Cornell Hotel and Restaurant Administration Quarterly*. 47(3), 272–85.

Christodoulidou, N. and Brewer, P. (2007) Electronic channels of distribution: challenges and solutions for hotel operators. *Hospitality Review*. 25(2), 92–100.

Christodoulidou, N., Connolly, D.J. and Brewer, P. (2013) An examination of the transactional relationship between online travel agencies, travel meta sites, and suppliers. *International Journal of Contemporary Hospitality Management*. 22(7), 1048–62.

Christou, E. and Sigala, M. (2006) A qualitative analysis of consumer attitudes on adoption of online travel services. *Tourism*, 54(4), 323–31.

Chung, T. and Law, R. (2003) Developing a performance indicator for hotel websites. *International Journal of Hospitality Management*, 22(1), 119–25.

Díaz, E. and Koutra, C. (2013) Evaluation of the persuasive features of hotel chains websites: a latent class segmentation analysis. *International Journal of Hospitality Management*, 34, 338–47.

Enz, C.A. (2003) Hotel pricing in a networked world. *Cornell Hotel and Restaurant Administration Quarterly*, 44(1), 4–5.

Enz, C.A., Peiró-Signes, Á. and Segarra-Oña, M.-D.-V. (2014) How fast do new hotels ramp up performance? *Cornell Hospitality Quarterly*, 55(2), 141–51.

Ert, E. and Fleischer, A. (2014) Mere position effect in booking hotels online. *Journal of Travel Research*. Online. Available HTTP: <http://jtr.sagepub.com/content/early/2014/11/20/0047287514559035. abstract>, accessed 14 December 2015.

Gan, L., Sim, C.J., Tan, H.L. and Tna, J. (2008) Online relationship marketing by Singapore hotel websites. *Journal of Travel & Tourism Marketing*, 20(3-4), 1–19.

Garcés, S.A., Gorgemans, S., Marínez Sánchez, A. and Pérez Pérez, M. (2004) Implications of the internet—an analysis of the Aragonese hospitality industry, 2002. *Tourism Management*, 25(5), 603–13.

Gazzoli, G., Kim, W.G. and Palakurthi, R. (2013) Online distribution strategies and competition: are the global hotel companies getting it right? *International Journal of Contemporary Hospitality Management*, 20(4), 375–87.

Green, C.E. (2008) *Demystifying Distribution 2.0*. McLean, VA: HSMAI Foundation.

Guo, X. and He, L. (2012) Tourism supply-chain coordination: the cooperation between tourism hotel and tour operator. *Tourism Economics*, 18(6), 1361–76.

Guo, X., Ling, L., Dong, Y. and Liang, L. (2013) Cooperation contract in tourism supply chains: the optimal pricing strategy of hotels for cooperative third party strategic websites. *Annals of Tourism Research*, 41, 20–41.

Ham, S., Gon Kim, W. and Jeong, S. (2005) Effect of information technology on performance in upscale hotels. *International Journal of Hospitality Management*, 24(2), 281–94.

Herrero, Á. and San Martín, H. (2012) Developing and testing a global model to explain the adoption of websites by users in rural tourism accommodations. *International Journal of Hospitality Management*, 31(4), 1178–86.

Hitchins, F. (1991) The influence of technology on UK travel agents. *Travel and Tourism Analyst*, (3), 88–105.

Hobson, P. and Cai, L.A. (2004) Making hotel brands work in a competitive environment. *Journal of Vacation Marketing*, 10(3), 197–208.

Jeong, M., Oh, H. and Gregoire, M. (2003) Conceptualizing website quality and its consequences in the lodging industry. *International Journal of Hospitality Management*, 22(2), 161–75.

Kärcher, K. (2006) The emergence of electronic market systems in the European tour operator business. *Electronic Markets*, 13/14, 10–11.

Kim, J., Bojanic, D.C. and Warnick, R.B. (2009) Price bundling and travel product pricing practices used by online channels of distribution. *Journal of Travel Research*, 47(4), 403–12.

Kimes, S.E. and Wagner, P.E. (2001) Revenue management system as a trade secret. *Cornell Hotel and Restaurant Administration Quarterly.* 42(5), 8–15.

Koo, B., Mantin, B. and O'Connor, P. (2011) Online distribution of airline tickets: should airlines adopt a single or a multi-channel approach? *Tourism Management*, 32(1), 69–74.

Law, R. and Hsu, C.H.C. (2006) Importance of hotel website dimensions and attributes: perceptions of online browsers and online purchasers. *Journal of Hospitality & Tourism Research,* 30(3), 295–312.

Law, R. and Jogaratnam, G. (2013) A study of hotel information technology applications. *International Journal of Contemporary Hospitality Management.* 17(2), 170–80.

Law, R., Leung, K. and Wong, R. (2013) The impact of the Internet on travel agencies. *International Journal of Contemporary Hospitality Management.* 16(2), 100–7.

Law, R., Leung, D., Au, N. and Lee, H.A. (2012) Progress and development of information technology in the hospitality industry: evidence from the Cornell hospitality quarterly. *Cornell Hospitality Quarterly*, 54(1), 10–24.

Lee, H.A., Guillet, B.D. and Law, R. (2013) An examination of the relationship between online travel agents and hotels: a case study of Choice Hotels International and Expedia.com. *Cornell Hospitality Quarterly*, 54(1), 95–107.

Lee, S.W. and Kim, D.J. (2004) Driving factors and barriers of information and communication technology for e-business in SMEs: a case study in Korea. *Proceedings of the IADIS International Conference on e-Society*, Ávila, Spain. 163–71.

Ling, L., Guo, X. and Liang, L. (2011) Optimal pricing strategy of a small or medium-sized hotel in cooperation with a web site. *Journal of China Tourism Research*, 7(1), 20–41.

Ling, L., Guo, X. and Yang, C. (2014) Opening the online marketplace: an examination of hotel pricing and travel agency on-line distribution of rooms. *Tourism Management*, 45, 234–43.

Minghetti, V. (2003) Building customer value in the hospitality industry: towards the definition of a customer-centric information system. *Information Technology and Tourism* 6(2), 141–53.

Murphy, H.C. and Chen, M.-M. (2014) Online information sources used in hotel bookings examining relevance and recall. *Journal of Travel Research.* Online. Available HTTP: <http://jtr.sagepub.com/content/early/2014/11/14/0047287514559033.full.pdf+html>, accessed 14 December 2015.

Murphy, J., Forrest, E.J., Wotring, C.E. and Brymer, R.A. (1996) Hotel management and marketing on the internet: an analysis of sites and features. *Cornell Hospitality Quarterly*, 37(3), 70–82.

Myung, E., Li, L. and Bai, B. (2009) Managing the distribution channel relationship with e-wholesalers: hotel operators' perspective. *Journal of Hospitality Marketing & Management.* 18(8), 811–28.

O'Connor, P. (1999) *Electronic Information Distribution in Hospitality and Tourism.* Wallingford: CAB International.

O'Connor, P. (2002) An empirical analysis of hotel chain online pricing strategies. *Journal of Information Technology and Tourism*, 5(3), 65–72.

O'Connor, P. (2008) Distribution channels and ecommerce. In Oh, H. & Pizam, A. (eds) *Handbook of Hospitality Marketing Management.* New York: Elsevier. pp. 186–208.

O'Connor, P. and Frew, A.J. (2002) The future of hotel electronic distribution. *Cornell Hospitality Quarterly*, 43(3), 33–45.

O'Connor, P. and Frew, A.J. (2003) An evaluation methodology for hotel electronic channels of distribution. *International Journal of Hospitality Management*, 23, 179–99.

O'Connor, P. and Picolli, G. (2003) Marketing hotels using Global Distribution Systems revisited. *Cornell Hotel and Restaurant Administration Quarterly*, 44(5-6), 105–14.

Okumus, F. (2004) Potential challenges of employing a formal environmental scanning approach in hospitality organizations. *International Journal of Hospitality Management*, 23(2), 123–43.

Paraskevas, A., Katsogridakis, I., Law, R. and Buhalis, D. (2011). Search engine marketing: transforming search engines into hotel distribution channels. *Cornell Hospitality Quarterly*, 52(2), 200–8.

PhoCusWright (2014) *U.S. Online Travel Overview*, 14th edn. Sherman, CT: PhoCusWright.

Poon, A. (1993) *Tourism, Technology and Competitive Strategies.* Wallingford: Cab International.

Sahadev, S. and Islam, N. (2013) Why hotels adopt ICTs: a study on the ICT adoption propensity of hotels in Thailand. *International Journal of Contemporary Hospitality Management.* 17(5), 391–401.

Sigala, M. (2013) The information and communication technologies productivity impact on the UK hotel sector. *International Journal of Operations & Production Management.* 23(10) 1224–45.

Sigala, M. and Buhalis, D. (2002) Changing distribution channels in the travel industry—new channels, new challenges. *Information Technologies & Tourism*, 5(3), 185–6.

Thakran, K. and Verma, R. (2013) The emergence of hybrid online distribution channels in travel, tourism and hospitality. *Cornell Hospitality Quarterly*, 54(3), 240–7

Toh, R.S., Raven, P. and DeKay, F. (2011) Selling rooms: hotels vs. third-party websites. *Cornell Hospitality Quarterly*, 52(2), 181–9.

Vallespín Arán, M. and Molinillo, S. (2014) El futuro de la intermediación en el sector turístico. *Revista De Análisis Turístico*. 17(1), 13–25.

Vich-i-Martorell, G (2003) The internet and tourism principals in the Balearic Islands, *Tourism and Hospitality Research*, 5(5), 25–44.

22

Pricing and revenue management in hotel chains

Aurelio G. Mauri

(UNIVERSITÀ IULM, ITALY)

Introduction: Pricing and revenue management in the new technological framework

Pricing and revenue management are, at the present time, two crucial issues for hotel chains. Revenue management can be defined as a collection of coordinated techniques and business practices, strictly connected to pricing, utilised for increasing profitability, centrally in service activities (Mauri, 2012a). Revenue management was first employed by the airline sector and was later implemented in the hotel sector. Finally, revenue management techniques have become widespread and have been applied in other conventional and unconventional service industries: car rentals, cruises, restaurants, golf courses, casinos, spas, etc. (Anderson and Xie, 2010). In general, revenue management techniques are applicable to any business that has a relatively fixed capacity of perishable inventory with differentiated demand, has a high fixed-costs structure and involves varying customer price sensitivity.

In the current business environment, characterised by increasing digitalisation, globalisation and tougher competition, price has augmented its central and crucial role. Nowadays, ICT (Information and communications technology) offers new, effective managerial instruments (Law et al., 2014) that can be used for applying pricing policies but also in make pricing decisions more complex and difficult to manage. In particular, technological improvements have offered sellers an unprecedented chance to track and analyse customer behaviour and to obtain useful information about customers' preferences, and greater knowledge of their price sensitivity and their willingness to pay (Hinz et al., 2011). As a result, differential pricing, also known as price discrimination, has been utilised more and more, as it is an effective means that permits sellers to improve their profits and to reduce the so-called consumer surplus, held by buyers. Concerning competition, now it is also simpler to monitor (for example through specific tools named rate shoppers) and deal with competitors' prices by operating continuous modifications of prices (dynamic pricing). In summary, new technologies have made dynamic pricing (Abrate et al., 2012) not only extensively possible but also commercially practicable and more profitable (Elmaghraby and Keskinocak, 2003). Furthermore, it is useful to pay attention to the various psychological dimensions of price, and their impacts on perceived value, fairness and brand loyalty (Grewal et al., 2003).

Price: Concept and relevance. Value-based pricing

In recent years, price and pricing policies have become a central issue in economic studies, despite the fact that in the past this topic has traditionally received limited academic investigation. At present, it is of little doubt that pricing has a decisive impact on a firm's performances. Price determines revenue and, as a consequence, profit, but also plays a considerable role in influencing demand and affecting competition. Briefly defined, price is 'the amount of money charged for a good or a service'. More broadly, 'price is the sum of the values consumers exchange for the benefits of having or using the product or service' (Kotler et al., 2010). Price is one of the four elements of the traditional concept of the marketing mix. Internal and external factors influence a firm's pricing decisions. Internal factors include the company's marketing objectives, marketing strategy, costs and organisational considerations. External factors embrace the nature of the market, demand characteristics, competition and other environmental elements.

Pricing decision approaches can be categorised into the following three groups (Phillips, 2005):

i. Cost-based pricing approaches: firms determine prices primarily with regards to data made available by cost accounting. The attention is put on the company itself and on its cost structure. A key tool is the cost-volume-profit (CVP) analysis;

ii. Competition-based pricing: this method is based on analysis of competitors. Firms use observed price levels of competitors as primary sources for setting their prices;

iii. Customer value-based pricing: decision makers try to assess the value a product delivers to one or more different types of customers and use it as the main factor for setting prices.

While traditional approaches were commonly based on costs, in recent years academics and practitioners have highlighted the crucial role of value perceptions by customers and consequently the rising importance of value-based pricing (Nagle et al., 2011). Pricing policy is crucial both at a strategic as well as a tactical level. From a theoretical point of view, pricing strategies determine long-term price structures and levels, while pricing tactics only affect short-term decisions (Morris and Calantone, 1990). Although in business practice this difference is not always so clear and the two terms are sometimes even considered synonymous. Phillips (2005) underlines that now companies must be able to face the real time pricing environment, managing pricing more rapidly.

Price discrimination/differentiation

According to economic literature, price discrimination occurs when prices vary across customer segments in manners that cannot be fully explained by differences in marginal costs (Armstrong and Vickers, 2001). In other words, price differences are due more to demand factors than to costs that do not differ correspondingly. Price discrimination has been studied both by economists and, more recently, by marketing scholars. While the label 'price discrimination' is the one most established, especially in economics, some authors prefer to use 'price differentiation' to indicate the same concept, maybe as the term 'price discrimination' reminds them of something unfair (Phillips, 2005).

The literature states that price differentiation can be a profitable pricing approach (Png, 2002). In fact, discriminatory pricing tries to understand and to get close to the reservation price of each market segment. The reservation price for a potential purchaser can be defined as the maximum price the buyer is willing to pay in order to purchase a product (good or service) and depends on the total consumer benefit. A consumer surplus is generated when there is a difference between the consumer's reservation price and the price the consumer has to pay for the product. Price discrimination often reduces consumer surplus and consequently enhances corporate profits.

In order to practically apply price discrimination, the following criteria must be fulfilled:

a. different market segments must have diverse value assessments;
b. different segments must be identifiable and price differentiation must be profitably applicable;
c. there should be no opportunity for clients belonging to one segment who have paid a lower price to resell their purchases to clients from other segments (arbitrage);
d. customers should not be confused or upset by the use of different prices (perceptions of unfairness).

In the lodging sector price differentiation requires appropriate market segmentation and can be applied by establishing barriers (called rate fences) between market segments. 'Rate fences' are the rules and criteria that hotels, or other services firms, can use to separate customer segments whose services value may differ (Mauri, 2012b). In fact, in order to entice different customers to actually pay different prices, hotels must introduce barriers that bring clients to purchase services following diverse patterns. To minimise 'buy-downs', e.g. customers who actually pay a lower rate when they would have been willing to pay a higher price, it is essential to adopt proper rate fencing (Vinod, 2004). Price fences can be classified in two groups: physical fences and non-physical fences (Hanks et al., 1992). Physical rate fences include physical location of and view from the rooms, size and furnishings, presence of amenities and extra services. Non-physical rate fences include consumption characteristics (i.e., time or duration of use, frequency or volume of consumption), transaction characteristics (i.e., booking time) and buyer features. It is also important to observe that different rate fence types may be combined. Adequate fencing and framing (the way prices are presented) are fundamental in generating perceptions of fairness or unfairness by customers, which may affect revenue management results. In fact, customers may perceive revenue management as an opportunistic behaviour of the corporation and then consider these practices as unfair. As a result, customers' trust and loyalty towards the hotel brand may deteriorate (Mauri, 2007).

The adoption of revenue management in the hotel sector: from yield management to revenue management

In the introductory period of employment the techniques and practices used to increase profitability of services firms were called yield management. In particular, as aforementioned, the first field of usage of yield management tools has been the airline sector starting in the 1960–1970s. Nevertheless, the crucial milestone for the development of yield management was the deregulation of the American airline industry (The Airline Deregulation Act of 1978). At that moment, new low-cost carriers entered the market and traditional airlines had to face serious economic problems due to tougher competition. Consequently, they had to improve their efficiency and effectiveness to be able to reduce prices, and started developing yield management tools.

Despite the fact that the hospitality industry has much in common with the airline industry, being both services and travel industries, hotels have adopted revenue management techniques only after a certain delay. There were various reasons this occurred, as obstacles to the spread of revenue management use in the lodging business were detected by Mainzer (2004). First, the lodging sector, in comparison with airlines, was highly decentralised and fragmented: there were a few major corporations and numerous individually managed hotels or minor corporations. Still now, despite the current trend towards the growth of hospitality groups within the lodging industry, a large proportion of hotels is still individually managed, especially in European countries. Second, the ownership and management structures of the hospitality industry were and are much more diverse and complex. In particular, because of the trend towards the split between 'bricks and brains', frequently a hospitality chain or brand is not the owner of the hotel property. Through franchising agreements, lease and management contracts, the three basic elements of real estate property, management and brand may be differently combined. Consequently, the number of companies to be integrated was greater. Third, hotels presented new issues to be considered in revenue management decisions such as the length of stay (regarding multiple-night stays) and the chance of getting revenue flows from ancillary services (the so-called multiplier effect) (Kimes, 1989). For example, referring to the first issue, accepting a hotel guest for the last room on a single day, even at the highest rate, could block a guest willing to stay multiple nights (Cross et al., 2011) and then inhibit potential higher revenue. However, airlines also have to face a similar problem with multiple flight-legs (the so-called 'network effect'), when some flights (more precisely named 'flight segments') are combined in a unique journey for a passenger. Coming to ancillary revenue, these days this topic has become particularly important, for instance regarding Food and Beverage, Spa and Gaming.

Anyway, notwithstanding these difficulties, by the late 1990s virtually all the world's major hotel groups had implemented revenue management systems (Cross et al., 2011). On the other hand, the situation of small groups and individual hotels was and still is differentiated concerning intensity and quality of usage of revenue management techniques. Marriott International was one of the first players in adopting and adapting yield management techniques by the hospitality industry. CEO J.W. 'Bill' Marriott's interest was stimulated by a chance discussion with Bob Crandall, ultimately Chairman and CEO of American Airlines. The success of revenue management implementation at Marriott was rapidly followed by the adoption of yield management at major North American hotel chains. Hilton, Holiday Inn and Sheraton successfully implemented these techniques in the 1990s (Cross et al., 2011). Furthermore, since 'yield' was considered an airline term, Marriott and other groups adopting these practices preferred to define them as 'revenue management' (Cross, 1997).

In a first phase, revenue management systems were based on predicting customer demand and optimising available price. Later, in the 2000s, because of demand slowdown, hotels understood the crucial role of managing rates themselves. The objective then became to optimise prices. This approach was based on forecasting demand, price elasticity and competitive rates. At present, the use of revenue management in the hotel business is largely connected to dedicated software developed by a number of ICT and consultancy companies.

Revenue management in the hotel business

Revenue management can be defined as an articulated business process implemented in order to maximise revenue and profits. A process is a structured, measured set of decisions and activities designed to accomplish a goal. Consequently, proper application of revenue management requires other sub-processes and activities, which can be assorted in phases (Mauri, 2012a).

Academics and practitioners have comprehensively studied revenue management and useful literature reviews are available (Chiang et al., 2006; McMahon-Beattie and Yeoman, 2013; Guillet and Mohammed, 2015; Wang et al., 2015). Authors have proposed some alternative structures and sequences of phases for illustrating the revenue management process (Ivanov, 2014). First steps can be represented by demand modelling, segmentation, and customers profiling, followed by demand forecasting, capacity allocation and pricing optimisation.

The revenue management process involves cycling through these steps at recurrent intervals. The frequency with which new cycles are performed depends on various factors such as the amount and availability of data, the rapidity of business condition changes, the type of forecasting and optimisation methods and systems adopted and, finally, the importance of the resulting decisions (Talluri and van Ryzin, 2005). In the present publication we would like to underline and deal with two central topics of the process: customer segmentation and demand forecasting.

Revenue management exploits differences in purchasing behaviours and value assessments by diverse market segments. Consequently, pricing and capacity allocation to the various market portions are the key levers. Market segmentation, executed by sub-dividing a market into distinct and homogeneous subgroups of customers, plays a crucial role in the effective implementation of revenue management strategies. In particular, market segmentation is functional to price setting. Moreover, segmentation is applied within the demand modelling framework that comprehends the product offering, the value definition and the analysis of the competitors. Effective revenue management requires matching a customer's needs with rooms offered (and other services offered too) from a strategic as well as from a tactical point of view, and then to set correct and profitable prices. Rooms constituting hotel inventory must be properly classified and codified according to their main characteristics (such as location of the room within the building, view, size and type, bed configuration and other relevant aspects). Also rates must be codified, with a decreasing order beginning from the rack rate (the highest rate that can be charged). Different prices can be related to guest characteristics, reason of stay, time of booking and length of stay, quantity of purchases, booking channel, etc.

The hotel industry has traditionally divided demand into two broad segments: group and transient, where the group segment includes conferences and corporate events. The transient segment represents all individual bookings (Koushik et al., 2012). Furthermore, the transient demand can be divided into retail and negotiated segments (Lee et al., 2011). However hotel chains are currently facing traveller motivations and behaviour that are increasingly fragmented and diverse and consequently more difficult to segment into clearly distinct customer groups. It will then be possible to predict a trend toward micro-segmentation grounded in advanced data mining techniques (Amadeus, 2010).

The second key aspect for successful revenue management is an appropriate forecast of demand (Frechtling, 2001). Forecasting techniques are employed to appreciate future demand, starting from historical data and then considering a number of factors, in addition to current bookings. The capability of correctly predicting demand is very important, and must be based on precise and analytical registrations of historical data regarding bookings and hotel stays.

Advanced forecasting techniques can simulate the effects of rate changes and capacity constraints usage. A framework for forecasting methods in hotel revenue management is given by Chen and Kachani (2007). Hotels organise demand forecasting, predicting the number of arriving guests for each day of arrival, for each length of stay and each rate class.

Demand forecasting has to consider bookings, walk-ins, cancellations, early and late checkouts, recaptures and eventually postponed arrivals. In the current practice, typical operational tools are hotel pick-up reports and booking (or pace) curves. Pick-up can be defined as the number of reservations collected from a given point in time to a different point in time over the booking process. The current effort is aimed at making forecasting price sensitive (Eister and Cross, 2012).

Specific and current issues of revenue management for hotel chains

As revenue management is rapidly evolving, for larger hotel chains, it is increasingly difficult to understand the rate with which all the aspects involved are developing. The application of revenue management in the lodging sector and especially in hotel chains meets, at present, the following crucial issues:

Distribution channels and revenue management

Structural and operative changes have strongly affected tourism distribution with the affirmation of multi-channel distribution and the phenomena of disintermediation and re-intermediation. The multi-channel sales environment makes managing pricing policies more complex and also conflicts among different channels may arise. In fact, the so-called 'price parity' (i.e. maintaining homogeneous rates for the same product) among different distribution channels has become a key concern for managers. Hotels must also face the challenge of metasearch websites and guest review websites.

Integration between revenue management and customer relationship management (CRM)

Although the profitability results of revenue management tools are evident, the integration between revenue management and customer relationship management is quite complex and it is becoming a crucial concern within a long-term view (Wang, 2012). In fact, it is important to evaluate the compatibility of traditional (called time-based or transaction-based) revenue management practices with customer relationship management, and avoid actions which may produce perceptions of unfairness, especially by loyal and profitable clients. Hospitality and travel firms must try to adapt their structures and processes in order to be more customer-centred, adopting a long-term view and integrating revenue management with loyalty programmes.

Learning from the airlines experiences (Vinod, 2008), with the purpose of increasing revenue management effectiveness, hotel chains can invest in data mining, business intelligence and advanced data analytics to comprehend customer characteristics, behaviours and preferences in order to increase customer retention, acquire new customers and maximise the revenue-generation potential from the customer base. In this regard the availability of complete, but also clean and consistent data is fundamental, also taking into account social media data and user-generated content (such as guest reviews).

Social media and revenue management

Social media may affect various steps in the revenue management process. Companies can increase their knowledge of consumers' features, behaviour and willingness to pay, that facilitates price strategy definition and demand forecasting. This helps improving segmentation, differentiation and personalisation of services provided. Then, social media is increasingly included in pricing strategies adopted by hotel chains, who may provide special rates, coupons and dedicated offers to members. Furthermore, through social media, customers frequently comment on the value-for-money (Christou and Nella, 2012; Maier, 2012) and thus other customers and prospective customers can enhance their information and compare different travel companies' offers.

In summary, social media offers various opportunities for revenue management application. However, to be able to exploit its full potential, companies should develop an integrated and strategic approach, based on the cooperation of all the firm's functions and departments (Minazzi, 2015).

There are also three important points:

Revenue management, brand proliferation and brand portfolios in the hotel sector

The use of revenue management by hotel chains and groups, instead of single unit hotels, highlights some matters related to the multi-unit, multi-brand environment. In fact, a crucial aspect in applying pricing and revenue management in hotel chains is represented by multi-branding. Most large firms operating in the lodging sector own and manage a set of different brands: i.e., they have a brand portfolio.

The hotel sector, especially in North America, but also in the other continents, has accelerated its evolution from an industry made up of small and independent hotel owner-operators to a market dominated by major international groups and institutional investors. The development of new product/market combinations has changed the set of the hotel groups' competitive relationships with other players, implying the encounter of new competitors as well as of some former competitors that have undertaken a similar expansion path from the traditional market. Consequently multimarket competition among hotel corporations takes place (Karnani and Wernerfelt, 1985). This variety's increment may also be useful for developing more complex pricing strategies, based on price discrimination, able to extract more consumer surplus. This is due to:

- the capability of applying better and more precise segmentation and of customising pricing strategies;
- the opportunity for achieving a better consistency between the hotel brand and the destination where it is located;
- the chance of facing competitors with multi-point competition.

However, on the other side of the coin some disadvantages may arise:

- overlapping/cannibalisation of brands; in fact an exaggerated hotel brand number may lead to cannibalisation among hotel brands, i.e. cannibalising of market share of one product (brand) by other products of the same company (Ivanov, 2007).
- confusion; in fact travellers may well become quite confused, frustrated, or even immune to brand differentiation;
- loss of brand consistency – an important aspect of successful branding (many hotels are franchised or managed by companies independent of the hotel chain's parent company).

Revenue management systems software

These days technological issues have become a central topic in hotel chain decisions, with the challenge of continuous new advancements, like the current emergence of cloud computing, that makes available IT (information technology) resources (i.e. databases and software) over the internet.

Within hospitality corporations and groups, revenue management is applied through expert software with automated and sophisticated demand forecast and optimisation systems. It is possible to distinguish between a 'decision' revenue management system and a 'recommendation' system. A decision system automatically executes a number of actions in the transaction system without intervention from the revenue manager. On the other hand, a recommendation system provides advice on the actions to be deployed. In this regard Schwartz and Cohen (2004) note that 'despite the increasing reliance on computers, human judgment is still indispensable in setting revenue-management rules' but they also note that 'judgment of revenue managers is prone to bias'. Generally, in hotel systems, computers and human decision makers interact and the computer-generated predictions and recommendations are evaluated and, in some cases, modified by revenue managers (Selmi and Dornier, 2011). However, for small and middle sized firms, it is feasible to implement revenue management by making use of more basic software, for instance employing spreadsheets for collecting historical data and demand forecasting (Cleophas and Frank, 2011).

A revenue management system can be composed of various software modules, and can assume different configurations depending on the historical IT solutions chosen and on the latitude of new functionalities added with integrative modules, that should be properly integrated (Mauri, 2012a).

Each hotel group has followed different paths in developing their own revenue management system. For example Pekgün et al. (2013) analyse the development of a revenue management system and software within the Carlson Rezidor Hotel Group, while Eister and Cross (2012) describe the evolution of revenue management by IHG. The experience of Marriott, especially regarding pricing groups, is illustrated by Hormby et al. (2010).

Technology integration is a crucial issue – the hotel revenue management software cannot exist as a standalone application. The solution should seamlessly be integrated firstly with the Property Management System, to provide for unified bookings, analytics and reporting functions, as well as with other corporate and third-party technologies and add-on modules. It should also interconnect with multiple data streams in addition to sales and distribution channels (Starfleet Media, 2014).

Several IT suppliers of dedicated software systems offer product solutions and support for the implementation of more advanced revenue management systems. We can mention a few: Amadeus, Booking Analytics, Duetto, IDeaS, Infor EzRMS, JDA, MaximRMS, Oracle Micros, PriceMatch and Rainmaker. The selection of the consulting partner and/or the technology solution provider is an important decision that must be made through an analytical and thorough process (Starfleet Media, 2014). Various modules, composing a revenue management system, can be recognised (Mauri, 2012a). These modules can be variously combined within software solutions available in the market. In particular it is possible to observe:

- the Property Management System (PMS); is a comprehensive software application used to manage some basic objectives such as coordinating the operational functions such as inventory, rate and reservations, billing, labour, accounting, room management, etc. The PMS can be considered the central data infrastructure of the hotel (Kokaz Pucciani and

Murphy, 2011). At present, there are many PMS providers available on the market that offer various solutions with a large number of functionalities based on the changing needs of hotels. Opera is the most used PMS. For hotel chains, the property management software is configurable to each property's specific requirements and can operate in either single-property or multi-property mode, with all properties sharing a central database. The Multi-Property functionality can help hotel chains to reduce hardware and software investments and costs, and labour expenses, by managing multiple properties through a single database and a unique hardware/software platform;

- the Central Reservation System (CRS) and the booking engine; the CRS is a computerised system utilised by hotel chains for centralising reservations of all their properties onto one system. The CRS allows one to store and retrieve information (rates, availability, reservations) and conduct transactions. It is connected with the website and with the mobile booking engines. The CRS and the PMS interface with one another in order to synchronise the data in both systems. Additionally the CRS may provide connectivity to Global Distribution Systems (GDS), Switches, Online Travel Agents (OTA) and reservation call centres. Some hotel chains have their own CRS, like Marsha (Marriott), Holidex (IHG) and Tars (Accorhotels) while other hotels use a third party CRS;

- the Revenue Management System (RMS); this may develop various functions (demand modelling, demand forecasting, optimisation and controls) providing proper information to the revenue manager or automatically executing price and availability changes;

- the Channel Manager; this is a software solution that allows hotels to manage availability, restrictions and rates across a multitude of sales channels rapidly and efficiently, that can also be integrated in the RMS. In fact, because of continuously pricing modifications, hotels need to update rates and inventory information, while minimising errors, across all distribution channels;

- the Rate Shopper; this is the tool that helps hotels to analytically monitor in real time their competitors' room rate decisions (the so-called competitive set) through the various booking channels. Another useful thing that the rate shopper can do is provide rate types with corresponding descriptions to enhance the analysis. It can also be integrated in the RMS, other possible integrative modules, such as Customer Relationship Management System (CRM) and Online Reputation Management.

Revenue management organisational aspects

A multi-unit organisation, such as a hotel chain or group has to make decisions regarding centralisation versus decentralisation of revenue management decision-making (Talluri and van Ryzin, 2005). Consequently the discussion regarding centralisation versus decentralisation of hotel chains decisions and operations is relevant (Espino-Rodríguez and Taylor, 2006).

Normally hotel chains have a centralised revenue management department. The corporate revenue management team supports the hotel revenue managers by providing systems, strategy and guidance. However, the revenue management centralisation of hotel chains differs from the highly centralised structure in the airline industry. The complex organisational structure of hotel revenue management presents significant challenges with respect to training, adoption, and consistent execution of strategies and system use (Koushik, et al., 2012).

A problem that arises is whether the hotel chain should focus on the optimisation of the revenues of the chain as a whole, of the hotels in a region or of the individual properties. This creates problems because of the different ownership of the hotels in the chain that may be managed by different operators. Therefore, the revenue optimisation decisions of the chain would have an impact on the revenues of the individual hotels and the incomes of their owners. Then conflicts may arise between the revenue management actions of the individual hotels and the overall revenue management strategy of the hotel chain. Another aspect is the access to corporate clients' data by an affiliated hotel, and the chance of storing and recovering this data in case the hotel leaves the group.

Finally, we can mention that, as a consequence of the increased attention given to pricing and revenue management by hoteliers, the business roles and professional competence of dedicated human resources has become a central issue. Furthermore, along with technical tools and abilities, social drivers can also impact revenue management performance (Queenan et al., 2011).

Conclusion

The dynamics that have characterised the tourism industry in the last few decades have significantly affected the way hotels and hospitality groups are organised, operate, deal with customers and face competition. Revenue management techniques are widespread in the lodging sector, increasing hotel profitability and operational performance. These techniques are constantly evolving with the endless progress of information and communications technology.

Revenue management exploits differences in purchasing behaviours by diverse market components, to reduce consumer surplus and increase hotels' profits. Dynamic and customised pricing, in conjunction with capacity allocation to various customer segments, are key levers. We must remember that two processes, which combine and interact, are fundamental in order to achieve market success: the creation of customer value (through the offer of appreciated services) and the value appropriation (i.e. extracting profits) (Mizik and Jacobson, 2003).

Updated systems and software, and the adequate collection of insightful data regarding clients and their behaviours, are fundamental for applying revenue management successfully. Data integration of guests' information, collected at a number of contact points, including front-line personnel, call centres, websites, social media, etc., allows hotel chains to improve individual customer satisfaction and to maximise yield on each customer simultaneously. Furthermore, as hotel guests usually do not just purchase a single service (the room) but they require other ancillary services that represent additional (and sometimes relevant) sources of revenue, it is important to look at the total value generated by customers.

References

Abrate G., Fraquelli, G., and Viglia, G. (2012) Dynamic pricing strategies: evidence from European hotels. *International Journal of Hospitality Management*, 31(1), 160–8.

Amadeus (2010) Hotels 2020: Beyond Segmentation Strategies for growth in an era of personalization and global change. Online. Available HTTP: <http://www.amadeus.com/web/amadeus/en_1A-corporate/Hotels/Resources-and-downloads/Research-reports/1319578304477-Page-AMAD_DocumentsPpal?assetid=1319609444141&assettype=Categorizable_P&industrySegment=1259068355773>.

Anderson, C.K. and Xie, X. (2010) Improving hospitality industry sales. Twenty-five years of revenue management. *Cornell Hospitality Quarterly*, 51(1), 53–67.

Armstrong, M. and Vickers, J. (2001). Competitive price discrimination. *Rand Journal of Economics*, 32(4), 1–27.

Chen, C. and Kachani, S. (2007) Forecasting and optimisation for hotel revenue management. *Journal of Revenue and Pricing Management*, 6(3), 163–74.

Chiang, W.C., Chen, J.C. and Xu, X. (2006) An overview of research on revenue management: current issues and future research. *International Journal of Revenue Management*, 1(1), 97–128.

Christou, E. and Nella, A. (2012) Web 2.0 and pricing transparency in hotel services. In Sigala, M., Christou, E., Gretzel, U. (eds), *Social Media in Travel, Tourism and Hospitality. Theory, Practice and Cases*. Surrey: Ashgate.

Cleophas, C. and Frank, M. (2011) Ten myths of revenue management – a practitioner's view. *Journal of Revenue and Pricing Management*, 10(1), 26–31.

Cross, R. (1997) *Revenue Management: Hard-core Tactics for Market Domination*. New York: Broadway.

Cross, R.G., Higbie, J.A. and Cross, Z.N. (2011) Milestones in the application of analytical pricing and revenue management. *Journal of Revenue and Pricing Management*, 10(1), 8–18.

Eister, C. and Cross, D. (2012) Pricing as a competitive weapon: how IHG's price optimization capability revolutionized pricing for hospitality, hospitality research summit (CHRS), October 8 and 9. Online. Available HTTP: <http://revenueanalytics.com/wp-content/uploads/2014/03/CHRS-Pricing-as-a-Competitive-Weapon-201209131.pdf>, accessed 3 December 2015.

Elmaghraby, W. and Keskinocak, P. (2003) Dynamic pricing in the presence of inventory considerations: research overview, current practices, and future directions. *Management Science*, 49(10), 1287–309.

Espino-Rodríguez, T.F. and Taylor, J.S. (2006) The perceived influence of centralising operations in chain hotels. *Tourism and Hospitality Research*, 6(4), 251–66.

Frechtling, D. (2001) *Forecasting Tourism Demand*. Oxford: Butterworth-Heinemann.

Grewal, D., Iyer, G.R., Krishnan, R. and Sharma, A. (2003) The Internet and the price–value–loyalty chain. *Journal of Business Research*, 56(5), 391–8.

Guillet, B.D. and Mohammed, I. (2015) Revenue management research in hospitality and tourism. Management, *International Journal of Contemporary Hospitality Management*, 27(4), 526–60.

Hanks R.B., Noland R.P. and Cross R.G. (1992) Discounting in the hotel industry, a new approach, *Cornell Hotel and Restaurant Administration Quarterly*, 33(3), 40–5.

Hinz, O., Hann, I. and Spann, M. (2011) Price discrimination in e-commerce? An examination of dynamic pricing in name-your-own-price markets. *MIS Quarterly*, 35(1), 81–98.

Hormby, S., Morrison, J., Dave, P., Meyers, M. and Tenca, T. (2010) Marriott International increases revenue by implementing a group pricing optimizer. *Interfaces*, 40(1), 47–57.

Ivanov, S. (2007) Conceptualizing cannibalisation: the case of tourist companies. *Yearbook of International University College*, 3, 20–36.

Ivanov, S. (2014) *Hotel Revenue Management: From Theory to Practice*. Varna: Zangador.

Karnani A. and Wernerfelt B. (1985) Multiple point competition. *Strategic Management Journal*. 6(1), 87–96.

Kimes S.E. (1989) The basics of yield management. *Cornell Hotel and Restaurant Administration Quarterly*, 30(3), 14–9.

Kokaz Pucciani, K. and Murphy, H.C. (2011) An investigation of data management and property management systems in hotels. *Tourism and Hospitality Management*, 17(1), 101–14.

Kotler, P., Bowen, J.T. and Makens, J.C. (2010) *Marketing for Hospitality and Tourism*, 5th edn. Upper Saddle River: Pearson.

Koushik, D., Higbie, J.A. and Eister, C. (2012) Retail price optimization at intercontinental hotels group. *Interfaces*, 42(1), 45–57.

Law, R., Buhalis, D. and Cobanoglu, C. (2014) Progress on information and communication technologies in hospitality and tourism. *International Journal of Contemporary Hospitality Management*, 26(5), 727–50.

Lee, S., Garrow, L., Higbie, J., Keskinocak, P. and Koushik, D. (2011) Do you really know who your customers are? A study of US retail hotel demand. *Journal of Revenue and Pricing Management*, 10(1), 73–86.

Maier T.A. (2012) International hotel revenue management: web-performance effectiveness modelling – research comparative. *Journal of Hospitality and Tourism Technology* 3(2), 121–37

Mainzer, B.W. (2004) Fast forward for hospitality revenue management. *Journal of Revenue and Pricing Management*, 3(3), 1–5.

Mauri, A G. (2007) Yield management and perceptions of fairness in the hotel business. *International Review of Economics*, 54(2), 284–93.

Mauri, A.G. (2012a) *Hotel Revenue Management: Principles and Practices*. Milano: Pearson.

Mauri, A.G. (2012b) Hotel revenue management and guests' perceived fairness. theoretical issues and empirical findings from a multiple-year survey. Smashwords. Online. Available HTTP: <http://www.smashwords.com/extreader/read/256716/1/hotel-revenue-management-and-guests-perceived-fairness-theor>, accessed 3 December 2015.

McMahon-Beattie, U. and Yeoman I. (2013) Revenue management in tourism In McCabe, S. (ed.) *The Routledge Handbook of Tourism Marketing*. Abingdon: Routledge, pp. 370–80.

Minazzi, R. (2015) *Social Media Marketing in Tourism and Hospitality*. Switzerland: Springer International Publishing.

Mizik, N. and Jacobson, R. (2003) Trading off between value creation and value appropriation: the financial implications of shifts in strategic emphasis. *Journal of Marketing*, 67(1), 63–76.

Morris, M.H. and Calantone R.J. (1990). Four components of effective pricing. *Industrial Marketing Management*, 19(4), 321–9.

Nagle, T.T., Hogan, J.E. and Zale, J. (2011) *The Strategy and Tactics of Pricing: A Guide to Growing More Profitably*, 5th edn. Englewood Cliffs: Prentice Hall.

Pekgün, P., Menich, R.P., Acharya, S., Finch, P.G., Deschamps, F., Mallery, K. and Fuller, J. (2013) Carlson Rezidor hotel group maximizes revenue through improved demand management and price optimization. *Interfaces*, 43(1), 21–36.

Phillips, R. (2005) *Pricing and Revenue Optimization*. Palo Alto: Stanford University Press.

Png, I. (2002) *Managerial Economics*, 2nd edn. Malden: Blackwell Publishers.

Queenan, C.C., Ferguson, M.E. and Stratman, J.K. (2011). Revenue management performance drivers: an exploratory analysis within the hotel industry. *Journal of Revenue and Pricing Management*, 10(2), 172–88.

Schwartz, Z. and Cohen, E. (2004) Hotel revenue-management forecasting: evidence of expert-judgement bias, *Cornell Hotel and Restaurant Administration Quarterly*, 45(1), 85–98.

Selmi N. and Dornier R. (2011) Yield management in the French hotel business: an assessment of the importance of the human factor, *International Business Research*, 4(2), 58–66.

Starfleet Media (2014) The 2015 Smart Decision Guide to Hospitality Revenue Management. Online. Available HTTP: <http://info.duettoresearch.com/rs/duetto/images/Smart%20Decision%20Guide%20-%20Hospitality%20Revenue%20Management%20-%20Duetto.pdf>, accessed 3 December 2015.

Talluri, K.T. and van Ryzin, G.J. (2005) *The Theory and Practice of Revenue Management*, New York: Springer.

Vinod, B. (2004) Unlocking the value of revenue management in the hotel industry. *Journal of Revenue and Pricing Management*, 3(2), 178–90.

Vinod, B. (2008) The continuing evolution: customer-centric revenue management. *Journal of Revenue and Pricing Management*, 7(1), 27-39.

Wang, X.L. (2012) Relationship or revenue: potential management conflicts between CRM and revenue management. *International Journal of Hospitality Management*, 31(3), 864–74.

Wang, X.L., Yoonjoung Heo, C., Schwartz, Z., Legohérel, P. and Specklin, F. (2015). Revenue management: progress, challenges, and research prospects. *Journal of Travel and Tourism Marketing*, 32(7), 797–811

23

Integrated marketing communications of hotel chains

Vladimir Zhechev

(UNIVERSITY OF ECONOMICS – VARNA, BULGARIA)

Introduction

Today's turbulent economic environment, associated with insistent competition and fluctuating demands, challenges hotel chains to walk the tightrope of market success in a much better planned and more precise way. Capturing the attention of increasingly demanding customers encompasses a wide array of processes revolving around design and implementation of persuasive integrated communication programmes. The capability of marketing associates to cut through the publicity clutter, their unbiased and timely communication with target audiences, as well as their ploys for emulating the success of most influential players from various industries are factors of crucial importance for competent marketing communications.

For some years now hotel chains have relied on promotional functions orbiting around mass media communications. That inevitably resulted in the dependence on advertising agencies for the delivery of wide-spanning marketing communications. Such endeavours established grounds for three main challenges: (1) Public relations (PR) engaged with publicity, image making and relationship building with target groups without being considered as an integral part of marketing communications; (2) Sales promotions were project-based and on that occasion – short-term incentives; (3) Marketing and promotion functions were kept well apart from each other and therefore had separate objectives, budgets, etc.

In the 1990s some hotel chains started recognising the need for strategic integration of promotional tools. The period witnessed the growing role of sales promotions, direct marketing, PR, which all contributed to the changing character of advertising as chief means of marketing communications. Hotel chains began to identify integrated marketing communications (IMC) as a process, which transforms intangible and tangible inputs into outputs (O'Cass and Weerawardena, 2009). The process itself requires coordination of different communication techniques and elements and by virtue of this it disengages mass media as a central communication medium.

IMC shaped its logic and practical application as a mechanism that provides opportunities for optimisation of communication techniques to arrive at better communication effectiveness, which also stimulates brand performance (Luxton et al., 2015).

With the growing competitiveness between market players in the hospitality industry and the flexible and timely response to communication actions of main rivals, hotel chains need to address IMC challenges by designing strategies that can transform communication resources into effective outcomes such as awareness, recognition, brand value, brand equity, etc. An essentially important issue here is the need to ensure all forms of communication work consistently and in consonance with each other. They must also correspond to the hotel chain's marketing strategy as this can create a consistent and consolidated image of all members of the chain. In order to be able to synchronise all forms of communication, hotel chain executives must assure compliance and mutual understanding of communication objectives across the business of all members of their networks.

Essentials and objectives of IMC for hotel chains and chain members

Shimp (2010: 10) defines integrated marketing communications as the process of planning, design, integration and coordination of all points of encounter with customers, which may have direct or indirect impact on the purchasing decision. The hotel industry, unlike product industries, requires a special priority for integration of channels as the service quality, brand image, location, among others, are chief consideration factors for customers (Loredana and Micu, 2014). A key challenge to hotel chain executives is how to deliver multiple messages and arrange consistency of communication channels so that a uniform communication mix is established.

IMC objectives for hotel chains can be defined as the following:

- Achieving higher sales (depending on the season, demands, economic situation, etc.);
- Increasing the visitor flow into affiliated hotels (requires special attention to possible cannibalisation);
- Improving the brand image – an emphasis should be put on consistency of message design and delivery;
- Encouraging frequent visits – frequency varies greatly from hotel to hotel as customer value is normally shaped by internal conceptions and macroeconomic impacts;
- Broaden corporate and individual hotels' brand awareness – individual hotels must also invent innovative experiences for their customers to raise not only theirs, but the chain's overall awareness (Konovalova and Jatuliaviciene, 2015; Verma and Jain, 2015);
- Creation of a unique sales proposition (USP is fundamental for customers seeking variety);
- Managing unique positioning (key source of competitive advantage, but requires emphasis on effectiveness of information accessibility and delivery);
- Motivating desirable customer attitude and loyalty (depends on the design of reward systems that are clear to the customers, have a comprehensible progress map, and incorporate value-enhancing service characteristics).

IMC objectives can be categorised into economic and communication oriented and they are an integral part of the design of effective marketing communications.

Alternatively, Barger and Labrecque (2013) discuss some IMC objectives in the social media, which can be applied to hotel chains, and can therefore be divided into short term and long term.

Short-term objectives

1. Gaining consideration – given that customers are progressively seeking advice and/or recommendations online, hotel chains can track down keywords linked to their service(s) and respond with appropriate presentation of relevant information.
2. Encouraging trial – hotel chains can use social media as a medium for launching sales promotions. The latter can take the form of discount vouchers, coupons, online contests, etc. that can encourage proponents to try different services.
3. Stimulating repurchase – hotel chains can reward customers for signing up for their social media pages by offering them short-term incentives (such as discount vouchers/codes). This way they can drive more customers to social media websites and by virtue of this, enhance their repeat purchases.

Long-term objectives

1. Improving customer satisfaction – social media can serve as direct instruments for the provision of feedback (satisfaction, complaints and recommendations). If the corporation and its individual chains treat complaints promptly, this can diminish dissatisfaction and enhance the overall customer experience. Alternatively, this can provide organisations with the opportunity to track down issues at an early stage and respond accordingly.
2. Establishing awareness – among the advantages of social media hotel chains can benefit from is content sharing. Hotel visitors are likely to share their moments and experiences if they are entertaining, amusing and/or dissatisfactory. Social media provides opportunities for raising awareness at an enormous pace.
3. Building relationships – hotel chains can seek to promote brand loyalty and sharing of positive experiences of customers by means of social media. They can regularly post content prompting visitors to comment/respond/associate themselves with it, which expands communications immensely.
4. Creation of communities – hotel chains can run communities of brand advocates or these can be self-administered. Communities are especially important as they drive new flows of visitors to the websites (and respectively – the affiliated hotels) and provide assistance with generation of strategic alternatives, marketing research, support in forums, blogs, etc.

IMC objectives can be set according to the communication channel and they should correspond to the marketing strategy of the hotel chain. They must comply with the S.M.A.R.T. rule (be specific, measurable, achievable, realistic and time-framed) and should strive to establish and maintain a reliable brand image.

Conceptual model of IMC in the context of hotel chains

IMC allow hotel chains to bring into line all communications about their brands and services, and based on that – to deliver reliable messages to target audiences. IMC must comply with the marketing strategy of the hotel chain, but they also need to maintain a uniform positioning strategy. Figure 23.1 presents a conceptual model of integrated marketing communications for hotel chains.

Figure 23.1 is divided into three main contexts: (1) internal network context, (2) consumer-centred context and (3) external context. *The internal context* encompasses the

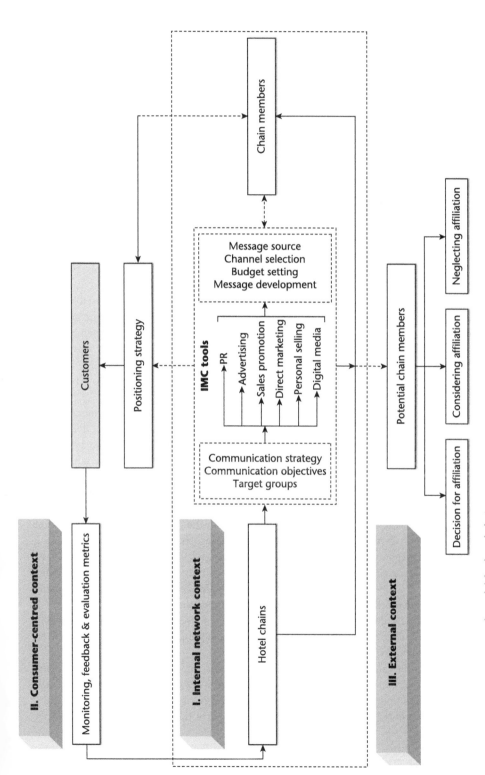

Figure 23.1 IMC conceptual model for hotel chains.

hotel chains and chain members (other affiliated hotels). In between them are IMC tools – PR, advertising, sales promotion, direct marketing, personal selling (traditional) and digital media (contemporary). Hotel chains can exploit the advantage of each one of them separately, but when used in combination they must employ an amalgamation of resources that can positively impact the customers' decision-making. There are three options here: (1) use the IMC tools and go through the steps of establishment of effective marketing communications to facilitate the job of chain members, who can adopt the chain's communication instruments; (2) repeat (1), but circumvent chain members and get directly to the positioning strategy; (3) skip the steps of effective communication and delegate the right of chain members to design and promote their own positioning strategy to instigate desirable customer results.

If the first option is chosen, first of all the chain must define target groups; set communication objectives; formulate communication strategy. After these steps have been taken, the chain must decide on the message design, content and source, before it chooses a positioning strategy. The latter must be transmitted through different interrelated communication channels so that the right target groups are reached. Option 1 has one major advantage – it offers opportunities for collaborative design and use of integrated communication tools. However, the latter can be limited if the chain operates hotels of a very different class.

In cases where option 2 is selected, the hotel chain takes all steps required for establishment of effective marketing communication, but does not check them with the chain members. The subsequently chosen positioning strategy shall be adopted by the chain members and they have to pursue it in their future communications with customers. This option can smooth the communication efforts of affiliated hotels, but may simultaneously deprive them of the independence to choose an individualised positioning strategy, tailored to their strategic orientation.

Option 3 stipulates that positioning strategies are handed over to the affiliated hotels without involving the general framework for effective communications. The decentralisation of communication and positioning has its advantages, the biggest one being the autonomy of individual hotels to fine-tune their own sales propositions, which can differ greatly.

The consumer-centred context incorporates choice of a positioning strategy, reaching the customers, monitoring and collection of feedback, and application of evaluation metrics. Initially, the hotel chain or affiliated hotels must decide on the differentiation that they want to achieve in the customer's mind. Common positioning strategies include emphasising benefits, attributes, application, users, etc. Once the strategy is in place, it must be broadcast to the target audience through the means of different communication channels (TV, radio, digital media, outdoor advertising). After that, since every IMC campaign must bring essential results, hotel chains must collect feedback and apply proper metrics of performance, which can include, but are not limited to: sales and leads generated, loyalty, WOM (more thoroughly discussed in monitoring, feedback and evaluation). By analysing the results, hotel chains can reformulate their approach to the management of IMC.

The last one is *the external context*. It includes an important party involved in IMC – the potential hotels that can join the chain. Given the rapid expansion of global chains, new affiliates also become part of target audiences of key players in hospitality. In this situation, both hotel chains and their individual affiliates can influence the decision of external parties to join the business network. Based on their strategic orientation and the effectiveness of communication efforts, among other factors, external hotels can take three decisions: (1) affiliate directly; (2) consider affiliation; (3) neglect affiliation.

The conceptual model presented attempts to visualise the process of IMC in the context of the hotel chain. We will next try to reveal the specifics of the IMC tools and their strategic implications for hotel chains as well as discussing in more detail the steps in the design of effective marketing communications.

Integrated marketing communication tools and strategic implications for hotel chains

Rakic and Rakic (2014) add digital marketing communications to the traditional tools of integrated marketing communications:

- *Advertising*. Every paid form of non-personal presentation of ideas, products, services by a conspicuous sponsor (hotel chain/chain members). Some hotel chains respond reactively to competitive advertising actions by looking for quick remedies to unstable demand or the success of current players and new entrants. Advertising can be used as a source of differentiation for hotel chains that persistently integrate communications into uniform messages. Visual aids, coupled with other communication tools, can reach the target audience effectively by avoiding ambiguity and accentuating important service attributes such as location, staff, facilities, etc.
- *Personal selling*. Personal interaction between hotel chain (members) and potential customers aiming to raise awareness, establish relationships with prospects and closing deals. Hotel chains can use personal selling to reinforce their corporate and individual affiliates image, stimulate purchase behaviour, and provide useful/not well-acknowledged information about the hotel locations.
- *Sales promotion*. A range of short term incentives that make every effort to promote initial interest and continuous visits to the hotel chain member establishments. Hotel chains must clearly identify target audiences and arrange individualised interaction with them. Additionally, sales promotion is incentive-based and should therefore lead to extra income generation by encouraging long-term visits instead of one-offs. In some countries hotel chains introduce continuous sales promotions which lead to customers getting used to these incentives and encouraging them to buy only when such promotions are currently running.
- *Direct marketing*. Direct communication with pre-selected customers to initiate interaction and obtain feedback. Direct marketing normally uses e-mail, telephone, mail, etc. as means of contact. In view of the specifics of the hotel industry, chains must accentuate calls-to-action (telephone, website) as decisions for travel may be the result of impulsive reaction. Monitoring and responding to feedback is also crucial, but corporations must try to avoid aggravating potential customers and ignoring the right of clients to opt-out (especially important with the rise of collective buying websites).
- *PR*. Incorporates all events that inform media channels, communities, authorities, political parties and other social groups about the hotel chain, nature of business and the guiding principles for functioning. Generally, the information does not directly aim at encouraging sales, but it rather seeks to build a positive image of the chain and its members. Hotel chains must remember PR enjoys better credibility than most other IMC tools, but any campaign must produce visible results (low employee turnover, help to local communities, intelligent waste management, etc.).
- *Digital marketing communications*. Using websites, directories, blogs, databases, mobile devices, online broadcasting of media and others to foster more effective communications,

feedback and relationship management with prospects. Hotel chains must be very careful with how they gather, store, use and distribute customer information online. Privacy policy is an emerging issue and some corporations such as Taj Group have launched separate pages on their websites to explain accurately how they track customer preferences and ensure data security.

Chaffey (2009) contrasts the characteristics of digital media marketing communications with those of the traditional media. The author provides an interpretation of the six Is of e-marketing, which can help hotel chains understand new media features that can reinforce the effectiveness of communication in the hospitality industry:

(1) *Interactivity*: new media channels, unlike traditional ones, exploit the 'pull mechanism'. That is to say that hotel chains can encourage two-way communication and explore opportunities for online sales promotions and other incentives that can generate revenue and broaden brand awareness. Nevertheless, hotel corporations must be cautious especially with disturbing business customers to respond to offers, messages, etc.

(2) *Intelligence*: using main websites and individual member pages, hotel chains can take advantage of the internet as a comparatively inexpensive method of conducting research and collecting customer data and feedback. Such establishments can use analytic tools to determine the most (and least) visited pages; respond to customer requests/complaints; monitor the average time it takes to respond to email enquiries; and track down important demographic, geographic and psychographic characteristics of customers through polls and rankings. As already mentioned, chains must try to reassure their visitors as to their online privacy.

(3) *Individualisation*: digital marketing communications allow hotel chains to customise the message that target audiences receive (unlike traditional media, where customers are showered with a single message). Individualisation can be achieved through means of launching extranets to key customers; tailoring hotel offerings to the profile of the visitor; displaying unique information to visitors and suggesting destinations according to the age, marital status, past visits, purchase frequency, etc. of customers.

(4) *Integration*: official websites, blogs, social media pages, etc. can be used as 'direct-response tools' to offers and promotions of hotel chains. Digital marketing communications can reinforce the final buying decision. For example, some hotel chains use magazines to give away discount vouchers that need to be registered online before the customer can take advantage of them. The latter process is described as 'mixed-mode buying' and allows integration of channels.

(5) *Industry restructuring*: two main terms need to described here: (1) reintermediation and (2) disintermediation. The first term refers to introduction of intermediaries between the hotel chain and its customers, while the second implies minimising intermediaries in the communication process. The important considerations here revolve around presence on specialised websites such as: tripadvisor.com, hotels.com, hotwire.com and maintaining/increasing popularity significantly or centralising the publicity function in-house by delegating and coordinating the communication activities of channel members.

(6) *Independence of location*: digital media offers opportunities to enter international markets which have been previously explored by the hotel chain. Hotels do not need to operate a foreign sales subsidiary to generate sales. The latter can also cause channel conflicts if the hotel chain promotes itself through other agents as this can limit their profits.

Table 23.1 Efficiency and effectiveness metrics for hotel chains' online presence

Areas	Efficiency	Effectiveness
Financial results	• Channel costs • Channel profitability	• Online contribution (direct) • Online contribution (indirect) • Profit contributed
Customer value	• Online outreach (unique visitors as % of total visitors) • Cost of acquisition or cost per sale • Customer propensity to defect	• Sales and sales per customer • New customers • Online market share • Customer satisfaction ratings • Customer loyalty index
Operational processes	• Conversion rates • Average value of stay • Email active %	• Fulfilment times • Support response times
Innovation and learning	• Novel approaches tested • Internal e-marketing education • Internal satisfaction ratings	• Novel approaches deployed • Performance appraisal review

Source: Adapted from Chaffey (2009).

Understanding the advantages of digital marketing communications can also help hotel chains design marketing objectives for their online presence. Chaffey (2009) proposes several metrics for efficiency and effectiveness in four key areas: financial results, customer value, operational processes, and innovation and learning (Table 23.1).

By using these metrics in the abovementioned areas, hotel chains can evaluate their capability of operating digital marketing channels. Since online revenue contribution continuously increases its share in total sales revenue, it is important to link communication strategies to the actual performance of every channel. And if digital marketing channels turn out to be the largest source of revenue, then effectiveness and efficiency metrics must be employed to assess their potential to deliver financial, operational and customer value.

Steps in the design of effective marketing communications for hotel chains

Effective marketing communications must be aligned with the mission, vision and the marketing strategy of the hotel chain. An important aspect of design is that there needs to be uniformity among communication messages. This way hotel chains can build trust and achieve consistency in target customers' perceptions (Jerman and Zavrsnik, 2011).

1. Identification of the target group

Hotel chains' objectives on this ground can conditionally be divided into: (1) target groups to be approached with promotional purposes and (2) individual hotels/investors to be approached for affiliation. Generally, target groups can consist of individual tourists, tourist groups, tourism and hospitality organisations, investors, suppliers, employees, local communities, etc. who can influence the decision-making process. Communication for hotel chain affiliation tends to be broader in scope compared to the messages broadcast by individual hotels, thus target groups must be well chosen.

2. Definition of promotional objectives

Promotional objectives can be divided into: (1) economic and (2) communication objectives. The first of these can incorporate: total sales volume, volume growth, market share, etc. Communication objectives can aim at: awareness, acceptance, preference, trial, repeated purchase and sustaining loyalty. If the hotel chain aims strategically at affiliation then promotional objectives can encompass: total establishments joined, individual hotels attracted by region, raising awareness, building recognition and others.

3. Selection of communication tools

Communications must be integrated in such manner that they do not interrupt each other. They should follow a unified logic and messages must be transmitted according to promotional objectives. The selection process itself depends predominantly on the strategy of the hotel chain and the budget allotted for the purpose. If the chain aims at a broader audience, then it may opt for advertising as it offers the widest reach. If the target is attraction of narrowly selected (groups of) customers, the hotel chain may choose direct marketing and/or personal selling. In situations where there are budget restrictions, means of sales promotion can be employed to encourage trial visits.

4. Communication message development and budget setting

There are a few widely adopted approaches to message development:

- Rational approach – emphasises the attraction of target groups to the functional benefits of the hospitality service (quality, pricing, physical attributes of the establishments, etc.). Hotel chains must also consider convenience of location, infrastructure and amenities as they may play a crucial role under the specifics of this approach;
- Emotional approach – instigates positive/negative emotions to encourage purchasing (humour, joy, happiness, fear, pride, prestige, satisfaction, etc.). Attractiveness of location, luxuriousness, waterfront facilities, exclusive travel options, etc. are among the accents to be considered in the framework of this approach;
- Moral approach – prompts a sense of ethical attitude and righteousness (social causes, corporate social responsibility). Hotel chains can emphasise the importance they place on health and safety, charities, and the work–life balance of their employees, among others, to fuel a principled attitude.

After selecting the approach to message development, the hotel chain must take decisions on:

- Message content – executives can take two approaches to designing the content of the message: (1) they can summarise the different attributes, benefits, location, past customers, and other distinguishing advantages of the hotel chain and its services or (2) they can include facts, achievements, real-life situations and milestones – this way they guide current and potential customers to make judgements about their success, superiority, advantages, etc.
- Message structure – another important issue related to the magnetism of the message is the need to structure and synthesise the delivered information in an effective way. Because of marketing clutter, customers tend to remember definite and unambiguous

Table 23.2 Hotel chains' approaches and format of message design

Hotel chain	Slogan/buzzword	Approach to message development	Message format characteristics	Country/ continent of origin
Rosewood hotels	A sense of place	Emotional	Cosmopolitan, heritage, privacy, uniqueness	Dallas, USA
Aman Resorts	Come journey with us	Emotional	Exotic, sincerity, serenity, experience (staff-customer ratio – 4:1)	Singapore, Asia
The Peninsula hotels	An inimitable legend of hospitality	Emotional	Sculptures, art, unique transportation (helicopters, boats, Rolls Royce)	Hong Kong, Asia
The Rezidor Hotel Group	'Yes I can!'	Moral/rational	Planet, people, together, ethical	Belgium, Europe
Ramada Hotels	Everything except excess	Rational	Discount, deal, bonus, practicality	New Jersey, USA
Melia Hotels International	Welcome back	Moral/rational	Culture, sustainability, innovation, consistency ('we do what we say')	Spain, Europe

statements that can potentially be used in the beginning and repeated at the end of the message.

- Message format – this should be attention-grabbing and the layout must be idiosyncratic, symbolising the house style, colour scheme and logo of the hotel chain. It's a good idea to include real-life stories of customers which convey humour, joy, comfort, lavishness, calmness and others corresponding to the target audience of the chain and/or its individual members. Some hotel chains employ celebrity endorsements as a strategy to attract potential visitors, others use images of different events (conferences, weddings, show programmes, annual award ceremonies, etc.) to grab the attention of customers (Table 23.2).

Table 23.2 visualises some of the world's most distinct hotel chains and their ploys to grasp their target audience's attention, based on their official (and affiliated) website experience (links to the web pages from which the information was retrieved are available in Bibliography). Important points that hotel chain managers must bear in mind include: (1) it is essential to develop messages that do not put across contradicting approaches (e.g. emotional and rational); (2) it is imperative to use attributes that conform with the hotel chain's mission and corporate values; (3) it is vital to use imagery that exhibits not only the most well-appointed spots as this may lead to wrong customer expectations and future interpretations of the chain's integrity.

Consequently, most common mistakes in message design can be categorised as follows:

- Ambiguous message – customers have different understandings of the message;
- Message is too long – customers have difficulty following it to the end (limits comprehension);

- Inconsistency between visual aids and the text which is displayed/broadcast;
- Distracting imagery – using symbols, signs, objects, people that distract the audience from the actual content that is of importance for the hotel chain.

Another important task under this step is budget setting. In practice there are three well-known budgeting methods for IMC (adapted from Ivanov and Zhechev, 2011):

- 'residual income method' – everything that the hotel chain can afford after deducting all other expenditures. This way the budget is tied to the financial resources of the hotel chain, but sales volume is not taken into consideration. Marketing expenditures do not correlate to the real business needs of the hotel chain;
- 'percentage of sales method' – IMC expenditures are defined as a percentage of actual or forecasted sales volumes. By deploying this method hotel chains can report the relationships between expenditures–sales/price–revenue (Sau-Yee and Hyunjung, 2014). A drawback of the method is the unequal distribution of expenditures for IMC when sales are decreasing, which might be the moment for counter-competitive actions;
- 'purposive method' – the budget is set on the basis of specific hotel chain's needs and objectives. In other words, the budget is attached to the marketing objectives of the hotel chain, which on the other hand, can cause difficult budget planning throughout reporting periods.

5. Choice of a communication channel

Communication channels represent the pathway through which messages reach the target audience. Messages can be transmitted through the various traditional means – printed media, radio and TV broadcasting, cinema and cinema commercials (Durankev, 2014), but also through more innovative channels such as: social media, blogs, mobile marketing, specialised forums, webinars, online newspapers, virtual conferences, etc.

The following lines discuss some critical issues of channel selection for hotel chains and are structured according to the IMC tools of the IMC conceptual model.

Advertising

According to Hollensen (2007) advertising campaigns media selection need to consider taking either a mass or target approach. Mass media can generally be effective if the major portion of the general public are potential clients of the hotel chain. However, given the multiple channels through which various hotel chains reach their target audiences, it is vital for them to realise that customers will keep hold of limited information about a comparatively high number of communication messages. For this purpose, chain executives can reflect on the following metrics for choosing media:

- Outreach – represents the total number of buyers to which can be delivered at least one message within a given time frame (OTS – opportunity to see);
- Frequency – the average times each customer is exposed to the message within a given time frame. It is critical to seek for integration of the message delivery. Given the specifics of the hotel industry, it is effective to build up a stronger and concise image through integration rather than deliver a series of messages that the customer cannot logically construe;

- Influence – depends predominantly on the relevance between the media and the channel (magazines like Forbes are used as a communication medium by upscale hotel chains as the former are geared to prosperous people);
- Gross rating points (GRP) per channel – this can be calculated through multiplying outreach by frequency. It shows the 'critical mass' of media work. Hotel chains can base their media planning on 'cost per 1000 GRPs'.

Television allows broad outreach and the capability to display scenes, sound, colours, etc. simultaneously. The processing of imagery can be effective predominantly when it exhibits exactness, clarity and time frame. The memory-enhancing attributes of television can foster consumer choice of a particular hotel from the chain based on location, facilities, desirability by others, etc. However, TV commercials normally incur high expenditures for broadcasting, low targeting options and high probability of skipping the message.

Radio transmission is significantly less expensive than television, but the influence is only through voices, sounds and it is often hard to memorise it as customers are normally driving, cooking, etc. while being exposed to it. However, many hotel chains do use radio transmission as a proxy to drive customers to their official website to support their buying decision. The cognitive understanding of hotel chain offers, their locations across the globe, their services, etc. can be reinforced by voice broadcasting on radio channels.

- Outdoor advertising – usually put out on roads, sports grounds, airports, stadiums, highways, building facades, vehicles, etc. Hotel chains principally intend to make potential customers memorise corporate and affiliated brands. Its effectiveness depends on the liveliness of the spots, where it is put on display. It may attract the attention of many people, but is considered appropriate for budget to mid-scale hotel chains. Outdoor advertising can help the reactivation of associations with the hotel chain and can also navigate customers to the desirable attributes of an offer.
- Newspapers and magazines – hotel chains can rely on specialised readership of tourism and hospitality newspapers and magazines to raise awareness and attract visitors. Some establishments prefer local issues, while others opt for internationally distributed printed media in accordance with their targets. Newspapers and magazines do not exert as persuasive an influence as they used to due to the fact that they are mutually exclusive information sources with the hotel chain websites. On the other hand, they can positively impact brand recall and result in better positioning by virtue of coupled communication efforts.
- Cinema – offers hotel chains the opportunity to gain broad exposure, but while cinema commercials can be very influential and less expensive, product positioning in films tends to be an exclusive option for hoteliers. Product positioning when the advertiser is not explicitly shown is referred to as stealth marketing (see for example: Zhechev, 2015).

Public relations

Hotel chains can benefit from multiple advantages of PR. On the one hand, it is a tool for reinforcing corporate and individual hotel's brand image. Some of the PR methods that hotel chains can exploit are:

- Charities;
- Sponsorship in competitions;

- Funding of university tourism and hospitality student contests;
- Press releases for new achievements, staff treatments, corporate social responsibility activities.

Hotel chain executives must understand that PR is a powerful word-of-mouth instrument for gaining customers. Nonetheless, integrity must be abided by as customers will add the PR methods to their sum of associations. In this respect, encouraging such initiatives continuously can help build more persuasive communications.

Sales promotions

Executives of hotel chains may also consider encouraging visitors through short-term discounts, free nights when a longer holiday is purchased, premium rewards for first purchasers, gifts at the hotels, vouchers for future visits, etc. The effectiveness of sales promotions depends primarily on tailoring them to the specific needs of target customers (as most prestigious hotels have to be careful not to give incentives to too many customers which might limit the perceived exclusivity of the property in the mind of frequent visitors).

Direct marketing

Among the most widely recognised methods of hotel chains' direct marketing are direct mail, telemarketing and internet marketing. All of them require adequate design of customer profiles and models so that the right prospects are approached. An important consideration for hoteliers is to maintain consumer privacy (most hotel chain websites use 'cookies', which should be exploited carefully, because at some point, due to sponsored suggestions, customers may feel they are being 'tricked').

Personal selling

Some of the preconditions for personal selling effectiveness for hotel chains are: (1) selection of the right mix of customers; (2) ensuring their awareness and preparation; (3) clear and memorable message accentuating customer satisfaction; (4) use of visual aids; (5) patient attention to customer requests/inquiries; (6) securing future contacts/feedback. It is also very important to keep a record of individual customers and their progress with the hotel chain (affiliated members) over time. Nevertheless, personal selling and accurate customer data are not sufficient for building a sustainable competitive advantage. For instance, the hotel industry is communication intensive and thus customers should not come upon emotionally intensive behaviour.

To sum up, printed media offers flexibility, carefully targeted customers and relatively low expenditures of publication. On the downside, there are factors such as: short lifecycle and narrow outreach. Broadcasting media has several advantages, such as multiple message transmissions and high market coverage, but these are very expensive to finance. Outdoor advertising has the major objective of establishing awareness and recognition of the hotel chain, while its effectiveness depends on the location, direction and number of customers passing by. Its advantage is its long lifecycle and long-term influence; however it can only display limited information, and the control over certain target groups is limited. Cinema commercials boast high perceptional impact, but are sometimes expensive to launch. Public relations tend to have a two-fold influence: fostering corporate image and spreading the word.

Sales promotions can only be short-term encouragements to reward repeat visits and/or customer loyalty (Ramakrishnan, 2012), while direct marketing can stimulate sales promotions through careful selection of target customers to be reached. Personal selling allows delivery of information to customers and opportunities for making direct purchases, but also collecting feedback at the points of interaction.

Choice of message source

This step involves choosing the person (or group of people) to present the hotel chain (and affiliated hotel) to target groups. The message can be delivered by:

- the owner of the chain (reputation, gravity, magnitude);
- internal appointment – someone with good presentation skills (comprehensible, memorable, compelling);
- individually hired actors/celebrities (endorsement, brand image, exclusivity, prestige);
- singers – at special corporate events (popularity, fame, attractiveness).

Selecting the right people to talk about the hotel chain is a vital step towards effective positioning.

Positioning and repositioning strategies for hotel chains: a key source for competitive advantage

Hotel chains may find achieving a competitive advantage through means of lower prices or better customer value a daunting task in the contemporary development of the hospitality industry. Some chains have started looking for new alternatives for adding customer value (Shakhshir, 2014).

In marketing theory and practice, positioning is broadening the scope of its strategy to maintain competitive advantage and is a key element in building a communication strategy. The standpoint of various scholars and practitioners in the field is that communications aim at the creation, improvement and modification of perceptions of customers towards products/services/brands. In view of this, the basis for assessment of ROI of positioning should be the degree of positive/negative impact on company performance.

Positioning is conceptualised as a complex, multi-layered construct, which strives to positively fine-tune the tangible characteristics of the hospitality service to its intangible perceptions on the market. More thoroughly examined, positioning can be viewed as a strategic approach of hotel chains to create positive perceptions in the customer mind through application of intangible corporate resources, which can lead to the generation of competitive advantage. Application of positioning strategies can be practically executed through the various IMC tools (advertising, public relations, sales promotions, direct marketing and personal selling).

Positioning strategies can be formulated and implemented in numerous ways, depending on: (1) the characteristics of the hotel chain brand(s) (functionally dominated, emotionally oriented, etc.); (2) the competition; (3) types of customers; (4) service category/class; (5) corporate goals and others. Regardless of the way a positioning strategy is launched, its ultimate aim is to improve the perceptions (and image) of the particular hotel chain.

Kotler (2012) outlines that companies are required to display very precise reasons for buying so as they can secure effective positioning. The author describes the following positioning strategies that can serve as possible sources of competitive advantage to hotel chains:

- *Attribute positioning*: accentuates specific attributes of the hotel chain;
- *Benefit positioning*: emphasises benefit(s) of the service(s) offered;
- *Use/application positioning*: the hospitality service is optimally positioned for certain periods/application;
- *User positioning*: the centre of attention is a specific target group that the hotel chain wants to attract;
- *Competitor positioning* (also called 'positioning against competition'): the difference and/ or superiority of the hotel chain is explicitly displayed to achieve distinction;
- *Category positioning*: the hotel chain manifests itself as a category leader;
- *Quality/price positioning*: the hotel chain and its services are positioned according to a specific price/quality ratio (high class/high price; value for money, etc.).

The practical exhibits of the aforementioned strategies are presented in Table 23.3.

Table 23.3 demonstrates that an important aspect of hotel chain positioning is how different it is to other similar establishments. Depending on the competitive market environment, marketing executives and hotel chains can adapt a particular positioning strategy, so that they can benefit from important psychological advantages that it can bring to the minds of customers.

On the contrary, Kotler (2012) also addresses some issues related to potential positioning mistakes:

- *Underpositioning*: failure to demonstrate particular benefits and/or reasons to buy;
- *Overpositioning*: assuming a very narrow positioning strategy that can fail to capture customers' attention;
- *Confusing positioning*: declaring few benefits that are not congruent with each other;
- *Irrelevant positioning*: claiming reasons to buy/attributes/benefits, etc. that are not valued highly by target audiences;
- *Doubtful positioning*: presentation of dubious benefits that customers may doubt the chain can deliver.

Many hotel chains concede such positioning errors, which can have financial, market and image impacts (Ram et al., 2007). Therefore a successful positioning strategy must correspond closely to the image that is depicted in the customer's mind and that is concomitantly linked to hotel chains' attributes/benefits/customer value delivery and others. Failure to do so is a commonplace nowadays given the overcrowding of communication channels and ever growing demands of customers. One way to modify the current brand image of a hotel chain is through application of a repositioning strategy.

Gilligan and Wilson (2012: 414) propose four repositioning strategies, which might be adequate given the dynamic development of hospitality markets, changes in competitive landscapes, and the growing need for precise catering for customer demands:

1. *Gradual repositioning* – ongoing adjustment to the changes in the market environment. An example is Hilton's entry into the mid-priced segment through Garden Inn, which is a direct rival of Marriott's Courtyard.

Table 23.3 Positioning strategies of hotel chains and their strategic orientation

Positioning strategy	Strategic orientation	Hotel/hotel chain	Application and remarks
Attribute positioning	Specific hotel chain self-importance	Westin Hotels & Resorts (Starwood hotels)	Westin Hotels & Resorts claims to be the oldest hotel management company with a history stretching back to 1930. Westin relies on upscale properties and is associated with avant-garde luxury.
Benefit positioning	Benefits of the service	JW Marriott Marquis Dubai Hotel (Marriott International)	The chain runs the tallest hotel of the world, which is over 350m. It is a distinct benefit that reinforces the chain's operations in Dubai.
Use/application positioning	Best for particular time period or particular service	Four Seasons Resort & Residences Whistler	Ranked the best hotel spa in Canada for 2014 with an overall score of 93.82.*
User positioning	Association with target groups	Viceroy Hotel Group	Lifestyle luxury hotel brands deemed to be primarily visited by the movie scene and music celebrities. For instance, L'Ermitage Beverly Hills hotel was listed first on Forbes travel guide as a place 'where celebs go'.
Competitor positioning	Positioning away or superior to competition	InterContinental Hotels Group	It has been the largest hotel chain in the world since 2004, when it acquired over 4,500 properties. The corporation currently operates in over 100 countries and it boasts high awareness of its globally renowned brands such as: InterContinental, Holiday Inn, Crowne Plaza, etc.
Category positioning	Category leadership	Karisma Hotels & Resorts	The chain has introduced Gourmet Inclusive® experience, which is described as 'a new concept in luxury vacations'. The chain tries to position itself as a category leader with innovative concept and finest Michelin-star trained chefs.
Quality/price positioning	Quality/price ratio variations	Accor Hotels	The corporation offers a wide range of budget (Formule 1, Ibis budget), mid-range (Mercure) and upscale hotels (Mercure Grand, Sofitel). The chain maintains the balance of price vs. quality through a wide range of properties and associated customer value.

* The award was granted by Travel and Leisure on the 19th annual poll. Online. Available HTTP: <http://www.travelandleisure.com/travel-guide/whistler/hotels>, accessed 18 May 2015.

2. *Radical repositioning* – such strategy is highly sought after in situations, whereby there are significant inconsistencies between customer wants and a hotel chain's ability to deliver them. NH Hotel Group aims at strategic repositioning since it incurred a debt of over EUR 1 billion. The far-reaching reorientation encompasses: new room appointments, rate increases and improvement of the overall customer experience (retrieved from: http://www.hotelnewsnow.com 18 May 2015).

3. *Innovative repositioning* – exploring a new strategic position that has market potential not currently explored by other rivals. For instance, Marriott operates Autograph Collection® hotels (Marriott Autograph Collection, retrieved from: http://www.marriott.com 18 May 2015), which is a group of specialist independent hotels, that emphasise local culture and arts. These hotels are normally located in cities with rich cultural heritage (e.g. Milan, Rome, London, Dublin, etc.).

4. *Zero positioning* – the hotel chain preserves unchanged attributes/benefits/customer value over a long period of time. Great Hotels of the World have selected only a few five star hotels in the island of Cyprus with the concept of saving the luxury holiday experience for mostly leisure and business travellers (Great Hotels of the World, retrieved from: http://www.ghotw.com on 18 May 2015).

Provided the opportunities that the abovementioned repositioning strategies may bring, hotel chains must watch out for the following strategic implications of their efforts to create and maintain a desirable position in the customer mind:

- Track down the positioning strategies of direct rivals and their outreach;
- Identify points-of-difference and points-of-parity with main competitors that can help design a new promising positioning strategy;
- Ensure positioning focus is understood and preserved by all member hotels;
- Build a positioning strategy that is strictly tailored to the needs of the chain in general and that does not interfere with individual hotels' target groups;
- Adjust communication tools across the chain and transmit them in an orderly manner so that common goals are pursued;
- Maintain control over the implementation of the strategy and monitor feedback effects.

Volatile market conditions have shifted customer demands, and positioning offers good counteraction opportunities for offsetting these trends. Essentially, it can reinforce the competitive advantage of hotel chains and lead to better revenues.

Despite the proven benefits of positioning as a strategy for establishing and maintaining a competitive position in the minds of customers, in recent years there have been criticisms of its universality. For example Zhelev (2010) argues that positioning is based on the marketing activities of the supplier and/or the user experience. This indicates that the communication strategy of the hotel chains is not a mandatory component in the design of a position in customer minds. Alternatively, based on this assumption, lasting impressions of customers are not only an outcome of differentiation (product, service, and/or related to entry into new segment/niche).

Monitoring, feedback and evaluation metrics

Integrated marketing communications can be considered effective once they have accomplished the objectives, mentioned in step 2. After an integrated marketing communication campaign has been launched, the marketing executives must decide on its effectiveness based on the results achieved and feedback provided. Barger and Labrecque (2013) propose some metrics for evaluation that can be informative for hotel chains:

- *Volume of visitors and leads generated* – not only does volume show the revenue changes, but it also serves as an important indicator of the chain's progress in building brand awareness;
- *Engagement* – the number of times information about the chain is shared (recommendations, comments and replies). Can easily be tracked down through websites and social media;
- *Loyalty* – number of customers who stay with the chain and chain members regardless of competitive offerings and who actively promote the brands to other prospects;
- *ROI* – revenue gained less the cost of the campaign;
- *Response time* – the time it takes to respond to customer requests, enquiries and complaints.

Other metrics can also be applied:

- *ROCI* – return on capital invested (income flows divided by returns);
- *Consumer behaviour measures* – frequency, recency, number of positive/negative recommendations, positive reviews posted online (Mayzlin et al., 2014), etc.
- *Intraorganisational metrics* – employee commitment, employee flexibility, staff-to-visitor ratio.

Evaluation of hotel chain's sales force effectiveness is also crucial for its market success. Four critical questions can be addressed to assess the sales force performance (adapted from Hollensen, 2007):

1. Is the sales force adapted for successful market coverage? (Key issues: sales force organisation by geography, concentration of individual hotels; size; territory representation.)
2. Are proper sales people appointed to the right positions? (Key issues: background and education; country of residence; age; gender; experience with international hotel chains; experience in the hospitality industry; emotional intelligence; cultural understanding; sales techniques.)
3. Is there any assistance provided? (Key issues: tutorials; seminars; training; hotel visits; handbooks; market focus; key accounts; coaching; job shadowing.)
4. Do rewards result in desired motivation of sales force? (Key issues: management by objectives; commissions; non-monetary incentives; team building; job enrichment; job rotation; empowerment.)

Addressing these questions can help hotel chains manage a sales force that is able to assist visitors at the different stages of the buying process.

Levels of IMC design – critical aspects for building effective integration

On a strategic level, Schultz and Schultz (1998) propose a four pillar model of IMC, which can serve as guideline to hotel chains that aim to build effective integration of their communications. It is especially important for newly established and developing hotel chains as it represents an integrative framework and establishments must demonstrate proficiency on all four levels:

- *Level 1: Tactical coordination* – initially the IMC focus on tactical coordination of different marketing communication tools (advertising, PR, digital media, etc.) to achieve consistency. The authors define the uniformity of the message delivered through different tools as 'one sight, one sound'. The idea behind it is the reception of a consistent message.
- *Level 2: Redefining the IMC scope* – the hotel chain must view marketing communications from a customer viewpoint (preferred channels/message forms). Executives should keep an eye on all sources of information for their corporate and individual hotel brands. The scope of IMC is broadened to other hotel chain employees, suppliers and external stakeholders so that communication programmes are more closely connected to target audiences.
- *Level 3: Information technology application* – information technologies provide better capabilities for hotel chains in terms of tracking customers' online behaviour, monitoring and identifying prospects, collecting customer information and storing in databases, analysis of empirical data, management of customer relationships and many others.
- *Level 4: Financial and strategic integration* – on this level hotel chains emphasise allocation of resources and ability to manipulate collected data so that they can more precisely examine the relationships between the investments in IMC and return on investment.

If a hotel chain realises the desired ROI this would mean that it has achieved tactical coordination, has targeted the most profitable prospects (through the best contact points) and has applied the right mix of IT tools to explore relationships with customers to the fullest extent.

Conclusion

Integrated marketing communications play a strategic role in the development of contemporary hotel chains. The way the latter are perceived, their brands, services and employees are mostly dependent on how IMCs are exploited. The key to long-term relationships with customers is communication which satisfies both them and hotel chains (and their affiliated establishments). This can be achieved by following the steps of establishing effective marketing communications.

Transmitting the benefits of using a particular hotel chain's services through the most appropriate IMC tools and channels can lead to better corporate and brand effectiveness. In view of that, the changing role of digital communications poses challenges to hotel chains as to their ability to strike a balance between traditional and online communications. For this reason, the conditions of application of different IMC tools have to be continuously tested and fine-tuned.

Finally, investigating the links between the integration of marketing tools and financial performance can help chains analyse the returns on marketing communication investments. Additionally, it is imperative that hotel chains apply metrics to study corporate and market level performances. By doing so, IMC can become a means of effective organisation, realisation and control of a hotel chain's strategy.

References

Aman Resorts (2015) About us. Online. Available HTTP: <http://www.amanresorts.com/aboutus. aspx>, accessed 19 May 2015.
Barger, V. and Labrecque, L. (2013) An integrated marketing communications perspective on social media metrics. *International Journal of Integrated Marketing Communications*, 5(1), 64–76.

Chaffey, D. (2009) *E-Commerce and E-Business Management: Strategy, Implementation and Practice.* Fourth edition. Harlow, UK: Prentice Hall.

Durankev, B. (2014) *Communication Policy.* 2nd edition. Sofia, Bulgaria: University of National and World Economy.

Gilligan, C. and Wilson, R. (2012) *Strategic Marketing Planning.* Oxford, UK: Butterworth-Heinemann.

Great Hotels of the World (2015) Cyprus: find and book only the best. Online. Available HTTP: <http://www.ghotw.com/list/country/home/cyprus.htm>, accessed 18 May 2015.

Hollensen, S. (2007) *Global Marketing: A Decision Oriented Approach.* 4th edn. Harlow, UK: Prentice Hall.

Hotel News Now (2015) NH Hotels turnaround on track. Online. Available HTTP: <http://www.hotelnewsnow.com/Article/15317/NH-Hotels-turnaround-on-track-CEO-says>, accessed 18 May 2015.

Ivanov, S. and Zhechev, V. (2011) *Hotel Marketing.* Varna: Zangador.

Jerman, D. and Zavrsnik, B. (2011) *Model of marketing communications effectiveness in the business-to-business markets.* Proceedings of the International Scientific Conference, Juraj Dobrila University of Pula, Department of Economics & Tourism 'Dr. Mijo Mirkovic', pp. 875–97.

Konovalova, T. and Jatuliaviciene, G. (2015) Innovation development perspectives in a hotel industry by example of Radisson hotel chain in Ukraine. *Regional Formation and Development Studies*, 15, 73–85.

Kotler, P. (2012) *Kotler on Marketing: How to Create, Win, and Dominate Markets.* New York, USA: The Free Press.

Loredana, T. and Micu, C. (2014) The evolution of the performance indicators specific to the hotel offer in Europe. *Agricultural Management*, 16(4), 65–70.

Luxton, S., Reid, M. and Mavondo, F. (2015) Integrated marketing communication capability and brand performance. *Journal of Advertising*, 44(1), 37–46.

Mariott Hotels (2015) Autograph Collection Hotels. Online. Available HTTP: <http://www.marriott.com/hotel-development/Autograph-Collection.mi>, accessed 18 May 2015.

Mayzlin, D., Dover, Y. and Chevalier, J. (2014) Promotional reviews: an empirical investigation of online review manipulation, *American Economic Review*, 104(8), 2421–55.

Melia Hotels International (2015) Sustainability at Melia Hotels International. Online. Available HTTP: <http://www.meliahotelsinternational.com/en/corporate-responsibility>, accessed 19 May 2015.

O'Cass, A. and Weerawardena, J. (2009) Examining the role of international entrepreneurship, innovation, and international market performance in SME internationalization. *European Journal of Marketing*, 43(11/12), 1325–48.

The Peninsula Hotels (2015) More moments. Online. Available HTTP: <http://www.peninsula.com/en/moments>, accessed 19 May 2015.

Rakic, B. and Rakic, M. (2014) Integrated marketing communications paradigm in digital environment: the five pillars of integration. *Megatrend Review*, 11(1), 187–203.

Ram, H., Yoram, M., and Jaffe, E. (2007) From blueprint to implementation: communicating corporate identity for the hotel industry. *International Journal of Contemporary Hospitality Management*, 19(6/7), 485–94.

Ramada Worldwide (2015) Meetings and events. Online. Available HTTP: <http://www.ramada.com/meeting-events/main>, accessed 19 May 2015.

Ramakrishnan, R. (2012) An exploratory study of marketing, physical and people related performance criteria in hotels. *International Journal of Contemporary Hospitality Management*, 24(1), 44–61.

The Rezidor Hotel Group (2015) Home page. Online. Available HTTP: <http://www.rezidor.com/phoenix.zhtml?c=205430&p=index>, accessed 19 May 2015.

Rosewood Hotels (2015) A sense of place™. Online. Available HTTP: <http://www.rosewoodhotels.com/en/gallery on 19 May 2015>.

Sau-Yee, L. and Hyujung, I. (2014) Drivers of customer–brand relationship quality: a case of mainland Chinese hotel loyalty program members, *Journal of Travel & Tourism Marketing*, 31(7), 763–82.

Schultz, D. and Schultz, H. (1998) Transitioning marketing communication into the twenty-first century. *Journal of Marketing Communications*, 4(1), 9–26.

Shakshir, G. (2014) Positioning strategies development. *Annals of the University of Oradea: Economic Science Series*, 23(1), 979–88.

Shimp, T. (2010) *Advertising, Promotion and Other Aspects of Integrated Marketing Communications*, 8th edn. Mason, USA: Cengage Learning.

Travel and Leisure (2015) Hotels in Whistler. Online. Available HTTP: <http://www.travelandleisure. com/travel-guide/whistler/hotels>, accessed 18 May 2015.

Verma, Y. and Jain, V. (2015) How experiential marketing is used in Indian luxury hotels, *Romanian Journal of Marketing*, 1, 1–11.

Zhechev, V. (2015) *Stealth marketing strategy – origins, manifestations and practical application.* Proceedings from the 'Horizons in the human resources and knowledge development' conference, Burgas, 2015.

Zhelev, S. (2010) *Positioning: Between The Needed, The Possible and The Actual.* Sofia, Bulgaria: University of National and World Economy.

24

Managing customer relationships in hotel chains: a comparison between guest and manager perceptions

Haywantee Rumi Ramkissoon (CURTIN UNIVERSITY, AUSTRALIA) *and Felix T. Mavondo* (MONASH UNIVERSITY, AUSTRALIA)

Introduction

Customer relationship management, especially in the increasingly competitive environment of chain hotels, has spurred significant interest in the marketing literature. While the concept has long been discussed in the literature, it is still negotiable in terms of its definition and meaning (Buttle, 2004). Originating from IT industries in the mid-1990s (Boulding et al., 2005), the concept of customer relationship management has emerged into a management philosophy in hotel chains (Lo et al., 2010). As the basis of the economy changes (Pine and Gilmore, 1999), the customer demands superior customer value in terms of best quality service, and best price among other elements. While the experience of the product is unique to the consumer (Jewell and Crotts, 2002), the key objective is to co-create value (Prebensen et al., 2014; Ramkissoon and Uysal, 2014) between the customer and hotel management (Nasution and Mavondo, 2008; Payne and Frow, 2005). Hence, in addition to understanding consumers' cognitive aspects, chain hotel managers now seek to maintain a long-term affective attachment with their customers (Cai and Hobson, 2004; Kim et al., 2008). This allows an evaluation of their positioning strategy vis-à-vis their competitors (Prasad and Dev, 2000).

Loyalty programmes in chain hotels are commonly used, aiming at customer retention and generating business returns. Major hotel chains such as Hilton, Intercontinental and Best Western have been successful in attracting approximately 92 million memberships (Dekay et al., 2009) to their loyalty programmes, e.g. Hilton HHonours, IHG Rewards Club, Best Western Rewards. Customers accumulate free rewards and value-added benefits when making repeated purchases (Xiong et al., 2014) including discounted room rates, preferential room allocation, point redemption for meals, flights and flight upgrades, early check-ins, and late and fast check-outs. Loyalty is seen as both behavioural and attitudinal (Kandampully and Suhartanto, 2000) with the former focussing on customers' repeat purchases with regard to brands over time (Bowen and Shoemaker, 1998) while the latter indicates the intention to recommend and repurchase (Getty and Thompson, 1994). Chain hotels are making rigorous efforts to manage customer relationships through customer segmentation (Prentice, 2013) and membership tier provision (McCall and Voorhees, 2010). A number of studies reflect that most research has focussed on customer loyalty from either a managerial perspective, i.e., service providers (e.g., Clark et al., 2009) or the customers' perspective (e.g., Lai, 2015; Xie and Chen, 2014). Central to customer loyalty however is service delivery and perceived value.

The interaction between customers and employees is critical to superior customer service delivery. This may be guided by customer orientation of the organisation and management support for employee training and sensitivity. Hospitality researchers (e.g., Kashyap and Bojanic, 2000) argue that perceived value has both a direct and indirect influence on revisit intentions. The literature evidences a number of studies in four and five-star hotels, with only a few in mid-scale and budget chain hotels. As tactics and strategies used in the hospitality sector become more complex (Rauch et al., 2015), this calls for additional research on the essential values in relationship management, influencing customers to enrol in hotel loyalty programmes across different classes of hotels, with more emphasis in mid-scale and budget chain hotels.

This study bridges the gap in the literature by examining differences between managers' and customers' perceived value across different categories of chain hotels. It aims to answer the following research question, using a case study with data collected from hotel managers and customers in premium, standard and budget hotels in Indonesia.

Do customers and chain hotel managers attach the same value across different categories of chain hotels?

This chapter sets out to make some important practical and theoretical contributions to the literature. Understanding differences in perceived value in managers' and customers' perspective is important, particularly to chain hotel managers in crafting value opportunities to increase the latter's emotional attachment to chain hotels. This has implications for the alignment, investment and profitability of the organisations. Furthermore, it opens doors for additional research avenues on promoting service quality across different hotel classifications.

Literature review

Perceived value

Central to the concept of managing customer relationships is the concept of value. The nature of service relationships encompasses high levels of involvement from both the provider and consumer (Palmatier et al., 2006) necessitating the importance of their perceived value. The concept of value has been applied across disciplines such as marketing, social sciences, product management, information systems, tourism and hospitality with diverse meanings (e.g., Nasution and Mavondo, 2008). Zeithaml (1988) considers perceived value to be the consumer's overall assessment of the effectiveness of a product based on what is given and received. He further assigns four different meanings to value: '(1) value is low price; (2) value is whatever one wants in a product; (3) value is the quality that a customer receives for the price paid and (4) value is what the customer gets for what they give' (Zeithaml, 1988, p. 3). Lepak et al. (2007) defines value as 'the specific quality of a new job, task, product or service as perceived by users in relation to their needs such as the speed or quality of performance on a new task or the aesthetics or performance features of a new product or service' (2007: 2–3).

Customer value: differing perspectives

With the growing competition in the hospitality sector, customers' perceived value continues to attract significant interest of researchers (e.g., Guillet et al., 2014; Nunkoo et al., 2013).

Customer value can fundamentally differ for hotel managers and consumers. Measurements of hotel ratings emphasising service quality can be very subjective and vary greatly (Callan, 1995; Su and Sun, 2007) across several countries. Generally, it is expected that the luxury hotels develop and implement effective products and services to provide superior value. Examples of some facilities include world class restaurants, modern facilities such as swimming pools, special needs rooms, health clubs and personal trainers among others.

The higher prices of premium hotels compared to standard and budget hotels are justified by provision of superior customer value. Customer quality experience serves as the primary guideline for managers for providing customer value. Since managers perceive customer service as a product, the customer's intangible experience is seen as the core of many hospitality products and services (Lewis and Chambers, 2006). Luxury hotel operations invest in integrated administrative packages and more sophisticated forms of communication (Baum and Devine, 2007). For instance the use of information technology in marketing of goods, and handling customers' complaints has become increasingly common in luxury hotels in the Antalya region in Turkey (Aksu and Tarcan, 2002). Employees' skills sets remain a vital operational tool across all categories of hospitality providers. Quality-based market strategies in premium hotels, however, necessitate that staff are more highly skilled (Klidas et al., 2007; Lloyd et al., 2005). With luxury hotels expanding in India, Mohsin et al. (2013) recommend that the Indian hotel industry recognise the need for appropriately trained staff and staff satisfaction for long-term benefits.

From a managerial perspective, the hospitality sector needs to focus on the long-term management of customer value, and develop, attract and maintain customer relationships (Yuan and Wu, 2008). In their study on Chinese luxury hotel staying behaviour, Chen and Peng (2014) suggest hotel managers should advertise in magazines, underlining the hotels' luxurious experience in its provision of luxury goods to customers. Attending trade shows could benefit hotel managers in identifying potential customers who think luxury hotels are pleasant and desirable (Wong et al., 2014). Hoteliers need to focus on customer engagement (van Doorn et al., 2010), emphasising service quality to meet the needs and expectations of customers (Haywood, 1983; Nasution and Mavondo, 2008). Mohsin and Lockyer (2010) state that the survival of luxury hotels in India depends largely on service quality. Customer value has to be planned for, and resources deployed to achieve customer desired value. Choi and Chu (2000), in their study of Asian travellers in Hong Kong hotels, noted that customer satisfaction was primarily derived from value (Choi and Chu, 2000). While value in the hospitality sector is generally largely delivered through service quality and the atmosphere of the hotel, organisations with a commitment to provide superior customer value focus on additional factors. The latter include customers' emotional attachment, prestige and behavioural price, which help enhance their competitive advantage (Nasution and Mavondo, 2008; Nateh et al., 2013).

Achieving customer loyalty is a key challenge for most hotel managers. They struggle to face the challenges of maintaining a positive relationship with customers (Kandampully and Suhartanto, 2000; Torres and Kline, 2000). Researchers (e.g. Kim and Oh, 2009) emphasise that manager communication is an important concept in determining customer orientation, which can in turn deliver customer satisfaction (Ramkissoon et al., 2013; Ramkissoon and Mavondo, 2014) and loyalty. What management delivers to its customers is vital to its success (Ahmad and Saber, 2015; Essawy, 2012). It is paramount for hotel employees to understand which part of the service encounter is most important to customers (Anderson et al., 2008).

Assessed from a consumer's perspective, value is the key link between cognitive elements of perceived quality (Paswan et al., 2007; Seric and Gil-Saura, 2012), value for money

(Ye et al., 2014) and behavioural intentions to return to the hotel (Liu and Jang, 2009). With hotels reflecting different levels of performance with the star ratings (Pine and Phillips, 2005) such as cleanliness of rooms, price, friendliness of staff and location (Kim et al., 2008; Lockyer, 2003; 2005), the customer uses these comparison factors to assess quality. When evaluated below tolerance level, the customer may switch to another service provider (Stein and Ramaseshan, 2015). Satisfied customers are more likely to recommend and repurchase the services (Petrick, 2002; Ramkissoon and Uysal, 2011) and in the long run build customer loyalty (Dekay et al., 2009).

More recently, researchers have found that loyalty in hotels could in turn have a positive influence on citizenship behaviour (e.g., Zoghbi-Manrique-de-Lara et al., 2014). Some evidence suggests that consumers' positive emotional responses to how management handles customers' complaints are tied to their intentions to return to the hotel (Karatepe, 2006). Customers exhibiting citizenship behaviour show tolerance and provide constructive feedback to hotel managers (van Doorn et al., 2010). The fundamental role of trust between the actors is emphasised in this exchange relationship (Nunkoo and Ramkissoon, 2012; Zafirovski, 2005).

In the highly competitive market with customers largely emphasising the quality of service experience (Volo, 2010) delivered by hotel organisations, researchers have called for further studies on both managers' perceived customer value across different classifications of hotels i.e., premium, standard and budget hotels. This would provide practical guidelines to the hotel managers on aligning their provision of services and facilities to meet customers' needs, in an attempt to attract new customers and retain old ones.

The case study: discussion and implications

The tourism industry is a growing and important sector in Indonesia. The main aim of the Indonesian tourism industry is promoting Indonesia to attract more foreign currency earnings (Nasution and Mavondo, 2008). Indonesia remains a very popular tourist destination in the South East Asia Region with tourists visiting from the neighbouring countries for cultural festivals. Also, Indonesia's improved flight connections have attracted a growth in tourist arrivals in 2014 (Indonesia Investments, 2014). For the purpose of this study, data was collected from Indonesia's hotel sector which is an important contributor of foreign exchange in the country.

Data from hotel managers was collected with a self-administered questionnaire sent to 801 chain hotels of different classifications (budget, standard, premium) across 29 provinces in Indonesia. These 801 chain hotels were the ones the researchers had full information on at the time. This allowed them to directly address correspondence to specific individuals at the chain hotels. Out of 801, 247 chain hotels responded to the survey. A usable sample of 231 questionnaires was retained for the final analysis with an effective response rate of 29 per cent. Responses covered almost all provinces in Indonesia, suggesting the sample was adequately representative of the population. Another self-administered questionnaire was collected from 385 hotel guests in Java, Indonesia. A total of 50 questionnaires were distributed to hotel guests at 7 participating hotels with the assistance of the hotel managers. The researcher collected the completed questionnaires the following month. The perceived value scale (18 items) was adapted from Petrick (2002), measuring quality, reputation, monetary value and prestige on a 7 point Likert scale (1=strongly disagree; 7=strongly agree). The customer questionnaire was identical to the relevant section for the management questionnaire to permit comparisons.

Table 24.1 Differences in customer value across chains as seen by stakeholders

	Budget hotels	Standard hotels	Premier hotels	F-ratio	Differences
Managers	5.34	5.73	6.23	15.267***	P>S>B
	N = 68	N = 134	N = 29		
Customers	3.89	5.03	4.94	32.20***	P and S>B
	N = 45	N = 81	N = 259		
Mean differences between managers and customers	1.45	0.70	1.19		
t-value	16.11***	11.67***	9.15***		
	M>C	M>C	M>C		

Note: The rows compare chains of different classifications. The columns are t-tests of differences between managers' evaluation of customer value and those perceived by customers.

Results in Table 24.1 indicate that managers of different classes of chain hotels significantly differ in the level of customer value they perceive they deliver to their customers. Premier chain hotel managers' perceived customer value is significantly different to the standard chain hotel managers'. Furthermore, standard chain hotel managers' perceived customer value is significantly different from those of budget chain hotels.

Interestingly however, customers' received value reflects different results to those of hotel managers across all three categories of chain hotels (premium, standard and budget). Customers of budget hotels believe they receive significantly inferior or lower customer value than those in standard and premier chains. Surprisingly those in standard hotels believe they are receiving very good customer value although this is not significantly higher than premier hotels. This may suggest standard hotels offer more value for money or are perceived as communicating their value offerings better than premier chain hotels.

Comparing the differences between managers and customers at the same hotels shows that managers across all classes of hotels think they are offering superior customer value, but their customers receive much lower value. The managers' score for premium hotels was 6.23 out of 7 while the received value score from customers was about 4.94 on the same scale. The differences are significant with the biggest discrepancies occurring among budget hotels followed by premier hotels (see Table 24.1). The standard hotels have narrower differences again suggesting better communication or service delivery or both.

The gap between managers' perception and customer-received value across the three categories of hotels reflect some important challenges to be met by managers. One of the main challenges may have to do with employee skills and training effectiveness. There is increasing debate about the level of skills required for hospitality workers (Baum and Devine, 2007). Hotel management need to focus on empowering staff, with a focus on customer-oriented organisational culture. This implies instilling staff with the company values and knowledge to shape their attitudes to achieve the desired behaviours.

Managers need to assess the potential benefits and requirements of enhancing hospitality staff skills to deliver higher levels of service quality. As much as technology has contributed to many more sophisticated forms of communication, new employees in the hospitality world 'must be trained to be loyal, flexible, tolerant, amiable, and responsible . . . at every successful tourism establishment, it is the employees that stand out . . . technology cannot substitute for welcoming employees' (Poon, 1993, p. 262). Our findings are in line with Poon's (1993) work.

Managers may need to build on their staff training to increase the quality of service across the different hotel classes to bridge the gap between their perceived customer value and customers' received customer value.

Findings suggest that managers of budget hotels have a specific need to review their strategies and align service delivery with their customers' expectations for their organisations to persist and be profitable. We also reinforce the notion that training in premium hotels needs to be constantly encouraged to move up-market to provide more value added services. This is essential to achieve product and competitive differentiation in Indonesia's premium hotels with the fast growing competition from different countries. This implies provision of high quality services and facilities that are not easily emulated, maintaining high occupancy rates and effective customer relations. A similar view is shared by Wu et al. (2008) in their evaluation of the tourist hotel industry performance in Taiwan.

Each of the hotel classes needs to maintain effective communication with their customers, which is often challenging with the intangible nature of hospitality services (Ibrahim, 2015). The differences in managers' and customers' perceived customer value across all three hotel categories may be the result of a lack of congruence between management's communication and messages received by guests and potential customers. Managers should focus more effort on developing two-way communication between hotel staff and customers. This exchange of information will assist managers to better understand the needs and expectations of their customers, and may help in achieving service excellence and customer loyalty.

Conclusion

This study assesses differences between managers' and customers' perceptions of customer value across different classes of hotels in Indonesia. The findings suggest that differences persist across all three (premium, standard and budget) Indonesian chain hotels. The tourism sector in Indonesia plays a vital role as a foreign exchange earner. Hotel associations and the Indonesian government will benefit from improving the service quality across these different hotel classifications.

Chain hotels need to concentrate on positioning as a key technique by which they can make their products and services more desirable to customers. Hotel managers need to constantly monitor customer expectations, aligning service delivery with their findings. Managers would benefit from investing in research to identify customer values, the drivers of customer value and customer needs. This would be beneficial for investing resources appropriately and gaining a competitive advantage. There is a need to conduct an evaluation of the hotels' resources such as employees' and management's efficiency on a regular basis. Such intangibles offer sustainable economic benefits (Galbreath, 2005), thus building customer loyalty and customer retention.

Creating and integrating value-added components through innovative product development and investment in customer understanding and customer linking activities will additionally help to promote Indonesia's tourism and hospitality sectors, thereby maintaining and enhancing destination competitiveness in the market. While it is essential for hotel chains to recognise the need for product diversification with higher investments in premium hotels to generate high revenues, it is important to maintain a balanced portfolio of hotel classes to cater for the different market segments.

The findings of this study could be extended by in-depth analysis of individual hotel chains by studying each branch and comparing managers and customers at each branch. This could be used by the hotel chain for benchmarking performance. Future researchers may consider this approach since it eliminates confounding factors like advertising intensity, organisational culture and atmospherics.

Despite its contributions, the limitations of this study are also evident. It includes only managers and customers across premium, standard and budget hotels in Indonesia. Given the contextual nature of the present study, our findings may be representative of Indonesia's hospitality sector. Thus, the study findings may not be generalizable. However, the classification of hotels in this study is representative of many experiences in other countries and the findings may be representative. Future studies can compare hotels across different regions and countries to provide additional insights on managers' and customers' perceived customer value in hotel chains.

Secondly, the selection of customers to participate in the study was done by hotel staff. This could bias the results through choosing agreeable customers rather than through random allocation. Thus, the customer responses could be more positive than in a random sample. The findings of this study suggest this was not a serious problem but should be considered in future research designs. Perhaps in the current study this was minimised by having all responses in sealed envelopes to prevent access to the questionnaires by staff once they were completed.

Finally, future researchers may consider not only managers but also frontline employees as possible participants. Frontline employees have direct interaction with customers and at times this is the only interaction the customers ever have with the hotel. Thus, their service delivery and evaluation of service quality is critical to the hospitality industry. This is important in view of the many part-time and casual positions in the industry. Understanding service delivery from the employees' perspective may point to the need for further training and other prerequisites for quality customer service delivery.

References

Ahmad, S. and Saber. H. (2015) Understanding marketing strategies with particular reference to small and medium-sized businesses in the United Arab Emirates. *Tourism & Hospitality Research*, 15(2), 115–29.

Aksu, A. and Tarcan, E. (2002) The Internet and five-star hotels: a case study from the Antalya region in Turkey. *International Journal of Contemporary Hospitality Management*, 14(2), 94–7.

Anderson, S., Klein Pearo, L. and Widener, S. (2008) Drivers of service satisfaction: linking customer satisfaction to the service context and customer characteristics. *Journal of Service Research*, 10, 365–81.

Baum, T. and Devine, F. (2007) Skills and training in the hotel sector: the case of front office employment in Northern Ireland. *Tourism & Hospitality Research*, 7, 269–80.

Boulding, W., Staelin, R. and Ehret, M. (2005) A customer relationship management roadmap. What is known: potential pitfalls and where to go. *Journal of Marketing*, 69, 155–66.

Bowen, J. and Shoemaker, S. (1998) Loyalty, a strategic commitment. *Cornell Hotels and Restaurants Administrative Quarterly*, 2, 12–25.

Buttle, F. (2004) *Customer Relationship Management. Concepts and Tools*. Oxford: Butterworth-Heinemann.

Cai, L. and Hobson, J. (2004) Making hotel brands work in a competitive environment. *Journal of Vacation Marketing*, 10(3), 197–208.

Callan, R. (1995) Hotel classifications and grading schemes: a paradigm of utilisation and user characteristics. *International Journal of Hospitality Management*, 14(3), 271–84.

Chen, A. and Peng, N. (2014) Examining Chinese consumers' luxury hotel staying behaviour. *International Journal of Tourism Research*, 39, 53–6.

Choi, T. and Chu, R. (2000). Levels of satisfaction among Asian and Western travellers. *International Journal of Quality & Reliability Management*, 17(2), 116–32.

Clark, R., Hartline, M. and Jones, K. (2009) Hotel employees' commitment to service quality. *Cornell Hospitality Quarterly*, 50(2), 209–31.

Dekay, F., To, R. and Raven, P. (2009) Loyalty programs: Airlines outdo hotels. *Cornell Hospitality Quarterly*, 50(3), 371–82.

Essawy, M. (2012) The implementation of relationship marketing by independent Egyptian hotels. *Tourism and Hospitality Research*, 12(4), 175–87.

Galbreath, J. (2005) Which resources matter the most to firm success? An exploratory study of resource-based theory. *Technovation*, 25(9), 979–87.

Getty, J. and Thompson, K. (1994) The relationship between quality, satisfaction, and recommending behaviour in lodging decision. *Journal of Hospitality & Leisure Marketing*, 2(3), 3–22.

Guillet, B., Liu, W. and Law, R. (2014) Can setting hotel rate restrictions help balance the interest rate of hotels and customers? *International Journal of Contemporary Hospitality Management*, 26(6), 948–73.

Haywood, K. (1983) Assessing the quality of hospitality services. *International Journal of Hospitality Management*, 2, 165–77.

Ibrahim, M. (2015) Evaluating hotel websites as a marketing communication channel: a dialogic perspective. *Information Development*, 1–10.

Indonesia Investments (2014) *Foreign tourist arrivals in 2013–2014*. Online. Avaialble HTTP:<http://www.indonesia-investments.com/news/todays-headlines/foreign-tourist-arrivals-to-indonesia-jump-22.6-in-january-2014/item1716>, accessed 3 December 2015.

Jewell, B. and Crotts, J., (2002) Adding psychological value to heritage tourism experiences. *Journal of Travel and Tourism Marketing*, 11(4), 13–28.

Kandampully, J. and Suhartanto, D. (2000) Customer loyalty in the hotel industry. *International Journal of Contemporary Hospitality Management*, 12(6), 346–51.

Karatepe, O. (2006) Customer complaints and organizational responses: the effects of complaints' perceptions of justice on satisfaction and loyalty. *International Journal of Hospitality Management*, 25(1), 69–90.

Kashyap, R. and Bojanic, D. (2000) A structural analysis of value, quality and price perceptions of business and leisure travelers. *Journal of Travel Research*, 39(1), 45–51.

Kim, W. and Oh, C. (2009) Customers' responses to customer orientation of service employees in full-service restaurants: a relational benefits perspective. *Journal of Quality Assurance in Hospitality and Tourism*, 10, 153–74.

Kim, W., Jin-Sun, B. and Kim, H. (2008). Multidimensional customer-based brand equity and its consequences in midpriced hotels. *Journal of Hospitality & Tourism Research*, 32(2), 235–54.

Klidas, A., van den Berg, P. and Wilderom, C. (2007) Managing employee empowerment in luxury hotels in Europe. *International Journal of Service Industry Management*, 18(1), 70–88.

Lai, I. (2015) The roles of value, satisfaction and commitment in the effect of service quality on customer loyalty in Hong-Kong style tea restaurants. *Cornell Hospitality Quarterly*, 56(1), 118–38.

Lepak, D., Smith, K. and Taylor, M. (2007) Value creation and value capture: a multilevel perspective. *Academy of Management Review*, 32(1), 180–94.

Lewis, R. and Chambers, R. (2006) *Marketing Leadership in Hospitality*. New York: John Wiley.

Liu, Y. and Jang, S. (2009) The effects of dining atmospherics: an extended Mehrabian-Russell model. *International Journal of Hospitality Management*, 28(4), 494–503.

Lloyd, C., Warhurst, C. and Dutton, E. (2005) The weakest link? Product market strategies, skill and pay in the hotel industry. *Work, employment and society*, 27(2), 254–71.

Lo, A., Stalcup. D. and Lee, A. (2010) Customer relationship management for hotels in Hong Kong. *International Journal of Contemporary Hospitality Management*, 22(2), 139–59.

Lockyer, T. (2003) Hotel cleanliness – how do guests view it? Let us get specific, a New Zealand study. *International Journal of Hospitality Management*, 22, 297–305.

Lockyer, T. (2005) The perceived dimension of price as one hotel selection dimension. *Tourism Management*, 26, 529–37.

McCall, M. and Voorhees, C. (2010) The drivers of loyalty program success. *Cornell Hospitality Quarterly*, 51(1), 35–52.

Mohsin, A. and Lockyer, T. (2010) Customer perceptions of service quality in luxury hotels in New Delhi, India: an exploratory study. *International Journal of Contemporary Hospitality Management*, 22(2), 160–73.

Mohsin, A., Lengler, J. and Kumar, B. (2013) Exploring the antecedents of intentions to leave the job: the case of luxury hotel staff, *International Journal of Hospitality Management*, 35, 48–58.

Nasution, H. and Mavondo, F. (2008) Customer value in the hotel industry: what managers believe they deliver and what customers experience. *International Journal of Hospitality Management*, 27, 207–13.

Nateh, B., Agbemabiese, G., Kodua, P. and Braimah, M. (2013) Relationship marketing and customer loyalty: evidence from Ghanaian luxury hotel industry. *Journal of Hospitality Marketing & Management*, 22(4), 407–36.

Nunkoo R. and Ramkissoon, H. (2012) Power, trust, social exchange and community support. *Annals of Tourism Research*, 39(2), 997–1023.

Nunkoo, R., Gursoy, D. and Ramkissoon, H. (2013) Developments in hospitality marketing and management: social network analysis and research themes. *Journal of Hospitality Marketing & Management*, 22(3), 269–88.

Palamatier, R., Dant, R., Grewal, D. and Evans, K. (2006) Factors influencing the effectiveness of relationship marketing: a meta-analysis. *Journal of Marketing*, 70(4), 136–53.

Paswan, A., Spears, N. and Ganesh, G. (2007) The effects of obtaining one's preferred service brand on consumer satisfaction and brand loyalty. *Journal of Services Marketing*, 21(2), 57–87.

Payne, A. and Frow, P. (2005) A strategic framework for customer relationship management. *Journal of Marketing*, 69(4), 169–76.

Petrick, J. (2002) Development of a multidimensional scale for measuring the perceived value of a service. *Journal of Leisure Research*, 34, 119–34.

Pine, B. and Gilmore, J. (1999) *The Experience Economy: Work is Theatre and Every Business a Stage*. Aurora, Ohio: Strategic Horizon.

Pine, R. and Phillips, P. (2005) Performance comparison hotels in China. *International Journal of Hospitality Management*, 24, 57–73.

Poon, A. (1993) *Tourism, Technology and Competitive Strategies*. Wallington, Oxon: CABI.

Prasad, K. and Dev, C. (2000) Managing hotel brand equity: a customer-centric framework for assessing performance. *Cornell Hotel and Restaurant Administration Quarterly*, 41(3), 22–31.

Prebensen, N., Chen, J. and Uysal, M. (2014) Co-creation of tourist experience: scope, definition and structure. In Prebensen, N., Chen, J. and Uysal, M. (eds.), *Creating Experience Value in Tourism*, Wallington UK: CABI, 1–10.

Prentice, C. (2013) Service quality perceptions and customer loyalty in casinos. *International Journal of Contemporary Hospitality Management*, 25(1), 49–64.

Ramkissoon, H. and Mavondo, F. (2014) Pro-environmental behaviour: the link between place attachment and place satisfaction, *Tourism Analysis*, 19(6), 673–88.

Ramkissoon, H. and Uysal, M. (2011) The effects of perceived authenticity, information search behavior, motivation and destination imagery on cultural behavioral intentions of tourists. *Current Issues in Tourism*, 14(6), 537–62.

Ramkissoon, H. and Uysal, M.S., (2014) Authenticity as a value co-creator of tourism experiences. In Prebensen, N., Chen, J. and Uysal, M. (eds.), *Creating Experience Value in Tourism*, Wallingford UK: CABI, pp. 113–24.

Ramkissoon, H., Smith, L. and Weiler, B. (2013) Testing the dimensionality of place attachment and its relationships with place satisfaction and pro-environmental behaviours: a structural equation modelling approach. *Tourism Management*, 36, 552–66.

Rauch, D., Colins, M., Nale, R. and Barr, P. (2015) Measuring service quality in mid-chain hotels. *International Journal of Contemporary Hospitality Management*, 27(1), 87–106.

Seric, M. and Gil-Saura, I. (2012) ICT, IMC and brand equity in high-quality hotels of Dalmantia. An analysis from guest perceptions. *Journal of Hospitality Marketing & Management*, 21, 821–51.

Stein, A. and Ramaseshan, B. (2015) Customers' referral behaviour: do switchers and stayers differ? *Journal of Service Research*, 1–11.

Su, C. and Sun, L. (2007) Taiwan's hotel rating system: a service quality perspective. *Cornell Hotel and Restaurant Administration Quarterly*, 48(4), 392–401.

Torres, N. and Kline, S. (2000) From satisfaction to delight: a model for the hotel industry. *International Journal of Contemporary Hospitality Management*, 18(4), 290–301.

van Doorn, J., Lemon, K., Mittal, V., Nass, S., Pick, D., Pirner, P. and Verhoef, P. (2010) Customer engagement behaviour: theoretical foundations and research directions. *Journal of Service Research*, 13, 253–66.

Volo, S. (2010) Bloggers' reported tourist experiences: their utility as a tourism data source and their effect on prospective tourists. *Journal of Vacation Marketing*, 16(4), 297–311.

Volo, W., Chen, J., Fan, L. and Lu, J. (2012) Tourist experience and wetland parks: a case of Zhejiang, China. *Annals of Tourism Research*, 39, 1763–78.

Wong, J., Li, T., Peng, N. and Chen, A. (2014) Conceptualizing trade show visitors' consumption behaviour. *International Journal of Tourism Research*, 16, 325–8.

Wu, W., Hsiao, S. and Tsai, C. (2008) Forecasting and evaluating the tourist hotel industry in Taiwan based on Grey theory. *Tourism & Hospitality Research*, 8, 137–52.

Xie, L. and Chen, C., (2014) Hotel loyalty programs: how valuable is valuable enough. *International Journal of Contemporary Hospitality Management*, 26(1), 107–29.

Xiong, L., King, C. and Hu, C. (2014) *International Journal of Contemporary Hospitality Management*, 26(4), 572–92.

Ye, Q., Li, H., Wang, Z. and Law, R. (2014) The influence of hotel price on perceived service quality and value in e-tourism: an empirical investigation based on online traveler reviews. *Journal of Hospitality & Tourism Research*, 38(1), 23–39.

Yuan, Y. and Wu, C. (2008) Relationships among experiential marketing, experiential value and customer satisfaction. *Journal of Hospitality & Tourism Research*, 32(3), 387–410.

Zafirovski, M. (2005) Social exchange theory under scrutiny: a positive critique of its economic-behaviorist formulations. *Electronic Journal of Sociology*. Online. Available HTTP: <htpp://www.sociology.org/content/2005/tier2/SETheory.pdf>, accessed 3 December 2015.

Zeithaml, V. (1988) Consumer perception of price, quality and value: a means-end model and synthesis of evidence. *Journal of Marketing*, 52(3), 2–22.

Zoghbi-Manrique-de-Lara, P., Suarez-Acosta, M. and Aguiar-Quintana, T. (2014) Hotel guests' responses to service recovery: how loyalty influences guest behaviour. *Cornell Hospitality Quarterly*, 55(2), 155–64.

25

Fostering service quality in hotel chains through a focus on employee development and performance

Vincent P. Magnini (VIRGINIA TECH UNIVERSITY, USA) *and*
Carol J. Simon (INDEPENDENT HOTEL CONSULTANT, USA)

Introduction

The purpose of this chapter is to provide a state-of-the-art review of how hotel chains go about fostering cultures in hotels in which high-levels of service quality are consistently provided at the frontline. Developing such cultures involves compartmentalising initiatives into three stages: 1) The pre-training stage entails recruiting and selecting frontline associates who are capable of performing at high levels. 2) The training stage involves arming the frontline associates with the knowledge and skills to deliver a top-rate service. 3) The post-training stage encompasses engendering a culture on an ongoing basis in which associates have both the ability and the motivation to deliver high quality experiences for guests.

Before discussing the three stages, it is prudent to ask the following question: How do executives at a chain's headquarters know if a given hotel is providing guests with acceptable service quality? First, nearly all chains survey a sample of recent hotel guests and compare survey results to a benchmark. Marriott brands, for example, term the survey results 'guest satisfaction scores' (GSS scores). Hilton, on the other hand, refers to the survey data as 'satisfaction and loyalty tracking' (SALT scores). Another example, Starwood Corporation, terms the survey results 'guest experience index' (GEI scores). For branded hotels, the survey results of a given hotel property are then compared and ranked among other properties within the brand. If a 10-point Likert-type scale is used on the survey mechanism (1 = strongly disagree; 10 = strongly agree), rather than creating benchmarks based on raw scores on the Likert-type scales, many hotel chains instead rate hotels based on the percentage of 9s and 10s that they receive for the items. The logic that supports this practice is that a guest who provides a 7 or 8 to an item may or may not remain loyal, but providers of 9s and 10s will likely repurchase and/or spread positive word-of-mouth.

If a hotel property consistently performs at or near the bottom of its brand with such scores then the corporate headquarters will initiate a series of actions. While specifics vary among companies, often the hotel is placed in universal service default which is a warning to managers and owners of the property that if the scores do not trend in a positive direction then the brand affiliation can/will be removed from the property. Often the headquarters will suggest, and in some cases require, that the hotel offers service training modules to associates and managers during universal service default. Removing the brand affiliation is often the final action taken after a series of efforts to improve service scores. If a hotel is managed by a third party management company and is in constant service default, the brand can put all future projects on hold for this company until the hotel rectifies its service defaults. Such an action exhibits the emphasis the brands put on service.

Other than guest surveying, hotel properties also monitor their rankings on consumer-generated-blog websites, such as Trip Advisor, to gauge their service performance. Tools such as Revinate in the USA and TrustYou in Europe are increasingly being used by hotel properties to text-analyse trends in consumers' blog postings and to examine how properties compare on these trend lines. Social media has a tremendous impact on what guests are saying about the hotels they stay in (Ayeh et al., 2013). All third party reservation sites now encourage their customers to leave feedback about the hotel with the service component being part of the ratings. Studies have shown that when a hotel gets continuous negative comments it has a direct negative impact on hotel revenues (Aureli et al., 2013; Kim et al., 2015).

Lastly, as has been the case since the advent of hotel chains, inspections from corporate headquarters are still employed to assess service quality at individual units. Some brands perform announced inspections, some carry out unannounced inspections, and some perform both. Relatedly, mystery (a.k.a. secret) shoppers are also sometimes utilised to assess service quality at hotel properties.

With the common methods for measuring service quality in hotel chains addressed, this chapter now moves to the pre-training phase of fostering a service quality culture in a hotel chain.

Pre-training measures to foster service quality

High levels of customer service delivery in hotels begin with recruiting and selecting the right personnel. Regarding the ability to attract a quality pool of applicants, hotel managers should meet regularly and brainstorm ways by which to increase the size and quality of the applicant pools for their vacant positions. The tactics stemming from such sessions will be unique to the marketplace of a given hotel. For *Hotel A* it might be advantageous to partner with or recruit through a local University or trade school, but for *Hotel B* it might be most useful to recruit legal foreign workers. Regardless of tactics, all hotels must routinely examine how to draw the best possible applicant pools for their open positions.

While recruitment tactics are hotel and market specific, there are three tactics in particular in which all properties should engage. First, open job positions should be posted on all the mainstream (and industry-specific) employment websites. Second, employee referral systems should be in place: employees should be encouraged to recruit the colleagues they feel might be suitable for open positions. Third, if a job position is trainable and does not require ad-hoc knowledge of technical skills, managers should recruit applicants as they themselves move as customers through other service environments and witness toprate service.

Once a quality applicant pool has been compiled, the best possible selection procedures must be applied in order to identify the leading candidate. Regarding selection, behavioural interviewing is now an essential component of hotel associate selection. A behavioural interview is comprised of: 1) situational questions that pose hypothetical scenarios to which the respondent is asked how s/he would respond; and 2) past behaviour questions that ask the candidate to describe his/her actions when faced with particular circumstances. Examples of behavioural interviewing questions are widely available on the internet. Well-crafted behavioural interviewing questions often mandate that the respondent consider: 1) a situation/ task; 2) an action; and 3) results (S-T-A-R) (Whitacre, 2007).

Because high quality service delivery often depends upon teamwork among associates, as suggested by Kaufman (2012), the following item can be included in the behavioural interview: 'Tell me how you achieved one of your greatest service successes' (Kaufman, 2012). Respondents who include more 'us', 'our' and 'we' than 'I', 'my' and 'me' are more likely to be team players if selected.

A type of interviewing known as 360 degree interviewing can also be useful in fostering a service culture in a hotel. That is, some hotel firms mandate that candidates be interviewed by a host of individuals – not only the executives who the candidate would report to, but also be interviewed by associates who would report to or work alongside the candidate if selected (Michelli, 2008). This 360 degree-style interviewing can be useful in gauging the candidate's level of emotional intelligence by allowing the ability to observe the candidate from multiple perspectives.

If multiple interviews are conducted, if possible, it is advantageous to spread them across more than one day (Magnini, 2013). Multiple-day interviewing helps assess the candidate's dependability as well as his/her service-oriented demeanour at different points in time. Panel interviewing in which the candidate meets with more than one interviewer at once is useful in gauging conversational ability – a key customer service trait (Dixon et al., 2002).

If a written portion is utilised as a component of the interview, sentence completion tasks are useful in assessing a candidate's service-related capabilities. Kaufman (2012) suggests using sentence stems such as the following:

1) It's not my _____.
2) I don't have _____.
3) Our policy isn't _____.
4) I'm sorry, but _____.

Sentence completion tasks are particularly useful because they generate spontaneous responses (Brinthaupt and Erwin, 1992) and they offer a glimpse at what the candidate views as relevant (McGuire and McGuire, 1988). For example, in response to stem no. 1 above, would it be better to select someone who states 'it's not my job' or 'it's not my place to judge, I just want to make it right'?

Finally, it is prudent to note that well-developed and refined selection procedures not only help identify the leading candidates, but also increase the likelihood that the leading candidates will accept the job offers from the firm. That is, a hotel's selection practices both consciously and subconsciously shape applicants' perceptions of the firm (Judge et al., 2000).

Training measures to foster service quality in hotel chains

A solid, consistent, and effective training programme is critical to dependably providing high quality service in a hotel. This section, therefore, draws upon findings from bodies of literature outside the hospitality area to provide some insight into how service quality training might be designed.

When and how should frontline employee customer service training be delivered?

First, hotel associates should receive customer service training as soon as possible following the beginning of their employment. That is, ideally the gap between initial hiring and training received should be as short as pragmatically possible. The need to deliver the training early is driven by the concept of social proof which is founded upon the notion that individuals look to each other to determine how they should behave in particular situations (Cialdini, 2001). Therefore, allowing untrained employees to interact with guests in the service environment will create an atmosphere in which sub-par service habits are acceptable. In addition to social proof, the theory of planned behaviour (TPB) also lends support to the notion that employees should receive training early. TPB contends that future behavioural intentions are, in part, driven by subjective norms (whether persons surrounding the decision-maker participate in the given behaviour) (Ajzen, 2006; Rhodes and Courneya, 2003). Consequently, fostering a situation in which hotel associates are transacting with guests without having received customer service training creates an environment in which sub-par transactional habits can be both exhibited and mimicked.

In terms of training delivery mode, consistent with the findings of a meta-analysis conducted by Arthur et al. (2003), a live trainer is typically more effective than technology-based delivery options for several reasons. First, a live trainer can incorporate examples unique to the hotel itself making the training more engaging for the recipients. Second, a live trainer can more readily hone-in on specific areas of coverage as deemed necessary for the given hotel or departmental context. Third, a live trainer can read the audience and adjust training delivery accordingly. While the use of technology-based modes such as CD-ROMS or webinars allow for more flexibility in terms of the scheduling of the training, this research contends that the use of a face-to-face trainer is the most ideal delivery mode for customer service training. In full-service hotel chains, often the live trainer works in the hotel's human resource office. In limited-service chains, often the trainer is a travelling corporate representative. Combinations of the previous two evidently exist; for example, a corporate trainer will visit a full-service location on occasion. Each chain has a unique manual with its own theme by which the trained content is packaged for delivery. For example, Hotel Indigo, a boutique chain by InterContinental, employs a training theme titled *Be Inspiring*. It is prudent to note that in many hotels, third party trainers are invited from time to time to augment the chain's content in an effort to keep training fresh, fun, and current.

Next, with regard to ongoing training, shadowing experienced associates is a pragmatic solution practised by many hotel firms including those within the high-end Ritz-Carlton brand (Michelli, 2008). Such shadowing can serve as a means for refining one's service skills and further building an arsenal of service tools. Daily shift meeting (a.k.a. shift huddles) can also be a very useful format for ongoing training. In such huddles, pet peeves of managers can be discussed, associates can be praised and can share recent stories of exceptional service, and a company value can be reinforced (Magnini, 2013).

What content areas should frontline employee customer service training include?

A customer service training system that stresses the dramaturgical metaphor of service delivery should yield better results than a training system that does not. The dramaturgical metaphor contends that employees are the actors, the guests are the audience, and the stage consists of anywhere in which the actors can be seen or heard by the audience. Popularised by Disney, this dramaturgical metaphor is a useful guide for social interactions (Goffman, 1959), particularly in service environments with high human components (Deighton, 1994; Grove and Fiske, 1983). Firms that incorporate an on-stage/off-stage component in their service training for their frontline associates will likely achieve higher customer service standards than firms that do not have an on-stage/off-stage training component.

Delivering high quality service relies, in part, on the verbal refinement of the hotel associates (Noe et al., 2010). As a consequence of the role of verbal communication, verbal coaching should be a component of the service training system. Weak verbal communication habits should be identified and discussed – such as responding with 'no problem' when a guest says 'thank you'. Relatedly, associates can be trained and coached to demonstrate strong verbal communication habits. For example, associates should be taught techniques that they can employ to more easily recall guests' faces and names (Magnini and Honeycutt, 2005).

Next, because most human communication occurs through the use of nonverbal cues and gestures (Pease and Pease, 2004; Zaltman, 1997), customer service training should include a body language component. Hotel associates should be taught how to avoid displaying negative cues, such as placing their hands in their pockets, and should also be taught how to more naturally and frequently display positive cues such as eye contact and smiling (Magnini, 2013; Noe, et al., 2010). Role playing during the training sessions helps to reinforce the importance of such cues. As well, when an associate is on the telephone, the tone of the voice and positive word selection plays an important part on how the guest perceives customer service. Many times this sets the tone for their entire experience, most of it prior to their even stepping foot into the hotel.

During service training, hotel associates should be told about the importance of triggering surprises (a.k.a. script deviations) for guests during their stays. Due to modern information overload, guests often only pay full attention during a service experience when something happens that they do not expect (Magnini, 2015). During this component of the training, photos of guests moving through various areas of the hotel can be shown and trainees can brainstorm ways with which to surprise the guests in those areas.

Relatedly, because a service failure is a negative script deviation, trainees should be taught that they have a guest's full attention when a problem transpires. Service failure recovery scenarios are, therefore, a key means to drive guest satisfaction and loyalty. Under the proper conditions, it is possible for a guest's post-failure satisfaction with the hotel to be higher than his/her pre-failure satisfaction (Magnini et al., 2007).

The satisfaction mirror concept should also be discussed and reinforced in the customer service training programme for hotel associates. The satisfaction mirror concept posits that there is a significant positive bidirectional relationship between associate satisfaction and guest satisfaction (Heskett et al., 1997). While the associate satisfaction → guest satisfaction component is rather obvious, the guest satisfaction → associate satisfaction link is a message that should be stressed to associates. Essentially, human attitudes and emotions are contagious; consequently, if guests are highly satisfied (by receiving top-rate service) then they will place less strain on the associates. Stressing this logic in training sessions provides additional motivation for associates to demonstrate high levels of service.

Post-training measures to foster service quality

Evidently, good selection and training practices do not guarantee high levels of service quality. With regard to employee training in general, some research finds that employees who receive training often do not perform differently from ones who do not (Hu et al., 2002; Puck et al., 2008). For example, Burke and Hutchins (2007) report that 40 per cent of trainees do not incorporate trained skills immediately after the training; 70 per cent fail to do so one year after the training; and ultimately only 50 per cent of training investments yield organisational improvements.

The term *training transfer* describes the degree to which trained skills are (or are not) internalised and displayed by the recipients of the training (Saks and Belcourt, 2006). One of the leading determinants of training transfer is perceived peer support among associates (Saks and Belcourt, 2006). Consequently, all frontline hotel associates must receive service training so that they are educated at the same level and are all held to the same standards of service performance.

Another key determinant of training transfer is the extent to which the associates perceive that managers genuinely believe in the training and its content (Saks and Belcourt, 2006). Several studies have found that in order for training transfer to occur, associates must genuinely feel that the organisation supports and buys into the value of the training (Clark, 2002; Ford and Weissbein, 1997; Tracey et al., 1995). All management actions send signals to associates regarding this level of buy-in and commitment (Baldwin and Magjuka, 1991; Santos and Stuart, 2003). Because much of the employee training in the hotel business is intended to teach attention to detail, hotel managers should signal their attention to detail to their staff. Such signalling can come in the form of picking up lint and specks of dirt on the carpet, cleaning scuff marks on walls, or simply displaying detail in one's attire (Magnini, 2013).

As indicated in Figure 25.1, when training is delivered, a hotel associate can either reject the content, pay lip-service to the content (only demonstrate it when a manager is watching), or be committed to the content (consistently display it). The extent of acceptance of the training content is highly related to peer support and manager support.

Also regarding perceived managerial commitment, research indicates that when a firm invests in training, doing so signals to employees that managers value the training (Min et al., 2013;

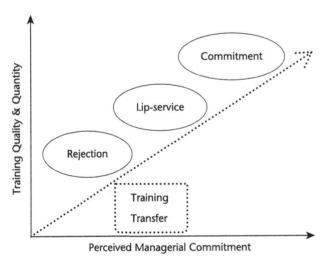

Figure 25.1 Potential associate reactions to service training.

Source: adapted directly from Magnini (2013).

Santos and Stuart, 2003). Therefore, if a service employee perceives that his/her firm has a heavy investment in his/her training and that this investment exceeds the norms practiced in the industry, then s/he will be more likely to internalise and demonstrate the training content. Because perceptions of training investment aid training transfer, hotel managers should use available opportunities to communicate the firm's commitment to training. For example, the emphasis on training can be described in the company's written strategic positioning documents and on electronic media.

Trained customer service skills are also more likely to be demonstrated by associates if they are rewarded for doing so. Creative contests and incentive programmes should be customised in hotels for this purpose. Successes should be shared with the entire hotel, having a central place for the associates to view this information. In addition, when an associate is identified by a guest or co-worker for demonstrating outstanding service, this person should be singled out by the hotel management and, if warranted, the corporate offices. Positive competition and recognition amongst individuals or departments will continue to keep customer service in the forefront.

In the spirit of reinforcement and feedback, whenever a frontline associate receives a formal performance evaluation, the evaluation form should include a section addressing customer service skills. Most hotel firms formally evaluate associates either once every six months or once per year, but many hotel chains still do not formally include customer service skills as a part of the written evaluation form.

Furthermore, in Western cultures, employees who feel empowered will be more likely to demonstrate high levels of customer service than ones who do not. Empowered employees are often more likely to go the extra mile in customer service situations such as service failure recovery scenarios because empowered workers are more likely to be satisfied with their jobs (Chiang and Jang, 2008; Gazzoli et al., 2010; Laschinger et al., 2004; Liden et al., 2000). In fact, empowerment typically has a stronger influence on the job satisfaction of customer contact employees than on non-contact employees (Lee et al., 2011).

Lastly, if associates are to deliver high quality service, they need the systems and supplies to do so. Although this final point appears to be obvious, often when a hotel struggles to provide adequate service, focus groups with the hotel's employees find that they do not have the supplies that they need to do their jobs effectively. Moreover, the paths of service that they are asked to follow are inefficient and do not match the flow of service needed to perform effectively.

An agenda for future research

In the assessment of the authors of this chapter, the issue of service quality in general has not received adequate attention in the extant body of hospitality literature. Moreover, it is reported that the topics receiving attention in the services literature do not align well with the questions that are most pressing in industry (Kandampully et al., 2014). For example, a reader of this chapter could search a database such as Google Scholar and find dozens of studies in the hospitality literature that examine standardised scales such as SERVQUAL, but such repeated examinations of these standardised scales are of little use to hospitality chains. All major chains that the authors of this chapter are aware of have developed surveying instruments much more tailored to their unique needs [such as Marriott's GSS, Hilton's SALT, and Starwood's GEI surveys referenced in the introduction section of this chapter]. Likewise, the concept of total quality management (TQM) is of little use to today's hotel chains because most now embrace more modern concepts such as return-on-quality that weigh the returns on quality initiatives against each other (Magnini, 2013). Despite the practitioner shift to a return-on-quality paradigm, the hospitality literature contains little coverage of this concept. In summary, there are many current areas of hospitality service quality in which practice is wiser than theory: stated differently, practice has outpaced the academic research. Therefore, this chapter offers a number of recommendations regarding future research extensions.

Regarding the pre-training stage of fostering a service culture, many hotel chains currently utilise various forms of personality inventory tests to gauge job candidates' service orientations. There has actually been considerable debate since the 1950s regarding whether such personality inventory tests are valid and reliable predictors of service performance (Stabile, 2001). Thus, future research is warranted that examines whether the hotel industry places an overreliance on such tools in the selection process and whether more valid and reliable tools can be developed.

In the past several years, a number of hotel chains have instituted 100 per cent money-back guarantees for guests who are not completely satisfied with their stays. While corporate headquarters concede that such policies are abused by some patrons, they contend that overall the practice is useful in that it draws out much useful guest feedback and signals the integrity of the brand to guests and associates. Emerging research, however, finds that when hotel associates must yield to opportunistic or illegitimate guest complaints, such situations place an undue quantity of emotional labour on the associates (Baker et al., 2012). Therefore, it would be informative for theory-development and practice alike to research further into the area of money-back guarantees and the influences of such policies on service performance and quality.

As another avenue for future research, it is prudent to note that service quality at many hotels is simply mediocre because mediocre service is an acceptable benchmark in the balanced scorecard that the owners have derived for the managers. That is, as long as the hotel earns service scores from guests that are in the average range within the brand, then the owner is fine with those results and would rather focus on short-term financial results achieved by measures such as reduced staffing. While it is little more than common sense that high quality service will lead to long-run financial success due to increased loyalty and positive word-of-mouth, many owners still incentivise managers with balanced scorecards that are disproportionally focused on short-run financial goals. For example, many hotels are owned by real-estate investment groups in which short-run financial goals are often the key focus for operations. The issue described in this paragraph has not received any attention in the hospitality literature, but begs attention because of the implications for service quality standards across the industry.

Finally, in most countries around the world, service quality in hotels is signalled to potential guests through star rating systems for which standards are established and monitored by the respective governments. In the US, however, quality is signalled instead through branding. Thus, research is warranted that further examines such forms of quality signalling. For example, how is quality signalled to consumers when a hotel is branded in a country that relies on a mandatory star system? Conversely, how is service quality signalled to consumers when a hotel uses an optional star system in the US where most consumers are trained to afford attention to branding?

References

Ajzen, I. (2006) Constructing a TPB questionnaire: conceptual and methodological consideration. Online. Available HTTP: <https://people.umass.edu/aizen/pdf/tpb.measurement.pdf>, accessed 4 December, 2015.

Arthur, W., Jr., Bennet, W., Jr., Edens, P. and Bell, S. (2003) Effectiveness of training in organizations: a meta-analysis of design and evaluation features. *Journal of Applied Psychology*, 88(2), 234–45.

Aureli, S., Medei, R., Supino, E. and Travaglini, C. (2013) Online review contents and their impact on three and four-star hotel reservations: some evidence in Italy. In *Information and Communication Technologies in Tourism 2014*. Cham, Switzerland: Springer International Publishing, pp. 381–93.

Ayeh, J.K., Au, N. and Law, R. (2013) 'Do we believe in TripAdvisor?' Examining credibility perceptions and online travelers' attitude toward using user-generated content. *Journal of Travel Research*, 52(4), 437–52.

Baker, M.A., Magnini, V.P. and Perdue, R.R. (2012) Opportunistic customer complaining: causes, consequences, and managerial alternatives. *International Journal of Hospitality Management*, 31(1), 295–303.

Baldwin, T.T. and Magjuka, R.J. (1991) Organizational training and signals of importance: linking pretraining perceptions to intentions to transfer. *Human Resource Development Quarterly*, 2, 25–36.

Brinthaupt, T.M and Erwin, L.J. (1992) Reporting about the self: issues and implications. In T.M. Brinthaupt and R.P. Lipka (eds), *The Self Definitional and Methodological Issues*, Albany: State University of New York Press, pp. 137–71.

Burke, L. and Hutchins, H. (2007) Training transfer: an integrative literature review. *Human Resource Development Review*, 6(3), 263–96.

Chiang, C. and Jang, S. (2008) The antecedents and consequences of psychological empowerment: the case of Taiwan's hotel companies. *Journal of Hospitality and Tourism Research*, 32(1), 40–61.

Cialdini, R.B. (2001) *Influence: Science and Practice*, 4th edn. New York: Allyn and Bacon.

Clark, N. (2002) Job/work environment factors influencing training effectiveness within a human service agency: some indicative support for Baldwin and Ford's transfer climate construct. *International Journal of Training and Development*, 6(3), 146–62.

Deighton, J. (1994) Managing services when the service is a performance. In R.T. Rust and R.L. Oliver (eds), *Service Quality*. Thousand Oaks, CA: Sage Publications.

Dixon, M., Wang, S., Calvin, J., Dineen, B. and Tomlinson, E. (2002) The panel interview: a review of the empirical research and guidelines for practice. *Public Personnel Management*, 31(1), 397–428.

Ford, J.K. and Weissbein, D.A. (1997) Transfer of training: an update review and analysis. *Performance Improvement Quarterly*, 10(2), 22–41.

Gazzoli, G., Hancer, M. and Park, Y. (2010) The role and effect of job satisfaction and empowerment on customers' perception of service quality: a study in the restaurant industry. *Journal of Hospitality and Tourism Research*, 34(1), 56–77.

Goffman, E. (1959) *The Presentation of Self in Everyday Life*. Garden City, New York: Doubleday.

Grove, S. and Fiske, R. (1983) The dramaturgy of service exchange: an analytical framework for services marketing. In L.L. Berry, G.L. Shostack and G.D. Upah, (eds) *Emerging Perspectives on Services Marketing*, Chicago, IL: American Marketing Association.

Heskett, J.L., Sasser, E.W. and Schlesinger, L.A. (1997) *The Service Profit Chain*. New York, NY: The Free Press.

Hu, W., Martin, L. and Yu, J. (2002) Cross-cultural impact and learning needs for expatriate hotel employees in Taiwan lodging industry. *Journal of Human Resources in Hospitality and Tourism*, 1, 31–45.

Judge, T., Higgins, C. and Cable, D. (2000) The employment interview: a review of recent research and recommendations for future research. *Human Resource Management*, 10(4), 383–406.

Kandampully, J., Keating, B., Kim, B., Mattila, A. and Solnet, D. (2014) Service Research in the hospitality literature: insights from a systematic review. *Cornell Hospitality Quarterly*, 55(3), 287–99.

Kaufman, R. (2012) *Uplifting Service*. New York: Evolve Publishing.

Kim, W.G., Lim, H. and Brymer, R.A. (2015) The effectiveness of managing social media on hotel performance. *International Journal of Hospitality Management*, 44, 165–71.

Laschinger, H., Finegan, J., Shamian, J. and Wilk, P. (2004) A longitudinal analysis of the impact of workplace environment on work satisfaction. *Journal of Organizational Behavior*, 25(4), 527–45.

Lee, G., Kim, B., Perdue, R. and Magnini, V. (2011) Time-varying effects of empowerment on job satisfaction for customer-contact versus non-customer-contact groups. *Proceeding of the 16th Annual Graduate Student Research Conference in Hospitality and Tourism*. (electronic proceedings).

Liden, R., Wayne, S. and Sparrowe, R. (2000) An examination of the mediating role of psychological empowerment on the relations between job, interpersonal relationships, and work outcomes. *Journal of Applied Psychology*, 85(3), 407–17.

Magnini, V. (2013) *Performance Enhancers: Twenty Essential Habits for Service Businesses*. Mustang, Oklahoma: Tate Publishing.

Magnini, V. (2015) *Surprise! The Secret to Customer Loyalty in the Service Sector*. Business Expert Press: New York, New York.

Magnini, V. and Honeycutt, E. (2005) Face recognition and name recall: training implications for the hospitality industry. *Cornell Hospitality Quarterly*, 46(1), 69–78.

Magnini, V., Ford, J., Markowski, E. and Honeycutt Jr, E. (2007) The service recovery paradox: justifiable theory or smoldering myth? *Journal of Services Marketing*, 21(3), 213–25.

McGuire, W. and McGuire, C. (1988) Content and process in the experience of self, in L. Berkowitz (ed.), *Advances in Experimental Social Psychology*, Vol. 21. Academic Press, New York, pp. 97–144.

Michelli, J. (2008) *The New Gold Standard*. New York: McGraw Hill.

Min, H., Magnini, V. and Singal, M. (2013) Perceived corporate training investment as a driver of hotel expatriate manager adjustment. *International Journal of Contemporary Hospitality Management*, 25(5): 740–59.

Noe, F., Uysal, M. and Magnini, V. (2010) *Tourist Customer Satisfaction: An Encounter Approach*. London: Routledge.

Pease, A. and Pease, B. (2004) *The Definitive Book of Body Language*. New York, New York: Bantam Dell.

Puck, J.F., Kittler, M.G. and Wright, C. (2008) Does it really work? Re-assessing the impact of pre-departure cross-cultural training on expatriate adjustment. *International Journal of Human Resource Management*, 19, 2182–97.

Rhodes, R. and Courneya, K. (2003) Investigating multiple components of attitude, subjective norm, and perceived control: an examination of the theory of planned behaviour in the exercise domain. *British Journal of Social Psychology*, 42, 129–46.

Saks, A.M. and Belcourt, M. (2006) An investigation of training activities and transfer of training in organizations. *Human Resource Management*, 45(4), 629–48.

Santos, A. and Stuart, M. (2003) Employee perceptions and their influence on training effectiveness. *Human Resource Management Journal*, 13, 27–45.

Stabile, S.J. (2001) Use of personality tests as a hiring tool: is the benefit worth the cost? *University of Pennsylvania Journal of Labor and Employment Law*, 4, 279.

Tracey, J.B., Tannenbaum, S.I. and Kavanagh, M.J. (1995) Applying trained skills on the job: the importance of the work environment. *Journal of Applied Psychology*, 80, 239–52.

Whitacre, T. (2007) Behavioral interviewing – find your star. *Quality Progress* 40(6), 72–73.

Zaltman, G. (1997) Rethinking marketing research: putting people back in. *Journal of Marketing Research*, 34(4), 424–37.

26

Intercultural human resource management in hotel chains

Cherylynn Becker and Wei Wang

(UNIVERSITY OF SOUTHERN MISSISSIPPI, USA)

Introduction

In the current global economy, interactions amongst individuals from various nations across the world are now occurring on a daily basis. Although hotels, by the nature of the service they provide, may be considered pioneers in offering and providing global services and managing culturally diverse workforces, many changes have occurred in the business environment of recent years that require increased attention to the issue of cultural differences. Global travel, whether for business or for pleasure, is no longer limited to an educated, upper segment of society that expects, anticipates and delights in experiencing cultural differences as a positive attribute of international travel. Given the labour intensity of hotels and the difficulty associated with staffing unskilled, minimum wage positions, the increasing use of foreign nationals to fill many positions has created a multi-cultural and multi-linguistic workforce in many regions of the world where historically, homogeneous workforces had provided the dominant model. For the hotel industry of the twenty-first century, cultural diversity is a reality that influences the effectiveness of an organisation's customer relationships, managerial practices and workforce motivation and performance. One of the biggest challenges impacting international human resource management is that of culture.

Culture defines the important assumptions and values that members of any particular social system share (Hofstede, 1980a). Values provide emotional standards for what is right, what is wrong and what is fair and just (Rokeach, 1968, 1973). Values, and guide attitude and behaviour, vary from culture to culture. Although differences in values may not be visible to an outsider, they may be inferred from what is rewarded or punished within a social system. Disparities amongst cultural values provide the basis for many cross-cultural misunderstandings in politics, in social settings and in business environments. Although, for example, values governing politeness appear to exist in all cultures (Maude, 2011) what constitutes politeness may differ dramatically across cultures. As every individual is born into and socialised within a particular culture, it is normal that individuals turn to their own culture's values as a standard and almost instinctively perceive behaviours guided by divergent value systems as unexpected or even wrong. Cultural values provide the dominant influence on how an individual relates to the workplace, performs his or her job, and interacts with bosses, subordinates and customers. Cultural values affect how employees react to human resources strategies and ultimately determine whether a strategy that is effective at motivating employees in one culture has the potential to motivate, or conversely, to undermine productivity in another. In the absence of at least a rudimentary understanding of how cultural values differ from one nation to another, the potential for cultural conflict is great. In the organisational setting, the responsibility for ensuring that employees have sufficient cultural awareness to communicate effectively with individuals from different cultural backgrounds falls under the purview of the human resource department. In this role, human resource specialists are required to reevaluate and modify traditional criteria for selecting, evaluating and rewarding employees in a manner that is sensitive to cultural differences. Training is imperative for effective management of the global workforce as well as for successful service delivery to a culturally diverse customer base. Within the international hotel segment, multi-cultural understanding is considered paramount for success and it is not uncommon to find standalone departments devoted to multi-cultural training and development activities. The purpose of the present chapter is to introduce the core concepts associated with developing and maintaining a culturally aware workforce. The chapter is organised to address the following concerns: (1) the identification and descriptors associated with the values specific to the major and dominant cultural perspectives, (2) the identification of employment classifications associated with a multi-cultural workforce, (3) the human resource interventions or activities specifically oriented towards effective management of a culturally diverse workforce.

Fundamental differences among cultures

The current understanding of the underlying elements associated with differing cultural values across nations can be traced back to Hofstede's landmark study (Hofstede, 1980b) which has continued to provide the dominant framework for identifying and evaluating the core dimensions and contrasting values that provide the foundation for understanding cultural differences. In a research agenda spanning over 30 years, Hofstede's research identified five major dimensions of culture: individualism-collectivism, power-distance, uncertainty avoidance, masculinity-femininity, long-term/short-term orientation (Hofstede, 1997). These dimensions facilitate a relative assessment of the foundational values that underlie meaningful differences in how divergent cultures evaluate behaviours and goals as good or bad, and right or wrong. Although some argue that contemporary society is moving towards a global culture, repeated measurement of the cultural dimensions have not substantiated such a trend except to note that as countries increase in wealth, their scores on individualism rise. A summary of the key issues pertaining to Hofstede's framework are briefly summarised in the section below.

The individualism-collectivism dimension addresses the orientation towards whether individuals are independent and considered to be primarily responsible for themselves or whether they are first and foremost members of a group to which they owe their loyalty and allegiance. In individualist countries such as the United States, Australia and Great Britain, managerial goals emphasise individual achievement and a results-oriented workplace (Hofstede, 1983). Workers in such cultures strive to be outstanding and expect to be rewarded for individual achievements. People in collectivist countries, such as those found in Asia, the Middle East and South America, are integrated into cohesive groups, where a person's first loyalty is to protect group members. Members from collectivist cultures can find individual recognition in the workforce to be offensive because they believe that outstanding achievements by any individual are only secured through the support and contributions of the whole.

Power-distance is used to express the degree to which members of a society accept an unequal distribution of power or status among its members. People from societies with a high power distance such as India, Mexico and Japan, accept and expect a hierarchical order in which some are more powerful and have greater status than others based upon birthright and social connections rather than achievement. In societies where power distance is low such as the United States, Israel or Denmark, people are considered to be equal and any power differentials that exist must be justified on the basis of performance. In high power distance countries, managers are more likely to behave autocratically and subordinates are more likely to exhibit deference and avoid conflict with superiors. In low power distance societies, workers feel more equal and expect to provide input into decision-making activities. Workers in these environments are comfortable challenging authority figures, an act which would be a sign of disrespect in a high power-distance environment.

Uncertainty avoidance expresses the degree to which members in a social system are comfortable with ambiguity and uncertainty. Societies high in uncertainty avoidance such as Germany, Japan and South Korea experience high levels of anxiety when faced with ambiguity and have a strong need for rules. In the workplace, individuals from these countries tend to fear failure and take fewer risks. They have a preference for job security and retirement pensions and tend to excel in precision technology. Nations scoring low on uncertainty avoidance, such as the United States and the United Kingdom, are much more comfortable with risk and are more likely to excel in innovation.

The contrast between masculine versus feminine cultures is the most highly visible among the five cultural dimensions. Masculine societies are highly competitive. They value achievement, assertiveness and material rewards as symbols of success. Masculine nations such as Japan, Kuwait and Italy project distinctive roles for the genders. Feminine societies such as Sweden or the Netherlands are more nurturing and emphasise concern for people, quality of life and gender equality over and above the acquisition of monetary rewards.

The fifth cultural dimension, long-term/short-term orientation, emerged from a concentration on the powerful influence of Confucianism in the Asian countries of the Far East. These cultures are oriented toward long-term values in that they revere persistence, savings and the concept of future rewards which do not necessarily provide immediate benefit. Countries with short-term orientations such as the United States, Saudi Arabia and Canada are more likely to be oriented toward the historical context of the past and the present (Hofstede, 1984). Cultures with a short-term orientation tend to strive for quick results and measure business success on a short-term basis. A sixth dimension, indulgence versus restraint, was also recently added to Hofstede's framework (Minkov and Hofstede, 2011).

Although Hofstede's model has been criticised at times for various shortcomings, recent large scale studies provide evidence to support the validity of his findings (Schwartz, 1994, 2004; House and Javidan, 2004). Through replication and extension, Hofstede's continuing research serves to confirm the long-term validity of his original findings (Hofstede, 2010). Although it appears that Hofstede's model has not been well integrated into organisational cultural training activities of the past, technological development leading to readily available assessment tools suggests that his foundational studies offer great potential in the area of cross-cultural awareness training for the future. Outside of Hofstede's original cultural dimensions and the subsequent augmentations offered by recent researchers, Hall's (1976) characterisation of culturally based communication styles as either high or low context continues to make a meaningful contribution in the area of cross-cultural communication.

It provides an effective complement to Hofstede's approach which is grounded in understanding value differences.

Hall, an American anthropologist, is acknowledged as the 'father of cross-cultural communication' and is noted for his contribution of introducing the importance of the non-verbal aspects of cross-cultural communication (Leeds-Hurwitz, 1990). Throughout the 1950s, Hall was employed by the US State Department at the Foreign Service Institute where he taught inter-cultural communications to foreign-service personnel. His conceptualisation of cultural communication styles as either high or low context continues to make an important contribution to training in cross-cultural communication skills today. High context cultures are generally associated with collectivist cultures and are the dominant communication style for Asia, South America and much of the Middle East. Communication in these cultures is relationship oriented and developing trust is the initial step in developing a business relationship. In high context cultures, communication is facilitated by intuition and feelings displayed more by facial expression, gesture and posture than by words. On the other hand, low context cultures, such as those found in most Western European countries and the United States, communicate with words emphasising logic, facts and precision. Low context cultures are task oriented and people from these cultures tend to be impatient with the expectation of investing time into building a relationship before entering into a business transaction.

Worker classifications in the global workforce

Human resource departments play a central role in securing and maintaining an adequate global workforce, initially through recruitment and selection, and subsequently with follow through in development and training. Within the context of the international hotel corporation, several potential types of employees exist. Expatriate employees are generally sent from the home country to manage operations in a different county. Expatriates most commonly take the form where the employee is of the same nationality as the corporate headquarters of the firm. Known as parent country nationals (PCNs) these employees have the advantage of a high degree of familiarity and understanding of the corporate mission and its organisational policies and practices. PCNs offer the advantage of being able to provide the most effective approach for communicating with personnel in the home office. PCN expatriate assignments may be used in the absence of locally qualified personnel, as a form of managerial development, or to accelerate the parent organisation's efforts to establish a presence in a new region of the world. Traditionally the movement of expatriate management was unidirectional with managers moving 'from developed to developing countries' (Maude, 2011: 145). This is changing as more developing countries are expanding into developed nations. According to existing research, initial costs associated with expatriate assignments are high: 'at least 3 times the base salaries of domestic counterparts' (Shaffer et al., 1999). When poorly selected and inadequately prepared for living in an unfamiliar cultural environment, PCNs are subject to high levels of stress and poor performance. According to research secured through feedback from 144 recruitment consultants in 40 countries, the primary reason for expatriate failure is a lack of cultural fit (Korn/Ferry, 2009).

A second type of employee is termed a host country national (HCN). This term is used to describe employees that share the nationality of the host country in which an individual property is located. As compared to PCNs, HCNs cost less to hire and have the advantage of knowing the local language, sharing the local culture and understanding the socioeconomic and political factors associated with the local environment. While clearly the choice of using HCNs avoids many of the stumbling blocks encountered by PCNs, individuals selected for

HCN assignments will need preparation to facilitate an understanding of the cultural values that drive corporate policy and the expectations of corporate executives from the parent company. Although published research in this area is scant (non-existent), recent inquiries to US-parented hotel operations in mainland China reveal that in preparation for HCN assignments, selected managerial employees undergo training stateside where they work side by side with US managers and are familiarised with US national culture as well as corporate values and expectations.

A third type of employee is described as a third-country national (TCN). Third-country nationals have been born and raised in a country other than the parent country or the host country. A manager born and raised in India, working for Marriott at a property located in Hong Kong provides a good example of this type of employee. In terms of advantages TCNs may be less expensive to maintain than a PCN and in some instances may be better informed about the host environment. This is especially true when care is taken to assign TCNs to locations where the cultural values more closely align with those from the home country in which the TCN was raised. Although third-country nationals are often employed in managerial assignments, they are used extensively in minimum wage positions in hotels located across the United States to fill positions in housekeeping, grounds maintenance and janitorial services. Although many US hotels that employ TCNs in low skilled positions rely solely upon third party contractors to recruit, secure legal right-to-work documentation and provide translation services, properties with aspirations for higher service quality standards do their own recruiting and are much more intimately engaged in the process of facilitating the performance of these employees.

The King and Prince, a resort hotel located on the coast of Georgia, US, associated with an 18-property chain, responded to labour shortages by hiring Hispanic immigrants. Many could not speak English and early attempts at training and supervising these employees were not successful. An initial effort to integrate these employees into the existing workforce also failed due to resistance encountered both by long-time employees and by the Hispanic recruits themselves. The solution was found by outsourcing to Spanglish Unlimited, a North Carolina consulting company that provided cultural awareness training to native US employees so that they better understood the challenges faced by their Hispanic co-workers, and an educational programme for the Hispanic employees that implemented bilingual job aids and schooled these employees on the standards and expectations inherent to service delivery expected of a high quality US resort (Brown, 2008).

Another source for TCNs is supplied through the recruitment and acquisition of interns and graduates associated with hospitality management programmes located in colleges and universities across the world. Many of these require mandatory internships as part of their degree programmes and offer placement assistance for their students. Many countries offer special right-to-work visas for foreign national students and recent graduates of degree and certificate granting post-secondary academic programmes.

Generic training guidelines for a multi-cultural workforce

Ideally a hotel's human resource department is responsible for employee development and employee training. The concepts differ in that development focuses on educational and experiential learning activities that prepare employees for future assignments, whereas training emphasises the skills and competencies employees need for successful performance in their current jobs. When addressing issues related to multi-culturalism, a one-fits-all strategy is unlikely to be either efficient or effective. Training needs differ dramatically depending upon the position, the employee, and the degree to which the employee is required to interact with customers, or alternatively with representatives from local businesses or local government agencies. A web-based search revealed that an ever increasing population of international agencies with expertise in multi-cultural training is available to provide outsourced assistance to organisations that lack the internal resources to develop these programmes in house. The United States of America-China Chamber of Commerce is an example of a non-profit organisation that has developed a cross-cultural training workshop designed specifically for the hospitality industry in anticipation of an ever increasing number of Chinese tourists within the US. The workshop offered by this group can be customised to meet a hotel's individual needs and can be provided at a cost of less than $100 per employee (Cross Cultural Training for Hospitality Industry, 2014). Although the effectiveness of multi-cultural training programmes is clearly maximised when programme content is modified to fit the responsibilities associated with an expatriate's job, some guidelines appear rudimentary across all levels of employment. The guidelines listed below focus on areas associated with generic competencies aimed at increasing employees' social skills and confidence in inter-cultural interactions with co-workers as well as with a culturally diverse clientele:

- Understanding of value differences across cultures
- Knowledge of appropriate greetings, leave-takings and apologies across cultures
- Awareness of appropriate/offensive nonverbal behaviours across cultures
- Elementary literacy in the host country language
- Effective use of active listening

Managerial training guidelines for a multi-cultural workforce

Whereas organisational investment in selection activities and multi-cultural training may be constrained for positions associated with unskilled and short term employees, the criteria for selecting and training managerial employees facing multi-cultural assignments should be much more stringent. Existing research suggests the selection of expatriate managers provides a crucial first step for human resource input and that its application limits the potential for failure. Researchers have identified a number of individual characteristics that should be considered when making expatriate managerial assignments. These include openness to change and new ideas (Huang et al., 2005), cross cultural communication skills (Tung, 2004), willingness to adapt to local cultural norms (Caligiuri and Cascio, 1998), likeability (Leung and Bond, 2001) and cultural sensitivity (Puck et al., 2008). Although English is most often the dominant language for international business, local language skills enhance relationship building and cultural understanding, and have been shown to be a strong predictor of success among expatriate employees.

Effective selection of candidates for expatriate positions can be enhanced through the use of a number of assessments that are commercially available. These include but are not limited to the Cross Cultural Adaptability Index (Kelley and Meyers, 1999) available through General Dynamics Information Technology, the Multicultural Personality Questionnaire (Van der Zee and Van Oudenhoven, 2000) available through Tamas Consulting, and the Intercultural Adjustment Potential Scale (Matsumoto et al., 2001) available through Humintell. These assessments are designed to identify personal characteristics such as tolerance for ambiguity, emotional resilience and learning motivation, all of which have been demonstrated to lead to expatriate management success. Once selected, training of the candidates is usually initiated through the development of skill sets in cross-cultural competence. At a minimum, it is fundamental that candidates for expatriate management have a clear awareness of the biases inherent in their own cultural viewpoints, the knowledge and understanding associated with cultural differences and cross-cultural communication skills that include at least a rudimentary ability to use the language of the host country where they will be located.

Post-selection development activities for expatriate managers

Given that an organisation applies the criteria above during the selection process, further training provides situation specific examples that assist an expatriate manager in avoiding common cultural mishaps that may have far reaching and negative implications. Too often management policies that serve as standards in the home country environment cannot be effectively imported into host country environments. In a study conducted by Magnini (2009), it is reported that the largest percentage of expatriates (94.7 per cent) turned 'to local nationals for cultural advice' (p. 516). Compensation and performance evaluation, participative management and contract negotiation offer a few examples of areas of expatriate responsibility where conflict tends to occur most often. Examples addressing each of these areas are briefly addressed below. The likelihood of problems will be exacerbated in situations where the cultural distance between the home country and the host country is great.

Pay for performance, for example, is widely accepted in the United States and across most of the northwestern European countries. In highly individualistic cultures, pay for performance, which allocates higher pay for higher levels of work performance, is considered to be justified because these cultures believe that individuals who work harder and produce more should be compensated to reflect their individual contributions. Collectivist cultures on the other hand attribute performance excellence by an individual to be an artefact of the organisational system; where input from co-workers, supervisors and management are the most important elements leading to an individual's ability to achieve outstanding levels of performance. Past attempts by Western expatriate managers to implement pay for performance compensation schemes into collectivist cultural settings have historically resulted in negative consequences reducing worker morale and increasing absenteeism and turnover (Maude, 2011).

Participative management, a hallmark of low power distance cultures, is often resisted by workforces in countries where power distance is high and status differentials preclude contributions from lower level employees as these may be viewed as disrespectful challenges to a superior's rightful authority. Individuals from high power distance countries may view requests for their input as evidence that their leaders are incapable of making decisions, and thus undeserving of leadership status.

Contract negotiations in cross-cultural settings require different skills and a much wider range of knowledge than domestic negotiations. When two or more countries come together, each is accompanied by a different set of traditions, policies and laws. Western managers from low context, individualistic cultures are oriented towards establishing legally enforceable contracts within the shortest time frame possible. In contrast, high context cultures expect negotiations to be relationship oriented and built on trust which can only be acquired over time. Research shows that individuals from different cultural backgrounds are predisposed towards different patterns in negotiation style (Sebenius, 2002), further contributing to complexity and increasing the potential for conflict. Effective negotiation in a cross-cultural context is highly dependent upon information about each party's goals and the way these are tied to the core ideological perspectives of the culture they represent. Cross cultural negotiators must possess sufficient cultural awareness to be able to see the issues from the perspective of their partners.

Organisational culture

Although the dominant attributes of national culture associated with the home country will be visible within the organisational culture of a multinational firm, a strong organisational culture can have a unifying effect particularly with regard to surface attributes associated with cultural norms. In branded international hotel chains standardised greetings, service attitudes, and behavioural norms have the ability to offset some of the challenges associated with operating in diverse cultural settings. These advantages appear mainly on the side of customer interactions and customer perceptions of service quality. On the other hand, the psychological contract existing between employee and employer, the criteria that inspire motivation, and the conditions that lead to employee commitment and loyalty will only be unlocked through an in-depth knowledge and understanding of the values inherent in the cultural identity associated with an individual's upbringing. To this end, hospitality organisations need to expand training to move beyond the symbolic and observable features of culture, and incorporate an understanding of the norms and values that underlie differences in human behaviour.

To date the prevailing perspectives in management theory have been generated by Western nations based upon the dominant values in Western cultures. As a result well-intentioned expatriate managers facing assignments in nations with divergent cultural values encounter many roadblocks. In summary it is hopeful that through knowledge, training, and careful selection of candidates for international assignments the potential for conflict and misunderstanding can be minimised for the future.

References

Brown, N. (2008) Awareness training bridges cultural gaps. *Hotel Motel Management*, 223(2), 16.

Caligiuri, P. and Cascio, W. (1998) Can we send her there? Maximising the success of western women on global assignments. *Journal of World Business*, 33(4), 394–416.

United States of America–China Chamber of Commerce (2014) Cross cultural training for hospitality industry. Online. Available HTTP: <http://www.usccc.org/#!cross-cultural-training-for-hospitality/c1il>, accessed September 23, 2014.

Hall, E.T. (1976) *Beyond Culture*. Garden City, NY: Anchor Press/Doubleday.

Hofstede, G. (1980a) Culture and organizations. *International Studies of Management & Organization*, 10(4), 15–41.

Hofstede, G. (1980b) *Culture's Consequences: International Differences in Work Related Values*. Beverly Hills, CA: Sage.

Hofstede, G. (1983) The cultural relativity of organizational practices and theories. *Journal of International Business Studies*, 14(2), 75–89.

Hofstede, G. (1984) *Culture's Consequences: International Differences in Work-Related Values* (Vol. 5). Newbury Park, CA: Sage.

Hofstede, G. (1997) *Cultures and Organizations: Software of the Mind*. New York: McGraw Hill.

Hofstede, G. (2010) Comparing regional cultures within a country. *Journal of Cross-Cultural Psychology*, 41(3), 336–52.

House, R.J. and Javidan, M. (2004) Overview of GLOBE. In R.J. House, P.J. Hanges, M. Javidan, P.W. Dorfman and V. Gupta (eds), *Culture, Leadership, and Organizations: The GLOBE Study of 62 Societies*. Thousand Oaks, CA: Sage, pp. 9–28.

Huang, T.J., Chi, S. and Lawler, J. (2005) The relationships between expatriates' personality traits and their adjustment to international assignments. *International Journal of Human Resource Management*, 16(9), 1656–70.

Kelley, C.M. and Meyers, J.E. (1999) The cross cultural adaptability inventory. In S.M. Fowler and M.G. Mumford (eds), *Intercultural Source Book: Cross Cultural Training Methods*, 2. Boston and London: Intercultural Press, pp. 53–60.

Korn/Ferry (2009) Executive recruiter index, 10th edition. Korn/Ferry International. Online. Available HTTP: <http://aneliteresume.com/uncategorized/kornferry-international-executive-recruiter-index/>, accessed 29 August, 2015.

Leeds-Hurwitz, W. (1990) Notes in the history of intercultural communication: the foreign service institute and the mandate for intercultural training. *Quarterly Journal of Speech*, 76, 262–82.

Leung, S.K. and Bond, M.H. (2001) Interpersonal communication and personality. *Asian Journal of Social Psychology*, 4(1), 69–86.

Magnini, V.P. (2009) An exploratory investigation of the real-time training modes used by hotel expatriates. *International Journal of Hospitality Management*, 28(4), 513–18.

Matsumoto, D., LeRoux, J., Ratzlaff, C., Tatani, H., Uchida, H., Kim, C. and Araki, S. (2001) Development and validation of a measure of intercultural adjustment potential in Japanese sojourners: the intercultural adjustment potential scale (ICAPS). *International Journal of Intercultural Relations*, 25, 483–510.

Maude, B. (2011) *Managing Cross Cultural Communication*. New York: Palgrave Macmillian.

Minkov, M. and Hofstede, G. (2011) The evolution of Hofstede's doctrine: cross cultural management. *An International Journal*, 18(1), 10–20.

Puck, J., Mohr, A. and Rygl, D. (2008) An empirical analysis of managers' adjustment to working in multinational project teams in the pipeline and plant construction sector conditions. *International Journal of Human Resource Management*, 19(12), 2252–67.

Rokeach, M. (1968) *Beliefs, Attitudes and Values: A Theory of Organization and Change*. San Francisco, CA: Jossey-Bass Inc Pub.

Rokeach, M. (1973) *The Nature of Human Values* (vol. 438). New York, NY: Free Press.

Schwartz, S.H. (1994) Beyond individualism/collectivism: new cultural dimensions of value. In U. Kim, H.C. Triandis, C. Kagitcibasis, S. Choi and G. Yoon, *Individualism and Collectivism: Theory, Method, and Application*. Thousand Oaks, CA: Sage, pp. 85–119.

Schwartz, S.H. (2004) Mapping and interpreting cultural differences around the world. In V. Vinken, J. Soeters and P. Ester, *Comparing Cultures: Dimensions of Culture in a Comparative Perspective*. Leidin & Boston: Brill, pp. 43–73.

Sebenuis, J.K. (2002) The hidden challenge of cross-border negotiations. *Harvard Business Review*, March, 76–85.

Shaffer, M.A., Harrison, D. and Gilley, K. (1999) Dimensions, determinants, and differences in the expatriate adjustment process. *Journal of International Business Studies*, 3(1), 557–81.

Tung, R.I. (2004) Female expatriates: the model global manager? *Organizational Dynamics*, 33(3), 243–53.

Van der Zee, K.I. and Van Oudenhoven, J.P. (2000) The multicultural personality questionnaire: a multidimensional instrument of multicultural effectiveness. *European Journal of Personality*, 14(4), 291–309.

27

Information systems management in hotel chains

Fernando José Garrigós Simón (UNIVERSITAT POLITECNICA DE VALENCIA, SPAIN),
Yeamduan Narangajavana (UNIVERSITY JAUME I, SPAIN) *and*
Roberto Llorente (UNIVERSITAT POLITECNICA DE VALENCIA, SPAIN)

Introduction

The use and management of information systems (IS) in hotels has been continuous since 1947, when the Westin hotel introduced 'Hoteltype'; allowing teletype machines to enable instantaneous confirmations of reservations (Bilgihan et al., 2011). In 1963, the Hotel Milton of New York started to use a computer in order to automatise the management of rooms (Martinez et al., 2006). Advances such as computer reservations systems (CRS) (for example the first one 'Holidex', from Holiday Inn, in 1965) were developed in the 1970s to manage, for instance, the inventory of free sleeping rooms inside the hotels or the hospitality chains (Buhalis and Law, 2008). In addition, the development of global distribution systems (GDS) in the late 1980s and their connections with CRSs, permitted connections. First with travel agencies (firms such as WizCom or Thisco (Martinez et al., 2006; Buhalis and Law, 2008)), and later, with other virtual intermediaries and final users, permitting better distribution and management of inventories.

Nowadays, these and other new tools: the development of the World Wide Web, the internet, and the spread of social networks and virtual communities, have transformed the ways in which hospitality enterprises operate, with IS investments playing a critical role in managing hotels strategically (Bilgihan et al., 2011). In the new framework, both the product and supply and demand chains are becoming more and more digitalised (Garrigos-Simon et al., 2014a). Moreover, many operations inside the hotels are being automatised and improved through the use of new and sophisticated IT systems. In addition, the emergence of the Web 3.0, the development of social networks and the transformation of the role of the customers are promoting the development of sophisticated customer relationship management, crowdsourcing techniques (Garrigos 2010, Garrigos et al., 2011, 2012) and the use of Masscapital, defined as 'the capabilities from all the individuals or organisations, related closely or not to the own company or organisation, which can help it to innovate or improve any of their activities or processes' (Garrigos-Simon et al., 2014b: 27). Furthermore, emerging technologies are also creating new opportunities for hotel chains. In this new arena, the relevance of IT is not only important but critical for the success and survival of hotels.

In this chapter, we are going to analyse some of the most important tools related to IS used by hotels to improve their activities, apart from the traditional CRSs and GDSs. First, we will emphasise some tools used separately to improve the operations and other functions in these enterprises. Secondly, we will focus on the integration of the ISs within the hospitality chain. Thirdly, we will develop mechanisms used to integrate the whole of the value chain. Then, we will focus on the importance of integrating the customers and other stakeholders in the IS, with techniques such as customer relationship management and advanced techniques related to Web 3.0. The chapter will finish with the analysis of some other new technologies which are being introduced in hotels, and recommendations for the implementation of IS.

Mechanisms to improve operations and other functions in the firm

Managers in hospitality and tourism have attempted to apply IT to improve customer service, enhance operational efficiency and ultimately increase revenue (Law et al., 2014). In addition, IT has been used for the internal re-engineering of hospitality firms (office systems, reservation systems ...), to improve management and enhance learning, knowledge and even creativity.

Specifically, IT tools are being used to improve the diverse inventories and to automatise routine operations in hotels, such as reservations, the management of checking-in and out, cleaning, self-service, preparation of meals, security processes, personal monitoring processes, or even diverse services to satisfy customers (Garrigos and Narangajavana, 2006). According to these authors, robots can be used for cleaning, or the preparation of meals; diverse codes can operate the doors of the rooms or monitor the behaviour of employees.

Actually, hotel chains are usually the pioneers in introducing and adopting new technologies in the hotel industry. Hence, examples of specific, i.e. not a comprehensive IT data gathering strategy but technologically advanced implementations in the hospitality sector can be found continuously in chains such as Intercontinental Hotels, Marriott Hotels or Starwood Hotels. For instance Intercontinental Hotels (2015) is creating several digitally driven innovations to provide personalised and interactive experiences for guests (e.g. mobile folio and mobile check-in and check-out, a translator app, or technologies to drive meaningful interactions with guests). Marriott Hotels (2015) is piloting keyless entry applications, or creating continuous innovations and devices in its in-room entertainment platform. Finally, Starwood Hotels (2015) is developing systems to cut water use, energy use, or reduce emissions; or mobile apps for meetings and events.

Moreover, authors such as Garrigos and Narangajavana (2006), or Buhalis and Law (2008), relate the relevance of the use of IT to improving business intelligence (especially the knowledge of markets, competitors or products) as well as the management and strategy of hotels. Application of IT data gathering leading to an enhanced business intelligence is found at industrial level, applied to optimise the economic impact of products and/or services. Concerning industrial products, data gathering leads to a mitigation of uncertainty regarding external provision chain elements or supply/demand estimation, as noted by Calof et al. (2015). In the case of retail services, business intelligence targets optimise customer satisfaction as indicated by Zaarour and Melachrinoudis (2015). Obviously, these experiences are also critical in the hospitality industry.

Considering hospitality services, and although some IT applications can be used simultaneously by customers, managers and employees, most hotel IT applications have been designed purely for employees, essentially for front of house, back of house, or both (Bilgihan

Table 27.1 Different IT applications in hotels

Front office applications:	*Back office applications:*
• Reservation systems	• Personnel and human resources management
• Check-in/check-out	packages
• Room status and housekeeping management	• Purchasing modules
• In-house guest information functions	• Accounting modules
• Guest accounting modules	• Inventory modules
	• Sales and catering
	• Generating financial reports
	• Updating statistics
	• Tools for business intelligence
Restaurant and banquet management systems:	*Guest-related interface applications:*
• Preparation of meals	• Call accounting system
• Cleaning systems	• Security processes
• Menu management systems	• Electronic locking system
• Sales analysis	• Energy management systems
• Beverage control systems	• Guest-operated devices (e.g., in-room
	entertainment)
	• Auxiliary guest services (e.g., voice mail)

Source: Adapted from Bilgihan et al. (2011).

et al., 2011). These technologies have been divided by Ham et al. (2005) and Bilgihan et al. (2011) into four categories (see Table 27.1).

However, and apart from the innovations designed for employees, nowadays, some authors emphasise the relevance of applications addressed to customers, such as amenities and some self-service devices in hotels. Examples include Intercontinental Hotels (2015) and Marriott Hotels (2015), as noted before. The use of self-service technologies benefits firms in terms of cost saving, but also by drawing the customer into a proactive or coproductive role. In this vein, Bilgihan et al. (2011), for instance, stress the importance of the hotels' development of online techniques or kiosks for check-in, Wi-Fi hotspots and internet access, in-room entertainment amenities, accessible electrical outlets, guest control panels, or specific IT applications for individual customer segments such as meetings and incentive travellers, or leisure travellers. With a similar perspective, Cobanoglu et al. (2011) defined some select hotel technology amenities, and empirically demonstrated the importance of 'Business essentials for travellers', 'In-room technologies', and 'Internet access' as predictors of hotel guest satisfaction. Apart from these, Garrigos and Narangajavana (2006) stressed the relevance of IT in order to develop creativity, generate knowledge and improve communications. In addition, Law et al. (2014) underline the relevance of integrating smart-phones, tablets and other mobile and hand-held technologies in enhancing tourism experiences, as well as the possibility of using mobile technology, virtual reality and 3D technology in e-business. Buhalis and Law (2008) also highlighted the importance of incorporating innovations such as interoperativity and ontology building (built on semantic web technologies, enabling tourism information systems to interact electronically and dynamically with partners by the most convenient method and to deliver the right information at the right time to the right user at the right cost), the use of multimedia, the application of mobile and wireless technologies, wireless local area networks, worldwide interoperability for microwave access, web design in both functionality and usability, accessibility and ambient intelligence.

The relevance of ambient intelligence, for instance, with the implementation of mobile communication and radio-frequency identification devices (RFID) in hospitality, is analysed by Collins (2010). We should add, apart from the development of the design and the quality of the webs: the use of Search Engine Optimisation and Search Engine Marketing in order to maximise efficiency in the distributions of hotels and also the use of revenue and yield management, or even dynamic price techniques (Narangajavana et al., 2014). They are used to set up prices and manage the sale and the inventory of rooms and other resources in the hotels.

Finally, Web 2.0 advances also offer new and numerous opportunities to firms to actively engage their customers in new service development processes (Sigala, 2012). Hence, she provides examples of activities, and Web 2.0 applications, which can support activities to engage customers in all stages of new service development processes. The importance of the use of the semantic web or Web 3.0 tools was also developed by Garrigos et al. (2011, 2012). Finally, Law et al. (2014) stress that the new innovations (such as new technologies in virtual reality and 3D technology), apart from improving operations, can also help managers better formulate new business models and marketing strategies. Nevertheless, while the interaction of technologies inside and outside the borders of hotel firms is critical, there are some specific problems, related mainly with a lack of a wide and complete marketing and management perspective in the use and implementation of these tools.

Connections between the different parts of the organisation

One of the most important potentials of IS/IT in the hospitality industry is the endeavour to incorporate the value chain in an integrated information system (Azevedo et al., 2014). In this vein, Sigala et al. (2004) demonstrated how hotels which combined technologies with other resources achieved better results than those which used technology for automation or in separate packages. We highlight two mechanisms used by hotels for internal information integration: Enterprise Resource Planning Systems (ERP) and connections with the Property Management System (PMS).

ERP systems are conceived as solutions-oriented to manage an organisation's resources and functions, and so the internal value chain, avoiding the problems of using separate tools with no connection between them. The mechanism acts as a central database or integrated system which aggregates and connects the information collected from various systems or functions within the organisations, or even integrates the various business processes of organisations, permitting the treatment and sharing of information between these diverse systems in real time, converting the data collected from all the sources into one easily accessible and user-friendly data set, and also providing decision-makers with an overview of the organisation's situation, globally and in each of its departments (Luck and Stephenson, 2009).

ERPs contribute significantly to developing business competitiveness as they improve many different aspects (Shang and Seddon, 2002; Azevedo et al., 2014). Decision-making and planning are supported through better control of tasks and departments, which is permitted by centralised information capable of data analysis. Operational tasks improve through automatisation, the reduction of costs and time-frame, gains in productivity and in the quality of customer service. The strategic situation advances due to integration through the value chain, integration of partners, and the fostering of innovation and new alliances. The organisation structure develops through the integration of departments and processes, and enhancement of communication and motivation of employees. And there are even technological benefits resulting from the reduction of the maintenance costs of systems and individual applications, enhancing the introduction of new applications. For instance, Vianna et al. (2014: 3367) recently explored the ERP adoption in the hotel industry, noting that they are 'strategic tools to get a better market position, reduce costs and raise process efficiency and service quality'. In addition they established that 'the main reason for adopting ERP is the need for better-centralised control in a naturally decentralised network of hotel units'.

However, ERP requires correct implementation, especially the connections between the diverse tools or functional systems within the organisation; an aspect which has some problems in the hospitality sector. As Azevedo et al. (2012) state, in the hospitality sector, ERPs do not cover a large part of the processes. Also, there is some dispersion of software applications with different origins, with the difficulty of the construction and management of interfaces between them.

In the hospitality industry, the major ERP suppliers have concentrated on those processes, such as the back office, which are similar to other industries, with SAP being the market leader for larger hotels (Azevedo et al., 2012). According to these authors, although other IS specific solutions have been adopted for some specific front office processes of hotels such as reservations, stock and supply, food and beverage, or point of sale management, most of them come from suppliers who do not offer integration with the back office and the implemented ERP System. The problem is that the integration of processes usually requires manual inter-vention which can lead to redundant information and inconsistent data, resulting in a negative impact on the quality of the service provided to the client (Martinez et al., 2006; Azevedo et al., 2012). This also reduces the organisation's ability to relate to its business partners, such as major online tour operators, missing the critical advantages of the capabilities brought by the use of internet and new technologies.

Another popular tool used in the hospitality sector, is the Property Management System (PMS) (used to manage physical properties containing diverse rooms individually associated with one or more users), which has been widely used since the first one implemented by the Waikiki Sheraton in 1970, in order to improve front office and back office processes (Martinez et al., 2006). According to these authors, these systems permit: 1) the management and registration of the reservation of rooms from diverse channels such as the CRS or GDS; 2) the management of check-in and check-out and the charges or expenses for clients; 3) the management of the rooms and their situation at every moment; 4) the management of the historical data from customers; or 5) the management of the relationships with travel agencies.

Systems to manage energy, leisure in the rooms, electronic room keys, telephone systems, or catering (with catering IS to manage the banquets and conferences, pricing and costs, stocks and recipes in the restaurants), are also interconnected through the PMS (O'Connor, 1996). Other mechanisms, which can be related to PMSs are, for instance, the Radio Frecuency Identification sytems (RFIDs), which can improve service quality (Öztaysi et al., 2009), and also operations within the hotels. Hence, RFID minibars connected to the PMSs can provide instant reports, inform room service of the inventories of the beverages in the rooms, and can also post charges to guests' folios. Moreover, energy management systems connected to the PMS could help front-desk agents to remotely set the temperatures in the rooms (Bilgihan et al., 2011).

Connections with the supply chain

The concept of supply chain management (SCM) is related to the efficient management of the operations of the supply chain; in our case, the hospitality supply chain. The process consists of the creation and improvement of the nodes or networks of firms related to a supply chain, or the enhancement of the participation, interaction, coordination and integration of all the agents or enterprises involved in the chain, in order to maximise the value offered to the customers, in this case, the tourist. This permits the fulfilment of the business objectives of the different enterprises within this tourism supply chain.

Studies of SCM in the tourism industry are very limited (Zhang et al., 2009). We could define a hospitality supply chain as a network of organisations engaged in different activities ranging from the supply of the different components of hospitality: products such as food/drinks and other culinary manufacturers, equipment manufacturers, furniture and decoration materials manufacturers, water/energy/telecommunications suppliers, maintenance suppliers, suppliers of fungible elements (serviettes, paper, cleaning products, etc.), suppliers of cleaning products, linens and other value added services (restaurants, spa, shops, hairdressing), to the distribution and marketing of the final hospitality products, involving a wide range of participants in both the private and public sectors. Obviously, the hospitality supply chain is connected to a wider tourism supply chain which could include other tourist agents such as transportation, tour operators and travel agencies.

Although SCM is often viewed as a supply perspective, the key concept resides in an interchange of information and knowledge in both directions: a backward flow of information, from the firms in touch with the target customers to the suppliers; but also a forward flow of goods or services and information from the suppliers to the firms which deliver the end products or services to customers. In this sense, the process attempts to emphasise the identification of the needs of the target customer, by the firms which are in touch with these customers, and the sharing of this information in real time with the 'first supplier' (the suppliers that procure the raw materials for the suppliers of the suppliers) in order to allow all the suppliers to better design, produce and deliver the needed items at the right moment: just in time. In addition, the flow of information and flow of goods moves from the first suppliers to the firms which are in touch with customers, allowing them to better forecast possible problems in the supply chain, and also to set up prices appropriately.

As Zhang et al. (2009: 351) state, 'IT is found to be an effective means of promoting collaboration between and among supply chain members and enhancing supply chain efficiency through providing real-time information regarding product availability, inventory levels, shipment status, and production requirements.' SCM can permit authorised tour operators or travel agencies to access a hotel chain's intranet to monitor, manage and control their capacities such as checking on room rates and availability for their customers. SCM reduces the operating cost of diverse firms (i.e. of producing products not demanded by customers, or producing and delivering them at inappropriate moments, with the costs of storage or the losses of spare products) and facilitates collaborative planning and forecasting among supply chain members (Li, 2007). It also enhances firm cooperation and common objectives and decision-making processes and increases competitiveness, efficiency and flexibility throughout the entire supply chain. In addition, SCM also increases the value for customers, as it offers customers, in this case tourists, products designed specifically to meet their requirements, with competitive prices (due to the reduction of cost of production, better development of products and improvements in logistics, etc.).

The failure to integrate across a value chain has problems such as poor general management of inventories and the needs of customers, and other costs related to the manual need to integrate information (Azevedo et al., 2012). In order to solve some of these problems, on the supply side, George et al. (2011) point to the use of techniques linked to IT in the hospitality industry, such as procurement, as a path to enhance revenue performance and reduce the costs associated with the supply function. Moreover, Barlow (2002) provides insights into how to improve inventory performance using a Just-in-Time approach in hotels. However, managers should also take into account the problems and opportunities surrounding the integrations in the value chains.

Connections with customers and other stakeholders

Research has increasingly emphasized the importance of the exchange rather than the transaction.... Essentially, the aim is to build and strengthen long-term customer relationships.

(Narangajavana et al., 2014: 29)

In the new arena, 'Customer Relationship Management (CRM) has a special relevance for service companies, in which contact with customers is intense, and loyalty is a source of competitive advantage' (Garrido and Padilla, 2012: 56). In the hospitality industry, due to the situation of growing customer-acquisition costs, rising customer expectations, price-sensitive travellers, more sophisticated clients, uncertain markets and less brand loyalty, CRM is widely considered to be one of the most effective ways to facilitate developing and expanding the customer base which, in turn, will assist in enhancing profitability and guest loyalty (Mohammed and Rashid, 2012). Hence, authors such as Hu et al. (2010) summarise how hotel chains have sought numerous ways to build relationships with their customers, using for instance loyalty programs, and the timing of rewards. In addition, Luck and Stephenson (2009) relate relationships between CRM and technology, and some similar concepts such as 'database marketing' to provide a better portrait of customers and their buying habits for marketing and promotional purposes. Moreover, Sigala (2012) stresses that by exploiting the customer intelligence of Web 2.0, firms can better understand and address customer needs and market trends. This is essential, according to her, as it reduces innovation failure rates, and improves market understanding and orientation.

With another perspective, Öztaysi et al. (2009) investigated the possibility of utilising RFID for improving service quality. The customer data acquired from the tool can be used to personalise or customise products and services, tailored to customer preferences (e.g. meal and drink preferences, access control, preferred lighting and room temperature, preferred hotel activities and cashless payment).

Moreover, Garrigos et al. (2011, 2012) emphasised broadly that in the new context of Web 3.0, intelligent machines read, understand, interrelate, and can manipulate data from cyberspace, permitting this process to be adapted by different users or firms according to their needs. According to these authors, in the Web 3.0 era, firms will be able to use the information gathered by organisations before, during, or after their contact with customers, via techniques such as data warehousing, data mining or customer relationship management, but also by using diverse pieces of information from several social networks, or the net in general. At this point, the management of processes outside the hotels is also important, emphasising aspects such as crowdsourcing processes or by enhancing the work of community managers. Sigala (2012) stresses that firms can use online social communities for actively co-operating and interacting with individual customers or customer communities in order to generate and evaluate new ideas, design and test new products and develop/support social innovation communities aiming to create and maintain customer bonds with the firm, its services and processes.

Hence, information about customer responses to previous offers, the personal characteristics of customers, or even about their general behaviour, can be used in order to market a hotel's products, services and special offers more effectively and to provide an improved and personalised service to customers (Luck and Stephenson, 2009). In addition, the management of external information and the management of social networks and virtual communities not only creates close bonds with customers, but also provides more precise information about their needs (Garrigos, 2010, Garrigos et al., 2011). This information, together with the use of cocreated processes, for instance through crowdsourcing techniques, is especially crucial for adapting and personalising products, brands and services by and for different users or firms according to their own needs (do what the user wants you to do, and behave as the user wants you to behave). They can be used when tourists want, allowing instant cross-marketing and other applications (Garrigos et al., 2011, 2012). Also, this information can be used to align business strategies, develop strategies and tactics or even to concentrate on knowledge management, being vital for effective and efficient decision-making and future tailored actions. For instance, Luck and Stephenson (2009: 13) provide examples of hotel chains which have acquired and stored customer data to improve the experience of customers and competitiveness.

To sum up, IS/IT in the hospitality industry can facilitate the understanding of customer needs and consequent adaptation (Azevedo et al., 2012). As a result, organisations can increase sales, obtain higher quality products, gain access to information and employee satisfaction, and above all, ensure long-lasting customer retention and loyalty (Mohammed and Rashid, 2012).

The future use of new technologies

Apart from traditional IS, new technologies are opening new possibilities for hotels. Here we present just a few of them.

Passive Wi-Fi tracking

Passive Wi-Fi tracking technology aims to continuously locate customers' mobile phones in the hotel premises. The tracking is completely passive for the user and is performed by the hotel Wi-Fi Access Points (AP). The Wi-Fi tracking permits univocal identification of each mobile phone, and the location of the phone in the premises (Musa and Eriksson, 2012).

The operating principle relies on the typical mobile phone configuration, where the Wi-Fi networking module actively sends a unique ID code when searching for available Wi-Fi networks. This permits the in-premises APs to identify and locate the user. It is worth noting that this is done without the customer's mobile phone actually being connected to the network. Passive Wi-Fi tracking spatial resolution can be enhanced by triangulation using data from simultaneous tracking using several APs (Kim et al., 2011).

Facial recognition

Facial recognition technology aims to acquire facial information as a first step to enable location and automated mood detection. Facial recognition capabilities have been improved in recent years by the continuous increase in camera resolution and the increase in processing power and analysis algorithms (Zhao et al., 2003).

Facial information is usually gathered via wall-mounted high-definition cameras. The customer's gender, age and mood can be evaluated from facial information (Gutta et al., 2000). Once facial information is gathered, the surveillance cameras can locate the customer at different places, thus effectively tracking the customer's activity in the hotel. As a further step, facial cues can be analysed as responses to ads or selection screens in the hotel (Kulkami et al., 2009).

RFID premise access systems

Access to the hotel premises is a key aspect which can be addressed using different technologies. RFID uses a radio signal to establish communication between two devices, a keylock transmitter (RFID reader) and a small card (RFID tag) receiver. Hotel customers carry the RFID tag. RFID tags are nowadays very small, and have built-in logic (microchip or state machine), memory and radio subsystems.

Passive and semi-active RFID systems are present in the market. In these systems, the RFID reader (keylock) is the only element using electrical power. The electromagnetic signal is generated by the RFID reader, which 'resonates' in the RFID tag and bounces back to the RFID reader to establish communication. Active RFID systems use RFID tags powered by batteries. A communication range of 100m is possible in this case (Rieback et al., 2006).

Data mining and Big Data analysis

Data mining addresses data analysis of the pervasive information gathered from the customer in the hotel by algorithmic processing in information systems in order to find patterns, regularities or irregularities in very large amounts of recurrent information (Rajaraman and Ullman, 2011). These patterns permit identification of the key processes the hotel management must pay special attention to. Further users of data mining in large and medium hotel chains automatically process electronic customer feedback to gauge the success of the business plan in place (Cooper et al., 2006).

Moreover, Big Data relates to the pervasive use of data-acquisition systems and algorithms in order to gather a very large number of parameters describing the customer activity. The information gathered can rely on conventional accounting activity, specific biometric data gathered at different places on the Hotel premises or even Internet-related data gathered from conventional social media networks like Facebook, Twitter, Google+ and the like. All this data is correlated, i.e. 'stitched', linking user activity, user presence and services used by the customer in order to be employed in data mining analysis to identify behaviour tendencies which, in turn, will be used to finely tailor the services offered by the hotel administration.

IP-TV distribution network

TV distribution in large premises, such as hotels, requires advanced technology. This distribution is carried out by an integrated reception system, which collects the RF signals (carrying TV, satellite and radio) from one or a small number of aerials and satellite dishes and distributes these signals to a large number of rooms employing coaxial cabling (Zahariadis et al., 2002). Advanced implementation relies on optical fibre with the advantage of reduced maintenance costs.

Another method for distributing TV is IP streaming using the LAN infrastructure network deployed in the hotel. In this case, specific TV receivers capable of decoding IP streaming are required alongside a computer encoder for converting the signal to IP data streams adequate for an IP-TV set (Obrist et al., 2009).

Conclusions and further considerations

Understanding and correct management of new developments in IS is critical for the success of hotel chains. ISs have evolved from interrelated components which collect, process, store and disseminate information to support decision-making, coordination, control, analysis and visualisation in an organisation, to dynamic, interoperable mechanisms of collecting, processing and disseminating intelligence within and outside organisations (Buhalis and Law, 2008). Moreover, the focus on the customer is overcoming the traditional uses of IS to improve operational mechanisms and increase efficiency. This work has emphasised some of the tools that managers should be aware of when considering the use of IS for hotels.

However, it is necessary to stress that the implementation of these tools and systems cannot only consider the importance of technology alone. The transformation of the organisations and their culture is also essential to help IS improve performance in the hotel industry (Theodosiou and Katsikea, 2012).

Martínez et al. (2006) and Azevedo et al. (2014) point out that new customer demands require companies to respond properly to all requests which can affect the quality of service, making the use of technology a strategic issue. However, the success of CRM and other programs related to customers does not depend only on technology. Internal organisational transformations are required (Mohammed and Rashid, 2012; Garrido and Padilla, 2012). In addition, and looking also outside hotel firms, the potential of new technologies cannot be conceived without the participation of people, who live, interact, learn and create via the web, social networks and personal relationships that are vital for firms (Garrigos et al., 2011, 2012). In this arena, and according to Garrigos et al. (2011, 2012), it is also crucial to look at the relevance of social networks, and the use of community managers and crowdsourcing techniques, as mechanisms to improve both marketing and strategic management processes. Moreover, Garrigos-Simon and Narangajavana (2014b) stress the importance of the use of Masscapital, conceived as 'the capabilities from all the individuals or organisations, related closely or not to the own company or organisation, which can help it to innovate or improve any of their activities or processes', that includes the participation of customers and other stakeholders, not only supplying knowledge, but also other resources and capabilities, in order to improve different processes in the organisations, which could be essentially enhanced with the use of the new technologies.

The use of all these internal and external elements, helped by the use of new technologies, is essential for the proper use of IS in strengthening the corporate image, promoting collaboration with experts, customers and suppliers. It represents a flexible source of information and knowledge about the latest innovations, tastes and preferences of consumers and other stakeholders, as well as an important source of capabilities and resources available to hospitality organisations.

References

Azevedo, P.S., Romão, M. and Rebelo, E. (2012) Advantages, limitations and solutions in the use of ERP systems (Enterprise Resource Planning): A case study in the hospitality industry. *Procedia Technology*, 5, 264–72.

Azevedo, P.S., Romão, M. and Rebelo, E. (2014) Success factors for using ERP (Enterprise Resource Planning) systems to improve competitiveness in the hospitality industry. *Tourism and Management Studies*, 10, 165–68.

Barlow, G.L. (2002) Just-in-time: implementation within the hotel industry – a case study. *International Journal of Production Economics*, 80(2), 155–67.

Bilgihan, A., Okumus, F. and Kwun, D.J.W. (2011) Information technology applications and competitive advantage in hotel companies. *Journal of Hospitality and Tourism Technology*, 2(2), 139–53.

Buhalis, D. and Law, R. (2008) Progress in information technology and tourism management: 20 years on and 10 years after the Internet – the state of eTourism research. *Tourism Management*, 29(4), 609–23.

Calof, J., Richards, G. and Smith, J. (2015) Foresight, competitive intelligence and business analytics – tools for making industrial programmes more efficient. *Journal of the National Research University Higher School of Economics (Foresight-Russia)*, 9(1), 68–81.

Cobanoglu, C., Berezina, K., Kasavana, M.L. and Erdem, M. (2011) The impact of technology amenities on hotel guest overall satisfaction. *Journal of Quality Assurance in Hospitality & Tourism*, 12(4), 272–88.

Collins, G. (2010) Usable mobile ambient intelligent solutions for hospitality customers. *Journal of Information Technology Impact*, 10(1), 45–54.

Cooper, D.R., Schindler, P.S. and Sun, J. (2006) *Business Research Methods.* New York: McGraw-hill

Garrido Moreno, A. and Padilla Meléndez, A. (2012) Estrategias CRM en empresas de servicios: recomendaciones directivas para su implementación. *Dirección y Organización*, 46, 56–66.

Garrigós, F.J. (2010) Interrelationships between professional virtual communities and social networks, and the importance of virtual communities in creating and sharing knowledge. In S. Dasgupta, S. (ed.) *Social Computing: Concepts, Methodologies, Tools, and Applications*, Vol. 3 (6.6), 1674–96. New York: Information Science Reference Publishing.

Garrigós, F.J. and Narangajavana, Y. (2006) *Capacidades Directivas y Nuevas Tecnologías en el Sector Turístico.* Castellón, Spain: Athenea, Publicaciones de la Universitat Jaime I.

Garrigos F.J., Gil, I. and Narangajavana,Y. (2011) The impact of social networks in the competitiveness of the firms. In Beckford, A.B. and Larsen, J.P. (eds) *Competitiveness: Psychology, Production, Impact and Global Trends.* Hauppauge: Nova Science Publishers Inc.

Garrigos F.J., Lapiedra, R. and Barberá, T. (2012) Social networks and Web 3.0: their impact on the management and marketing of organizations. *Management Decision* 50(10), 1880–90.

Garrigos-Simon, F.J., Narangajavana, Y. and Galdón-Salvador, J.L. (2014a) Crowdsourcing as a competitive advantage for new business models. In Gil-Pechuán, I., Palacios-Marqués, D., Peris-Ortiz, M.,Vendrell, E., Ferri-Ramirez, C. (eds), *Strategies in E-Business.* New York: Springer US, pp. 29–37.

Garrigos-Simon, F.J. and Narangajavana, Y. (2014b) The use of Masscapital in education. In F. Garrigos, et al. (ed.), *INNODOCT/14 Strategies for education in a New Context*, Valencia, Spain: Ed.Universitat Politecnica de Valencia.

George, B.P., Williams, A.J. and Henthorne, T.L. (2011) E-procurement in the hospitality industry: an exploratory study. *International Journal of Procurement Management*, 4(1), 37–55.

Gutta, S., Huang, J.R., Jonathon, P. and Wechsler, H. (2000) Mixture of experts for classification of gender, ethnic origin, and pose of human faces. *Neural Networks, IEEE Transactions*, 11(4), 948–60.

Ham, S., Kim, W.G. and Jeong, S. (2005) Effect of information technology on performance in upscale hotels, *International Journal of Hospitality Management*, 24(2), 281–94.

Hu H-H., Huang C-T. and Chen, P-T. (2010) Do reward programs truly build loyalty for lodging industry? *International Journal of Hospitality Management*, 29, 128–35.

Intercontinental Hotels (2015) Hospitality Net. Online. Available HTTP: <http://www.hospitalitynet.org/news/global/154000320/4070756.html>, accessed 15 July 2015.

Kim, B., Bong, W. and Kim, Y.C. (2011) Indoor localization for Wi-Fi devices by cross-monitoring AP and weighted triangulation. In Proceedings of the Consumer Communications and Networking Conference, Las Vegas 9-11 January, IEEE, pp. 933–36.

Kulkarni, S.S., Reddy, N.P. and Hariharan, S.I. (2009) Facial expression (mood) recognition from facial images using committee neural networks. *Biomedical Engineering Online*, 8(16), 1–12.

Law, R., Buhalis, D. and Cobanoglu, C. (2014) Progress on information and communication technologies in hospitality and tourism. *International Journal of Contemporary Hospitality Management*, 26(5), 727–50.

Li, L. (2007) *Supply Chain Management: Concepts, Techniques and Practices Enhancing Value Through Collaboration.* Singapore: World Scientific.

Luck, D. and Stephenson, M.L. (2009) An evaluation of the significant elements of customer relationship management within the hotel industry. *Tourism Today*, 9, 7–26.

Marriott Hotels (2015) Hospitality Net. Online. Available HTTP: <http://www.hospitalitynet.org/news/4069999.html>, accessed 15 July, 2015.

Martinez J., Majo J. and Casadesus, M. (2006) El uso de las tecnologías de la información en el sector hotelero. VI Turitec Proceedings. Málaga, Spain, pp. 47–58. Online. Available HTTP: <http://www.turitec.com/actas/2006/L04usotecnologias.pdf>, accessed 15 July, 2015.

Mohammed, A.A. and Rashid, B. (2012) Customer Relationship Management (CRM) in Hotel Industry: a framework proposal on the relationship among CRM dimensions, marketing capabilities, and hotel performance. *International Review of Management and Marketing*, 2(4), 220–30.

Musa, A.B.M. and Eriksson, J. (2012) Tracking unmodified smartphones using wi-fi monitors. In Proceedings of the 10th ACM Conference on Embedded Network Sensor Systems, pp. 281–94, Nov 6–9, 2012, Toronto, Canada.

Narangajavana, Y., Garrigos-Simon, F.J., García, J.S. and Forgas-Coll, S. (2014) Prices, prices and prices: a study in the airline sector. *Tourism Management*, 41, 28–42.

Obrist, M., Miletich, M., Holocher, T., Beck, E., Kepplinger, S., Muzak, P. and Tscheligi, M. (2009) Local communities and IPTV: lessons learned in an early design and development phase. *Computers in Entertainment* (CIE), 7(3), article 44.

O'Connor, P. (1996) *Using Computers in Hospitality*. London, UK: Cassell.

Öztaysi, B., Baysan S. and Akpinar, F. (2009) Radio frequency indentification (RFID) in hospitality. *Technovation* 29(9), 618–24.

Rajaraman, A. and Ullman, J.D. (2011) *Mining of Massive Datasets*. Cambridge: Cambridge University Press.

Rieback, M.R., Crispo, B. and Tanenbaum, A.S. (2006) The evolution of RFID security. *IEEE Pervasive Computing*, 5(1), 62–69.

Sigala, M. (2012) Web 2.0 and customer involvement in new service development: a framework, cases and implications in tourism. In M. Sigala, E. Christou and U. Gretzel (eds), *Social Media in Travel, Tourism and Hospitality: Theory, Practice and Cases*. Surrey, UK: Ashgate Publishing, Ltd., pp. 25–33.

Sigala, M., Airey, D., Jones, P. and Lockwood, A. (2004) ICT paradox lost? A stepwise DEA methodology to evaluate technology investments in tourism settings. *Journal of Travel Research*, 43(2), 180–92.

Shang, S. and Seddon, P. (2002) Assessing and managing the benefits of enterprise systems: the business manager's perspective. *Information Systems Journal*, 12, 271–99.

Starwood Hotels (2015) Online. Available HTTP: <http://www.starwoodhotels.com/corporate/about/investor/news.html>, accessed 15 July 2015.

Theodosiou, M. and Katsikea, E. (2012) Antecedents and performance of electronic business adoption in the hotel industry. *European Journal of Marketing*, 46(1/2), 258–83.

Vianna, R.H.P., Fonseca, F., Mello, A.M. and Nascimento, P.T. (2014) ERP adoption in the hotel industry: how software implementation becomes development. In Proceeding of International Conference on Management of Engineering and Technology (PICMET), 27–31 July, 2014, Kanazawa, Portland IEEE pp. 3367–75.

Zaarour, N. and Melachrinoudis, E. (2015) Performance optimization in retail business using real-time predictive analytics. In Proceedings of the International Conference on Applied Operational Research, ICAOR (p. 46), Vienna, Austria, 15–17 July 2015.

Zahariadis, T., Pramataris, K. and Zervos, N. (2002) A comparison of competing broadband in-home technologies. *Electronics & Communication Engineering Journal*, 14(4), 133–42.

Zhang, X., Song, H. and Huang, G.Q. (2009) Tourism supply chain management: a new research agenda. *Tourism Management*, 30(3), 345–58.

Zhao, W., Chellappa, R., Phillips, P.J. and Rosenfeld, A. (2003) Face recognition: a literature survey. *ACM Computing Surveys* (CSUR), 35(4), 399–458.

28

Financial management, control and reporting in hotel chains

Liliya Terzieva

(NHTV UNIVERSITY OF APPLIED SCIENCES, BREDA, NETHERLANDS)

Introduction

Nowadays, despite the recent and continuous technological innovations, businesses and organisations continue to face a growing range of challenges no matter where they operate or what industry they are in (Nijs, 2014). This is especially so in the field of hospitality, which is the sector referred to as the most impacted by current changes, and at the same time, the sector which is most standardised (Nijs, 2014). To survive and thrive in such fast-changing times, hospitality businesses and organisations recognise the necessity to transform their way of thinking and acting, where finance is not an exception.

The forms of integration existing in the hotel industry are diverse, from simple business associations to hotel chains, where, at the same time, different degrees of relationships can be identified. The phenomena of hotel association and integration are relatively recent, arising in the United States after the Second World War. Chains are a specific form of hotel concentration, involving both unified as well as third party management of a certain number of establishments, according to diverse models, but having in common the same management and the same production processes but not necessarily the same objectives, since they depend on the competitive set and the target markets (Colomina et al., 2014).

Sound financial management is at the core of any successful hospitality business, especially when it comes to hotel chains: by following basic accounting principles, hotel owners and managers have the information they need to identify trends before they can have a negative impact on the business even if the accounting data is time-lagged. They can reduce expenses, readily accommodate anticipated peak business times, and scale back operations during slow periods.

The objective of the current chapter is to explore financial matters and accounting in hotel chains and what differentiates them from other hospitality companies. In the first part of the chapter the specifics of financial management in hotel chains are defined, whereby a clear distinction is made between the financial management of hotel chains and independent hotel properties. In the next section, the relations between financial statements within the hotel chains are discussed, as well as the differences between the ratios of a single hotel property and a hotel chain. The reporting and financial control mechanisms are an essential part of any hotel chain contract and there are a number of issues that should be taken into consideration, which is exactly what the next part of the chapter is about. Apart from the above, another critical issue in hotel chains is analysed, namely financial control. It is presented in terms of how the actual extent of control, determined by the particular entry mode, enables the hotel chain to apply its policies towards the individual properties; as well as how the financial reports further affect the financial management of the whole chain. The case study at the end of the chapter focuses on the hotel chain (Hyatt Regency) accounting system and how it differs from any single property accounting systems. We also discuss the hotel chain's involvement in the property's accounting procedures and how it impacts the property's financial management.

Financial management: implications for hotel chains

Hospitality financial management's main function is fairly similar to financial management in every organisation. It is intended to ensure that the financial resources of a hotel or other hospitality company are controlled and well organised, as hotels have to balance their revenues with continuous and non-continuous expenses (Beck et al., 2011). However, there are some unique issues in hotel financial management. According to Guilding (2003), these include: functions' interdependency, high sales volatility, high product perishability, high fixed costs and labour-intensive activities. Hotel chains have been 'accused' by certain financial experts of a certain depersonalisation and uniformity in their service and an abuse of their dominating position in the market in contrast to small and medium-sized independent hotels (Colomina et al., 2014). However, their multiple advantages far exceed these drawbacks (Harris and Mongiello, 2012).

Management methods and the business structure of chains are diverse. Some chains are managed by the owners or participate actively in the management of the hotels belonging to the group. Others rent or sign management or franchise contracts with establishments owned by others. In fact, the same chain might carry out different methods at the same time, but in all cases, to a greater or lesser extent, they assume risks and are responsible for the control of management (Gonzalez and Jareno, 2014).

In fact, in small hotel companies, the role of a financial and managerial accountant can be performed by a single person. In addition, the same person can be entrusted to perform the work of an analyst. In this case, the accounting service becomes the source or the so-called 'right hand' to a hotel management. It combines the operations of recording, classification and summary presentation of transactions but also planning, analysis and controlling. Business communication, organised through a direct connection between accounting and management, has many advantages over using the services of an external organisation. However, due to the complex functions performed by one person only, omissions are possible (Hales, 2011).

The financial management of hotel chains differs considerably from that of a single hotel. One very important factor is geographical diversification. Thus, hotel chains reduce business risk through product variety and geographical diffusion. Geographical dispersion enables chains to enlarge the range of their offer and at the same time encourages the creation of new units abroad if necessary. This combination of expansion and diversification as the direction of growth has enabled the world's most famous hotel chains to enter the international hotel business, that is, to grow from national into international companies (Šušić, 2009; Ivanova, 2013). Another characteristic specific to hotel chains where financial practices do not comply with local laws and regulations, is financial personnel dispersion, thus there are financial professionals in each of the hotel members of the hotel chain, who need to be aligned and managed accordingly. Complex management structure also needs to be taken into account, since within the hotel chain there exists a multi-level management system, which encompasses internal as well as external challenges. Risk also needs to be included amongst the specific features since the synergy between headquarters and financial management requires a continuous collaboration and a fully aligned policy.

Recently the role of financial managers in either hotel chains or third party management companies, is becoming increasingly proactive (Nijs, 2014). Not only do they have to reflect on a company's financial history, taking into account each and every component of the system, but they also need to make decisions for both short-term and long-term planning. In order to be able to do so, the following two main competencies are important:

1. More consolidated analysis of the three key basic financial statements: balance sheet, profit and loss account (income statement) and cash flow.
2. Complex and integrated calculation and interpretation of financial ratios: operating, liquidity, solvency, activity and profitability.

As Cunill (2006) states, from a financial perspective in hotel chains, the following main financial strategies are being implemented:

• *Expansion*: a business strategy in which growth is obtained by increasing the number of hotels of a given chain, where customers can obtain the same services. Unlike relocation, business expansion entails opening up new hotels in different physical locations while still maintaining the current business locations.

• *Cost reduction*: obtained, basically, through the standardisation of the processes and the introduction of new technologies. In addition, businesses have the intention of achieving objectives, such as the creation of shareholder value, the increase of asset turnover or others, such as an increase in profitability and maintaining a specific level of income.

• *Diversification of financial sources*: re-investment of profits and an increase in solid financial resources. It can be deduced that the businesses are concerned with making their expansion compatible with an adequate financial balance. This compatibility is demonstrated by the fact that some businesses combine their expansion strategy with the re-organisation of their hotel-portfolio. To do so, transactions are carried out, consisting of the selling of hotels owned by the chain in order to later incorporate them in that chain by means of management and rental contracts.

Relations between financial statements within the hotel chain

In the activity of every business a number of varied economic operations, as regards character, content and dimension, are in process. These are namely the operations that can cause a change in the business's property. With the help of the method of balance summary these processes can be spotted and registered, and a balance should be made after the occurrence of each and every one of the processes mentioned above.

When analysing the accounting and financial management of a hotel chain, a very important aspect is differentiating a hotel chain from a management company (Section I, Chapter 1). As explained in detail in Section II of this book, different contractual forms can be used by hotel chains, which form different governance structures, that in turn impact the financial and operational management of the hotel chains. Commonly used are (Ghorbal-Blal,

2008) franchises, management contracts, leases, rentals, and full or partial equity participations or a combination of the above:

- *Franchise contract*: since this agreement normally includes the sales, marketing and quality control system of the chain and in this case, the chain does not manage the hotel, the hotel owner controls its daily operations and physical assets. What is important in terms of financial relations, the chain only retains control over the codified assets, while the tacit control over assets is often shared with the hotel or royalties are collected (Holiday Inn, Choice International, etc).
- *Lease contract*: the hotel chain temporarily, or for a certain period of time rents an object and pays a certain amount of money for that.
- *Management contract*: seen from the financial point of view, here, the management company can, but does not have to be an investor, but manages a hotel for agreed compensation.

The largest number of management companies, which manage objects of famous hotel chains, have their origin in the USA. The big corporate chains have in their structure management companies who manage different hotels. For example, corporate chain Marriott International, apart from the hotels in its ownership, on various grounds also manages around 900 hotels which are not in its ownership. The biggest management companies that own most of their hotels are: Extended Stay Hotels (around 700 hotels), Interstate Hotels & Resorts (owns and manages around 230 hotels) etc. (Roth and Fishbin, 2015). Unlike corporate chains, management companies tend to be less oriented towards the international hotel business, which, however, has been changing in recent years.

Taking into consideration the specifics of the hotel chains mentioned above, we need to note the differences in the accounting of hotel chains and their financial management, e.g. hotel chains' revenues are generated mainly from franchising and management fees. Actually the type of expansion form/entry mode presupposes the sources of revenues – to be generated either more from fees than from operations or vice versa. In this regard, the structure of revenues and costs has to be analysed. For hotel chains that own part of their property, for example Accor with 29 per cent (Accor, 2014) their revenues consist of both fees and operational revenues. On the contrary, for hotel chains, which do not own a single property from their portfolio, their revenues are generated only from fees. Moreover it is also valid for the franchise that it provides a significant number of selling points in its own and other countries without large investments. The company expands on the market with minimum financial risk. Leading corporate hotel chains are the biggest providers of franchise. The best examples are corporate chains: Wyndham Hotel Group (out of 7,043 hotels, 7,016 are franchised), Choice Hotels International (all the hotels are franchised), InterContinental Hotels Group (86 per cent are franchised) etc. (Šušić, 2009).

Financial statements of hotel chains contain a lot of financial information and the analysis of this information requires more than simply reading the reported facts. The most significant is the interpretation of the reported facts, which is accomplished through financial ratio analysis. In the context of hotel chains the financial ratios are referred to as 'sustainable growth indicators' (Tidikova, 2014). Based on the general financial statements, relations are explored by means of financial ratio analysis, referring mainly to the liquidity, solvency and profitability.

In general when referring to single hotels there are five major classifications of ratios: operating, liquidity, solvency, activity and profitability (see Table 28.1).

Table 28.1 Financial ratios

Type of Financial ratio	Sub-ratios
Operating ratios assist in the analysis of the hotel chain's operations.	Revenue ratios, market segmentation ratios, labour cost ratios, expense ratios, retail ratios and undistributed operating expense ratios.
Liquidity: the extent to which a company is capable of meeting its short-term payment obligations.	The current ratio, the quick ratio, the cash ratio, the net working capital.
Solvency: the extent to which a company is capable of settling its long-term debt.	Debt ratio, equity capital ratio, capitalisation ratio, interest coverage ratio and cash flow to debt ratio.
Activity ratios measure management's effectiveness in using its resources.	Retail inventory turnover ratio and property, equipment turnover ratio and asset turnover ratio.
Profitability: when there is an acceptable return on capital.	Profit margin analysis, effective tax rate, return on assets, return on equity capital and return on capital employed.

Source: Adapted from Schmidgall (1989).

The hotel-specific ratios are Occupancy Percentage, Average Daily Rate (ADR), Revenue Per Available Room (RevPAR), Revenue Per Available Customer (RevPAC) and Cost Per Occupied Room (CPOR). Taking the evolutionary perspective, Schmidgall (1989) discusses that within an in independent hotel, the financial ratios that general managers of single hotels used to consider being the most useful, were the operating and activity ratios, while owners gave profitability ratios more importance. However, today, General Managers use the Balanced scorecard reward systems.

When referring to hotel chains, financial ratios play a very important role as well (Tidikova, 2014). Apart from the key indicators provided by the Average Daily Rate (ADR), and the Revenue Per Available Room (RevPAR), Solvency and the Profitability ratios (of the general model presented above) are calculated and analysed in depth not only annually but also at given specific regular periods of time (e.g. quarterly). The profitability ratios provide detailed information on the possibilities for investment and the necessary measures to be taken towards tax reduction, enlarging the EBIT and raising investing and operating profit. When it comes to solvency, financial leverage provides the information for managerial decisions to be made on changing the share of the equity and possibilities for becoming more risky by using debt financing, for example.

The sustainable growth indicators relating to hotel chains and as a further consolidation and integration of general financial ratios (as referred to above) consist of seven main indicators: *earnings before interest and taxes, revenue, assets, equity, taxes, interest rate* and *dividends*. These provide data on the sustainable growth rate within the hotel chain. There are two limitations to financial ratios in the context of hotel chains:

1. Over-dependency on financial ratios: just taken into account on their own, they may be less meaningful unless compared to those of previous accounting periods (this is the reason why hotel chains use STAR reports in many parts of the world), budgeted results, industry averages, or similar properties.

2. Financial ratios do not measure the hotel chain's intellectual capital assets such as brand name, potential for growth, and intellectual or human capital when assessing a hotel chain's true worth (Šušić, 2009).

Reporting and financial control

When referring to hotel chain reporting, there always comes the issue of 'hierarchy or network' no matter whether the hotel chains are multinational companies, 'where multiple centres of excellence exist' or domestic ones (Delany, 2000). Apart from the entry mode of franchising, in network organisations, where headquarters report to shareholders and units report to headquarters, the centre-to-units and units-to-centre communication channels bring direction and coordination and crucial information in order to implement a global strategy (Rutherford and O'Fallon, 2011). The reporting system adopted is an essential part of the accountability process – in that it enables the flow of information upon which the senior managers monitor units' performances and consequently evaluate their managers. The reporting system, therefore, is assumed to feature a coherent orientation with the autonomy-versus-control choice of organisation.

A hotel chain is usually classified as operating under a management contract or as a franchise or a marketing consortium. Hotel chains usually make certain rules regarding standards, rules, policies, procedures of affiliation, etc. In general, the more centralised the organisation, the stronger the control over the individual property. Some chains own affiliated properties, but many do not. Some chains have strong control over the architecture, management and standards of affiliated properties while other hotel chains only concentrate on advertising, marketing, or purchasing.

Over the years, in many hotels, the ownership structure has become increasingly complex. Consequently, the daily operations are run by either managers or owners, who take active responsibility for the oversight of their business. Thus, as hotel employees, the managers are required to run the hospitality business with asset management tools, with the aim of achieving a positive financial performance, driven by the need to increase the return on the owners' investment (Anson, 2012).

As discussed above, hotel chain expansion plays a key role in the entire chain policy, thus reports and control are an essential part of it. As Ghorbal-Blal (2008) states: 'Control, in its simplest form, is a cybernetic process that ensures actions to be performed according to principles' (p. 33). The main ways in which control is exercised are by means of: separation of duties, awareness of systems and people, and measurement and awareness of risk.

However, when referring to financial control, which is the main objective here, the extent of financial control is actually determined by the particular entry mode, which either enables the hotel chain to apply a customised or a rather integrated controlling policy towards its individual properties. The latter differs when referring to a marketing consortium. For example, where in the latter more independence is granted, then more advantages in terms of flexibility can be seen (e.g. Best Western). While within a franchise system compliance of controlling mechanisms in the entire entity needs to be observed to the least detail.

As Gonzalez and Jareno (2014) discuss, within the framework of the centralised accounting control (franchise, lease contracts and some forms of management contracts) most of the accounts are prepared at the property of the given hotel chain and then almost all information is either transmitted to head office (the hotel corporation), where it is processed by specialised staff, or inspected by auditors of the third party management companies. This approach has grown in recent years with the rapid rise in technology and easy transmission of data, and is particularly appropriate for the comparatively simple and standardised operations within the hotel chain system (Gonzalez and Jareno, 2014). Where centralised systems are used there is little need for a financial control department because all information is simple and very tightly managed. The hotel chain management will then have to perform a so-called 'self-audit' by completing checklists that list a range of procedures daily and periodically, which ensures that checks are taking place (Colomina et al., 2014; Ghorbal-Blal, 2008). By self-accounting (marketing consortia), what is important is that the local property (hotel chain) does all of its own accounts – gathers all the revenues, including all debts, pays all invoices, produces final profit and loss and balance sheets and then pays its own taxes. In this case a lot of on-site control staff in the various areas is necessary.

Taking into consideration the differences of the specific hotel chains, and especially their international distribution, when it comes to financial reporting and accounting systems, it is of considerable importance to analyse when the hotels within the chain need to stick to the local accounting rules (legislation and procedures) and when they can impose rules in addition to those mandated by law and set for the entire chain. Differences can be noted between the annual reporting documents of NH Hotel Group, where the local specifics play a dominant role, and ACCOR Group, where the uniformity of the system is more important (Gonzalez and Jareno, 2014). There are also regulations determined for the financial relations between the headquarters and the properties, where increased synergy can be seen in exchanging good practices as proven also by the reports and analysis of Puetz-Willems (2015) and Roth and Fishbin (2015). When it comes to who is responsible for the financial reports, a recent trend is that the General Management and/or the Chief Executive Officer develops the strategic policy and the key financial/performance indicators. Thus the Chief Accountant or the External Financial and Auditing Bureau makes the analysis and draws the conclusions, which are included in the further development of the hotel chain policy (Puetz-Willems, 2015).

Case study: Hyatt Regency hotel chain

Being part of the Hyatt Corporation (and one of the ten Hyatt Brands) and observing its standardised financial systems, the Hyatt Regency hotel chain manages a semi-centralised financial operation flow (Hyatt Hotels Corporation, 2015). The aims of the business property are numerous and diverse, as regards theme and concept; which is why the business accounts are not used in isolation, but within a system. For this reason, different kinds of business accounts are used, and each of them is a means of classifying: grouping the positive and the negative effects that appear as a result of any economic operation, as a result of which the current changes in the business entities, and their current state, are traced (Hyatt Hotels Corporation, 2015).

Two central financial reporting and controlling figures have been appointed:

• Director of Finance, who manages the operations of the Auditing/Accounting Department as well as collaborating with General Management in designing and developing the Strategic Policy.

• Assistant Director of Finance, who coordinates, organises and actively oversees the operations of the Auditing/Accounting department. Management of cash flow, necessary reporting and approval of all accounting functions are also requirements of the position.

The headquarters of Hyatt – Global Hyatt Corporation has a dominant and decisive role within the financial management system of the Hyatt Regency hotel chain since all properties are required to use a centralised regulation and reporting system (Hyatt Hotels Corporation, 2015), that defines:

- Owed and leased hotels segment;
- Management and Franchise fees (geographical distribution);
- Selling, General and Administrative expenses (Openings and future expansion, Share repurchase, Corporate finance/asset recycling, Balance sheet/other items, Annual information).

With the Shared Services Centre (SSC), Hyatt takes a centralised approach whereby all processing and administration activities that do not need to be processed locally are outsourced to the main centre in Mainz. These include accounts receivable, accounts payable and general ledger accounting, such as the posting, checking and payment of all supplier bills. To relieve individual hotels from these time-consuming, labour-intensive tasks, Hyatt uses multi-client-enabled accounting software, allowing any number of hotels to be incorporated and managed within the system. Specifically, the hotel data converges on the Epicor centralised solution (Hyatt Hotels Corporation, 2015). The entire accounting information is system-atised in accounts as regards their importance for consumers. The chart of accounts generated is a list of accounts, where the economic operations connected with the assets, the owner's equity, the income and expenditure are all registered. These are synthetic and analytical accounts and subsidiary accounts which are given an index with a corresponding number and name.

The controlling at the Hyatt Regency single hotel property is organised within a self-accounting unit, consisting of:

- Financial controller
- Assistant controller
- Revenue controller (income auditor)
- Credit controller and sales ledger staff
- Purchase ledger (accounts payable)
- General cashier
- Food and beverage controller
- Computer services controller
- Payroll check

In contrast to a single property accounting system, the centralised system is more efficient in time and long-term management prospects, while a drawback can be seen in the customisa-tion that some of the properties need to acquire, e.g. dependent on the location and the organisational and customer culture model expected.

In terms of how the centralised financial management influences the general management of the Hyatt Regency hotel chain, the following benefits can be defined:

- Adequate investment policy development possibilities
- Up-to-date relevant accounting information
- Financial analysis and ratio calculation regardless of time
- Systematised and integrated financial and economic overview of both the entity as well as the individual properties
- Automated regime of working

Moreover within the Hyatt Regency system there has been established the 'human-oriented' cost control. It is exactly the human that is the foundation and soil of management and operation. At the same time the subject of cost control and implementation is the staff of the hotel, therefore there is the need of active participation of all staff besides accountants and cost controllers. The 'human-oriented' management idea aims to fully recognise the human value, find out human potentiality, stimulate human vigor, improve human characters effectively and achieve the optimum combination, giving full play to enthusiasm (Harris and Mongiello, 2012). As a result, the effectiveness of cost control is continuously being raised as well as the customisation in terms of 'experience-boutique-emotion triangulation' as complexity growth indicator (Nijs, 2014) is further improved.

Conclusions and further research

Modern hotel financial management is the core of hotel management, closely related to all departments, with every link involving capital flow from hotels; from purchasing to processing, selling, financial collection, and then back to purchasing. As society is currently evolving with a speed no one is able to recognise from previous times (due to interconnectivity, globalisation, the increasing importance of experiences, etc.), the research on financial management in hospitality and in hotel chains in particular is extremely well developed (Tsai et al., 2010). There is to be noted a search for and strive for new business models that generate sustainability and at the same time consistency in growth and development (Roth and Fishbin, 2015). As Puetz-Willems (2015) argues, hotel chains, as business organisations, can be seen from a highly critical perspective, entering the market of lifestyle and boutique experiences translated into multi-national and multi-cultural financial implications. It is no longer possible to only relate financial outcomes and reports to prescribed or centrally planned models as collective, co-creative, cross-case comparative and multi-disciplinary modes start emerging on the hospitality scene. Therefore it is no wonder that today's financial management, as well as reporting and control, has been shifting towards more complex and open (not predetermined) systems of developing and defining performance that makes sense not only within closed (hotel corporation) communities but also within every layer of the multi-spectrum of life (Beck et al., 2011).

References

Accor (2014) Consolidated financial statements and notes. Online. Available HTTP: <www.stock proinfo.com/doc/2014/FR0000120404_2014_20141231_US_1F.pdf>, accessed 4 April, 2015.

Anson, M. (2012) Asset owner versus asset managers: agency cost and asymmetries of information of alternative assets. *The Journal for Portfolio Management*, 38(3), 89–103.

Beck, J., Knutson, B., Cha, J. and Kim, S. (2011) Developing revenue managers for the lodging industry. *Journal of Human Resources in Hospitality & Tourism*, 10(2), 182–94.

Colomina, C.I.M., Guerrero, C.V., Priego, J.B. and Palacios, C.A. (2014) An analysis of strategic information published by large Spanish hotel chains. Manuscript submitted for publication. Online. Available HTTP: <http://eprints.ucm.es/6840/1/0416.pdf>, accessed 10 December, 2014.

Cunill, O.M. (2006) *The Growth Strategies of Hotel Chains: Best Business Practices by Leading Companies.* New York: The Haworth Hospitality Press.

Delany, E. (2000) Strategic development of the multinational subsidiary through subsidiary initiative-taking. *Long Range Planning*, 33, 220–44.

Ghorbal-Blal, I. (2008) *An exploration of the construct of control in expansion strategies of hotel chains: a multiple case-study.* Doctoral thesis, Virginia Polytechnic Institute and State University.

Gonzalez, C. and Jareno, F. (2014) Financial analysis of the main hotel chains of the Spanish tourism sector. *Regional and Sectoral Economic Studies*, 14(2), 90–108.

Guilding, C. (2003) Hotel owner/operator structures: implications for capital budgeting process. *Management Accounting Research*, 14(3) 179–99.

Hales, J.A. (2011) *Accounting and Financial Analysis in the Hospitality Industry*. New Jersey: Pearson.

Harris, P. and Mongiello, M. (2012) *Accounting and Financial Management. Developments in the International Hospitality Industry*. Oxford: Routledge.

Hyatt Hotels Corporation (2015) Financial reports. Online. Available HTTP: <http://investors.hyatt.com/investor-relations/financial-reporting/annual-reports/default.aspx>, accessed 20 April, 2015.

Ivanova, M. (2013) Affiliation to hotel chains as a development opportunity for Bulgarian hotels. (Unpublished Doctoral dissertation.) University of Economics-Varna, Bulgaria. Online. Available HTTP: <http://ssrn.com/abstract=2346377>.

Nijs, D. (2014) *Imagineering the Butterfly Effect, Transformation by Inspiration*. Amsterdam: 11 International Publishing.

Puetz-Willems, M. (2015) Hotel industry 2015: between mainstream and mindset. *Hospitality Inside Special, Berlin: ITB*. Online. Available HTTP: <http://www.hospitalityinside.com/downloads/article_3_hospitalityInside_SPECIAL_ITB_2015_engl_FINAL.pdf>.

Roth, H. and Fishbin, M. (2015) Global hospitality insights: top thoughts for 2015. Report EYG no. DF0196. EY Hospitality. Available HTTP: <http://www.ey.com/Publication/vwLUAssets/ey-global-hospitality-insights-2015/$FILE/ey-global-hospitality-insights-2015.pdf>, accessed 31 March, 2015.

Rutherford, D.G. and O'Fallon, M.J. (2011) *Hotel management and Operations*. (5th ed.). Hoboken, New Jersey: Wiley.

Schmidgall, R. (1989) Financial ratios: perceptions of lodging industry general managers and financial executives. *FIU Hospitality Review*, 7(2), 1–9.

Šušić, V. (2009) The development and territorial allocation of hotel chains in the world. *Economics and Organization*, 6(3), 313–23.

Tidikova, G. (2014) *The Impact of Sustainable Growth Indicators on Hotel's Financial Management*. Jyväskylä: JAMK.

Tsai, H., Pan, S. and Lee, J. (2010) Recent research in hospitality financial management. *International Journal of Contemporary Hospitality Management*, 23(7), 941–71.

29

Legal aspects of hotel chain management and operations

Vivien Ulu (ANGLIA RUSKIN UNIVERSITY, UK) *and*
Dirisa Mulindwa (UNIVERSITY OF SUNDERLAND, UK)

Introduction

The chapter provides an analysis of hotel management contracts with a focus on grievance areas of the contracts. Although the chapter does not deal with total property lease and franchise agreement in which the financial risk is placed on the operator and not the owner of the property or the brand owner respectively in any detail, section one of this chapter provides a brief overview of the related legal issues in franchise and total property lease. In the wake of growing legal disputes arising from hotel management contracts particularly from the USA and given the global nature of the hotel industry there is a need to examine the nature of the legal relationships in hotel chain management/operations. This is discussed in section 2 to provide a needed reality check on the legal issues. Section 3 focuses on the major contractual terms using experiences of hospitality legal practitioners and decided cases, while rights, responsibilities and liabilities arising from hotel management agreements (HMAs), in particular from the law of agency and fiduciary duties, are explored in section 4. Legal issues identified and the applicable legal principles covered in sections 3 and 4 are addressed in section 5 under drafting options and legal considerations. In section 6 the chapter offers an analysis of the current legal position of HMAs based on decided cases. The chapter concludes in section 7 with an analysis of the future of hotel management contracts, in particular HMAs.

Nature of legal relationships in hotel chain management and operations contracts

Today we have become accustomed to the tri-furcation of the hotel industry including franchises, leases and hotel management agreements (Moseley, 2005). The structure chosen will often depend on the nature and scale of investment by the hotel owners; it will also depend on land ownership. In many cases, where the hotel owners would rather minimise the obligations and responsibilities that are associated with land ownership, they usually prefer the HMA. Managing hotels on the owner's behalf inevitably gives rise to a wide range of complex commercial and legal issues.

Legal relationships in each of these structures vary depending on the extent to which pertinent rights, responsibilities and risks are transferable from one party to the contract to the other. The nature of these contracts is briefly examined below to put the discussion on the legal relationships created in context.

In a franchise, a branded hotel, mostly part of big chains such as Hilton, Marriott, Sheraton (as franchisors) enters into an agreement with a third party (the franchisee) to allow the franchisee to use its brand, operating systems, central reservation systems and marketing plan to run the hotel. The franchisee is charged a fee for the use of these facilities and bears the responsibility of funding the operations and running the business, in accordance with franchisor standards (Rushmore, 2002; Braun, 2004; Hayes and Ninemeier, 2005). A detailed discussion of franchise is provided in Chapter 12 of this text. In a total lease, a hotel management company/operator (referred to here as HMC) enters into contract to use the property of a third party (known as the lessor) to run the hotel business. The 'lessor' is neither involved in the management of the hotel nor in the funding of the hotel operations, but is paid rent for the premises which often includes furniture, fixtures and equipment (FF&E). Typically, financial risk in the hotel operation is therefore borne by the HMC (Rushmore, 2002). A detailed discussion of lease contract is provided in Chapter 15 of this text. The HMA model is where the owner of a hotel (this can also be a franchisee or lessee) enters into contract with a third party handing over the running of the hotel to this third party (Beals and Denton, 2005; Barth, 2012). The third party, typically an HMC, is paid for this service. In return, the hotel owner derives benefit from the expertise and experience of the HMC (Johnson, 1999; Butler and Braun, 2014). The financial risk involved in running the hotel remains that of the owner as operators are not responsible for funding the operations (deRoos, 2011; Butler and Braun, 2014).

There are two categories of HMC, first-tier and second-tier hotel management companies. Typically, hotel chains with brand names fall into the first tier while non-brand management companies fall under second tier. With a second-tier management agreement, the owner of a hotel property can obtain a brand name by entering into franchise agreement with a brand owner (Rushmore, 2002). In many respects an HMA with a first-tier hotel is a fused franchise agreement where the HMC provides services that a franchisor would have offered to the franchisee but this time the brand owner equally undertakes the management duties that would have fallen on the franchisee.

Whereas legal issues occur in all the above chain hotel–owner relationships, the focus of this chapter is on the HMA. In a franchise, the legal relationship between the hotel owner and the brand is founded on the contractual terms of the franchise agreement. In general, from a legal perspective, no agency is created between the parties, though it should be noted that economics theories explaining the continuing use of share contracts such as franchise place the franchisor as the principal and franchisee as the agent for that purpose (Lafontaine, 1992). Similarly, with a total lease contract, the legal relationship is governed by the tenancy agreement and generally, no agency is created between the parties (Rushmore, 2002). It is also common for a franchisee or a lessee to enter into another contract with a third party – handing over the running of the hotel to the HMC, so in this case the relationship will be governed by the management agreement (Brewer, 2003; Butler and Braun, 2014). The franchisee or lessee is in a tripartite contract. First contract is between the franchisor/lessor and the second contract is with a managing company/operators.

On the other hand, in the HMA, apart from the contractual terms, the relationship between the hotel owner and the operator is typically governed by the law of agency or the law relating to personal services or on independent contractor terms (Rushmore, 2002).

Under such agreements, the hotel operator works for the owner but with almost exclusive control over the property. The hotel owner's role is that of a sleeping partner until problems are encountered.

Terms in hotel management contracts

In the twenty-first century, hotel management agreements have become fine-tuned to the extent that legal issues are well developed and even the formats seem more and more similar. The relationship between hotel owners and operators has become sophisticated to the point where many contracts are now heavily negotiated documents covering a number of issues. The emergence of disputes between the two parties to these agreements has led to some issues becoming more important while at the same time new issues continually need to be addressed from both sides.

The significance of the provisions in the terms of the agreement is that rights, responsibilities and liabilities of the parties are defined therein (Johnson, 1999; Hayes and Ninemeier, 2005). Hotel management agreements are usually long and have become more complex in recent years, but the major dispute areas include the contract duration, fees, control, competition clause, dispute resolution and choice of law.

Contract duration

A contract term specifies the duration of the agreement; typically this will contain the initial and renewal terms. The success of the hotel is in both the operator and owner's interest, however in practice differences have emerged between the two parties over the terms of management agreements entered into as part of a 'sale and manage back' transaction. Operators usually prefer long initial terms and the ability to exercise several long renewal periods; on the other hand, the hotel owners prefer shorter periods with no specific renewal rights. With a franchise, 5–20 year terms are common (deRoos, 2011; DLA Piper, 2012), while the initial terms for a lease can be between 10–20 years, it is also common to have less than 10 years or over 20 years lease term, typically with two options for renewal for up to 5 years (deRoos, 2011).

Hotel management agreements are usually long-term arrangements. First-tier/hotel chain operators will often demand contract terms of a minimum of 10 years with provisions for extensions. Second-tier operators are often unable to negotiate lengths as long. Termination before the expiry of the duration of HMAs has been the subject of numerous litigations in the industry (Detlefsen and Glodz, 2013; Green and Hanif, 2013). The norm is that HMCs include a period of non-cancellation of the agreement. Therefore, hotel owners need to be careful that the Agreement does not frustrate their ability to exit should a suitable opportunity arise. The processes for allowing such exits in many cases require detailed negotiation and drafting to ensure that both parties are comfortable with the position. Owners can also incorporate a buy-out clause where a non-performing operator's contract can be terminated before the expiry of the contract for an agreed payment.

Right to terminate and power to terminate

Terms on termination will grant a right to the parties to terminate with cause (Green and Hanif, 2013). In practice it is not common to find a hotel management agreement with a provision that empowers the owner to terminate either at any time or on sale of the hotel without cause. On the few occasions the operator may agree to such a provision to be included in the agreement, the termination is conditional upon payment of compensation to the operator. In HMA, the norm is that the use of this right will result in a payment of two to three times the yearly management fee (deRoos and Berman, 2014).

A right to terminate arises from provisions specified in the agreement such as deficit-performance (Chen, 2009), but non-performance on the grounds of force majeure is excluded (McKendrick, 1995). However, in most cases, HMAs establish agency relationship and where agency is waived in the terms of agreement, the relationship will fall under personal services agreement, consequently the contract can be terminated at any time notwithstanding provisions to the contrary (Butler and Braun, 2014; McCarthy, 2013) as in the cases below.

In *FHR TB, LLC, et al. v. TB ISLE RESORT, LP., Case 1:11-cv-23115-DLG 62 FLSD Docket 10/14/2011* (hereafter referred to as 'Turnberry'), the Court described the situation succinctly when it stated that the use of this power by the hotel owner was tantamount to 'Yes, we're violating the notice and cure provisions of HMA, but we have the power to do this whenever we want because the agency is revocable, so go ahead and sue us if you don't like it' (Turnberry, p. 5).

Other important court decisions on the issue of termination include: *Rc/Pb, Inc. v. The Ritz-Carlton Hotel Company, L.L.C., Case No: 50 2011CA010071* (hereafter referred to as 'Ritz-Carlton'). In Ritz-Carlton, the owner of the hotel terminated the HMA with Marriott notwithstanding that the HMA contained a non-terminable provision. The court held that the owner had a right to terminate the contract on the grounds of breach of the HMA prior to the expiry of term.

Equally, in *Woolley v. Embassy Suites, Inc., 227 Cal. App. 3d 1520, 278 Cal.Rptr. 719 (Cal. Ct.App. 1991)*, the agreement provided that the contract could be terminated with cause, on notice, and made provision for any dispute arising between the parties to be referred first to arbitration. Woolley (the hotel owners) gave notice to terminate the HMA as per this provision. Embassy Suites (the HMC) obtained an injunction from a trial court restraining Woolley from terminating the contract until after the arbitration of the matter. Woolley appeal against the injunction was upheld.

However, termination outside the provisions of the HMA could result in a wrongful termination and, in turn, in damages (deRoos and Berman, 2014; Butler and Braun, 2014).

The courts, however, make exception on the use of the power to terminate in situations where the agency is coupled with an interest.

Agencies coupled with an interest

An exception to the position that agency is terminable at any time is where the agency is held to be coupled with an interest. For example, financial investments by an operator in the hotel will be regarded as an interest in the agency. For instance, in *Pacific Landmark Hotel, Ltd. v. Marriott Hotels, Inc., 23 Cal.Rptr. 2d 555 (Cal.Ct.App. 1993)* (hereafter referred to as *Pacific Landmark*), the trial court granted an injunction order to Marriott (the HMC) to bar the owners from terminating the operating contract before the expiry of the term. However, the owners' appeal against the decision was upheld, as Marriott could not establish a valid interest in the hotel, the basis of the Marriott claim being an investment and loan made by an affiliate. The court stated that the interest held by a separate entity other than the agent would not suffice, but affirmed that if an agent had proprietary right in the subject of the agency, in this case the hotel, that would make the HMA non-terminable. Doubts have been expressed as to whether other courts would follow this decision to deny the existence of an agency coupled with interest if the investment is by an affiliate of an HMC.

The decision in Turnberry (at 40–41) provides some clarity on the position. In that case the court stated that an investment interest held by the owner of a managing company (Fairmount) did not amount to proprietary interest; such an interest must be deemed as an interest held by a separate entity other than Fairmount. The court opined that for an argument that proprietary interest exist in the agency to stand that interest must be vested in the agent itself and not in another entity, thus affirming the decision in Pacific Landmark.

Use of waivers

An operator can avoid agency issues by entering into the agreement as an independent contractor, in this case the operator will neither work as an agent nor as employee of the owner. Legally such a party will be regarded as being in the business for itself; however, the courts may still find agency if the relationship can be construed as such.

Further, where an agency relationship cannot be established, the HMA will be deemed as a personal services agreement. Management services agreements are classified by law as personal services contracts. As in agency, none of the parties to a personal services contract can be forced to continue with the agreement. This means that a hotel owner, even if an agency cannot be established, can still terminate the contract at will and even if the termination amounts to a breach of the contract (Butler, 2013). The operator's relief will then be a remedy of damages for breach of contract. This position finds support in the decision of the court in *Marriott Intl., Inc. v Eden Roc, LLLP* 2013 *NY Slip Op 02013*, decided on 26 March, 2013 (hereafter referred to as 'Eden Roc').

Fees

Fees are the remuneration paid to the operator for the provision of services under the HMA. It is an expense for the hotel owners since it reduces their share of the return from the hotel business; on the other hand, this remuneration should motivate the operator to perform well. In a franchise, the franchisee pays an initial fee for the rights to use the trade name, service marks, goodwill and other franchise services; this could be a set fee or based on room charges or a royalty fee (based on gross revenues). Additionally, the franchisee pays fees (on gross revenues) for other services including marketing, reservation and loyalty programmes (deRoos, 2010; Rushmore et al., 2013). With a lease, a minimum rent is often capped and guaranteed. It is also possible to provide for 100 per cent variable rent payment based on room revenue. In this case, unlike an ordinary lease, the financial risk is shared between the parties (deRoos, 2011).

The typical fee structure in an HMA is based on a percentage of revenue and profit (deRoos, 2010); fees can be capped or made subject to attaining specific standards. Provisions for forfeiture of fees and restitutions of fees paid can also be incorporated. It should be noted that in the HMA the relationship between the operator and the owners is governed not only by management agreement but also by parallel arrangements such as licence, royalty or service agreements. Therefore, to come to the actual value hotel owners pay to the operator, it is also important to include the fee requirement of these parallel contracts. Legal issues develop from disagreements over how much is paid in fees particularly when all the parallel contracts are included. Management agreements need to be drafted in such a way that restricts the operator from incurring certain types of expenditure that may result in increased revenue and create a higher base fee which may not correspond to increased profits.

Control

Control is about defining the responsibilities of both the operator and the owners. With a lease, the lessor has less control over the lessee's handling of the property. Although the financial risk for repair and replacement of FF&E is on the lessee, the lessor bears the liability for property structural maintenance and other major repairs (deRoos, 2011; Rushmore, 2002). With a franchise, although the franchisee has control of the management of the hotel, the franchisor maintains significant control over the franchisee through responsibility to run the hotel in accordance with franchisor standards (deRoos, 2011).

Hotel management agreements usually specify the responsibilities of each party. Control of operations and managing of the hotel property are assigned to the HMCs. However, some HMAs will include a control clause covering areas requiring owners' consent including budget and operational review meetings. The owners may have greater control over the handling of the hotel property through contractual asset-management provisions. However, tensions usually arise when the question of who should be responsible for the residual risk is posed, in addition to who is responsible when action is required for tasks that are not assigned in the agreement.

Competition clause

A common provision in HMA is to place restrictions on operators from operating competing hotels, so the important issue here relates to the question of scope restrictions. The question, for example, is whether or not an agreement to manage an upscale hotel will be a ground for restricting the HMC from establishing or managing a budget facility in close proximity. Given the problems that arise from complying with a non-compete clause and the agency issues, provisions on geographical non-competition may be considered insufficient for the purpose of avoiding disputes on non-compete grounds. Such provisions must specify in detail the nature and the scope including non-competition by affiliates or through ownership changes of hotels in proximity. The termination of the HMC in the Ritz Carlton case discussed earlier was based on non-compliance with the operator's non-compete duties (Stroock, 2008). More recently, an approach to non-compete is to allow an HMC to operate other hotels in the HMA territory under a different name. With a franchise, non-compete is possible but not the norm and therefore there is no guarantee that a franchisee will obtain a territorial protection as a term of the contract (deRoos, 2011; Butler and Braun, 2014).

Dispute resolution

Typical provisions on how disputes are to be resolved include clauses on use of alternative dispute resolution (ADR), choice of law and subordination, non-disturbance and attornment agreements (SNDA). In many cases, disputes between hotel owners and operators are settled out of court and even disputes that begin life in courts are often withdrawn and settled out of court (McDaniel, 2008). Where ADR proceeding is employed effectively it can offer speedier resolution of the matter, less cost, access to opinions of industry experts, and often relationships between parties will be preserved, but the process in some cases can fail to offer any of these advantages. In the context of HMA, an arbitration clause is only useful if the operator contract has not been terminated. For an in-depth exploration of ADR see Blake et al. (2013); Mackie et al. (2007); and Boulle and Nesic (2001).

It is common to specify the law applicable to the agreement. A choice of law clause allows the parties to select the law deemed more favourable to giving effect to the express terms of the agreement. HMCs in the United States, for example, wishing to avoid agency law, may opt for the law of the State of Maryland. Also, HMAs typically incorporate SNDA to the effect that on insolvency of the owner, the lenders or new owners will recognise the legal rights of the operating companies (Eisen, 2012; Butler and Braun, 2014).

Rights and liabilities

Under normal circumstances, where none of the parties in a contract is a fiduciary to the other, each party acts in its own best interest within the terms of the contract. However, the HMA does not operate under this circumstance; the hotel management agreement creates a different type of legal relationship between the hotel owner and the hotel operator – an agency/fiduciary relationship (Moseley, 2005). The law of agency was considered viable in HMAs, as on insolvency of the owner the HMC sought protection from liabilities in the law of agency on the ground that it is merely acting as an agent of the principal and not for itself. This position informed the terms of the agreement and gave boost to operators deploying HMAs as a preferred business model.

This relationship has also been one of the main issues of contention between the two parties in the HMA, but it has repeatedly been held by the courts to create an 'agency' relationship. In the United Kingdom, the English common law has over the years developed legal principles that would apply to most agency situations. For instance, an agent is considered as a fiduciary with many responsibilities such as full disclosure, a duty of loyalty and non-competition (Carvalho, 2008). Generally, in an agency relationship, the principal consents to the agent acting on his/her behalf and gives authority to the agent to affect legal relationship between him/her and third parties. Consequently, the principal becomes liable to the third parties. A third party is any person other than the principal and his/her agent.

In the context of an HMA, a hotel operator is the agent of the hotel owner (the principal) and is therefore authorised to act on behalf of the owner in relation to the operation of the hotel. More importantly, agency grants the HMCs the authority to create legal relationships between the owners and third parties. In other words, a hotel owner is liable to third parties for the actions of the operator in this regard. Also important is that agency relationship is a fiduciary relationship, it operates on trust; both the operator and the hotel owner are bound by law to act in good faith in dealing with each other (Anson, 2010). In the context of a franchise, as earlier stated, generally no agency is created between the hotel chain/franchisor and franchisee by the franchise agreement; however where the franchisee gives the franchisor authority to act on its behalf in other respects and to create legal relations with third parties, for example in the central reservation system, purchasing agreements, competing with the franchisee even where there is no territorial protection, agency and fiduciary duties may be implied by law (Brewer, 2003). A similar agency position may arise in a total property lease although generally no agency is created between the lessor and the lessee.

Typically, parties to commercial transactions ought to be guided by the principle of caveat emptor (legal principle of buyer beware) hence ordinarily, the bargains a party to a contract can obtain will largely be determined by the bargaining position of each party. However, if agency and in turn fiduciary relationship is established as explained above, an agent is required by law to place the interest of the principal above his/her own interests. It is instructive to state that while an agent in a strong bargaining position can negotiate and waive aspects of the business transactions that are not in its interest, fiduciary duties can hardly be waived.

Instances of breach of fiduciary duties

- Agent negotiating discounts with suppliers and failing to pass this on to the principal.
- Non-disclosure of gains made from purchases, charging higher prices for supplies than its own business, allowing third parties to charge higher prices or restricting the choice of suppliers in order to benefit from the transaction.
- Competing with the principal by operating a similar business in the same location.
- Use of data and employee – the principal's rights may also be breached by the manner in which the operator uses information generated from operation of the hotel such as guest data and using the hotel as training ground for employees deployed at operator's other hotels.

Some of these grievance areas have been the cause of termination of HMAs (Moseley, 2005). For example in Ritz-Carlton, the operator (Marriott) was found to have breached its fiduciary duties to Ritz-Carlton by operating for a third party a similar upscale hotel (the Four Seasons) and in close proximity. The two hotels were approximately 7 kilometers apart. Equally, in *2660 Woodley Road Joint Venture v. ITT Sheraton Corp., 369F2d, 732, U.S. Court of Appeals, Third Circuit (2004)*, Sheraton (as the operator/agent of the owner) was found to have acted in a manner that placed its interest above that of the principal by, for example, failing to pass on discounts received from supplies to Woodley and competing with the principal by operating a similar business.

Also in *Town Hotels Limited Partnership v. Marriott International, Inc., 246 F.Supp. 469 (S.D. W. Va. Feb. 25, 2003)* the dispute with the management company (Marriott) and the owner concerned negotiating and receiving sponsorship funds, payments and rebates from the supplier without passing these on nor disclosing these arrangements to the hotel owner. The court found a breached of the agent's fiduciary duty and stated that Marriott in receiving these payments failed to put the interest of the principal above its own personal interest.

Drafting options – legal considerations

Some of the rights and duties implicit in management contracts that come with an agency relationship can be waived by a fully informed written consent, but others cannot be waived. Some operators have negotiated and included clauses that seek to waive agency relationship in the HMAs. And other operators like Marriott try to avoid the 'agency' label in their management agreements. However, it should be noted that couching HMAs in a manner that disclaims agency relationship by using terms such as independent contractor may not offer comfort to operators as courts tend to look into the substance of the agreements; therefore if the relationship purports to be an agency, the court will find agency irrespective of the wording of the contract. For practical purposes, HMAs will have to be couched in unequivocal terms to avoid the issues raised here.

The legal position is that personal services agreements cannot be specifically enforced. This means that where the terms are couched in such a manner that the operator is found not to be the agent of the owner but to act for itself, a dissatisfied owner can still terminate the contract prior to the end of the term, given that the owner cannot be forced to continue with the relationship. Consequently, the contract will still be terminable under the principles of law governing personal services contract, as management agreements are legally classified as personal services contracts. The position stated here finds support in the decision of the court in *Marriott Intl., Inc. v. Eden Roc, LLLP 2013 NY Slip Op 02013* decided on March 26, 2013 (hereafter referred to as Eden Roc) and in *FHR TB, LLC, et. al. v. TB ISLE RESORT, L.P., Case 1:11-cv-23115-DLG 62 FLSD Docket 10/14/2011*, (hereafter referred to as Turnberry). In Turnberry, the court upheld the ousting of the management company notwithstanding the contract had up to 50 years of life and was stated as non-terminable. However, in *M Waikiki LLC v. Marriott hotel services Case 1:11-cv-06488, NYS/2011*' although the facts were similar to Turnberry in that the owner of the hotel terminated an irrevocable management contract with a 30 years span to go, in this case, the court ordered a reinstatement of the ousted operator (Berzon and Hudson, 2011; Butler and Braun, 2014).

From the above cases, whether or not a contract which expressly states that it is irrevocable will be held as such will depend on court interpretation. The terms of the contract and the governing law of the management contract appear immaterial. The two cases discussed were governed by the same law of New York State, but the courts arrived at different decisions. It remains to be seen whether or not the decision in Eden Roc will provide consistency on the legal position and needed judicial precedent on this matter. In that case the court stated that even if the relationship between the hotel owner and the operator were not governed by agency, the HMA being a personal services contract would still be revocable at will.

The legal position on HMAs from analysis of decided cases

Provisions placing obligations on the parties to give notice prior to revocation of the contract or to submit disputes to arbitration or making early termination subject to arbitration approval will not restrict the court from giving effect to a revocation in breach of these provisions. In the Turnberry case, revocation action contravened a similar provision when without notice, or arbitration hearing, Turnberry owners expelled Fairmount (the HMC) and yet the revocation was allowed by the court. Turnberry arbitrarily revoked the HMA in question without any formal notice of its intention, alleging that Fairmount 'mismanaged and inadequately marketed the resort'. But the HMA term provided for an initial 25 year term and for five more extensions of 5 years – effectively a term of 50 years. Equally, the contract term stated that the hotel owner was under obligation to give 30 days' notice to the operator prior to revocation of the contract. Terms of the HMA also required that the operator was given an opportunity to remedy any breach of the term. In other words, the right to terminate would arise after the 30 days' notice has been honoured and the operator had failed to remedy the breach. However, the HMA specifically chose New York State Law as the applicable law which grants owners the power to revoke at will. The legal position as stated in Turnberry 'is that the principal has the power to revoke the agency even if the revocation is wrong, even if it breaches the contract and even if the revocation creates liability for damages'.

The courts also distinguished 'between powers, rights and duties arising under the contract creating the agency such as in HMAs and powers, rights and duties arising under the agency, thus while a principal has the power to revoke the agency at will, the principal will be liable to the agent for breach of the contract' (Turnberry at 34). A distinction between power to revoke and the right to revoke an agency was also made by the court in Pacific Landmark.

Power to revoke is exercisable outside the contract term while the right to terminate arises under the contract terms. A right to revoke will provide contractual conditions under which the right can be exercised while the power to terminate exists without conditions (Turnberry at 35, 37).

- A provision stating that the agency is coupled with an interest will not suffice. The agent must have actual interest in the property, as a mere description that agency is coupled with an interest will not suffice (Moseley, 2005). Operator's financial achievements will not constitute a valid proprietary interest.
- Provisions granting the operator a right to acquire the hotel property if the hotel is to be sold will not suffice as a proprietary right as stated in the Turnberry case, nor a right to invest in future development of the hotel. Legally, both the right of first offer and right to invest in future development of the property are contingent rights not actual rights. With the right of first offer and right to invest in developments, agent's interest can only be triggered if the property is up for sale or if the opportunity arises for developing the property respectively, therefore the rights cannot be regarded as existing proprietary interest (Skoblo and Haragovitch, 2012; Smith, 2012). Equally, where the proprietary right is vested in an affiliate of the agent such an interest will not suffice. The position in law is that the property interest must be held by the agent itself not an affiliate, as property interest and agent must be vested in one entity (Turnberry at 41 and Pacific Landmark case, the appeal court decision). The rationale for this is that three separate entities are involved where an affiliate or a subsidiary has a vested interest. The principal, the agent and the affiliate or subsidiary but the agency is between two of the entities, the hotel owner and the operator. In Pacific Landmark case, although a subsidiary of Marriott owned 5 per cent in Pacific and granted $8million loan to the hotel owner, the court held that Marriott agency was not coupled with an interest; the proprietary right being vested in a separate entity (*Pacific Landmark case* at 620, 624–27).
- In addition, provision for the parties to obtain a remedy of specific performance for anticipatory or actual breach of the agreement or termination prior to expiry of the term may not be upheld by the courts. In Turnberry, the HMA contained provisions barring early termination and provided for specific performance. These provisions failed to sway the court to grant an injunctive relief or specific performance.
- Equally a provision to waive an owner's power to terminate by stating that damages will not be adequate remedy for injury to the operator's reputation may not prevent the courts from allowing the termination. In Turnbery, the HMA contained a provision to the effect that damages will not be an acceptable compensation for termination outside the contract term.
- Any provision to restrict the courts from making judgments that are in conflict with the express terms of the HMAs may not stand. For example, a provision to the effect that the express terms of the agreement shall supersede any contrary implied term of the HMAs governing law (Turnberry at 13).

Conclusion

The future of HMAs fundamentally lies with the implications of the power to terminate and the legal position on the remedy of injunctive relief. The determination from the cases used in this chapter demonstrated implication on HMAs, now and into the future. The question as to whether or not the court will grant an injunction order to reinstate an operator, pending the outcome of an arbitration proceeding or to allow first an attempt to resolve the dispute before an arbitration panel, must be reconsidered. The position at present is that such an injunction will be denied unless the operator can prove that the agency is non-terminable. These court decisions have also redefined not only the expectations of both the hotel owners and the operators but also the relationship between the two parties involved in the hotel management contract. These decisions have also demonstrated that what in the past was considered as irrevocable contracts that the courts would enforce with an order for specific performance, can now be revoked, albeit with the risk of damage awards. Case law establishes that a hotel owner, as a general rule, has the power to revoke the HMA at will. The exercise of this power outside the terms of the agreement will amount to a breach of the contract and will give the operator a right to damages whether under agency or personal services contract.

The cases in this chapter have also demonstrated that regardless of how the hotel management contract is written, if it creates a principal agency relationship and responsibilities, such a contract will be subject to the Law of Agency. Whereas the agency mechanism in HMAs was initiated by hotel chain operators to enable them to have total control of the hotel with minimal financial risks, over the years it has turned into a 'beast' in the legal ecosystem of hotel management. Where disagreements occur, the fiduciary duties of the operator go under a microscopic scrutiny and have been central in some of the high profile law suits in the industry.

The challenge for both the hotel operators and owners is to develop ways and means to allow disagreements to be resolved amicably. Otherwise, there could be significant increase in litigation relating to hotel management contracts. Undoubtedly, it is in the interest of both parties in the HMA to include in the hotel management contract mechanisms that seek to resolve disputes internally before either party is able to refer the dispute externally.

References

Anson, W.R. (2010) *Principles of the English Law of Contract and of Agency in Its Relation to Contract*, US: Gale Ecco, Making of Modern Law.

Barth, S. (2012) *Hospitality Law: Managing Legal Issues in the Hospitality Industry*, 4th edn. New York: John Wiley & Sons.

Beals, P. and Denton, G. (2005) The current balance of power in North American hotel management contracts. *Journal of Retails & Leisure Property*, 4(2), 129–45.

Berzon, A. and Hudson, K. (2011) Marriott Loses Trendy Waikiki hotel as owner changes locks overnight. Wall Street Journal. Online. Available HTTP: <http://online.wsj.com/news/articles/SB100014240 5311190419940457653714048896155 6?mg=reno64wsj&url=http%3A%2F%2Fonline.wsj.com%2F article%2FSB1000142405311190419940457653714048896155 6.html>, accessed 30 July, 2014.

Blake S., Browne J. and Sime S. (2013) *The Jackson ADR Handbook*, Oxford: Open University Press.

Boulle, L. and Nesic, M. (2001) *Mediation: Principles, Process, Practice*. London: Butterworth-Heinemann.

Braun, R. (2004) *Hotel Franchise Agreements: Opportunities and Pitfalls*. Global Hospitality Group. Online. Available HTTP: <http://www.hotelonline.com/News/PR2004_3rd/Sept04_FranchiseAgreements. htm>, accessed 28 July 2014.

Brewer, W. III (2003) Franchisees and shareholders: the next wave of hotel litigation. *Cornell Hotel and Restaurant Administration Quarterly*, 44(3), 77–88.

Butler, J. (2013) Marriott loses Appeal in Eden Roc Case: why all long-term hotel management agreements are now terminable, *Hotel Lawyers*. Online. Available HTTP: <http://www.mondaq. com/unitedstates/x/231718/Hotels+Hospitality/Marriott+loses+appeal+in+Eden+Roc+case+ Why+all+longterm+hotel anagement+agreements+are ow+terminable>, accessed_30 July 2014.

Butler, J. and Braun, R. (2014) *The Hotel Management Agreements and Franchise Agreement Handbook*. 3rd edn. Los Angeles: JMBM Global Hospitality Group.

Carvalho, A. (2008) Contracting out of fiduciary relationships is engagement letters: the citigroup. *Trust and Trustees*, 14(6), 406–41.

Chen, T. (2009) Performance measurement of an enterprise and business units with an application to a Taiwanese hotel chain. *International Journal of Hospitality Management*, 28(3), 415–22.

deRoos, J.A. (2010) Hotel management contracts – past and present. *Cornell Hospitality Quarterly*, 51(1), 68–80.

deRoos, J.A. (2011) Gaining maximum benefit from franchise agreements, management contracts, and leases. In M.C. Sturman, J.B. Corgel and R. Verma (eds), *The Cornell School of Hotel Administration on Hospitality: Cutting Edge Thinking and Practice*. New Jersey: John Wiley & Sons, pp. 293–307.

deRoos, J. A. and Berman, S. (2014) Calculating damage awards in hotel management agreement terminations. *Cornell Hospitality Reports*, 14(16), 6–16.

Detlefsen, H. and Glodz, M. (2013) Historical trends – hotel management contracts, Chicago: HVS. Online. Available HTTP: <http://www.hotelnewsresource.com/pdf11/HVS022013.pdf>, accessed 30 July 2014.

DLA Piper (2012) Hotel franchising in Europe. DLA Piper. Online. Available HTTP: <https://www.dlapiper.com/~/media/Files/Insights/Publications/2012/02/Hotel%20franchising%20in%20Europe/Files/Hotel_Franchising_in_Europe/FileAttachment/Hotel_Franchising_in_Europe.pdf>, accessed 30 July 2014.

Eisen D. (2012) Management contracts put under the microscope. Online. Available HTTP: <http://www.hotelmanagement.net/operator-owner/management-contracts-put-under-the-microscope-17184>, accessed 19 August 2014.

Green S. and Hanif S. (2013) Major issues in hotel management agreements. Charles Russell Speechlys. Online. Available HTTP: <http://www.charlesrussellspeechlys.com/updates/publications/real-estate-construction-new/major-issues-in-hotel-management-agreements/>, accessed 12 July, 2014.

Hayes, D.K and Ninemeier, J.D (2005) *Hotel Operations Management*, 2nd edn. London: Pearson.

Johnson, K. (1999) Hotel management contract terms. *Cornell Hotel and Restaurant Administration Quarterly*, 40(2), 34–39.

Lafontaine, F. (1992) Agency theory and franchising: some empirical results. *The RAND Journal of Economics*, 23(2), 263–283.

Mackie K., Miles D., Marsh W. and Allen T. (2007). *The ADR Practice Guide: Commercial Dispute Resolution*, 3rd edn. London: Tottel.

McCarthy, A. (2013) United States: hotel management agreement termination disputes: is there shelter from the storm? Mondaq. Online. Available HTTP: <http://www.mondaq.com/unitedstates/x/269982/Hotels+Hospitality/Hotel+Management+Agreement+Termination+Disputes+Is+There+Shelter+from+the+Stor>, accessed 30 July 2014.

McDaniel, K.C. (2008) *Current Issues in the Negotiation of Hotel Management Agreements. Modern Real Estate Transaction*. Philadelphia: American Law Institute and the American Bar Association.

McKendrick, E. (1995) *Force Majeure and Frustration of Contract, GB*, 2nd edn. London: Informa Law from Routledge.

Moseley, D. (2005) Hotel management agreements: industry trends and today's issues. Paper presented at the Third Hospitality Law Conference, USA. Online. Available HTTP: <http://hospitalitylawyer.com/wp-content/uploads/Management_Contracts-Article4.pdf>, accessed 30 July 2014.

Rushmore S. (2002) *Hotel Investments Handbook*, New York: HVS International. Online. Available HTTP: <http://www.hvs.com/emails/rushletter/Hotel%20Investments%20Handbook/Hotel%20Investments%20Handbook.pdf>, accessed 12 July, 2014.

Rushmore. S, Choi, J.I., Lee, T.Y. and Mayer, J.S. (2013) *2013 United States Hotel Franchising Fee Guide*. New York: HVS publication. Online. Available HTTP: <http://www.hvs.com/article/6306/2013-united-states-hotel-franchise-fee-reference-guide/>, accessed 10 December, 2015.

Skoblo, A. and Haragovitch, A. (2012) The hotel operator's fiduciary duty to the owner. *The Moscow Times*. Online. Available HTTP: <http://www.themoscowtimes.com/business/business_for_business/article/tmt/472173.html>, accessed 30 July 2014.

Smith, H. (2012) *A Legal Guide to Investing in the UK for Foreign Investors*. 4th edn. London: Herbert Smith LLP.

Stroock (2008) Non-competition clauses and their effect on multi-brand hotel competition: an update. *Stroock Hospitality Industry Practice Group Special Bulletin*. Online. Available HTTP: <http://www.stroock.com/SiteFiles/Pub648.pdf>, accessed 10 December, 2015.

Cases

1. *FHR TB, LLC, et al. v. TB ISLE RESORT, LP., Case 1:11-cv-23115-DLG 62 FLSD Docket 10/14/2011.* Online. Available HTTP: <http://hotellaw.jmbm.com/files/2014/03/Fairmont-v-Turnberry-Court-decsion-10-14-11-and-opinion-.pdf>.
2. *Marriott Intl., Inc. v. Eden Roc, LLLP 2013 NY Slip Op 02013.* Decided on March 26, 2013.
3. *M Waikiki LLC v. Marriott hotel services Case 1:11-cv-06488, NYS /2011*
4. *RC/PB, INC., v. The Ritz-Carlton Hotel Company, L.L.C., CASE NO: 50 2011CA010071*
5. *2660 Woodley Road Joint Venture v. ITT Sheraton Corp., 369F2d, 732,* U.S. Court of Appeals, Third Circuit (2004)
6. *Town Hotels Limited Partnership v. Marriott International, Inc., 246 F.Supp. 469* (S.D.W.Va. Feb. 25, 2003).
7. *Pacific Landmark Hotel, Ltd. v. Marriott Hotels, Inc., 23 Cal.Rptr. 2d 555* (Cal.Ct.App. 1993).
8. *Woolley v. Embassy Suites, Inc., 227 Cal. App. 3d 1520, 278 Cal.Rptr. 719* (Cal.Ct.App. 1991).

A productivity analysis
of a chain of hotels

Carlos Pestana Barros (UNIVERSITY OF LISBON, PORTUGAL) *and*
Luiz Pinto Machado (UNIVERSIDADE DA MADEIRA AND CEFAGE CENTRE FOR ADVANCED
STUDIES IN MANAGEMENT AND ECONOMICS, UNIVERSITY OF ÉVORA, PORTUGAL)

Introduction

The analysis of hotel efficiency and productivity is a well-established line of research in tourism, which was initiated by Baker and Riley (1994), who analysed the hotel industry with ratios, and later Anderson et al. (1999) who analysed hotels in the USA with a DEA model. Brown and Ragsdale (2002) applied the DEA analysis of hotels in the USA, whilst Huang and Chang (2003) applied DEA models to Taiwanese hotels; Barros (2004) analysed the Portuguese ENATUR hotels chain; Chiang et al. (2004) continued the analysis of Taiwanese hotels and Barros (2005a,b) then analysed the ENATUR hotels with a DEA model. This initial phase used DEA and stochastic models that were innovative at the time of publication, but are nowadays somewhat out-of-date. These papers initiated policy prescriptions for improving efficiency and productivity in the hotel industry.

Following on from these initial papers in tourism efficiency and productivity, a huge number of papers have been published on hotels, using alternative DEA and SFA models, and alternative hotel samples (Cracolici et al., 2007; Barros, 2005a; Peypoch and Solonandrasana, 2008; Lionetti, 2010). Efficiency is defined as being the position of the hotel in the frontier of production possibilities. Some hotels are efficient and stay at the frontier, while others are inefficient and stay below the frontier. The only way to exit a position of inefficiency, below the frontier, is to implement adjustment measures in order to improve efficiency and thus avoid technical bankruptcy. Productivity is the rate at which goods or services are produced relative to the inputs used. A common measure of productivity is the ratio of output per unit of labour used for production (Barros, 2005a,b). Productivity change is the change in total output relative to the change in total inputs, and it is composed of technical efficiency change (managerial practices and scale effects) and technological change (innovation and investment in new technologies). The analysis of efficiency is common (Baker and Riley, 1994; Wijeysinghe, 1993; Brotherton and Mooney 1992; Donaghy et al., 1995), but the analysis of productivity is rare (Hu and Cai, 2004; Jones and Siag, 2009).

The previous studies on ENATUR, which was formerly a public company, reported significant levels of inefficiency, suggesting that structural changes were needed to improve performance. It is worth noting that during the period of analysis of the study of Barros

(2004), ENATUR was still a hotel chain operated by the State, but as from September 2003 it became a concession of the Pestana Hotels private hotel group, which is Portugal's premier international tourism and leisure group, currently with a portfolio of nearly 95 four- and five-star hotels worldwide.

The International Monetary Fund, as well as the World Bank, the Central European Bank and the European Union, all use privatisation as part of their structural adjustment programmes. The main objective of privatisation is to improve organisational efficiency (Bishop et al., 1994; Boyco et al., 1996). Hence, the privatisation of ENATUR was motivated by continuous significant losses and followed a line of privatisations that was in operation all over the world, and was recommended by various regulatory institutions of world economies.

The motivation of the present research is to analyse productivity in a chain of hotels, focusing again on ENATUR and the changes undertaken by incorporating it into the Pestana hotel chain. This chapter uses data envelopment analysis (DEA) and aims to calculate Malmquist indices for three measures of interest: productivity growth, technical progress (catch up) and efficiency change (innovation). Productivity growth is the overall measure of productivity, which is also referred to as the Malmquist index, and it is defined as being the sum of technical progress and efficiency change. Technical progress and efficiency change can be decomposed into their constituents and in the present case, efficiency change is decomposed into its constituents, namely: OBTECH (output-biased technological change), which is a measure of output changes caused by technological progress, IBTECH (input-biased technological change), which is a measure of input changes due to technological progress, and MATHECH (residual efficiency change), which is the residual change in technological progress, a change that is not attributed to inputs or output changes which is therefore a measure of innovation. These components of technological progress enable the capture of the causes of technological progress. Therefore, the methodology adopted in this context is generic and it permits the decomposition of the innovation that is measured by technological change, and also obtains a clear description of the ENATUR hotels, which are closer to the industry frontier, due to stiff competition. Finally, the increase in competition and globalisation among hotels signifies that this is an activity in a very competitive sector, and that productivity is a central issue in this context, as only efficient hotels can survive in a competitive environment, as they are the ones that capture a higher market share and have better financial results.

Empirical setting

Pousadas de Portugal intends to 'accommodate visitors and provide them with food in accordance with the style of each region' (Pousadas de Portugal, 2014). It is unknown who originally designed the concept and the model of the system of management and operation of the Pousadas, but it is probable that the concept was modelled on the Spanish 'Paradores', which is an initiative of the National Tourist Board, a public body of the kingdom of Spain, which was created by King Alfonso XIII in 1928, to restore, preserve and disseminate the historical, cultural and ethnographic heritage of Spain. In current Portuguese, the term 'Pousada' evokes the idea of a break or a pause. In a certain way, it devolves the sense of art and pleasure in travelling. Although not identical in all aspects, the perception of the concept of the Pousada seems to deserve some consensus among the economic players and society of the 1940s. The Pousadas chain were thought of as being small tourist establishments, with a philosophy of economic exploitation from attracting potential tourists, based on the reproduction of local and regional idiosyncrasies. Originally the project was to build ten hotels in locations with regional characteristics, with a capacity of 10 to 15 rooms, assuming that they would be built by the State and that their management would be subcontracted to individuals, under the overall supervision of the chain (Abrantes, 2012).

The first unit of the network was inaugurated in 1942 in Elvas (on the Portugal/Spain border), in the Alentejo region, which currently has the largest number of 'Historic Pousadas'. Other 'Regional Pousadas' were inaugurated, always with a limited number of rooms, and special attention was given to the cuisine of each region. In the 1950s, the concept of the Pousada was extended, with the emergence of the 'Historic Pousadas', which were installed in historic buildings and monuments, such as castles, convents and monasteries. As a result of the political, social and industrial change that occurred after the revolution of April 1974, mainly in 1975, the Pousadas de Portugal hotels underwent severe upheaval. Some were practically abandoned by their operators, whilst others maintained the status quo, or reverted to self-management, but all, without exception, experienced moments of economic and financial difficulty, to which were added the difficulties of a downturn in the demand for tourism. Thus, the Portuguese authorities found the need to create conditions that would allow for a balanced system of management, based on maintaining the profitability of the existing tourist infrastructure. The government decided to set up a department to manage publicly operated tourism and to supervise the management of all State companies involved in tourism. Hence, in 1976, it passed a law creating ENATUR – the National Tourism Company, EP.

The Portuguese Government and ENATUR (since 1976) held the assets of the Pousadas and managed them for the best part of six decades. In 2003, ENATUR had 44 hotels, of which 18 were in historic buildings, and also two restaurants. In 1995 the American Society of Travel Agents (ASTA) and the Smithsonian Foundation, awarded the Pousadas de Portugal their annual award for institutions around the world that had the most significant role in defending the environment and cultural heritage for tourism purposes. In 2003, the Portuguese Government addressed a situation of accumulated net losses for over a decade, and decided to privatise the company and assign the management in line with the widespread privatisation of State-owned organisations across the world.

Other privatisation initiatives have taken place in different industries, such as banking, telecommunications and energy, and new processes of privatisation are planned for the transport, postal delivery and television industries. In September 2003, Pestana Pousadas Group (GPP) assumed the responsibility for operating ENATUR for a period of 15 years, with an equity share of 49 per cent, whilst the State agency, Turismo de Portugal, held 51 per cent. As part of the Ministry of the Economy, Innovation and Development, Turismo de Portugal is the national tourism authority and it is responsible for the promotion, enhancement and sustainability of tourism. Starting with a 300-bedroom hotel in the island of Madeira in Portugal in 1972 (which was operated by the Sheraton in the first decade), the Pestana family owns the Pestana Group, which has grown steadily and is currently comprised of nearly 95 four- and five-star hotels worldwide, with two brands: Pestana Hotels & Resorts and the Pousadas de Portugal.

The company is now Portugal's largest international tourism and leisure group and is one of the largest in Europe, ranking 25th. Currently it employs 7,000 collaborators worldwide, with eight business divisions operating under the Pestana brand: Hotels & Resorts, Pousadas de Portugal, Holiday Ownership, Gaming, Travel, Golf and Residence, Industry and the International Business Centre of Madeira (Pestana Hotel Group, 2015). Table 30.1 summarises the key characteristics of the ENATUR hotels under analysis.

Table 30.1 Characteristics of the analysed ENATUR hotels (average from 2000 to 2013)

Number	Location	Hotel name	Number of rooms	Number of employees
1	Marão	S. Gonçalo	35	31
2	V. do Minho	S. Teotónio	20	24
3	Gerês	S. Bento	32	42
4	Guimarães	Nª. Sª. Oliveira	32	29
5	V.N. Cerveira	D. Dinis	35	34
6	Guimarães	Sta. Marinha	24	28
7	V. do Castelo	M. Sta. Luzia	33	27
8	Amares	Sta. M. do Bouro	32	39
9	Braga	S. Vicente	51	24
10	Manteigas	S. Lourenço	29	19
11	Bragança	S. Bartolomeu	28	23
12	Alijó	B. de Forrester	26	20
13	V. Pouca da Beira	C. Desagravo	16	28
14	Óbidos	Castelo	28	22
15	Murtosa	Ria	36	35
16	Condeixa	Sta. Cristina	21	18
17	Ourém	Conde de Ourém	21	22
18	Proença a Nova	Amoras	21	24
19	Viseu	Viseu	28	24
20	Freixo	Freixo	12	14
21	Setúbal	S. Filipe	25	25
22	Palmela	Palmela	44	30
23	Queluz	D. Maria I	25	31
24	Elvas	Sta. Luzia	29	29
25	Évora	Loios	16	21
26	Estremoz	Sta. Isabel	21	20
27	S.Clara a Velha	Sta .Clara	15	16
28	Marvão	Sta. Maria	29	27
29	Torrão	Vale do Gaio	12	17
30	Sousel	S. Miguel	10	12
31	S.T. do Cacém	Q. da Ortiga	19	19
32	Alvito	C. de Alvito	16	19
33	Beja	S. Francisco	33	30
34	Crato	Flor da Rosa	39	37
35	Arraiolos	Nª. Sª. Assunção	29	12
36	V. Viçosa	D. João IV	13	14
37	Alcácer do Sal	D. Alfonso II	18	21
38	S.B. Alportel	S. Brás	32	24
39	Sagres	Infante	19	21
40	Tavira	C. Graça	14	14
41	Estoi	Estoi	16	24
42	Faial Açores	Sta. Cruz	48	22
43	Terceira/Angra	S. Sebastião	27	19

Source: values computed based on the data obtained ENATUR.

Literature review

The competitiveness of industry and firms has been one of the most important themes of research in the fields of economics and business studies. The competitiveness of a country is derived from the performance of its enterprises (Barros, 2004). Although the concept of the competitiveness of nations was initially proposed by economists (e.g., Porter, 1998), the term has also gained importance as a subject of study among management scholars during the last decade. Most empirical studies on competitiveness at industry level have been related to manufacturing and related sectors, and only recently have some researchers started to examine the international competitiveness of the service sector, with a particular focus on tourist resorts and the hotel industry, which deserves a systematic and critical review (Tsai et al., 2009). Competitiveness is related to efficiency and productivity. Efficiency is the position of the hotels in the frontier of production possibilities (Varian, 1987), with some hotels in the frontier and others below it, signifying that those below it are less efficient than those hotels situated on the frontier. Productivity is defined as being a change in the frontier of best practice for two consecutive years. Therefore efficiency and productivity are related.

Destination competitiveness is a destination's ability to perform better than other destinations in the delivery of goods and services. A large number of variables are linked to the notion of destination competitiveness. They can be quantitative, such as: the number of visitors, market share, tourist expenditure, employment, value added by the tourism industry; or qualitatively measurable variables, such as: richness of culture and heritage, the quality of tourism services, etc. (Omerzel, 2006).

At a national or regional level, competitiveness is the result of the performance of companies at an operational level and it is viewed in terms of the size of an enterprise's market share (Begg, 1999; Porter, 1998; Krugman, 1996).

With regards to privatisation, Barros (2004) argued that when the company was still State-owned:

> The role of the government as a provider of tourism services restricted the expansion of the private sector. The planned privatisation of ENATUR is a sound public policy, insofar as it maintains the historical and architectural heritage, while allowing the chain to be managed from a market-oriented, commercial perspective. . . . reflects the drive away from nationalised industry on which the country embarked some years ago, and owes much to European integration. . . . The Single Market Programme is a vital component of the plan of convergence of EU national economies in prices and costs, and its emphasis is on competitiveness. The introduction of the Euro has removed the possibility of national governments using currency devaluation to correct their public deficits, whilst the Maastricht Treaty places restrictions on the deficits in financing public services, including State-owned hotels. These policies oblige EU-member governments to privatise industries.

The analysis of hotel efficiency is restricted to a small number of studies. Among the earliest, Baker and Riley (1994) propose the use of ratios to analyse the performance of the hotel industry. Wijeysinghe (1993) suggests the use of break-even analysis to discern the effectiveness of tourism management. Brotherton and Mooney (1992) and Donaghy et al. (1995) apply yield management to analyse the efficiency of hotel management.

Such studies are clearly very few for such an important tourism issue in the market context, particularly when compared with other fields of research, such as banking

(Berger and Humphrey, 1997). Moreover, Anderson et al. (1999) present a stochastic frontier model. The present chapter intends to enlarge on the economics of tourism in this specific respect and to call the attention of other researchers to this neglected area.

Hathroubi et al. (2014) proposed a performance evaluation of Tunisian hotels, taking into account their environmental management practices, and concluded that environmentally responsible attributes may enhance a hotel's efficiency. Their findings identify several drivers of efficiency in Tunisian hotels. The principal driver is visible environmental policies, such as the hotel's respect for the natural surroundings in which it is situated. Managers benefit if they help conserve the authenticity of the hotel site. Thus this result adds an element to the previous analysis of Lee et al. (2010). These authors highlighted the fact that a 'green' hotel's overall image can contribute to more favourable behavioural intentions. It seems that the authenticity of the location of the hotel adds real economic value, as it is the first efficient driver. Moreover, hotels that use clean or renewable energies and those that have implemented ISO 140001 certification, are more efficient. These results are consistent with previous studies, such as that of Scalon (2007), which stresses the real need to establish this certification. Thus, environmentally friendly approaches help hotels save money, improve their competitiveness, and earn environmentally-concerned consumer certification, all of which enable them to be more efficient.

Perrigot et al. (2009) studied the eventual superiority, in terms of performance, of plural form chains, compared to the predominantly franchised or company-owned ones. Instead of working in an internal benchmarking perspective (unit level), their study is built on an external benchmarking perspective and is innovative, as most previous authors have just focused on the unit level.

They argue that the first contribution when applying DEA at chain level is the comparison of several organisational forms for chains (plural form, predominantly franchised and predominantly company-owned), and also their different impact on chain performance. Researchers and practitioners are interested in such a comparison, and in knowing more about plural form efficiency in comparison to predominantly franchised and company-owned chains. The second contribution of the DEA application at chain level is strategic, and concerns the development of an external benchmarking. This is particularly useful for chain managers when they have to adapt their chain and their managerial practices to the competitive environment in which they operate.

The paper highlighted the advantage, in terms of performance, and more specifically efficiency, of mixing both franchising and company ownership within the same hotel chain. Indeed, plural form hotel chains have higher overall and technical efficiency scores than predominantly franchised ones, and higher overall efficiency scores than predominantly company-owned ones. Moreover, plural form hotel chains are often referred to as benchmarks for the efficiency improvement of inefficient hotel chains.

Although the hotel industry performed relatively well in 2009, the average occupancy rate, average room rate, average revenue per available room and total gazetted hotel room revenue all declined significantly in comparison to 2008. Brown and Dev (2000) suggest that operation productivity by hotels changes when there is a change in economic conditions. Hence, it is important to obtain a measurement of efficiency for evaluating the performance of the hotel industry in Portugal over a given time period. With such a measurement, information about the hotel sector and its contribution to the country's economy can be obtained.

Methodology

This chapter estimates the total factor productivity change for ENATUR hotels using DEA, estimating a productivity Malmquist index, (Malmquist, 1953). Furthermore, we aim to analyse the decomposition of the technological change for the same companies in order to see whether they show Hicks-neutral technological change. Finally, we plan to see whether the regulation does not change ENATUR hotels' productivity ranking, in order to see if it is effective in the short run.

The Malmquist index (MALM) is traditionally decomposed in technical efficiency change (EFFCH) and technological change (TECH). Technical efficiency change (EFFCH) is further decomposed in pure efficiency change (PURE) and scale efficiency change (SCALE). PURE change is attributed to managerial effects and scaled to the company dimension in terms of its relevant attributes, such as total assets. Therefore, technical efficiency change reflects the managerial and scale effects of the company. Scale effects are those that are related to the scale of activities, enabling big companies to earn a return that is not open to small companies. Technological change is decomposed into several elements. Färe and Grosskopf (1996) proposed the decomposition of technical efficiency change into its following components: OBTECH-output biased technological progress, that describes the technological change in outputs produced (the output change may be Hicks-neutral technological change or not); BTECH-input biased technological progress that describes the technological change in inputs usage (again it may be a Hicks-neutral technological change, or not); and MATECH-magnitude of technological progress, which is a residual technological change that includes technological change effects which are not reflected in input usage or output produced. The results of the Malmquist index are invariable, relative to the decomposition of their components. The decomposition of TECH in its constituents permits the identification of the type of changes observed in OBTECH, IBTECH and MATECH. In traditional microeconomics, technological progress, which is defined in isoquants with respect to outputs, is Hicks-neutral when the marginal rate of transformation between two outputs is constant, holding the mix of outputs constant (Varian, 1987). Hicks-neutral technological progress is illustrated by a parallel shift of the production possibility set. In the real world, the shift may not be parallel and the change in the production frontier will not be homothetic. In the case of our research, some auditing companies will move up the production possibility set, whilst others will shift down. Therefore this decomposition is important in opening up the black box of productivity. The input-biased technological progress between the inputs is analysed holding the input mix constant, and the output-biased technological progress between the two outputs is analysed holding the output mix constant.

The reciprocal of the Shephard (1970) input distance function serves as a measure of Farrell (1957) input efficiency. Linking input efficiency indexes across time allows us to estimate the Malmquist productivity index. This index can be decomposed into change in resource use due to efficiency change and also change in resource use due to technological change:

$$MALM = EFFCH \times TECH$$

Furthermore, the chapter adopts the approach of Färe and Grosskopf (1996) in decomposing technological change into an index of output-biased technological change, an index of input-biased technological change, and also an index of the magnitude of technological change.

$$TECH = OBTECH \times IBTECH \times MATECH$$

In the next section, the input technical efficiency is calculated and the components of the Malmquist input-based productivity index for the ENATUR hotels examine the bias in the use of inputs and the production of outputs found in the technological change index.

Theoretical background

The theoretical framework of the present research is that of the resource-based theory of Barney (1986) and Teece et al. (1997). This theory explains the competitive advantage of a hotel, based primarily on the application of a bundle of valuable tangible or intangible resources that are at the hotel's disposal. Valued resources are rare and inimitable, and are non-substitutable, an example being location. Within the framework of the resource-based view, the chain is a common resource of ENATUR. Capabilities are a special type of resource, which is specifically an organisationally embedded non-transferable hotel-specific resource, whose purpose is to improve the productivity of the other resources possessed by the hotel, Ludwig and Pemberton (2011). Based on this theory, there are three research questions:

- What is the productivity change in ENATUR that is homogeneous, following the network structure of ENATUR, or heterogeneous?
- Has productivity improved after privatisation?
- Is technological change Hicks neutral, or not?

These research questions will be answered below.

Data and results

The data set was obtained from ENATUR, on request. The sample used in this paper consists of 43 ENATUR hotels during the 14 year period from 2000 to 2013. DEA has a proportional rule which requires that the number of observations be three times higher than the sum of inputs and outputs: 602 > 3 × (3+3), (Vassiloglou and Giokas, 1990; Dyson et al., 2001). This condition is fulfilled in the present research. The DEA frontier identifies outputs and inputs. These variables were chosen based on the literature review of Barros (2005a,b) and are presented in Table 30.1. The outputs used are: sales, number of guests and nights spent. The inputs are: the number of full time workers, the number of rooms and operational cost.

In this section, the results will be presented in a sequential way, firstly for the average Malmquist index, which measures overall productivity change for the period analysed 2000–2013 in Table 30.2. In the same table, the components of the Malmquist index are presented, together with those of efficiency change (EFFCH) and technological change (TECH) and finally, the components of technological change are also presented, namely, input-biased technological change (IBTECH), output-biased technological change (OBTECH) and magnitude of technological change (MATECH).

The Malmquist indices of the ENATUR hotels firms are presented in Table 30.2. Values of the Malmquist index, efficiency change, technological change, output-biased technological progress, input-biased technological progress and magnitude of technological progress less than one, all indicate productivity increase, or increases in efficiency, or technological progress.

Table 30.2 Malmquist Index average for the ENATUR hotels: 2000–2013, ranked according to their geographic location, from north to south

Units	Hotels	MALM	EFFCH	TECH	OBTECH	IBTECH	MATECH
1	S. Gonçalo	0.897	1.019	0.880	1.094	1.267	1.0191
2	S. Teotónio	0.024	1.002	0.024	1.093	1.013	0.022
3	S. Bento	0.048	0.234	0.205	1.015	1.048	0.211
4	Nª.Sª. Oliveira	0.048	1.000	0.048	1.000	1.049	0.050
5	D. Dinis	0.024	1.001	0.024	1.099	1.025	0.022
6	Sta. Marinha	1.000	1.008	0.992	1.043	0.904	0.859
7	M. Sta. Luzia	0.008	1.006	0.007	0.212	1.025	0.033
8	Sta. M. do Bouro	0.018	1.004	0.018	1.098	1.023	0.016
9	S. Vicente	0.035	0.028	1.250	1.340	1.036	0.966
10	S. Lourenço	0.016	1.000	0.016	1.000	1.016	0.016
11	S. Bartolomeu	0.004	1.091	0.003	1.073	0.969	0.002
12	B. de Forrester	0.049	0.122	0.402	0.810	1.012	0.502
13	C. Desagravo	0.056	0.140	0.400	1.084	0.945	0.348
14	Castelo	1.048	1.000	1.048	1.000	0.952	0.997
15	Ria	0.012	0.069	0.174	1.011	1.024	0.176
16	Sta .Cristina	1.028	1.010	1.017	1.094	0.980	0.911
17	Conde de Ourém	0.026	0.120	0.217	0.260	1.061	0.885
18	Amoras	0.076	0.148	0.514	1.180	1.076	0.468
19	Viseu	0.012	0.018	0.667	1.290	0.999	0.516
20	Freixo	0.058	0.140	0.414	1.000	1.036	0.428
21	S. Filipe	1.018	0.980	1.039	1.099	1.003	0.948
22	Palmela	0.033	1.053	0.031	1.086	1.048	0.029
23	D. Maria I	0.978	1.009	0.969	1.000	0.942	0.912
24	Sta. Luzia	0.034	0.132	0.258	1.094	0.961	0.226
25	Loios	0.026	0.026	1.000	0.912	0.975	1.069
26	Sta. Isabel	0.018	0.112	0.161	0.321	1.063	0.533
27	Sta. Clara	0.002	1.000	0.002	1.000	1.002	0.002
28	Sta. Maria	0.052	0.142	0.366	0.412	0.976	0.867
29	Vale do Gaio	0.004	1.000	0.004	1.000	1.005	0.004
30	S. Miguel	0.026	0.116	0.224	1.099	0.975	0.198
31	Q. da Ortiga	0.061	0.140	0.436	0.240	1.047	1.902
32	C. de Alvito	1.036	1.046	0.990	1.099	1.058	0.953
33	S. Francisco	0.032	0.128	0.250	0.280	1.033	0.922
34	Flor da Rosa	0.044	0.142	0.310	1.000	0.961	0.297
35	Nª.Sª.Assunção	1.004	0.614	1.635	1.098	0.964	1.435
36	D. João IV	0.317	0.814	0.389	1.315	0. 563	0.166
37	D. Afonso II	0.634	0.715	0.886	1.145	0.715	0.553
38	S. Brás	0.894	0.832	1.074	1.167	0.219	0.201
39	Infante	0.714	0.452	1.579	1.318	0.318	0.380
40	C. Graça	0.216	0.317	0.681	1.189	0.173	0.099
41	Estoi	0.893	0.621	1.438	1.217	0.219	0.258
42	Sta. Cruz	0.563	0.563	1.000	1.512	0.187	0.123
43	S. Sebastião	0.513	0.816	0.628	1.218	0.561	0.289
	Mean	0.316	0.579	0.550	0.991	0.901	0.484
	Median	0.049	0.621	0.402	1.086	1.002	0.348
	Std. Dev	0.408	0.414	0.477	0.312	0.271	0.452

Note: MALM = EFFCH × TECH, TECH = OBTECH × IBTECH × MATECH, numbers may not multiply on account of rounding up errors.

Table 30.3 Productivity change over some years

Year	MALM	EFFCH	TECH	OBTECH	IBTECH	MATECH
2000	0.120	1.095	0.110	0.066	1.015	0.657
2005	0.829	0.800	1.036	0.329	0.016	0.254
2010	0.420	1.094	0.384	0.420	1.013	1.196
2011	0.140	1.099	0.127	1.098	0.410	0.047
2012	0.120	0.106	1.132	0.160	0.088	0.014
2013	1.190	0.949	1.254	0.209	0.013	0.1581

Values of the Malmquist index, efficiency change, technological change, output-biased technological progress, input-biased technological progress and magnitude of technological progress that are greater than one, all indicate productivity regression, decreases in efficiency, or technological regression.

Table 30.2 provides the answer to the first research question, proving that efficiency change in ENATUR hotels is mixed, with some hotels presenting productivity improvement, whilst others present a decrease in productivity. Table 30.3 facilitates the answer to the second research question, showing that privatisation does not explain the productivity change in ENATUR hotels, as it increases and decreases over the privatisation period. The decomposition presented in Tables 30.4 and 30.5 provides the answer to the third question, and confirms that, whether the Hicks-neutral technological change is Hicks neutral or not (as is the case with the values of IBTECH, OBTECH and MATECH), one cannot accept the Hicks neutrality hypothesis.

It can be seen that the total productivity change score in Table 30.2 (the Malmquist index presented in column 1), is on average 0.316 (MALM<1), which signifies that there was a slight increase in productivity change during the period. Santa Clara is the most efficient hotel in the period, followed by Sao Bartolo and Vale do Gaio. However, there is a small group of hotels that display productivity regression, namely Santa Marinha, Nossa Senhora de Assunção, São Filipe, Santa Cristina, Castelo do Alvito and Castelo. These ENATUR hotels display a decrease in productivity over the period, which is explained by efficiency change (EFFCH) and/or a decrease in technological change (TECH).

Furthermore, there is no Hicks-neutral technological change in ENATUR hotels during the period, some being IBTECH > 1, whilst others were IBTECH < 1. The same pattern is observed for OBTECH > 1 and OBTECH < 1.

Table 30.4 Input-biased technological change

ENATUR hotels for which:				
	$\left(\frac{x_1}{x_3}\right)^{t+1} > \left(\frac{x_1}{x_3}\right)^{t}$	$\left(\frac{x_1}{x_3}\right)^{t+1} < \left(\frac{x_1}{x_3}\right)^{t}$	$\left(\frac{x_2}{x_3}\right)^{t+1} > \left(\frac{x_2}{x_3}\right)^{t}$	$\left(\frac{x_1}{x_3}\right)^{t+1} < \left(\frac{x_2}{x_3}\right)^{t}$
IBTECH>1	10 (x_1-saving)	10 (x_1-using)	8 (x_2-saving)	6 (x_2-using)
IBTECH<1	3 (x_1-using)	0 (x_1-saving)	2 (x_2-using)	0 (x_2-saving)
Neutral	2		2	

Table 30.5 Output-biased technological change

ENATUR hotels for which:			
$\left(\dfrac{y_1}{y_3}\right)^{t+1} > \left(\dfrac{y_1}{y_3}\right)^{t}$	$\left(\dfrac{y_1}{y_3}\right)^{t+1} < \left(\dfrac{y_1}{y_3}\right)^{t}$	$\left(\dfrac{y_2}{y_3}\right)^{t+1} > \left(\dfrac{y_2}{y_3}\right)^{t}$	$\left(\dfrac{y_2}{y_3}\right)^{t+1} < \left(\dfrac{y_2}{y_3}\right)^{t}$
OBTECH>1 9 (y_1-producing)	2 (y_1-producing)	3 (y_2-producing)	4 (y_2-producing)
OBTECH<1 4 (y_1-producing)	4 (y_1-producing)	2 (y_2-producing)	4 (y_2-producing)
Neutral 5		6	

Discussion and conclusion

This paper estimates the Malmquist input-based index of total factor productivity for ENATUR hotels that were in operation from 2000 to 2013. Productivity change is first partitioned into an index of efficiency change (catch up) and an index of technological change (innovation). Next the index of technological change is partitioned into output-biased technological change, input-biased technological change and the magnitude of technological change. Therefore, the three implications of this study are the following: firstly, it is found that, based on the Malmquist index, the average productivity (0.253) increase over the period for the sample of ENATUR hotels analysed is due to an average increase in efficiency change (0.566) and the average increase in technological change (0.457). However, among these average values there are hotels that display improvement in productivity. Secondly, productivity oscillates up and down along the period, which signifies that central management does not affect productivity in a consistent way. Therefore, productivity growth depends on both the ability of the hotels to catch up and to innovate, and also the quality of management does not exercise a notable effect on ENATUR hotels. Thirdly, and this is a distinctive characteristic of this paper, the values of output-biased technological change, input-biased technological change and the magnitude of technological change, all show that there is no Hicks-neutral technological change in hotel chains, and therefore the Malmquist index with technological change is adequate for hotel chains.

Revisiting the research questions, we are able to say that, with regards to the first question, the hotels in the chain are heterogeneous, with some of them improving productivity, whilst others decrease in productivity. This may result from the distinct location of these hotels around the country. Answering the second research question, we can see that productivity has improved after privatisation, but not in a systematic way, as it decreases in some years, and therefore, although it oscillates up and down, productivity has increased after privatisation. Finally, in relation to the third question, although traditional microeconomics books assume Hicks-neutral technological change, which means that isoquant changes in production are parallel when the marginal rate of transformation between two outputs is constant (Varian, 1987), in this research, there is no evidence of Hicks-neutrality. In the real world, the shift may not be parallel and the change in the production frontier will not be homothetic. In this case, some hotels will shift up the production possibility set, whilst others will shift down.

From these results the policy implication is that ENATUR hotels need to improve their productivity and that this improvement should be focused on efficiency change (catch up) and an index of technological change (innovation). Efficiency change (catch up) improvements signify changes in managerial practices and changes in the scale of operations, which means that active managerial practices aimed to increase scale are needed to improve efficiency change. Technological change improvement signifies investment and the implementation of new procedures, as well as methods that increase technological change. There was some improvement in these investments, but more active policies are needed. The results seen from technological change, input-biased technological change and the magnitude of technological change all signify that there is some common policy for ENATUR hotels, although each hotel is driven by its local context. In this context, we observe that some hotels reduced staff, while others increased their staff. This heterogeneous behaviour signifies that management practice is limited. In the competitive context of these hotels being located in distinct places, no common policies are possible. However, each hotel should adopt a productivity improvement focus that results in an improvement in the Malmquist index, as a result of changes in efficiency change and technological change. Simultaneous changes in efficiency change and technological change are needed to improve productivity in a sustainable way. The changes required in efficiency are clear: better management practices and an improvement of scale. The changes in technological change are not so clear, but input-biased technological change should result if costs decrease, and output-biased technological change should result in an increase in profit. The magnitude of technological change is residual and therefore no policy can be proposed. However, the use of this methodology is in line with the resource-based theory of Barney (1986) and Teece et al. (1997), which justifies that hotel chains are heterogeneous in terms of resources and capabilities, based on their location and their managerial practices, and thus heterogeneity is expected to interfere with productivity. Given that this methodology is used for the first time in this area, it is difficult to have a direct comparison between the productivity results of this study and other related studies in the area. Focusing on Table 30.2, this research uses the same inputs and outputs that are adopted in the published literature, but it uses an extended period and also focuses on productivity. However, it is possible to discuss whether related studies have converged to reach similar conclusions in terms of the impact of the selected variables on efficiency. DEA does not identify the causes of inefficiency, but identifies which units are inefficient, and therefore enables one to derive some conclusions. Three reasons are identified as being the major causes of inefficiency, namely: the scale of ENATUR hotels, a lack of commensurate investment and inadequate managerial practices. Managerial practices and scale are behind in terms of efficiency change and investment is behind for technological change. Some hotels have less productivity on account of their location and attract lower business and therefore do not permit an efficient use of the resources available. Other hotels that have positive technological change are inefficient, on account of the lack of investment over the period studied.

References

Abrantes, A. (2012) Relatório profissional. Tese de Mestrado e Turismo, conferido pela Universidade Lusófona de Humanidades e Tecnologias (Masters thesis).

Anderson, R., Fish, M. Xia, Y. and Michello, E. (1999) Measuring efficiency in the hotel industry: a stochastic frontier approach. *International Journal of Hospitality Management*, 18, 45–57.

Anderson, R., Fok, R. and Scott, J. (1999) Hotel industry efficiency: an advanced linear programming examination. *American Business Review*, 18(1), 40–48.

Baker, M. and Riley, M. (1994) New perspectives on productivity in hotels: some advances and new directions. *International Journal of Hospitality Management*, 13(4), 297–311.

Barney, J. (1986) Strategic factor markets: expectations, luck and business strategy. *Management Science*, 32(10), 1231–41.

Barros, C.P. (2004) A stochastic cost frontier in the Portuguese Hotel industry. *Tourism Economics*, 10, 177–92.

Barros, C.P. (2005a) Measuring efficiency in the hotel sector. *Annals of Tourism Research*, 32(2), 456–77.

Barros, C.P. (2005b) Evaluating the efficiency of a small hotel chain with a Malmquist productivity index. *International Journal of Tourism Research*, 7, 173–84.

Begg, J. (1999) Cities and competitiveness. *Urban Studies*, 36, 795–807.

Berger, A. and Humphrey, D. (1997) Efficiency of financial institutions: international survey and directions for future research. *European Journal of Operational Research*, 98, 175–212.

Bishop, M., Kay, J. and Mayer, C. (1994) Introduction: privatization in performance. In M. Bishop, J. Kay and C. Mayer (eds), *Privatization and Economic Performance*. New York: Oxford University Press.

Boycko, M., Shleifer A. and Vishny, R.W. (1996) A theory of privatisation. *Economic Journal*, 106, 309–19.

Brotherton, B. and Mooney, S. (1992) Yield management progress and prospects. *International Journal of Hospitality Management*, 11, 23–32.

Brown, J. and Ragsdale, C. (2002) The competitive market efficiency of hotel brands: an application of data envelopment analysis. *Journal of Hospitality and Tourism Research*, 26(4), 332–60.

Brown, J.R. and Dev, C.S. (2000) Improving productivity in a service business: evidence from the hotel industry. *Journal of Service Research*, 2(4), 339–54.

Chiang, W., Tsai, H. and Wang, L. (2004) A DEA evaluation of Taipei hotels. *Annals of Tourism Research*, 31, 712–15.

Cracolici, M.F., Nijkamp, P. and Cuffaro M. (2007) efficiency and productivity of Italian tourist destinations: a quantitative estimation based on data envelopment analysis and the Malmquist method. In A. Matias, P. Nijkamp and P. Neto (eds), *Advances in Modern Tourism Research*. Heidelberg: Physica-Verlag, pp. 325–43.

Donaghy, K., McMahon, U. and McDowell, D. (1995) Yield management: an overview. *International Journal of Hospitality Management*, 14, 1339–50.

Dyson, R.G., Allen, R., Camanho, A.S., Podimovski, V.V., Sarrico, C. and Shale, S. (2001). Pitfalls and protocols in DEA. *European Journal of Operational Research*, 132(2), 245–59.

Färe, R. and Grosskopf, S. (1996) *Inter-temporal Production Frontiers: With Dynamic DEA*. Boston/London/Dordrecht: Kluwer Academic Publishers.

Farrell, M.J. (1957) The measurement of productive efficiency. *Journal of the Royal Statistical Society*, 120(3), 253–81.

Hathroubi, S., Peypoch, N. and Robinot, E. (2014) Technical efficiency and environmental management: the Tunisian case. *Journal of Hospitality and Tourism Management*, 21, 27–33.

Hu, B. and Cai, L. (2004) Hotel labor productivity assessment: a data envelopment analysis. *Journal of Travel & Tourism Marketing*, 16(2–3), 27–38.

Huang, S. and Chang, T. (2003) Using data envelopment analysis to measure hotel managerial efficiency change in Taiwan. *Tourism Management*, 24(4), 357–69.

Jones, P. and Siag, A. (2009) Re-examination of the factors that influence productivity in hotels: a study of the housekeeping function. *Tourism and Hospitality Research*, 9, 224–34.

Krugman, P. (1996) Making sense of the competitiveness debate. *Oxford Review of Economics and Policy*, 12, 17–25.

Lee, J.S., Hsu, L.T., Han, H. and Kim, Y. (2010) Understanding how consumers view green hotels: how a hotel's green image can influence behavioural intentions. *Journal of Sustainable Tourism*, 18(7), 901–14.

Lionetti, S. (2010) Tourism productivity: incentives and obstacles to fostering growth. *Tourism Analysis*, 14(6), 781–91.

Ludwig, G. and Pemberton, J. (2011) A managerial perspective of dynamic capabilities in emerging markets: the case of the Russian steel industry. *Journal of East European Management Studies*, 16(3), 215–36.

Malmquist, S. (1953) Index numbers and difference surfaces. *Trabajos de Estatística*, 4, 209–42.

Omerzel, D.G. (2006) Competitiveness of Slovenia as a tourist destination. *Managing Global Transitions*, 4(2), 167–89.

Perrigot, R., Cliquet, G. and Piot-Lepetit, I. (2009) Plural form chain and efficiency: insights from the French hotel chains and the DEA methodology. *European Management Journal*, 27, 268–80.

Pestana Hotel Group (2015) Institutional. Online. Available HTTP: <http://www.pestana.com/en/contents/institutional>, accessed 2 December 2015.

Peypoch, N. and Solonandrasana, B. (2008) Aggregate efficiency and productivity analysis in the tourism industry. *Tourism Economics*, 14(1), 45–56.

Porter, M. (1998) *The Competitive Advantage of Nations*. London: Macmillan.

Pousadas de Portugal (2014) Pestana Pousadas de Portugal. Online. Available HTTP: <www.pousadas.pt>, accessed 10 December, 2015.

Scalon N. (2007) An analysis and assesment of environmental operating practices in hotel and resort properties. *International Journal of Hospitality Management*, 26, 711–23.

Shephard, R.W. (1970) *Theory of Cost and Production Functions*, Princeton: Princeton University Press.

Teece, D.J., Pisano, G. and Shuen, A. (1997) Dynamic capabilities and strategic management, *Strategic Management Journal*, 18(7), 509–33.

Tsai, H., Song, H. and Wong, K.K.F. (2009) Tourism and hotel competitiveness research, *Journal of Travel & Tourism Marketing*, 26(5), 522–46.

Varian, H. (1987) *Intermediate Microeconomics: A Modern Approach*. New York: W.W. Norton & Co.

Vassiloglou, M. and Giokas, D. (1990) A study of the relative efficiency of bank branches: an application of data envelopment analysis. *Journal of Operational Research Society*, 41(7), 591–97.

Wijeysinghe, B. (1993) Breakeven occupancy for hotel operation. *Management Accounting*, 712, 23–33.

31

Competitiveness and performance of chain hotels

Manuel Becerra (UNIVERSITY OF QUEENSLAND, AUSTRALIA),
Rosario Silva (IE BUSINESS SCHOOL, SPAIN) *and*
Oksana Gerwe (IE BUSINESS SCHOOL, SPAIN)

Introduction

The empirical literature on the effect of chain affiliation on hotel performance provides mixed evidence and it is not clear yet if (and when) being part of a hotel chain has positive consequences for its competitiveness in market and financial performance. For instance, Ingram and Baum (1997a) observed lower failure rates for the members of hotel chains due to economies of scale and knowledge transfer between chain hotels. Recent research also shows a positive effect of chain membership on the room prices of member hotels (Becerra et al., 2013). On the contrary, other studies have not detected significant revenue or performance differences between chain and independent hotels. For instance, Israeli (2002) analysed how chain affiliation affected a hotel's yield (i.e., the ratio between revenue realised and revenue potential) in Israel and concluded that chain affiliation cannot be regarded as a strategic resource (Israeli, 2002). In addition, O'Neill and Carlbäck (2011) in their analysis of the effect of economic expansion and recession on chain versus independent hotels found that chain hotels had higher occupancy rates while independent hotels actually had higher average daily rate and revenue per available room. Regarding net operating income, they did not find any significant difference between affiliated and independent hotels during the years of economic expansion, and only during years of economic recession they found that chain hotels had significantly higher net operating income (O'Neill and Carlbäck, 2011).

Given these mixed results, we designed an empirical study to investigate the effect of being part of a hotel company on room prices and, most critically, profits. Furthermore, we also wanted to distinguish between merely being part of a hotel company versus hotels that also belong to a hotel chain using a common brand. Thus, we are able to separate the organisational benefits of being part of a hotel company from the external benefits of using a shared brand to attract customers through a chain. This distinction is critical to our understanding of hotel performance because a hotel's brand name has been identified as one of the key attributes on which consumers make their purchase decision (Kim and Kim, 2005).

In our analysis, we first distinguish between fully independent hotels and those that belong to a hotel company. The latter can be divided into two further categories: chain hotels and company-managed hotels, following the definitions provided in Chapter 1 of this Handbook. Thus, a chain hotel is part of a group of hotels that share a common brand and have some degree of common management in contrast to a company-managed hotel, which is managed by one company but does not share a common brand among its company-managed hotels. It should be noted that the previous literature does not make this distinction clearly and authors often use the term chain hotels to refer to both chain hotels and company-managed hotels, which we explicitly distinguish.

We conduct our study of how being part of a hotel company impacts both price and net profit per room in a large dataset of Spanish hotels (27,050 hotel-year observations) during the 5 years from 2004 to 2008. Even though profit maximisation is often regarded as a critical financial goal in running a hospitality firm, it cannot be successfully achieved without paying attention to top-line factors, such as price per room, which drives revenue maximisation and ultimately the hotel's bottom line (O'Neill and Mattila, 2006). We also analyse empirically different moderators that influence the effect of being part of a hotel company on hotel room prices and financial performance, such as the size of the company, the type of hotel, and its overall level of quality as reflected by its number of stars. The results from our panel analysis confirm that hotels that belong to a company indeed charge higher prices and achieve greater performance versus independent hotels; however, this positive effect depends on the type of hotel and its level of quality. The results also confirm that chain hotels charge higher prices and profits than independent hotels, and set higher prices in contrast to company-managed hotels that do not use a common brand. We discuss these findings after first formulating our expectations in the following section.

The effect of being part of a hotel company on hotel room prices and performance

The literature on hotel pricing, especially in the stream of research about hedonic pricing, has investigated how different hotel characteristics, including chain affiliation, influence a hotel's ability to exercise a particular pricing strategy (Becerra et al., 2013; Israeli, 2002; Ivanov, 2014; Papatheodorou, 2002; Thrane, 2007). However, as mentioned above, the results in this stream of research are mixed. For example, Israeli's (2002) study of the effects of chain affiliation on prices in the hotel industry in Israel for the years 1999–2000 showed positive, negative, and sometimes statistically insignificant effects of chain-affiliation, depending on the geographic location under analysis. Similarly, the study of chain-affiliated Mediterranean resorts demonstrated opposite effects of chain membership on room prices depending on whether the resort was located in the centre or in the periphery (Papatheodorou, 2002); chain hotels in central locations were characterised by price discounts, while peripheral hotels with chain affiliation were charging a price premium (Papatheodorou, 2002). In contrast, Thrane (2007) found that single room rates of Norwegian chain hotels in 2005 were about 15 per cent higher than for non-chain members, ceteris paribus, but this effect was not significant for double room prices. Ivanov (2014) also provides evidence of positive and insignificant effects. In a hedonic pricing model of 146 hotels in Sofia (Bulgaria), he found that chain affiliation had positive and statistically significant impact on weekend rates but not on weekday rates. Finally, in their cross-sectional study of Spanish hotels for the year 2005, Becerra et al. (2013) also observed that chain hotels charged higher prices and they further provided a smaller discount over listed prices than independent hotels.

We posit that the combination of local presence with central management and resource sharing across the hotel company create unique strategic advantages for the company as a whole and for each individual hotel (Ingram and Baum, 1997a). Being part of one hotel company generates a certain degree of market power versus competitors that arguably translates into the ability for company hotels to charge a price premium. Furthermore, there is clear evidence in the literature that multimarket competition (i.e., firms that compete against the same set of players across different markets) reduces rivalry and facilitates mutual forbearance (Silva, 2015), so that these firms will compete relatively less on prices because they realise their mutual interdependence in their interactions across different geographical markets. These benefits of being part of a hotel company can be exploited by hotel members regardless of whether the hotels within the company decide to use a common brand or not, which may trigger additional marketing benefits of sharing a brand that we will analyse later on. We can thus formulate our baseline hypothesis:

Hypothesis 1: Company hotels charge higher prices than independent hotels.

In addition to the positive effect on room prices of being part of a company hotel through market power and mutual forbearance, research in the hospitality industry has explored several advantages that hotel companies can provide to its hotels to improve their financial performance, including economies of scale, easier access to resources, and knowledge transfer (Ingram, 1996; Ingram and Baum, 1997a, 1997b). According to Ingram and Baum (1997a), replication of standardised services, facilities, operations, equipment, and buildings generate economies of scale for the company and lead to cost savings for the member hotels. Being part of a company can provide its hotel with privileged access to slack resources and serve as a protective buffer against environmental uncertainty (Ingram and Baum, 1997a). Furthermore, the possibility of following collective action can also be a potential source of market power for hotels from the same company (Ingram and Baum, 1997a). For instance, hotel companies can have more power for reducing input costs, such as food or subcontracted labour, than independent hotels.

Possibly even more importantly, company hotels also have a critical advantage over independent hotels in terms of knowledge generation and exploitation. The possibility of standardisation facilitates knowledge transfer between the company hotels, ensuring dispersion of good practices and avoidance and correction of the inferior ones. Hotel companies provide an excellent setting for the creation and distribution of knowledge from operations, as their multi-unit structure makes it possible to 'conduct controlled experiments' and evaluate their effects on hotel performance (Ingram and Baum, 1997b: 2). Thus, knowledge created in one hotel can be quickly and efficiently transferred to other company hotels through centralised leadership and corporate headquarters of the company. In this way, hotel companies facilitate the proper exploitation of rents from knowledge-based resources (Garcia-Almeida et al., 2011), which should have a direct impact on each hotel's profits.

There is already some empirical evidence that company hotels indeed enjoy a knowledge advantage. Knowledge seems to travel faster across organisations that are embedded in a network (Darr et al., 1995). In the hotel industry, Baum and Ingram (1998) found that hotels do assimilate the experience of local hotels that belong to the same company. Orfila et al. (2005) also found that the innovation rate was higher in hotels belonging to the same company than in independent hotels, which may be a result of the advantage of hotel companies in the generation and transfer of knowledge among their members. In light of these arguments, we formulate the following hypothesis:

Hypothesis 2: Company hotels have greater profits per room than independent hotels.

Notwithstanding the arguments above regarding independent versus company hotels, we should further distinguish between company hotels that are part of a chain and those that are not. As we previously defined, chain hotels are company hotels that use a common brand, such as AC Hotels or NH in Spain, whereas company-managed hotels use their own hotel names without any umbrella name.

In the hotel industry, consumers tend to rely on brand names as a critical attribute, if not the most critical one, when choosing their accommodation in a given location. This is probably due to the value that is being communicated by a familiar brand and its unique image (Dubé and Renaghan, 2000). Prasad and Dev (2000) argue that branding is an effective way for hotel chains to distinguish themselves from competition in the mind of the consumer. Thus, the brand may become an important source of differentiation, since different brands reflect different preferences in the consumer's mind (Becerra et al., 2013). To the extent that this is so, hotel chains should be able to exploit their presence across different locations more effectively than can individual hotels and those hotels that are managed by the same company but do not share a brand.

Moreover, in a hotel chain that offers to the consumer a promise of standardised reliable quality across the chain, the use of the same brand name reinforces the guarantee of homogeneity in the type and quality of its service (Ingram, 1996). The standardisation, quality assurance and lower transaction costs (e.g., search costs) of purchasing a familiar brand name can be valuable attributes that a chain offers to the customer (Wu, 1999). This, in turn, may increase the consumer's willingness to pay and consequently the ability of the hotel to charge a price premium for the additional value that a brand name communicates. Hence:

Hypothesis 3: Chain hotels charge greater prices than company-managed hotels.

The use of a common brand characteristic of a hotel chain should also reinforce the positive performance consequences of company membership that we discussed earlier. The brand name is considered as a valuable, unique, and inimitable resource, which, according to strategy scholars, may generate a sustainable competitive advantage (Barney, 1991). Brand name acts as an intangible resource that leads to superior performance to the extent that the brand is regarded as a strategic resource for the hotel. Thus, hotel chains may enjoy the additional external benefits associated with this intangible resource on top of the organisational benefits of being part of a company.

When hotel companies adopt a common brand name, they actually contribute to development of a reputational advantage through their joint efforts. A hotel guest can have greater confidence that a chain will provide quality service because it has the incentive to ensure future business across the hotels that share the brand (Ingram, 1996). In this case, standardised and consistent services act as a commitment signal that chain association transmits to the consumer (Ingram and Baum, 1997a).

Although being part of the same chain often leads to increased revenues and cost savings, the literature also recognises that it can increase some costs. For instance, Holverson and Revaz (2006) enumerate the extra costs that franchises assume, such as the initial fee, the annual royalty, the reservation service, and marketing fees, as well as the costs for training programmes, technology maintenance, and loyalty programmes. Despite the financial and time investments required to build a strong new brand name valued by consumers (Tauber, 1988), we hypothesise that chain hotels will nevertheless be able to benefit from a superior competitive position and, thus, may be expected to obtain greater profits than company-managed hotels that do not share a common brand. Hence:

Hypothesis 4: Chain hotels have greater profits per room than company-managed hotels.

Methodology

Data

We used the Official Hotel Guide published by the Instituto de Estudios Turísticos to build a panel of hotels for the 5-year period 2004–2008 in Spain, which has one of the most competitive hotel industries in the world. Our initial panel dataset contained 43,172 hotel-year observations, but due to missing data, the final dataset for this study was reduced to 27,050 hotel-year observations for the analysis of pricing.

To obtain financial information for individual hotels, we first used the Census of Hotels 2005 from Alimarket to obtain the name of the company that owned the hotels in our dataset. Second, we collected the financial data of each company from SABI (Sistema de Análisis de Balances Ibéricos) database, discarding all the companies that were diversified in other activities or had missing data. This step reduced the dataset substantially because there were public data about individual hotel performance for a limited number of hotels. For that reason, the second sample for the profitability analysis was reduced to 1,275 hotel-year observations.

Variables

Our analysis is based on two dependent variables. First, we obtain the *Price of a double room* directly from the Guide for the peak season, which we convert into logarithm form because the frequency distribution of prices is highly skewed to the right. Second, we compute the *Yearly net profit per room* as the dependent variable of our profitability analysis from the SABI database by dividing Net Profit (or losses) by the number of rooms in the hotel.

We also compute the following independent variables for our empirical analysis:

Company hotel. This is a dummy variable that represents whether the hotel is part of a hotel company as reported in the Official Guide, regardless of whether or not it uses the company brand. We further break down this variable into two categories in some of the regression analyses, depending on whether the hotel uses an umbrella brand or not. Thus, we use *Chain hotel* as a dummy variable equal to one when the hotel uses the parent company name, such as NH or Barceló, or a common brand that it shares with at least one other hotel of the same chain, such as Novotel or Tryp. On the other hand, we assign a value of one to the dummy *Company-managed hotel* when a specific company hotel does not share its brand with other hotels that belong to its company and it uses a completely different name.

To confirm that our results are not confounded by other hotel features, we include several control variables in our regression model:

- *Hotel size.* The variable refers to the total number of rooms of each hotel, which allows us to control for any economies of scale. Larger hotels may have greater potential to lower average costs and, therefore, to reduce prices or increase margins.
- *Age.* We also controlled for the age of the hotel to account for the possibly greater pressure on older hotels to lower their prices (i.e., new hotels can be more attractive for

customers because of their modern design and new facilities) or increase their costs (e.g., larger maintenance costs).

- *Beach* is a dummy variable that takes the value of one if the Guide indicates that the hotel is near a beach within the city.
- *Mountain* is a dummy variable that indicates whether the hotel is located near a mountain area.
- *Company size.* The total number of rooms that belong to the hotels that are managed by its company in each year. This variable is used to capture the degree of market power of each company. Ingram and Baum (1997a) suggest that larger hotel companies may enjoy market power since they may be able to buy cheapest inputs, to collude successfully on prices or to influence laws.

The Official Hotel Guide classifies the hotel services in six different groups: *business services* (i.e., audiovisual equipment, meeting rooms, etc.), *general facilities* (i.e., parking, medical services, etc.), *services for families* (i.e., family rooms, children's animation, children's playground, etc.), *leisure and sports services* (i.e., discotheque, gym, golf, spa, etc.), *amenities* (minibar, hairdryer, etc.) and *services for people with physical or sensory needs.* These variables allow us to control whether the hotel is focused on a particular type of services. Customers' preferences between different hotels are influenced in part by the availability of some services and facilities (Dubé and Renaghan, 2000). Therefore, the type of services that the hotel provides may influence its attractiveness to different customer segments (i.e., families, business, leisure, etc.) and hence its prices.

- *Stars dummies.* The number of stars (one to five stars) is generally considered a good proxy for hotel quality (Núñez-Serrano et al., 2014). In Spain, the number of stars is assessed by the corresponding agency based on current regulations as obtained from the Official Guide.
- *Year dummies.* To control for unobserved effects associated with changes in our empirical setting over time, we include year dummies (year fixed effects).
- *City dummies.* To control for any unobservable differences across 2,031 cities in the sample (109 cities for the analysis of Profit per room), fixed city effects were also included.

Model specification

We performed pooled regression analysis to test for the effect of being part of a hotel company and chain affiliation on room prices and room profits. After we test our four hypotheses, we conduct additional analyses to understand better how various hotel features may moderate these effects. Although the Hausman test suggested that regression analysis with hotel fixed-effects was appropriate, we decided not to use fixed effects because the variability of the independent variables (company hotel and chain hotel) was negligible across time, which would eliminate them from the analyses if we used fixed-effects regressions. We discuss the implications of our methodological choices later in the discussion section.

Results

The results from the pooled regression analysis are shown in Table 31.1. Models 1 and 2 report the regression of LogPrice and ProfitRoom respectively on the company hotel variable and the entire set of control variables, including hotel size, age, type of hotel

Table 31.1 Regression analysis room prices and yearly profits per room

	(1)	(2)	(3)	(4)
	LogPrice	ProfitRoom	LogPrice	ProfitRoom
Company hotel	0.12***	2104.08***		
Company-managed hotel			0.09***	1496.06*
Chain hotel			0.14***	3437.67***
Hotel size	−0.00***	3.30	−0.00***	3.73
Age	−0.00***	5.77	−0.00***	9.79
Beach	0.03***	−1599.66	0.03***	−1611.52
Mountain	−0.02**	−3781.52	−0.02**	−3859.60
Business	0.02***	−34.40	0.02***	−45.57
Facilities	−0.01***	210.31	−0.01***	202.67
Families	0.00	−106.99	0.00	−123.05
Leisure	0.02***	−212.08	0.02***	−231.12
Amenities	0.02***	262.79	0.02***	269.72
Special needs	−0.00***	38.08	−0.00***	47.77
Star1	−0.42***	804.13	−0.42***	878.70
Star2	−0.27***	−426.14	−0.27***	−442.28
Star4	0.25***	−1082.65	0.24***	−988.17
Star5	0.60***	−3675.02*	0.60***	−3140.67
2005	0.02***	103.81	0.02***	140.61
2006	0.01***	98.24	0.01***	141.40
2007	0.12***	−491.82	0.12***	−439.97
2008	0.14***	−590.54	0.14***	−540.76
Constant	4.44***	−699.38	4.44***	−790.66
R-Sq.	0.81	0.09	0.81	0.09
F test	1,956.56***	1.50*	1,866.44***	1.54*
N	27,050	1,275	27,050	1,275

* $p < 0.10$, ** $p < 0.05$, *** $p < 0.01$. City dummies not shown (2,031 for LogPrice and 109 for ProfitRoom).

(e.g., beach hotel), and services provided, (e.g., services for business), plus the three sets of dummy variables (number of stars, year, and city). The control variables are highly significant for the pricing regressions, but not for profits per room. For instance, hotels with a larger number of rooms as well as older hotels usually charge lower prices; also room prices have increased during the period under investigation; obviously, room prices increase significantly with the number of stars. Interestingly, there is not one single hotel feature systematically associated with higher profits per room, with the critical exception of being a company hotel.

The key finding is captured by the significant coefficient of the company hotel variable. Hotels that belong to a hotel company, regardless of whether or not they are affiliated to a chain, charge significantly higher prices, after controlling for many features of the hotel, such as number of stars, city in which it is located, and services provided. Thus, there is clear support for Hypothesis 1, as indicated by the significant coefficient ($\beta = 0.12$; $p < 0.05$) for the company hotel variable in Model 1. Furthermore, company hotels also have greater profits per room, on average around 2,100 euros per room per year. This confirms Hypothesis 2, so that being part of a hotel company is significantly associated with greater profits, as we expected.

Table 31.2 Interaction analysis

	(5)	(6)	(7)	(8)	(9)	(10)
	LogPrice	LogPrice	LogPrice	ProfitRoom	ProfitRoom	ProfitRoom
Company hotel	0.12***	0.30***	0.16***	1,965.13**	4,835.35	2,978.88***
Hotel size	-0.00***	-0.00***	-0.00***	3.37	3.26	3.78
Age	-0.00***	-0.00***	-0.00***	5.70	7.98	4.77
Beach	0.03***	0.03***	0.03***	-1,608.15	-1,457.36	-1,586.23
Mountain	-0.02**	-0.03**	-0.02**	-3,786.13	-4,533.32	-3,695.08
Business	0.02***	0.02***	0.02***	-36.61	55.16	-16.20
Facilities	-0.01***	-0.01***	-0.01***	213.02	184.59	222.26
Families	0.00	-0.01***	-0.00	-108.95	-37.84	-83.39
Leisure	0.02***	0.03***	0.02***	-212.03	-262.60	-185.83
Amenities	0.02***	0.02***	0.02***	264.90	402.90*	239.49
Special needs	-0.00***	-0.00**	-0.00***	37.84	-62.26	38.37
Star1	-0.42***	-0.40***	-0.41***	825.91	432.68	1,226.40
Star2	-0.27***	-0.26***	-0.26***	-429.39	-286.61	-28.17
Star4	0.25***	0.25***	0.30***	-1,086.55	-1,062.04	-574.60
Star5	0.60***	0.63***	0.71***	-3,802.12	-4,453.17**	-4,852.94**
Company*Company size	0.00**			4.96		
Company*Business		-0.00			-433.51	
Company*Facilities		-0.01***			250.87	
Company*Families		0.02***			-686.21	
Company*Leisure		-0.02***			388.82	
Company*Amenities		-0.01***			-772.95**	
Company*Special needs		-0.00			420.06**	
Company*Star1			0.01			-2,464.92
Company*Star2			-0.01			-7,718.28*
Company*Star4			-0.10***			-2,129.09
Company*Star5			-0.19***			2,283.40
Constant	4.44***	4.39***	4.42***	-726.40	-1,372.02	-869.37
R-Sq.	0.81	0.81	0.81	0.09	0.11	0.10
F test	1,859.19***	1,506.38***	1,632.80***	1.94***	2.17***	2.04***
N	27,050	27,050	27,050	1,275	1,275	1,275

* $p < 0.10$, ** $p < 0.05$, *** $p < 0.01$. City dummies not shown (2,031 for LogPrice and 109 for ProfitRoom). Year dummies not shown.

We replicated the analysis, but distinguished between independent hotels and the two types of company hotels: chain hotels (i.e., company hotels with a common brand name) and company-managed hotels (i.e., company hotels without a common brand name). Overall, the results are quite similar, but much stronger for chain hotels. As we can see in Models 3 and 4 in Table 31.1, the coefficients for the two critical variables, chain hotels and company-managed hotels are generally significant. Note that the results are stronger for chain hotels. These hotels charge significantly higher room prices (LogPrice in Model 3; $\beta = 0.14$; $p < 0.05$) and they also have higher profits per room (ProfitRoom in Model 4), actually having over 3,400 euros higher profits than independent hotels. Regarding company-managed hotels, they also charge higher prices ($\beta = 0.09$; $p < 0.05$, in Model 3) and higher profits per room ($\beta = 1,496$; p-value < 0.10).

We also tested for significant differences in the coefficients for chain hotels and company-managed hotels for room prices and profits, as Hypotheses 3 and 4 suggest for LogPrice and ProfitRoom respectively. The two coefficients in Model 3 are significantly different from each other (0.09 and 0.14; $F(1, 24999) = 62.52$; $p < 0.01$), but they are not in Model 4 (1,496 and 3,437; $F(1, 1123) = 2.26$; $p > 0.10$). Thus, we only found clear support for Hypothesis 3. The higher profits per room of chain hotels (mean = 4,058 euros) was only marginally higher than for company-managed hotels (mean = 1,813 euros) using a Bonferroni t-test of difference in means. These t-tests also showed significant mean differences with chain hotels versus independent hotels (4,058 vs. 825), but not between company-managed hotels versus independent hotels (1,813 vs. 825).

Table 31.2 provides additional insight into the variables that moderate the observed differences in room prices and profits between company hotels and independent hotels. As shown in the interaction between company hotel and company size, company hotels are able to charge significantly higher prices as their company grows in size, though it does not seem to affect room profits. In addition, there are significant differences in the effect that company membership has on prices and profits depending on the type of services they offer (interactions in Models 6 and 9) as well as the number of stars (interactions in Models 7 and 10). Future research may want to investigate in greater depth why these differences exist.

Conclusion

Our study provides strong empirical support for the idea that company hotels charge higher prices, which further allows them to generate greater profits per room with respect to independent hotels. Furthermore, our results confirm that chain hotels obtain higher prices and profits versus independent hotels and higher prices with respect to company-managed hotels that do not share a common brand. Thus, chain management seems to improve hotel performance, which we argue is due to a combination of internal factors (e.g., economies of scale and knowledge management) as well as external factors (e.g., market power and brand management).

One word of caution, however, is necessary regarding the causality implications of the differences in room prices and profits that we have detected. Though we control for a large number of hotel features, including also fixed-effects for years and locations, few hotels change from being independent to being part of a company and a chain, or vice versa in our panel dataset. Further longitudinal research is necessary to understand the extent to which this change actually affects room prices and performance.

References

Barney, J. (1991) Firm resources and sustained competitive advantage. *Journal of management, 17,* 99–120.

Baum, J.A.C. and Ingram, P. (1998) Survival-enhancing learning in the Manhattan hotel industry, 1898–1980. *Management Science,* 44, 996–1016.

Becerra, M., Santaló, J. and Silva, R. (2013) Being better vs. being different: differentiation, competition, and pricing strategies in the Spanish hotel industry. *Tourism Management,* 34, 71–79.

Darr, E., Argote, L. and Epple, D. (1995) The acquisition, transfer and depreciation of knowledge in service organizations: productivity in franchises. *Management Science,* 41, 1750–62.

Dubé, L. and Renaghan, L.M. (2000) Creating visible customer value: how customers view best-practice champions. *The Cornell Hotel and Restaurant Administration Quarterly,* 41, 62–72.

García-Almeida, D.J., Bernardo-Vilamitjana, M., Hormiga, E. and Valls-Pasola, J. (2011) Cultural compatibility in internal knowledge transfers: an application to hotel chain growth. *The Service Industries Journal,* 31, 1645–57.

Holverson, S. and Revaz, F. (2006) Perceptions of European independent hoteliers: hard and soft branding choices. *International Journal of Contemporary Hospitality Management,* 18, 398–413.

Ingram, P. (1996) Organizational form as a solution to the problem of credible commitment: the evolution of naming strategies among US Hotel Chains 1896–1980. *Strategic Management Journal,* 17, 85–98.

Ingram, P. and Baum, J.A. (1997a) Chain affiliation and the failure of Manhattan hotels, 1898–1980. *Administrative Science Quarterly,* 42, 68–102.

Ingram, P. and Baum, J.A. (1997b) Opportunity and constraint: organizations' learning from the operating and competitive experience of industries. *Strategic Management Journal,* 18, 75–98.

Israeli, A.A. (2002) Star rating and corporate affiliation: their influence on room price and performance of hotels in Israel. *International Journal of Hospitality Management,* 21, 405–24.

Ivanov, S. (2014) *Hotel Revenue Management: From Theory to Practice.* Varna: Zangador.

Kim, H.B. and Kim, W.G. (2005) The relationship between brand equity and firms' performance in luxury hotels and chain restaurants. *Tourism Management,* 26, 549–60.

Núñez-Serrano, J.A., Turrión, J. and Velázquez, F.J. (2014) Are stars a good indicator of hotel quality? Asymmetric information and regulatory heterogeneity in Spain. *Tourism Management,* 42, 77–87.

O'Neill, J.W. and Carlbäck, M. (2011) Do brands matter? A comparison of branded and independent hotels' performance during a full economic cycle. *International Journal of Hospitality Management,* 30, 515–21.

O'Neill, J.W. and Mattila, A.S. (2006) Strategic hotel development and positioning. *Cornell Hotel and Restaurant Administration Quarterly,* 47, 146–54.

Orfila, F., Crespí, R. and Martínez, E. (2005) Innovation activity in the hotel industry: evidence from the Balearic Islands. *Tourism Management,* 26, 851–65.

Papatheodorou, A. (2002) Exploring competitiveness in Mediterranean resorts. *Tourism Economics,* 8, 133–50.

Prasad, K. and Dev, C.S. (2000) Managing hotel brand equity: a customer-centric framework for assessing performance. *The Cornell Hotel and Restaurant Administration Quarterly,* 41, 22–31.

Silva, R. (2015) Multimarket contact, differentiation, and prices of chain hotels. *Tourism Management,* 48, 305–15.

Tauber, E.M. (1988) Brand leverage: strategy for growth in a cost-control world. *Journal of Advertising Research,* 28, 26–30.

Thrane, C. (2007) Examining the determinants of room rates for hotels in capital cities: the Oslo experience. *Journal of Revenue & Pricing Management,* 5, 315–23.

Wu, L. (1999) The pricing of a brand name product: franchising in the motel services industry. *Journal of Business Venturing,* 14, 87–102.

Section IV
The individual hotel's perspective

Section IV deals entirely with the perspective of the individual hotel that was, is, or plans to be affiliated to a hotel chain. The objective of Chapter 32 by Mats Carlbäck is to examine the reasons why independently owned firms in the hotel industry would consider affiliating and consequently give up the freedom and independence that is commonly perceived as central for entrepreneurs. By using the concept of agency theory, strategic entrepreneurship, lifestyle entrepreneurs and resource-based views of the firm in a hospitality context the chapter helps us to gain a better understanding of the hotel owners' decision process. The independent hotel owner has to compare the pros and cons of affiliation and compare different affiliation alternatives against each other and therefore gain a better understanding of whether affiliated hotels perform better. This will enhance the prospects for both the affiliations themselves and the hotels contemplating affiliating. But the results show that it is not the pure performance enhancing factors which are most desired by the currently independent hoteliers. Most important are technical innovations, central sales and marketing, purchasing systems, loyalty systems, access to information and better ways to explore new possibilities for the future, while factors such as higher profitability and increased value are less important.

In Chapter 33, Stanislav Ivanov and Maya Ivanova elaborate on the choice of type of affiliation to a chain by the individual hotel. This chapter discusses the preferred types of affiliation by hotel managers and owners, and the factors that influence their preferences by using Bulgaria as a case study. The authors find that hoteliers in the country perceive two of the non-equity forms of affiliation (namely, franchise and management contract) as equally appropriate for the business environment in the country as the ownership-based forms (full ownership and joint venture), and much more appropriate compared to the other two non-equity modes (lease and marketing consortium). These findings suggest that if hotel chains look for local partners in the country they should attract them by offering franchise agreement and/or management contract.

In Chapter 34 by Dimitris Koutoulas, the process of selecting the proper hotel chain to join is analysed from the perspective of the owner of an individual hotel. Such a high-stakes decision comes with an inherent risk due to the large costs of hotel chain participation and the usually long-term legal commitment. This risk can be mitigated if a hotel owner follows a structured approach during the hotel chain selection process such as the one presented in this chapter. The recommended approach has two distinct dimensions: the criteria that a hotel can employ for choosing a chain to join and the steps the hotel should follow during the selection process. A set of 19 criteria is suggested for application during the selection process, to make sure that the hotel chain participation is clearly beneficial for the hotel owner. The criteria have been grouped into two categories, i.e. criteria reflecting the hotel's characteristics, market position and the objectives of the hotel owner as well as criteria reflecting the characteristics and the policies of the hotel chains under consideration. Based on these criteria, a step-by-step approach should be employed during the chain selection process that includes three distinct phases. Phase 1 comprises the pre-selection of hotel chains in accordance with the aforementioned criteria, thus resulting in a shortlist of the chains best fitting the hotel's profile and ambitions. Initial negotiations with the selected chains are conducted during Phase 2, with the chains being ranked according to their suitability for the hotel's strategic aims. The final negotiations are then made with the highest-ranking chain(s) during Phase 3 leading to a signed contract.

Chapter 35 by Florian Aubke and Christian Walter deals with the management of the affiliation process. The decision of a property owner to affiliate with a brand is a multi-step process. This chapter describes the final step of this process, the implementation of the brand affiliation. Setting off with a brief description of the affiliation search and negotiation process, the authors discuss aspects of due diligence and the implementation phase. Due diligence is carried out by the new operator or their representatives and focuses on three main aspects, namely the legal framework in which the hotel currently operates, the real estate/technical framework which assesses the technical status of the building and the operational framework which assesses the current operations of the hotel. The subsequent implementation phase is characterised by both hard and soft issues. Soft issues refer to changes in management and other human resources. More context-specific hard issues discussed in this chapter include: compliance with brand standards, changes to the technical infrastructure, merging of old and new property management systems, sales and marketing as well as quality control and compliance. To conclude, the authors stress that the owner seeking the affiliation is well advised not only to rely on professional support during the affiliation search process, but to have the entire affiliation process accompanied.

The final chapter in the section (Chapter 36) by Dirisa Mulindwa and Vivien Ulu discusses the hotel affiliation evaluation and the decisions that the hotel owners/managers should take: to remain in the chain, leave the chain, or rebrand. There are many reasons for reflagging hotels including the property changing ownership, termination of the existing affiliation, expiration of the existing agreement, etc. Usually management contracts and franchise agreement are long term contracts that bind the hotel owner to a brand for many years or even decades. However, when the initial contracts are signed and the affiliation is established, hotel owners usually start the process of evaluating the impacts of that affiliation to a hotel chain on the performance of their properties. The findings from the evaluation leave the hotel owners with the question of whether to remain with the current affiliation or leave. Furthermore if the decision is to leave, hotel owners also have to decide on whether to brand or rebrand their hotels by affiliating to another hotel chain or take the independent route. This chapter discusses the evaluation process and the decisions hotels managers have to take regarding their properties when they come to end the existing affiliation. Each decision is presented and discussed to show what the hotel owners need to consider before making decisions that are going to affect the hotel's performance for many years.

32

Independent or flagged? The decision to affiliate to a chain

Mats Carlbäck

(SCHOOL OF HOSPITALITY, CULINARY ARTS AND MEAL SCIENCE, ÖREBRO UNIVERSITY, SWEDEN)

Introduction and background

To be or not to be affiliated is a greatly discussed and debated topic in today's hotel industry. Chains, consortia and franchise operations, both smaller and larger, are becoming increasingly dominant in the global hotel market. The industry has for centuries been dominated by small-scale businesses, often run by a family, but today this trend is changing (Rushmore, 2001a,b). The market is developing and hoteliers are seeking new ways to achieve growth and development, where different types of affiliations will play an important role. Independently owned hotels are being incorporated in larger organisations for expansion possibilities or just to survive in times when the competition is becoming increasingly fierce. The trend to affiliate in the hospitality sector is swelling and this creates a contradictory and complex situation. The independent owner-operated firms have previously been identified as the most efficient form of running a company (Abdellatif et al., 2010; Astrachan, 2010; Jensen and Meckling, 1976), but a large part of these independent hotels are affiliating with the scope to enhance the performance potential for the future. Why are independently owned firms in the hospitality sector affiliating, and what are they seeking when they choose to give up their freedom and independence to become a part of something much larger?

The objective in this chapter is to examine the reasons why independently owned firms in the hotel industry would consider affiliating and hence giving up the freedom and independence that is universally perceived as being important for entrepreneurs. By establishing the reasons for affiliating from a hotel perspective it should also be possible to identify and understand if the affiliations are offering what the hotels require from the chain. The concepts of agency theory, strategic entrepreneurship, lifestyle entrepreneurs, and resource-based views of the firm in a hospitality context will contribute to a better understanding of the hotel owners' decision process. Can the hotel owners develop on their own? Or would they be better off in an affiliation context? And how could the affiliations enhance the membership to attract new members and create a better product for current and potential members, thereby strengthening the brand name?

Interestingly, the old axiom 'location, location, location' is now often replaced by 'flag, flag and what flag' (Taylor, 1995) as an answer to the question: 'What are the three most important factors for a successful hotel operation?' Lately, the flag associated with affiliations has become one of the most important strategic issues in the hotel industry (O'Neill and Mattila, 2010). In the UK, independent mid-market hotels are facing considerable competitive pressure, as both corporately owned branded hotels and branded budget hotels are so strong (Imrie and Fyall, 2001). Imrie and Fyall (2001) conclude that operators of independent mid-market hotels either sell to a hotel chain, alter their product, create economies of scale or simply do nothing and wait for the inevitable. So, the owners of independent hotels will have to choose between the prospects of trying to succeed alone, or alternatively, let some of the independence and liberty slip away in order to gain competitive advantage by joining some kind of organisation. Consequently, the independent hotel owners have to compare the pros and cons of affiliation *and* compare different affiliation alternatives against each other. A clear understanding of whether affiliated hotels perform better and how this is achieved would enhance the prospects for both the affiliations and the hotels contemplating affiliating. If affiliating could lead to better performance on a long term basis, this needs to be addressed in terms of how it is communicated and utilised in order to attract more hotels into this business format. But in a global perspective the affiliations still play a limited role, even if the presence of affiliations is increasing in most markets. Brand penetration was over 70 per cent in the 'commercial lodging industry' in the United States, 40 per cent in Canada, and just under 25 per cent in Europe with an observed upsurge (Rivet, 2011). Statistics from Rivet (2011) show that only 15 per cent of the world's hotel portfolio are considered to be affiliated, previously identified by Sangster (2000). The global trend points in one direction, but the true figure regarding the amount of hotels belonging to an affiliation points in another direction. The independent businesses have been researched broadly and it has been argued that this business format is the most efficient, due to limited effects relating to agency problems or costs (Jensen, 1983; Jensen and Meckling, 1976). Recent research has indicated that this situation might not be the case. Independently owned businesses could actually be less effective as the power and knowledge in decision-making, employee selection process, and managerial incentives lie within a small ownership structure (Schulze et al., 2001).

This presents us with an interesting and challenging paradox – a growing number of independently owned hotels are changing from a perceived efficient business format, with freedom and independence, to a more unknown future as affiliated entities. Why are they doing this and for what reasons? One way to deal with this complex and abstract issue is to translate the flag into brand value. It will create possibilities of viewing the issue from different perspectives, with alternative theories. Further, it will present opportunities to measure and evaluate the value of the flag. The hospitality industry is growing and has become an industry where investors seek a return on their invested capital. The larger hospitality corporations play an important and influential role in most countries today (Bailey, 2007; Imrie and Fyall, 2001; Martorell Cunill, 2006).

Hotel affiliations bring a package of useful tools for business operators in the hotel industry (Holverson and Revaz, 2006; Xiao et al., 2008). The large operations develop and maintain central reservations systems, yield/revenue management programs, cumulative purchasing power, loyalty programs, global distribution systems, brand awareness, and sales and marketing activities. This is something that independent business operators will have problems matching, but these benefits come at a sometimes considerable cost (Rushmore, 2001b). To operate independently presents advantages such as giving the owner freedom to operate differently and to promote the hotel property based on its uniqueness in addition to money saved on franchise royalty and marketing fees. Rushmore (2005) states that hotels with

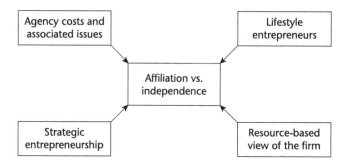

Figure 32.1   Theoretical approaches for identifying the independent hotel owner's decision-making process regarding affiliating (Carlbäck, 2012).

certain attributes, such as exclusive locations or historic value, could manage well on their own without brand affiliation. Hotels with unique features can generate rate premiums due to their distinctiveness. Every owner/manager must therefore evaluate the cost of affiliation because it can be costly at times (Rushmore, 2001a,b), and assess whether the affiliation fulfils the need of the individual business owner (Carlbäck, 2008).

Theoretical background

The issue of affiliating or not could be analysed from various perspectives. In this chapter we will use the following theoretical perspectives to get a better understanding of the phenomena. Each section will be followed by a brief conclusion related to the latest findings.

Agency theory

Owner operated firms are often perceived as the most efficient form to run a company and will normally perform better than non-owner-operated businesses (Abdellatif et al., 2010; Astrachan, 2010; Astrachan and Shanker, 2003; Jensen and Meckling, 1976). One explanation for this is the agency perspective (Jensen, 1983; Jensen and Meckling, 1976) as the constellation for an independent, owner operated firm per definition will lack many of the issues relating to agency costs and agency problems. This will be specifically valid in the hotel industry, where most of the independent firms are owner operated. But Schulze et al. (2001) are challenging this theory as independent, owner operated businesses will face other issues that could make it less efficient than non-owner-operated firms. Agency costs arise when the interests of the firm's manager are not aligned with those of the firm's owner(s). It could be perks, shrinking and making self-interested decisions. These costs could be controlled and limited by the owner, depending on how well they can control the costs or monitor the spending and decision-making of hired managers/external parties, which in these circumstances could be an affiliation. Many of the reasons behind an establishment's decision to remain independent could be explained by agency-related issues. Letting other parties into the business could cause conflicting situations for a non-owner-operated company. The affiliations would also require access to information from the member, even in the case of marketing organisations. Franchise chains, on the other hand, will ensure a complete control of most business aspects and in all cases the owner will have to let go of some of the control.

The flow of information could be asymmetric and decisions based on such information could be biased, which could cause problems, not only for the business owner but also for the affiliation. The affiliation options will consistently involve agency costs, which could affect the value of the firm (Jensen and Meckling, 1976), even though affiliations could add value to the firm's intangible asset value, according to American research (O'Neill and Xiao, 2006). As the flag in itself is becoming more important, this relationship becomes more of a focal point. Schulze et al. (2001) show that the previous notion that no agency costs exist in an independent owner-operated firm has been challenged and therefore must be taken into consideration. An independent owner-operated business may incur agency costs, often comparable to those of affiliated firms. The independent owner operated firm could be affected by costs associated with adverse selection, hiring the wrong staff and with recruitment taking place within the family or close network, poor access to information and other factors affecting the performance (Schulze et al., 2001). Agency issues were identified as one aspect related to the decision to affiliate or not, even if few practitioners in the hotel industry would be aware of this (Carlbäck, 2012). The most important factor was connected to control rights, i.e. few independent hotel owners were willing to let any aspect of the control of the business go to someone outside the organisation, in this case an affiliation. This was the case even if less control theoretically could lead to growth and increased profit (Carlbäck, 2012). The perception among the independent hoteliers is also that an independent, owner-operated business is the most efficient way to run hotels, with few agency issues affecting the efficiency (Carlbäck, 2012).

Strategic entrepreneurship

Webb et al. (2010) explain the term strategic entrepreneurship as exploring future business domains while exploiting current domains, something that presents a vital and difficult question for most business owners and entrepreneurs. The balancing act between taking advantage of what one has got (exploiting), and potential possibilities (exploring), would be part of any business owner's agenda. The question of affiliation would be part of the equation – to exploit the possibilities and remain independent or to explore new domains with the help of an association.

Webb et al. (2010) apply the discussion of strategic entrepreneurship to family-owned and other independent properties, which would be comparable to the hospitality industry. As parts of this discussion, Webb et al. (2010) propose trying to find a balance between exploitation and exploration. Would the hotel have enough competitive advantage to build on in their current situation or would it be necessary to take new measures to be able to keep this in the future? The competitive advantage is an important factor in the hotel industry and something to build strategies on (Oh and Kim, 2004). It will be important to establish the identity of the firm, i.e. values and tradition, which could obstruct any affiliation plans. One important part of Webb et al.'s (2010) description of strategic entrepreneurship is continuous innovation – something directly related to the hotel industry, not least in the technological arena. At present there is a great evolution connected to the use of social media, smart phones and the internet. Large, multinational firms have an advantage in the development of innovations, backed by financial muscles, and with departments dedicated to such tasks. Siguaw et al. (2000) show different adoption of technology with a comparison between chains and independents, where the chains are more likely to adopt (Dittman et al., 2009; Siguaw et al., 2000). But there was no significant difference regarding guest and service strategy priority between chains and independent hotels (Siguaw et al., 2000). Independent hotels do have a clear picture of what to exploit from their current situation, but find it a larger challenge to explore new directions for the future (Carlbäck, 2012). Joining an affiliation could be one alternative, but few hotel owners had a clear picture of how this would affect their entrepreneurial situation.

Lifestyle entrepreneurs

According to a survey by Mieyal Higgins (2006), individual hotels produced better profits than hotels belonging to various chains. The independent hotels could hold their own business and did not depend on ups and downs in the economy. One reason could be the goal of building something for the family, which was ranked highly in a study by Andersson et al. (2002). In the same study the top goals for owner-managers were presented as challenge/stimulus, business opportunity, lifestyle and long-term financial gains (Andersson et al., 2002). One conclusion might be that stronger forces drive the independent business owner more than financial rewards – way of life, social life, working together as a family, enjoying work, freedom, etc.

In the same study, several of the business owners agreed with the statement that 'enjoying the job is more important than making lots of money' and they would rather keep the business modest and under control, than expanding to make lots of money. Getz and Petersen (2005) argue that growth is frequently neither desired nor achieved among owner-operated businesses. The reasons could be that growth is hard to achieve, due to lack of capital, and might be avoided due to higher risks, more work and more debt (Getz and Petersen, 2005). Several studies show the importance of creating a decent lifestyle and being able to support oneself and create a fair way of life as opposed to growth and huge financial awards (Carlbäck, 2012; Andersson et al. 2002). Few hoteliers would give up their freedom and independence to become part of something larger, albeit with potential growth opportunities.

Resource-based view of the firm

A hotel owner's decision to affiliate can depend on many factors – several have been discussed above. It is also important to take a look at the theory surrounding the resource-based view of the firm (Astrachan, 2010; Astrachan and Shanker, 2003; Barney, 2001) as this will affect the decision to remain independent or not. This theory stipulates that firms achieve and maintain a competitive advantage based on a combination of tangible and intangible recourses (Barney, 2001; Moores, 2009), something closely related to the question of independence versus affiliation. What resources do the independent hotels hold today and what resources could be lacking in the future within this environment? An internal due diligence process would be required to identify what resources are at hand if the independent hotel would like to retain its competitive advantage or find opportunities to create such an advantage. What resources could be developed inside the firm or what resources would come with affiliation (Oh and Kim, 2004)? But the question is whether it is possible for the independent hotel to add resources to the current operation and if this would be feasible, in economic terms. If not, affiliation could be a better alternative. An option and a current trend in the hotel industry, for the firm with limited resources, could be outsourcing (Espino-Rodríguez and Padrón-Robaina, 2004; Lamminmaki, 2006). A hotel with limited resources to develop a competitive advantage with, for example, F&B, could use outsourcing as an alternative (Lamminmaki, 2011).

Carlbäck (2012) finds that a majority of independent hotel owners think they have the necessary resources within the company to create growth and development, with two exceptions; technical innovations and sales and marketing activities, areas where the affiliations normally have a strength.

Brand value attributable to affiliation (BVAA)

When translating the issues of affiliating into a value, i.e. intangible asset value, transparency could be affected. In the hospitality literature, research has been carried out to attempt to identify the value of the brand, which would be part of the firm's intangible asset value (O'Neill, 2004; O'Neill and Belfrage, 2005). The issue of measuring the value of the brand could be subtracting brand-attributable expenses from brand-attributable revenue. For many stakeholders in the hospitality industry it would be advantageous to define and calculate brand value as a foundation for decision-making between different hotel brands. But it is also important to be able to estimate whether hotel affiliation is warranted and when. All branded hotels, due to their global distribution systems, loyalty programmes, and name recognition, have a relatively higher operating volume compared to individual hotels, with the brand expected to add value to individual hotel properties (Häggström, 2012).

Initially, it is necessary to define brand value and explain in what ways it differs from brand equity. Brand value and brand equity are two closely related but different concepts. Tiwari (2010) explains the differences in brand value as being the net present value of future cash flows from a branded product less the net present value of future cash flows from a similar unbranded product, i.e. what the brand is worth to management and shareholders (Tiwari, 2010) – in this case the hotel owners. Brand equity is a set of perceptions, knowledge, and behaviour on the part of customers that creates demand and possibly a price premium for a branded product, i.e. what the brand is worth to the company based on the customer's perception. Every company has a brand, whether it is affiliated or not. The small, independent hotel will have a brand to promote in the same way as 'W' in New York. Several articles describe the importance of brand, both in an affiliation context and as a stand-alone-unit (Bailey and Ball, 2006; Carlbäck, 2012, 2013; O'Neill and Xiao, 2006). The brand value attributable to the affiliation (BVAA) will be positive, if the cash flow associated with the brand is positive – the contribution from the brand produces a surplus. The BVAA would be the brand value attributable to membership in any kind of affiliation compared to a similar product without membership in an affiliation.

O'Neill and Carlbäck (2011) analysed longitudinal data of more than 51,000 hotels operating in the United States during a full economic cycle. From the findings it was possible to draw conclusions regarding the performance of affiliated hotels compared to independent operations under various economic conditions. Affiliated properties experience higher occupancy rates during the different phases of the economic cycle, while independent hotels experience higher average daily rate (ADR) and room revenues per available room (RevPAR) during the same time. When affiliated hotels are faced with various payments attributable to the brand, royalty payments and other membership-related fees, these do not have a deleterious effect on net operating income (NOI) compared to NOI for independent hotels. Independent hotels appear to be unable to bring their ADR and RevPAR premiums to the bottom line despite their savings in affiliation expenses. The results indicate similar NOI for affiliated hotels and independent hotels during economic expansion, but significantly higher NOI for branded hotels during economic recession. Intangible asset value of hotel brands may not be static, but may vary by time. Sources of such intangible value of brands attributable to affiliation may include shared resources, guest loyalty programmes, and yield management systems. These results contribute insight to the complex hotel owners' decision of choosing between a brand affiliation and an independent operation.

Valuation methods of brand

Based on the discussion above, where the brand value created could constitute an important tool as a foundation for decision-making, it stresses the importance of measuring or evaluating the brand value. Most studies indicate that apart from the actual real estate, the building where the hotel is operating, the most significant part of the remaining value is attributable to intangible assets – mainly the brand (Bailey and Ball, 2006; O'Neill and Belfrage, 2005; Tiwari, 2010; Tollington, 2002). Different methods have previously been used in order to separate the BVAA from the market value of a hotel property. This could be a more complex task than first anticipated as fees and royalties differ considerably, just like the benefits received from the brand, i.e. the attributable revenue streams, rooms booked, etc. One widely used method is the Rushmore method (Häggström, 2012; O'Neill and Belfrage, 2005; Rushmore, 2005), where management and franchise fees are removed from hotels' operating cash flow and the remaining value is directly traceable to the real estate.

The accurate value of a hotel affects a number of parties, including hotel owners, operators, brokers, management companies, and financiers. O'Neill and Belfrage (2005) have suggested methods for appraising intangible assets within hotels and creating new frameworks for hotel valuation. By identifying the contribution associated with the ongoing affiliation as well as incremental costs, and including the investment for converting the property in accordance with the stipulated standards for the affiliation, an easy-to-use model for computing the brand value attributable to affiliation (BVAA) is developed (Carlbäck, 2015). The model includes the initial investment needed to fulfil the standards stipulated by the affiliation to be part of the organisation, a factor which independent hotel owners viewed as a major issue in considering whether to affiliate (Carlbäck, 2012). This study produces an indicative valuation method (the BVAA calculation method) usable both for evaluating the brand value associated with a specific brand and for separating intangibles from the market value. From an affiliating process prospect, the possibility of putting a value on the flag representing the affiliation would facilitate the decision process for independent hotels entering into such a venture. Would affiliating add value to my business or would it mainly add expenses?

Conclusion

To be or not to be affiliated depends on the various factors discussed above, both hard and soft values. A summary of identified advantages and disadvantages of being affiliated is presented in Table 32.1 in an attempt to visualise the factors that could affect such strategic business decisions.

The factors presented in Table 32.1 could be used as a framework for analysing the affiliation decision process from a strictly strategic business development perspective. But one must not ignore the underlying factors expressed by concerned hoteliers. Would lost freedom and independence be off-set by possible, but uncertain financial and strategic gains? Would the reasons why an entrepreneur entered into a project as risky as running a hotel in the first place prevail as the hotel becomes a part of a larger organisation such as an affiliation, or would that diminish the entrepreneurial spirit? As long as the challenge of determining the

Table 32.1 Summary of advantages and disadvantages of being affiliated based on literature review

Identified advantages of independence	Identified advantages of affiliating
• Freedom	• A flag to fly
• Better control over decision	• Economies of scale
• Independence	• Increased net profit
• Avoidance of certain agency related costs	• Availability of tools, systems, loyalty cards, and channels
• No fees or royalties	• Brand value
• Shorter line decisions	• Central sales and marketing
• Marketing based on unique features of business	• Access to information
• Easier exploitation of internal resources	• Continuous innovation
	• Easier exploration of new possibilities

value of the actual flag (the membership in an affiliation) is neither calculated nor analysed, the decision process will be left to less rigid forms, and to a certain degree, speculations. Loss of freedom, independence and interference in the decision-making process need to be compensated by substantial improvement regarding the operational aspects connected to affiliation. And it is within the operation-enhancing factors we find the ones most sought after by currently independent hoteliers – technical innovations, central sales and marketing, purchasing systems, loyalty cards, access to information, and better ways of exploring new possibilities for the future. Less focus is put on pure economic advantages, such as better profitability and increased value. The entrepreneurial spirit and the wish to deliver something good seem to dwarf the wish for excessive profits and growth. Something both the hotel owners and affiliations should be aware of.

References

Abdellatif, M., Amann, B. and Jaussaud, J. (2010) Family versus non-family business: a comparison of international strategies. *Journal of Family Business Strategy*, 1(2), 108–16.

Andersson, T.D., Carlsen, J. and Getz, D. (2002) Family business goals in the tourism and hospitality sector: case studies and cross-case analysis from Australia, Canada, and Sweden. *Family Business Review*, 15(2), 89–106.

Astrachan, J.H. (2010) Strategy in family business: toward a multidimensional research agenda. *Journal of Family Business Strategy*, 1(1), 6–14.

Astrachan, J.H. and Shanker, M.C. (2003) Family businesses' contribution to the U.S. economy: a closer look. *Family Business Review*, 16(3), 211–19.

Bailey, R. (2007) *UK hotel industry brand equity: its meaning and uses for brand management.* (Unpublished doctoral thesis.) Sheffield Hallam University, Sheffield.

Bailey, R. and Ball, S. (2006) An exploration of the meanings of hotel brand equity. *The Service Industries Journal*, 26(1), 15–38.

Barney, J. (2001) Resource-based theories of competitive advantage: a ten-year retrospective on the resource-based view. *Journal of Management,* 27(6), 643–50.

Carlbäck, M. (2008) Are the chain operations simply with it? Five aspects meal model as a development tool for chain operations/franchise organizations. *Journal of Foodservice*, 19, 74–79.

Carlbäck, M. (2012) Strategic entrepreneurship in the hotel industry: the role of chain affiliation. *Scandinavian Journal of Hospitality and Tourism*, 12(4), 349–72.

Carlbäck, M. (2013) Brand value attributable to affiliation in the Swedish hospitality industry – an explorative study. Unpublished manuscript, Gothenburg, Sweden.

Carlbäck, M. (2015) Brand value attributable to affiliation (BVAA) – a method for measurement in a consortium context. Unpublished manuscript, Gothenburg, Sweden.

Dittman, D.A., Hesford, J.W. and Potter, G. (2009) Managerial accounting in the hospitality industry. In C.S. Chapman, A.G. Hopwood and M.D. Shields (eds), *Handbook of Management Accounting Research*. New York: Elsevier Ltd., pp. 1353–69.

Espino-Rodríguez, T.F. and Padrón-Robaina, V. (2004) A resource-based view of outsourcing and its implications for organizational performance in the hotel sector. *Tourism Management*, 26(5), 707–21.

Getz, D. and Petersen, T. (2005) Growth and profit-oriented entrepreneurship among family business owners in the tourism and hospitality industry. *International Journal of Hospitality Management*, 2005(24), 219–42.

Häggström, R. (2012) *Intangible assets and hotel value*. PhD Thesis, Gothenburg University, Gothenburg.

Holverson, S. and Revaz, F. (2006) Perceptions of European independent hoteliers: hard and soft branding choices. *International Journal of Contemporary Hospitality Management*, 18(5), 398–413.

Imrie, R. and Fyall, A. (2001). Independent mid-market UK hotels: marketing strategies for an increasingly competitive environment. *Journal of Vacation Marketing*, 7(63), 63–74.

Jensen, M. (1983) Organization theory and methodology. *Accounting Review*, 56, 319–38.

Jensen, M. and Meckling, W. (1976) Theory of the firm: managerial behaviour, agency costs, and ownership structure. *Journal of Financial Economics*, 3, 305–60.

Lamminmaki, D. (2006) *Outsourcing in the Hotel Industry: A Management Accounting Perspective*. Oxford: Butterworth-Heinemann.

Lamminmaki, D. (2011) An examination of factors motivating hotel outsourcing. *International Journal of Hospitality Management*, 30(4), 963–73.

Martorell Cunill, O. (2006) *The Growth Strategies of Hotel Chains* (Vol. 1). New York: The Haworth Hospitality Press.

Mieyal Higgins, S. (2006) Independents relish individuality (Cover story). *Hotel & Motel Management*, 221(21), 1–38.

Moores, K. (2009) Paradigms and theory building in the domain of business families. *Family Business Review*, 22(2), 167–80.

Oh, H. and Kim, B.Y. (2004) How do hotel firms obtain a competitive advantage? *International Contemporary Hospitality Management*, 16(1), 65–71.

O'Neill, J.W. (2004) An automated valuation model for hotels. *Cornell Hotel and Restaurant Administration Quarterly*, 45(3), 260–68.

O'Neill, J.W. and Belfrage, E.E. (2005) A strategy for estimating identified intangible asset value: hotels affiliation contribution. *The Appraisal Journal*, 73(1), 78–86.

O'Neill, J.W. and Carlbäck, M. (2011) Do brands matter? A comparison of branded and independent hotels' performance during a full economic cycle. *International Journal of Hospitality Management*, 30(3), 515–21.

O'Neill, J.W. and Mattila, A.S. (2010) Hotel brand strategy. *Cornell Hospitality Quarterly*, 51(1), 27–34.

O'Neill, J.W. and Xiao, Q. (2006) The role of brand affiliation in hotel market value. *Cornell Hotel and Restaurant Administration Quarterly*, 47(3), 210–23.

Rivet, V. (2011) *The Challenges of Repositioning an International Brand: A Case Study on the Hospitality Industry*. Escola de Administração de Empresas de São Paulo, Sao Paolo.

Rushmore, S. (2001a) Six things to consider before obtaining a hotel franchise. *Hotels Magazine*. Online. Available HTTP: <http://www.hvs.com/article/1521/six-things-to-consider-before-obtaining-a-hotel-franchise/>, accessed 11 December, 2015.

Rushmore, S. (2001b) Hidden costs of franchise agreements. *Hotels Magazine*. Online. Available HTTP: <http://www.hvs.com/article/1533/hidden-costs-of-franchise-agreements/>, accessed 11 December, 2015.

Rushmore, S. (2005) A case for being independent. *Canadian Lodging Outlook*. Online. Available HTTP: <http://www.hvs.com/article/1732/canadian-lodging-outlook-may-2005/>, accessed 11 December, 2015.

Sangster, A. (2000) European hotel branding. *Travel & Tourism Analyst*, 6, 63–81.

Schulze, W.S., Lubatkin, M.H., Dino, R.N. and Buchholtz, A.K. (2001) Agency relationships in family firms: theory and evidence. *Organizational Science*, 12(2), 99–116.

Siguaw, J.A., Enz, C.A. and Namasivayam, K. (2000) Adoption of information technology in U.S. hotels: strategically driven objectives. *Journal of Travel Research*, 39(2), 192–201.

Taylor, P.S. (1995) Choosing a flag. *Lodging Hospitality* (July), 24–27.

Tiwari, M. (2010) Separation of brand equity and brand value. *Global Business Review*, 11(3), 421–34.

Tollington, T. (2002) *Brand Assets.* Chichester: John Wiley & Sons Ltd.

Xiao, Q., O'Neill, J. and Wang, H. (2008) International hotel development: a study of potential franchisees in China. *International Journal of Hospitality Management*, 27(3), 325–36.

Webb, J., Ketchen, D. and Ireland, R. (2010) Strategic entrepreneurship within family-controlled firms: opportunities and challenges. *Journal of Family Business Strategy*, 1, 67–77.

33

The choice of type of affiliation to a chain by the individual hotel

Stanislav Ivanov and Maya Ivanova

(VARNA UNIVERSITY OF MANAGEMENT, BULGARIA)

Introduction

As elaborated in previous chapters of this handbook, the process of a hotel chain's expansion involves two parties, namely the hotel chain and the individual hotel. Despite possessing high financial and bargaining power, the hotel chains expand predominantly by using non-equity modes (see Chapters 12–15) and, therefore, need proper partners, in order to expand their networks and enhance their market visibility, market share and financial performance. In this regard, independent hotels are considered valuable partners and 'clients' for the hotel chains (Dev, 2012). Understanding the viewpoint of individual hotels (Cho, 2005; Connell, 1997; Xiao et al., 2008) would facilitate the chains in their marketing strategies and efforts to attract new members. This chapter discusses the preferred types of affiliation by hotel managers and owners, and the factors that influence their preferences by using Bulgaria as an exemplary case study.

Theoretical background

A large body of literature is dedicated to the choice of entry mode of international hotel chains (Chen and Dimou, 2005; Martorell-Cunill, Mulet-Forteza and Otero, 2013; Contractor and Kundu, 1998a, among others), but only a few papers focus on the viewpoint of the individual hotel (Cho, 2005; Connell, 1997). Most hotel chains declare their *preferred type of affiliation* for new hotels and it may seem to their potential partner hotels that the type of affiliation is predetermined by the hotel chain and the individual hotel has only the right to accept the proposed type or not. However, the increased competition among hotel chains in recent years presses them to negotiate with each individual potential partner hotel about the type of affiliation that is most appropriate for both of them (Butler and Braun, 2014). Moreover, most hotel chains use plural forms of expansion (see Brookes and Roper, 2012; Perrigot et al., 2009), which is another opportunity for the individual hotel to choose among various types of affiliation. Therefore, individual hotels find themselves in a position to negotiate and bargain for the most appropriate type of affiliation for them (Butler and Braun, 2014).

The most popular classification of entry modes (from the viewpoint of the hotel chains) or types of affiliation (from the hotel's perspective) divides them into equity or hierarchal modes (full ownership and partial ownership, or joint venture), and non-equity or contractual modes (management contract, franchise, marketing consortium and lease), depending on the capital involvement of the hotel chain (Contractor and Kundu, 1998a). As each type was elaborated in detail in Chapters 11–15, here we will only briefly discuss the literature dealing with the perspective of the individual affiliated hotel and will outline key factors that determine the choice of the type of affiliation by the hotel's managers and owners.

The equity modes presume financial involvement of the chain with the hotel. In *full ownership* the chain holds the entire capital of the hotel and does not have a partner. Therefore, we cannot talk about individual hotel managers' perceptions about the affiliation process, because the decision by the hotel to be affiliated to the chain is not market-based, as it is fully owned by the chain. In a *joint venture* the chain has partial ownership of the capital of the hotel (Contractor and Kundu, 1998a; Cunill, 2006). The joint venture presumes long-term involvement of the chain in the proper management of the hotel, because of its capital stake in it (Contractor and Kundu, 1998a) and in many cases it is accompanied by a management contract and/or franchise. The financial, managerial and control links between the hotel and the chain are very strong (Quer et al., 2007). However, the different perspectives of the partners might ruin the relationship. Hotel chains' long-term focus on brand equity and consistent service quality might not be in line with their local partners' desire for short-term profits. Conflicts between the partners might arise from various sources (disagreements about investments in and renovations of the property, number and salaries of personnel, dividends, marketing strategy of the hotel, price levels, etc.) and end up in the sale of the chain's or local partner's stake in the property (Cunill, 2006). In general, joint venture is applied more for large investment projects (e.g. resort complexes) and luxury hotels where the local company pursues the financial support by and/or the long-term commitment of the chain. Small-sized, low category properties would find it difficult to attract the attention of the chains to invest in them. It should be noted that in some countries (like China and UAE) foreigners are not allowed to be majority shareholders in a business. Thus joint venture becomes the appropriate type of affiliation for small and medium sized hotels in these countries as well. Furthermore, in some developing countries, a government entity is the local partner of the hotel chain. In this case, both the chain and its local partner would focus on the long-term development of the hotel rather than the short-term profits and their interests would be aligned. Nevertheless, conflicts between partners might arise.

Each of the non-equity types of affiliation determines a separate and quite distinct stream in the research literature elaborated in Chapters 12–15 of this handbook. *Management contracts* are discussed with regard to the legal obligations, terms and litigation for both parties involved (DeRoos, 2010; Johnson, 1999; Eyster, 1997) – the individual hotel and the management company (or hotel operator). The hotel operators could be independent or brand operators (Butler and Braun, 2014). The independent operators are not bound to a certain brand and may manage properties flagged under different brands, while branded operators flag the property with their own brand. The hotels' perspective in most cases is less examined with the notable exception of Butler and Braun's (2014) handbook, which primarily considers the perspectives of the hotel owners, developers and investors.

As a successful business model, the *franchise* is popular with the service industries, especially in hospitality (Cunill and Forteza, 2010). Unlike management contracts, franchise literature is abundant with case studies on the franchisee's viewpoint (Altinay et al., 2014; Hodge et al., 2013; Peterson and Dant, 1990; Knight, 1986), but the hotel franchisee's perspective is presented in only a few papers (Cho, 2005; Connell, 1997; Xiao et al., 2008). This entry mode is often cited to be the prevailing mode in the hotel industry (Cunill and Forteza, 2010), and also the most preferable from the individual hotel's perspective (Guillet et al., 2010). Franchising has been discussed in the light of factors that determine its appropriate use/ suitability for the hotel chains (Contractor and Kundu, 1998b; Alon et al., 2012).

The *marketing consortium*, in contrast to the above, is usually explored from the individual hotel's perspective. Roper (1992) makes a thorough analysis of the marketing consortium, putting a stable ground from an academic perspective. Further, Holverson and Revaz (2006) discuss the marketing consortium as a 'soft' version of hotel chain affiliation. In all papers the marketing consortium is illustrated as providing the highest level of independence of the hotels within the chain, therefore recommended as the most appropriate type of affiliation for those hotels, avoiding stronger commitment with a chain (Chatoth and Olsen, 2003), at the same time enhancing their marketing positions (Morrison, 1994).

The *lease contract* has received least attention in the literature, and it is discussed mostly in a comparison to another type of affiliation (Huang and Chathoth, 2011; Ghorbal-Blal, 2008; Cunill, 2006; Lelacqua and Smith, 2012). Although in some occasions the lease is classified like an equity mode (Martorell-Cunill et al., 2013), we consider it as a non-equity type of affiliation, because the hotel chain does not possess the hotel property. The lease contract is recognised as a possible option for affiliation by a limited number of hotel owners, because it does not allow the owner any involvement in the property management (Ghorbal-Blal, 2008).

Type of affiliation influences the strength of connection between the hotel chain and its members, but also the relationship scheme of the venture. Therefore, the agency theory (Eisenhardt, 1989) and relationships within an agent model are relevant and thoroughly discussed in this field (Chen and Dimou, 2005; Ramon Rodriguez, 2002). Within the context of agency theory, roles of the principal and the agent pertain either to the chain, or to the individual hotel, depending on the type of affiliation. For instance, in the franchise contract the hotel chain is the principal and the hotel owner is the agent, while in the management contract this is the opposite. The terms of the contract (fees, duration, termination, rights and obligations of the parties, and other contract terms) govern the principal–agent relationship and have a huge impact on the choice of type of affiliation. These contract terms are determined mainly by the hotel chains, but also negotiable with the partner hotel, and are specific for each type of affiliation. The individual hotels have to take such terms into consideration, when evaluating their future costs and relations with the chain.

The rights and obligations, deriving from different affiliation contracts, bring other concerns to the individual hotel managers and owners, not directly connected with finance and fees. For example, in franchising, the principal is the hotel chain, providing all the operational guides in the hands of the individual hotel (the agent) in the form of service operation manuals, but also requiring it to adhere to the standards of the brand. The hotel owner has more freedom regarding the operational control, but less chance of sharing tacit knowledge from the chain compared to the management contract, as the chain representatives do not take part in the management of the hotel (Dev, 2012). On the other hand, the management contract leaves the whole operational management in the hands of the chain, but the terms regarding termination are often stricter. Considering the above, the willingness of the owner regarding stricter operational control might result in choice of franchise or marketing consortia, whereas gaining more tacit knowledge in hotel management through closer consultations with its representatives might incline the hotel owner to prefer a management contract.

The individual hotel's managers and owners should evaluate their abilities to enter into a particular contract where certain limitations on their operational freedom would be raised. This highlights the importance of the experience and skills of hotel managers in the choice of type of affiliation (Xiao et al., 2008), because they will ensure the professional attitude and expertise in establishing and maintaining good relations with the chain, as well as in implementing properly the chains' standards and requirements.

In conclusion, hotel managers and owners would prefer different types of affiliation of their properties to hotel chains depending on various factors – their knowledge, skills, experience and willingness to maintain control of hotel's operations, the type of affiliation used predominantly by the chain and the consultations provided by its representatives, and the specific contract terms – fees, duration and termination. Knowing the preferences of individual hotels' managers and owners would help hotel chains' brand representatives attract more accommodation establishments to their hotel chain networks. The next section of the chapter evaluates the importance of each of these factors in the context of the Bulgarian hotel industry.

The choice of type of affiliation to a chain by the individual hotel: the preferences of hotel managers and owners in Bulgaria

Overview of chain-affiliated hotels in Bulgaria

Bulgaria has experienced an explosive growth in the number of accommodation establishments and their bed capacity in recent years – from 1,433 establishments with 183,439 beds in 2000 to 3,163 establishments with 314,257 beds in 2014 (NSI, 2001, 2015), but nevertheless the market penetration of hotel chains in the country remains very low – less than 5 per cent of all accommodation establishments are affiliated to a hotel chain (see Table 33.1 and Ivanova, 2010; Ivanova and Ivanov, 2014). As of 1 May 2015, the authors identified 132 chain hotels in the country: 52 hotels affiliated to 33 foreign hotel chain brands and 80 hotels belonging to 18 domestic chains. Non-equity type of affiliation (franchise, management contract and marketing consortium) prevails among hotels affiliated to foreign chains, while hotels affiliated to domestic chains are owned by the chains. Both domestic and foreign chains prefer to affiliate with higher category properties (4–5 stars), although domestic chains have a greater tendency to have 2- and 3-star hotels under their brands as well. Foreign chains affiliate with mostly very large properties (over 150 rooms), while Bulgarian chains also have a significant share of small (up to 50 rooms) and midsized properties (51–100 rooms). Finally, Table 33.1 reveals that foreign chains affiliate mostly urban and seaside hotels, while domestic chains focus on the leisure market and have predominantly seaside and mountain hotels. Therefore, there is appears to be significant market potential for affiliation of the accommodation establishments in Bulgaria to hotel chains.

Methodology

This chapter presents part of the results of a large survey on hotel chains and individual hotels in Bulgaria. The survey aimed to critically evaluate:

• The view point of the hotel chains regarding: the most appropriate type of entry mode in the context of Bulgarian hotel industry, the factors considered when choosing an entry mode, requirements towards individual hotels.

Table 33.1 Types of affiliation of accommodation establishments in Bulgaria

	2012[a]		2014[b]		2015[c]	
	Foreign chains	Domestic chains	Foreign chains	Domestic chains	Foreign chains	Domestic chains
Total number of accommodation establishments affiliated to hotel chains	108		124		132	
Total number of accommodation establishments	2,758		2,923		3,163	
Hotel chains market penetration	3.91%		4.24%		4.17%	
Number of chains operating in the country	28	12	33	14	33	18
Number of affiliated accommodation establishments	47	61	55	69	52	80
Full ownership or joint venture	2	56	2	67	1	75
Franchise	14	–	19	–	17	–
Management contract	15	10[d]	16	7[d]	21	10[d]
Marketing consortium	22	–	23	–	16	–
Number of accommodation establishments affiliated to hotel chains by category						
1 star	–	–	1	–	1	–
2 stars	1	4	1	8	1	9
3 stars	5	15	5	13	4	18
4 stars	30	33	36	38	35	43
5 stars	11	9	12	10	11	10
Number of accommodation establishments affiliated to hotel chains by size						
Up to 50 rooms	9	12	10	17	8	21
51–100 rooms	8	22	8	22	9	23
101–150 rooms	6	6	7	7	5	9
Over 150 rooms	24	22	30	23	30	27
Number of accommodation establishments affiliated to hotel chains by location						
Urban	21	10	26	11	23	16
Seaside	21	27	24	34	25	40
Mountain	4	23	4	23	3	23
Rural/Countryside	1	1	1	1	1	1

Source: adapted from Ivanova and Ivanov (2015b) and expanded by the authors.

Note: Several hotels belong to two foreign hotel chains simultaneously (to one chain through franchise/management contract and to another one through marketing consortium).

a As of 01st December 2012

b As of 01st October 2014

c As of 01st May 2015

d Some of the management companies and the hotel owner companies belong to the same holding, have the same or connected physical persons as the owners. Numbers reflect the officially stated type of affiliation on the websites of the hotel and the hotel chain, although the authors suspect that all or most hotels affiliated to domestic chains are owned by the chains or connected companies. See Ivanova and Ivanov (2014) for further details.

- The view point of the individual hotels regarding: advantages/disadvantages of chain affiliation, the most appropriate type of affiliation to a chain in the context of Bulgarian hotel industry, the factors considered when choosing a type of affiliation, preferred attributes of the chain, their managers' perceptions of chain requirements towards individual hotels.

Some of the findings are reported in other publications (Ivanova and Ivanov, 2014, 2015a, 2015b). This chapter presents only the results of the survey among individual hotels. Data were collected during the period June–November 2012. Three groups of hotels were contacted:

- *Hotels currently affiliated to foreign hotel chains.* At the time of data collection the population included 47 hotels, all of which were contacted and 36 returned completed questionnaires yielding a 76.6 per cent response rate.
- *Hotels formerly affiliated to hotel chains.* The opinion of this group of respondents was considered important for the research due to their previous experience as chain members. The size of this population was difficult to determine precisely. The authors successfully identified 24 properties in Bulgaria that were part of a chain. Nineteen of them had left the hotel chains in the last 5 years, and 5 properties between 5 and 10 years before data collection. All formerly affiliated hotels were contacted, but not all of their managers could answer the survey questions because they had either not been working in these hotels at the time the hotels left the chains, or they did not want to complete the questionnaire due to confidentiality concerns. That's why only 7 responses were received (response rate 29.2 per cent).
- *Independent hotels that have never been affiliated to a chain.* The authors successfully identified the contact details of 2,120 of the accommodation establishment (hotels, family hotels, aparthotels, etc.). Current or former chain members were removed from the list. From the remaining 2,049 independent hotels that have never been affiliated to a chain, 103 responses were received (response rate 5.03 per cent).

In total, the sample included 146 accommodation establishments from 2,120 contacted properties (6.89 per cent response rate). Similar low response rate from the Bulgarian hotel industry has been reported in other studies as well (Ivanov, Stoilova and Illum, 2015; Ivanov, Ivanova and Iankova, 2014; Ivanov, 2014).

Only hotels affiliated to foreign hotel chains were contacted due to their non-equity type of affiliation. Hotels belonging to domestic chains were either fully or partially owned by the domestic chains and the decision to be part of the chain was not based on market principles but on ownership. Furthermore, most of their marketing activities were centralised in the domestic chains' headquarters and that's why their opinion was not considered relevant for the research. Responses from the Bulgarian chain headquarters reflected the view points of the chains, not the hotels, and were thus excluded from this analysis. Questionnaires were distributed by email to the people responsible for marketing and management of the property – general manager, marketing manager, front office manager, or owner (if possible). At least two reminders to participate in the survey were sent to each respondent group.

The questionnaire to the individual hotels included several blocks of questions. The first block related to respondents' perceptions of the advantages of chain hotels, measured on a five-point scale (where 1 = completely unimportant and 5 = completely important). The same scale was used for the next two blocks of questions: factors, influencing a hotel's choice of type of affiliation to a chain, and the hotel manager's preferred attributes of the chain. The fourth block measured respondents' opinion regarding the appropriateness of the various types of affiliation of hotels to chains in the context of Bulgaria (1 = completely unsuitable, 5 = completely suitable). Finally, data were also collected on hotels' star category, size (number of rooms), location (urban, seaside, mountain, rural/countryside) and chain affiliation (current member, former member, independent property that has not been part of a chain).

The authors adopted ANOVA to identify differences in respondents' answers on the basis of their properties' chain affiliation, category, size and location. The Tukey's HSD and Scheffe's post-hoc tests were used to further analyse the differences identified with ANOVA. As both tests identified the same differences with the same levels of significance, only the Tukey's HSD test results are reported.

Findings

Respondents are quite unanimous regarding their evaluations about the suitability and applicability of the different types of chain affiliation for hotels in Bulgaria (see Table 33.2). They perceive full ownership (m = 2.71), joint venture (m = 2.66), franchise (m = 2.80) and management contract (m = 2.71) as nearly equally applicable in the context of Bulgarian hotel industry. The paired samples t-test has not identified any statistically significant difference in managers' perceptions about the suitability of these four types of affiliation. Marketing consortium (m = 2.18) and lease (m = 1.73) are considered as least suitable and the differences with the other four types are statistically significant (paired samples t-test p <0.01 for all pairs). Accommodation establishments' chain affiliation, category and location have no impact on their managers' perceptions about the suitability of the types of chain affiliation. However, in this context, size does matter: the largest properties are more likely to favour manage-ment contract (Tukey's HSD test p <0.05) and franchise (p <0.05) compared to the smallest properties. This result is expected, considering the fact that hotel chains prefer properties under franchise or management contract to have a relatively large number of rooms (Ivanov and Zhechev, 2011). This proposition has been confirmed in the context of Bulgaria: hotels under

Table 33.2 Most suitable type of chain affiliation for hotels in Bulgaria

Type of affiliation	Total mean	Standard deviation	F-statistic			
			Chain affiliation	Category	Size	Location
Full ownership by the chain	2.71	1.876	1.521	0.527	0.935	0.733
Joint venture	2.66	1.805	1.077	1.383	0.335	1.884
Franchise	2.80	1.848	1.154	1.908	2.427*	1.562
Management contract	2.71	1.853	2.064	1.447	2.462*	0.381
Marketing consortium	2.18	1.814	0.886	0.008	0.365	0.821
Lease	1.73	1.620	0.864	1.052	0.651	1.134

Source: adapted from Ivanova and Ivanov (2015b).

Note: mean responses (m) on a 5-point scale (1 = extremely unsuitable, 5 = extremely suitable). Grouping of respondents: Chain affiliation (current foreign chain members, former foreign chain members, independent accommodation establishments that have never been part of a chain), Size (up to 50, 51–100, 101–150 and over 150 rooms), Location (seaside, rural, mountain, urban), Category (1–2, 3 and 4–5 stars).
*Significant at 10% level.

Table 33.3 Factors influencing the choice of type of affiliation to a chain

Factors	Total mean	Standard deviation	F-statistic			
			Chain affiliation	Category	Size	Location
Contract fees	3.55	1.694	5.724***	2.624*	1.163	0.495
Contract duration	3.55	1.670	6.776***	5.089***	1.656	0.783
Contract termination terms	3.64	1.677	7.405***	4.686**	2.547*	0.641
Other contract terms	2.91	1.718	2.928*	1.498	1.312	0.355
Willingness of hotel owner to keep operating control on hotel's activities	3.45	1.702	0.631	0.397	0.161	0.257
Consultations by chain representatives	3.69	1.578	2.680*	0.895	0.027	2.953**
Experience and skills of hotel managers	3.78	1.565	1.247	0.875	0.155	1.064
Predetermined chain strategy for affiliating hotels	3.37	1.722	3.771**	4.070**	2.170*	1.369

Source: adapted from Ivanova and Ivanov (2015b).

Note: mean responses (m) on a 5-point scale (1-extremely unimportant, 5-extremely important). Grouping of respondents: *Chain affiliation* (current foreign chain members, former foreign chain members, independent accommodation establishments that have never been part of a chain), *Size* (up to 50, 51–100, 101–150 and over 150 rooms), *Location* (seaside, rural, mountain, urban), *Category* (1–2, 3 and 4–5 stars).
*Significant at 10%-level; ** significant at 5%-level; *** significant at 1%-level.

franchise, management contract or joint venture in the country have much higher capacity than the average hotel or the properties in marketing consortia (Ivanova and Ivanov, 2014).

Respondents evaluate the various factors, influencing the choice of type of affiliation to a chain with nearly the same importance (Table 33.3). Experience and skills of hotel managers (m = 3.78), possibility for consultations by chain representatives (m = 3.69), contract termination terms (m = 3.64), contract fees (m = 3.55) and contract duration (m = 3.55) are the main factors mentioned by respondents that determine their choice of type of affiliation. If managers of the hotel have extensive experience, the owner of the hotel might prefer that they manage it, rather than transferring the management of the property to the chain. Therefore, they would favour a franchise or marketing consortium instead of a management contract or lease. On the other hand, a management contract provides greater opportunities for competent consultations by chain representatives compared to marketing consortium, for example, because chains' representatives are directly involved in the management of the property, unlike marketing consortia. Contract fees, duration and termination terms would vary by type of affiliation as well.

Surprisingly, hotel owners' willingness to keep the operating control on hotel's activities (m = 3.45) is not one of the top factors considered by respondents, although the authors expected the opposite. Moreover, respondents are very uniform in their evaluations of this factor and no statistically significant differences were identified in their answers on the basis of hotel size, category, location or chain affiliation (Table 33.3). Experience and skills of hotel managers are reported as more important than owners' willingness to control and the differences between the two factors are statistically significant (paired samples t-test:

t = −3.024, p <0.05). This emphasis on managerial skills rather than the willingness to control might explain why affiliation types with highest level of control by the chain (full ownership, joint venture, management contract) are evaluated as similar or more suitable for the context of Bulgarian hotel industry than affiliation types that provide more operational control for the owner like franchise and marketing consortium (Table 33.2).

The ANOVA shows that chain affiliation influences managers' evaluations of most of the factors: contract termination terms (F = 7.405, p <0.01), contract duration (F = 6.776, p <0.01), contract fees (F = 5.724, p <0.01), predetermined chain strategy for affiliating hotels (chain's entry mode) (F = 3.771, p <0.05), other contract terms (F = 2.928, p <0.10) and consultations by chain representatives (F = 2.680, p <0.10). Tukey's HSD test reveals that managers of independent hotels overestimate the importance of contract fees, duration, termination terms (p <0.01 for all three) and chain's predetermined strategy for affiliation of properties (p <0.10), compared to managers of chain hotels. It seems that chain members' managers' experience taught them that the contract terms (fees, duration and termination) are not so rigid and that chains are more flexible than managers of independent properties think.

Accommodation establishments' category influences managers' opinions regarding contract duration (F = 5.089, p <0.01), contract termination terms (F = 4.686, p <0.05), predetermined chain strategy for affiliating hotels (F = 4.070, p <0.05) and contract fees (F = 2.624, p <0.10). More specifically, managers of lower category properties are more concerned about contract fees (Tukey's HSD test p <0.10), duration (p <0.01), termination terms (p <0.01) and predetermined chain strategy for affiliating hotels (p <0.05) than managers of luxury properties. This might signal that managers of lower category properties consider that they have low bargaining power and do not see chances of negotiating these conditions with the chains.

Size of the accommodation establishment has a small impact on its managers' opinion about the factors, influencing their choice of type of affiliation. The ANOVA indicates only minor statistically significant differences regarding contract termination terms (F = 2.547, p <0.10) and chain's predetermined strategy for affiliating hotels (F = 2.170, p <0.10). In both cases managers of the smallest hotels (up to 50 rooms) put greater importance on the respective factor than managers of 101–150-room properties do (p <0.10 for both). A similar small impact is identified for the location of accommodation establishments. Managers of urban properties put less emphasis on potential consultations by chain representatives than managers of seaside properties (p <0.05), probably due to the all-year round employment in urban hotels, allowing them to hire highly qualified full-time staff rather than relying on seasonal workers like most of the seaside properties.

Conclusion

From a managerial perspective, research results clearly indicate that Bulgarian hoteliers consider two of the non-equity forms of affiliation (namely, franchise and management contract) as equally appropriate for the business environment in the country as the ownership-based forms (full ownership and joint venture), and much more appropriate compared to the other two non-equity modes (lease and marketing consortium) (Table 33.2). These findings suggest that if hotel chains look for local partners they should attract them by offering franchise agreement and/or management contract. The application of plural forms of affiliation is recommended as this strategy would provide more options of types of affiliation for the individual hotel managers and increases the probability that they find a type suitable for the properties they manage. Furthermore, when approaching potential partner hotels and during the affiliation negotiations with them, hotel chain managers need to emphasise the support the chain representatives would provide to the individual hotel managers, and, of course, the benefits the chain affiliation would bring to the hotel's marketing and financial performance. However, they should also think about greater flexibility in the contract fees/duration/termination as these factors are of great importance to individual hotel managers. Future research on the perspective of the managers of the accommodation establishments should be undertaken in other geographic and cultural settings. It may turn out that the hoteliers in different countries put different weights on factors influencing the choice of type of affiliation, or other factors considered by the industry representatives.

References

Alon, I., Liqiang, N. and Wang, Y. (2012) Examining the determinants of hotel chain expansion through international franchising. *International Journal of Hospitality Management*, 31(2), 379–86.

Altinay, L., Brookes, M., Yeung, R. and Aktas, G. (2014) Franchisees' perceptions of relationship development in franchise partnerships. *Journal of Services Marketing*, 28(6), 509–19.

Brookes, M. and Roper, A. (2012) Realising plural-form benefits in international hotel chains. *Tourism Management*, 33(3), 1–12.

Butler, J. and Braun, R. (2014) *The Hotel Management Agreements and Franchise Agreement Handbook*. 3rd ed. Los Angeles: JMBM Global Hospitality Group.

Chathoth, P. and Olsen, M. (2003) Strategic alliances: a hospitality industry perspective. *International Journal of Hospitality Management*, 22(4), 419–34.

Chen, J. J. and Dimou, I. (2005) Expansion strategy of international hotel firms. *Journal of Business Research*, 58(12), 1730–40.

Cho, M. (2005) Transaction costs influencing international hotel franchise agreements: the case of Holiday Inn Seoul. *Journal of Vacation Marketing*, 11(2), 121–33.

Connell, J. (1997) International hotel franchise relationships – UK franchisee perspectives. *International Journal of Contemporary Hospitality Management*, 9(5/6), 215–20.

Contractor, F.J. and Kundu, S.K. (1998a) Modal choice in a world of alliances: analyzing organizational forms in the international hotel sector. *Journal of International Business Studies*, 29(2), 325–57.

Contractor, F.J. and Kundu, S.K. (1998b) Franchising versus company-run operations: modal choice in the global hotel sector. *Journal of International Marketing*, 6(2), 28–53.

Cunill, O.M. (2006) *Growth Strategies of Hotel Chains: Best Business Practices by Leading Companies*. New York: The Haworth Press.

Cunill, O.M. and Forteza, C.M. (2010) The franchise contract in hotel chains: a study of hotel chain growth and market concentrations. *Tourism Economics*, 16(3), 493–515.

DeRoos, J.A. (2010) Hotel management contracts – past and present. *Cornell Hospitality Quarterly*, 51(1), 68–80.

Dev, C. (2012) *Hospitality Branding*. New York: Cornell University Press.

Eisenhardt, K. (1989) Agency theory: an assessment and review. *The Academy of Management Review*, 14(1), 57–74.

Eyster, J. (1997) Hotel management contracts in the US: the revolution continues. *Cornell Hotel and Restaurant Administration Quarterly*, 38(3), 14–20.

Ghorbal-Blal, I. (2008) *An exploration of the construct of control in expansion strategies of hotel chains: a multiple case-study*. Doctoral thesis, Virginia Polytechnic Institute and State University.

Guillet, B.D., Zhang, H.Q. and Gao, B.W. (2010) Interpreting the mind of multinational hotel investors: future trends and implications in China. *International Journal of Hospitality Management*, 30(2), 222–32.

Hodge, C., Oppewal, H. and Terawatanavong, C. (2013) Determinants of franchise conversion: a franchisee perspective. *European Journal of Marketing*, 47(10), 1554–75.

Holverson, S. and Revaz, F. (2006) Perceptions of European independent hoteliers: hard and soft branding choices. *International Journal of Contemporary Hospitality Management*, 18(5), 398–413.

Huang, R.S. and Chathoth, P.K. (2011) Leasing as a modal choice in China's company-run budget hotels: an exploratory study. *Tourism Planning and Development*, 8(1), 37–50.

Ivanov, S. (2014) *Hotel Revenue Management – From Theory to Practice*. Varna: Zangador.

Ivanov, S. and Zhechev, V. (2011) *Hotel Marketing* (in Bulgarian). Varna: Zangador.

Ivanov, S., Ivanova, M. and Iankova, K. (2014) Sustainable tourism practices of accommodation establishments in Bulgaria: an exploratory study. *Tourismos*, 9(2), 175–205.

Ivanov, S., Stoilova, E. and Illum, S.F. (2015) Conflicts between accommodation establishments and travel agencies. *Tourism and Hospitality Research*, 15(1), 54–70.

Ivanova, M.G. (2010) Potential of Bulgarian accommodation establishments to join hotel chains (in Bulgarian). *Proceedings of the Development Alternatives for Contemporary Tourism Conference*, 25 June 2010, University of Economics-Varna, Bulgaria, 363–73.

Ivanova, M. and Ivanov, S. (2014) Hotel chains' entry mode in Bulgaria. *Anatolia*, 25(1), 131–35.

Ivanova, M. and Ivanov, S. (2015a) Affiliation to hotel chains: requirements towards hotels in Bulgaria. *Journal of Hospitality Marketing & Management*, 24(6), 601–08.

Ivanova, M. and Ivanov, S. (2015b) Affiliation to hotel chains: hotels' perspective. *Tourism Management Perspectives*, 16, 148–62.

Johnson, K. (1999) Hotel management contract terms. *Cornell Hotel and Restaurant Administration Quarterly*, 40(2), 34–39.

Knight, R. (1986) Franchising from the franchisor and franchisee points of view. *Journal of Small Business Management*, 24(3), 8–15.

Lelacqua, L. and Smith, T. (2012) Hotel contracts – to lease or not to lease? Online. Available HTTP: <http://www.hvs.com/article/5925/hotel-contracts-to-lease-or-not-to-lease>, accessed 11 December, 2014.

Martorell-Cunill, O., Mulet-Forteza, C. and Otero, L. (2013) Choice of market entry mode by Balearic hotel chains in the Caribbean and Gulf of Mexico. *International Journal of Hospitality Management*, 32(1), 217–27.

Martorell-Cunill, O., Gil-Lafuente, A., Socias Salva, A. and Mulet-Forteza, C. (2013) The growth strategies in the hospitality industry from the perspective of the forgotten effects. *Computational and Mathematical Organization Theory*, 20(2), 195–210.

Morrison, A. (1994) Marketing strategic alliances: the small hotel firm. *International Journal of Contemporary Hospitality Management*, 6(3), 25–30.

National Statistics Institute (NSI) (2001) *Tourism*. Sofia: NSI.

National Statistics Institute (NSI) (2015) Accommodation establishments by statistical zones, statistical regions and by districts in 2014. Online. Available HTTP: <http://www.nsi.bg/en/content/7067/annual-data>, accessed 2 May 2015.

Perrigot, R., Cliquet, G. and Piot-Lepetit, I. (2009) Plural form chain and efficiency: insights from French hotel chains and the DEA methodology. *European Management Journal*, 27(4), 268–80.

Peterson, A. and Dant, R. (1990) Perceived advantages of the franchise option from the franchisee perspective: empirical insights from a service franchise. *Journal of Small Business Management*, 28(3), 46–61.

Quer, D., Claver, E. and Andreu, R. (2007) Foreign market entry mode in the hotel industry: the impact of country- and firm-specific factors. *International Business Review*, 16(3), 362–76.

Ramon Rodriguez, A. (2002) Determining factors in entry choice for international expansion. The case of the Spanish hotel industry. *Tourism Management*, 23(6), 597–607.

Roper, A.J. (1992) *Hotel consortia: strategies and structure. An analysis of the emergence of hotel consortia as transorganisational forms*. Unpublished doctoral thesis, University of Huddersfield, UK.

Xiao, Q., O'Neill, J. and Wang, H. (2008) International hotel development: a study of potential franchisees in China. *International Journal of Hospitality Management*, 27(3), 325–36.

34

Selecting a partner chain by the hotel

Dimitris Koutoulas

(UNIVERSITY OF PATRAS, GREECE)

Introduction

Joining a hotel chain makes sense if there is a significant value to be gained by the hotel owner. Value may be derived from a variety of factors such as better brand recognition; improved guest satisfaction due to superior service delivery also resulting in improved online ratings on TripAdvisor and similar platforms; higher room rates; improved occupancy; efficient booking generation through cutting-edge booking technology and a strong web presence; improved revenue management; gaining tacit knowledge and useful practices from the more experienced chains; access to centralised contracts with suppliers, intermediaries and customers; access to a wider customer base; access to previously untapped markets either in geographical terms (i.e., getting into the reach of visitors from specific countries or other continents) or in terms of specific market segments such as the meetings market; and a variety of several other factors (Holverson and Revaz, 2006; O'Neill and Carlbaeck, 2010). A more in-depth analysis on this subject can be found in Chapter 32 of the present book.

If joining a chain doesn't lead to an improvement in performance that offsets the costs associated with chain affiliation, then it obviously isn't worth taking this decision. Time, however, is an important part of the equation, as it takes a few years for the aforementioned benefits to be realised in full. The hotel owner should know when to expect each benefit, with the hotel chain taking on contractual responsibility according to a clear timetable. This should help in dealing with the absolutely reasonable impatience of a hotel owner, who wants to see some return on investment after spending a significant amount of money to join a chain.

There is always the risk of choosing a hotel chain affiliation that doesn't deliver the expected benefits. The costs of participation may not be recovered if the growth in bookings is small, if there is no improvement in average daily rates (ADR) and revenue per available room (RevPAR), or if the hotel doesn't improve its position in regard to its competitive set (Estis Green and Lomanno, 2012) etc.

In most cases where this has happened, hotel owners are stuck with a long-term and highly complex contract they cannot easily terminate (deRoos, 2010). Therefore, the decision to join a hotel chain brings with it an obvious risk of making the wrong choice (and a very costly one). This risk can be mitigated if a hotel owner follows a structured approach during the hotel chain selection process.

Such a selection process is described in the present chapter. The chapter's first part is a review of the literature that has been written on the topic of selecting a hotel chain and negotiating the terms of chain participation. The second part comprises the *criteria* that a hotel can employ for choosing a chain to join. The third part analyses the recommended *steps* a hotel can follow as part of the selection process.

Literature review

Literature about how hotels select a chain and negotiate their chain participation is very limited. One of the earlier contributions by Rainsford (1994) stresses that it was during the early 1990s, following years of turbulence in the hospitality sector, that hotel owners began to request management contracts be tied to performance clauses. According to Rainsford's research, the five most important criteria for selecting a hotel management company as determined by the sampled hotel owners are as follows (Rainsford, 1994: 30):

- Past performance as determined by previous contracts with the owner's firm
- Past performance as determined by actual management results for other clients
- The management company's reputation for integrity
- Accessibility of senior management to the owner or owner's representative
- Marketing strength of the management company's corporate staff as measured by those staff members' experience in hotel marketing

Joining a chain through a management contract is a highly complex form of affiliation. Schlup (2004), Rouse (2004) as well as Turner and Guilding (2010) emphasise the inherent conflict of interests, as hotel owners want a high profit and return on investment as well as the appreciation of the hotel real estate, whereas hotel operators want to maximise their income from fees and enhance their brand value. This has led to owners pushing for performance-based fees by asking for lower base fees and agreeing to increased incentive fees reflecting the profits actually earned. Owners are also asking for more transparency regarding the various charges made by the operating company to member hotels and have managed over the years to negotiate a larger degree of control over their hotels, for instance through the approval of budgets, senior staff appointments and long-term contracts with suppliers.

Kim (2008), analysing the case of Korean hotels operating under a management contract, elaborates on how the profitability of management contracts has improved over the years. According to Bader and Lababedi (2007: 172), hotel owners recently 'have become more sophisticated in their selection of operators and in the negotiation of contract terms, often with the help of specialist advisory firms'. A major priority of hotel owners in selecting and negotiating a management contract with a hotel operator is flexibility with regard to the duration of the contract. Due to a shift of market power from hotel operators to hotel owners, there has been a drop in the average length of terms from 20 years to 15 years.

Territorial exclusivity, i.e., a hotel being the sole hotel chain member in a certain geographic area, has also been a source of friction between hotel owners and hotel chains, as chains try to limit their members' ability to block new member hotels opening in their vicinity (Kalnins, 2005). However, the growing market power of hotel owners gave them the ability to enforce more favourable contracts in this regard.

Hotel owners opting for franchises, in particular, are looking for technologically advanced reservation systems and strong brands. An early survey from the UK has shown that British franchisees were motivated to join hotel chains 'by a need to access international reservations systems and to become part of a more internationally recognised and technologically advanced chain' (Connell, 1997: 219).

Research about the views of hotel franchisees conducted in China by Xiao et al. (2008), several years later reveals which aspects of a franchisor's offerings are considered of greater importance. The interviewed potential franchisees assign greater value to a strong brand name and a reservation system, with operating systems, marketing and promotion support and support for hotel openings being of lesser importance. They also seem to favour the strength of the brand name and attractive franchise fees over the flexibility of a short-term franchise agreement.

A conclusion that can be drawn is that a major factor for selecting a hotel chain is making the proper deal. Hotel owners these days are very demanding concerning the contractual terms of joining a hotel chain and will prefer those chains that agree to a contract that balances the interests of both parties involved.

Criteria for choosing a hotel chain

Joining a hotel chain is – or should be – a long-term commitment crucial to implementing the hotel owner's strategy. Several criteria should be applied during the selection process in order to ensure that (a) there is no mismatch between the hotel and the hotel chain resulting in low return on investment, and (b) that the cooperation is clearly beneficial for the hotel owner.

The criteria can be grouped into two categories:

- Criteria reflecting the hotel's characteristics, market position and the objectives of the hotel owner
- Criteria reflecting the characteristics and the policies of the hotel chains under consideration

The first set of criteria is crucial for understanding what each hotel owner is looking for in a hotel chain and helps in narrowing down the choice of potential hotel chain partners. The second set is then applied for ranking the pre-selected hotel chains.

The criteria will be presented in the form of questions. The first set comprises a total of seven criteria.

Criterion No. 1: What is the owner's ambition and overall strategy for their hotel?

This is the starting point for any consideration of joining a hotel chain. Depending on the owner's overall strategy for their hotel asset, there is just a limited number of hotel chains that would offer the required positioning, market reach and operational expertise for that particular case. For instance, if the hotel aims at establishing itself as the area's most expensive hotel, the owner should find a hotel chain with a well-established reputation as a leading luxury hotel operator among a limited number of companies fitting the bill, with Four Seasons, Ritz-Carlton and Mandarin Oriental being among the most obvious choices. A different set of hotel chains would be taken into consideration, should the hotel aim at becoming the premier choice for conventions or families or backpackers.

Criterion No. 2: Who will be operating the hotel?

A crucial decision to be made before getting in contact with potential hotel chains is whether the owner wants to operate the hotel or prefers to entrust their property to a more experienced hotel operator. Depending on the decision taken, different types of hotel chain affiliation will apply. The potential affiliation options are as follows:

Hotel to be operated by the owner – affiliation options to consider:

- Franchise agreement
- Marketing consortium membership

Hotel to be operated by a hotel chain – affiliation options to consider:

- Management contract
- Leasing contract

Hotel to be operated by a third-party management company (without their own hotel brand) – affiliation options to consider (on top of the initial management contract):

- Franchise agreement
- Marketing consortium membership

Criterion No. 3: What are the main product characteristics of the hotel?

Characteristics include the location and type of hotel (city, resort, boutique, convention, etc.), the star rating and the price level, the number of rooms, the departments and the range of amenities such as meeting rooms, spa, sports facilities, etc. Thus, a three-star city centre hotel with 50 rooms and an owner interested in maintaining the management of the hotel will look for a different hotel chain to join than a large five-star beach resort with extensive leisure facilities and several meeting rooms owned by a company lacking any hotel operations expertise. Brands to consider in these cases would be Best Western and Starwood's Westin, respectively.

Criterion No. 4: Which market segments is the hotel interested in growing?

Several hotel brands are well positioned in specific market segments, such as luxury travel, family holidays, couples-only holidays, all-inclusive holidays, meetings and conventions, etc. Some hotel chains have also built a large market share in specific origin markets through their marketing activities and loyalty programmes, thus delivering a large number of bookings from those particular countries or continents, as in the case of French and German resort operators such as Club Méditerranée or TUI's Club Robinson. If the hotel in question is targeting such market segments, then it should look for hotel chains with an established customer base in those markets.

Criterion No. 5: What are the operational and financial results of the hotel, so far?

Operational performance achieved in previous years by the hotel is a critical point, as the aim of joining a hotel chain should be, among others, the improved performance, for instance in regard to hotel occupancy, average daily room rate and revenue per available room (RevPAR). Similarly, an improvement should be sought in financial performance, for instance in relation to revenues, gross operating profits, etc. This criterion obviously does not apply to newly built hotels without any previous performance history.

Criterion No. 6: What kind of competition is the hotel facing?

The hotel's competitive set is an important consideration in the decision of which hotel chain to join. Are competing hotels members of hotel chains or independent properties? Which competitors outperform the other hotels in that particular destination? Are competing hotels better positioned in specific market segments that we would like to grow? Depending on the answers to these questions, the appropriate shortlist of hotel chains can be prepared.

Criterion No. 7: Is the hotel owner interested in committing to a long-term partnership or is more flexible cooperation being sought?

Depending on the answer to this question, a hotel owner will consider different hotel chains to join based on the affiliation options available. Management contracts are of a more long-term nature, whereas marketing consortia represent a highly flexible option requiring just an annual commitment from their member hotels.

The second set of criteria deals with the characteristics and the policies of the hotel chains to be considered for membership. It comprises twelve criteria.

Criterion No. 8: Which hotel brands are appropriate for our hotel's product characteristics and possess the required operational skills?

Depending on the hotel's location type (urban, resort, etc.), size, star rating etc., the owner should prepare a list of chains comprising similar hotels. Special attention should be given to hotel chains that possess operational expertise and a spotless reputation in regard to particular services or amenities our hotel is offering, such as butler floors (a signature service of Starwood's St. Regis brand), spas (a playing field of highly reputable Asian hotel operators such as Six Senses and Banyan Tree), golf courses (with Marriott being highly involved in golf resorts), gourmet cuisine (a stand-out feature of members of Relais and Châteaux) or meeting facilities.

Criterion No. 9: Which hotel brands are well positioned in specific market segments?

In accordance with Criterion No. 4 above, the hotel should consider joining a hotel chain with an established customer base in a specific market segment that the hotel is aiming at. Market segments can refer to specific guest types (e.g. families with children, single travellers, couples, senior travellers, LGBT travellers, etc.), special travel interests such as spas and water sports, specific countries or regions of origin, etc.

Criterion No. 10: Which is the presence of the hotel chains under consideration in our greater geographical area?

With a growing number of hotel corporations operating multiple hotel brands, it is important to consider all those brands when assessing the presence of a hotel chain in our hotel's catchment area. Hotels belonging to a hotel chain may face internal competition from the parent corporation's hotel network, either from nearby hotels carrying the same brand or from hotels carrying a sister brand, yet utilising the same marketing infrastructure such as the corporation's reservation platform or loyalty programme. Such 'cannibalisation' should be considered before joining a hotel chain.

Criterion No. 11: Which hotel chains have the desired marketing skills and infrastructure?

There are significant differences among hotel chains in regard to marketing. Some chains stand out for their strong brand (e.g. The Leading Hotels of the World), a high share of direct bookings (Accor), a sophisticated web presence (Jumeirah), an extensive network of sales offices in several countries (InterContinental), high-quality advertising campaigns (Peninsula), etc. The hotel should join a chain guaranteeing a growth in income through higher occupancy, improved room rates, higher turnover across the hotel's profit centres, etc.

Criterion No. 12: What is the cost of joining a hotel chain?

Joining a hotel chain is a costly affair and is frequently associated with a very complex cost structure, especially in the case of management contracts. There are several cost components such as base fees, license fees, incentive fees, marketing fees, commissions, technical fees, FF&E contributions, etc. Hotels should insist that chains are very clear about what is and what is not covered by the quoted fees, and that there are no hidden costs. Of particular interest is which services concerning marketing (such as loyalty programme participation), staff training and quality control incur extra costs.

Criterion No. 13: What is the hotel chain's vision about the future of our hotel?

Should the hotel chain take over the management of our hotel, it should be in a position to understand the local hotel market, to ensure customer satisfaction, to enhance hotel performance and reputation and to incorporate all these aspects in a clearly formulated strategy. This criterion is of lesser importance should the owner maintain the management of their hotel.

Criterion No. 14: What is the hotel chain's approach to asset management?

Should the hotel chain take over the management of our hotel, it is expected to have a clear asset management strategy and to handle our property in such a way, that it will enhance the value of the asset during the contract's duration and at its end. This criterion does not apply in the case of an owner-operated hotel.

Criterion No. 15: What are the hotel chain's plans concerning staffing?

If the hotel chain is expected to take over the management of our hotel, it should be very clear about its staffing plans, especially concerning senior management positions. The hotel chain should provide guarantees that top-talent managers will take charge of the day-to-day business.

Criterion No. 16: Would the hotel chain consider investing in our hotel?

Owners may appreciate a hotel chain's willingness to invest into a hotel by taking up an equity position, i.e. becoming a minority shareholder by paying, for instance, for a renovation or expansion of the hotel in the case of a management contract. Such a move, which shows a chain's long-term commitment to the success of a particular hotel and its willingness to share the risks with the owner, is quite rare and is usually made when a chain wants to win over a hotel that is of strategic importance to that chain's hotel network.

Criterion No. 17: How flexible is the hotel chain in regard to adjusting the contract to the hotel owner's needs and preferences?

Hotel chains used to be quite inflexible in changing the provisions of their standard contracts. Due to increased competition over recent years, hotel chains have become more accommodating to individual requests by owners. Hotel chains are now more willing to agree to contracts with a shorter duration, to guarantee performance by tying their remuneration to the achievement of financial goals, to guarantee territorial exclusivity, to step back from vendor exclusivity clauses, to involve the owner in budgetary approvals, etc. (Bader and Lababedi, 2007; deRoos, 2010).

Criterion No. 18: Does the hotel chain understand the local market conditions?

A hotel chain entering a new country may have limited knowledge of local market conditions and a limited understanding of cultural differences (Martorell Cunill, 2006). Therefore, before choosing a chain, the hotel owner should assess the chain's ability to operate successfully in the hotel's country. Negotiations with the hotel chain will reveal any lack of understanding of the local market.

Criterion No. 19: Which is the exit strategy from a hotel affiliation?

Hotel chains are not making it easy for hotels to terminate their contract earlier than agreed, by including clauses incurring penalties or requiring legal action for quitting the contract. It is, therefore, important for a hotel owner to negotiate an agreement that would allow for early termination if the hotel chain does not achieve the agreed goals.

The above two sets of questions can be used as guidelines for hotel owners in deciding which chains to approach for initial talks and in making their final selection.

The proposed step-by-step hotel chain selection process

The nineteen criteria introduced in the previous section are being utilised in the hotel chain selection process presented below, for minimising the risk of choosing the wrong hotel chain and for ensuring the best possible match between owner and brand. Each criterion is being applied at a different stage of this step-by-step procedure.

More specifically, the chain selection process proposed in the present chapter comprises three distinct phases:

> *Phase 1 – Pre-selection*
> Criteria to be applied: No. 1 to No. 11
> The outcome: a shortlist of suitable hotel chains

> *Phase 2 – Contact and initial negotiations*
> Criteria to be applied: No. 12 to No. 16
> The outcome: a clear frontrunner

> *Phase 3 – Final negotiations*
> Criteria to be applied: No. 17 to No. 19
> The outcome: a signed contract

Phase 1 is the first step in selecting a hotel chain to join. Based on the aforementioned criteria and the answers given to the respective questions, a hotel owner can draft a list of hotel chains fitting the profile of the hotel. This list should then be reviewed in detail before deciding on a shortlist of chains that will be contacted by the owner.

During Phase 2 all chains on the shortlist will be contacted through a request for proposal (RFP). The aim of these contacts is to reconfirm the information gathered during Phase 1, to explore the conditions and costs of becoming a chain member, to understand the modus operandi of each chain, to detail how the hotel will be integrated into the chain's day-to-day business and to discuss the benefits the hotel should expect from joining that particular chain. This phase also includes some initial negotiations for specifying the terms of cooperation in more detail. The result of Phase 2 will be the ranking of the contacted chains after eliminating the less attractive companies. Thus the hotel will have a clear picture which hotel chain tops the list as the most appropriate partner.

Phase 3 includes the detailed negotiations with the chain topping the list. Should there be no agreement, the hotel owner can work down the list until a suitable partner is found, and the proper deal can be made.

Due to the complex nature of management contracts and franchise agreements, negotiations are also complex and demanding. Even though some hotel chains may initially hint that their contracts are standardised and cannot be altered, in fact *everything* on a contract is negotiable (see, for instance, Butler and Braun, 2014). A very important point that the hotel owner should insist on is having the location of the hotel as the place of jurisdiction for the contract. Contract termination clauses should cover not just the event of unsatisfactory performance, but also the potential sale of the hotel by the present owner.

The agreement should also prevent the owner losing control of what is happening at the hotel in the case of a management contract. The owner should be involved in crucial decisions such as the approval of budgets, the renovation of the hotel, the hiring of senior staff members or critical decisions about marketing.

In any case, all hotel owners are well advised to employ the services of legal and business experts during the selection process, considering the complexity of both the negotiations and the contract to be signed.

In general, the owner should opt for a hotel operator willing to agree on lower base fees in return for higher incentive fees, thus proving the operator's commitment to delivering good operating and financial results. Another important aspect besides the financial details of the agreement is making sure that the hotel chain and the company owning the hotel represent compatible corporate cultures, and that there is good chemistry between the parties at an interpersonal level. After all, it's about entrusting your property's reputation, profitability and future success to somebody you have never worked with before, and who you expect to deliver operational excellence, highly sophisticated marketing savvy normally out of reach of an individual hotel and instant recognition of your business through a well-established brand.

References

Bader, E. and Lababedi, A. (2007) Hotel management contracts in Europe. *Journal of Retail & Leisure Property*, 6(2), 171–9.

Butler, J. and Braun, B. (2014) *The HMA and Franchise Agreement Handbook*. Los Angeles: Global Hospitality Group.

Connell, J. (1997) International hotel franchise relationships – UK franchisee perspectives. *International Journal of Contemporary Hospitality Management*, 9(5/6), 215–20.

deRoos, J.A. (2010) Hotel management contracts: past and present. *Cornell Hospitality Quarterly*, 51(1), 6880.

Estis Green, C. and Lomanno, M.V. (2012) *Distribution Channel Analysis: a Guide for Hotels*. McLean, VA: HSMAI Foundation.

Holverson, S. and Revaz, F. (2006) Perceptions of European independent hoteliers: hard and soft branding choices. *International Journal of Contemporary Hospitality Management*, 18(5), 398–413.

Kalnins, A. (2005) *The Effect of New Hotels and Brand Conversions on Revenues of Existing Hotels*. Ithaca, NY: Center for Hospitality Research Reports, Cornell University.

Kim, S.Y. (2008) Hotel management contract: impact on performance in the Korean hotel sector. *The Service Industries Journal*, 28(5), 701–18.

Martorell Cunill, O. (2006) *The Growth Strategies Of Hotel Chains*. New York : Haworth Hospitality Press.

O'Neill, J. and Carlbaeck, M. (2010) Do brands matter? A comparison of branded and independent hotels' performance during a full economic cycle. *International Journal of Hospitality Management*, 30(3), 515–21.

Rainsford, P. (1994) Selecting and monitoring hotel-management companies. *Cornell Hotel and Restaurant Administration Quarterly*, 35(2), 30–5.

Rouse, C. (2004) *Legal agreements and contracts*. In Ransley, J. and Ingram, H. (eds), *Developing Hospitality Properties and Facilities,* 2nd edn. Oxford: Elsevier Butterworth-Heinemann, pp. 95–111.

Schlup, R. (2004) Hotel management agreements: balancing the interests of owners and operators. *Journal of Retail and Leisure Property*, 3(4), 331–42.

Turner, M. and Guilding, C. (2010) Hotel management contracts and deficiencies in owner-operator capital expenditure goal congruency. *Journal of Hospitality and Tourism Research*, 34(4), 478–511.

Xiao, Q., O'Neill, J.W. and Wang, H. (2008) International hotel development: a study of potential franchisees in China. *International Journal of Hospitality Management*, 27, 325–36.

35

Managing the affiliation process

Florian Aubke (MODUL UNIVERSITY VIENNA, AUSTRIA) *and*
Christian Walter (PKF HOTELEXPERTS)

Introduction

The affiliation process is a key element in the development of a new hotel project or the redevelopment of an existing hotel. In this context, affiliation refers to the flagging of a hotel under a brand name, as opposed to operating the business as an independent hotel. Essentially, it describes the separation of ownership of the hotel property and the operation thereof, a move which is increasingly common worldwide (deRoos, 2002). Strictly speaking, affiliation also includes the entry into marketing consortia, sometimes referred to as soft branding (Holverson and Revaz, 2006). The latter represents a special form of affiliation and will thus only be touched upon briefly in this chapter.

The affiliation processes for hotel developments or existing hotels tend to differ in terms of the initial situation, approach and objectives. Following the lines of thought set out in this book, the authors will focus their attention on the affiliation process for an existing hotel in the form of a management contract. Through this agreement, the brand provider also operates the hotel, which is not the case under a franchise agreement (in which merely the right to use a brand is acquired). Since the scope of this chapter does not allow for an in-depth discussion of all possible affiliation possibilities (Section II of this book elaborates in detail on the various affiliation options), the authors outline the key steps of the affiliation process for the following stylised case:

> *A private owner/manager of a hotel decides to step down from the operator's role and wishes to enter into an affiliation. He intends to keep the property in the long term and thus seeks a branded operator for his business.*

A systematic and structured approach to the affiliation search is the key to success. Hereby, the motives of the owner relating to his role in the business after affiliation drive the affiliation search. The objective of this chapter is to outline such a systematic approach to managing the affiliation process. It is acknowledged that this process is neither universal nor necessarily internationally applicable. Local differences in hotel business culture and regulatory frameworks for affiliation contracts exist and govern the details of affiliation forms and thus the process for finalising such affiliations. The authors draw on their experience in managing affiliation processes in Central and Eastern Europe as well as previous publications on this topic (see Walter, 2014). Interested readers are also directed to the seminal work of Steven Rushmore (Rushmore, 2001).

The affiliation process starts with the conscious decision of the owner to transform their property from an independent hotel to a branded hotel. This decision may have been made by the current owner, who may or may not remain the operator of the property, or involve an acquisition by the new owner, of the property. The reasons for deciding to affiliate are manifold and have been covered in depth in preceding chapters. The main reason to affiliate with a brand is to increase the hotel's performance (see e.g., Love et al., 2012; O'Neill and Belfrage, 2005), and, as a result, the value of the property (see e.g. O'Neill and Xiao, 2006) by means of:

1) Transferring management.
2) Enhancing operational efficiency through the hotel chain's management expertise and various synergies within the group.
3) Strengthening the competitive position through the hotel chain's brand.
4) Increasing market share through the hotel chain's sales, distribution and marketing.

At this point, if not earlier, the owner is well advised to seek assistance in managing the affiliation process. In recent times, it has become common practice to involve a third party to either consult or entirely represent the owner in this process (Armitstead and Marusic, 2006). This institutionalisation of the affiliation management process has mainly been triggered by the increasing complexity of the industry, namely the growing number of potential hotel chains and their brands (Lomanno, 2010). Economic challenges and additional intricacies of the financial markets – particularly after the economic crisis in 2009 – have further complicated the management of the affiliation process in terms of both depth and breadth. Lastly, managing the process with the objective of satisfying all parties involved requires not only in-depth knowledge and a broad skills set, but also a network of relevant contact persons at potential affiliation companies.

The complexity of the affiliation process dictates the need for a systematic and structured approach. The process described herein is best termed stylised, as local contingencies relating to legal frameworks, financial regulations and cultural habits have to be ignored.

Fundamentally, this process is separated into two essential phases, the *affiliation search* and the *negotiation phase*. Due to the complexity of each phase, the first phase is separated into a pre-selection and a selection activity (please refer to Chapter 34 of this book for details of the selection process); the negotiations also commonly take place in two rounds. Upon successful completion of the contract negotiations, the changes in management and brand need to be implemented. Figure 35.1 below shows the key components of each of the five steps. Although a fallback option is only visualised for the last step, it should be noted that, at any point in time during the process, the deal may be cancelled, as a result of which it becomes necessary to continue the search or the negotiations with another affiliation partner. In essence, fallback options should be built into the process from the beginning.

Phase 1: Affiliation search

The intrinsic motives of the current owner of the property define the scope and direction of the affiliation search. Does the owner already have preferences for certain hotel chains?

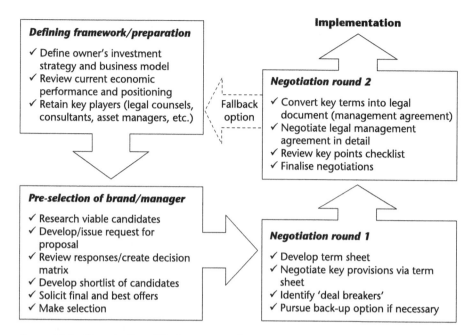

Figure 35.1 Steps in the affiliation process (management contract).

Source: Own figure, based on Crandell et al. (2004).

Is the wish to flag the property with a certain brand name based on rational economic criteria, or more driven by emotions? What is the current economic situation of the property? Is it performing well relative to comparable properties in the market or is it struggling? Or is the business considered underperforming and a turn-around is therefore necessary? Is the objective of the owner to create the best mix of economic parameters (e.g., management contract fees) and prospective business volume (e.g., brand profile and image of the hotel chain)?

The structured approach comprises the following steps:

1) Conduct a thorough business analysis and formulate the economic situation and possible outlook for the business in a concise and objective manner.
2) Based on this, define a catalogue of criteria which a hotel chain as an affiliation partner should fulfil.
3) Use this catalogue to identify a critical mass of possible affiliations for the property.

The critical mass is generated by means of the above questions and should yield a list of 10–15, but not more than 25–30 appropriate affiliation partners. Generating such a number of possible affiliations may pose a challenge if the hotel is highly specialised. The broader the alternative uses of the hotel property are, the wider the choice of possible affiliations. Furthermore, the historic performance of the hotel is indicative of the range of possible affiliations, since not every hotel chain is specialised or interested in turn-around projects.

This step in the affiliation search, the initial identification of possible affiliation partners, represents a good opportunity to consider the current product and positioning. During a highest-and-best-use analysis, external advisors can review the positioning of the property in the market and, if necessary, suggest adaptations to the real estate which improve the overall quality (and thus performance). Such analysis and subsequent adaptations[1] are likely to broaden the range of possible affiliations and increase the attractiveness of the project for hotel chains.

Assuming that at this point a workable list of potential hotel chains has been created by the owner or his representative, a first contact with the hotel chain is initiated. This commonly occurs by submitting a brief yet concise and appealing request for proposal (RFP) to the respective contact person of each of the hotel chains. This RFP should contain relevant information on the existing property, its historic performance, future outlook, source markets and key financial indicators, plus planned developments which will increase the attractiveness and value of the real estate. This RFP is essentially a sales document and should be presented accordingly. However, one should provide only enough information to allow the hotel chain to assess the proposal among many others. An owner who discloses too many details at this early point gives away negotiating power during later stages in the affiliation process. Furthermore, owners are well advised to consider the selection criteria of international hotel chains. Ivanova and Ivanov (2015) asserted that hotel chains are primarily interested in task-related criteria such as the hotel building itself. It is plausible to argue that other criteria such as the hotel's image and performance as well as human resources are of lesser importance to hotel chains as these will fall under the control of the new operation.

This phase of the affiliation search is completed once all hotel chains have responded to the initial contact. Assuming that sufficient hotel chains have expressed interest in an affiliation, the owner now submits additional documents about the project to the hotel chains. The information entailed here usually includes:

- Details about the hotel property (including floor plans, room plans and other facilities)
- Maps and photographs of the location and surroundings
- An excerpt of the feasibility study
- Information on the competitive set
- Information on the owner of the property
- A structured term sheet template

As with the initial proposal, this document is still considered a sales tool, and the audience comprises development managers rather than architects and financial experts. The aim of this proposal should be to reinforce the interest of the affiliation partners in the project. Thus, technical and financial details are best packaged and prepared in a condensed manner, with an effective message forming the foundation of this document.

It may also be advisable to include an initial, brief term sheet (a summary of the key elements of the affiliation contract) as this forms the basis for a binding offer and allows for comparability of term sheets.

It has become common practice to evaluate the decision criteria in a systematic manner. In order to do so, the advisors who accompany the process will apply a decision support tool in which each criterion is first weighted in importance and then rated based on the hotel chain's offer. This approach provides an objective evaluation of the offers and should result in a shortlist of affiliation partners with which more in-depth negotiations can begin.

Phase 2: Contract fundamentals and negotiations

The affiliation contract is not only the most important legal document for the owner and operator, it also defines the pillars upon which the partnership is built for a period of typically

20 or more years. The following five issues form the essence of any affiliation contract (deRoos, 2010, p. 70):

- The legal framework
- Investments by the affiliation partner
- Term, renewal and contract termination rights
- Fees and system reimbursable charges
- Reporting and controlling

The complexity of the contract commonly leads to a two-step negotiation process, as outlined in Figure 35.1. During the first round of negotiations, the parties agree on the general terms of the agreement; in the second round, these general terms are transferred to a legal document and the details of the agreement are negotiated. The contract negotiation phase ends with the signed contract, unless the negotiations are interrupted before due to severe disagreements.

At the outset of the contract negotiations, all parties are – at least theoretically – on a level playing field (Crandell et al., 2004). In practice, the bargaining power tends to be imbalanced, therefore the appointment of an experienced owner's representative is advisable. The owner is seeking an operator to manage the property and maximise investment returns, and the operator seeks opportunities to enhance fee revenues and maximise the number of branded properties. The bargaining power of the owner increases with experience, but is largely determined by the attractiveness of the property. On the other hand, the bargaining power of the operator is determined by the strength of the brand and a good track record of successfully managed properties.

During the first round of contract negotiations the parties attempt to find a consensus on the following positions:

The legal framework defines the entities in the affiliation agreement. Far from being a single document which outlines who is owner and who is operator, this legal framework may comprise numerous sub-agreements which regulate issues such as pre- and post-opening management, brand license, royalty or franchise agreements, employment agreements, etc. The common practice of creating operating and owning entities is to limit liability and to provide lenders with a foreclosure path. The legal framework defines which entity functions as the employer and which entity is the holder of licences and other permits necessary for running the business as a hotel. It further defines the principal-agent relationship. This is essential as the principal in an agency relationship has the right to terminate the contract if the agent breaches its fiduciary duty to the principal (Wilson, 2001). Another major component of the legal framework defines the dispute-settlement mechanisms – the most common being arbitration. Lastly, the legal framework clarifies the matter of property rights. For a long time it was common practice to accept that the real estate and physical personal property remained with the owner. More recently, contract terms are framed in such a way that operators hold ownership of assets such as guest history and marketing data. In essence, this allows operators to withhold information from the owner and even control cash flows in the event that the owner does not fulfil its capital obligations (Eyster and DeRoos, 2009).

Investments by the affiliation partner define the degree to which the operator invests in the business. The deal structure may foresee such investment by the owner, which strengthens the owner's position in the affiliation. Investments by the operator may take the form of key money, mezzanine loans, cash-flow guarantees or equity investments. Such investments from the operator are seen as a sign of commitment and usually have a favourable effect for the operator on the remaining fee structure.

Term, renewal and contract termination rights are issues of utmost importance as they provide contingencies for dispute resolution. Affiliation contracts are often signed for more than 15 years, plus renewal options. Therefore, clauses which define the rights to terminate the contract before the agreed end of the term are in the interest of all parties. Since termination without cause is usually not accepted by operators (unless a break clause stipulating a penalty payment from the owner to the operator in lieu of liquidated damages is agreed upon), the most common form is performance-related termination rights. Here, owner and operator will need to negotiate in detail what constitutes poor performance and the metrics and benchmarks that will be applied. Also, the continuance of the operator agreement in the case of foreclosure, sale of the property or any other changes in ownership are subject to negotiation.

Fees and system reimbursable charges define the revenue streams of the operator. Whilst simple in theory, this section of the contract has become increasingly complex in recent years. The practice of combining a base fee and a performance/incentive fee satisfies the interests of both the owner and the operator. The fee structure is vastly different in a management agreement compared to a franchise agreement. Here, the reader is directed to the respective chapters in this edition in which both affiliation forms are discussed in detail. In general, the base fee comprises a straightforward percentage of the gross revenue, where the parties will need to negotiate the detailed definition of gross revenue. The incentive fee structure is more complex as this essentially shifts the financial risk of operating the business. More controversial in negotiations are the system reimbursable charges. These are fees charged by the operator for centralised services of the hotel chain, such as marketing, regional sales and revenue management, loyalty programmes, reservation systems and the like. The controversies surrounding these charges (and, as a result, affecting the negotiation) relate to questions of fair cost allocations of these overheads and how operators can adjust these charges over the contractual term (Bader and Lababedi, 2007; DeRoos, 2010; Eyster, 1997; Goddard and Standish-Wilkinson, 2001).

Reporting and controls represent the last of the key issues to be negotiated. The financial reporting is commonly a straightforward issue. It is accepted that the operator manages the business on behalf of the owner, thus the owner has a right to receive timely and accurate reports in order to fulfil his legal accounting requirements. In contrast, budgets are a more controversial issue during the negotiation process. Historically, owners maintained the right to approve budgets for operating, FF&E and capital expenditures. There is a tendency, however, to curtail the rights of the owner in favour of the operator, for example by changing the owner's right from approving to simply reviewing the budget. Given the large amounts of money at stake with capital expenditures, it is in the interest of owners to at least agree with the operator on long-term capital expenditure budgets to allow for strategic cash planning.

A careful negotiation of the legally binding document is paramount for setting the stage for the long-term relationship between the parties involved. The bargaining power of each party defines the outcome of the negotiations.

Once the negotiation phase has been successfully completed, the implementation phase starts. In order to successfully implement an affiliation, a thorough analysis of the status quo is required, which is the due diligence outlined below.

Due diligence

Figure 35.2 exemplifies the issues covered in a due diligence process. The due diligence process is carried out by the new operator or their representatives and focuses on three main aspects; namely the legal framework in which the hotel currently operates, the real estate/technical framework which assesses the technical status of the building and the operational framework which assesses the current operations of the hotel.

During the affiliation process presented above, the due diligence audit forms the final step of the negotiation before the agreement is set out in a final contract and the implementation phase is initiated. However, due to the fact that a due diligence process requires substantial resources and the operator is allowed to investigate the status of the existing business in detail, a letter of intent is signed by all parties, substantiating the interest of a future agreement.

1. Legal framework		2. Real estate/Technical framework	
1.1	Legal issues	2.1	Legal documentation for real estate
1.2	Corporate law	2.2	Licences/permits
1.3	Licences/permits	2.3	Real estate contracts
1.4	Contracts	2.4	External approval certificate
1.5	Insurance cover	2.5	Technical documentation/facility management
1.6	Legal disputes		
1.7	Labour law	2.6	Real estate evaluation/fixtures and fittings
1. 8	Finances and taxation	2.7	Construction plans/illustrations

3. Operational framework

3.1	General
3.2	Appraisal of fixtures and fittings
3.3	Appraisal of operating supplies
3.4	Hygiene
3.5	Administration
3.6	Data protection and backup
3.7	Business plan current year
3.8	Occupancy 3–6 months / reservations on-the-books
3.9	Documentation of sales and marketing
3.10	General upkeep and facility maintenance
3.11	Supplier contracts
3.12	Hotel IT systems
3.13	Emergency plan
3.14	Departmental operating processes
3.15	Human resources
3.16	Payroll administration
3.17	Staffing
3.18	Vacation planning
3.19	Employment contracts
3.20	Employee accommodation
3.21	Employee benefits
3.22	Finances
3.23	Signatory power/processes
3.24	Status of accounts receivable/accounts payable
3.25	Unsolved legal disputes
3.26	Cash journal
3.27	Cash at bank
3.28	Cash budget
3.29	Tax accountant
3.30	Accruals and prepayments
3.31	Managing director as mandated by trade law

Figure 35.2 Due diligence checklist.

Source: Reprinted with permission of Michaeler & Partner.[2]

If the due diligence is completed with favourable results, the final agreement is negotiated, signed and the implementation phase is initiated.

Phase 3: Implementation

The final step of the affiliation process is the implementation, i.e., the branding or flagging of the hotel. The implementation process may reach levels of complexity which cannot be elaborated on within the scope of this chapter. The implementation phase is driven by both hard and soft issues. Soft issues refer to changes in management and other human resources. These changes may cause friction among existing staff. Knowledge gained from the field of change management in organisations can assist in dealing with these issues (see e.g., Okumus and Hemmington, 1998, for research in the hospitality industry). More context-specific are the hard issues listed and further elaborated on below:

1) Adaptations to the property in compliance with brand standards (capital expenditures plan)
2) Changes to technical infrastructure
3) Merging of old and new PMS (ownership of guest data)
4) Public relations
5) Staffing
6) Sales
7) Marketing
8) Quality control and compliance

Most of the above issues are foreseeable, but nonetheless often cause arguments between owners (as previous managers) and new management. Therefore, both parties are well advised to address the above implementation issues during the contract negotiations. In many cases, real assets are negotiated, such as guest history databases. For the owner, such data represent a real asset and, whilst he has a valid interest in transferring the knowledge to the new management, the data still has a monetary value for which he would expect to be compensated. Furthermore, there may be notable disruptions to operations due to the reflagging, sometimes with substantial financial consequences (Love et al., 2012). A structured due diligence process in the negotiation phase can prevent arguments during the implementation phase, as all parties should have an informed understanding of the status of the business and the requirements for the implementation phase. Next, the above steps of the implementation process should be elaborated on. Again, it should be noted that these steps only provide a guideline; the actual implementation process is highly context-related, and thus property-specific.

Adaptations to the property in compliance with brand standards/changes to technical infrastructure

The future operator will require that a set of brand standards are adhered to, and in most cases adaptations to the existing building are necessary. First of all, the relevant brand standards need to be identified and an agreement sought on those brand standards that actually need to be fulfilled. For this, a brand standard checklist of the operator is useful for defining those brand standards which are already in place, those which are implementable as well as those standards which cannot easily be fulfilled due to, for example, restrictions imposed by the building itself. Once the adaptation needs have been defined, a time schedule is drawn up including deadlines by when individual adaptations have to be completed. Since most adaptations require some investment (sometimes substantial), a capital expenditures (CapEx) plan accompanies the schedule. This CapEx plan defines the details of the financing options for the necessary investments (operational cash flow/equity financing/debt financing/ brand provider key money). Both the operator as well as the owner should carefully negotiate this CapEx plan. Capital expenditures are traditionally the preserve of the owner, so the operator will look very carefully at whether the owner is financially stable enough to carry out the necessary implementations.

For smaller items such as operating supplies, the operator may provide a list of recommended suppliers. For more substantial adaptations to the technical infrastructure and larger investments, a tender process is initiated, at the end of which proposals are compared, work is commissioned, monitored, documented and its successful completion signed off.

Merging of old and new PMS

The property management system (PMS) is the operational heart of the hotel. This is where historic as well as current data are stored and managed. For a branded operator, it is imperative that the property's PMS is aligned with the wider system, so an adoption of the PMS usually used by the operator may be deemed necessary. If the parties agree that a new PMS needs to be installed, a number of challenges have to be faced. First of all, it has to be determined whether the new PMS is compatible with the existing IT infrastructure, and whether adaptation in terms of hardware and/or software is needed to the IT infrastructure. Second, data migration from the old to the new PMS must be possible without any data losses. Third, a new PMS may require training for existing staff. Since all of these adaptations consume large amounts of resources, the investments again need to be planned carefully, and the operator may decide to transform the PMS in phases.

Public relations

A change in the hotel's affiliation will in most cases mean that the hotel operates under a new flag in the future. This constitutes a substantial change to the product and service, a change which needs to be dutifully communicated to the stakeholders of the organisation. In the form of a public relations plan, the communication of the brand affiliation to existing guests/clients and business partners (such as tour operators, travel agencies and wholesalers) needs to be considered. Other recipients of this communication include existing suppliers and contractors, existing staff as well as the marketplace and the general public. The preparation of press releases, press kits and media briefings support the public relations plan. Furthermore, the hosting of events targeted to inform relevant stakeholders may be considered.

Staffing

It is without doubt that a change in affiliation has an imminent effect on the employees of the hotel, since it is the employees who have to fulfil the brand promise (Punjaisri and Wilson, 2007). The current organisational chart has already been investigated as part of the due diligence process, but during the implementation phase decisions will need to be made on potential changes to this organisational chart. A change in affiliation in most cases results in a change of the top management team, thus the existing employees need to be informed and prepared for changes in the management structure. Transitional processes need to be implemented to train staff on new operational procedures; in many cases this is carried out by means of staff training programmes. The legal aspects of contract termination and re-hiring are highly context-specific, and thus are not elaborated on here.

Sales

The main reasons for a change in affiliation are the repositioning of the hotel in order to improve its performance (Hanson et al., 2009). Therefore, it is imperative to consider the sales and distribution strategy during the affiliation process. A new brand provider will utilise their own, proprietary distribution channels which the hotel needs to be integrated into. In line with the new affiliation, the previous pricing strategy may need to be remodelled. During this phase of the implementation, the consideration of revenue management policies and practices are paramount. Whilst partly covered in the process of adapting the IT infrastructure, the focus here is on computerised revenue management systems and their integration into the existing systems. If necessary, room categories are redefined and room inventories need to be reallocated accordingly. Should the branded operator apply a system-wide segmentation which deviates from the existing segmentation, capacity needs to be reorganised as well. Less technical in nature, a new affiliation requires an active sales approach, often in the form of a sales blitz or roadshows. Sales opportunities which arise as a result of the hotel's integration into a branded operator's system need to be identified, quantified and seized. Lastly, the integration into a larger system requires staff to become acquainted with relevant sales techniques and cross-selling opportunities.

Marketing

In line with the sales activities described above, a new affiliation requires considerable marketing activities which aim at repositioning the hotel and communicating the new affiliation to the public. A new marketing plan accompanies the affiliation implementation process. The marketing plan details the steps necessary to revamp the property website, the redesign of all relevant social media platforms as well as the print material. Most likely, the hotel's marketing activities will be integrated into the brand's overall marketing system, which requires an adaptation to potentially centralised marketing activities. During this adaptation process, some activities and services which historically happened in-house may become redundant (or require reorganisation) and marketing staff need to be trained in relevant new marketing techniques.

Quality control/compliance

Much has been said about the adaptations to meet brand standards of the new affiliation partner. However, it is not sufficient to simply implement the required standards, they need to be regularly monitored and complied with. In order to truly implement the brand provider's quality standards, the relevant standards need to be integrated in the operation's written documentation such as standard operating procedures and checklists. Staff affected will need to be made aware of any changes to standard operating procedures and new quality standards. The very same staff need to understand the quality control mechanisms installed by the brand provider and prepare for external quality control measures. In order to comply with brand standards in the future as well as contractual obligations stemming from the affiliation agreement (e.g., franchise agreement, management contract), internal systems of compliance evaluation need to be set up and implemented. Finally, since the affiliation brings with it new financial obligations in the form of relevant fees payable to the brand provider, the accounting department/financial controller needs to integrate these into the budgeting process and possibly initiate changes to the accounting procedures.

Concluding remarks

It needs to be emphasised that the affiliation decision and ensuing process have to be rooted in a comprehensive discussion of the business model and long-term strategy of the entrepreneur. Usually, there are several alternatives that come with their respective pros and cons, and partnering with a brand on the basis of a franchise or management agreement may just be one of many valid options. Only once the framework has become clear, can a process fit for reaching the pre-defined goals be developed. The process itself needs to be well structured, transparent and flexible enough to go one step back or to take alternative routes if need be. The affiliation process outlined in this chapter is stylised at best. Numerous contingencies define the actions to be taken. Whilst practical experience has shown that considerable overlaps exist in the implementation of the chosen affiliation options (management contract, franchise, manchise or tri-party agreements), the devil is in the details. In particular, the degree of utilisation of – and thus adaptations to – centralised systems for marketing and distribution activities can vary with respect to the chosen form of affiliation. In any case, the owner seeking the affiliation is well advised not only to rely on professional support in choosing the affiliation process, but also to have the affiliation process accompanied. As a closing remark, the authors also wish to point out that the affiliation process does not end with the successful takeover of the hotel's management by a third party. The affiliation process continues until the termination of the contractual relationship between the parties and sometimes demands a 180-degree change of perspective from the real estate owner: the owner is no longer the manager of the business but becomes an asset manager who needs to monitor and control the third-party management, as the third-party management is the facilitator of the owner's return-on-investment. Owners with previous operating experience may bring the necessary skill set of an asset manager along, whereas others may have to adopt certain tools to become a successful asset manager.

Notes

1 It should be noted that adaptations do not necessarily have to be implemented before the affiliation search begins. In fact, a proposal of the changes is often sufficient to attract hotel chains to the property. Furthermore, during contract negotiations, the parties involved may agree on a shared implementation scheme for the upgrade of the property.
2 The authors acknowledge the input by Mrs. Martina Maly-Gärtner in the development of this chapter.

References

Armitstead, M. and Marusic, M. (2006) Evaluating a deal in the hospitality industry. *Journal of Retail and Leisure Property*, 5(3), 197–203.
Bader, E. and Lababedi, A. (2007) Hotel management contracts in Europe. *Journal of Retail and Leisure Property*, 6(2), 171–9.

Crandell, C., Dickinson, K. and Kanter, F.I. (2004) Negotiating the hotel management contract. In Beals, P. and Denton, G.A. (eds), *Hotel Asset Management: Principles & Practices*. East Lansing, MI: University of Denver and American Hotel and Lodging Educational Institute, pp. 85–104.

deRoos, J.A. (2002) Alternative means of operating hotels: a critical look at single tenant leases versus management contracts. Online. Available HTTP: <http://scholarship.sha.cornell.edu/articles/222>, accessed 20 May 2015.

deRoos, J.A. (2010) Hotel management contracts – past and present, *Cornell Hospitality Quarterly*, 51(1), 68–80.

Eyster, J.J. (1997) Hotel management contracts in the U.S., *Cornell Hotel and Restaurant Administration Quarterly*, 38(3), 21–33.

Eyster, J. and deRoos, J. (2009) *The Negotiation and Administration of Hotel Management Contracts*, 4th edn. London: Pearson Custom Publishing.

Goddard, P. and Standish-Wilkinson, G. (2001) Hotel management contract trends in the Middle East, *Journal of Leisure Property*, 2(1), 60–80.

Hanson, B., Mattila, A.S., O'Neill, J.W. and Kim, Y. (2009) Hotel rebranding and rescaling: effects on financial performance, *Cornell Hospitality Quarterly*, 50(3), 360–70.

Holverson, S. and Revaz, F. (2006) Perception of European independent hoteliers: hard and soft branding choices. *International Journal of Contemporary Hospitality Management*, 18(5), 398–413.

Ivanova, M. and Ivanov, S. (2015) Affiliation to hotel chains: requirements towards hotels in Bulgaria. *Journal of Hospitality Marketing and Management*, 24(6), 601–8.

Lomanno, M.V. (2010) The continuing evolution of the U.S. lodging industry. *Cornell Hospitality Quarterly*, 51(1), 15–9.

Love, S.A., Walker, B.H. and Sutton, D.W. (2012) New option in hotel appraisals: quantifying the revenue enhancement value of hotel brands. *The Appraisal Journal*, 80(3), 223–34.

Michaeler and Partner (2015) Due diligence checklist. Unpublished internal corporate document.

Okumus, F. and Hemmington, N. (1998) Barriers and resistance to change in hotel firms: an investigation at unit level. *International Journal of Contemporary Hospitality Management*, 10(7), 283–8.

O'Neill, J.W. and Belfrage, E.E. (2005) A strategy for estimating identified intangible asset value: hotel affiliation contribution. *Appraisal Journal*, 73 (1), 78–86.

O'Neill, J.W. and Xiao, Q. (2006) The role of brand affiliation in hotel market value. *Cornell Hotel and Restaurant Administration Quarterly*, 47(3), 1–14.

Punjaisri, K. and Wilson, A. (2007) The role of internal branding in the delivery of employee brand promise. *Journal of Brand Management*, 15, 57–70.

Rushmore, S. (2001) *Hotel Investments Handbook 2002*. New York: The West Group. Online. Available HTTP: <http://www.hvs.com/emails/rushletter/Hotel%20Investments%20Handbook/Hotel%20Investments%20Handbook.pdf>, accessed 30 September 2014.

Walter, C. (2014) Die Herausforderungen bei der Internationalen Betreibersuche. In von Freyberg (ed.), *Hospitality Development: Hotelprojekte Erfolgreich Planen und Umsetzen*. Berlin: Erich Schmidt Verlag, pp. 171–90.

Wilson, R.H. (2001) Agency law, fiduciary duties and hotel management contracts. *Journal of Hospitality and Tourism Research*, 25(2), 147–58.

36

Hotel affiliation evaluation: remaining, leaving, or rebranding?

Dirisa Mulindwa (UNIVERSITY OF SUNDERLAND, UK) *and*
Vivien Ulu (ANGLIA RUSKIN UNIVERSITY, UK)

Introduction

In 2012, Smith Travel Research, an American research firm, noted that close to 2500 hotels changed their brand affiliation in 2011 (Hoyt and Freitag, 2013). This process of changing a brand name by hotels is referred to as reflagging, that is the hotel initially operated under a specific brand such as Hilton, Best Western or Marriott, but is now operating under a new name or brand. There are many reasons advanced for hotels reflagging including acquisition by new owners such as the case for the former Somerston hotels in the UK that were acquired by private equity firm Lone Star, who changed the name to Atlas Hotels. Besides the hotel reflagging due to new owners, a name or brand change could also be due to the expiration of the current contract. Furthermore, rebranding can happen if the owners or the chain are not satisfied with the hotel's performance under the brand.

Chapters 12 and 13 in this handbook have discussed the concepts of franchise and management contracts as strategic choices made by hotel chains that wish to expand, particularly in the new markets. This chapter takes a different perspective and focuses on the hotel owners' evaluation of the brand they are affiliated to, and the choices available to them when they decide to reconsider their association with the hotel chain. In general, the current chapter focuses on the process of evaluation of a hotel's performance after joining a chain, and the consequent decisions that a hotel owner could make regarding their properties – to remain with the chain until the end of the contract, to renegotiate with the chain, to terminate the contract or to rebrand.

The choice of either to affiliate or not to affiliate with a brand depends on the intent of the owner of the hotel property. When the choice is made to associate with a brand, the owner also decides on the type of affiliation. Whereas some owners may want to participate in the hotel's operations (self-managed franchises and independent hotels) others may want to hand over all the responsibilities of management to the 'experts' (management contracts and franchises with a third party manager). The owners who view their properties as real estate investment usually concede their properties to others to manage them on their behalf (Detlefsen and Glodz, 2013). Their choice of management could be a management contract either directly with the brand, or indirectly through a third party management company.

While owners who would like to get involved in the hospitality and business components of their property may either opt to remain independent or affiliate through a franchise.

Braun (2013) stated that hotel owners have four basic choices regarding the management of the properties. These include:

1) *Management by the brand* – where a hotel chain will agree with the owners to operate the hotel on their behalf under the chain's brand, and the owner essentially hands the property over to the manager with oversight rights, and obligations, defined in a management agreement.

2) *A franchise with a third party manager* – this is when the owner enters into an agreement with a chain hotel to operate under its brand, but at the same time enters into a second agreement with a third party manager who will actually operate the property.

3) *A self-managed franchise* – the owner obtains a license or franchise to operate under the brand, but manages the property itself.

4) *An unbranded/independent hotel* – property is operated either by a third party manager or by the owner (Braun, 2013).

However, regardless of the perspective of the owners, the decisions they make regarding the control of their hotel as well as its branding will have a big impact on the time and financial investment put in the property, as well as on the financial performance of the hotel. Apart from the fourth alternative, the other three mean that the property will be affiliated to a hotel chain. Regardless of how the hotel owners decide to affiliate with a brand, they have to evaluate its impact on their property's performance and the relationship they have with the brand. Rushmore (2011) argued that selecting to affiliate with a brand that is appropriate to the hotel's goals affects the property's ability not only to compete in the local market but also to generate profits. It should be noted that the success of a hotel property is based primarily on the cash flow generated, therefore hotel owners need to weigh the benefits of a brand affiliation against the total cost of such a commitment (Rushmore et al. 2013).

O'Neill and Mattila (2006) noted that brand affiliation has an effect on hotel revenue, because consumers equate brands with quality. If consumers assign a high value to a brand, they are willing to pay extra. O'Neill and Xiao (2006) found name recognition, brand affiliation and reputation for high quality service are some of the factors that contribute to the value of the hotel. The economic value of a brand lies in generating a higher demand for the products and services it stands for, and in securing this, demand for the future. For the hotel owners, the value of the brand they are affiliated to can be viewed as the net present value of the property's future cash flow (Rushmore et al, 2013). Brand names are intangible assets that have a huge impact on the financial performance of the hotel as well as enhancing the value of the real estate assets (Elgonemy, 2013).

Therefore, one of the significant decisions a hotel owner will have to make for their property is choosing the right brand, that will bring financial success as well as adding value to the property. Affiliation with a reputable and well-established brand is a strategic advantage to the hotel, that may enhance its financial value and create the need for the hotel owner to stay affiliated with the brand for a longer term (Dev, 2008). It should be noted that choosing a wrong brand could result in a reduction in current earnings and devalue the property, making it harder to finance or sell it.

Affiliation with a brand will offer hotel property services such as a well-managed website, loyalty programmes, marketing and reservation systems that could drive the hotel occupancy. However, Butler and Braun (2014) caution hotel owners to be wary of these services, to evaluate the costs associated with the affiliation, because while these services may justify the argument to affiliate with the brand, they could also bring huge costs and erode the direct benefits to the hotel owner. Therefore, owners affiliated to a hotel chain would to like evaluate the brand on a regular basis to establish if it is still serving the interests of their property both in the medium and long term.

Factors to be considered when evaluating an affiliation to a hotel chain

Firstly, the success of the affiliation will depend on the hotel management agreement or the franchise agreement, the two primary documents that set out the terms of the relationship between hotel owners and the brand (Crandell et al., 2009). For hotels managed by a brand, the owners retain more risk than the chain managing the hotel on their behalf, but the owners have limited control over the management and operation of the property; this control is often exercised through a performance test. Usually the management contracts are designed in such a way that the owners cannot terminate their affiliation to a brand without incurring heavy fines or termination fees. However, the outcome of this test could allow the owners to have the cause or the right to terminate the affiliation with a poorly performing hotel management (Migdal, 2007).

The performance test of the brand may kick in after the hotel's affiliation has been in existence for at least three years. The hotel owners need to start evaluating the property's performance by considering some of the key elements such as the profitability of the property, the daily occupancy rate as well as the hotel's performance compared with its competitors (Lababedi and Bader, 2007). Hotel properties rated by agencies such as Smith Travel Research, may carry out a comparative performance test to find out how their property compares with the hotels in the same market segment in the area where the hotel is located. This comparative test may consider factors such as 'the revenue per available room' (RevPAR), which should not be less than the annual average percentage of the competitors in a given fiscal year.

For hotel owners who associate with the chain through a franchise, their primary goal is to generate additional occupancy. Therefore, their evaluation of performance may consider if the affiliation to a chain has any impact on the hotel's revenue. They may also need to consider the chain's competitive advantage over other brands in generating customers and repeat guests.

The value of the brand the hotel is affiliated to is a key influence on the value of its assets. Some hotel chains have established a reputation of high performance, therefore consistently have stronger value. Love et al. (2012) argued that the value of the hotel's business does not depend on the hotel's operations alone, but also includes the effect of brand affiliation. Hotels affiliated to well-established brands tend to enjoy all the mass-marketed systems of identification and operations. Brands that add a high value to the hotel property are less volatile and hotel owners affiliated to them would prefer to remain with the same brand, while hotels owners affiliated to lesser brands are constantly seeking to leave and affiliate their properties to brands that would improve their performance.

Location or geographic exclusivity is another subject that is considered when evaluating an affiliation. This covers the geographical territory or zone of the hotel's customer base. Under normal circumstances hotel owners would not like the chain they are associated with to licence its brand to another hotel in the same location; this could be a street, the same city or part of the city, as this will have a significant impact on the value of their hotel. Hotel owners usually require a clause to be put into the agreement that the franchisor will allow the hotel to be the only one to operate in the area under its brand, at least for a period of time (Migdal, 2007; Rushmore, 2011). However, clashes over geographical exclusivity rights occur due to the need and desire for brand owners to continue to grow. In some cases the exclusivity clause in the franchise agreement may be worded in such a way that it may exclude announcement of any affiliation with any other hotel within the geographical territory (Migdal, 2007).

Butler (2008) presents an interesting case of location encroachment: in 2008, Ritz-Carlton Bali terminated its affiliation with Marriott International and Ritz-Carlton, when the franchisor and management contractors decided to give a licence to another hotel owner to operate a hotel under the Ritz-Carlton's Bulgari branded hotel, less than five miles from Ritz-Carlton Bali (see Butler, 2008). The above case demonstrates that for the affiliation to continue hotel owners need to evaluate the geographical exclusivity provision, because without a strong exclusivity clause in the agreement, there is no guarantee that brand owners will not grant a licence to a hotel next door with even more rooms, which will create direct competition.

Another factor to consider during the brand affiliation evaluation is the licence fee and its associated costs. Hotel owners who choose to affiliate their property to a brand either through management or franchise, will have to pay a license fee (royalty fee) to use the chain's brand and logo. Therefore, when evaluating a hotel's affiliation to a chain, one of the important economic considerations is the structure and amount of the franchise fees. According to Rushmore et al. (2013) the franchise fee constitutes the second biggest cost to the hotel after payroll. In many cases hotel owners find out that the cost of affiliation to the chain is more than just the licence fee, a long way into the affiliation, and that the franchise fee is just the cost of becoming part of the hotel chain. The hotel owners may still have to pay monthly fees for the use of the chain's central reservation system, in addition to the cost of loyalty programmes and marketing. There may also be costs to meet the chain's standards, either for straightforward refurbishment or rebranding. The assessment of these different fees is done through various formulas, which may include a percentage of rooms' revenue, and in some cases may include a percentage of the food and beverage revenue. Hotel owners need to evaluate these fees and decide whether the affiliation to the chain is economically viable, and will add value to the hotel as well as warranting the continuation of the property's association with the chain. The decision to continue with the affiliation will also be on the price-value relationship; if the hotel owners find it favourable they could stay with the brand.

Another contentious issue to consider during the evaluation of the hotel's association with the chain is the relationship between the hotel owners and the chain. O'Neil et al., (2013) noted that the relationship between a hotel and its brand is always a source of tension. Affiliation, whether through a management contract or franchise, provides a means for hotel owners to operate their properties under a well-known hotel chain. On the one hand, these affiliations help the hotel chain to expand in new markets without investing huge amounts of capital, while for the hotel owners, it helps them to add value to their properties because they are trading under a well-known and trusted brand. Therefore, good working relations between the two parties could make the whole affiliation system more effective (Berg, 1999). These relationships are based on the premises that an improvement in the hotel's performance is good business for the chain, and in return an improvement in the chain brand is good for the hotel owners. Both parties benefit when their guests are happy with the product – making guest satisfaction a key metric indicating success. Therefore the relationship is built on a common goal that both parties are in business to satisfy their guests and in the process make a profit; however, their interest and how they achieve profitability differ (Berg, 1991). For instance, whereas the hotel chain depends on the distribution of its brand and portfolio size as well as brand recognition, the hotel owners' interest would be in occupancy levels, room rates and creating real estate value for their property (O'Neil, 2004). Affiliations are usually long term, meaning that the two parties have to work together over a long period, therefore during this time there could be conflicts and breaks in the working relationship (DLA Piper, 2012). Some of them could be minor and easy to resolve while others could be difficult to resolve. The property owners need to evaluate the working relationship with the hotel chain, assess and find a convergence between their interest and those of the hotel chain.

This evaluation of the hotel's affiliation to the chain could help the owners when faced with the question 'what decisions should they make in relation to the future operations of their properties?' Such owners may have to make a choice out of the 2 alternatives available to them; (i) they may decide to remain with the current affiliation, (ii) or trigger the owners' right to terminate the affiliation. Alternatively, they may decide to remain with the affiliation and leave the brand at the end of the contract. When the property owners choose the second option, they also need to decide on whether they rebrand through another operator or take the independent route.

Remaining with the current affiliation

According to Elsenbaum and Perret (2010), hotel affiliations to brands either as a management contract or a franchise tend to be long-term (5–15 years for franchises and 15–25 years for managed contracts). Hotels do not usually change their affiliations over time. According to Hoyt and Freitag, (2013), a study by STR Global (an American hotel research company) noted that there has been only 90,000 changes in hotel affiliation over the last 30 years since 1987. During the period that was covered by the study, 60 per cent of the hotels that were surveyed kept their first affiliation. That is, they either remained with their brand or kept the independent status in all the lifetime of their operation. A small percentage of 20 per cent of all hotels had had at least 2 affiliations while 23 per cent had had at least 3 or more affiliations.

The value of a brand could be the main factor that keeps hotel properties with their affiliation. O'Neill and Xiao (2006) argued that the brand becomes embedded in the consumers' minds, driven by their perceptions of particular brands, that is, the quality of services or products offered by the business. Therefore, the brand the hotel owners may choose to adopt for their property usually influences the length of affiliation. Higher brands such as the Ritz-Carlton, Fairmont and Park Hyatt usually secure long-term contracts (Detlefsen and Glodz, 2013). This is important for hotel owners who seek to maximise the market value of their properties. These hotel owners usually develop long standing relationships with the brand. At the end of these long contracts hotels owners may choose to remain with the brand as the decision to change may incur, for the owner, very large costs to rebrand, a reduction in the hotel's value, and revenue in the short run. Hotel owners may consider the cost of buying a complete new inventory, as terminating the current affiliation means changing the brand logos on all hotel products, cleaning up the local image of the property and starting afresh.

Hotel owners dealing with less established brands would prefer short-term contracts initially, with provisions allowing them to renew or leave the brand if they feel that their goals are dissimilar to those of the affiliated brand (deRoos, 2011). If the management company fails to perform to the owners' satisfaction, they may decide at the end of the contract to leave and rebrand. Some of the reasons that may force hotel owners not to remain with their existing brands include the need to seek a new image for the hotel, the opportunity to get better returns, concessions and even negotiating better fees, but most important is the desire to improve the hotel's business and profitability.

The decision to leave the affiliation

Under normal circumstances hotel owners would prefer to remain affiliated to the same brand, because a change of brand name would lead to a drop in revenue (O'Neill and Mattila, 2010). However, factors such as the changing economic conditions, the hotel assets as well as the changes in the market that may occur during the initial term of affiliation, may force the hotel owners to rethink their relationship and affiliation to the existing brand. Besides, the external factors and internal differences regarding the property's performance, the cost of the affiliation and the relationship between the hotel chain and the property owners, could also lead the owners to evaluate their association with the brand.

On the other hand, the change may also be forced on the hotel owners, as their properties suffer wear and tear over the years, and may no longer be able to satisfy the basic requirements of the existing affiliation. The brand affiliated to may require the hotel undergo major renovation which may be costly. Therefore, before investing money in the required renovation, hotels owners may need to consider the options available to them, because the extensive refurbishment required by the brand owner may not necessarily translate into huge profits for the hotel (Major, 2014). In other words, the return on investment (ROI) may not be worth it, because of the existing market conditions. Therefore the hotel may need to think about rescaling or repositioning (choosing a new market segment), or rebranding (choosing a new affiliation); it may be more profitable than renovation to meet the new standards of the existing affiliation (Crandell et al., 2009). Hotel owners should always make choices that not only add value to their properties but also allow them to maximise their profits. They need to realise that a brand is not an obsolete necessity. In the end, regardless of the type of affiliation, it is the hotel owners who run the biggest risks. Therefore, hotel owners considering leaving their existing brand affiliation have a set of questions they need to answer, such as:

- How should the hotel be positioned?
- What type of investment is needed?
- If they change their affiliation, what value will this create for their customers?
- How will the new changes impact on both the customers' behaviour and the hotel revenues?

The answers to these questions require the hotel owners to take a holistic view of their property's existing situation, and where they want it to be in the future. Before committing resources to changing their affiliation, hotel owners need to determine the nature of the changes and whether the changes are worth making. Rushmore (2002) argued that the hotel owner needs to carry out a realistic self-analysis of the owned entity; this may include the business model, their capabilities and priorities, as well as their future vision, in order to make the right decisions regarding the future operations of their property. They need to decide whether to rebrand with another affiliation or turn their property into an independent hotel.

The decision to rebrand or to be independent is based on a number of factors. Hotel owners need to consider the model that would enable them to maximise the value of their hotel assets as well as correctly position their property. Generally it is assumed that small hotel owners would prefer to remain in control of their assets and would not like to surrender them to third parties. While on the other hand, owners of large hotels with ambitions to expand or scale up their business may decide to affiliate with a brand that could provide them with marketing, reservation and loyalty support.

Other factors such as location and cost-benefit analysis may also help the owners to decide on the business model they would like their property to adopt. Generally hotel properties located in urban or coastal resort destinations may opt to operate independent non-branded or non-affiliated hotels. Whereas hotels within secondary market locations, such as airports, may perform better when affiliated to a known brand (Yang et al., 2012). Next up is the consideration of the cost-benefit analysis; the hotel owners have to take into consideration the costs associated with affiliating to a brand, including expenses such as distribution fees, royalty fees and the information technology fees, in comparison to the incremental revenue or profitability that may be generated by their association with a particular brand. In addition to location and cost-benefit analysis, hotel owners may also need to consider their customer base; a hotel with a large proportion of local customers would be better off operating as an independent, and focus on building its own brand (O'Neill and Carlback, 2011; Eisenbaum and Perret, 2010).

Conclusion

The purpose of this chapter was to discuss the process of evaluation of a hotel's performance after joining a chain, or after expiration of the contract, and the different options available to hotel owners after the evaluation. Basically, there are two main options that hotel owners have to consider to determine the future of their properties; these are remaining with the brand or leaving. When they decide to leave, they again need to determine whether they would like to work with another brand or take the independence route. If the hotel owners decide on using another hotel brand, they need to seek brands that allow them more flexibility, and provide them with accountability and efficiency. Therefore they need to set higher standards, that could enable them to negotiate better deals with the affiliations. When choosing the brand to affiliate with their property, they need to consider the strength of the brand, and the value it will bring to the property, therefore they need to evaluate the benefits as well as the challenges of affiliating to a brand from a realistic perspective, to be able to make decisions that are going to affect their hotel properties for a long time.

References

Berg, P. (1991) Franchising '91: strengthening the relationship. *Hotel and Resort Industry Special Edition*, February, 38–49.

Berg, P. (1999) Friction in Franchise relationships. *Hotels, Special Report* March, 58–9.

Braun, R. (2013). To brand or not to brand the hotel. When should you choose a brand for your hotel? And when should the brand manage the hotel? *Global Hospitality Group Blog*. Online. Available HTTP: <http://hotellaw.jmbm.com/to_brand_or_not.html>, accessed 14 April 2015.

Butler, J. (2008) Ritz-Carlton breached contractual and fiduciary duties under hotel management agreement, giving rise to free termination, and $10.3 million in damages plus attorney's fee: when will hotel operators 'get it'? Online. Available HTTP: <http://hotellaw.jmbm.com/hotel_lawyer_ritzcarlton_breac_1.html>, accessed 10 June 2015.

Butler, J. and Braun, B. (2014) *The HMA and Franchise Agreements Handbook. Hotel Management and Franchise Agreements for Owners, Developers, Investors and Lenders*. 3rd edn. Los Angeles: Global Hospitality Group.

Crandell, C., Dickinson, K. and Kanter, F.I. (2009) Negotiating the hotel management contract. In Beals, P. and Denton (eds) *Hotel Asset Management: Principles and Practices.* East Lansing, MI: University of Denver and American Hotel and Lodging Educational Institute.

de Roos, J.A. (2011) Gaining maximum benefit from franchise agreements, management contracts, and leases. In Sturman, M., Corgel, J. and Verma, R. (eds) *The Cornell School of Hotel Administration on Hospitality: Cutting Edge Thinking and Practice.* Hoboken, New Jersey: Wiley, pp. 293–308.

Detlefsen, H. and Glodz, M. (2013) Historical Trends: Hotel Management Contracts. HVS Global Hospitality Service, London. Online. Available HTTP: <http://www.hospitalitynet.org/news/4059515.html>, accessed 12 December 2015.

Dev, C. (2008) The corporate brand: help or hindrance? *Harvard Business Review,* Reference no. R0802, 49–58.

DLA Piper (2012) Hotel franchising in Europe. Online. Available HTTP: <https://www.dlapiper.com/~/media/Files/Insights/Publications/2012/02/Hotel%20franchising%20in%20Europe/Files/Hotel_Franchising_in_Europe/FileAttachment/Hotel_Franchising_in_Europe.pdf>, accessed 12 December 2015.

Eisenbaum, M. and Perret, S. (2010) Hotel franchise fee guide – Europe. HVS Global Hospitality Service, London. Online. Available HTTP: <http://www.hotelnewsnow.com/media/File/PDFs/Reports/2010_Franchise_Fee_Guide_Europe.pdf>, accessed 12 December 2015.

Elgonemy, A. (2013) Clarifying misunderstandings about intangible assets of hotels. *Hotel Online.* Online. Available HTTP: <http://www.hotel-online.com/News/PR2013_1st/Feb13_IntangibleAssets.html>, accessed 15 May 2015.

Hoyt, A. and Freitag, J. (2013, 13th May) How long does a brand last? *Hotel News Now.* Online. Available HTTP: <http://www.hotelnewsnow.com/Article/10471/How-long-does-a-brand-last?>, accessed 14 April 2015.

Lababedi, A. and Bader, E. (2007) Hotel management contracts in Europe. *Journal of Retail and Leisure Property,* 6(2) 171–9.

Love. A.S., Walker, B.H. and Sutton, D.W. (2012) New options in hotel appraisal: quantifying the revenue enhanced value of brands. *The Appraisal Journal,* 80(3), 223–34.

Major, L. (2014) Effects of major renovations on hotel market penetration and net present value. HVS Global Hospitality Service, London. Online. Available HTTP: <http://www.hospitalitynet.org/file/152005338.pdf>, accessed 12 December 2015.

Migdal, N. (2007) Hotel law: emerging issues for the hospitality industry. Online. Available HTTP: <http://hotelexecutive.com/business_review/1647/hotel-law-emerging-issues-for-the-hospitality-industry>, accessed 12 December 2015.

O'Neill, J.W. (2004) An automated valuation model for hotels, *Cornell Hotel and Restaurant Administration Quarterly,* 45(3), 260–8.

O'Neill, J.W. and Carlback, M. (2011) Do brands matter? a comparison of branded and independent hotel performance during a full economic cycle. *International Journal of Hospitality Management,* 30(3), 515–21.

O'Neill, J.W. and Mattila, A.S. (2006) Hotel branding strategy: its relationship to guest satisfaction and room revenue. *Journal of Hospitality and Tourism Research,* 28(2), 156–65.

O'Neill, J.W. and Mattila, A.S. (2010) Hotel brand strategy. *Cornell Hospitality Quarterly* 51(1), 27–34.

O'Neill, J.W. and Xiao, Q. (2006) The role of brand affiliation in hotel market value. *Cornell Hospitality Quarterly,* 47(3), 210–23.

O'Neill, J.W., Dev, C.S, and Yanagisama, H. (2013) Hotel assets: an analysis of brand affiliation, franchise fees, hotel age and performance. *International Journal of Built Environment and Asset Management,* 1(2), 139–64.

Rushmore, S. (2002) *Hotel Investments: A Guide to Lenders and Owners.* New York: The West Group. Online. Available HTTP: <http://www.hvs.com/emails/rushletter/Hotel%20Investments%20Handbook/Hotel%20Investments%20Handbook.pdf>, accessed 30 September 2014.

Rushmore, S. (2011) Evaluating the total cost of a franchise, *Lodging Hospitality,* 5(10). Online. Available HTTP: <http://www.hvs.com/article/5265/evaluating-the-total-cost-of-a-hotel-franchise/>, accessed 12 December 2015.

Rushmore, S, Choi. J.I., Lee. T.Y. and Mayer J.S. (2013) 2013 United States hotel franchising fee guide. HVS Global Hospitality Service, London. Online. Available HTTP: <http://www.hvs.com/article/6233/hvs-us-hotel-franchise-fee-guide-2013/>, accessed 12 December 2015.

Yang. Y., Wong. K.K.F. and Wang, T. (2012) How do hotels choose their location: evidence from hotels in Beijing. *International Journal of Hospitality Management,* 31, 675–85.

Section V

Contemporary and future issues in hotel chain management

In the lead chapter of this section (Chapter 37), authors Seoki Lee and Sujin Song explore environmental awareness practices among hotel chains. Recently, the public, governments, and other stakeholders have been paying increasing attention to the impact of human activities on society and the environment. In the contemporary corporate world, expectations are that business operations should be responsible for any harm done to society and the environment, thus minimising such negative impacts. The hotel industry is not exempt from this significant trend. This chapter provides a brief history of sustainability issues in the hotel industry, presents current practices of hotel chains' environmental programmes, and discusses several issues regarding hotels' green strategies.

In Chapter 38, Irena Erbakanova discusses implications of hotel chains for higher education. Hotel chains and corporations of all types and sizes in different locations around the world consistently note concerns in recruiting, developing, and maintaining a competent, educated and well-motivated workforce at all organisational levels – managerial or operational. Thus, this chapter focuses on the two sides of the international and/or domestic labour market: demand for skills where hotel corporations and chains are, and the supply side, where different sources of workers stand and recruitment strategies take place, such as higher education institutions (HEIs). Therefore, the core discussion of this chapter is on the interactions between HEIs and the relationships hotel corporations build. Those relationships between hotel chains and HEIs might have many innovative forms and objectives, thus the aim of the first part of the chapter is to explain and illustrate them with practical examples. As those forms of partnerships and innovative strategies for recruitment, personnel training and development, on operational and managerial level have advantages and disadvantages for both sides of the contract/agreement, the second part of the chapter aims to explain them.

Next, in Chapter 39, Craig Webster addresses issues related to hotel chains, globalisation, and politics. Globalisation is a multifaceted phenomenon that has far-reaching impacts upon economies, societies, and political institutions throughout the world. In this piece, the author investigates the impact globalisation has had on the world, specifically on the hotel industry. The author investigates the trajectory of globalisation, illustrating the ways in which brands and chains have expanded rapidly in recent decades, and looks into the ways that hotel chains are perceived as agents of change by people of different ideological viewpoints. The author then looks into how the trajectories of the process of globalisation will likely impact upon international hotel chains in the near future.

In Chapter 40, Claudia Sima discusses how the customer is changing in the hotel industry. More specifically, this chapter set out to understand the key characteristics of the Baby Boom, Generation X, Generation Y, Generation Z, and Generation α as chain hotel customers and also to identify how the chain hotel industry is adapting to them. All five generations have interesting and complex profiles. Expressions such as 'latest technology', 'a stylish product', 'affordable', 'and a special customer experience' seem to dominate the narratives of these generations. However, each generation appears to understand these aspects in different ways as the chapter explores. With each new generation the focus seems to be more on individualised, personalised hotel experiences, stylish, yet affordable, technologically advanced, but with a human touch. This is a challenge as most existing chain hotels provide a standardised, globalised product, and originality and style come at a considerable cost to build and maintain. Product adaptation as well as product innovation appear to be the strategies employed by many major chain hotels with new services and new types of chain hotels specifically targeting each generation being developed. Marriott, for example, is attempting to target the leisure Generation Y traveller with a new budget hotel (MOXY), and the business Gen-Y with a new design-focused hotel brand (AC Hotels). The changes they are implementing now are to ensure their survival as Generation Y takes the main stage and Generations Z and α come of age.

In Chapter 41, Emmanouil Papavasileiou explores the changing employee landscape with regard to chain hotels. Despite the growing practitioner interest, systematic research into differences between the prevalent generations of workforce within the hotel sector is scarce. In this chapter, the author provides a systematic review of the evidence concerning inter-generational differences between employees in hotel chains. The chapter begins by outlining the theoretical framework of generational theory as applied within the organisational context. Subsequently, the discussion proceeds to the results of cross-temporal studies of generational differences across various nations and from different sectors. Emphasis is placed on studies that examine employees working in hotel chains. A summary of the inter-generational differences in a number of work-related aspects describes the profile of multigenerational symbiosis in the contemporary workplace of hotel chains. The concluding section discusses the implications of the analysis for researchers and practitioners concerned with the generational phenomenon within the sector.

In Chapter 42, Ulrike Gretzel discusses the new technologies that have implications for chain hotels. Advances in information and communication technologies are creating tsunamis of change that threaten to destroy hotel chains as we know them. This chapter specifically focuses on developments in social media, mobile technologies, robots, search and semantic technology, virtual meetings, Big Data, and sensor technologies. The analysis of these technologies shows both tremendous challenges but also enormous opportunities for hotel chains to create value and remain relevant. It becomes clear that consumers and individual hotel properties come to be ever more empowered due to ongoing and upcoming technological shifts and that hotel chains will have to up their game in terms of offering technologies and guidance that make sense at the chain level.

In Chapter 43, Matthew Krawczyk and Zheng Xiang address knowledge management and Big Data in hotel chains. Big Data is a research area with growing importance for the lodging industry. One example is how the increasing popularity of online consumer reviews has enabled researchers and practitioners to further understand traveller perceptions of marketing concepts such as branding. This chapter examines the concept and practice of Big Data as well as previous studies involving Big Data analytics in the hospitality industry. The chapter then presents a case study in which a large number of online reviews were used to determine the extent to which hotel brands are reflected in these reviews. A perceptual map based on correspondence analysis is used to show the similarities and dissimilarities between hotel brands within the semantic space of online reviews. The findings clearly suggest that while customers do not explicitly discuss brands, there are underlying factors at work that distinguish between lodging segments and hotel brands. This study points to a promising direction for the lodging industry to use Big Data analytics to improve their marketing and positioning strategies.

In Chapter 44, Anderson Gomes de Souza and colleagues explore the topic of brand extension. The purpose of this chapter is to discuss how the brand extension strategy can be used by hotel chains, demonstrating the particular case of a luxury restaurant group from São Paulo, Brazil, in expanding their business into the hospitality industry. Therefore, this chapter deals with the management of brands in the hotel industry as a whole, hence offering the readers a broader understanding of the subject. At the same time, it provides a general explanation about how the brand extension strategy can be applied to both hotel and restaurant chains, in order to highlight its relevance to the sector. The strategic branding management approach, as proposed in this chapter, may lead the reader to a new perspective in terms of the role of gastronomy in the hotel business. Accordingly, the case of a hotel chain in the city of São Paulo is examined. Considered the greatest and most prosperous Brazilian case − especially for its current outstanding position − the hotel chain addressed herein was first established in the market as a successful upscale restaurant brand. Surprisingly, such a success gave rise to a noteworthy luxury hotel chain in Brazil, which gives prominence to the case, reinforcing its position as a particular example of brand extension in the hotel industry.

In Chapter 45, Magdalena Kachniewska discusses the business and leisure equilibrium in contemporary hotel chains. The travel market is facing many challenges within tourism changing requirements: the growth of the independent traveller, a progressive shift away from organized holiday packages, combining several purposes with travelling, such as business, leisure, entertainment, and education. The result is what can be called "bleisure" and "edutainment" tourism. At the same time, changes in the experience and use of time make consumers in developed countries become harried in their futile attempt to increase even the productivity of their non-work time. Modern existence has also created a new challenge: finding an appropriate work–life balance. The bleisure trend represents a new type of work-related travel, one where guests have increased flexibility to relax and fulfil their personal needs as well as their professional requirements. It requires appropriate changes within hotel services, technology and design as well as new thinking about the loyalty programmes (weekend discounts or free accommodation for the accompanying person in a double room encourages guests to extend their stay and enjoy some time in a new destination). Thus, bleisure can be linked to higher revenues (additional services for businesspeople and accompanying persons, extra nights) as well as reduced seasonality (higher occupancy rates in weekends) and satisfied clients that will promote their image. The trend of incorporating leisure activities into business trips constitutes both a challenge and a chance for modern hotel chains.

Finally, in Chapter 46, Michael LaTour and Kathryn LaTour identify what it takes to build an integrated marketing communications mindset for hotel managers. Integrated Marketing Communications (IMC) is often misunderstood by hotel chain managers. No doubt this is due to all the confusing hype associated with the revolutionary changes brought about by the technology and the amount of data that has been created. The key to navigating all the data and tools available is a strategic mindset that is consumer centric. Despite all the technological changes, now more than ever, hotel chain managers need to bring all of this under a strategic umbrella to create more engagement with their customers as a means to enhance their overall customer experience.

37

Environmental awareness and practices among hotel chains

Seoki Lee and Sujin Song

(PENNSYLVANIA STATE UNIVERSITY, USA)

Introduction

The term sustainability has traditionally been about environmental issues, but recently the term is often used interchangeably with corporate social responsibility (CSR). This chapter uses the term primarily for environmental matters which help to have a more focused discussion. Recently, the public, governments, and other stakeholders have been paying increased attention to the impact of human activities on society and the environment. In the contemporary corporate world, expectations are that business operations should be responsible for any harm done to society and the environment, thus minimising such negative impacts. The hotel industry is not exempt from this significant trend and has certainly jumped on the bandwagon. According to Kang et al. (2012), hotel guests are willing to pay a premium for hotels' green efforts while TripAdvisor launched its GreenLeaders programme in 2013, working with Energy Star, the US Green Building Council, and the United Nations Environment Programme.

The business community and academia have widely embraced the concept of the triple bottom line (Elkington, 1997), which translates sustainable development as a concept into a tangible business model beyond traditional measures of profits (e.g., return on investment, and shareholder value), including environmental and social dimensions. These three dimensions are often referred to as the 3Ps – Profit, People, and Planet. Economic prosperity (Profit) proposes that firms should be profitable, but with total transparency towards all stakeholders and with ethics; social responsibility (People) proposes that firms should take care of the surrounding communities including employees, the local, national, and international communities; and last, environmental protection (Planet) proposes that the impact that any business has on the environment must be assessed and reduced as much as possible. Another major theory that supports firms' efforts in sustainability is stakeholder theory, which holds that firms should satisfy all relevant stakeholders, not only shareholders, to achieve long-term prosperity (Freeman, 1984). Stakeholders typically include the environment along with employees, community, consumers, government, and so on.

A brief history of sustainability in the hotel industry

Some early studies of environmental issues in the hotel industry were done by Stipanuk between 1930 and 1950, including topics such as product reuse, recycling, reducing fossil fuel usage, etc. Although Stipanuk noted that some environmental issues were of interest to the hotel industry, the environmental label was not yet in use to describe them. Then in 1962, Rachel Carson wrote a book, 'Silent Spring', a detailed exposition on the dangers of environmental pollution to human health. Many believe that this was the beginning of modern environmentalism in the US and a new wave of green-activist movements largely started then. Following such movements, in the late 1960s, the social aspects of sustainability emerged in the hotel industry, mostly focusing on customer relationships and employer responsibilities. The hotel industry also started to pay more attention to energy conservation after the energy crisis of 1973–1974.

In 1987, 'Our Common Future' (better known as the Brundtland Report) defined sustainability as 'development that meets the needs of the present without compromising the ability of future generations to meet their own needs'. The Brundtland Report greatly influenced how businesses incorporate environmental issues in their operations. In 1990, the International Ecotourism Society was established to promote sustainable travel by helping customers and travel professionals to better understand environmental issues. In 1992, the International Hotels Environmental Initiative (IHEI) was formed to enhance sustainability standards for hotels through a collaborative forum.

Since 1992, the hospitality and tourism industry started to place emphasis on efficient energy use, adoption of technology, and concerns for the environment. For example, Agenda 21 contained a forward by the World Trade and Tourism Council (WTTC) and the World Tourism Organisation (UNWTO), international guidelines for sustainable tourism by the Earth Council, and the Global Code of Ethic for Tourism (GCET) by UNWTO. In response to these guidelines, the lodging industry initiated the concept of 'Green Hotels', which has gained great popularity over the past two decades. The major hotel chains started various types of sustainability programmes, mostly focused on facility management measures such as water saving, energy saving, and waste reduction. In addition, sustainable procurement, indoor environment quality, and staff training programmes are emerging as areas of focus. Sustainability practices became especially important during the financial crisis of 2008–2009, due to the urgent need to cut down operational costs.

As time goes by, the hotel industry is beginning to embrace not only environmental issues, but also economic development and social issues related to employment, training, community, diversity, and human rights. In the 2000s, public attention to sustainability and CSR issues kept growing. For example, according to Kang et al. (2012), the number of news stories about CSR and environmental issues on a hospitality industry website, Hospitality Net, increased from 63 in 1999 to 139 in 2007. The CSR industry grew to a $20 billion market in 2008 (Kniss, 2008) and spending on sustainability by large US firms reached $28 billion in 2010 (DiGuili and Kostovetsky, 2014). Also, almost 60 per cent of Fortune 500 companies exclusively published CSR related reports in 2011 and more than one-third of large U.S. companies have incorporated third-party certifications for social and environmental standards into their operations (Kitzmueller and Shimshack, 2012; Lys et al., 2013). These days, most leading hotel chains incorporate environmental and CSR issues into their core business strategies, and also publish exclusive reports accounting for such issues.

Current practices in the hotel industry

Regarding sustainability in the hotel industry, facility management is an important area for hoteliers to focus on at a property level. In general, activities are often undertaken to optimise operational efficiency, thus reducing operational costs, through dealing with issues of energy, water, and waste. To improve energy efficiency, hotels may replace existing (often old and energy inefficient) equipment with new energy efficient equipment whenever possible. Hoteliers may invest in renewable sources of energy, such as solar, wind, etc. For water use, hotels may develop a programme to reduce the use of it (for example, towel and linen reuse programmes). Lastly, many hotels are already implementing a variety of strategies to reduce, reuse, and recycle waste. The hotel industry is a major contributor of waste in landfills, representing 23 per cent of commercial sector facilities (that is, around 45 per cent of all municipal solid waste) (Bacot et al., 2002). Singh et al., (2014) performed cost-benefit analysis of hotels' waste, using a waste-audit technique. They found that, on average, only about 12–13 per cent of hotels' waste is true trash and the remaining waste is reusable, recyclable or compostable. Furthermore, their cost-benefit analysis suggested that profits of about $24,000 per year can be generated through proper recycling of waste and consequently, greenhouse gas (GHG) emissions can be reduced by an amount equivalent to 90 passenger vehicles annually.

At a firm level however, environmental issues are not only limited to a facility management context. Many leading hotel chains now heavily invest in programmes to improve environmental conditions for their community and the world. For example, Marriott has committed $2 million to help protect the Juma rainforest reserve in the State of Amazonas, Brazil, while InterContinental Hotels launched the 'Hotel Carbon Measurement Initiative' global carbon standard for hotels in 2012 in the International Tourism Partnership (ITP)/World Travel and Tourism Council (WTTC) working group. Further environmental programmes and investments practised by leading US chain hotels are summarised and presented in Table 37.1.

The hotel industry inevitably consumes considerable amounts of energy, water, and non-durable products due to their distinctive operating characteristics. Most hotel groups worldwide have acknowledged the environmental issues related to their business, and attempted to solve deleterious environmental problems by putting enormous amounts of capital investment into environmental endeavours. In particular, although the level of awareness and the achievement in each hotel property were varied, considerable, and painstaking efforts in reducing energy consumption, water use, waste, and carbon were

Table 37.1 Summary of US chain hotels' environmental programmes and investments

1. Intercontinental Hotel Group	
Environmental performance and goals	• Achieved a 2.4% reduction in carbon footprint per occupied rooms between 2012 and 2013 and on track to achieve 12% target by 2017 • Achieved a 4.6% reduction in water use per occupied room in water-stressed areas between 2012 and 2013 and on track to achieve 12% target by2017

Environmental Programme	• IHG Green Engage
	  • An online environmental management tool which tracks the use of energy, carbon, water and the management of waste in the properties
	  – 2,646 hotels are now enrolled in IHG Green Engage

Source: http://www.ihgplc.com/index.asp?pageid=718#ref_cr   *(Continued)*

Table 37.1 (Continued)

---

2. Hilton Worldwide

Environmental performance and goals	• Hilton achieved 12.8%, 24.9%, 12.2%, 10.2% reduction of carbon output, waste output, energy usage, and water usage respectively • $253 million estimated utility cost savings since 2009 • Hilton Worldwide purchased 450 million kWh of renewable power to December 31, 2012 • 42,000 car's carbon output saved as a result of carbon reduction in 2012 • 270,000 pounds of soap donated to the Global Soap Project • Hilton aims to reduce energy, carbon, and waste by 20%

Environmental programme	• LightStay™
	  – Hilton Worldwide's proprietary sustainability management programme
	  – 27,000 homes could be powered by energy reductions resulting from LightStay™
	  – 8,000 best practice projects shared through this system
	  – 7,688 households' worth of waste reduced

Source: http://cr.hiltonworldwide.com/_pdf/Hilton_2012CRR_PDF_v22.0.pdf

---

3. Marriott International

Environmental performance and goals	• Marriott reduced energy consumption at their two data centres by 10.4% and water consumption by 2.5% in 2013 versus 2012 • Marriott educated more than 700 contracted suppliers on sustainable supply chain goals • In 2008, Marriott pledged $2 million to protect 1.4 million acres of rainforest in the Juma Sustainable Development Reserve • From 2010 to 2012, Marriott supported Conservation International's community-based conservation work to conserve fresh water resources in Southwest China

Environmental programme	• Global Green Council
	  – The executive-level Council evaluates the hotels' environmental practices, sets major sustainability business objectives by discipline, and measures progress
	  – 27,000 homes could be powered by energy reductions
	  – 8,000 best practice projects shared through this system
	• KiWi Power's DR programme
	  – In partnership with Exelon company, Marriott has developed a demand response (DR) programme across the US, enrolling 167 properties across five regions. Marriott reduced its overall energy usage by 83.5 MWh through participation in the DR program
	• Chilled Water Diagnostic Tool
	  – Chilled water systems can account for up to 40% of electricity use in Marriott hotels
	• Partnership with Siemens
	  – Audits energy usage and optimises management systems to monitor energy consumption

- Partnership with Clean the World®
  - Collects and recycles partially used soaps and other hygiene amenities
  - Over 91,000 pounds of soap and 61,000 pounds of amenities were donated to Clean the World's program
- Partnership with Arrow Value Recovery
  - Prevented nearly 1.7 million pounds of used technology from entering the solid waste stream, and extended the useful life of nearly 15,000 PCs, laptops and LCDs globally

Source: http://www.marriott.com/corporate-social-responsibility/corporate-responsibility.mi

---

4. The Ritz Carlton Hotel

Environmental performance and goals	• Further reducing energy and water consumption • Sourcing environmentally preferred products • Addressing environmental challenges through innovative conservation initiatives including rainforest protection and water conservation
Environmental programme	• The Ritz-Carlton Hotel is deploying a global programme to calculate carbon footprint, water footprint, waste diversion, and energy intensity at each individual hotel. This will allow meeting professionals to quantify the environmental footprint for overnight stays and meetings • The partnership with Jean-Michel Cousteau's Ambassadors of the Environment offers guests a meaningful experience that imbues them with a deep appreciation and respect for nature, as well as an understanding of how to live more environmentally responsibly back home

Source: http://www.ritzcarlton.com/en/CommunityFootprints/Default.htm

---

5. Wyndham Hotel Group

Environmental performance and goals	Through the various Wyndham Green programmes, main areas of focus include:
	• Reduce water and energy usage and recycle
	• Improve air quality
	• Minimise waste by recycling and reusing materials
	• Implement sustainable procurement practices
	• Performance in 2012:
	  – reduced its greenhouse gas emissions by 11.7%
	  – reduced its water usage 1.7% by square foot.
	  – approximately 21,000 Wyndham Worldwide associates, and more than 650 general managers and owners were educated about the Wyndham Green Programme

Environmental programme	• ENERGY STAR® tracking system
	  – Recycle and reuse paper, glass, plastic, batteries, cell phones, lights
	  – Recycle guest directories, and other property materials
	• EarthSmart® linen and towel programme
	• EPA WaterSense® certified products
	• Smart Uniform Programme – Uniforms made from recycled plastic bottles
	• Wyndham ClearAirSM rooms by Pure™

Source: http://www.wyndhamworldwide.com/corporate-responsibility

(Continued)

Table 37.1 (Continued)

---

6. Accor

Environmental performance and goals	• Tourism for Tomorrow Award 2010 given to Accor by the World Travel & Tourism Council (WTTC) to award the Group's best practices in sustainable tourism around the world
	• Nature (water, waste, biodiversity)
	  – 96% of hotels had installed flow regulators on showers and taps
	  – 219 hotels were equipped with rainwater recovery systems
	  – 86% of hotels recycled their waste
	  – 94% of hotels sorted and recycled batteries, fluorescent lamps and tubes
	  – 90% of hotels sorted and recycled paper and cardboard
	  – 88% of hotels used certified paper for printing
	  – 89% of hotels used locally adapted plants
	  – 72% used eco-friendly gardening products
	• Carbon (energy, CO_2 emission, renewable energy)
	  – 95% of hotels used low-consumption bulbs for 24/7 lighting
	  – For CO_2 reduction, 43% of the hotels are equipped with a timer for common area air conditioning
	  – 162 hotels around the world were equipped with solar panels to produce domestic hot water
	  – 232 hotels used biomass, geothermal and other renewable energies

Environmental programme	• PLANET 21
	  – Accor's new sustainable development programme
	  – Nature: reduce water use, expand waste recycling, protect biodiversity
	  – Carbon: reduce energy use, reduce CO_2 emissions, increase the use of renewable energy
	• Plan for the Planet
	  – More than 3.5 million trees had been funded and more than 1,400 hotels were taking part in Plant for the Planet

Source: http://www.accor.com/en/sustainable-development.html

---

7. Best Western

Environmental performance and goals	• Best Western offers environmentally friendly guestrooms design prototype • Best Western holds workshops and webinars for hotel owners and staff to share how-to's and best practices for going green • Best Western has replaced inefficient lighting and installed new cooling and heating systems as well as energy-efficient appliances • Since energy-saving efforts began, Best Western has saved 1.4M kWh of electricity • All North American hotels are required to use keycard sleeves made from recycled paper and printed with vegetable oil-based ink

Environmental programme	• Partnership with ENERGY STAR®
	    – A joint programme of the U.S. Environmental Protection Agency
	      and the U.S. Department of Energy
	• A Trip-Reduction programme
	    – This programme aimed at reducing single-occupant-vehicle trips
	    – This company's programme won an award at Phoenix's 2008
	      Valley Metro Clean Air Campaign Awards

Source: http://www.bestwestern.com/about-us/green-hotels/

prominent in the hotel industry. Also, establishing a strong and enduring relationship with suppliers who provide environmentally friendly and healthy local products is part and parcel of accomplishing a higher standard of sustainability management. For example, Marriott and Best Western, as some of the major hotel corporations, have strongly encouraged their managers and owners to have 'green supply chains' for sustainable procurement practices.

Furthermore, each hotel company has their own objectives and specific targets for each year, which were mostly a 10–20 per cent reduction in energy, water, and waste. To achieve this goal, the hotels tend to have either their own environmental management tools, and tracking systems, or a partnership with other environmental organisations. Wyndham Worldwide's Green Toolbox and ENERGY STAR system, Accor's PLANET 21, IHG's Green Engage, Hilton's LightStay, and Marriott's Global Green Council and Demand Response (DR) are paragons of those programmes that track the hotel's energy, water, and other environment-related consumptions. These investments in environmental programmes enabled hotels to thoroughly monitor and significantly reduce water and energy consumption.

Discussions

Despite all the hype of environmental issues in the corporate world, there are certainly several issues that hoteliers need to consider and contemplate. First, for hotel chains, financial implications from engaging in environmental issues are an important subject. Although everyone would agree that it is a good thing for hotels to be eco-friendly, not everyone would guarantee that such involvement or investment would turn out to be economically profitable as well. In fact, shareholder theory (Friedman, 1970) may argue that in general, a firm's investment in environmental issues would reduce the firm's value because such resources should be used for enhancing the firm's core business to increase owners' or shareholders' value of the firm. However, as discussed in the introduction, stakeholder theory would suggest the opposite: that a firm's investment in environmental issues would actually improve the firm's value, especially in the long-term, because such practices will satisfy the firm's multiple stakeholders (e.g., environment, community, consumers and/or government) (Freeman, 1984). For example, a firm's involvement in environmental issues improves the firm's image, thus consumers begin liking the firm better, which will lead them to purchase more products from the firm. For US hotel chains, Lee and Park (2009) examined the effect of hotels' investment in socially responsible activities and found a positive impact on hotels' value performance. Kang et al. (2012) also found that hotel guests are willing to pay a premium for hotels' environmental efforts, which shows a positive financial implication for hotels.

Even with some empirical findings regarding a positive financial implication of hotels' investments in environmental issues, caution should be exercised in claiming such a positive effect. Effects of hotels' investment in green issues may not occur immediately, but only in the long-term. Therefore, without a clear long-term perspective or vision held by the senior or top management team, it may be challenging for hotel chains to make a meaningful and substantial investment in environmental matters. This is why hotel chains need to develop a thorough green strategy incorporated into their competitive strategies. Moreover, whenever possible, hotel chains may strive to develop a green strategy that is related to their core business (that is, the hotel business) to enhance its positive impacts which Chandler and Werther (2014) call strategic CSR.

Another issue with hotels' investment in green initiatives is about how to quantify benefits of hotel chains' green investments. Many hotel operators have a difficult time with investment in environmental issues because it is hard for them to know how much of the resulting benefits are due to said investments. Investment in green activities may create financial implications for multiple stakeholders including customers, employees, the local community, and so on. For example, hotel chains' involvement in environmental issues may increase their brand image and reputation for their customers, consequently bringing positive financial implications. Hotels may also enhance the retention rate and productivity of their employees because eco-friendly engagement by their companies may make employees feel more proud of their work and thus become more satisfied with and committed to their companies. These financial implications through multiple stakeholders put hotel operators in a situation where they have a hard time to quantify exact financial benefits (i.e., dollar figures) from their investment in environmental issues. Moreover, many potential financial implications are long-term in nature. For instance, improvement in brand image or reputation due to hotels' investment in environmental issues may happen within a quarter or a year or over many years. The same thing can happen with other potential benefits from eco-friendly investment such as enhanced employees' retention rate or productivity. Although there are no clear solutions for these matters, one suggestion may be that hotel operators need to develop their green strategies from a long-term perspective, not a short-term.

Greenwash can be defined as 'the act of misleading consumers regarding the environmental practices of a company or the environmental benefits of a product or service' (Chandler and Werther, 2014). Many hotel customers may suspect hotels' green activities as a mere greenwashing marketing tool rather than a genuine effort, no matter what the truth actually is. To overcome or alleviate such negative sentiments by hotel customers, hoteliers may need to implement internationally recognised certifications. For example, Leadership in Energy and Environmental Design (LEED) comprises a suite of rating systems for the design, construction, and operation of high performance green buildings, homes and neighbourhoods. Developed by the US Green Building Council (USGBC), LEED is intended to provide building owners and operators with a concise framework for identifying and implementing practical and measurable green building design, construction, operations, and maintenance solutions. Another internationally recognised green certification is ISO 14001. The requirements of ISO 14001 are an integral part of the European Union's Eco-Management and Audit Scheme (EMAS). EMAS's structure and material requirements are more demanding, concerning performance improvement, legal compliance, and reporting duties. Travelocity also provides a list of certified green hotels called the 'Green Hotel Directory.'

Another interesting issue regarding hotels' sustainability practices is a comparison between chain and independent hotels. In general, chain hotels are known to be more effective in developing and implementing sustainability practices than independent hotels (Rahman et al., 2012). Chain hotels typically develop and implement green policies and practices at a corporate level, and maintain them throughout the entire chain (Alvarez et al., 2001). Chain hotels often possess more resources including a team dedicated to the environmental issue; therefore they can more likely develop effective green strategies/practices, and transfer successful green strategies/practices to individual units rather efficiently (Nicholls and Kang, 2012, Rahman, et al., 2012). Moreover, through a widely adopted franchising strategy, many hotel chains require franchisees to adopt the corporate standards (Bohdanowicz, 2006). On the contrary, independent hotels' managers and staffs tend to pay less attention to environmental issues (Enz and Siguaw, 1999; Kirk, 1998). Understanding the ever increasing environmental awareness of society, independent hotels should strive to compete against chain hotels with regards to environmental issues. With more resource constraints, independent hotels may seek third party certification and fully utilise well-established guidelines (such as, Green Seal's GS-33 standards).

Hotel chains may also consider the following recommendations when developing their green strategies. First, hotels should look for partnering with non-governmental organisations (NGOs) in developing their green strategies. Cooperation with NGOs will likely provide hotels with helpful experiences and thus create a positive synergy. Second, hotels should have an exclusive environmental management team that will take the lead on developing and executing environmental strategies. With the management team, systematic development and evaluations of green strategies can be established and maintained, not just in the short-term, but with long-term goals. Third, hotels should consider developing sustainability strategies that are closely related to their core operations, referred to as 'strategic CSR' by Chandler and Werther (2014). Although sometimes it may not be easy to develop a sustainability strategy that is directly related to hotels' core operations, they should still look for a way to use their core competencies to maximise outcomes from the implementation. It may also help to enhance recognition and awareness of such sustainability strategies for their customers and the public. Last, hotels should spend some resources on developing a system that can quantify costs of and benefits from implementing sustainability initiatives, especially the benefits. Such a system will surely help hotel managers to make good and financially solid decisions for their sustainability initiatives.

In terms of academic research, there are several recommendations that hotel researchers may consider for their future studies. First, although the hotel literature has examined various sustainability issues from a customer perspective, sustainability research on employees seems to be lacking. More studies on how hotel firms' sustainability initiatives are related to, or impact upon employees' attitudes and perceptions about their company are encouraged in the future. Second, the hotel sustainability literature seems to have focused more on a positive side of the sustainability issue while the other side has been somewhat ignored. Hotel researchers may need to investigate more potentially negative consequences of sustainability initiatives, not to discourage the hotel industry from investing in the sustainability issue, but to have a better understanding of all different and potential consequences of the sustainability strategy so that a better strategy can be developed. Last, hotel researchers are encouraged to develop a hotel specific framework or model for the sustainability issue, incorporating the idiosyncratic features of the hotel industry.

References

Álvarez Gil, M.J., Burgos-Jiménez, J. and Céspedes Lorente, J.J. (2001) An analysis of environmental management, organizational context and performance of Spanish hotels. *The International Journal of Management Science*, 29, 457–71.

Bacot, H., McCoy, B. and Plagman-Galvan, J. (2002) Municipal commercial recycling: barriers to success. *American Review of Public Administration*, 32(2), 145–65.

Bohdanowicz, P. (2006) Environmental awareness and initiatives in the Swedish and Polish hotel industries – survey results. *International Journal of Hospitality Management*, 25, 662–82.

Chandler, D. and Werther, W.B. (2014) *Strategic Corporate Social Responsibility: Stakeholders, Globalization, and Sustainable Value Creation*, 3rd edn. Thousand Oaks, CA: SAGE Publication Inc.

DiGuili, A. and Kostovetsky, L. (2014) Are red or blue companies more likely to go green? Politics and corporate social responsibility. *Journal of Financial Economics*, 111, 158–80.

Elkington, J. (1997) *Cannibals with Forks: The Triple Bottom Line of 21st Century Business*. Chichester: Capstone Publishing Ltd.

Enz, C.A. and Siguaw, J.A. (1999) Best hotel environmental practices. *The Cornell Hotel and Restaurant Administration Quarterly*, 40(5), 72–5.

Freeman, R.E. (1984) *Strategic Management: a Stakeholder Approach*. Englewood Cliffs, NJ: Prentice Hall.

Friedman, M. (1970, September 17) The social responsibility of business is to increase its profits. *New York Times*, SM17–SM20.

Kang, K.H., Stein, L., Heo, C.Y.H. and Lee, S. (2012) Consumers' willingness to pay for green initiatives of the hotel industry. *International Journal of Hospitality Management*, 31(2), 564–72.

Kirk, D. (1998) Attitudes to environmental management held by a group of hotel managers in Edinburgh. *International Journal of Hospitality Management*, 17, 33–47.

Kitzmueller, M. and Shimshack, J. (2012) Economic perspectives on corporate social responsibility. *Journal of Economic Literature*, 50(1), 51–84.

Kniss, B. (2008, 5 December) Corporate social responsibility becoming mainstream concept. *Canadian HR Reporter*. Online. Available HTTP: <http://www.hrreporter.com/userlogin?article=6566-corporate-social-responsibility-becoming-mainstream-concept>, accessed 5 December 2015.

Lee, S. and Park, S.Y. (2009) Do socially responsible activities help hotels and casinos achieve their financial goals? *International Journal of Hospitality Management*, 28(1), 105–12.

Lys, T., Naughton, J. and Wang, C. (2013) Pinpointing the value in CSR. *Kellogg Insight*, 71. Online. Available HTTP: <http://insight.kellogg.northwestern.edu/browse/issue/71/>, accessed 5 December 2015.

Nicholls, S. and Kang, S. (2012) Going green: the adoption of environmental initiatives in Michigan's lodging sector. *Journal of Sustainable Tourism*, 20(7), 953–74.

Rahman, I., Reynolds, D. and Svaren, S. (2012) How 'green' are North American hotels? An exploration of low-cost adoption practices. *International Journal of Hospitality Management*, 31(3), 720–7.

Singh, N., Cranage, D. and Lee, S. (2014) Green strategies for hotels: estimation of recycling benefits. *International Journal of Hospitality Management*, 43, 13–22.

38

Hotel chains and higher education institutions

Irena Erbakanova

(VARNA UNIVERSITY OF MANAGEMENT, BULGARIA)

Introduction

The fact that the hospitality industry is a 'people business' (Hayes and Ninemeier, 2009) is predetermining the importance of proper personnel recruitment and training in each hotel department in order to ensure that the product/service actually exists and is sold with the expected high level of professionalism required by the newest tendencies in the business. Indeed hotel chains and corporations of all types and sizes in different locations around the world consistently note concerns in recruiting, developing, and maintaining a competent, educated and well-motivated workforce at all organisational levels – managerial or operational (Cooper and Hall, 2008; Hayes and Ninemeier, 2009; Nickson, 2007; Whitelaw et al., 2009). It is inevitable here to mention that some hotel chains are multinational (MNC) and because they sell their product/service outside their home countries they face issues of building their applicant pool for their overseas units in a different environment (in terms of language, culture, economic and political systems, legislative frameworks and management styles) (Briscoe et al., 2012; Nickson, 2007) and on a larger scale in terms of international human resource management (IHRM). Thus, it can be said that there are two sides of the labour market (international and/or domestic) – demand for skills where hotel corporations and chains are, and the supply side where different sources of workers stand and recruitment strategies take place, such as: in-house job referral, company website, local and national press, employment agencies and professional/industry associations, personnel consultants, job fairs and higher education institutions (HEIs) (Boella and Goss-Turner, 2013; Nickson, 2007; Walker and Miller, 2010). The recruitment and selection processes adopted by different business companies in the hospitality industry are addressed in detail in the literature (Andrews, 2009; Boella and Goss-Turner, 2013; Hayes and Ninemeier, 2009; Lee-Ross and Pryce, 2010; Nickson, 2007; Riley, 1996), in the context of Human Resource Management (HRM) and IHRM (Briscoe et al., 2012; Dowling et al., 2008; Edwards and Rees, 2006; Harzing and Pinnington, 2011). Little academic attention, however, is paid to the Higher Education Institutions (HEIs) and the relationships hotel corporations build with them. Such relationships should not be neglected because as Brookes and Becket (2011) say, on the one hand 'HEIs are charged with the role of producing graduates capable of working within globalised economies' (p. 241) (part of which is the hospitality industry) and, on the other, the demand for graduates capable of working in the hospitality industry has been recognised by the hotel chains. Therefore, those innovative and diverse relationships, with examples of such in the industry and their advantages and disadvantages for the groups of stakeholders (hotel chains, HEIs, students and the local community), represent the core discussion in this chapter.

Hotel chains and HEIs: forms of cooperation

The relationships between hotel chains and HEIs might have many innovative forms and objectives (see Table 38.1), and therefore the aim of this part of the chapter is to illustrate and explain them. As was mentioned earlier, there are several groups of stakeholders – the hotel chains, the HEIs, the students and the local community. Their interactions, mainly triggered by the needs of the industry, shape the different forms of collaboration, that can be summarised as follows:

- Recruitment of educated personnel (placements, internships, apprenticeships, etc.) directly from the HEI by forming partnerships and/or contract agreements;
- Forming a separate HEI like Conrad N. Hilton College, whereas the demand for skills and the supply side are owned by the hotel corporation itself, or providing scholarships for education for students (Best Western);
- Hotel corporations' training centres and academies with qualification certificates for the public and/or current employees; Distinction has to be made between training and getting a certificate/diploma earned at EIs. InterContinental's IHG Academy, for example, provides qualification programmes in hospitality for local communities and for future employees only, therefore all those examples are specifically designated in Table 38.1.
- Provision of training and development opportunities for current employees (corporate online training platforms, corporate universities and academies, funds for education of employees such as Nordic Choice, etc.);
- Connecting lecturers at HEI with industry leaders and giving them opportunities to learn and gain operational experience today (Marriott on the move, 2014) and vice versa; industry leaders coming to the EI as guest lecturers;

In order to illustrate the above in Table 38.1 below particular practical examples are shown for 22 hotel corporations and chains from around the world.

Summarising the HEI–hotel chains interactions and linking them with the time frame of the education process, they can be structured as shown in Figure 38.1. It should be mentioned, that when current employees have to be considered, they may enter at the postgraduate level in the timeframe, because as Knowles et al. (2003) mention 'there are a number of points in the management hierarchy that are difficult to pass without a degree level qualification' (p.45). Thus, the employee might need to go 'back to school' in order to climb the career ladder.

Advantages and disadvantages of the partnerships

Those forms of partnerships and innovative strategies for recruitment, personnel training and development, on operational and managerial level, have advantages and disadvantages for both sides of the 'contract/agreement'. The other parties affected by those partnerships – the students and the local communities – must be consider as well. They also bear the positives

Table 38.1 Industry examples of connections between hotel chains and corporation and higher education institutions (current and future employees)

Hotel corporations & chains	Partnership with HEI internships/contract agreements	Hotel chain lecturers	Hotel chain education certificates and others
Hilton	10 partner HEIs all over the world		Conrad N. Hilton College of Hotel and Restaurant Management
Accor			Académie Accor – only for employees
Starwood	4 partner HEIs		Vita and Finance Futura – graduate management programme & eCornell professional hotel classes online
InterContinental Hotel Group	3 partner HEIs all over the world Online training programmes – for employees only	Chengdu Vocational and Technical College	The IHG Academy
Mandarin Hotel Oriental Group	11 partner HEIs all over the world		eCornell courses & in-house MBA programme with RMIT for senior employees
Marriott	Have internships but no partner institutions	Connecting teachers with industry leaders	
Wyndham hotels and resorts	University relations programme; Have internships but no specific HEI partner		
Best Western			Online training centre for employees; scholarships for higher education;
Carlson			Online corporate CWT University for employees only
Hyatt	10 partner HEIs all over the world		Regular visits to HEI
G6 Hospitality			G6 University iLearn@6
Louvre hotel group			Corporate University – U - for employees only
LQ Management			LQ University online
NH Hotel Group	Have internship programmes, no specific institution		NH University (corporate) & NH University Learning Lounge
Whitbread	Have internships but no specific partners		Apprenticeship and Advanced Apprenticeship
Travelodge Hotels			JuMP (Junior Management Programme) A-level students (18+) L2 Apprenticeship & L3 Advanced Apprenticeship

(Continued)

Table 38.1 (Continued)

Hotel corporations & chains	Partnership with HEI internships/contract agreements	Hotel chain lecturers	Hotel chain education certificates and others
			Hospitality Internship Programme
MGM			Management Associate Programme – full time employees are provided with $2,100 per year in tuition assistance to pursue a degree or certification in a HEI
Caesars Entertainment	President's Associate Internship – no partner institution		Web-based online learning curriculum – for employees only
Shangri-La Hotels and Resorts	Have partner institutions		The Shangri-La Academy
Nordic Choice			Nordic Choice Academy – for employees only
Four Seasons Hotels and Resorts	23 HEI in USA; 2 in Canada 7 in Switzerland; 1 in France; 1 in Egypt; 5 in China;	Yes in all partner institutions	Management Development Programme - Ugenius online learning resource – for employees only;
Club Méditerranée			Talent University – for employees only

Sources: Hilton Worldwide (2015); Starwood (2015); InterContinental Hotel Group (2015); Mandarin Hotel Oriental Group (2015); Marriott on the move (2014); Marriott (2015); Wyndham Worldwide (2015); Best Western (2015); Carlson (2015); Hyatt (2015); G6 Hospitality (2015); Louvre Hotel Group (2015); LQ Management (2015a, 2015b); NH Hotel Group (2015a); NH Hotel Group (2015b); Whitbread (2015); Travelodge (2015); MGM Resorts International (2015); Caesars Entertainment (2015); Shangri-La Hotels and Resorts (2015); Nordic Choice Hotels (2015); Four Seasons Hotels and Resorts (2015); Club Mediterranee (2015); author's elaboration.

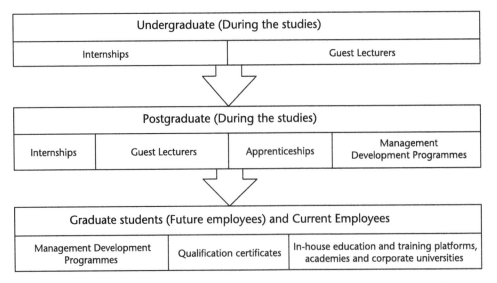

Figure 38.1 Forms of relationships between higher education institutions and hotel chains and corporations in an education process time frame.

and the negatives and in their own right can view those relationships as beneficial or not. Those issues are addressed further in this section of the chapter.

The most obvious advantage for hotel chains of forming a partnership/contract agreement with HEIs for recruitment of students is that it secures sources of educated labour in hospitality and tourism. The disadvantage for the hotel chains here can be seen in the context of the general reliability of the HEIs and the quality of education they provide. Reliability, though, can be easily checked by looking at the government data on the accreditation of the particular academic institution (Pearce, 2013). Quality and effectiveness, in terms of providing the curricula that corresponds to the business demand for particular skills, however, are a subjective matter, which has been addressed and researched by Harkison et al.(2011), Hsu (2011), Kavita and Sharma (2011), Pearce (2013) and Perman and Mikinac (2014). Although there has been a tremendous growth in the number of hospitality programmes all over the world (Knowles et al., 2003), due to the expansion of the hospitality and tourism industry, Hsu (2011), Kavita and Sharma (2011) and Perman and Mikinac (2014) stress the fact that the quality within the hospitality industry depends on the overall level of education of employed personnel, the efficient national policy of education and professional development, and how the education system has adapted to modern trends in hospitality and tourism. In other words, the quality of management and service, competitiveness and business success is highly determined by the combined efforts of academics and industry altogether. Kavita and Sharma (2011) add that hospitality leaders demand that students graduating within specific higher education programmes possess appropriate management skills and competencies, and that educational experience actually plays a critical role in shaping future business leaders. Developing a workforce with employable skills and competencies is a challenge for both educators and entrepreneurs (Kavita and Sharma, 2011). In order for them to benefit from their cooperation and therefore provide benefits for the students (by teaching them the 'right subjects') and for the local community (to make an employable labour market) they have to work towards one goal instead of working towards 'a goal' that no one would benefit from.

Here it should be to mentioned that the direct cooperation between both institutions in the form of guest lecturers coming in from the hotel chains to the HEIs, and bringing in lecturers from HEI to the hospitality industry (a strategy adopted by Marriott, for example, in 2014) will ensure the effectiveness of educators on the one hand (Harkison et al., 2011), and on the other, will create a 'new generation' with competent, competitive, practical and up-to-date knowledge of today's business workforce.

The recruitment from employment agencies or any other source of personnel mentioned previously in this chapter compels employers (hotel chains) to face not only fierce competition for staff but also the problem of poor image and the perception of little prestige in the hospitality industry as a working place (Andrews, 2009; Cooper and Hall, 2008; Jenkins, 2001; Whitelaw et al., 2009). When turning to a HEI partner who educates a quite significant number of students already showing a certain loyalty to the lodging industry by choosing to undertake hospitality-related studies, hotel chains can secure loyalty to their particular brand. This loyalty can be built on when representatives of the hotel chain appear in the academic institutions, cooperating in different ways, as, for example, at a job fair or as guest lecturers. Probably this will be the quickest way to match a particular vacant position with the right person who shares, and most importantly believes in, the company mission and vision. Ultimately such individuals are the most likely to give the required high-level of service and further their career to become 'great leaders'.

The next set of advantages and disadvantages of the relationships can be summarised in terms of reputation. It is a fact that both parties in the partnership very much rely on their image in order to operate effectively and efficiently in today's extremely competitive environment. Firstly, looking at the hotel chains, as noted by Briscoe et al. (2012), a challenge for multinational hotel chains in the recruitment process is to develop an employer reputation that attracts job candidates to the company, and, in order to achieve that, the potential candidates must perceive the company as a desirable place of work (Jenkins, 2011). One of the best ways to send this message is when hotel chain representatives actually visit the campuses of their HEIs partners during job fairs and/or when they visit classes as guest lecturers. As a result, the hotel chains can collect a desirable applicant pool (recruitment process) and then be able to have an efficient selection process, because both processes must operate effectively for optimal staffing decisions to be made and to save money and time (Dowling et al., 2008). On the other hand, HEIs very much rely on rankings (Times, Guardian, Eduniversal, QS, U Multirank, National universities rankings, etc.) and for a HEI to be ranked higher it has to provide evidence that there are a respectable number of employment opportunities for its students. The higher the ranking of the HEI, the more students are going to be attracted to study there. An example is Les Roches International School of Hotel Management (http://www.lesroches.edu/); the EI actually states on their website that they act as recruiters for Fairmont Hotels and Resorts, Mandarin Oriental Hotel Group, Shangri-La Hotels and Resorts, Hyatt, Hilton, Four Seasons Hotels and Resorts, The Ritz-Carlton, Marriott, InterContinental Hotels and Resorts, White Lodging, etc., so it is evident that the relationship is official and it can be assumed that it is working in favour of the HEI.

Thus when HEIs in a country have a good reputation and provide the curricula that corresponds to the business needs, which happens when working together with hotel chains in all forms of partnerships, there is no doubt that the local community, and equally the students, would benefit.

With regard to students, there is an idea that should not be overlooked. According to the work of Harkison et al. (2011) the industry (a part of which are the hotel chains) values experience more than qualification. However, the expense of a degree education might be quite significant, and therefore, in order to protect the interests of both sides, cooperation in terms of internships and placements between hotel chains and HEIs would be very beneficial (Knowles et al., 2003). The hotel chain would be able to find a graduate with significant operational experience and for the students it would be invaluable after the time and money they spend in HEI.

As was mentioned earlier in this chapter, some hotel corporations are multinational (MNCs) and one of the key issues in IHRM is the way in which MNCs staff their overseas units (Nickson, 2007; Riley, 1996). In most cases those businesses have a multinational workforce and are seeking people who are willing to move or, to use the relevant term, expatriates. According to Edwards and Rees (2006) recruitment is an extremely significant issue in IHRM for the reason that a failed expatriate assignment can be a catastrophic waste of money and time for a company and can result in a bad public image and reduced profits. Briscoe et al. (2012) add that attracting candidates to work internationally raises an important challenge for MNCs (such as multinational hotel chains and corporations) of how to find individuals interested in international work as well as those interested in a permanent international career. This brings us to the idea that the cooperation between HEIs and MNCs in terms of internships will produce a workforce that is ready to work in a multi-cultural environment in terms of customers and colleagues. Moreover, according to Brookes and Becket (2011) HEIs are also becoming multicultural by the internationalisation of hospitality programmes. For instance they enrol international students and thus, during the education process their graduates are already exposed to dealing with people with different cultural backgrounds when they have to work on assignments and projects with their foreign colleagues. Those individuals are used to travelling and working with different people or, as noted by Brookes and Becket (2011), they were able to develop cross-cultural competencies, so when the partnership has to take place, when the hotel chain has to select the right candidate, it would choose them from an applicant pool of desired individuals. Looking at Table 38.1, it is apparent that some multinational hotel chains such as Hilton, InterContinental Hotel Group (IHG), Hayat and Four Seasons Hotels and Resorts undertook a strategy of keeping expatriates to a minimum (for example just for management positions) by building partnerships with HEIs around the world. Therefore, the advantage for the international hotel chains of the partnership with a domestic HEI is that they can recruit local young professionals who understand the local market. It is clear that in the two cases the local community would be affected; when bringing expatriates in it might cause a conflict with the local population because of giving the vacant position to a non-local, and in to the contrary, when a MNC steps into the local market it provides job opportunities for local residents (if the company decides to recruit from the host country).

According to Perman and Mikinac (2014) investment in its personnel is a must for a tourism company striving to meet the guests' needs, since it thereby educates them to provide additional satisfaction to customers. Thus, in the cases where partnerships are formed in order to provide qualification programmes and online platforms for education of current staff members, it has to be considered that the most concerned employees will be those having graduated in hospitality and/or other tourism related studies, and those who graduated in another sphere but desire to work in the hospitality industry and are very motivated (Dredge, Airey and Gross, 2015). In-house education and qualification programmes will help both groups of individuals to achieve their career goals, to increase their qualifications and therefore to be more effective and productive for the company. Moreover, investment in personnel increases motivation and loyalty and as Perman and Mikinac (2014) state, satisfied personnel will demonstrate their satisfaction in the guests' presence which will ultimately affect the customers' satisfaction. The beneficiaries in the cases considering the future employees are the people from the local community that do not possess a diploma in tourism and/or hospitality and are willing to work in the industry, because companies such as LQ Management, G6 Hospitality, IHG, Shangri-La Hotels and Resorts are providing qualification programmes for such individuals. However, they give specific diplomas/certificates with special emphasis on the skills and knowledge applicable to the particular hotel chain or corporation, which might be considered a limitation with regards to general employment options in other hospitality companies. On the other hand, such certificates might actually improve employees' CVs and their competitiveness in the labour market. Nevertheless, undertaking such a programme promises a position in the respective company for the future employee undertaking the given qualification programme.

Conclusion

Hospitality industry leaders have to know that they need university graduates; they need qualified personnel to stay in the business. This fact is of greater importance for hotel chains, because in their case there are multiple properties at stake. Harkison et al. (2011) stress that qualified personnel have less training needs and learn faster. Thus, hotel chains need to collaborate and influence the HEIs. On the other hand, HEIs would not be able to survive the competition in the education market if they fail to be seen as institutions that educate students who are competitive on the labour market. Harkison et al. (2011) state that 'if educators know what industry requires, they can continually adjust curricula to support industry's expectations and needs, thereby improving the prospects and satisfaction of graduates'(p. 380). Moreover, relationships with hotel chains would also help HEIs to revitalise their programmes instead of just replicating the past (Morrison and O'Mahony, 2003). They will have graduates that would be able to reflect on and ameliorate industry and management practices (Morrison and O'Mahony, 2003) and the industry needs a breath of fresh air.

Each of the two sides of partnerships has to keep its values while, at the same time they have to support each other. On the one hand, hotel chains need to understand that behind professional education stand a lot of professionals, history and practice in shaping the students into proactive professionals, and on the other, HEIs need to understand the current needs and situation of the hotel business. As Morrison and O'Mahony (2003) mention, failing to liberate the hospitality programmes would result in university graduates with 'inherited and outmoded ways of thinking about the world' (p. 40).

The main focus of this chapter has been the innovative and diverse relationships between hotel chains and HEIs, the examples of such forms in the industry and their advantages and disadvantages were also discussed. However, a number of questions are still to be answered – how hotel chains and corporations actually choose HEI partners, will they form a checklist, will they use recommendations, will they focus on what the competition is doing or whom are they using, etc. and going even deeper in the matter, looking at Figure 38.1, investigating what is the level of influence of hotel chains and corporations on the curricula during the different stages of the education process and what are the terms (limitations) of those contracts/agreements.

References

Andrews, S. (2009) *Human Resource Management: A Textbook for the Hospitality Industry*, New Delhi: Tata McGraw-Hill Publishing Company Ltd.

Best Western (2015) Best Western for a Better World; Online. Available HTTP:: <http://www.bestwestern.com/about-us/better-world/education.asp>, accessed 4 February 2015.

Boella, M. and Goss-Turner, S. (2013) *Human Resource Management in the Hospitality Industry: A Guide to Best Practice*, 9th edn. Abingdon: Routledge.

Briscoe, D., Schuler, R. and Tarique, I. (2012) *International Human Resource Management: Policies and Practices*, 4th edn. New York: Routledge.

Brookes, M. and Becket, N. (2011) Internationalising hospitality management degree programmes, *International Journal of Contemporary Hospitality Management*, 23(2), 241–60.

Caesars Entertainment (2015) Training and development programs. Online. Available HTTP: <http://caesars.hodesiq.com/Link_nav/on-campus/graduates/training_development.asp>, accessed 13 February 2015.

Carlson (2015) Career opportunities. Online. Available HTTP: <http://www.carlson.com/jobs/hotels.do>, accessed 5 February 2013.

Club Mediterranee (2015) Club Med Job opportunities and career development. Online. Available HTTP: <http://www.clubmedjobs.co.uk/100-jobs-be-discovered/working-village/career-progression-club-med>, accessed 4 February 2015.

Cooper, C. and Hall, C.M. (2008) *Contemporary Tourism: An International Approach*, 1st edn. Oxford: Butterworth-Heinemann, Elsevier Ltd.

Dowling, P.J., Festing, M. and Engle, A.D. (2008) *International Human Resource Management*, 5th edn. London, UK: Thomson Learning.

Dredge, D., Airey, D. and Gross, M.J. (2015) *Routledge Handbook of Tourism and Hospitality Education*. Abingdon: Routledge.

Edwards, T. and Rees, Ch. (2006) *International Human Resource Management: Globalization, National Systems and Multinational Companies*. Essex: Pearson Education Ltd.

Four Seasons Hotels and Resorts (2015) Recruitment calendar and opportunities. Online. Available HTTP: <http://jobs.fourseasons.com/Students/recruitmentcalendar/Pages/Recruitmentcalendar.aspx>, accessed 6 February 2015.

G6 Hospitality (2015) Careers and development programs. Online. Available HTTP: <http://www.g6hospitality.com/career-opportunities/training-and-development>, accessed 6 February 2015.

Harkison, T., Poulson, J. and Jung-Hee, G.K. (2011) Hospitality graduates and managers: the big divide. *International Journal of Contemporary Hospitality Management*, 23(3), 377–92,

Harzing, A. and Pinnington, A. (2011) *International Human Resource Management*, 3rd edn. London, UK: SAGE Publications Ltd.

Hayes, D.K and Ninemeier, J.D (2009) *Human Resources Management in the Hospitality Industry*. Hoboken, New Jersey: John Wiley and Sons.

Hilton Worldwide (2015) Careers: Universities. Online. Available HTTP: <http://jobs.hiltonworldwide.com/en/universities/?cntry=united-states>, accessed 4 January 2015.

Hsu, C.C.H. (2011) *Global Tourism Higher Education: Past, Present, and Future*. Abingdon and New York: Routledge.

Hyatt (2015) Career paths. Online. Available HTTP: <http://www.hyatt.jobs/career-paths/rooms-operations/>, accessed 5 February 2015.

InterContinental Hotel Group (2015) Corporate responsibility report. Online. Available HTTP: <http://www.ihgplc.com/index.asp?pageid=754>, accessed 2 February 2015.

Jenkins, A.K. (2001) Making a career of it? Hospitality students' future perspectives: an Anglo-Dutch study. *International Journal of Contemporary Hospitality Management*, 13(1), 13–20.

Kavita, K.M. and Sharma, P. (2011) Gap analysis of skills provided in hotel management education with respect to skills required in the hospitality industry: the Indian scenario. *International Journal of Hospitality & Tourism Systems*, 4(1), 31–51.

Knowles, T., Teixeira, R.M. and Egan, D. (2003) Tourism and hospitality education in Brazil and the UK: a comparison. *International Journal of Contemporary Hospitality Management*, 15(1), 45–51,

Lee-Ross, D. and Pryce, J. (2010) *Human Resources and Tourism: Skills, Culture and Industry, Aspects of Tourism Texts*, vol.2. Bristol: Channel View Publications.

Louvre Hotel Group (2015) Careers and training. Online. Available HTTP: <http://www.louvrehotels.com/en/career/hotel-catering-training>, accessed 6 February 2015.

LQ Management (2015a) Careers and training. Online. Available HTTP: <http://www.lq.com/en/navigation/careers/training.html>, accessed10 February 2015.

LQ Management (2015b) LQ university information. Online. Available HTTP: <http://www.lquni.com/>, accessed 10 February 2015.

Mandarin Hotel Oriental Group (2015) Graduate Programmes. Online. Available HTTP: <http://www.mandarinoriental.com/careers/graduate-programmes/>, accessed 2 February 2015.

Marriott (2015) Career Paths. Online. Available HTTP: <https://www.marriott.com/careers/paths.mi>, accessed 30 January 2015.

Marriott on the move (2014) Teaching 'Hospitality 101'in China. Online. Available HTTP: <http://www.blogs.marriott.com/marriott-on-the-move/2014/09/opening-doors-to-teachers-in-china.html>, accessed 4 January 2015.

MGM Resorts International (2015) *College programs*. Online. Available HTTP: <http://www.mgmresortscareers.com/college/programs.aspx>, accessed 11 February 2015.

Morrison, A. and O'Mahony, G.B. (2003). The liberation of hospitality management education. *International Journal of Contemporary Hospitality Management*, 15(1), 38–44.

NH Hotel Group (2015a) Internships. Online. Available HTTP: <http://corporate.nh-hoteles.es/en/job/internships-and-fellowships>, accessed 9 February 2015.

NH Hotel Group (2015b) NH university information. Online. Available HTTP: <http://corporate.nh-hoteles.es/en/job/nh-university>, accessed 9 February 2015.

Nickson, D. (2007) *Human Resource Management for the Hospitality and Tourism Industries*. Oxford: Butterworth-Heinemann, Elsevier Ltd.

Nordic Choice Hotels (2015) Employee development programs. Online. Available HTTP: <https://www.nordicchoicehotels.com/work-with-us/our-employees/develop-your-skills>, accessed 6 February 2015.

Pearce, R. (2013) *International Education and Schools: Moving Beyond the First 40 Years*. London: Bloomsbury Publishing Plc.

Perman, L. and Mikinac, K. (2014) *Effectiveness of education processes in tourism and hospitality in the Republic of Croatia*. Conference paper, Tourism and Hospitality Industry 2014, Congress Proceedings Trends in Tourism and Hospitality Industry, 616–31.

Riley, M. (1996) *Human Resource Management in the Hospitality and Tourism Industry*, 2nd edn. Oxford: Butterworth-Heinemann.

Shangri-La Hotels and Resorts (2015) Career opportunities and Shangri-La Academy. Online. Available HTTP: <http://www.shangri-la.com/corporate/careers/shangrila-academy/>, accessed 13 February 2015.

Starwood (2015) Vita and Finance Futura. Online. Available HTTP: <http://www.starwoodvitafutura.com/framework>, accessed 30 January 2015.

Travelodge (2015) Career opportunities. Online. Available HTTP: <http://www.travelodge.co.uk/careers/>, accessed 11 February 2015.

Walker, J.R. and Miller, J.E. (2010) *Supervision in the Hospitality Industry, Study Guide: Leading Human Resources*, 6th edn. Hoboken, New Jersey: John Wiley & Sons.

Whitbread (2015) Careers and development programs. Online. Available HTTP: <http://www.whitbread.co.uk/careers/learning-development.html>, accessed 9 February 2015.

Whitelaw, P.A, Barron, P., Buultjens, J., Cairncross, G. and Davidson, M. (2009) *Training Needs of the Hospitality Industry*. CRC for Sustainable Tourism Pty Ltd.

Wyndham Worldwide (2015). Graduate programs. Online. Available HTTP: <http://careers.wyndhamworldwide.com/student-grads/recent-graduates>, accessed 10 February 2015.

39

Hotel chains, globalisation, and politics

Craig Webster

(BALL STATE UNIVERSITY, USA)

Introduction

The hotel industry has gone through expansion internationally and changes in terms of the scale of hospitality enterprises in recent decades. One of the major movements that plays a role in the expansion of hotel chains internationally since the 1970s is globalisation, something that is social, political, and economic in nature. Here, we delve into the literature that has been written on the topic of hotel chains, their global operations, and the politics of hotel chains in recent decades, looking into the trajectory of the globalisation of hotel chains in the future and the political environments in which they function, and will likely function in, in the future.

First, we look into the literature on the topic of politics and the globalisation of the tourism industry in general, and hotel chains in particular. Then we delve into the phenomenon of globalisation and its trajectory, linking how this has had an impact upon hotel chains and their holding companies in recent years. Following that, we briefly comment upon how ideology plays a role in the perception of hotel chains in the globalisation process. Then, we investigate the implications of the globalisation process for hotel chains and likely political issues that will play a role in terms of limiting and enabling the increasing global operations of hotel chains and their holding companies.

Literature on the topic

There is a large amount of literature that deals with the positive and negative impacts of globalisation. There are many who take a critical stance on globalisation (see for example: Rodrik, 2011; Stiglitz, 2003) while others view it as something beneficial for individuals, countries, and businesses (see for example; Bhagwati, 2007; Bhagwati and Cammett, 2005; Friedman, 2005). There seems to be a general agreement that globalisation refers to a phenomenon which encompasses economic, social, and political interactions between countries and societies. The economic aspect of it refers to the increasingly international economic exchanges and contacts, the social or cultural aspect deals with cultural and social sharing of ideas, and the political aspect deals with the creation of political linkages connecting countries.

For the past few years, the impact the political environment has had on the tourism industry has been of increasing interest, with many looking at the role that political actors play in the tourism industry. Webster and Ivanov (2012) and Webster, Ivanov and Illum (2011) investigate the ways in which the National Tourism Organisations function, using a very different philosophy of how the organisation will interact with the industry and market, based upon the prevailing ideology of the state's intervention in the economy. Some have looked into the way that political processes and planning play a role in the life cycle of coastal resorts, finding that political involvement in the economic activity of tourism can be beneficial, although different levels of government complicate the growth and trajectory of the tourism industry (Andriotis, 2006). Other scholarship generally deals with unravelling the complex relationship between the role of the state, society, and the economy in the regulation and encouragement of tourism (see for example; Anastasiadou, 2007; Bianchi 2006; Altinay and Bowen, 2006; Burns and Novelli, 2007; Robinson and Smith, 2006; Tribe 2006; Antonakakis et al., 2015).

There is also a great deal of literature dedicated to exploring the impact of globalisation upon the hotel and tourism industries. For example, Dwyer (2014) looks into the various ways that the tourism industry is influenced or may be influenced by globalisation. There are various other authors who consider how and in what ways the tourism industry is currently and will be impacted by globalisation (see for example, Cunill, 2006; Cunill and Forteza, 2010; Munar 2007). Many authors explore the benefits and challenges that globalisation offers the tourism industry. Ivanov and Webster (2013) use a statistical model, investigating the 167 countries for which data were available to see if globalisation was positively linked with increases in the per capita contribution of tourism to the economy. What they found is that there is no positive relationship between globalisation levels and per capita contribution of tourism to the economy, implying that globalisation may not actually be as beneficial as most would think. However, in their analysis on Indonesia, Sugiyarto et al. (2003) found that globalisation has a positive impact upon social welfare and growth in the Indonesian economy. At any rate, whether globalisation will have a net positive or negative impact upon tourism is not really under debate, as globalisation, almost by definition means an increase in the movement of people for tourism, although what is in doubt is whether the increased social and economic interactions will lead to desirable or undesirable externalities.

More specifically, there is a small but growing academic literature that deals with the issues raised by globalisation and the challenges and opportunities such a phenomenon offers the hotel industry. This is an expanding field, and there have been many who in recent years have considered how the process of globalisation offers challenges and possibilities to the modern hotel chain. There are some who look into the strategic and market opportunities that a globalised environment creates for hotel chains (see for example Whitla et al., 2007; Zhang, 2009; Gustavo, 2013; Harvey, 2007; Ottenbacher et al., 2006). Martorell-Cunill et al. (2014) make a very sophisticated analysis of the different strategies that hotel chains use when expanding abroad to be more globally competitive.

However, there are some that are interested in how large hotel chains enter into regions, competing with local chains. Rogerson (2014) shows that the large global chains in recent decades have entered into Africa to gain a large share of the market, explaining the difficulties which South African chains and others would have to consider in this competitive environment. However, there is also interesting and creative work to be done to investigate the way in which globalisation places stress upon the workforce. For example, Seifert and Messing (2006) ponder the way that globalisation has impacted upon the workplace of the cleaners in the hospitality industry, leading to a more difficult job for them. What is interesting about this research is that it makes a clear relationship between the prevailing ideology of neo-liberalism and the degradation of the workplace conditions of the cleaners in hotels.

Since globalisation is such a massive phenomenon that impacts upon businesses and governments everywhere, it is logical that the academic literature has focused upon it. In terms of the literature dealing with tourism, in general the focus of the literature deals with how globalisation impacts upon societies, governments and businesses. The very specific literature that deals with the hospitality industry is generally focused upon the strategies that hotel corporations use in terms of penetrating new markets and expanding other ones, while a minority deals with how the globalisation process has changed the workplace for the workforce in the hospitality industry. Now, we turn to a look at globalisation that delves into its development and trajectory, and consider the hierarchy of the global hotel holding companies.

Hotel chains and globalisation today

Because hotels are just one part of the global economy, it is important to reflect upon the general impact and trajectory of globalisation in recent decades. Figure 39.1 illustrates the trends in globalisation in recent decades, according to one major measure of global-isation, the KOF Index of Globalisation (see Dreher et al., 2008; Dreher, 2006). The vertical axis represents the mean score for globalisation for all the countries, with zero representing no globalisation and one hundred representing a fully globalised world. While this index may not be the 'perfect' way of measuring the complex social, economic, and political concept that we refer to as 'globalisation', we see that there is an empirical trend that probably coincides with our intuitive conception of the increasingly interrelated nature of commerce and politics since the early 1970s. The data illustrate that the world's political economy has increasingly globalised the environment that the current hotel corporations and chains function within. The data clearly show that the world is a more integrated unit socially, economically and politically, as the general trend towards globalisation seems to go in only one direction, especially since the early 1990s. This process has been assisted by technologies

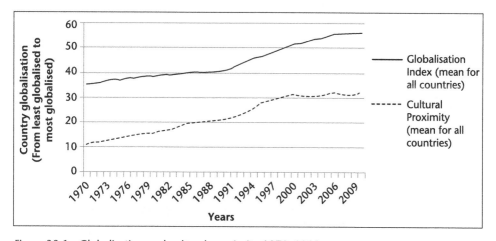

Figure 39.1 Globalisation and cultural proximity 1970–2011.

Source: KOF Index of Globalisation

and the creation and enhancement of political and economic institutions to create a more liberal global economy, whose ideology is usually referred to as neo-liberalism.

The sub-index by KOF, which measures cultural proximity, is also noteworthy. This variable is composed of three different statistics; one a measure of McDonald's restaurants per capita, one is a measure of IKEAs per capita, and one that is a measure of trade in books as a percentage of GDP. This indicator is especially telling as it indicates that it is largely composed of data that show that two major brands (McDonald's and IKEA) are rapidly expanding and infiltrating different markets around the world. Although the data are unfortunately also intertwined by a third variable (although this additional variable is weighted in ways so that it is only 10 per cent of the sub-index), the variable's direction is indicative of the increasingly global role that these two major brands play around the world, and there is no reason to believe hotel chains are becoming less global in outlook. As a matter of fact, as we note below, hotel chains are very global in their activities, although ownership is still overwhelmingly Western.

One of the most interesting aspects of hotel chains and the hotel business is that the biggest hotel corporations, the entities that own the chains and their brands, are disproportionately based in the USA, although their operations are just about as global as can be imagined. Table 39.1 illustrates the leading hotel corporations in the world, ordered by room capacity, according to the most recent data available. Although the largest hotel corporation with the largest hotel room capacity in the world is a UK company, IHG, seven of the ten top hotel corporations in the world are US-based companies. The other companies that are on the list are either French or Chinese.

What this means for the hotel business is that the hotel chains are dominated by American capital. The brands and chains that the American-based corporations own are quite familiar and international, even if the holding companies may not be known to all. For example, while 'Starwood Hotels and Resorts' may not be recognised in many households, Westin, Le Méridien, and Sheraton, chains owned by the corporation, are likely to be recognised by many consumers. There are many chains that are managed by massive hospitality holding companies. What this means for the consumer is that while the name of the holding company

Table 39.1 Top hotel corporations globally 2013

Corporation	Country	Number of hotels	Number of rooms	Number of countries present
InterContinental Hotels Group	UK	4602	675982	100
Hilton Hotels	USA	3992	652378	80
Marriott International	USA	3672	638793	72
Wyndham Hotel Group	USA	7342	627437	66
Choice	USA	6198	497023	35
Accor	France	3515	450199	92
Starwood Hotels and Resorts	USA	1121	328055	100
Best Western	USA	4024	311611	100
Home Inns	China	1772	214070	1
Carlson Rezidor Hotel Group	USA	1077	166245	110

Source: Hospitalitynet.org (2013); Accor (2015); Best Western (2015); Carlson Rezidor hotel group (2015); Choice hotels (2015); Hilton Hotels and Resorts (2015); Home Inns hotel group (2015); InterContinental Hotel Group (2014); Marriott International (2015); Starwood hotels and resorts (2015); Wyndham hotel group (2015).

of the hotel chain that she or he stays with may be unknown, the hotel chain's brand is known and likely conveys something regarding the quality and cost of the brand.

What is rather remarkable is that the Western corporations seem to be very global in outlook, rather than regional players, as McNeill (2008) noted. For example, IHG's major brands include InterContinental, Crowne Plaza, Holiday Inn, and Holiday Inn Express. Holiday Inn and Holiday Inn Express alone presently operate on all continents in the world. It is no surprise that IHG is so large globally, as many of its brands do not operate with a national nor even regional mind-set. But the same could be said of almost all of the top hotel corporations that seem to be interested in having a presence in almost every continent.

However, despite the fact that seven of the ten top hotel corporations in the world (measured by rooms) are US corporations, there is a major changing of the guard going on. At present Home Inns, a Chinese company, is only in ninth place, yet it is a growing organisation that was only formed in 2002. As a newcomer to the business, Home Inns began by only considering development in China. With its growth, we now see that it is one of the major players in the hotel industry, even though it has not yet made major efforts to expand beyond China. However, the growth of this corporation suggests that this juggernaut will soon be a major player in the industry internationally, as it is planning expansion in Asian markets and it experienced 21.2 per cent growth in 2013 (Hospitalitynet. org, 2013).

What this means in terms of globalisation is that while Western capital has dominated and continues to dominate the hotel industry and their chains, this may be coming to an end with the formation and export of a major hotel corporation from China. Although the major companies and their chains have the advantage of being in the field first and having brand names that are long established, the Chinese juggernaut challenges the domination of Western capital on the hotel industry. This illustrates to a large degree the globalisation of capital in a way that does not merely assert that globalisation is about the growth of operations of Western organisations abroad, but also that it offers opportunities for non-Western capital.

Another noteworthy fact to be found in the data is that the leading hotel corporations are holding companies that own various different chains, showing that multi-branding strategies are the rule among the top brands. While IKEA or McDonald's, for example, may be global brands, they do not attempt to expand market shares, generally, by creating different chains to cater to slightly different clientele. The diversification of what they sell is not so noteworthy. But then, this is part of the general strategies of hotel corporations, to use various brand names and chains within the corporation in order to place their product at different positions in the market, from the high-end to the budget market. For example, Accor owns the Sofitel brand to attract the luxury market, the Pullman brand for the upscale market, the Novotel brand for the midscale market, and the Ibis brand for the budget market. All the leading corporations seem to invoke this same strategy, using different brands/chains to infiltrate and grow within various markets in different countries. The exception to this so far is the Chinese upstart, a corporation that is not yet mature enough to follow this strategy.

We have seen that globalisation seems to be a trend. Therefore, it seems to be that the corporations that own the hotel chains should anticipate increasingly global expansion and competition. We have also seen that Western corporations dominate the field, although one Chinese corporation is challenging this hegemony. We now look into perceptions of the globalisation of hotel chains.

Craig Webster

Ideological perceptions of hotel chains

In general, there is an ideological lens through which one could view the role of the hotel chain in a globalisation process, as Table 39.2 illustrates. Using the ideological categories used by Webster et al. (2011), we see that liberals alone seem to be the group that is the most enthusiastic about the positive aspects of globalisation and the role of hotels, as one form of the multinational/transnational corporation in the spread of global capital. It is understandable that liberalism is the ideology of capitalism, as it views the expansion of capital as a positive force, bringing progress, economic efficiency, and spreading economic, political, and social ideas generally associated with progress.

However, the other prevailing ideologies of political economy have a very different view of the role and impact that such organisations bring to the world. While the Marxists (social democrats and communists) are generally in agreement that the spread of global capital will increase inequalities and likely bring economic displacement, environmental degradation, and political dissonance, they are largely in disagreement regarding the solution, as the social democratic approach tends to look for peaceful political solutions via the ballot box, putting substantial political regulations into effect, effectively regulating the economy to minimise undesired externalities of capitalism. The mercantilists, as economic nationalists, look at this more as a question of the ownership of the corporation, being suspicious of foreign ownership while coordinating free-market forces with strategic political decisions of the home country.

So, all in all, there is a question regarding the impact that hotel chains make internationally. However, whether a person views the hotel chain's international operation as a progressive force or a threat depends upon one's ideology. The proponents of globalisation (see for example Bhagwati, 2007; Bhagwati and Cammett, 2005; Friedman, 2005) are clearly liberals,

Table 39.2 Ideological views on hotel chains and globalisation

Ideology of political economy	Role of MNCs	Expected impacts	Prognosis
Liberalism	Positive	Creation of jobs, wealth, and amenities for tourists	Continued growth and development
Mercantilism	Mostly negative	Creating competition for local industries, unless the state plays a mitigating role	Continued growth and development of MNCs, leading to increased dissatisfaction/protectionist policies
Social democracy	Negative	Creating increasing inequalities between rich and poor and spreading Western values and values associated with the desires of global capital	Increased inequalities and negative externalities, leading to mass dissatisfaction with globalisation
Communism	Negative	Creating increasing inequalities between rich and poor and spreading Western values and values associated with the desires of global capital	Increased inequalities and negative externalities, leading to mass dissatisfaction/revolution

Source: based upon typologies in Webster, Ivanov and Illum (2011).

464

as the liberal thinking is the ideology that supports the project of globalisation, promising economic progress and political freedom. The opponents of globalisation view it in a very different way, noting the environmental degradation, growth of inequality, and other negative social, political, and economic outcomes. We now consider globalisation and factors involved in globalisation that may play a role in influencing the operation of global hotel corporation and their chains.

Key features impacting upon hotel chains globally

Globalisation as a one-way street?

One of the key aspects of the global political economy is that companies will increasingly have to compete in a global way. The way that global corporations have used the brands/chains that they own to penetrate markets in many countries and increase market share is something that they have had to do to remain competitive. That does not mean, though, that globalisation will not have reversals nor face impediments. For example, in 2015, Target, a leading US retailer, closed operations in Canada (Ziobro and Trichur 2015). While it would be expected that Canada could be easily penetrated by such a major corporation from the USA, the experiment seemed to have failed for Target. There may be failures of the launches of brands, although there will more likely be difficulties that require adjustments, as in the case of IKEA entering into the USA, following a strategy that treated the USA just like a European market (Twarowska and Kąkol, 2013). But these will likely be occasional hiccups as the barriers between countries and the legal barriers associated with them fade, as well as corporations becoming increasingly adept at modifying their products and services for different markets.

Globalisation is unstoppable, irreversible and inevitable, at least this is the ideological viewpoint that many people take (Soborski, 2012). We may see at some future time a period in which states begin to implement protectionist policies in reaction to political or economic crises and such protectionism may create issues for the globalised operations of the holding companies owning chains worldwide. So, while globalisation seems to have had a good run, political forces may be invoked at some period in the future to place impediments in the way of globalisation. When and if political forces act to thwart or limit interactions across borders, many industries could suffer, including the hospitality industry. So, it should be remembered that if globalisation is a positive force for global operations of hotel chains, there is still a possibility that it may be reversed.

Regional integration

Another aspect that the major chains will have to navigate, much of which works to its advantage, are regional integration projects that are taking place throughout the world, as Webster and Ivanov (2015) pointed out. While these integration projects are taking place in many places in the world, none is as advanced as the project that is the European Union. But the most bombastic plan is for a transatlantic free trade area including NAFTA (North American Free Trade Agreement) and the European Union, referred to as the 'Transatlantic Free Trade Agreement' (TAFTA) (European Commission, 2014). A massive economic region in which there would be a free flow of trade would enable global business between the two massive economic entities to grow substantially, erasing the many barriers to trade between the entities. While the implications for hotel chains may not yet be obvious, it is likely that there would be a realignment of industry and business in the EU and North America as a result of this massive change. However, much like the general trajectory of globalisation, it is possible that the blocks that are created may break down.

Asia's rise

One of the most undeniable features of the current global situation is the growth of China, as many well-known scholars have noted (see for example Jacques, 2012; Frank, 1998). The growth of the Chinese market may be a precursor to a change of guard in the global hierarchy. Already, there is strong evidence that US hegemony has faded, leading the way for Chinese hegemony in the world (Webster and Ivanov, 2015). Therefore, it would be expected for Chinese capital to be increasingly visible, with less of a noteworthy hegemony of Japanese, European, and US corporations in almost all fields. While China is playing a game of catch-up with the larger and more established firms of the West in the hospitality business, the meteoric rise of a Chinese group of hotels should not be a surprise, as China's economy continues to develop and export capital.

However, it is not just China's rise that is something to watch out for. Major western hotel groups may also face challenges from firms coming from the other members of the BRICS (Brazil, Russia, India, China and South Africa) or PINE (Philippines, Indonesia, Nigeria and Ethiopia) economies, as the growth of these two conglomerations of countries will be a major driver in future tourism (Webster and Ivanov, 2015). While it may appear that the hotel market is awash with many groups and chains and Western group and companies have the advantage of being the first to go truly global, this advantage may fade as we look into a future in which major global hotel chains are owned by many groups outside of the USA or Europe.

There would be two noteworthy ways in which non-Western groups could expand to become major giants, one is the way that Home Inns has done it, by creating a new brand to capture a significant chunk of a large market and then diversity brands. Another way is for a wealthy holding group to purchase a pre-existing brand/chain, much the way that the Holiday Inn brand moved from US to UK ownership. It is likely that with the growth of Asian economies, the wealth accumulated in the East will have the ability to make purchases of large chains/brands currently owned by Western groups. The Chinese economy is the harbinger with Home Inns, but other countries may soon enter into this Western-dominated sector of the global economy.

Other key demographic and political factors

One of the key aspects of the global political economy is that companies will increasingly have to compete in a global way, with implications for the management, clientele, and ownership of the chains. The fact that global chains will have to deal with a multitude of multicultural issues in terms of management as well as dealing with a multicultural clientele in a global operating environment is obvious. However, the difficulties go far beyond the fact that many Western ways of interacting with others may be perceived of as rude by Asians, and this incorporates pretty much every aspect of the operation of a hotel, as Wang and Wang (2009, p. 54) point out. There are key demographic data linked with this to keep an eye on, most specifically is the aging and declining populations of most of the Western countries and the rise of a middle class and wealthy class of Asians. The rise of Asia's wealth and the decline of most Western countries' populations will translate into meaningful strategic challenges for the global hotel chains business both in terms of the sensitivities of the next generation of guests and the demographics, abilities and tastes of the guests in the near future.

Conclusion

The top ten corporations that own the hotel chains control a great number of rooms globally (over four and a half million rooms). What is noteworthy about this is that these top ten corporations own the major brands that have penetrated almost all the major markets in the world. Almost all of the top ten corporations have operations that are global in scope, while they also have national and regional strategies that enable them to penetrate new markets and expand their market share.

One thing to think about is the extent to which the globalisation of hotel chains plays a role in spreading the values of the home country of the corporation. Inadvertently, hotel chains going global spread the culture and values of the home country of the owners of the corporation. In subtle ways, such as the furnishings, fixtures, foods, expectations of the workforce, and comforts of the hotel, suggestions regarding culture values can be spread. While many Westerners may not view this as a negative thing, as the spread of Western cultural values have traditionally been equated with progress, non-Westerners may not view the spread of these values in the same way. Certainly, if Chinese-owned hotel chains begin operating in Western countries, the subtle ways in which culture may be spread via these economic entities may become more obvious to those who are guests in the hotels as well as the staff employed by the Chinese owners.

For students and researchers it would seem that looking into the impacts of globalisation may be fruitful. Although many have considered/contemplated the strategies of the globally operating corporations that own chains, this line of research still offers many possibilities for researchers who want to learn more about the effectiveness of different types of strategies for different markets. However, there has been less research regarding how globalisation places demands and stresses upon workforces in globally competitive hotel chains. This would seem to be a fruitful thing to look at in the future.

Practitioners, especially in situations in which they are involved in making strategic decisions for hotel chains, should view globalisation not merely as an inevitable process that is unilinear and assured. Instead, they should appreciate that while it may be something that seems to be a permanent fixture of the operating environment during much of their lifetimes, it is the product of a prevailing ideology of people in key positions of political power. These people in positions of political power have shared this ideology and ensured that it is enshrined in various international agreements and it has been supported by various technological advances. However, there is a real risk of reversal. So globalisation should be appreciated for its opportunities and benefits, although a wise practitioner would understand that a business's dependence upon this may lead to the strategic inability to cope with a possible change or shock to this operating environment.

All in all, we have seen that the hotel chains operate in a global industry. It is global because the clientele is or can be global. But most importantly, the major corporations that own the chains are massive companies that own many different chains, all trying to penetrate new markets and expand upon markets in which they already have a market share. These major corporations and their chains also face global competition with the other major corporations in the global hospitality market. A major factor all these major chains should come to appreciate is that the trend of globalisation is a trend that requires multi-layered thinking for their business, incorporating strategies for capturing market shares in luxury to budget markets country by country, using different brands, while having regional and global strategies as well and keeping in mind the demographic changes that are easy to forecast. Globalisation makes old-fashioned country-specific thinking about hotel chains seem quaint, simple, and predictable, but not particularly relevant in the current globally competitive environment.

References

Accor (2015) Accor worldwide. Online. Available HTTP: <http://www.accor.com/en/group/accor-worldwide.html>, accessed 25 March 2015.

Altinay, L. and Bowen, D. (2006) Politics and tourism interface. *Annals of Tourism Research*, 33(4), 939–56.

Anastasiadou, C. (2007) Group politics and tourism interest representation at the supranational level: evidence from the European Union. In P. M. Burns and M. Novelli (eds), *Tourism and Politics: Global Frameworks and Local Realities*. Oxford: Elsevier, pp. 59–80.

Andriotis, K. (2006) Hosts, guests and politics: coastal resorts morphological change. *Annals of Tourism Research*, 33(4), 1079–98.

Antonakakis, N., Dragouni, M. and Filis, G. (2015) Tourism and growth: the times they are a-changing. *Annals of Tourism Research*, 50, 159–72.

Best Western (2015) About us. Online. Available HTTP: <http://www.bestwestern.com/about-us/>, accessed 25 March 2015.

Bhagwati, J. (2007) *In Defence of Globalization*. New York: A CFR Book. Oxford University Press.

Bhagwati, J. and Cammett, M. (2005) In defence of globalization. *International Journal*, 60(2), 592–5.

Bianchi, R. (2006) Tourism and the globalisation of fear: analysing the politics of risk and (in)security in global travel. *Tourism and Hospitality Research*, 7(1), 64–74.

Burns, P.M., and Novelli, M. (eds) (2007) *Tourism and Politics: Global Frameworks and Local Realities*. Oxford: Elsevier.

Carlson Rezidor hotel group (2015) Online. Available HTTP: <http://carlsonrezidor.com/home>, accessed 25 March 2015.

Choice hotels (2015) About Choice hotels. Online. Available HTTP: <http://www.choicehotels.com/en/about-choice/aboutchoicehotels>, accessed 25 March 2015.

Cunill, O.M. (2006) The internationalization-globalization of hotel chains. In *The Growth Strategies of Hotel Chains: Best Business Practices by Leading Companies*. New York: The Haworth Press, pp. 169–90.

Cunill, O.M., and Forteza, C.M. (2010) The franchise contract in hotel chains: a study of hotel chain growth and market concentrations. *Tourism Economics*, 16(3), 493–515.

Dreher, A. (2006) Does globalization affect growth? evidence from a new index of globalization. *Applied Economics*, 38(10), 1091–110.

Dreher, A., Gaston, N. and Martens, P. (2008) *Measuring Globalisation: Gauging its Consequences*. New York: Springer.

Dwyer, L. (2014) Transnational corporations and the globalization of tourism. In Lew, A.A., Hall, C.M., William, A.M. (eds), *The Wiley Blackwell Companion to Tourism*. Chichester, UK: John Wiley & Sons, pp. 197–209.

European Commission (2014) *In Focus: Transatlantic Trade and Investment Partnership*. Online. Available HTTP: <http://ec.europa.eu/trade/policy/in-focus/ttip/>, accessed 25 March 2015.

Frank, A.G. (1998) *ReOrient: Global economy in the Asian age*. Berkeley: University of California Press.

Friedman, T. (2005) *The World is Flat*. New York: Farrar, Straus and Giroux.

Gustavo, N. (2013) Marketing management trends in tourism and hospitality industry: facing the 21st century environment. *International Journal of Marketing Studies*, 5(3), 13–25.

Harvey, B. (2007) International hotels. *Journal of Retail and Leisure Property*, 6(3), 189–93.

Hilton Hotels and Resorts (2015) Hilton hotels and resorts locations. Online. Available HTTP: <http://www3.hilton.com/en/about/locations/index.html>, accessed 25 March 2015.

Home Inns hotel group (2015) Home inns hotel group reports fourth quarter and full year 2014 financial results. Online. Available HTTP: <http://media.corporate-ir.net/media_

files/IROL/20/203641/HMIN_4QFY2014_earnings_release_v17_clean.pdf>, accessed 25 March 2015.

HospitalityNet.org (2013) World ranking 2013 of hotel groups and brands. Online. Available HTTP: <http://www.hospitalitynet.org/news/4060119.html>, accessed 23 January 2015.

InterContinental Hotels Group (2014) Online summary of our annual report and Form 20-F 2014. Online. Available HTTP: <http://www.ihgplc.com/files/reports/ar2014>, accessed 25 March 2015.

Ivanov, S. and Webster, C. (2013) Tourism's impact on growth: the role of globalisation. *Annals of Tourism Research*, 41, 231–6.

Jacques, M. (2012) *When China Rules the World: The End of the Western World and the Birth of a New Global Order*. London: Penguin Books.

KOF Index of Globalisation (2014) Online. Available HTTP: <http://globalization.kof.ethz.ch>, accessed 19 January 2015.

Marriot International (2015) About Marriot international. Online. Available HTTP: <https://www.marriott.com/marriott/aboutmarriott.mi>, accessed 25 March 2015.

Martorell-Cunill, O., Gil-Lafuente, A.M., Socias Salvà, A. and Mulet Forteza, C. (2014) The growth strategies in the hospitality industry from the perspective of the forgotten effects. *Computational and Mathematical Organization Theory*, 20(2), 195–210.

McNeill, D. (2008) The hotel and the city. *Progress in Human Geography*, 32(3), 383–98.

Munar, A.M. (2007) Rethinking globalization theory in tourism. In P. M. Burns and M. Novelli (eds), *Tourism and Politics: Global Frameworks and Local Realities*. Oxford: Elsevier, pp. 347–67.

Ottenbacher, M., Gnoth, J. and Jones, P. (2006) Identifying determinants of success in development of new high-contact services: Insights from the hospitality industry. *International Journal of Service Industry Management*, 17(4), 344–63.

Robinson, M. and Smith, M. (2006) Politics, power and play: the shifting contexts of cultural tourism. In Robinson, M. and Smith, M. (eds.), *Cultural Tourism in a Changing World: Politics, Participation and (Re) presentation*. Clevedon: Channel View Publications, pp. 1–17.

Rodrik, D. (2011) *The Globalization Paradox: Democracy and the Future of the World Economy*. New York: W.W. Norton and Company.

Rogerson, J. M. (2014) Unpacking the growth of hotel chains in Africa: enterprises and patterns. *Mediterranean Journal of Social Sciences*, 5(14), 135–46.

Seifert, A.M., and Messing, K. (2006) Cleaning up after globalization: an ergonomic analysis of work activity of hotel cleaners. *Antipode*, 38(3), 557–78.

Soborski, R. (2012) Globalization and ideology: a critical review of the debate. *Journal of Political Ideologies*, 17(3), 323–46.

Starwood hotels and resorts (2015) Company overview. Online. Available HTTP: <http://www.starwoodhotels.com/corporate/about/index.html>, accessed 25 March 2015.

Stiglitz, J. (2003) *Globalization and its Discontents*. New York: W.W. Norton & Company.

Sugiyarto, G., Blake, A. and Sinclair, M.T. (2003) Tourism and globalization: economic impact in Indonesia. *Annals of Tourism Research*, 30(3), 683–701.

Tribe, J. (2006) Tourists, places and politics. *Tourism and Hospitality Research*, 7(1), 1–2.

Twarowska, K. and Kąkol, M. (2013, June) International business strategy- reasons and forms of expansion into foreign markets. Proceedings of the Management, Knowledge and Learning International Conference 2013, Zadar, Croatia. Online. Available HTTP: <http://www.toknowpress.net/ISBN/978-961-6914-02-4/papers/ML13-349.pdf>, accessed 25 March 2015.

Wang, J. and Wang, J. (2009) Issues, challenges, and trends, that facing hospitality industry. *Management Science and Engineering*, 3(4), 53–8.

Webster, C. and Ivanov, S. (2012) The political economy of tourism in the future. In J. Leigh, C. Webster, and S. Ivanov (eds) *Future Tourism: Political, Social and Economic Challenges*. Abingdon: Routledge, pp. 21–34.

Webster, C. and Ivanov, S. (2015) Geopolitical drivers of future tourist flows. *Journal of Tourism Futures*, 1, 58–68.

Webster, C., Ivanov, S. and Illum, S. (2011) The paradigms of political economy and tourism policy: NTOs and state policy. In J. Mosedale (ed.), *Political economy and tourism*. New York and Oxford: Routledge, pp. 55–73.

Whitla, P., Walters, P. G. and Davies, H. (2007) Global strategies in the international hotel industry. *International Journal of Hospitality Management*, 26(4), 777–92.

Wyndham hotel group (2015) Get to know us. Online. Available HTTP: <http://www.wyndhamhotelgroup.com/about-us/about-wyndham>, accessed 25 March 2015.

Zhang, Z. (2009) Impacts of globalisation on hotel companies' internal operation environment. *Canadian Social Science*, 1, 68–71.

Ziobro, P. and Trichur, R. (2015, January 15) Target to Exit Canada After Failed Expansion. *The Wall Street Journal*. Online. Available HTTP: <http://www.wsj.com/articles/target-to-exit-canada-1421328919>, accessed 25 March 2015.

40

Generations BB, X, Y, Z, α – the changing consumer in the hospitality industry

Claudia Sima

(UNIVERSITY OF CENTRAL LANCASHIRE, UK)

Introduction

A challenge for any competitive business is adapting to the fast changing needs of its customers. Chain hotels, in particular, are trying to anticipate and adapt to their current and future customer types and their personalities. A popular segmentation method for chain hotels is by generation: 'From the Builders Generation who literally and metaphorically built this nation after the austerity years post-depression and World War 2, to the Baby Boomers who redefined the cultural landscape, to Generation X who ushered in new technologies and work styles, and now to Generations Y and Z who in this 21st Century are redefining life stages and lifestyles' (McCrindle, 2014). As a result, new services and even new chain hotels are starting to emerge specifically targeting Baby Boomers (BB), Generation X (Gen-X), Generation Y (Gen-Y), Generation Z (Gen-Z), or most recently Generation α (Gen-α). Marriott, for example, is attempting to target the leisure Generation Y traveller with a new budget hotel (MOXY), and the business Gen-Y with a new design-focused hotel brand (AC Hotels). This is because research shows there are fundamental differences between generations in terms of how they think about travel and accommodation, how they purchase, how they use technology, what they look for in a hotel, how they think and react in general. The focus here is to identify some of the key characteristics and needs of the five generations as chain hotel customers and how the chain hotel industry is adapting to them. Table 40.1 presents a summary of the key issues characterising the selected five generations as chain hotel customers.

Baby Boomers – the 'ideal' chain hotel customer

Born after the Second World War, Baby Boomers are the ideal chain hotel customer. They are perceived as being highly loyal repeat customers, having considerable available income and time due to being retired or being close to retirement. Many chain hotels still perceive them as their main market (McMahon, 2005). As they have been around for quite some time, their habits have been well researched. They are the building block on which most major chain hotels around the world have built their business. However, even Baby Boomers' characteristics are changeable. Research shows they are easily influenced by Generation X

Claudia Sima

Table 40.1 An overview of generations and their key characteristics as hotel chain customers

Category	Estimated birth date	Age in 2015	Key characteristics as hotel chain consumers
Baby boomers	1943–1960	55–72 years old	• Loyal to brands • Desire face-to-face contact • Seek safety and security mainly • They like to experiment with technology • They are the building-block clientele of chain hotels
Generation X	1961–1980	35–54 years old	• Can become loyal to brands • Value individuality • Seek comfort and full service mainly • They need technology for all aspects of life • Their travelling habits supported the aggressive expansion of chain hotels over the last 30 years
Generation Y	1981–2000	15–34 years old	• Highly unlikely to be or become brand loyal • Social-media sociable • Seek style at an affordable price • They are addicted to technology • They are a challenge for established chain hotels and bring the promise of a new chain hotel business landscape
Generation Z	2001– 2010	5–14 years old	• They are the generation that has it all but owns nothing due to rising living costs; highly complex, value experiences and any source that can help them 'grow' as human beings • Emotional, environment-focused • Seek 'an experience' and 'continuous novelty' • Technology experts • They are an enigma for chain hotels • They want to be part of the dialogue when designing the chain hotel product
Generation α	2010–ongoing (2020)	<5 years old	• Likely to be focused on new experiences/ experiments • Likely to be highly experienced in travel and technology from a very young age • Likely to seek novelty, originality or a strong desire to manufacture it as they can access anything, anywhere, anytime • They will take technology for granted as they've never been without it • They will be offered a more diverse and complex product by chain hotels than ever before

Source: Adapted from Howard and Stonier (2001); McMahon (2005); Jaume (2015).

habits (McMahon, 2005). Fewer studies exist on how Baby Boomers are changing as chain hotel customers. They may not travel as much as before but they are more active than previous retired generations. Jaume (2015) argues that although they play catch-up in terms of technology, they are nevertheless knowledgeable, curious and keen to experiment with the latest gadgets like a self-check-in front desk. They are however always looking for personalised attention in the form of physical staff. They prefer booking with a human voice over the phone but do not mind booking online if a choice is not provided. This satisfies their need for trust, reliability, safety and security. They are highly sociable and prefer to interact with people face to face, however they do use some mainstream forms of social media. They look for quality content in both traditional and new media. In terms of adapting to this generation, most chain hotels have invested considerably in meeting the changing health, safety and mobility needs of Baby Boomers.

Generation X – the main market for chain hotels currently

Sandwiched between the Baby Boomers and Generation Y, Generation X is the best educated and the first technologically savvy generation in history. They are more tolerant and value individuality. These people tend to have realistic expectations and are family-oriented (Fitzpatrik, 2005). If Baby Boomers are starting to wind down and Generation Y is starting to power up, Generation X is in full swing and the main market for hotel chains around the world. As leisure travellers, they may have to juggle finances and family, but as business travellers their spending habits are considerable. Most are in the mid-stages of their careers and moving into their peak-earning years. According to McMahon (2005) they outspend all other generations, including Baby Boomers. Due to their lifestyles as well as having grown up in a rapidly changing technological, environmental, political and cultural landscape, their needs are changing and chain hotels are adapting quickly: 'Chains have started changing floor plans, menus, lighting and even the dialogue between client and concierge. Hyatt's menus are becoming healthier and more organic, and the chain is introducing Aveda shampoo and conditioner. Hilton hotels are adding MP3-friendly alarm clocks, allowing guests to awaken to their own music. Marriott has decided to redo its beds, favouring what one executive called a "fort effect" with six pillows and luxurious, 300-thread-count sheets' (McMahon, 2005). A common feature of many Generation X orientated hotels are rooms with spacious bathtubs and flat-panel television sets, yoga supplies and ergonomic desk chairs, swimming pools and bars on the rooftops, full service and comfort. Generation X will become brand loyal as long as they perceive their needs are met and chain hotels acknowledge their individuality.

In addition to healthier food choices and a better quality hotel experience, new Gen-X chain hotel brands are being introduced. Intercontinental, which operates Holiday Inn, is creating a new line of boutique hotels, called Hotel Indigo. The rooms have hardwood floors, satellite TV service and stereos. According to Peter Yesawich, 'It's reflective of the generation ... Gen Xers celebrate individualism. They're beginning to react to the numbing sameness of brands and are increasingly looking for accommodations that are an extension of their lifestyle – places with more personality and a unique tone' (McMahon, 2005).

Generation Y – the generation revolutionising the chain hotel industry

Often characterised as demanding, not brand-loyal and immune to traditional marketing channels (Schroer, 2015), Generation Y (Echo Boomers or Millennials) represent a large and lucrative market, but also a complex and contradictory consumer segment for hotel chains. Although agreement on profile and numbers does not exist, Generation Y workers make up roughly 25 per cent of the world population. It is one of the largest generational categories in the world. In contrast, Generation X is roughly 21 per cent, and Baby Boomers roughly 18 per cent of the world population (GenerationY.com, 2015). Adapting to the Y-generation demands is seen as an urgent priority that chain hotels cannot afford to miss out on; 'a number of hotel brands have the millennials in their sights, including Starwood's Aloft, W and Element brands; InterContinental's Hotel Indigo; Commune Hotels & Resorts' Tommie; Choice Hotels' Cambria Hotels & Suites; Hilton's Home2 Suites; TRYP By Wyndham; and independents such as Yotel, CitizenM; and Ace Hotels' (Langfield, 2014).

These companies tend to differentiate between the Gen-Y leisure traveller and Gen-Y business traveller and target one or both sub-segments. However, at this stage both have proved hard to win over. Hotel chains are finding that free internet, more electrical sockets, and social media marketing are not enough to make loyal customers of Gen-Y (Langfield, 2014). Some voices argue that the solution is personalisation through targeted loyalty schemes, efficient use of Big Data and a good understanding of the food and beverage needs of Gen-Y (Jhunjhunwala in Langfield, 2014). Others argue for tailored technology, streamlined hotel interior design, a twist in the service, value-added amenities and modern fitness facilities (Mettler, 2015). Although none of the international hotel chains have conquered the market, Mariott has made some progress. Marriott is attempting to target both the leisure Gen-Y with a new budget hotel (MOXY), and the business Gen-Y with a new design-focused hotel brand (AC Hotels). The hotel chain is very much focused on understanding the characteristics of Gen-Y.

In 2013, Marriott announced a new affordable hotel chain specifically targeting the Millennial leisure travellers called MOXY: 'Meet MOXY, Marriott's newest brand, focuses on the rapidly growing 3-star-tier segment. *MOXY's focus is on the millennial traveller*, who understands that style can be delivered at attractive prices'. (Moxy-hotels Marriott, 2015a). The company philosophy seems to be in-line with Gen-Y characteristics: 'Moxy offers a new way of travelling in which smaller is concentration, not reduction. In which affordability is not a sacrifice of *style*, nor a loss of *comfort*. When we say "less is more", we accentuate more. Not less.' (Moxy-hotels Marriott, 2015b). This generation is often characterised as credit-dependent and associated with lifestyle-debt (McCrindle, 2014). According to Schroer (2015) 'one in nine Gen-Yers has a credit card co-signed by a parent'. However, all purchases are satisfying life-style choices; they are not need-based but want-based. Therefore, Gen-Y has less financial stability than Gen-X, but a stronger attraction to stylish products and a stylish lifestyle. Cussen (2015) brings up a study by Towers Watson that underlines some 'notable trends in millennial spending, such as their propensity to buy designer clothes at discount stores such as Sam's Club and Costco as well as a tendency to purchase cheaper beers while investing in finer brands of wine'. Gen-Y seems to be characterised by an interesting paradox: financially vulnerable, with an addiction to fashionable lifestyles, but at discount prices. A budget hotel chain with a stylish atmosphere or a boutique hotel at an affordable price appears to be the ideal hospitality product for Gen-Y and Marriott hotel chain wish to position themselves as such with MOXY (Moxy-hotels Marriott, 2015a). Locations are chosen in accordance with the company philosophy and consumer profile. The first hotel opened in Milan, Italy in 2013 and the chain was introduced to the US in January 2015 with plans to expand rapidly to New York City, San Francisco, Seattle, New Orleans, Chicago, Munich, Frankfurt, Berlin, Copenhagen and London by the end of 2017. The hotel chain plans to expand in about 150 locations across Europe and the US (Mas, 2013; Moxy-hotels

Marriott, 2015a). The locations are chosen because of their stylish atmosphere and appeal to Gen-Y travellers.

The MOXY brand and discourse appears to celebrate and glorify Gen-Y lifestyle choices: 'Millennials are curious and adventurous, and much more self-sufficient than their parents were at that age. Especially when it comes to travel. Thanks to their intimate relationship with the web, millennials know how to help themselves. As long as there's free Wi-Fi . . . They see themselves as part of the tribe of the individual. Independent but connected. Daring (but never far from their devices). Smart but not superior. With a witty and playful sense of humour, that they know will get a giggle on Instagram and Twitter. Because sharing and recommendations are not only part of their identity – it's their social currency. Not just because they seek approval (to be part of the tribe). But also to set the trend – and boast about finding the best deals and the most exciting places in the world. That's why they choose Moxy' (Moxy-hotels Marriott, 2015b).

The choice of language is very important, as Gen-Y is also one of the most criticised generations. Wright (2013) writes: 'To be a millennial is to hear constantly about how awful your generation is.' Certainly Gen-Y do not like to be described as 'entitled', 'selfish', 'spoilt', and 'irresponsible' and keywords such as 'adventurous' and 'witty' resonate better. Certainly Marriott appears to have a strong understanding of this consumer category and 'every aspect of the hotel was thoughtfully researched and crafted to reflect and deliver on the changing lifestyles and expectations of this fast-growing customer segment' according to CEO of Marriott International, Arne Sorenson (Mas, 2013). Not much agreement exists on Gen-Y as previously mentioned, but three characteristics appear to characterise them: 'its digital media use, especially for entertainment, social networking and creative endeavours; it has positive attitudes towards diversity, flexibility, social issues and its own future; it has an orientation towards family and social groups '(Donnison, 2007). The MOXY brand is built around these characteristics. The company mantra: 'Smaller means concentration, not reduction' (Moxy-hotels Marriott, 2015b) is achieved by looking at the business from three perspectives: the guests, owners and operators. By focusing the product on self-service and new technology, such as mobile check-in and free Wi-Fi throughout the hotel, not only are the Gen-Y needs completely fulfilled, but costs are also kept down (Mas, 2013). The hotel recognises that Gen-Y members are self-sufficient, as such, a 165-room hotel is staffed by only 17 full-time staff (Moxy-hotels Marriott, 2015a). Room-service is replaced by self-service. The hotel design is also in line with the consumer profile: 'Moxy design and style is seriously considered, and playfully executed. From the communal NOW public space to smart, flexible bedrooms, Moxy is a bold, surprising design for the socially extroverted, energetic consumer.' (Moxy-hotels Marriott, 2015b). The design of the hotel recognises Gen-Y's desire to socialise and invests considerably in public areas transforming them into entertainment or 'fun' areas. The 17 square meter hotel room itself has as its main feature a '47 inch LED TV and technology features in the room (furiously fast and free WI-FI, screencast, usb ports)'. A fitness centre is available on the premises and meeting rooms have an informal design.

As can be seen from the description of the MOXY-Marriott hotel chain, the hotel concept itself is being re-imagined as a result of Gen-Y characteristics. The focus is less on the hotel room/bedroom but on the public areas where Gen-Y can socialise, either face to face or through social networks. It is less about facilitating the physical presence of the guest in the hotel, and more on facilitating his presence online through reliable, fast and free Wifi. It is less about face-to-face employee-guest contact and more about self-service and reliable technology. The marketing of the hotel chain is also re-imagined and value is placed on an

Instagram guestbook, avoiding traditional marketing. This recognises that most Gen-Ys are easily influenced by social media. Recent studies argue that peer pressure through social media has strong impacts on Gen-Y purchases and experiences. Millennials feel pressure to conform to the financial and life habits of their peers because of social media, where purchases and experiences are routinely posted for all to see and envy (Cussen, 2015). Therefore, the Gen-Ys hotel experience is less about him and more about/for his online entourage.

One major difference exists between the leisure Gen-Y and the business Gen-Y. According to Rushmore (in Langfield, 2014), the millennial leisure traveller is frugal but the millennial business traveller is indulgent. The average Gen-Y business traveller tends to overspend on his business trips but at the same time is always looking for value-added amenities and freebies. Availability and source of funds is the explanation. The AC Hotel chain brand is Marriott's strategy. The AC will be 'a design-focused brand inspired by the fashion houses of Europe that appeals to younger business travellers.'; and the hotels will have 'free Wi-Fi throughout, mobile check-in, 24-hour snack-stocked lounges, fresh, healthy, local food and drink brands, USB charging ports, lots of personalisation options and in-room technology that lets guests easily tap into their own entertainment plans, such as Netflix and HBO GO … Prices will be competitive with hotels in the top end of the upper-moderate tier' (Langfield, 2014).

Comparing the two brands both targeting Gen-Y, similarities can be found. Both the leisure and the business travellers are more independent and technology driven, and desire a product with personality – a concept hotel that is young, trendy and fun. However, while the leisure Gen-Y wishes for stylish, cheap, and fast service (for example: self-check in, or e-concierge), the business Gen-Y wants to be spoilt with choices and desires a very personalised product (for example: personalised check-in on a tablet in their room).

Generation Z – an 'enigma' for chain hotels

Each generation is more complex than the previous. Generation Z is no exception, 'they're smarter than Boomers, and way more ambitious than the Millennials' (Kingston, 2014). Considered 'the most complex shopper of all time' (Davies, 2013; FITCH, 2015), by 2020, today's 14–15 year olds will make up 40 per cent of US, Europe and other BRIC countries population, and 10 per cent of the rest of the world. A paradox in itself, the Z-consumer has a very short attention span but a sharp and hyper-informed eye, they live in a constant state of partial attention and information overload, 'logged into multiple platforms across a mosaic world of their own making' (Davies, 2013).

The adolescents of 2010–2018 are growing up in a complicated economic, socio-cultural and environmental landscape, marked by a prolonged global economic crisis and rising un-employment rates, social media outbursts, extreme technological innovations and accelerated consumerism, multiplied environmental catastrophes and accelerated resource depletion, a bigger than ever world population and growing social inequalities and disparities, alarmingly high rates of depression and anxiety, global obesity and a long string of health and terrorist scares, etc. They are the post-9/11, credit crunch generation, well aware of the implications of credit-type over spending. Advertising agency Sparks & Honey's research found a few key characteristics regarding generation Z: 60 per cent of 'Gen Zers' want jobs that have a positive social impact compared to 'Gen Ys'; 72 per cent of 'Gen Zers' want to start their own business; 56 per cent of 'Gen Zers' said they rather save than spend – in other words, they are opinionated, connected, resourceful and influential across multiple platforms. 'As savvy cynics, they trust their peers, not marketers' (Davies, 2013). They are also environmentally aware and inpatient to make a difference – 'educated, industrious, collaborative and eager to build a better planet' (Kingston, 2014). They constantly look for novelty, originality and 'the experience'. They value emotions but fail to reflect on them and see the bigger picture. Instead they are quick to act on them and make them known through social media platforms. They are the generation where the line public-private is more blurred than ever. For this highly demanding generation, when it comes to product development and marketing, chain hotels need to consider shifting from telling the hotel's story to starting a conversation about the Z-consumer's story and stressing the social and environmental benefits of the product and the difference the Z-consumer is making by purchasing; and from making the product better before sharing, to making it better with their input. 'Gen Zers' expect constant innovation, dialogue and want to be part of the innovation process, 'they are happy to have a beta product today, with the promise of a better one tomorrow; it will be better because they've co-created it' (Davies, 2013).

Considering that the need for originality, constant innovation and change defines the Z-generation, there might be a generation-gap issue and a wider chain hotel industry issue. Research conducted on UK and US hotels found that the hospitality industry is rather reactive when it comes to innovation (Robson and Ortmans, 2008; Enz, 2004). Most often hotels and restaurants implement changes only when forced to by a crisis or market circumstances. A lack of creativity and vision for the future, technology implementation and usage difficulties, as well as budget constraints might be good reasons to hold back on adopting new technologies or new methods of operating, however O'Connor (2003: 105) points out that there is an 'inbuilt tension in the innovation acceptance process' as 'most innovations fail relates to the fact that innovations are normally accepted and therefore recognised by the desired target audience when the audience can recognise the usefulness of the new idea'. Insufficient research exists on the reasons behind this 'reluctance to change' or how it is distributed across XYZ generations. Debates on the impacts of globalisation suggest that innovation – especially technological innovation – often leads to standardisation and a destruction of individuality, originality and sense of place. It could be argued that chain hotels are impacted by this process more than independent hotels. By their very definition and characteristics chain hotels are a representation of a globalised society.

A comparison between Premier Inn Preston Central and The Park Hotel Preston reveals that their prices, location and target markets are similar. However, the independent hotel provides a sense of place and personality with its old fashioned, staff-managed only check-in service. By its very description The Park Hotel stands out in terms of old fashioned hospitality and service: 'The Park Hotel is 3 Star AA Edwardian Manor House built in 1903. We are the only 3 star hotel that is independently owned and run in Preston, as such, we feel that we can offer a better, and more personal service for your stay, The Edwardian Mansion house dates back to 1903, and retains its wonderful period features' (TripAdvisor, 2014). On the other hand, the chain hotel with its innovative self-checking service enhances the 'anywhere in the world' feeling and may not appeal to Generation Z at all. It is the quirky, unique, independent hotel that would definitely attract a Baby Boomer, and may also be preferred by a Generation Z client. It could be argued the future of chain hotels is to adopt an independent hotel look and feel. Each hotel in the chain needs to look different and provide a unique atmosphere. Having a theme for each hotel in the chain and including Gen-Z in the design of the hotel product might need to be considered as this generation comes of age.

Generation α – a highly diverse generation in need of a highly diverse chain hotel landscape

Although there is no generally accepted agreement on the timeline and characteristics of all generations, the last generation to be acknowledged is Generation α. This generation is expected to be the most educated in history and the most technological (Schawabel, 2014). They will be bombarded with information and their cognitive, affective and conative abilities will be influenced and developed by the virtual world (including social media). They will be a highly diverse generation both in terms of personality types and abilities. In terms of the chain hotel industry, this generation will require and benefit from a more diverse chain hotel landscape as a result of adaptation to Gen-Y and Gen-Z.

Conclusion

This chapter set out to understand the key characteristics of the Baby Boom, Generation X, Generation Y, Generation Z and Generation α as chain hotel customers and also to identify how the chain hotel industry is adapting to them. All five generations have interesting and complex profiles. Expressions such as latest technology, a stylish product, affordable and a special customer experience seem to dominate the narratives of these generations. However, each generation appears to understand these aspects in different ways, as the chapter explored. With each new generation the focus seems to be more on individual, personalised hotel experiences, stylish yet affordable, technologically advanced but with a human touch. This is a challenge, as most existing chain hotels provide a standardised, globalised product, and originality and style come at a considerable cost to build and maintain. Product adaptation as well as product innovation appear to be the strategies employed by many major chain hotels, with new services and new types of chain hotels being developed that are specifically targeting each generation. The changes they are implementing now are to ensure their survival as Generation Y takes the main stage and Generations Z and α come of age.

References

Cussen, M.P. (2015) Money habits of the millennials. *Investopedia*. Online. Available HTTP: <http://www.investopedia.com/articles/personal-finance/021914/money-habits-millennials.asp>, accessed 8 September 2014.

Davies, C. (2013, November 6) How Gen Z shops: retail for a constant state of partial attention. *Chain Storage Wars*. Online. available HTTP: <http://www.chainstoreage.com/article/how-gen-z-shops-retail-constant-state-partial-attention>, accessed 6 March 2015.

Donnison, S. (2007) Unpacking the Millennials: a cautionary tale of teacher education. *Australian Journal of Teacher Education*, 32(3), 23–54.

Enz, C. (2004) Issues of concern for restaurant owners and managers, *Cornell Hotel and Restaurant Administration Quarterly*, 45(4), 315–32.

FITCH (2015) Gen Z shopping: Designing retail for the constant state of partial attention. Online. Available HTTP: <http://www.slideshare.net/FITCH_design/gen-z-fitch>, accessed 12 June 2015.

Fitzpatrick, M. (2005) Building Generation X loyalty. *Hospitality Upgrade* (Fall issue). Online. Available HTTP: <http://www.hospitalityupgrade.com/_files/file_articles/hufall05buildinggenxloyalty_fitzpatrick.pdf>, accessed 7 May 2015.

GenerationY.com (2015) Generation Y demographics. *Generation Y*. Online. Available HTTP: <http://www.generationy.com/details-about-generation-y-in-the-workforce/demographics/>, accessed 17 June 2015.

Howard, R. and Stonier, J. (2001) Marketing wine to generations. Online. Available HTTP: <http://www.winetitles.com.au/awmc/presentations/11_roz_howard/roz_howard.pdf>, accessed 9 September 2014.

Jaume, C. (2015, February 25) Millennials generation vs. Baby Boomers in the hospitality industry. *WinHotel*. Online. Available HTTP:, <http://www.winhotelsolution.com/blog/hotel-news/millennials-generation-vs-baby-boomers-hospitality-industry/>, accessed 7 May 2015.

Kingston, A. (2014) Get ready for Generation Z. *Maclean's – Rogers Media*. Online. Available HTTP: <http://www.macleans.ca/society/life/get-ready-for-generation-z/>, accessed 23 March 2015.

Langfield, A. (2014, May 20) Marriott bids for Gen Y business with AC Hotel. *CNBC*. Online. Available HTTP: <http://www.cnbc.com/id/101681146>, accessed 6 March 2015.

Mas, N. (2013, April 5) What IKEA and Marriott have in store for Gen Y. *HCBSH*. Online. Available HTTP: <http://www.howcoolbrandsstayhot.com/2013/04/05/what-ikea-and-marriott-have-in-store-for-gen-y/>, accessed 17 May 2015.

McCrindle (2014) Generations defined [Official company blog]. McCrindle Pty Ltd. Online. Available HTTP: <http://mccrindle.com.au/resources/Generations-Defined-Sociologically.pdf>, accessed 17 May 2015.

McMahon, S. (2005, April 24) Going the X-tra mile. *Union-Tribune San Diego*. Online. Available HTTP: <http://www.utsandiego.com/uniontrib/20050424/news_mz1b24going.html.>, accessed 17 May 2015.

Mettler, L. (2015, January 27) Millennial Appeal: 5 Ways Hotels Are Engaging Gen Y. *US News.* Online. Available HTTP: <http://travel.usnews.com/features/Millennial-Appeal-5-ways-hotels-are-engaging-Gen-Y/>, accessed 8 June 2015.

Moxy-hotels, Marriott (2015a) Hotel development. Online. Available HTTP: <https://hotel-development.marriott.com/brands/moxy/>, accessed 20 May 2015.

Moxy-hotels, Marriott (2015b) Meet MOXY! Online. Available HTTP: <http://www.marriott.com/Multimedia/PDF/Hotel_Development/MOXYHOTELSBrochure.pdf>, accessed 20 May 2015.

O'Connor, P. (2003) Innovation in hospitality. In Wood, R.C. (ed.), *Key concepts in hospitality*. London: Sage Publications, pp. 100–13.

Robson, S. and Ortmans, L. (2008) First findings from the UK Innovation Survey 2007. *Economic and Labour Review*, 2(4). 47–53.

Schawabel, D. (2014, June 25) 74 of the most interesting facts about the Millennial Generation. Dan Schawbel Consultancy. Online. Available HTTP: <http://danschawbel.com/blog/74-of-the-most-interesting-facts-about-the-millennial-generation/§hash.WpOcDSwZ.dpuf>, accessed 16 May 2015.

Schroer, W.J. (2015) Generations X, Y, Z and the others. *Social Marketing Newsletter.* Online. Available HTTP: <http://www.socialmarketing.org/newsletter/features/generation3.htm>, accessed 16 May 2015.

TripAdvisor (2014) The Park Hotel. Online. Available HTTP: <http://www.tripadvisor.co.uk/Hotel_Review-g528818-d285058-Reviews-The_Park_Hotel-Teddington_Greater_London_England.html>, accessed 12 January 2015.

Wright, J. (2013, June 14) Marriott reaches out to the millennial demographic with its imported AC Hotel chain. *Entertainment Designer*. Online. Available HTTP: <http://entertainmentdesigner.com/news/hotel-design-news/marriott-reaches-out-to-the-millennial-demographic-with-its-imported-ac-hotel-chain/§hash.hCX7vBa6.dpuf>, accessed 18 May 2015.

41

The changing employee across hotel chains – a generational approach

Emmanouil F. Papavasileiou

(UNIVERSITY OF PORTSMOUTH, UK)

Introduction

In a domestic, family-owned hotel chain in a Mediterranean country, the workforce, like many similar hospitality organisations, was mainly comprised of employees with no previous qualifications, who attained their roles after many years of working within the chain. However, the increase in the occupancy rate in both city and resort hotels, along with the decrease in the basic salary imposed by the recent financial crisis and the impending retirement of a large number of employees have led the owners to replenish the workforce composition by providing an opportunity for employment to a considerable amount of new graduates. While the latter cohort revealed a preference for a collaborative environment and experiential learning, the former was reluctant to transfer firm-specific knowledge. The owners understood that a generational gap between the two cohorts has created a resistive environment, which in turn has led to mistrust, conflict and dysfunctional behaviour. This situation has threatened the family-oriented environment of reciprocity and natural bonding between the workforce, which have been the foundation upon which employee relations have been built and developed for years within the chain. As a result, the hotel chain referenced above hired a team of HR professionals to help reinstate an environment of trust and mutual respect between preceding and succeeding generations in order for knowledge, skills, experiences and resources to be effectively transmitted within the organisation.

The previous chapter has illuminated aspects of the relationships developed in hospitality, emphasising the determinants of demand and of the hospitality experience. While this approach reflects the richness involved in the 'sacred' bond[1] between guest and host (drawing on generational theory), it is argued here that similar subjective features actually have a bearing within the workplace of the hosting establishments. Generational diversity is also applicable to the area of the *supply* of hospitality and warrants equal attention by academics and practitioners.

Generational diversity is an organisational reality in the hospitality industry. It is also a key concern for theory and practice in management. The workforce in hospitality has become more diverse in terms of their generational composition over the years, and will continue to become more diverse in years to come (Solnet et al., 2013; Zopiatis et al., 2012). Indeed, the impending retirement of a large cohort of the aging population, and their replacement in the workforce by a comparable cohort of young employees, is shifting the balance of generational dominance in the current hospitality workforce. King et al.'s (2011) interviews with general managers in Australia, Hong Kong and mainland China revealed that generational shift is amongst the most important issues faced by the sector. The opening vignette[2] illustrates how a crucial issue such as the distribution of knowledge and skills from older to new employees might be affected by this phenomenon. Within this context, hotel owners, executive teams and human resource professionals have renewed their focus on generations and particularly on enhancing their understanding of inter-generational differences. Emphasis has therefore been placed on finding new and innovative ways to appease the different demands and expectations of each generation, while still operating within the short-term cost restraints imposed by hotel executives (Solnet et al., 2013).

Despite the growing practitioner interest, systematic research into differences between the prevalent generations of workforce within the hotel sector is scarce. In this chapter, we provide a systematic review of the evidence concerning inter-generational differences between employees in hotel chains. We begin by outlining the theoretical framework of generational theory as applied within the organisational context. Subsequently, we will look at the results of cross-temporal studies of generational differences across various nations and from different sectors. Emphasis is placed on studies that examined employees working in hotel chains. A summary of the inter-generational differences in a number of work-related aspects describes the profile of multigenerational symbiosis in the contemporary workplace of hotel chains. The concluding section discusses the implications of the analysis for researchers and practitioners concerned with the generational phenomenon within the sector.

Theoretical background

Over the past decade, generational differences in the workplace have been broadly studied by a variety of disciplines including career development (Hess and Jepsen, 2009), human resource management (Benson and Brown, 2011), managerial psychology (Cennamo and Gardner, 2008; Dries et al., 2008; Real et al., 2010), nursing management (Takase et al., 2009) and hospitality management amongst others (Chi et al., 2013; Gursoy et al, 2013; Lu and Gursoy, 2013; Lub et al., 2012; Lub et al., 2011; Park and Gursoy, 2012). Within this multidisciplinary context, the term 'generation' is most commonly adopted to denote an 'identifiable group that shares birth years, age, location and significant life events at critical developmental stages' (Kupperschmidt 2000: 66). Accordingly, there is a general descriptive consensus that three generations[3] prevail in the current workforce, namely Baby Boomers (born 1946–1964), Generation X (born 1965–1980) and Millennials[4] (born after 1981). In each case, the classification of employees within these three generational cohorts is based on the belief that each cohort brings to work a distinct set of symbols, values, attitudes and practices, as a result of growing up within a certain historical and socio-cultural context and therefore experiencing the same formative events. This perspective is rooted in the foundational generation theory of Mannheim (1952).

As with Marxist theories of social class, Mannheim viewed generations as a means of understanding social structure, with an emphasis on the procedures of social change. Mannheim believed that all individuals, in a conscious or unconscious manner, belong to a specific social location, on the basis of their year of birth and their place in historical time. For Mannheim, generations, as a social location phenomenon, emerge not just by one (horizontal) dimension of birth cohort but also by a second (vertical) dimension of historical process. Although Mannheim recognised the significance of the biological process of birth, aging and death in the formation of generations, he further argued that the influence of the changing historical circumstances needs to be taken into account. As a product of the formative personal experiences of society members, history is a crucial determinant in the formation of generations (Vincent, 2005). Thus, the meeting point of birth cohorts and historical process creates a two-dimensional space, which Mannheim calls 'generational location' and objectively positions each generation across the pattern of social structure.

Generational differences in the workplace

Empirical support for the proposition that substantive and meaningful generational differences exist between employees in the current workplace, has recently been provided by a number of scholars (see Table 41.1). Amongst the earliest studies, Lyons et al. (2005) documented the differences in work values across four generations (Matures, Baby Boomers, Generation X and Millennials) of Canadian knowledge workers employed full-time in private, public and not-for-profit sector organisations with 500 or more employees. In particular, the results of univariate F tests for the individual work values indicated significant generational differences

Table 41.1 Studies of inter-generational differences in the workplace

Study	Occupation	Country	Cohorts	Variable
Lyons, Duxbury and Higgins (2005)	Knowledge workers	Canada	Matures (n = 48) Boomers (n = 370) Xers (n = 632) Millennials (n = 131)	Work values
Cennamo and Gardner (2008)	Multi (lawyers, sales, recruiters, IT developers, construction)	New Zealand	Boomers (n = 117) Xers (n = 288) Yers (n = 86)	Work values
Dries, Pepermans and De Kerpel (2008)	University employees and students	Belgium	Silent (n = 86) Boomers (n = 171) Xers (n = 205) Yers (n = 288)	Organisational security
Hess and Jepsen (2009)	Multi (administrative, managerial, sales/ marketing, human resources, customer service)	Australia	Boomers (n = 100) Xers (n = 107) Yers (77)	Employer obligations
Takase, Oba and Yamashita (2009)	Registered nurses	Japan	Boomers (n = 56) Xers (n = 97) Millennials (n = 162	Job orientations
Real, Mitnick and Maloney (2010)	Construction workers	USA	Boomers (n = 742) Xers (n = 1012) Millennials (n = 762)	Work ethic

Takase, Oba and Yamashita originally categorised the prevalent generations of nursing workforce in Japan into three cohorts: (a) those born between 1946–1959 and named as the 'Dankai generation' (meaning a mass generation) which is equivalent to the Baby Boomers (b) those born between 1960–1974 and labelled as 'Shinjinrui' (meaning a new mankind) which is equivalent to Generation X and (c) those born after 1975 and called 'Post Dankai juniors' which is equivalent of the Millennial Generation.

on four types of work values: intrinsic, altruistic, social and prestige. Pairwise comparisons of the generational cohorts revealed that both Baby Boomers (n = 370) and Millennials (n = 131) placed significantly less importance on intrinsic work values than did Generation Xers (n = 632). In addition, altruistic work values were significantly more important to Matures (n = 48) than to Generation Xers and Millennials. Baby Boomers also placed significantly more importance on altruism than did Millennials.

In terms of social work values, Millennials were significantly more important than Generation Xers, Baby Boomers or Matures. Notably, Generation Xers placed more importance on these type of work values than did Baby Boomers or Matures. Nonetheless, Lyons et al.'s (2005) findings revealed that prestige work values were significantly more important to Millennials than to Generation Xers, Baby Boomers or Matures. Generation Xers also placed more importance on prestige than did Baby Boomers.

Cennamo and Gardner (2008) in New Zealand also reported differences in work values within a sample of employees from various industries including law firms, media corporations, the construction industry, pharmaceutical distribution, information technology and recruitment. Generational cohorts differed on status and freedom work values. In particular, Generation Y (n = 86) valued freedom and status-related aspects of work more than Generation X (n = 288) and Baby Boomers (n = 117).

In neighbouring Australia, Hess and Jepsen (2009) revealed further inter-generational differences in the workplace. Participants were from a variety of occupational areas including administrative, managerial, human resources, sales/marketing and customer service, and represented a range of industries including insurance, finance, not-for-profit/government and manufacturing. Post hoc comparisons illustrated a significant difference between relational obligations for Generation X and Baby Boomers, with relational obligations placed higher for Baby Boomers than for Generation X.

In Europe, Dries et al., (2008) found significant differences across four generations (Silent, Baby Boomers, Generation X and Generation Y) of employees and students in a large Belgian university. One-way analysis of Variance (ANOVA) and further post-hoc tests revealed that members from the Silent Generation (n = 86) attached significantly more importance to organisational security than did Baby Boomers (n = 171) and people from Generation X (n = 205). Furthermore, Generation X had significantly lower scores than Generation Y (n = 288).

Inter-generational differences were also observed in job orientations (professional privilege, clinical challenges, social rewards and working conditions), between nurses in Japanese public hospitals. Takase et al. (2009) found that working conditions were of significantly lower importance for Baby Boomers compared to the younger generations. In addition, professional privilege and clinical challenges were of significantly more importance for Generation X compared to the Millennials.

Nonetheless, Real et al. (2010) documented inter-generational differences in work ethics with US construction workers. Post-hoc tests suggested that Millennials (n = 762) scored higher in hard work and centrality of work and lower in morality/ethics and wasting time than both Generation X (n = 1012) and Baby Boomers (n = 742). In addition, Millennials rated higher in aspects related to leisure, self-reliance and delay of gratification than Baby Boomers.

Generational differences across hotel chain employees

A growing body of cross-temporal evidence from employees working in hotel chains provides further compelling evidence of generational differences in the workplace (see Table 41.2).

Table 41.2 Studies of inter-generational differences in hotel chain employees

Study	Country	Context	Cohorts	Variable
Park and Gursoy (2012)	US	29 mid- and upscale hotels from a North American chain	Boomers (n = 236) Xers (n = 248) Millennials (n = 193)	Work engagement
Gursoy, Chi and Karadag (2013)	US	29 mid- and upscale hotels from a North American chain	Boomers (n = 257) Xers (n = 260) Yers (n = 200)	Work values
Lu and Gursoy (2013)	US	29 mid- and upscale hotels from a North American chain	Boomers (n = 236) Xers (n = 248) Millennials (n = 193)	Turnover intention
Chi, Maier and Gursoy (2013)	US	29 mid- and upscale hotels from a North American chain	Boomers (n = 109) Xers (n = 89) Yers (30)	Perceptions of younger and older managers
Lub, Blomme and Bal (2011)	Netherlands	An international hotel chain with 3 and 4 star properties	Xers (n = 37) Millennials (n = 65)	Employer obligations
Lub, Bijvank, Bal, Blomme and Schalk (2012)	Netherlands	20 establishments from a 4 star hotel chain	Boomers (n = 43) Xers (n = 130) Millennials (n = 186)	Commitment

Within the US, Dogan Gursoy and his associates have conducted a series of studies using data from customer contact employees and managers at a North American chain with 29 mid- and upscale hotels. Significant differences were identified between generational cohorts in a number of work-related variables. For example, Gursoy et al. (2013), consistent with previous studies from other occupations and industries (i.e., Cennamo and Gardner, 2008 and Lyons et al., 2005), found significant differences in work values between generational cohorts of front line and service contact employees (n = 717). In addition, using a sample of 678 customer contact employees and managers, Park and Gursoy (2012) and Lu and Gursoy (2013) documented generational differences in work engagement and turnover intention, respectively. Nonetheless, Chi et al. (2013), based on data from 228 managers, including the general managers and department managers, reported generational differences in the perceptions of younger and older managers.

In a similar vein, Xander Lub and his associates explored the phenomenon of generational differences among hotel chain employees in the Netherlands. Based on a sample of 102 employees from an international hotel chain with 3 and 4-star establishments, Lub et al. (2011) revealed inter-generational differences in relational obligation, supporting earlier findings from other occupations and industries (i.e., Hess and Jepsen, 2009). Later, using data from a wider sample of 359 employees working in a domestic 4-star chain with 20 establishments, Lub et al. (2012) found significant generational differences in the levels of organisational commitment.

Table 41.3 provides a summary of the results documented by the above studies. In terms of the perceptions of hotel chain employees about their younger and older managers across the three prevailing cohorts, managers from the Millennial generation appeared to have significantly more negative perceptions of their managers in comparison to managers from

Table 41.3 Inter-generational differences across hotel chain employees

Generations	Millennials vs. X-ers		Millennials vs. Boomers		X-ers vs. Boomers	
Importance	Low	High	Low	High	Low	High
	power[a] job security[b]	non-compliance[a] leadership[a]	work centrality[a] technology challenge[a]	non-compliance[a] leadership[a]	work centrality[a] technology challenge[a]	power[a] stimulating job[b]
Work-related outcomes	autonomy[b] work engagement[c] affective commitment[b] continuance commitment[b]	recognition[a] stimulating job[b] inter-organisational mobility[b] relational obligations[d]	work engagement[c] affective commitment[b] continuance commitment[b] job satisfaction[e]	recognition[a] work-life balance[a] relational obligations[b] turnover intention[e]		inter-organisational mobility[b] work-life balance[b][a]
Perceptions of other generations	connectedness[f] slacking[f]	competency[f]	connectedness[f] slacking[f]	competency[f]		

[a]Gursoy et al. (2013), [b]Lub et al. (2012), [c]Park and Gursoy (2012), [d]Lub et al. (2011), [e]Lu and Gursoy (2013), [f]Chi et al. (2013)

the older generations. In particular, the level of 'connectedness' (e.g., 'They try very hard to get to know employees', 'They are up to date', 'They push for better training' and 'They are very appreciative of their subordinates') was significantly lower than both Boomers and X-ers. By contrast, managers from the Millennial generation had more positive perceptions of their younger managers than the older generations.

Specifically, Millennials' level of competency (e.g., 'they know how to manage', 'they have lots of experiences', 'they respect life experiences', 'they know how hard employees work') was significantly higher than both Boomers and X-ers. Moreover, the level of 'slacking' for Millennials ('they lack people skills', 'they do not work very hard to try to prove themselves', 'they are not confident and hard workers', 'they are whipper-snapper babies', 'they need to gain a lot of experience') was significantly lower than the older generations.

In terms of the relationship between the new entrants in hotel chains and the preceding generations, as shown in Table 41.3, Millennials tend to place significantly more importance on relational obligations (e.g., 'work that makes me feel involved' and 'work that gives me the opportunity to learn'). Furthermore, it seems that Millennials valued certain aspects of work significantly more than their older counterparts. These were related to (a) non-compliance (e.g., 'I am likely to challenge workplace norms such as dress codes, flex-time, and employee-supervisor relations', 'I truly believe the cliché that rules were meant to be broken', 'I have low tolerance for bureaucracy and rules', 'I am deeply cynical about management'), (b) recognition (e.g., 'they treat younger employees like kids', 'No one respects younger employees because they are young') and (c) leadership (e.g., 'I work best when there is strong leadership', 'I work best when there is direction').

By contrast, the findings in Table 41.3 indicate that the level of work engagement, in terms of vigour, absorption and dedication, was significantly lower among Millennials. In the same vein, the youngest cohort of workers in hotel chains were significantly less committed than members of the older generations, in terms of affective (e.g., 'I feel strongly attached to the organisation') and continuance commitment (e.g., 'It would cost me too much if I were to leave the organisation shortly').

Nonetheless, the findings from pairwise comparisons between Millennials and members from the Boomer generation summarised in Table 41.3 indicate that Millennials were significantly less satisfied with their job. Millennials appeared to be significantly less willing to (a) 'work hard and long hours' and (b) 'wait for their turn for promotions and rewards' than their Boomer colleagues did. Similarly, they placed significantly more importance than Boomers on work–life balance (e.g., 'I work to live, not the other way around', 'My philosophy is to leave work at work', 'I will not sacrifice my leisure time for the company', 'My priorities are with my friends and my family, not the boss', 'I want to work as many hours as I have to but not a minute longer'). Turnover intention was also found to be significantly higher in Millennials versus Boomers.

In relation to Millennials versus Xers, Table 41.3 reveals that the younger generation were significantly more willing to take the opportunity to work within another department and/or get another job in the same hotel chain (intra-organisational mobility). Furthermore, Millennials believed that having a job that provides the opportunity to learn and/or to develop new skills and knowledge (stimulating job) is significantly more important than X-ers did. On the contrary, opportunities to engage in decisions and/or to organise tasks according to their own best judgment (autonomy) were less significant to Millennials versus the X-ers. Similarly, Millennials were significantly less interested compared to X-ers in having a permanent position and/or a contract that offers job security.

The summarised findings in Table 41.3 present further significant pairwise differences between the older generations. In particular, Boomers placed significantly more importance than X-ers on being 'in command' when in a group and on organising and directing the activities of others (power), whereas technology challenges were significantly less important (e.g., 'Technology makes my job harder', 'Using latest technology makes my job easier').

Conclusion

Generational differences in the workplace represent a part of the wider 'diversity literature' (Parry and Urwin, 2011). The wider diversity literature dictates that differences in the workplace arise from variety in race and ethnicity, cultural and national orientation, sexual orientation, gender and disabilities. Within the generational context, diversity is assumed to be manifested from the unique values and attitudes that each cohort brings to work. Our literature review results support the notion that substantive and meaningful differences in the workplace exist between generations from different cultures (i.e., USA, Canada, New Zealand, Australia, Japan and Belgium) and across a variety of occupations (i.e., nurses, knowledge workers, construction workers, university employees, recruiters, lawyers and IT developers). Specifically, evidence from a series of cross-temporal studies across employees working in hotel chains revealed significant inter-generational differences in a variety of work-related variables work such as organisational commitment, work values, work ethics, work orientations and relational obligations at work.

These results generate serious implications for managers, owners and human resource professionals within hotel chains. Generational diversity is a double-edged sword with challenges accompanying its management. From one side, when hotel chains manage their diverse workforce effectively, employees exhibit desirable behaviours, which contribute to the success of the organisation (Mamman et al., 2012; Ng, 2008; Richard, 2000). Conversely, failure to manage diversity has the potential to create conflict and dysfunctional behaviour (Shore et al., 2009), which represent impediments to the effectiveness of even the most sophisticated organisations (Zopiatis et al., 2012). Therefore, human resource managers within hotel chains need to be educated and informed about the potential benefits and risks of managing generational differences. A worthwhile avenue in this direction could be a values-based approach, which holds the potential of inspiring and motivating employees by developing meaningful tasks, congruent with their personal values (Anderson, 1997; Lyons et al., 2010). The theory of work adjustment (Dawis and Lofquist, 1984) dictates that the degree of an individual's satisfaction in the role of worker depends on the degree of the attainment of his/her work values. The assessment of employees' values is therefore of critical importance to organisational success because value correspondence − the fit between one's values and work outcomes − is related to one's choice of occupation/job and satisfaction within a specific work environment. Awareness should be transformed into targeted human resource practices, so that managers can have a roadmap to guide their efforts in effectively managing the different expectations and motivations of their multigenerational workforce.

The summarised findings of this study imply that human resource managers in hotel chains should place more focus on the distinct work identity of each generational cohort. In particular, there is a need for a shift from the 'one size fits all' practices that currently exist in human resources paradigms, to more trustworthy innovative initiatives and interventions that aim to enhance inter-generational comfort and synergies (Zopiatis et al., 2012, p.17). One way for human resource management professionals in hotel chains to identify and implement novel practices that provide a clear and cohesive connection between generations is by drawing more attention to the concept of 'reverse mentoring'. It is an inverted type of mentoring relationship whereby new junior employees are paired up with more experienced managers or employees to help the experienced worker acquire new learning (Chaudhuri and Ghosh, 2012, p.56). Unlike traditional mentoring practices where learning is dispensed hierarchically from an older mentor to a younger protégé, reverse mentoring provides an opportunity for the older employees to learn from their younger counterparts. However, Chaudhuri and Ghosh, (2012, p.57) caution that for this novel practice to be effectively implemented it has first to be firmly 'acknowledged that junior or new members who join the organisation have knowledge to share and are willing to do so with more senior managers'.

Exploration of generational differences across employees working in hotel chains is a relatively new undertaking. However our study, although limited to evidence from the US and the Netherlands, provides sufficient documentation that generations of employees working in hotel chains differ in a variety of work related variables. Thus, further research should build on our results and explore the causes and consequences of these differences.

Notes

1 The early Greeks had an international morality, which was bound up with the duties of hospitality (*xenia*), a personal relationship that cut across the usual boundaries of political feudal obligation. The great god Zeus himself, as Zeus Xenios, had set the rules of hospitality and punished offences against them. For Zeus, hospitality progressed through three 'gestures' (1) the admittance of the *xenos* (guest) into the house; (2) the bathing of the guest and his gift of a fresh change of clothes; and (3) the meal (see Roth, 1993).
2 The vignette has been created for illustrative purposes only and it is based on working experience.
3 Following the North American clustering (see Pary and Urwin, 2011).
4 Also known as Generation Y, Nexters, the Nexus Generation, Gen Me, and iGen.

References

Anderson, C. (1997) Values-based management. *Academy of Management Executive*, 11, 25–46.
Benson, J. and Brown, M. (2011) Generations at work: are there differences and do they matter? *The International Journal of Human Resource Management*, 22(9), 1843–65.
Cennamo, L. and Gardner, D. (2008) Generational differences in work values, outcomes and person-organisation values fit. *Journal of Managerial Psychology*, 23(8), 891–906.
Chaudhuri, S. and Ghosh, R. (2012) Reverse mentoring: a social exchange tool for keeping the boomers engaged and millennials committed. *Human Resource Development Review*, 11(1), 55–76.
Chi, C.G., Maier, T.A. and Gursoy, D. (2013) Employees' perceptions of younger and older managers by generation and job category. *International Journal of Hospitality Management*, 34, 42–50.
Dawis, R.V., and Lofquist, L.H. (1984) *A Psychological Theory of Work Adjustment: An Individual-differences Model and its Applications*. Minneapolis: University of Minnesota Press.
Dries, N., Pepermans, R. and De Kerpel, E. (2008) Exploring four generations' beliefs about career: Is 'satisfied' the new 'successful'? *Journal of Managerial Psychology*, 23(8), 907–28.
Gursoy, D., Chi, C. G.-Q. and Karadag, E. (2013) Generational differences in work values and attitudes among frontline and service contact employees. *International Journal of Hospitality Management*, 32, 40–8.
Hess, N. and Jepsen, D.M. (2009) Career stage and generational differences in psychological contracts. *Career Development International*, 14(3), 261–83.
King, C., Funk, D.C. and Wilkins, H. (2011).Bridging the gap: an examination of the relative alignment of hospitality research and industry priorities. *International Journal of Hospitality Management*, 30, 157–66.
Kupperschmidt, B.R. (2000) Multigeneration employees: strategies for effective management. *The Health Care Manager*, 19(1), 65–76

Lu, A.C., and Gursoy, D. (2013) Impact of job burnout on satisfaction and turnover intention: do generational differences matter?, *Journal of Hospitality and Tourism Research*, 20(1), 151–63.

Lub, X.D., Blomme, R.J. and Bal, P.M. (2011) Psychological contract and organizational citizenship behavior: a new deal for new generations? *Advances in Hospitality and Leisure*, 7, 109–30.

Lub, X., Bijvank, M.N., Bal, P.M., Blomme, R. and Schalk, R. (2012) Different or alike? Exploring the psychological contract and commitment of different generations of hospitality workers. *International Journal of Contemporary Hospitality Management*, 24(4), 553–73.

Lyons, S.T., Duxbury, L. and Higgins, C. (2005, May) *An empirical assessment of generational differences in work-related values*. Paper presented at the 2005 Administrative Sciences Association of Canada Conference, Toronto, Ontario, Canada

Lyons, S.T., Higgins, C. and Duxbury, L. (2010) Work values: development of a new three-dimensional structure based on confirmatory smallest space analysis. *Journal of Organizational Behavior*, 31, 969–1002.

Mamman, A., Kamoche, K. and Bakuwa, R. (2012) Diversity, organizational commitment and organizational citizenship behavior: an organizing framework. *Human Resource Management Review*, 22(4), 285–302.

Mannheim, K. (1952) *Essays on the Sociology of Knowledge*. London: Routeledge and Kegan Paul.

Ng, E.S. (2008) Why organizations choose to manage diversity? Toward a leadership-based theoretical framework. *Human Resource Development Review*, 7(1), 58–78.

Park, G. and Gursoy, D. (2012) Generation effects on work engagement among US hotel employees. *International Journal of Hospitality Management*, 31(4), 1195–202.

Parry, E. and Urwin, P. (2011) Generational differences in work values: a review of theory and evidence. *International Journal of Management Reviews*, 13(1), 79–96.

Real, K., Mitnick, A.D. and Maloney, W.F. (2010) More similar than different: Millennials in the U.S. building trades. *Journal of Business Psychology*, 25, 303–13.

Richard, O.C. (2000) Racial diversity, business strategy, and firm performance: a resource-based view. *Academy of Management Journal*, 43(2), 164–77.

Roth, P. (1993) The Theme of Corrupted Xenia in Aeschylus's 'Oresteia', *Mnemosyne*, 6(1), 1–17.

Shore, L.M., Chung-Herrera, B.G., Dean, M.A., Ehrhart, K.H., Jung, D.I., Randel, A.E. and Singh, G. (2009) Diversity in organizations: where are we now and where are we going? *Human Resource Management Review*, 19(2), 117–33.

Solnet, D., Kralj, A. and Baum, T. (2013) 360 degrees of pressure: the changing role of the HR professional in the hospitality industry. *Journal of Hospitality and Tourism Research*, 39(2), 271–92.

Takase, M., Oba, K. and Yamashita, N. (2009) Generational differences in factors influencing job turnover among Japanese nurses: an exploratory comparative design. *International Journal of Nursing Studies*, 46(7), 957–67.

Vincent, J.A. (2005) Understanding generations: political economy and culture in an ageing society. *The British Journal of Sociology*, 56(4), 579–99.

Zopiatis, A., Krambia-Kapardis, M. and Varnavas, A. (2012) Y-ers, X-ers and Boomers: investigating the multigenerational (mis)perceptions in the hospitality workplace. *Tourism and Hospitality Research*, 12(2), 101–21.

42

The new technologies
tsunami in the hotel industry

Ulrike Gretzel

(UNIVERSITY OF QUEENSLAND, AUSTRALIA)

Introduction

Hotel chains owe part of their existence to the efficiencies gained from developing and operating information systems that help individual properties manage and distribute their products in an efficient way, otherwise not available to single hotels because of the cost and their lack of expertise/technological innovativeness (Benckendorff et al., 2014). This technological backbone or technology-related raison d'être of hotel chains is now increasingly challenged by advances in information and communication technologies (ICTs) that empower individual properties and shift technology innovation and implementation to the hotel rather than the chain level. In addition, these emerging technologies are also encroaching on other areas of hotel chain expertise and responsibility, such as marketing. Social media players like TripAdvisor are adding transparency to the market and increasingly undermine traditional hotel chain branding efforts by providing ever more sophisticated ways for consumers to support their decision-making processes with the opinions of other consumers (Yoo et al., 2015). Further, ICTs have given rise to the sharing economy (Belk, 2014) that has the power to completely disrupt commercial models of hospitality. Couchsurfing and AirBnB take advantage of the connectivity provided through social media and complex reputation management systems that allow consumers to offer accommodation to other consumers. Smart tourism systems initiatives (emerging in Asia and Europe but increasingly spreading to other parts of the world) further challenge the role of hotel chains in the 'tourism food chain' in that they change value propositions and make linkages among the various actors in the tourism network dynamic (Gretzel, Werthner, Koo and Lamsfus, 2015). The hotel chain's importance for training is also under scrutiny as an ever greater amount of online educational resources such as MOOCs (Massive Open Online Courses) becomes available and make training and education much more accessible (Ryan et al., 2013; Murphy et al., 2014). This leaves hotel chains struggling to keep up with technological developments and at the same time means they have to increasingly justify their existence.

This chapter will explore the different technological waves that together are forming a technological tsunami that threatens to wipe out hotel chains, or at the very least force them to rethink their current approaches in order to survive in the new hospitality landscape that will emerge in its aftermath. Specifically, it will delve into advances in search technology,

Big Data, social media, robotics, virtual meeting technologies, developments in mobile technology and the concept of smart tourism to identify opportunities and threats for hotels in general, and specifically hotel chains. It also addresses stark contrasts in the way hotels manage technology-mediated guest experiences, ranging from social media-themed hotels to black hole/technology-free resorts. While some of these waves have taken shape already and are building up volume fast, others like robotics are still farther away on the horizon and are more difficult to describe in terms of what impact they will have.

Connecting the consumer with the product

Hotel chains have been crucial elements in the hotel distribution channel, linking hotel products to other distributors or the end-consumer. Werthner and Klein (1999) illustrated already, during the early stages of the internet, that web technologies have the potential to cut out hotel chains and their central reservation systems. Yet, websites with booking functions are hard to maintain and brand recognition still matters in a context of information overload and making high risk decisions on products that are difficult to describe. In addition, bargaining power is important when negotiating with the many cyber-intermediaries that have entered the tourism and hospitality marketplace. Not surprisingly, hotel chains were able to withstand the threats of Web 1.0. However, Web 2.0 (the social web) and Web 3.0 (the semantic web) (Gretzel, 2015) are new technological tsunamis bringing with them new technologies and new opportunities for consumers to find, evaluate and book individual hotel properties.

Social media lend consumers an incredibly powerful voice. This is often referred to as the megaphone effect of social media (McQuarrie and Philips, 2014). The hospitality industry is slowly adjusting to this shift in consumer power and the immense transparency regarding the availability and characteristics of hotel products. Social media have also empowered individual hotel properties, in that an online presence is made easy for technology laggards. Connections with consumers are facilitated through abilities to subscribe (follow or like). Moreover, regular updates and engaging visual contents allow hotels to build strong emotional affinity. The 'selfie' and immediacy culture of social media change what a brand is and does (Kozinets, 2014). Consumers expect authentic, rich, meaningful conversations and personal interactions. The challenge for hotel chain brands here lies in becoming empty labels, as it is much harder to provide such contents at the chain level. Creating standardised contents for individual properties to implement, as is done for traditional advertising, does not work in the social media context. Individual hotels need to maintain their own social media presence. Consequently, the chain now has to manage thousands of individual hotel brands under its chain brand. And on social media all brands are, to a great extent, co-created by consumers (Jenkins, 2014), which means also managing millions of traveller voices.

A related aspect of social media is reputation management. Ratings and reviews are widely used by travellers to inform their hotel decision-making (Yoo and Gretzel, 2008), and hotel performance has been directly linked to online reputation (Ye et al., 2009). Facebook and Twitter are used by many consumers to voice complaints, and interact with customer service representatives in real-time. The challenge for hotel chains lies in their reputation for being situated at the individual property level. There are no TripAdvisor ratings for a chain. Customer service requests need to be handled by individual hotel properties. This means that reputation has to be monitored and managed at the property level. Where chains can make a contribution in this area is by providing social media monitoring and management tools to help properties access the latest social media metrics without having to pay the cost-prohibitive prices for implementing such tools at the property level. They can also provide insights on reputation management best practice, and put in place quality standards for social media interactions (e.g., for responses to TripAdvisor reviews).

Hotel chains provide a great advantage to frequent travellers who collect loyalty points and would like to be able to use them across as many properties as possible. Their ability to partner directly with airlines and car rental companies adds great value to their loyalty programmes. However, following the 2.0 spirit, ever more platforms emerge that enable the exchange of points among consumers and across loyalty programmes. Thus, one can easily envision a future in which hotel chain-level programmes become meaningless.

While the social media tsunami already hit a while ago, the hotel industry is still underwater. Social media are constantly emerging with new platforms gaining popularity, and new application areas being discovered. Sharing economy platforms like AirBnB and Uber are the latest craze, visual platforms such as Snapchat and Instagram are gaining traction, and in China and South Korea platforms focusing on personal communication/private social networks (e.g., WeChat) are increasingly popular. Hotel chains have yet to use existing and emerging social media to their advantage, and find interaction models that work for social media contexts; all that while the Web 3.0 wave is already emerging on the horizon.

Scholars envision that the semantic web will bring new ways in which value can be added to data. New search algorithms and recommender systems form a new breed of intelligent systems with great impact on tourism and the hospitality industry (Gretzel, 2011). Google Travel has already implemented an intelligent hotel search that in many ways erodes the need for big hotel chain brands. The saving grace for hotel chains is that Google is essentially an advertising company, and big investments in organic as well as paid search are needed to maintain a successful online presence. However, for the consumer, these background investments are not visible. As a consequence, hotel chains might lose their 'face' and only provide services to their hotel members in the future.

Big Data as a big opportunity for hotel chains

IBM (n.d.) describes the Big Data phenomenon along four dimensions: volume, velocity, variety and veracity. This means that Big Data is not only big in terms of scale (see Chapter 43) but also available for analysis almost instantaneously. Variety explains that Big Data emerges from many different sources, and veracity implies that it represents data that is of much greater accuracy than, for instance, retrospective survey data. Big Data gains in value the bigger it gets. This indicates a clear advantage for hotel chains over individual properties. Cloud computing (data being stored and retrieved via web services) and advanced data analytics make it possible for hotel chains to act as data clearing houses, and provide key services to members. Benchmarking is extremely important for the hospitality sector (Wöber, 2000) and Big Data can greatly enhance benchmarking efforts. Having data available at the chain level for all properties facilitates analytics initiatives as individual properties might not otherwise be willing or capable of sharing data. The hotel chain can buy into even bigger data services to supplement chain-internal data, thereby again adding value through increasing volume and variety.

Big Data also provides great opportunities for hotel chains in terms of listening and responding to customers. As indicated above in the discussion of social media monitoring, real-time awareness of trends in the marketplace are important for marketing and customer service efforts. However, they are also increasingly used to forecast/predict demand and therefore allow for much more fine-tuned yield management approaches. Such predictions are potentially also available to consumers. While tools have so far only been implemented for flights (e.g., by the meta-search engine Kayak), Big Data certainly make it possible for consumers to gain greater insights into hotels' yield management practices. If that will be the case, the hotel industry will have to respond rapidly with more sophisticated yield management techniques and hotel chains can certainly play an important role in this scenario.

The mixed bag of mobile technologies

The term mobile technology encompasses a variety of technologies and devices that have tremendous implications for hotels. The wide adoption of smartphones and tablets, and the impact on traveller experiences and expectations have been recognised and conceptualised as a new era of travel (Wang et al., 2014). It can be expected that this mobile tsunami will continue to hit the hospitality industry in multiple waves.

At the very basic level, hotels had to realise that consumers increasingly use these mobile devices to access information, including hotel information. This requires websites to be optimised for mobile use in order to facilitate mobile information search. Hotels have responded to this with either separate mobile websites, optimisation of their general website, mobile apps, or they have ignored this trend all together. In this respect, the latest website design approach is to make websites as flexible as possible, in order to accommodate a multitude of mobile devices through so-called responsive website design (Gibbs and Gretzel, 2015). Responsive website design is, however, complex and costly, especially for large websites, such as those at the chain level. This means that while hotel chains are probably more likely to have the financial resources to invest in responsive website design, they also have to deal with the much greater investments needed. They are also more likely to have recently invested in other forms of mobile optimisation, or separate mobile sites/apps and might be locked into these technologies for a while. This has allowed small players to leapfrog and more quickly adopt responsive design than the large hotel chain corporations.

Hotel mobile apps represent a particular challenge for hotel chains. On one hand, mobile apps have greatly enhanced interaction possibilities with hotel consumers, and have been designed for a wide range of hotel functions to enrich the hotel guest experience (Dickinson et al., 2014). On the other hand, they have to be designed to accommodate various mobile devices separately and have to be maintained and updated, which comes with a hefty price tag. An analysis of the North American hotel mobile app landscape (Gibbs et al., 2014) shows that there is a lot of overlap and likely confusion in the app marketplace, with apps being available at both the individual hotel level and the hotel chain level. From a consumer point of view, it makes little sense to download a separate app for each and every hotel one stays at. This would speak to a need for app development and hosting at the chain level. However, if these apps are too general, they might have to compete with travel agency and destination apps. In addition, Gibbs et al. (2014) list features that only make sense at the property level, and actually require physical investments in the hotel infrastructure in order to be able to deliver services. This means that implementation at the chain level is impossible or would require ensuring buy-in at the individual hotel property level.

Mobile technologies increasingly being discussed in the context of hotels are near-field communication (NFC) and mobile wallets (Basili et al., 2014; Palumbo and Dominici, 2015). They continue the trend of self-service technology implementation in hotels (Beatson et al., 2007). Their implementation is particularly relevant for check-in/check-out automation, and gaining access to hotel rooms and other hotel facilities with a smartphone. They promise huge cost-savings and increased convenience for the hotel guest and employees. Because of the physical changes needed at doors, etc. this is again a technology that requires implementation at the individual property level. However, hotel chains can certainly provide invaluable implementation know-how and technology consulting in order to stay relevant in this domain. Although not a mobile technology per se but often linked to mobile technology through credentials being stored in smartphones, biometric technology poses similar opportunities and challenges. Privacy and security concerns have held back adoption despite its access control-related advantages (Murphy and Rottet, 2009). Whether we will see widespread adoption of these technologies by hotels depends largely on resolving these privacy and security issues. What also needs mentioning in this context is the need to acknowledge that not all hotel guests will have access to smart phones. Whether it is lack of adoption or unwillingness to pay for international roaming, hotels will have to provide multiple options for the foreseeable future.

Smart hotels

Smart tourism has become an important concept to describe technological developments based on sensor technologies supporting, among other things, the Internet of Things, Big and Open Data, and intelligent systems that reason and infer. Context-aware mobile tour guide applications with recommender functions are an example of a smart tourism technology. Höjer and Wangel (2015) argue that it is not so much the individual technological advances but rather the interconnection, synchronisation and concerted use of different technologies that constitute smartness. Gretzel, Sigala, Xiang and Koo (2015) define smart tourism as tourism that takes advantage of smart technologies in order to enhance touristic experiences. Consequently, a smart hotel is an establishment were a suite of smart technologies is used to inform operational decisions, ensure sustainability and enrich guest experiences. Smart destinations then constitute smart tourism ecosystems (Gretzel, Werthner, Koo, Lamsfus, 2015), focused on smart value creation at the concerted destination level. Besides their sensor-equipped physical layers, these smart destinations include dynamic business networks in which traditional consumer/producer and provider/distributor roles are blurred. What role hotel chains can or should play in such a scenario is not clear. The issues and potential advantages for hotel chains discussed in the contexts of Big Data and mobile technologies also hold true for smart tourism but 'smart' is currently a lot more clearly defined at the operational hotel property level than at the hotel chain level. A smart hotel senses, reasons and acts. It has a physical presence connected to a digital presence, both of which are interlinked with other actors as needed. A smart hotel chain will have to establish a clear value proposition relevant in such a complex digital ecosystem. And how hotel chains will deal with the dynamic nature and 'plug and play' attitude of smart destinations remains an unsolved puzzle.

Dancing with robots

Robots are a natural extension of the trend toward automated service and self-service technologies already implemented in many hotels. Vacuum and pool cleaning robots are household items these days, and stylish, interactive guest assistant robots have been designed for the headquarters of Santander bank in Spain (Hornyak, 2010). Hay (2012) conducted interviews with hotel managers who foresaw robots as taking over various service tasks in the hotels of the future, even fundamental service encounters such as being served food and drinks in hotel restaurants. Others have also speculated that robotic technology can and will increasingly takeover the delivery of services to tourists (Yeoman 2013). With robots becoming ever more autonomous, intelligent and humanoid, and guests increasingly used to interactions with automated systems as well as robots, one can easily imagine a hotel lobby of the future bustling with robots eager to clean, repair and serve guests. Such robots constitute important technological investments and, like investments in other hotel technologies such as central reservation systems, there is certainly a role to take on for the hotel chain. Robot 'manuals' to implement certain service standards, the look of robots to convey hotel chain branding, robot maintenance, etc. are important services to offer for the hotel chains of the future.

Virtual meetings

Many hotel chains rely heavily on business travel, with company contracts often being negotiated at the chain level. While technology has certainly not replaced the need to meet, due to several limitations related to immersion and social presence (Persson and Mathiasson, 2014), virtual meeting technologies are increasingly used by companies to be able to reduce meeting-related costs (Gustafson, 2012). As communication technologies become more sophisticated and more able to convey rich information (Dean et al., 2014) corporate travel will likely be further cut. Sophisticated meeting technology also poses a problem to hotel properties in that meetings that happen at hotels now need these technologies to bring in others who are not co-present. It is not only the investment in the latest meeting technology that constitutes a big investment for hotels but also the need to consider the cost of internet bandwidth taken up by such meetings.

Technology-free and technology-themed hotels

Another technology-related trend is that more and more consumers actually resent their technological dependence and need help in escaping from the technology. Offering technology-free zones or packages in hotels has become a new trend, in reaction to ever more pervasive technology use (Future Foundation, 2011). Pearce and Gretzel (2012) illustrate the benefits and risks of tourism experiences in technological dead zones or so-called black hole resorts for the tourism consumer. Greater relaxation, true escape from daily routines and more meaningful social interactions are only some of the benefits for travellers. However, there are also great advantages to be realised from the hotel perspective. Technology use in hotels, especially in lobbies, restaurants and relaxation areas can destroy the carefully crafted atmospheres hotels try to construct. Heavy technology users not only ruin the experience for themselves but also for others, and make it difficult for service personnel to have real interactions with them. Some hotels see such a great need in managing technology use at their properties that they offer rewards like discounted rates or special amenities to those that check their mobile phone in when they check into the hotel. This stands in stark contrast to hotels that facilitate technology use such as the 1888 Hotel Sydney, which brands itself as the Instagram hotel, or the Sol Wave House, which is a Twitter-themed property. The Instagram hotel seizes every opportunity to encourage selfies and offers maps for specific Instagram tours around the hotel while the Twitter hotel offers a Twitter-based app that makes it easier for its guests to connect. At the hotel chain level, there is thus a clear need to provide guidance for the strategic orientation towards or away from heavy technology use. This might be very difficult for chains that attract a variety of segments with very different technology preferences and needs. Also, while the hotel chain can set directions, these clearly have to be implemented at the property level.

Conclusion

Hotels have always been test laboratories for new technologies and hotel chains have been established in part to take advantage of consolidated electronic distribution systems. This close relationship between hotels/hotel chains and technology continues. Advances in information and communication technologies affect hotel chains in many ways, some positive and some very threatening. This chapter only presented a small range of technologies, selected based on their perceived importance for the strategic orientation and value of hotel chains. Many other technologies directly impact a hotel property's operations.

What becomes clear from the above discussion of the various tsunamis faced by hotel chains is that there is no way their business can continue as usual. Whether a hotel chain will be washed away by a technological tsunami or whether it will be able to ride on top of its waves is clearly a function of its ability to innovate, and carve out unique selling propositions. It seems, however, that there are more advantages to be gained on the management side of things and not so much on the direct marketing and branding to consumers. In the age of AirBnB in which consumers are willing to pay money to sleep in somebody's spare room in order to have a cheaper and/or more authentic travel experience, one has to seriously question the future of a chain brand like Hilton or Intercontinental.

References

Basili, A., Liguori, W. and Palumbo, F. (2014) NFC Smart Tourist Card: Combining Mobile and Contactless Technologies towards a Smart Tourist Experience. In *WETICE Conference (WETICE), 2014 IEEE 23rd International*. IEEE, pp. 249–54.

Beatson, A., Lee, N. and Coote, L.V. (2007) Self-service technology and the service encounter. *The Service Industries Journal*, 27(1), 75–89.

Belk, R. (2014) You are what you can access: sharing and collaborative consumption online. *Journal of Business Research*, 67(8), 1595–1600.

Benckendorff, P.J., Sheldon, P.J. and Fesenmaier, D.R. (2014) *Tourism information technology*, 2nd edn. Oxford, UK: CAB International.

Dean, J., Apperley, M. and Rogers, B. (2014, January) Refining personal and social presence in virtual meetings. In *Proceedings of the Fifteenth Australasian User Interface Conference-Volume 150*. Australian Computer Society, Inc., pp. 67–75.

Dickinson, J.E., Ghali, K., Cherrett, T., Speed, C., Davies, N. and Norgate, S. (2014) Tourism and the smartphone app: capabilities, emerging practice and scope in the travel domain. *Current Issues in Tourism*, 17(1), 84–101.

Future Foundation (2011) *Beyond 2020: the future of travel*. Online. Available HTTP: <https://nvision.futurefoundation.net/default.aspx>, accessed 8 December 2015.

Gibbs, C. and Gretzel, U. (2015) Drivers of responsive website design innovation by destination marketing organizations. In Tussyadiah, I. and Inversini, A. (eds), *Information and Communication Technologies in Tourism 2015*. Berlin: Springer Verlag, pp. 581–92.

Gibbs, C., Saltzman, J. and Gretzel, U. (2014) Adoption and Features of North American Hotel Mobile Applications. *3rd International Tourism Conference*. Montego Bay, Jamaica, November 9–11, 2014.

Gretzel, U. (2011) Intelligent systems in tourism: a social science perspective. *Annals of Tourism Research*, 38(3), 757–79.

Gretzel, U. (2015) Web 2.0 and 3.0. In Cantoni, L. and Danowski, J.A. (eds), *Communication and Technology*, Handbooks of Communication Science (HOCS) series. Berlin: De Gruyter Mouton, in press.

Gretzel, U., Sigala, M., Xiang, Z. and Koo, C. (2015) Smart tourism: foundations and developments. *Electronic Markets*, 25(3), 179–88.

Gretzel, U., Werthner, H., Koo, C. and Lamsfus, C. (2015) Conceptual foundations for understanding smart tourism ecosystems. *Computers in Human Behavior*, 50, 558–63.

Gustafson, P. (2012) Managing business travel: developments and dilemmas in corporate travel management. *Tourism Management*, 33(2), 276–84.

Hay, B. (2012) Future timelines for the extinction and adoption of new technology in hotels with particular reference to the future use of service and sexual service robots: a manager's perspective. In *CAUTHE 2012: The new golden age of tourism and hospitality; Book 1; Proceedings of the 22nd Annual Conference*. La Trobe University. Online. Available HTTP:: <http://eresearch.qmu.ac.uk/2672/1/eResearch_2672.pdf>, accessed 5 April 2015.

Höjer, M. and Wangel, J. (2015) Smart sustainable cities: definition and challenges. In Hilty, L.M. and Aebischer, B. (eds), *ICT Innovations for Sustainability, Advances in Intelligent Systems and Computing*. New York: Springer, pp. 333–49.

Hornyak, T. (2010) Ferrari-red robots greet visitors to Santander Bank. Online. Available HTTP: <http://www.cnet.com/news/ferrari-red-robots-greet-visitors-to-santander-bank/>, accessed 5 December 2015.

IBM (n.d.) The Four V's of Big Data. Online. Available HTTP: <http://www.ibmbigdatahub.com/infographic/four-vs-big-data>, accessed 1 February 2015.

Jenkins, H. (2014) Participatory culture: from co-creating brand meaning to changing the world. *GfK Marketing Intelligence Review*, 6(2), 34–9.

Kozinets, R.V. (2014) Social brand engagement: a new idea. *GfK Marketing Intelligence Review*, 6 (2), 8–15.

McQuarrie, E.F. and Philips, B.J. (2014) The megaphone effect in social media: how ordinary consumers become style leaders. *GfK Marketing Intelligence Review*, 6(2), 16–20.

Murphy, H.C. and Rottet, D. (2009) An exploration of the key hotel processes implicated in biometric adoption. *International Journal of Contemporary Hospitality Management*, 21(2), 201–12.

Murphy, J., Kalbaska, N., Williams, A., Ryan, P., Cantoni, L. and Horton-Tognazzini, L.C. (2014) Massive open online courses: strategies and research areas. *Journal of Hospitality and Tourism Education*, 26(1), 39–43.

Palumbo, F. and Dominici, G. (2015) Unraveling the complexity of tourist experience with NFC technology and mobile wallets. In Erçetin, Ş.Ş. and Banerjee, S. (eds), *Chaos, Complexity and Leadership 2013*. Springer International Publishing, pp. 189–96.

Pearce, P.L. and Gretzel, U. (2012) Tourism in technology dead zones: documenting experiential dimensions. *International Journal of Tourism Sciences*, 12(2) 1–20.

Persson, J.S. and Mathiassen, L. (2014) Investigating multimodal communication in virtual meetings: the sharing of dynamic representations. *Communications of the Association for Information Systems*, 34(1), 79.

Ryan, P., Williams, A. and Murphy, J. (2013) Current and Future Trends in Hospitality and Tourism Higher Education. Paper presented at the 11th Asia-Pacific CHRIE Conference in Macau, China. Online. Available HTTP: <http://www.consulted.biz/Papers/Ryan,%20Williams%20%26%20Murphy%20-%20Current%20and%20Future%20Trends.pdf>, accessed 10 March 2015.

Wang, D., Xiang, Z. and Fesenmaier, D.R. (2014) Adapting to the mobile world: a model of smartphone use. *Annals of Tourism Research*, 48, 11–26.

Werthner, H. and Klein, S. (1999) *Information Technology and Tourism: a Challenging Relationship*. Vienna, Austria: Springer.

Wöber, K.W. (2000) Benchmarking hotel operations on the Internet: a data envelopment analysis approach. *Information Technology and Tourism*, 3(3), 195–211.

Ye, Q., Law, R. and Gu, B. (2009) The impact of online user reviews on hotel room sales. *International Journal of Hospitality Management*, 28(1), 180–2.

Yeoman, I. (2013) Is I Robot fantasy or reality? Blogpost. Online. Available HTTP: <http://www.tomorrowstourist.com/robot.php>, accessed 17 September 2013.

Yoo, K.H. and U. Gretzel (2008) Use and impact of online travel reviews. In O'Connor, P., Höpken, W. and Gretzel, U. (eds). *Information and Communication Technologies in Tourism*. Vienna, Austria: Springer, pp. 35–46.

Yoo, K.H., Sigala, M. and Gretzel, U. (2015) Exploring TripAdvisor. In Egger, R., Gula, I., Walcher, D. (eds). *Open Tourism: Open Innovation, Crowdsourcing and Collaborative Consumption Challenging the Tourism Industry*. Berlin: Springer. In press.

43

Big Data analytics for the lodging industry

A case study of perceptual mapping of hotel brands using online customer reviews

Matthew Krawczyk and Zheng Xiang

(VIRGINIA TECH UNIVERSITY, USA)

Introduction

Big Data analytics has become one of the most prominent concerns for businesses in recent years, with a majority of firms believing it is crucial for success (Columbus, 2014). Big Data refers to the huge amounts of information being generated through multiple digital sources. These include internet browsing, smartphone processes, social media, financial transactions and many other areas that generate and transmit data (George et al., 2014). The concept of analytics refers to the extraction of key information from these sets of data using sophisticated statistical and technological methods (Chaudhuri et al., 2011). In the context of Big Data, analytics are methods by which a large quantity of data can be analysed, visualised and interpreted with the goal of identifying novel patterns and new business insights. As the lodging industry strives to develop sustainable competitive advantages, the advent of Big Data analytics offers a promising direction for developing tools to support and improve decision-making at both the operational and strategic level, particularly in today's data-rich business environment. For example, a recent survey of revenue managers has shown that data analytics is becoming the number one desired skill set for incoming lodging managers, which underlines the growing importance of technological acumen for those who seek a successful career in the hospitality industry (Kimes, 2011).

The definition of Big Data is often misinterpreted and its actual implementation is not always clear to hospitality industry practitioners (Boyd and Crawford, 2012). Despite the capabilities of large hotel chains to capture and store huge amounts of customer-specific data, the purposes and methods of using Big Data are not fully understood or developed. In order to show how Big Data can help both scholars and practitioners to generate new insights, this chapter will discuss the role of Big Data analytics in the lodging industry by presenting a case study which identifies the consumer perception of hotel brands as represented in online reviews. This chapter is organised as follows: first, a brief review of what Big Data analytics refers to will be presented, followed by specific examples, as well as the limitations, of how Big Data is currently being utilised in the hospitality and tourism industry. Next, a case study is used to illustrate how Big Data can be utilised to create perceptual mapping of hotel brands based upon a large quantity of online customer reviews. Finally, the chapter concludes with future directions for research, and implications for both theory and management.

What is Big Data analytics?

The tremendous growth of new data sources has inspired the so-called Big Data analytics approach to discover and address business problems that cannot be easily solved using conventional methods (e.g., Abrahams et al., 2012; Mayer-Schönberger and Cukier, 2013). Big Data is present in a wide spectrum of fields, ranging from hard sciences such as biology and chemistry, to more socially oriented disciplines including communication, finance and sociology (Chen et al., 2012). While analysis of data is not a new concept, Big Data analytics differ from traditional knowledge construction in three key aspects (McAfee and Brynjolfsson, 2012): first, the sheer *volume* of data has increased tremendously due to the advancement of technologies such as mobile devices and more capable personal computers. The volume has increased to the point where traditional statistical and computing methods are no longer adequate. In order to identify latent patterns and existing trends in this mass of data, new database concepts such as MapReduce have been developed in order to handle the constantly growing amount of data. Second, contributing to the amount of data is the *velocity* of incoming data. With every computer and cell phone user contributing significant data points on an hourly basis, the speed of data being created has reached unprecedented levels. Finally, the *variety* of data presents issues for the previous methods of storing and processing data. With both structured data such as figures in financial transactions, and unstructured data such as those present in online reviews and social media applications, understanding how to apply Big Data analytics for businesses becomes a much more complex challenge than analysis of numerical databases alone (McAfee and Brynjolfsson, 2012).

In response to the changing nature of data, analytic methods have evolved to meet business and academic needs. Statistics are still the central field by which data analysis is conducted; however, tools for processing, classification and clustering of data have changed considerably. The use of algorithms and machine-learning techniques has provided one of the key foci for the study of Big Data. Data is first broken down into smaller chunks and then classified according to the design of the algorithm, allowing for a huge volume of data to be handled in an efficient manner (Cohen et al., 2009). The increase in online content has also given rise to text analytics, which refers to analytical approaches applied to corpuses of unstructured text (Aggarwal and Zhai, 2012). Text analysis of unstructured data represented by online consumer content yields an unsolicited look at consumer perceptions (Pang and Lee, 2008). The changing paradigm of this type of communication is encouraging businesses to change their approach from one-way messages to a conversation between potential consumers and the firm (Lusch et al., 2010). Due to the unstructured nature of this type of data, specific statistical methods must be utilised in order to discern the meaning of what has been written. One approach using text analytics is sentiment analysis, which has been defined as 'the computational detection and study of opinions, sentiments, emotions, and subjectivities in text' (Duan et al., 2013). Typical tasks of sentiment analysis include 1) finding relevance of a source of data for a specific topic or purpose; 2) pre-processing collected data, e.g. tokenising online review content into single words and extracting relevant information from them; and 3) identifying the sentiment surrounding the product or company from these data (Schmunck et al., 2014).

The use of Big Data analytics has been championed through the case of Google and its tracking of pandemic diseases, although its validity has since been challenged due to inaccurate results (Tarran, 2014). These methods are more than just an alternative approach to research;

indeed, they represent a distinct change in the very nature of how we understand the world around us (Boyd and Crawford, 2012). To this end, Big Data analytics tend to follow an exploratory approach, although they are not exclusive of hypothesis testing. This approach contrasts the opinion of some professionals, who argue that the advent of Big Data will make traditional research methods archaic. This belief states that, due to the volume and velocity of Big Data, conventional understanding of human behaviour has become moot and all of the important questions can be answered with enough data (Boyd and Crawford, 2012). However, the subjectivity associated with the processing, analysis, and interpretation of data gathered and the application of knowledge construction still requires much scientific rigor.

Big Data analytics in hospitality and tourism

Recognition by the service industry of the potential of Big Data analytics is nothing new. Multiple sources have promoted Big Data techniques as being key to a more thorough understanding of current and potential customers, as well as being the methods by which to improve efficiency of the business. One of the earliest examples of the utilisation of analytic techniques comes from the gaming industry, in which Harrah's was instrumental in demonstrating that tracking and understanding actual individual consumer preferences could lead to the customisation of a better experience and, subsequently, increase loyalty and related revenues for the company's casinos (Loveman, 2003). Their pioneering work in collecting real behavioural data from individuals led the way for casinos as a whole to make better decisions regarding staffing and game availability. Also, this type of personalised information has enabled the identification of more specific rewards for frequent casino guests based on subsidiaries such as dining options and spa treatments (Ellis, 2014). The theme park industry has also begun to realise the potential of Big Data analytics, tracking guest movement throughout the park via wristband sensors. By monitoring eating and visitation habits of individuals, park management can create a better flow for crowds of people as well as interact on a more personal level with individuals (Palmeri, 2014).

Hotels are able to leverage Big Data for a variety of purposes. So far the two most common practices are customisation of the guest experience and revenue management. Similar to the gaming industry, the tracking of a guest's actions as they enjoy the subsidiary services of the hotel property allows for an immediate response from management. If a guest has shown an affinity for the hotel's restaurants, dining offers can be built in as incentives for return patronage. Knowledge of requests for room types, amenities and even preferences of pillows allow hotels to cater to individual guests for a unique stay. One example of utilisation of Big Data found that guests desired more bathroom storage and additional kitchen features. The analysis of thousands of one hotel chain's online reviews enabled the acknowledgement and subsequent implementation of these ideas, which were met with very positive guest feedback (IBM, 2013). Moreover, the increasing use of social media allows for feedback to hotel management, who can then provide service recovery for issues that might have otherwise gone unnoticed. From the perspective of a revenue manager, Big Data can be used to gain information about booking preferences for travellers as well as to optimise rate structures. The collection of customer information can be accomplished through using large sets of reservations to create aggregate figures, that allow revenue managers to gain an understanding of the property's lead times, realised daily rate revenues and geographic dispersion of incoming guests (Coleman, 2014).

The advent of Web 2.0 brought about a huge amount of consumer generated data in a variety of forms including customer reviews, individual blogs and message boards, to name just a few. They constitute a new and exciting source of information by which we can better understand a vast range of consumer behaviour such as purchasing preferences, motivations for selecting specific services and responses to personal experiences (Pang and Lee, 2008). In particular, online consumer reviews are used by industry professionals in an effort to understand the perception of their properties and services. With customer feedback being essential to understanding the perception of the hotel, many management teams actively follow social media sites in order to better understand the positives and negatives associated with a stay at their property. However, online reviews represent substantially more than just the face value of what is written. When many reviews are considered together, a clearer picture of the general attributes associated with each brand name, as well as how hotel chains are considered similar or dissimilar to each other, can be developed. Previous research has added credence to this concept, showing the ability of online hotel reviews to differentiate rival properties via sentiment analysis, with a clear distinction between the individual hotels (Crotts et al., 2009). Multiple studies have examined online hotel reviews and helped to confirm their appropriateness as a source of unsolicited customer feedback for use in measuring guest satisfaction (Jeong and Jeon, 2008). Other works discuss how user-generated content (UGC) is a reliable source for indicating customer perceptions of hotel quality on a deeper level than an overall rating, giving indications of the varying dimensions comprising the levels of service and product offered by the hotel (García-Barriocanal et al., 2010; Giannakos et al., 2012). A more recent article highlights how consumer reviews can be used to delineate the hotel experience and identify related dimensions that may not be readily evident (Xiang et al., 2015). To date, the great majority of studies involving UGC focus on consumer satisfaction or perceptions of quality from the traveller's hotel stay. However, firms are also able to use this type of review data as a means to understand the market structure as reflected from the customer's point of view. The following case study illustrates the usefulness of Big Data analytics in constructing perceptual mapping of hotel brands based upon a large quantity of online customer reviews.

Case study: perceptual mapping of hotel brands using online customer reviews

Chain hotels use branding as a means to increase the market value of their properties, as well as to signal to customers the nature of the services and products being offered (O'Neill and Xiao, 2006). Subsequently, understanding the position of the brand in the consumer's mind is of vital importance to hotel executives, who can leverage the perception of the brand to compete more effectively for the traveller's consideration (Dev et al., 1995). Brands can be considered intangible assets that can be used by consumers to distinguish a firm from its competitors (Brucks et al., 2000). In the context of the lodging industry, brands are used to measure firms on the weight of their value proposition, indicated by the level of service and product offered (O'Neill and Xiao, 2006). This proposition influences current and potential consumers to consider the firm for purchase, as the brand builds associations in the minds of travellers (O'Neill and Matilla, 2010). An understanding of how a hotel brand is perceived by consumers allows managers to position the firm appropriately in order to better portray their core competencies.

Previous research has examined the concept of hotel branding strategy using perceptual mapping to compare competing firms based on similarities and dissimilarities in attributes such as quality of service, facilities offered and physical features (Dev, 2012; Lewis, 1990). While contributing to a better understanding of the topic, some of these studies have used a priori conditions to explore the issue; this approach yields results based on the researchers' design and can be driven by hypotheses as a result. Also, the majority of these studies used surveys and panel methods to collect data, which are prone to potential response bias as a result of targeted questionnaires and sampling methods. It is argued that the Big Data analytics approach allows for exploration of consumer-generated content without a set of predefined conditions that constrain the research goal; instead, it lets the data speak for itself and the researcher guides this process using his/her domain knowledge to ensure the validity of the research findings. It is thus hoped that, in this case study, a deeper analysis of a large number of online reviews can lead to a generalisable glimpse into travellers' perceptions of hotel brands as identified by their experiences staying at the hotel.

A large set of data was collected from hotel reviews posted on Expedia.com during an eleven day period using a web crawler. These data encompassed hotels from across the United States and included both major hotel chains and independent hotels for a total of 60,648 reviews related to 10,537 hotel properties. For the purposes of this study, only large hotel chains were considered and brands comprised of less than 15 properties were categorised as independent. Hotels were classified according to the brand they were associated with, for example 'Embassy Suites' or 'Days Inn'. Star rating was determined from the rating given on Expedia.com. Five-star and one-star properties represented only 0.4 per cent of the total population and were not present in the data set for every chain, so they were removed from consideration. After removing independent properties and sorting the remaining hotels by their parent company (i.e. Westin was grouped as Starwood, Hampton Inn as Hilton, etc.), a data set consisting of a total of 4,246 properties remained. Some chains (e.g., Marriott and Hilton) had properties in both midscale and upscale categories; however, only the related sub-brands were used in the analysis for their respective categories. Expedia's star rating was used as an indication of the level of amenities and service at the hotel and provided a base upon which to classify hotel properties. Two- and three-star properties were categorised as midscale properties, and four star hotels were grouped together as upscale. This classification was determined with the goal of creating some type of parity across multiple large hotel chains and did not necessarily reflect the true level of service at each property.

Analysis of online reviews followed a standard process of text mining which usually involves several steps of data cleaning, domain identification and statistical association analysis (for details of this process refer to Xiang et al., 2015). First, data cleaning aimed to stem words (coding the several forms of a word into a central form representing the same 'root'), identify and correct misspellings, and remove stop words common to all reviews, such as adverbs and conjunctions. Next, the domain was identified by creating a dictionary of words representing unique concepts. This domain was cross-validated with multiple experts in the field to ensure concept validity. The result had many words that were mentioned infrequently and were only applicable to specific properties based on geographic location ('New York') or features specific to particular brands (i.e. 'Heavenly Bed'). Thus, they could not be compared across multiple hotel properties and were removed. Finally, the frequency of the remaining words was calculated for reviews within each property. These words and their frequencies were used in a correspondence analysis to build a perceptual map to show how each hotel brand was associated with these words. Correspondence analysis was selected for its ability to map categorical data in a common space based on unknown dimensions as well as its frequent use in marketing studies (Greenacre, 2010). Based on the results of initial analysis, a cutoff point of 0.025 per cent frequency of the total word set was selected, as inclusion of words beyond this value did not significantly add to the resulting map.

To understand similarities and differences within each segment, three correspondence maps were created for the midscale, upscale and the combination of the two segments, respectively. The words included in these maps were determined first by including the fifty most frequent words that were identified through the text analysis. Words were added, ten at a time, until the perceptual structure no longer significantly changed, resulting in the inclusion of 100 words to define each correspondence map. The terms and words on the maps reflect frequencies of terms that were common to each chain. Thus, a term that is located in close proximity to a chain reflects a high use of the term in that chain's reviews. The word does not have an associated valence, but shows certain features and concerns common to each chain's properties in the data set. Due to limited space only Figure 43.1 is presented here, showing the combination of the midscale and upscale segments mapped together.

The correspondence maps show some interesting patterns in the perceptual space involving competing hotel brands. First, it is very interesting to note that, in these online reviews, customers did not make explicit references to hotel brands. That is, when they shared their stories about their stay at a specific property, they rarely mentioned the name of the hotel or the brand. Second, while there was a noticeable difference in the position of each brand on all three maps, similarities could be observed among direct competitors. For example, both midscale and upscale brands for Hilton and Marriott were shown to be very similar in consumer perceptions, while La Quinta, Choice, Best Western and Wyndham were all grouped closely together in the midscale map. On the combined map (Figure 43.1), there exists a clear distinction between brands which offer a larger upscale presence and others which are predominantly midscale-oriented. Supporting this distinction were the locations of certain words; 'value', 'cheap' and 'pay' were associated with midscale brands, suggesting a customer perception of value for money. Words such as 'staff', 'spacious', and 'quality' were all mapped closely to upscale brands, perhaps showing an increased concern for a higher standard of products and services. Terms that were paired concepts also were reflected in the correspondence map; 'cheap' and 'expensive' are located at opposite ends of the X axis. In general, it seems that hotel chains have been quite successful in creating distinguishable images within their segments as reflected in the perceptual maps. However, whether these are desirable positions in the market remains a challenging question for hotel chains to answer.

From the perspective of academics, the results showed similar patterns in hotel market structure as identified in previous literature (Dev et al., 1995). This finding is important as it shows the appropriateness of this type of data for answering questions related to consumer perceptions. By confirming the structure of the industry as defined by both firms and previous research, this study shows the usefulness of Big Data analytics for the study of market positioning. The results also show that, while consumers do not explicitly discuss brand-specific concepts, attributes of hotel brands are clearly embedded in these online reviews, although in an implicit way. Consumer emotions that could be tied to individual brands and indicators of brand attributes were found to be very sparse. Instead, relatively innocuous words such as 'room', 'bed' and 'desk' were some of the most commonly used terms in reviews. This finding was not surprising, given the unsolicited nature of online reviews and the lack of prompt for brand information from consumers. Nonetheless, the findings suggest that these patterns emerge to form a clear picture of hotel brands as perceived in the market once these online reviews are aggregated and examined together.

Conclusions and future research

Big Data analytics research in the hospitality and tourism field has been few and far between, with many research opportunities to explore in the future. Hotel practitioners are hoped to benefit through the use of Big Data analytics to take advantage of the wealth of data at their fingertips. Obviously, Big Data analytics will continue to develop to include a wide spectrum

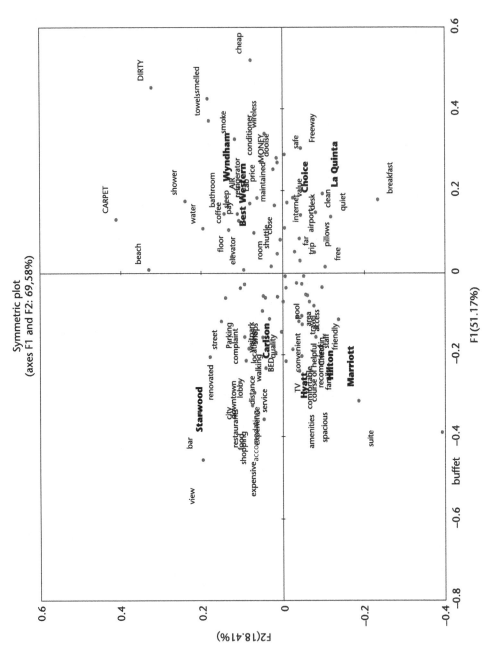

Symmetric plot
(axes F1 and F2: 69,58%)

F1(51.17%)

F2(18.41%)

Figure 43.1 Correspondence map of midscale and upscale segments combined.

of sources and analytical approaches. For example, mobile technology can also be used to understand the patterns of guests as they move through upscale and luxury properties, allowing for better planning of amenities as well as addressing the needs of the guest before check-out (Kim et al., 2012). In this chapter, the case study highlights one application of analytics, although many other questions are left unanswered. Nonetheless, this study shows that the ability to compare one's brand with others using customer sentiment is an important tool to ensure that your firm is being perceived the way you prefer. Taken a step further, the review data could be classified through factor analysis, and the underlying dimensions creating the separation in brands could be better understood. Also, these dimensions could be used to predict the classification of a property into a brand, adding new value to this type of analysis. Potentially, future studies in Big Data can lead to a better understanding of the market structure of the lodging industry in the eyes and minds of the consumers (Lee and Bradlow, 2011; Netzer et al., 2012).

References

Abrahams, A.S., Jiao, J., Wang, G.A. and Fan, W. (2012) Vehicle defect discovery from social media. *Decision Support Systems*, 54(1), 87–97.

Aggarwal, C.C. and Zhai, C. (2012) *Mining Text Data*. New York: Springer.

Boyd, D. and Crawford, K. (2012) Critical questions for Big Data: provocations for a cultural, technological, and scholarly phenomenon. *Information, Communication and Society*, 15(5), 662–79.

Brucks, M., Zeithaml, V.A. and Naylor, G. (2000) Price and brand name as indicators of quality dimensions for consumer durables. *Journal of the Academy of Marketing Science*, 28(3), 359–74.

Chaudhuri, S., Dayal, U. and Narasayya, V. (2011) An overview of business intelligence technology. *Communications of the ACM*, 54(8), 88–98.

Chen, H., Chiang, R.H. and Storey, V.C. (2012) Business intelligence and analytics: From big data to big impact. *MIS Quarterly*, 36(4), 1165–88.

Cohen, J., Dolan, B., Dunlap, M., Hellerstein, J.M. and Welton, C. (2009) *MAD skills: New analysis practices for Big Data*. Proceedings of the VLDB Endowment, 2(2), 1481–92.

Coleman, K. (June 23, 2014) Business intelligence provides answers to hotel revenue management questions. Online. Available HTTP: <http://www.hospitalitynet.org/column/154000392/4065891. html>, accessed 10 December 2015.

Columbus, L. (Oct 19, 2014) 84% of enterprises see Big Data analytics changing their industries' competitive landscapes in the next year. *Forbes Magazine*. Online. Available HTTP: <http://www. forbes.com/sites/louiscolumbus/2014/10/19/84-of-enterprises-see-big-data-analytics-changing-their-industries-competitive-landscapes-in-the-next-year/>, accessed 10 December 2015.

Crotts, J.C., Mason, P.R. and Davis, B. (2009) Measuring guest satisfaction and competitive position in the hospitality and tourism industry: an application of stance-shift analysis to travel blog narratives. *Journal of Travel Research*, 48(2), 139–51.

Dev, C. (2012) *Hospitality Branding*. Ithaca: Cornell University Press.

Dev, C.S., Morgan, M.S. and Shoemaker, S. (1995) A positioning analysis of hotel brands: based on travel-manager perceptions. *The Cornell Hotel and Restaurant Administration Quarterly*, 36(6), 48–55.

Duan, W., Cao, Q., Yu, Y. and Levy, S. (2013) Mining online user-generated content: using sentiment analysis technique to study hotel service quality. In *System Sciences (HICSS), 2013 46th Hawaii International Conference*. IEEE, pp. 3119–28.

Ellis, B. (2014) Turning big data into actionable data. Online. Available HTTP: <http://hotelexecutive. com/business_review/4079/turning-big-data-into-actionable-data>, accessed 10 December 2015.

García-Barriocanal, E., Sicilia, M.A. and Korfiatis, N. (2010) Exploring hotel service quality experience indicators in user-generated content: a case using Tripadvisor data. In *Proceedings of the 5th Mediterranean Conference of Information Systems (MCIS)*. Association of Information Systems (AIS), Tel-Aviv, Israel, p. 33.

George, G., Haas, M R. and Pentland, A. (2014) Big Data and management. *Academy of Management Journal*, 57(2), 321–6.

Giannakos, M.N., Pateli, A. and Pappas, I. (2012) Investigation of the hotel customers' perceptions: a study based on user-generated content of online booking platforms. In *Proceedings of 2nd Advances in Hospitality and Tourism Marketing and Management Conference, (AHTMMC'12)*. Online. Available HTTP: <http://users.ionio.gr/~mgiannak/AHTMMC_2011.pdf>, accessed 10 December 2015.

Greenacre, M. (2010) *Correspondence Analysis in Practice*. London: Chapman & Hall/CRC Press.

IBM News Report (Nov. 04, 2013) IBM big data and analytics translates into big hotel room bookings for Denihan hospitality group. Online. Available HTTP: <http://www-03.ibm.com/press/us/en/pressrelease/42343.wss>, accessed 10 December 2015.

Jeong, M. and Jeon, M. (2008) Customer reviews of hotel experiences through consumer generated media (CGM). *Journal of Hospitality and Leisure Marketing*, 17(1-2), 121–38.

Kim, T., McFee, E., Olguin, D.O., Waber, B. and Pentland, A. (2012) Sociometric badges: using sensor technology to capture new forms of collaboration. *Journal of Organizational Behavior*, 33(3), 412–27.

Kimes, S.E. (2011). The future of hotel revenue management. *Journal of Revenue and Pricing Management*, 10(1), 62–72.

Lee, T.Y. and Bradlow, E.T. (2011). Automated marketing research using online customer reviews. *Journal of Marketing Research*, 48(5), 881–94.

Lewis, R.C. (1990) Advertising your hotel's position. *Cornell Hotel and Restaurant Administration Quarterly*, 31(2), 84–91.

Loveman, G. (2003) Diamonds in the data mine. *Harvard Business Review*, 81(5), 109–13.

Lusch, R.F., Liu, Y. and Chen, Y. (2010) The phase transition of markets and organizations: the new intelligence and entrepreneurial frontier. *IEEE Intelligent Systems*, 25(1), 71–5.

Mayer-Schönberger, V. and Cukier, K. (2013) *Big Data: a Revolution that will Transform How we Live, Work, and Think*. Massachusetts, US: Eamon Dolan/Houghton Mifflin Harcourt.

McAfee, A. and Brynjolfsson, E., (2012) Big Data. The management revolution. *Harvard Business Review*, 90(10), 61–7.

Netzer, O., Feldman, R., Goldenberg, J. and Fresko, M. (2012) Mine your own business: market-structure surveillance through text mining. *Marketing Science*, 31(3), 521–43.

O'Neill, J.W. and Mattila, A.S. (2010) Hotel brand strategy. *Cornell Hospitality Quarterly*, 51(1), 27–34.

O'Neill, J.W. and Xiao, Q. (2006) The role of brand affiliation in hotel market value. *Cornell Hotel and Restaurant Administration Quarterly*, 47(3), 210–23.

Palmeri, C. (March 07, 2014) Disney bets $1 billion on technology to track theme-park visitors. Online. Available HTTP: <http://www.businessweek.com/articles/2014-03-07/disney-bets-1-billion-on-technology-to-track-theme-park-visitors>, accessed 10 December 2015.

Pang, B. and Lee, L. (2008) Opinion mining and sentiment analysis. *Foundations and Trends in Information Retrieval*, 2(1-2), 1–135.

Schmunk, S., Höpken, W., Fuchs, M. and Lexhagen, M. (2014). Sentiment analysis: extracting decision-relevant knowledge from UGC. In Xiang, Z. and Tussyadiah, I. (eds) *Information and Communication Technologies in Tourism, Proceedings of the International Conference in Dublin, Ireland, January 21–24, 2014*. Switzerland: Springer International Publishing, pp. 253–65.

Tarran, B. (Oct. 03, 2014) Tim Harford, and the perils of Big Data. Online. available HTTP: <http://www.statslife.org.uk/science-technology/1748-tim-harford-and-the-perils-of-big-data>, accessed 10 December 2015.

Xiang, Z., Schwartz, Z., Gerdes, J. and Uysal, M. (2015) What can big data and text analytics tell us about hotel guest experience and satisfaction? *International Journal of Hospitality Management*, 44(1), 120–30.

44

Brand extension: from a restaurant chain to a hotel chain

Anderson Gomes de Souza, Maria de Lourdes Barbosa and Mariana Bueno de Andrade Matos

(UNIVERSIDADE FEDERAL DE PERNAMBUCO – UFPE, BRAZIL)

Introduction

Branding has become one of the most dominant trends in the global hospitality industry. In the US, the penetration ratio of hotel chains in the tourism market has increased sharply during the past years (Forgacs, 2006). Following market growth worldwide, several organisations have sought to expand their business into new and unexplored markets. Accordingly, hotel companies have become multi-brand organisations at the same time as they seek ways to strengthen their major brand, in order to establish market differentiation (Richter, 2004; Gardini, 2014).

The high frequency with which new brands, goods and services appear is a reflection of the fact that companies need to differentiate themselves from, and position themselves against competitors. Under such circumstances, brand value becomes an essential asset for the survival of these organisations (Sinclair and Keller, 2014). Brand value is a specific attribute, and it contributes to the formation of images in the consumer's mind, being a brand's equity strategy, according to Keller (2003a). In this context, brand extensions emerge as one of the core strategies used to build up brand value and its distinction in the market.

Therefore, the main reasons to adopt the brand extension strategy are related to the improvement of consumers' acceptance toward a certain company whenever a new product is launched, besides the likelihood of implementing an economy of scale, which might help strengthen and revitalise an existing brand (Aaker, 1998; Keller, 2003b). Thus, brand extension leads to reciprocal effects that may increase or decrease the value of the major brand (Swaminathan et al., 2001), and hence, influence consumer's overall evaluation.

Brand extension strategy is, to some extent, a quite common practice in the hotel sector, where new enterprises tend to be introduced to the market by taking advantage of the success of a chain (Gardini, 2014), thus using the power of the latter as a lever to succeed. A great example of the successful adoption of this strategy can be attributed to the Holiday Inn chain.

During the last decades, the major brand 'Holiday Inn' has extended its original concept to include the Holiday Inn Express, Holiday Inn Select, The Inn at Resorts, Crowne Plaza by Holiday Inn and the Staybridge Suites by Holiday Inn. The purpose behind the strategy adopted by the chain is to penetrate, and hence compete within different market segments, with distinctive price levels.

However, not surprisingly several companies in the hospitality industry, such as restaurants, have also directed their attentions to the relevance of brand extension (Mukherjee, 2014). According to Muller (1998), some businesses in the gastronomy sector, for instance, have restructured their orientation in order to enhance brand presence in the market. Consequently, the adoption of this strategy often results in great opportunities for expanding the company's brand into new categories of services, which includes the lodging market.

Based on what has been presented, this chapter explores the case of an upscale restaurant brand, established in São Paulo, Brazil, whose prominence and prestige in the market led to the expansion of business into a luxury hotel chain, which has recently entered the international market. Thus, it becomes noticeable that the process of brand extension is likely to occur in an integrative way within the hotel industry. However, rather than being an example, the case presented herein proves to be a singular event where the brand extension process occurred from the restaurant to the hotel brand, in opposition to the pathway frequently adopted by firms in the lodging sector.

Branding: the creation of value for hotel chains

Brands constitute the greatest expression of a firm's attempt to establish market distinction between themselves and several rivals competing within a specific sector. They reflect and reinforce the identity of a product/company, helping customers and clients make conscious choices, based on the promises that give rise to their expectations toward certain goods/ services being acquired (Tuškej et al., 2013). In this sense, brands connect to the consumption logic as it can be responsible for determining consumer's behaviour.

The importance of branding for the hotel industry relies on the fact that achieving differentiation in such a competitive market can only be possible by adding great value to the services offered. Thus, rather than strictly translating a firm's positioning strategies, it is quite evident that hotel brands have become a powerful tool for increasing consumers' attitudes toward the set of characteristics that define certain enterprises (Mahasuweerachai and Qu, 2015).

Creating a distinctive hotel brand is not as simple as it might seem. That is probably the reason why hotel chains employ massive efforts to strengthen their image in order to maintain and enhance their position. After all, brand is now part of a business's assets. And so, the impression that the market holds about a company determines and assures its own sustainable survival (Sinclair and Keller, 2014).

The emergence of the concept of 'brand equity', during the 1980s, called the attention of marketing scholars and practitioners to the role played by the brand in a company's success. According to Keller (2003a), the aforementioned term is not exclusively related to the functional features of a single product, rather it expresses the commercial value that derives from the consumer's perception toward a particular organisation.

Moreover, Keller and Machado (2006) state that brand equity means a set of intangible attributes that a given brand is capable of transferring into a company's offer, being represented by the positive associations consumers tend to make with the brand. By acknowledging this, hotel chain managers make plans and seek ways to control their firms' brand image in order to obtain a certain level of prestige, as well as distinguishing their offer in the hospitality market.

Another critical issue when it comes to hotel chains' branding decisions is with respect to brand positioning. Aaker (1996) points out some benefits that a well-conceived brand can bring to a company. First, when the brand is already established in the market it becomes easier for the organisation to cope with some orientation matters. Consequently, new opportunities for expanding brand reach appear and, hence, increase the chain's potential of competitiveness. Furthermore, a solid position also gives the company a chance to broaden their own business, as will be discussed later in this chapter.

In that sense, positioning a hotel chain's brand represents a strategic decision in several aspects. It implies the effective definition of relationship strategies, distribution channels and target markets, among other managerial priorities (Furrier, 2008). However, in every situation it must be recognised by the organisation that successful brands should be strongly connected to reality. That is, they have not only to satisfy consumers' needs, but further, match their expectations in terms of functional and emotional attributes.

Consequently, the creation of value demands that cautious decisions are made in order to enhance the company's opportunities for expansion. Therefore, the subsequent topic will address some issues concerning the strategies usually adopted by hotel chains to expand their offer system to different markets. It is nevertheless surprising that branding questions appear to be so closely related to most of these decisions.

Hotel chains' branding strategies

Marketing strategies are used in different ways by various organisations according to certain characteristics, such as their size, culture, objectives and competitive position in the market. Notwithstanding, companies decide to adopt not a specific strategy, but a combination of them in accordance with their needs and, consequently, the market in which they operate (Serralvo, 2008).

Some of the core brand strategies used by firms in the market are 'multi-brands', 'co-branding', 'trading-down/trading-up' and 'brand extension'. Multi-brand strategy occurs when two or more brands of similar products are owned by one company. This strategy is widely employed by the beauty industry to launch new products (Serralvo, 2008). Leuthesser et al. (2003) state that co-branding occurs when two different companies (with different brands) decide to work together in order to create a new product. Such a strategy, also known as 'brand alliance' or 'composite branding', aims to combine forces to reach a stronger position for their product in the market.

The trading-down or trading-up strategy is likely to be adopted when a certain brand decides to decrease (or increase) its position (e.g. the launch of new products aiming to reach different target audiences, for instance shifting from a luxury to a popular market). Finally, brand extension strategy occurs when a new product, directed to a new target market, uses a well-established brand name as a 'parent brand', as stated by Aaker and Keller (1990).

Among the aforementioned strategies, brand extension has been the one most frequently adopted by the hotel industry. Accordingly, the value added by the major brand helps a new product reach a larger share of the intended audience and, hence, succeed in the market (Mollahosseini et al., 2011). The greatest feature of this strategy is related to the product launch costs reduction, since the brand is already well recognised in the market. A great example of a successful adoption of brand extension in the hotel industry is the Holiday Inn chain. The company has been extending its brand to several secondary brands in the sector, such as the Holiday Inn Express, Holiday Inn Select, Holiday Inn Sunspree Resorts, Crowne Plaza by Holiday Inn and so forth. It results in a wider range of markets served by the chain, which certainly rely on the image associated with the major brand, adding credibility and value to the services offered (Kim, 2010).

However, it is important to point out that despite being the most commonly used strategy in the hotel industry, brand extension also presents some risks for companies. According to Serralvo (2008), a negative event (or experience) in any of the hotels belonging to the same brand is likely to affect the entire chain, thus causing harm to its long-standing reputation. Another situation that must be considered herein is that the major brand can also lose its position in the market if customers fail to associate it with a particular service. That would lead to the dilution of the brand, decreasing its presence in the market.

Nevertheless, hotel chains have largely adopted the brand extension strategy not only in terms of extending their market share exclusively, but also by aiming to diversify the range of services offered in the hospitality sector. A very clear example of this is the expansion of several hotel chains into the food and beverage business. According to Kim (2010), some hotel chains have been relying on their major brand in order to expand the company business into these sectors, thus achieving higher profitability levels (Mahasuweerachai and Qu, 2015).

By adopting this strategy, hotel chains seek to extend their well-established brand reputation to the restaurants belonging to the same chain. Although this is a practice largely employed by the hotel industry, brand extension can also follow a different pathway. That means, in some cases – to a certain extent still rarely – a restaurant brand can be extended to a hotel chain.

The extension of brands into hotel chains

Brand extension has largely been one of the core strategies used by companies in the hospitality sector since the 1980s. By doing so, firms tend to use a well-recognised brand name in order to establish new product categories or classes (Keller and Aaker, 1992). Accordingly, they increase brand equity not only because customers more easily recognise the chain to which the hotel belongs, but also due to the credibility acquired by the company over the years.

A successful brand positively influences the launch of a new service category, for instance, from the moment a company considers the fact that brand extension may decrease the risks perceived by consumers (Aaker, 1990). Consequently, customers' positive attitudes toward a hotel chain results in the need for less investments in marketing promotions, which helps reduce the organisation's overall costs. Well-established chains, such as Marriott, Hilton and Accor have followed the aforementioned pathway and succeeded (Jiang et al., 2002).

Moreover, lately the hospitality industry has been faced with the fact that firms, outside the sector, have also attempted to get into the hotel business. The new scenario shows that brands, such as Armani (http://www.armanihotels.com), Bulgari (http://www.bulgarihotels.com) and Salvatore Ferragano (http://www.lungarnocollection.com), originally powerful within the fashion world, have been using their strong reputation to expand their business into the hospitality sector. It is also noteworthy that, recently, some other companies (e.g. EasyJet (http://www.easyhotel.com) and Virgin Airlines (http://www.virginhotels.com) have invested a great amount of money in new businesses, such as cafeterias, restaurants and, also, hotels.

All the aforementioned brands have focused exclusively on the luxury market. But what drives those successful companies to invest in such a complex sector as hospitality? Although it must be recognised that it is a very bold decision, the strategy seems to have been succeeding so far. And the only explanation for this may be the strong connections, made by consumers, between the new businesses and their major brands. Therefore, brand extension strategy points to a great opportunity for successful companies to enhance and perpetuate the concept of a well-established identity of product quality in a given market. The next section will look at a particular case of brand extension in the hotel sector, in which instead of a hotel chain originating a restaurant, a restaurant gave rise to a successful hotel chain in Brazil.

The case of a Brazilian hotel chain

The Fasano Restaurant (http://www.fasano.com.br) is currently one of the most valuable Brazilian gastronomy brands. Its historical trajectory began over a century ago and, during this time span, it has become an outstanding reference for luxury in Brazil. The credibility built by the group, on the basis of its distinctive features, has helped consolidate its identity, which consequently led its managers to extend the brand in order to enter the competitive hotel industry.

It has been argued in this chapter that the extension of hotel chains' brand is a phenomenon, to certain extent consolidated in the lodging market. It basically evolves multi-brand organisations competing with each other to increase their market share, based on brand equity (Richter, 2004). In this sense, several hotel chains have developed multiple brands aiming to serve multiple markets (Jiang et al., 2002). Accordingly, the value of brands is based on its awareness, quality perception and the overall satisfaction of the customers (Aaker, 1991).

Most of the hotel brands currently found in the market are nothing but extensions of certain well-established chains. Intercontinental Hotel, Wyndham Hotel, Marriott International, Hilton Hotels, Accor, among others, are great examples of chains that clearly adopt the brand extension strategy in order to expand their businesses. Moreover, market experience has shown that such a strategy is effective not only in terms of segmentation. Thus strong hotel chains' brands provide the basis for the creation of secondary, yet competitive services for a company.

When it comes specifically to the Food and Beverage department – F&B, the services arising from the extension of a major brand (hotel chain) represent a significant portion of a company's profitability (Mandelbaum, 2001). Therefore, it is not surprising that brand extension has been largely applied within the hotel industry as a means to expand businesses into the food and beverage segment. Kim (2010) argues that, particularly in Korea, such a practice has proved to be extremely successful, given the positive responses that have been observed, by hotel chains, from the market. Thus, brand extension in the hospitality industry seems to have become a natural path to be followed by most companies.

However, the Brazilian lodging sector faced a different sort of situation. While most hotel chains expand their market share by extending a complex and diverse service, such as hotels, to a more specific and focused one (restaurants), the Fasano followed the opposite direction. That is, Brazil shows a very singular case in which a restaurant brand gave rise to a successful hotel chain. In that sense, the Fasano case stands out for having started its career by providing a much focused service – F&B, and later extending their offer into a more complex and multifaceted luxury hotel service.

It is important, therefore, to explore how the Fasano brand was first created so that it becomes possible to understand its extension process. The brand was founded in 1902, when the Italian citizen of Milan, Vittorio Fasano, moved to São Paulo, Brazil, to take over his family's coffee importing business. A few years after his death, in 1947, his youngest son, Ruggero, decided to resume the family's business.

In 1982, the third generation of the family took control of the business. Fabrizio Fasano, Vittorio's grandson, then invited his son, Roger, to start a new business in town. In 1984 the brand became even more prominent within the Brazilian gastronomy scene, being considered a reference of quality, distinction and luxury. Such a context led, by the 1990s, to a rapid expansion process of the Fasano Group, with the emergence of new businesses in the food and beverage sector.

After dedicating over a hundred years to the gastronomy activities, with a strong consolidation of their business in that field, the heir of the group decided to extend the family's brand to the hotel industry, taking advantage of the secular experience and reputation built by the family. Thus, in 2003, the very first hotel establishment of the chain was founded. The Hotel Fasano, located in São Paulo, came about as part of a partnership between the Fasano Group and João Paulo Diniz, heir of the Pão de Açúcar Group. The latter was a Brazilian national leader in the field of food and grocery retailing, also the largest retail company in Latin America, with over 2,143 establishments in the market.

However, the partnership that had been sealed in 1998 ended in March 2007, when the Hotel Fasano was taken over by the JHSF Group (http://jhsf.com.br), a leading upscale real estate company in Brazil. The JHSF Group's businesses include commercial and residential property sales, the development and management of malls, besides its intensive presence in the international executive aviation industry. With the merger, JHSF now controls 50 per cent of the Fasano Hotel Chain. JHSF was the first company in their segment to incorporate a hospitality business into its activities. This initiative has added even more value to their projects, by associating its image with an internationally well-recognised brand.

Carrying on the expansion strategy of the chain, in 2007, the Hotel Fasano began operating in the city of Rio de Janeiro, also in Brazil. Just a few years later, the successful partnership with the JHSF Group led to an international penetration of the chain. In 2010, the first establishment was finally settled abroad, in Punta del Este (La Barra), Uruguay. Following the Fasano chain pattern, the hotel is considered one of the finest establishments of Uruguay. Back to the Brazilian market, in 2011, the chain launched the Hotel Fasano Boa Vista, located in Boa Vista, less than 100 km away from the city of São Paulo. As part of their internationalisation strategy, the Fasano chain intends now to compete within the North American hospitality market. Their primary plans are to settle their business initially in New York City, possibly expanding it to other parts of the country.

Both credibility and value aggregated to the Fasano brand were important features of the group over the years. Its outstanding position in the hospitality sector is constantly reinforced by the awards the chain has received over its career. The Year's Luxury Hotel (4 Wheels Magazine Award), Leading Showcase (Leading Hotels of the World), Trendiest Hotel in Brazil (Trip Advisor), among others, are examples of the grandiosity reached by the chain.

The presentation of the group's history contributes to a better understanding of the Fasano restaurants brand, which allowed them to build up the credibility that led to its extension into the Fasano hotels brand. The brand extension model proposed by Aaker and Keller (1990) reinforces the need for the companies to work on aspects such as similarity, perceived quality, credibility, perceived risk and innovation. However, Hem et al. (2003) point out the first two factors as being of special interest when it comes to the services industry, which is the case of restaurants and hotels.

The similarity between the major brand and its extensions is an essential element for the hospitality sector. According to Aaker and Keller (1990), when a company decides to expand its brand into different products, but still maintaining the similarity of what is offered, as in the case of restaurants and hotels, customers tend to evaluate the firm's brand more positively. The emphasis given by the Fasano Group to keeping a certain similarity between their restaurants and hotels services proves that the company has been trying to improve its chances of winning the trust of its consumers, as recommended by Ruyter and Wetzels (2000).

With regard to the perceived quality, Völckner and Sattler (2006) developed a model in which they show that three main factors may affect the success of a brand extension process: (a) major brand's strength (related to the quality of personal interactions), (b) physical environment of the major brand (the influence of environment on the assessment of consumers), (c) perceived quality and similarity with the major brand. Therefore, it is important to note that when consumers recognise the quality of the major brand, the likelihood of succeeding in a brand extension process increases sharply (Aaker and Keller, 1990). Thus, perceived quality becomes an essential factor, especially when it comes to the services sector, due to its characteristics, including intangibility, simultaneity and heterogeneity.

Through the successful history of development and management presented herein, the Fasano Hotel chain shows that its brand has been strongly consolidated throughout its existence. The business that initially was intended to operate as a complex of restaurants, extended its activities and succeeded as a renowned luxury hotel chain. Certainly, this success originated from the well-established Fasano brand that, undoubtedly, managed to transfer their food and beverage experience and reputation to hotel operations. The outcome of this strategy can be easily observed in the synergy that characterises the luxury image held by the Fasano chain within the hospitality market.

Considerations

This chapter dealt with brand extension in the hospitality industry, addressing issues such as value and brand strategy. From this discussion, it was found that the long-term success of a specific case of brand extension is related to the success of the brand of the company that gave birth to it. Branding remains a research topic of relevance for studies in tourism and hospitality. It has proved to be important for both researchers and practitioners in terms of providing new insights on how to develop successful brands in the sector.

According to what has been presented in this chapter, brand extension strategy has been largely employed by hotel chains worldwide. Several cases show that the brands representing hotel establishments tend to give rise to new enterprises, which take advantage of the image held by the brands. However, such a strategy is not exclusively adopted when a certain chain decides to set up a new hotel project, but sometimes the power of the brand is used to endorse other services also related to the hospitality industry.

A growing number of tourism companies, such as food and hotel chains (e.g. Holiday Inn, Marriott, Virgin Group, Accor, Pizza Hut, Carlson Rezidor Hotel Group, Walt Disney and so forth) have expanded their brands over the years. In this sense, the Brazilian case of the Fasano chain has showed that a restaurant brand can also give rise to the emergence of a successful hotel chain. Since its foundation, in 2003, the Hotel Fasano chain has proved to be an exceptional case, revealing that brand extension in the hospitality industry is not always a one-way road. Instead, it announces the possibility that a prosperous hotel chain can arise from any existing and successful brand in the market – in the case discussed in this chapter, a restaurant brand.

Therefore, the hotel industry must be open to new opportunities. It means that all of those directly involved with the sector need to find ways to take advantage of the diverse scenarios.

The purpose of this chapter was to arouse the interest of hotel managers, students and scholars about alternative ways to approach the brand extension subject when it comes to hotel chains. Marketing strategies find a fertile field in the hotel industry. Thus, everyone in the sector should be prepared and willing to thrive in such a promising business.

References

Aaker, D. (1991) *Managing Brand Equity*. New York: Simon & Schuster.

Aaker, D. (1996) *Criando e Administrando Marcas de Sucesso*. São Paulo: Futura.

Aaker, D. (1998) *Marcas-Brand Equity: Gerenciando o Valor da Marca*. 2nd edn. São Paulo: Negócio.

Aaker, D. and Keller, K. (1990) Consumer evaluations of brand extensions. *Journal of Marketing*, 54(1), 27–41.

Aaker, D.A. (1990) Brand extensions: the good, the bad, and the ugly. *Sloan Management Review*, 31(4), 47–56.

Forgacs, G. (2006) *Brand asset and a balancing act in the hotel industry*. Online. Available HTTP: <http://www.hotel-online.com/News/PR2004_3rd/Jul04_BrandAsset.html>, accessed 10 December 2015.

Furrier, M. (2008) Posicionamento e reposicionamento de marcas. In: F. Serralvo et al. (eds), *Gestão de Marcas no Contexto Brasileiro*. São Paulo: Saraiva, pp. 163–209.

Gardini, M. (2014) The challenge of branding and brand management: perspectives from the hospitality industry. In H. Pechlaner and E. Smeral (eds), *Tourism and Leisure: Current Issues and Perspectives of Development*. Wiesbaden: Springer Fachmedien Wiesbaden, pp. 247–68.

Hem, L., Chernatony, L. and Iversen, N. (2003) Factors influencing successful brand extensions. *Journal of Marketing Management*. 19 (7/8, August), 781–806.

Jiang, W., Dev, C. and Rao, V. (2002) Brand extension and customer loyalty: evidence from the lodging industry. *Cornell Hotel and Restaurant Administration Quarterly*, 43(4), 5–16.

Keller, K. (2003a) *Strategic Brand Management: Building, Measuring and Managing Brand Equity*. 2nd edn. Upper Saddle River: Prentice-Hall.

Keller, K. (2003b) Brand synthesis: the multidimensionality of brand knowledge. *Journal of Consumer Research*. 29(4), 595–601.

Keller, K. and Aaker, D. (1992) The effect of sequential introduction of brand extensions. *Journal of Marketing Research*, 29(1), 35–50.

Keller, K. and Machado, M. (2006) *Gestão Estratégica de Marcas*. São Paulo: Pearson.

Kim, C. (2010) *Brand Extensions for Hotels' Food and Beverage Expansion to the Outside of Property: a Case of Westin Chosun Hotel in Korea*. UNLV, Korea.

Leuthesser, L., Kohli, C. and Suri, R. (2003) 2+2=5? A framework for using co-branding to leverage a brand. *Brand Management*, 11(1), 35–47.

Mahasuweerachai, P. and Qu, H. (2015) The effect of multiple hotel brand extensions. *Tourism and Hospitality Research*, 15(1), 27–38.

Mandelbaum, R. (2001) The changing role of hotel F&B. Online. Available HTTP: <http://www.hotel-online.com/News/PR2001_1st/Jan01_F&BRoles.html>, accessed 10 December 2015.

Mollahosseini, A., Kermaniand, Z. and Abassi, A. (2011) Identification and investigation of effective factors on consumer's primary attitudes formation towards brand extension of Pegah company of Kerman. *Journal of Business and Retail Management Research*, 5(2), 71–81. Online. Available HTTP <http://connection.ebscohost.com/c/articles/64446964/identification-investigation-effective-factors-consumers-primary-attitudes-formation-towards-brand-extension-pegah-company-kerman>, accessed 10 December 2015.

Mukherjee, J. (2014) Market development by multinational brands: empirical evidence from Indian fast food retailing business. *Vision: the Journal of Business Perspective*, 18(1), 1–7.

Muller, C. (1998) Endorsed branding: the next step in restaurant-brand management. *Cornell Hotel and Restaurant Administration Quarterly*, 39(3), 90–6.

Richter, A. (2004) ISHC top 10 list signals shifting priorities. Hotel Interactive. Online. Available HTTP: <http://www.hotelinteractive.net/article.aspx?articleid=3934>, accessed 10 April 2015.

Ruyter, K. and Wetzels, M. (2000) The role of corporate image and extension similarity in service brand extensions. *Journal of Economic Psychology*, 21(6), 639–59.

Serralvo, F. (2008) *Gestão de Marcas no Contexto Brasileiro*. São Paulo: Saraiva.

Sinclair, R. and Keller, K. (2014) A case for brands as assets: acquired and internally developed. *Journal of Brand Management*, 21(4), 286–302.

Swaminathan, V., Richard, F. and Srinivas, R. (2001) The impact of Brand Extension Introduction on choice. *Journal of Marketing*, 65(4), 1–15.

Tuškej, U., Golob, U. and Podnar, K. The role of consumer-brand identification in building brand relationships. *Journal of Business Research*, 66(1), 53–9.

Völckner, F. and Sattler, H. (2006). Drivers of brand extensions success. *Journal of Marketing*, 70(2), 18–34.

45

Bleisure: business and leisure equilibrium in contemporary hotel chains

Magdalena Kachniewska

(WARSAW SCHOOL OF ECONOMICS, POLAND)

Introduction

Changes in the experience and use of time have been among the most spectacular trends in modern times (Haller et al., 2013). Relatively recent changes that occurred in production, the ever growing industrialisation and eventually greater earnings, resulted in two opposites. On the one hand, growing rationalisation of work produced more free time with new possibilities for spending time, enjoying leisure, improving recreation, creating culture and travelling abroad (Nahrstedt, 1998). On the other hand, nearly everyone in Western society suffers from a frightful shortage of time. Time is physically limited, compared to the abundance of commodities, made available by the progress in technology and productivity. This lack of time is apparent not only from the quick tempo of our lives and from our crowded schedules but also from the manner in which the modern family spends its time.

The well-researched acceleration of time was brought forward by scientific and technological inventions in the areas of communication, transportation and industrial production (Toffler, 1970; Schor, 1993; Sennett, 1998; Rosa, 2005; Seidel and Verwiebe, 2006). Economic science has always claimed that increased welfare will offer more leisure time. But today, nothing seems to be as scarce as time. One of the causes for this miscalculation by economists is their neglect of the time aspect of consumption (Linder, 1970; Goudzwaard, 1979). In modern industrial societies people allocate a significant fraction of their disposable time to consumption activities. There can be little doubt that the pattern of combination of time and commodities basically affects lifestyles and consumptive behaviour (Schipper et al., 1989; Jalas, 2002; Sanne, 2005; Cogoy, 2007). A curtailment of action events such as time for eating, sleeping and communication results in an increasing 'time consciousness' when conducting such actions (Garhammer, 1999, 2002; Towers et al., 2006). Consequently, it has been observed since the early 1970s that consumers in rich countries have become harried in their futile attempt to increase even the productivity of their non-work time (Linder, 1970). Cogoy (2010) states that time is an input as necessary as are commodities, since no pleasure, or 'utility', can be derived from consumption without making use of a portion of the permanent flow of time, and the pattern of combination of time and commodities significantly determines the outcome (Becker, 1965, 1976; Michael and Becker, 1973; Gronau, 1977, 1986; Juster and Stafford, 1991).

For the modern leisure class that time became more harried inadvertently. In their haste to buy gadgets to increase the yield of their leisure time, they were often blind to the maintenance requirement of many goods. For example, many who have acquired a swimming pool have been unhappily surprised to find themselves obliged to clean it. Having a garden means mowing the lawn. Similarly, they may have over-committed themselves to recognition-enhancing activities that tend to overrun estimated time—life balance. And employers have to meet their demands. Major companies, embroiled in the battle to attract the very best graduates, are doing whatever they can to lure them in. Instead of stressing higher salaries, some international companies highlight the opportunity for flexible hours, the chance to work from home, and the offer of up to a year of 'family leave' to look after children or elderly parents. One of the most interesting elements of modern social packages is a possibility to blur business travels and leisure.

The consumption-related nature and consequences of globalisation bring ongoing diffusion of new forms of retailing, customers' behaviour and consumption styles (Keillor et al., 2001). Thanks to social media development, new customers are better informed, have more disposable income and are more active. Contemporary tourists like to change their itinerary during the trip and to combine several purposes with travelling, such as business, leisure, entertainment and education. The result is what can be called 'bleisure' and 'edutainment' tourism.

More and more business travellers extend their stay at their destination for leisure purposes. The new trend of 'bleisure travel' increases on a global level. Many companies refer to this recent phenomenon where the business trip leads to a short vacation, with some rest and relaxation, also known as RandR. The trend is going to change modern hospitality, however it reflects wider changes in society.

The origin and determinants of bleisure trend

The Collins Dictionary (2009) defines bleisure as 'the blurry line between business and leisure trips', however the contamination of 'business' and 'leisure' first appeared in a Carlson Hotels press release in 2007 (Carlson.com, 2014). The same term (sometimes referred to as 'bizcation' or 'busitainment') was coined in 2008 by The Future Laboratory (LS:N Global, 2008) to reflect wider changes in different aspects of consumer behaviour. For a generation weaned on the internet ('digital native', Generation Y, Millenials) and formed in a cloud of mixed multimedia, the freedom and ability to choose from various options across the board are key. Consequently, traditional distinctions – such as the boundary between work and life – are no longer relevant.

Generation Y bloggers define the origin of the 'bleisure' term also as the contamination of business and pleasure. 'If your boss is your Facebook friend and Twittering is part of your day job, you can't determine whether your last holiday was for work or pleasure' (LS:N Global, 2008: 9). The typical representative of the Millennials generation 'does not want home to feel like work – they want work to feel like the playground' (CRET, 2014). They look for a compromise between the demands of a busy career and a healthy home life and they're creating a very lucrative new market.

The growing market for products and services that bridges the boundaries between business and social life influences almost every aspect of our life. It can easily be observed in so-called 'between spaces': while driving a car or sitting in a train or a taxi, we consult our clients or issue orders to our secretaries; at an airport we call our friends or check Twitter and Facebook statuses. Virtual worlds offer an alternative and uncategorised environment in which to work and play. Telecommunication and mobile services change the way people work, learn, teach, shop, the way they are entertained, cared for, in terms of social, legal and medical services and – of course – travel (Kachniewska, 2014). Digitalisation leads to questions about managing virtual workforces (distance-work and distance-learning).

According to the Future Laboratory Report (LS:N Global, 2008) newspapers, magazines and TV channels were the first to reposition themselves to tap into this new 'bleisure market'. In 2007, *The Economist* relaunched its lifestyle magazine, *Intelligent Life*, for members of the bleisure generation. *The Wall Street Journal* introduced its *WSJ* weekend magazine in September 2008, strengthening the business newspaper's coverage of leisure pursuits. The *Financial Times* targets 'the bleisure class' with its lifestyle-heavy *FT Weekend*. In Poland, the most popular newspapers and magazines have developed not only digital versions and tablet device editions, but they started multi-channel communication with internet users, including a presence in social media and mobile applications where the news and games blur. New technologies and crowdsourcing techniques enable the readers to participate in a two-way communication process: they become prosumers when providing news, photographs and information, and 'part-time marketers' when sharing posts in social media, discussing brands and reviewing services. One of the most significant shifts in editorial content has taken place on CNN. Once a purely business channel, it now runs a host of shows including CNN Business Traveller, design360 and My City-My Life, which have a clear lifestyle focus. CNN has become the ultimate 'bleisure channel' (LS:N Global, 2008).

The bleisure trend is also about fashion, technology and design. In January 2008, for instance, Louis Vuitton gave its interpretation of the modern work/life balance of today's male professionals: luxury wear for the bleisure age. Paul Helbers, men's studio director for the French luxury brand, cited bleisure lifestyle as the key influence in the autumn/winter 2010 collection. The trend was noticeable in the clothing shown on the runway, with a mix of formality and comfort that allows wearers to slip effortlessly from the boardroom to the bar.

Getting the right balance between work and leisure is important to a person's well-being. In a survey conducted by YouGov, over three-quarters (76 per cent) of adults in the UK reported that having a good work–life balance was an important indicator of a good employer (http://yougov.co.uk). People live in a digital world where they are always on, 24/7, 365 days a year. For a lot of them, this means constantly being connected to the office, thus removing the need to work traditional hours in a traditional environment. As a result, people are becoming more experimental in their working behaviour. Many businesses are keen to advocate a better work–life balance for their employees: e.g. relaxing the rules on allowing casual clothing every day or inviting employees' families to join them on a business trip. It is obvious that hotel chains – especially those concentrated on servicing business guests – need to facilitate companies in providing employees with quality time.

Bleisure trend in tourism and hospitality

The emerging post-industrial society can be characterised by the dominance of the service industry, higher disposable income and more conscious consumers (Arva and Deli-Gray, 2010). Perhaps the most important developments set to change the face of tourism are of demographic and social character; however they are based on solid economic ground. New customers and new tourists are not only more affluent, so less price conscious and more quality orientated, but they are also seeking activity, participation, fantasy and experience.

These new types of tourists are more interested in the aesthetic aspects of life and are seeking a highly differentiated, personalised experience.

These 'postmodern tourists' look for the possibility to compose tourism packages personally and to modify them during the trip according to their personal needs and interests (Kachniewska, 2014), thus becoming Toffler-defined prosumers (Toffler, 1970). They are not likely to invest a great deal of time in pre-planning a travel schedule in detail. For all these reasons, they need pragmatic and logistic information within easy reach (available anytime and anyhow) during their travel. Information and communication technologies (ICT) have created innovative ways for providing value to clients. The adoption of mobile devices has grown tremendously and their characteristics of mobility and connectivity support on-demand services that are tailored to users and their specific situations.

For the first time, in the twenty-first century, hundreds of millions of people will be living in a consumer economy (Bourdieu, 1984). The purchase of consumer goods becomes an increasingly important expression of one's values and identity. On the other hand, there are growing questions about consumerism. In affluent, developed-world countries, studies show that more money does not equal more happiness (Trivedi, 2011). Whereas material goods are likely to thrive in less-developed economies, having rich personal experiences is increasingly important for people in more-developed countries. The main focus in contemporary tourism development has shifted from the delivery of 'tourism products' to the provision of 'tourism experiences'. It represents one instance of a broader transformation of the overall economy into the experience economy (Pine and Gilmore, 1999). The essence of tourism in today's world is the development of travel experiences for a range of individuals who wish to see, understand and experience the nature of different destinations and the way people live, work and enjoy life.

The growing importance of health and beauty makes tourism suppliers provide appropriate services (health clubs, sporting facilities, alternative menu in restaurants and 'body assistance' in SPA centres). In parallel, a growing shortage of leisure time makes it a most precious commodity. More and more consumers are now considering carefully what to commit their leisure time to, including how to get uninterrupted rest (Belk, 1995). This means that decisions on time commitment are being made not in terms of the cost of leisure activities but on the basis of the most desirable way to spend scarce hours. Thanks to mobile devices and m-applications, contemporary tourists can combine several purposes with travelling.

Bleisure travel brings added value to the equation by increasing the benefits the traveller receives from the journey. Certainly there are cost savings, as the primary traveller will often have transportation and accommodation costs covered by an employer or business, but the appeal goes beyond money: evenings, which business travellers normally spend in the company of strangers or the TV, become opportunities to explore and enjoy a new destination when accompanied by family or friends and a rush to the crowded airport on a Friday afternoon becomes a relaxing wind-down from the week when anticipating leisure activities.

The trend of incorporating leisure activities into business trips was noticed in the early 2000s and even late 1990s. This trend has two components: one that involves more instances in which spouses or children tag along on business trips for a few added-in days of family fun, and another that entails solitary leisure and sports activities that are fitted into business trips, often by younger travellers who are being sent farther away from home, and for longer durations (Tala et al., 2011).

What encourages the blending of business trips and leisure? On the demand side, mainly globalisation and merging lifestyles: more and more travellers extend their professional visits with a leisure trip, and bring family or friends with them to enjoy the facilities and culture of the destination. Combining business travel with a mini-family vacation is a growing trend in a tight economy, according to a 2010 survey of 549 business travellers by Homewood Suites (Raines, 2011). Sixty-seven per cent of frequent business travellers said that they sometimes or often combined a business and leisure trip. That was up from 51 per cent in 2000. In Poland, 71 per cent of business travellers going abroad extend their professional visits, usually (almost 90 per cent of them) bringing their family or friends with them (CRET, 2014).

On the supply side, the main determinant is a growing sophistication of hotel chains' loyalty programmes. Originally based on collecting credit points, nowadays they need some revival. 'Hotel stand-by' (the prolonged stay), weekend discounts or free accommodation for an accompanying person in a double room encourages guests to extend their stay and enjoy some time in a new destination. In this way, bleisure means added benefits to all the parties: hotel chains, employers and employees. Bleisure can be linked to higher revenues (additional services for the businessperson and accompanying persons, extra nights) as well as reduced seasonality (higher occupancy rates in weekends) and satisfied clients that will promote their image.

Employees are less tired and less frustrated – they can save money while having some time with their families. Without much incremental expense (they do not have to pay for their air ticket, which is one of the main expenses of travel), tacking on a mini-vacation to a business trip is a great way to get some rest and relaxation. Last but not least, the employers benefit from the creating of a better company image, related to the concept of corporate social responsibility (CSR). More efficient and productive employees constitute additional advantage.

Whether you spend holidays in a new destination or you take a business trip every month to the same city, the unique experience could make you extend your stay or come back with the family. It does not matter whether you have pre-planned the trip, if you are a typical Millennial you will probably like to taste something new and extraordinary. Both the properly trained hotel staff and modern technology (including contextual information m-applications) could influence your decisions concerning visiting plans and leisure.

'Bleisure generation': cash-rich, time-poor and always on

Bleisure trend developments represent a new type of work-related travel, one where guests have increased flexibility to relax and fulfil their personal needs as well as their professional requirements. With 6.7 million adults prolonging their business trip (Anonymous, 2014), the trend looks set to continue, and with 70 per cent of these travellers remaining in the same hotel for an extended trip, hotels are updating and adapting to suit the new 'bleisure' customer. Apparently, glamorous business travels tend to lose appeal for those who find themselves away from home, family and friends on a regular basis. A bleisure trip helps tackle the problem in an interesting way – a potentially stressful business trip can become a shared pleasure.

There are three things that really matter to bleisure travellers: context, flexibility and mobility. Context is all about orientation. Corporate travellers want information to help them navigate their surroundings. Location-based push notifications, constant feedback from peer networks and the ability to seamlessly navigate are all key; which involves a lot of crossover with social media.

Flexibility is a facet of control. Hospitality managers need to start thinking about the traditional travel policy very differently. For example, Four Seasons is one of many hotel chains trying to push innovation in the mobile space: a technologically savvy traveller might receive a notification on his/her mobile device upon landing in New York, 'We would like to check you in.' Upon confirming the check-in, the hotel would send him/her a key code so the traveller could bypass the front desk and go straight to their room.

Mobility might be the most important, as millennial business travellers want to be connected at all times – 41 per cent of business travellers would refuse to go to a location where they were not connected (CRET, 2014). Similar characteristics can be found in a little older generation, too. With no fixed working hours or place of work, subscribers to the 'bleisure lifestyle' are free to work and play wherever the Wi-Fi takes them. According to a survey by Pullman Hotels, and looking at the behaviours of 2,200 seasoned inter-national travellers, company-owned mobile devices are indeed very much at the heart of their everyday travel behaviours (Gonzalo, 2013):

- 43 per cent of international travellers always take their mobile professional devices with them on holiday or weekend trips;
- The Chinese and the Brazilians are 'blurring' champions and the most connected travellers. 79 per cent and 71 per cent respectively have at least one mobile professional device (compared with 60 per cent in the other countries);
- French and German travellers are the ones that blur their professional and private lives the least;
- The French have a very negative opinion of the use of mobile professional devices. Most notably, 59 per cent of them believe it to be a source of stress;
- 43 per cent of the survey sample acknowledges that they work before going to their workplace.

Gonzalo (2013) states that although these statistics point towards a very real potential conflict between personal time and business, it also underlies another phenomenon where business travellers are now more upfront about going on business trips with their spouse and even children. According to a US report published by Orbitz in 2012, polling 600 American business travellers, 72 per cent said that they take extended executive trips that have a leisure component. Forty-three per cent had a significant other accompany them on a business trip (Du Tre, 2013). According to the National Business Travel Monitor, in 2000, more than two-thirds of frequent American business travellers, a sharp jump from previous years, reported that they combined leisure activities with business trips (Sharkey, 2001).

The bleisure generation, cash-rich, time-poor and always on, is an important target market. The increase in frequency of corporate travel in recent years has resulted in an explosion of requirements to adhere to the habits and quirks unique to this specific group of travellers. Understanding and meeting their needs is essential to stay competitive and capitalise on what can be an extremely lucrative segment of the market, bearing in mind that there is a shift in the behaviour of corporate travellers who now want to engage in both business and leisure activities. Millennials brought up on intuitive search and booking platforms are finding themselves forced into outdated hotel experiences that fail to meet expectations and antiquated travel-management platforms dictated by corporate travel policies. Hoteliers and travel managers need to embrace the leisure experience and put it in a context that's congruent with managed travel.

The CRET survey in Poland (2014) found that most people travel with at least some of their personal technology. Eighty-three per cent would not travel without their personal gadgets, with more than half of the survey group citing their laptop or digital camera as a must-have when travelling. Films and pictures taken during the trip in 76 per cent are shared via social networks. Being online is not only about permanent work, it means keeping in touch with home and family. Years ago people used to keep photos of their children in wallets, nowadays people are increasingly using their Facebook profiles as online showcases of home. Containing images of users' favourite rooms, objects, books, pets, friends and family, these virtual home capsules are forever suspended in the ether, waiting to be accessed at the click of a mouse. Thus, wireless internet access in every hotel room is an indispensable element of hotel offerings; Wi-Fi access in the hotel lobby is not a good solution. The wired internet (and the plug) in the hotel room is useless, when you travel just with a smartphone. R. Solomons (IHG CEO) decided to make internet free for all members of IHG's loyalty program, including those without elite status. He explained it clearly: 'You can get free Internet almost everywhere. You can get it for spending 99 cents at McDonald's, or at Starbucks or frankly, in some cities, anywhere on the street. So you are kidding yourself to charge. It's just recognising what the consumer wanted' (Mayerowitz, 2014).

Hotel chains and the bleisure market

According to a recent survey of Accor-Poland with 4,600 travellers, when choosing a hotel, people look for a central location (48 per cent), prioritise friendly and efficient service (74 per cent) as well as convenience (58 per cent) as the hotel is a hub for managing their busy schedules (Orbis-Accor Polska, 2012). Busy not only because of the business purpose of their visit, but also because of intensive 'social programme': evenings with friends or family combined with shopping or visiting the city. New hotel guests require effortless service, seamless experiences and easy hospitality supported by new technologies giving them power, independence and control. At the Four Seasons Hotel St. Louis, for example, managers witnessed a notable drop off in the usage of the property's concierge desk because corporate travellers were using online tools to research the destination before and upon arrival. The desk has since been converted to a coffee bar, which has generated a significant uptick in traffic.

Generation Y also might have different expectations about the hotel product in general. They appreciate diversification, they want more boutique-style, and social-type hotels for their travel experience (CRET, 2014). Pullman Hotels and Resorts tries to attract this generation with its new meeting rooms, dubbed the Business Playground with a poker-inspired table. It's a result of the brand's extensive guest study which found that 85 per cent of travellers think that owning equipment enabling them to work remotely has changed the organisation between their private and professional lives, and 79 per cent of them think this change is positive (LS:N Global, 2008). Boutique design hotels are replacing the drab minimalism of old rooms with multifunctional spaces linked together by wireless technology. With the incorporation of spa features into bathroom fixtures and a growing availability of in-room wellness services, business no longer has to be something you do in order to pay for leisure.

Hoteliers are looking for ways to identify and reach hybrid customers. ACCOR's fast expanding Pullman brand is updating their portfolio with a focused new brand symbol and marketing campaign. A part of it is pairing business and leisure, with a yin-yang inspired design. With the motto 'Work hard, play hard,' the hotel chain is targeting a new generation of business travellers who are 'hyper-connected and mobile'. According to G. Champetier, Accor global chief marketing officer, 'to differentiate ourselves in this market every trip must be an enriching experience that enhances performance and creativity at work without losing sight of the enjoyable and social dimension of travel' (Valecillo, 2013).

After decades in which business travellers said that what they do is a chore and a bore, serious and stressful, nowadays they begin to admit that they enjoy business trips (Tala et al., 2011). A theatre visit, a spa visit or a mini-break with family transform a stressful business trip into a romantic getaway or a bonding family treat. With the proliferation of spas, gyms and treatment facilities, expectations of business travellers have increased to include high standards of comfort and service away from home as they travel along with their partners. Apart from these, low-cost flights available to cities and the spread of boutique-style accommodation into commercial metropolitan zones ensure a pleasant trip.

With one in four Polish business travellers being accompanied by a partner, friend or child on a business trip and a further 27 per cent expected to follow a similar trend in the future, the trend seems to be quite strong (CRET, 2014). Hotel chains try to find their place in the new tourism value chain and the bleisure trend gives them the opportunity. Highly efficient, a bleisure traveller walks out of an afternoon meeting to reach a weekend break destination. A potentially stressful business trip or marketing meeting can become a shared pleasure with a family, such as a cultural city break in one of the world's great cathedrals, a stunning art gallery, a performance at the new opera house or a midweek football match. The high level of competition makes hotel chains include bleisure offers into their packages.

When booking corporate travel, agencies often overlook the leisure capabilities of a hotel. A business traveller might need a hotel with good wireless capabilities and close proximity to the airport, 'but by offering a place with a state-of-the-art gym, unique rooftop bar and an excellent cigar selection, your traveller might be more than happy to go for a hotel beyond the usual airport stay or a large chain branch' (Lukey, 2014). The majority of consolidated booking portals offers a wide range of choices and real-time availability as well as flexibility to alter the booking if needed, as travel schedules are often unpredictable. The big data analysis potential goes beyond this simple opportunity: as booking portals are becoming more advanced, it is now possible to greatly customise and filter the searches, ensuring the client's request for a nearby golf course or the best restaurant in town can be met. Lukey (2014) suggests one simpler but impressive advantage the traveller will certainly like: being able to print out the booking confirmation in the destination's local language. This would make it much easier to communicate to the taxi driver and explain to him where to go.

Another impressive example comes from the Sheraton Hotels & Resorts chain, which announced in 2010 the launch of a new $20 million dollar, multi-media marketing campaign created to highlight the brand's $6 billion revitalisation effort (Starwood News, 2014). The 'Rediscover Sheraton' campaign encouraged travellers to take a new look at Sheraton, which features an enhanced guest experience. A key insight that directed the creative vision for the campaign was the growing trend of travellers blending business and leisure and the demand for socially driven designed spaces and amenities. As part of the brand's overhaul, every aspect of the new Sheraton guest experience was designed to promote social interaction and bring people together. The campaign depicted this through clever headlines and striking imagery that unite seemingly disparate concepts to capture attention: 'Who brings business suits and bathing suits together', 'Who brings power walks and power talks together' and 'Who brings bottom lines and bottom ups together' (Starwood News, 2014).

The burgeoning trend of the smart corporate traveller extending work trips into holidays has not gone unnoticed by American Express and Starwood which recently partnered to launch The Starwood Preferred Guest® Credit Card from American Express helping smart travellers do just that (NerdWallet, 2014). Research by the two companies found that six out of ten business travellers currently collect rewards and points on travel-related schemes and credit cards. Of these, four out of ten use the rewards as a means to subsidise or upgrade their holidays (SPG, 2014). The Card makes this process that much easier: every full pound spent on the card earns one Starpoint that can be redeemed on a flexible range of rewards, such as complimentary nights at Starwood hotels and resorts, on both weekdays and weekends; room upgrades; flights on over 350 leading airlines without blackout dates including BA; Virgin Atlantic and American Airlines; or special experiences such as VIP concert tickets that can be booked through the SPG® Moments online auction (SPG, 2014). Thus, a loyalty programme is partly combined with so called gamification (Zichermann and Cunningham, 2011) and enables guests to extend their stay or to invite friends or relatives for a weekend.

The bleisure trend is changing the way we think about hotel services. While most hotels offer wake up calls, The James Hotel in Chicago has taken it a step further with a new service called 'Shut Down' calls. These calls are made in the evening to remind guests to shut off their laptops and cell phones and go out and enjoy the sights or just relax. This service is just one part of their 'Weekday Bleisure' package, which is designed for the business person who enjoys a little relaxation and fun while traveling for meetings and business ventures.

QHotels offer a free stay for a business person's partner and up to two children aged 12 and under (QHotels Press Release, 2014). Polish Orbis Hotels (Accor Group) try to lure guests with a diverse culinary experience (Valecillo, 2013). Pullman Saigon Centre offers impressive amenities as well as floor to ceiling windows that offer spectacular views of the city's skyline (Valecillo, 2013). Sofitel makes it a point of honour to celebrate its French heritage via numerous cultural events, linked to literature, fashion and art. These include celebrating international festivals such as the Fête de la Musique in their hotels and organising travelling photo exhibitions. The chain tries to gain on three strategic pillars inspired by French 'Art de vivre': a focus on design and innovation; the celebration of gastronomy and wines as well as a passion for culture and events (Sofitel.com, 2014). Each Sofitel has a local story that is linked to France: in Warsaw, Sofitel stresses the Polish-French ties of Maria Sklodowska-Curie and Frederic Chopin as well as the glamour of the city, which used to be called 'the Paris of North' (Sofitel.com, 2014).

The challenge that evolves is due to mobile professional devices and the evolution of travel technologies. This is where understanding online marketers, mobile and social media practitioners can gain a competitive edge, as can be seen with many luxury hotel chains such as Hilton, Marriott and Four Seasons. Many of these luxury hotels mine social media to enhance the customer experience prior, during and after the stay in their establishment.

Younger business travellers are showing different behaviours from the older ones, according to a recent survey organised by Expedia with 8,500 travellers in 24 countries (Gonzalo, 2013):

- 18–30 year olds take more leisure trips (4.2 mean) than those 31–45 (2.9 mean) and 46–65 (3.2 mean).
- In North America, 54 per cent of 18–30 year olds bring a significant other on a business trip, versus 36 per cent of 31–45 and 16 per cent of 46–65.
- Globally, 42 per cent of 18–30 year olds say they would spend more of the company's money on high-end meals, compared to 26 per cent of 31–45.

Not surprisingly, the study also found that younger business travellers are much more vocal on review sites such as TripAdvisor or Yelp; not necessarily because they are more outspoken, but perhaps more simply because this generation was brought up with sharing platforms as part of their daily life. It means that they can become important advocates of the hotel chain if they are really satisfied with the service.

The Meetings, Incentive, Corporate & Events (MICE) segment of the travel industry tends to blur with more traditional leisure travel behaviours, needs and wants. There is certainly an opportunity here, and it will be interesting to see how this trend unfolds and which destinations make the most of it. Hotels try to inspire business travellers to stay longer by offering a cultural experience and family discount. When travelling alone, a business person can be offered advice on how to arrange a short weekend visit for his/her family members.

MGM Resorts International pioneered a new way to reach traditional business travellers by aligning its 'M life' loyalty programme with Hyatt Hotels Corporation's 'Gold Passport' programme (MGM Resort International, 2014). One of the most common ways of extracting leisure revenue from business guests is motivating meeting-and-convention attendees, who will often bring their families, to stay over after their event. Although MGM Grand has been doing this informally for years, it is no longer an afterthought, but a formal form of add-on business. The hotels often include stay-over rates and packages in their meeting proposals. Similarly, Universal Orlando Resort in Florida, which includes four hotels operated by Loews Hotels & Resorts, offers its group room rate to meeting attendees for three days before and after an event. Hotel representatives observe a significant increase in the number of companies that encourage meeting attendees to include their families in the experience. Because of Orlando's status as the world's No. 1 family vacation destination and Universal's unique amenities, which include theme parks and the CityWalk dining and entertainment venue, the company has the unique ability to take advantage of the bleisure trend.

In Chicago, the Radisson Blue Aqua is leveraging meeting business for leisure revenue. Like Universal Orlando, it offers group rates, subject to availability, for three days before and after a conference. The same practice has been adapted in Warsaw city business hotels which suffer a low season during the summer holidays: not many industry conferences are scheduled in the summer, and hotels encourage the guests to bring the family with special rates and activities.

Work and holiday blur on trips abroad, as the ways of doing business demand a more flexible approach. Nowadays consumers demand that hotels meet a wide-ranging set of criteria that embraces spaces to work and meet in, as well as those for engaging with the cultural life of the city and to relax and refresh. However, due to the complicated structure of the tourism product, the proper development of experience tourism needs the cooperation of different stakeholders, including local governments, tourism destination organisations and local citizens. European cities and most big American cities can reap the rewards from the bleisure trend. A close cooperation of hotel chains, travel agencies and cultural institutions seems to be the only way to arrange an exciting experience for a demanding bleisure tourist. Moreover, in the future, a key tactic will become the aggressive and creative exploitation of mobile technology to motivate spontaneous activity, such as extending a business trip for a few days of leisure to enjoy destinations (PhoCusWright, 2013).

There is also another trend connected with bleisure trips: more and more often business travellers choose serviced apartments instead of hotels. One of the advantages that serviced apartments have in comparison to hotels is that they are often found in the main business hubs of cities, compared to hotels which are more likely to be found on a high street. This allows guests to immerse themselves more easily in the feeling of the city. The bleisure travellers do not want to feel like tourists but instead want to blend in with the city.

Last but not least, further legal trend evolution in comparison with traditional packages is necessary as the relationship between travel law, leisure and business seems inoperable. Employers need the tools protecting them from possible abuse; hoteliers need clear rules concerning proper invoicing and settlements with corporations. Research conducted by Jurys Inn shows that one in five business travellers view an overseas working trip as an ideal holiday opportunity. In the United States, where annual leave days are fewer, many employers are more tolerant of these extended stays. However, it remains a murkier area in the UK and a topic that is hotly contested in the business community (PayandBenefits, 2013).

Central to this debate is what is reasonable for employees to claim when taking bleisure trips and how to ensure that they don't lead to spiralling costs for businesses. It seems perfectly reasonable for an employee who is staying in a beautiful and unexplored city to want to make the most of their visit. However, it's also equally justifiable for finance teams to be suspicious when it comes to the resulting expenses. With this in mind, it has never been more important for businesses to ensure that they have a robust travel expenses policy in place, ensuring both employers and their workforce know where they stand. By doing this, firms can harness the bleisure trip as a motivational tool for their workforce.

To tackle any grey areas, all employers need to ensure that they have clear guidance in place. Without this, travel costs and any associated subsistence and accommodation could soon spiral out of control.

Summary

The travel market is facing many challenges from tourism's changing requirements: the growth of the independent traveller, a progressive shift away from organised holiday packages, combining several purposes with travelling, such as business, leisure, entertainment and education. The result is what can be called 'bleisure' and 'edutainment' tourism. Hotel chains have to be more sensitive to the changes in customers' needs. Existing products have to be tailored and new products have to be developed to suit the 'new' customer. Modern existence has created a new challenge: finding an appropriate work–life balance. The trend of incorporating leisure activities into business trips constitutes both a challenge and a chance for modern hotel chains.

References

Anonymous (2014) New bleisure travel trend. Online. Available HTTP: <http://www.celebrityangels.co.uk/article/new_bleisure_travel_trend_emerges_tt9>, accessed 6 March, 2014.

Arva, L. and Deli-Gray, Z. (2010) New types of tourism and tourism marketing in the post-industrial world. *Applied Studies in Agrobusiness and Commerce*, 5, 33–37.

Becker, G.S. (1965) A theory of the allocation of time. *Economic Journal*, 75, 493–517.

Becker, G.S. (1976) *The Economic Approach to Human Behaviour*. Chicago/London: The University of Chicago Press.

Belk, R.W. (1995) Studies in the new consumer behaviour. In D. Miller (ed.), *Acknowledging Consumption*. London: Routledge, pp. 58–95.

Bourdieu, P. (1984) *Distinction: A Social Critique of Judgement of Taste*. London: Routledge and Kegan Paul.

Carlson.com (2014) Carlson Rezidor hotel Group opens Park Inn by Radisson. Online. Available HTTP: <http://www.carlson.com/news-and-media/news-releases.do?article=7683378>, accessed 23 April, 2014.

Cogoy, M. (2007) Enjoyment of life, the structure of time, and economic dynamics. In L. Bruni and L. Porta (eds), *Handbook on the Economics of Happiness*. Cheltenham: Elgar, pp. 170–84.

Cogoy, M. (2010) Consumption, time and the environment, *Review of Economics of the Household*, 8, 459–77.

Collins Dictionary (2009) Bleisure. Online. Available HTTP: <http://www.collinsdictionary.com/submission/5426/Bleisure>, accessed 16 May, 2014.

Creative Cities and Experience Tourism Research Group [CRET] (2014) *Modern MICE in Poland*. Unpublished manuscript.

Du Tre, C. (2013) Bleisure travel. Online. Available HTTP: <http://growingsocialmedia.com/bleisure-travel/>, accessed 8 June, 2014.

Garhammer, M. (1999) *Wie Europa er ihre Zeit nutzen. Zeitstrukturen und Zeitkulturen im Zeichen der Globalisierung*. Berlin: Edition Sigma.

Garhammer, M. (2002) Pace of life and enjoyment of life. *Journal of Happiness Studies*, 3, 217–56.

Gonzalo, F. (2013) The growing trend of bleisure travel. Online. Available HTTP: <http://www. socialmediatoday.com/content/growing-trend-bleisure-travel>, accessed 18 April, 2014.

Goudzwaard B. (1979) *Capitalism and Progress: A Diagnosis of Western Society*. Toronto, Canada: Wedge Publishing Foundation and Grand Rapids.

Gronau, R. (1977) Leisure, home production and work. The theory of the allocation of time revisited. *Journal of Political Economy*, 85, 1099–1123.

Gronau, R. (1986) Home-production, a survey. In O. Ashenfelter and R. Layard (eds), *Handbook of Labour Economics*, vol. 1. Amsterdam: North Holland, pp. 273–304.

Haller, M., Hadler, M. and Kaup, G. (2013) Leisure time in modern societies: a new source of boredom and stress? *Social Indicators Research*, 111, 403–34.

Hirschman, A.O. (1973) An alternative explanation of contemporary hurriedness. *Quarterly Journal of Economics*, November, 634–37.

Jalas, M. (2002) A time use perspective on the materials intensity of consumption. *Ecological Economics*, 41, 109–23.

Juster, F.T. and Stafford, F.P. (1991) The allocation of time: empirical findings, behavioural models, and problems of measurement. *Journal of Economic Literature*, 29, 471–522.

Kachniewska, M. (2014) Tourism value added creation through a user-centric context-aware digital system. *University of Szczecin Scientific Journal*, 836: *Economic Problems of Tourism*, 4(28), 103–18.

Keillor, B., Amico, M. and Horton, V. (2001) Global consumer tendencies. *Psychology and Marketing*, 18, 1–19.

Linder, S.B. (1970) *The Harried Leisure Class*. New York: Columbia University Press.

LS:N Global (2008) *The Future Laboratory: Trend Briefing Report*. Online. Available HTTP: <http://www. thefuturelaboratory.com/download/forms/2008.10.06.tba.booking>, accessed 11 June, 2014.

Lukey, C.H. (2014) How to cater to the bleisure traveller. Online. Available HTTP: <http://www.ttgasia. com/article.php?article_id=21734>, accessed 12 Sept, 2014.

Mayerowitz S. (2014) *InterContinental Hotels CEO on Free Wi-Fi, Bleisure Travel and Brand Power*. Online. Available HTTP: <http://skift.com/2014/07/01/intercontinental-hotels-ceo-on-free-wi-fi-bleisure-travel-and-brand-power/>, accessed 23 August, 2014.

MGM Resort International (2014) M life. Online. Available HTTP: <https://www.mgmresorts.com/players-club/>, accessed 22 October 2014.

Michael, R.T. and Becker, G.S. (1973) On the new theory of consumer behaviour. *Swedish Journal of Economics*, 75, 378–96.

Nahrstedt, W. (1998) Modernization by leisure, culture and tourism. In W. Nahrstedt and T. Pančić Kombol (eds), *Leisure, Culture and Tourism in Europe: The Challenge for Reconstruction and Modernisation in Communities*. Bielefeld: Institut für Freizeitwissenschaft und Kulturarbeit (IFKA), pp. 413–20.

NerdWallet (2014) Starwood American express: the best hotel credit card. Online. Available HTTP: <http://www.nerdwallet.com/blog/credit-cards/starwood-american-express-review/>, accessed 8 January, 2015.

Orbis-Accor Polska (2012) Reports. Online. Available HTTP: <http://www.orbis.pl/accor-reports>, accessed 22 November 2014.

PayandBenefits (2013) New trend in business travel. Online. Available HTTP: <http://www. payandbenefitsmagazine.co.uk/pab/>, accessed 16 November, 2014.

PhoCusWright (2013) Targeting bleisure business. Online. Available HTTP: <http://www.hotelnewsnow. com/Article/13721/Targeting-bleisure-business>, accessed 23 November, 2014.

Pine, B.J. and Gilmore, J.H. (1999) *The Experience Economy*. Boston, MA: Harvard Business School Press.

QHotels Press Release (2014) Bleisure: our family friendly business package. Online. Available HTTP: <http://www.qhotels.co.uk/bleisure-our-family-friendly-business-package/>, accessed 7 December 2014.

Raines L. (2011) 'Bizcations' provide fun on budget in tight times. Online. Available HTTP: <http:// www.ajc.com/news/business/bizcations-provide-fun-on-budget-in-tight-times/nQt9c/>, accessed 5 November, 2014.

Rosa, H. (2005) *Beschleunigung. Die Veranderung der Zeitstrukturen in der Moderne*. Frankfurt am Main: Suhrkamp.

Sanne, C. (2005) The consumption of our discontent. *Business Strategy and the Environment,* 14, 315–23.

Schipper, L., Bartlett, S., Hawk, D. and Vine, E. (1989) Linking lifestyle and energy use: a matter of time. *Annual Review of Energy,* 14, 273–320.

Schor, J.B. (1993) *The Overworked American. The Unexpected Decline of Leisure.* New York: Basic Books.

Seidel, N. and Verwiebe, R. (2006) Der Wandel von Zeitstrukturen in der tertiaren Gesellschaft. *Berliner Debatte Initial,* 17, 97–109.

Sennett, R. (1998) *Der Flexible Mensch. Die Kultur des Neuen Kapitalismus.* Berlin: Berlin Verlag.

Sharkey J. (2001) Leisure activities are increasingly being fitted in to help make life on the road less of the grind. *New York Times.* Online. Available HTTP: <http://www.nytimes.com/2001/04/18/business/business-travel-leisure-activities-are-increasingly-being-fitted-help-make-life.html>.

Sofitel.com (2014) Le art de vivre. Online. Available HTTP: <http://www.sofitel.com/gb/luxury-hotel-experience/art-de-vivre.shtml>.

SPG (2014) Podróż do środka świata. Online. Available HTTP: <http://www.starwoodhotels.com/preferredguest/about/index.html?IM=aboutspg_spghp_acctbox&language=pl_PL>, accessed 7 November, 2014.

Starwood News (2014) sheraton hotels & resorts launches multi-million marketing campaign to support $6 billion brand revitalization. Online. Available HTTP: <http://development.starwoodhotels.com/news/8/68-sheraton_hotels_resorts_launches_multi-million_marketing_campaign_to_support_6_billion_brand_revitalization>, 9 March 2014.

Tala, M., Schiopu, A. and Brindusoiu C. (2011) Bleisure: a new trend in tourism industry. *Forum Ware International, Special Issue: Excellence in Business, Commodity Science and Tourism,* 1, 235–39.

Toffler A. (1970) *Future Shock.* New York: Random House.

Towers, I., Duxbury, L., Higgins, Ch. and Thomas, J. (2006) Time thieves and space invaders: technology, work and the organization. *Journal of Organizational Change Management,* 19(5), 593–618.

Trivedi, M. (2011) Regional and categorical patterns in consumer behaviour: revealing trends. *Journal of Retailing,* 87(1), 18–30.

Valecillo F. (2013) Accor unveils 'bleisure' plan for pullman [html]. Online. Available HTTP: <http://www.worldpropertychannel.com/europe-vacation-news/pullman-hotels-resorts-accor-european-expansion-bleisure-6900.php>, accessed 6 November, 2014.

YouGov Global (2010) Online. Available HTTP: <http://research.mena.yougov.com/en/sectors/travel-and-leisure>, accessed 21 June 2014.

Zichermann, G. and Cunningham, C.H. (2011) *Gamification by Design: Implementing Game Mechanics in Web and Mobile Apps.* Sebastopol, CA: O'Reilly Media Inc.

46

Building an integrated marketing communications mindset for hotel managers

Dedicated to the memory of Michael S. LaTour (March 1954 – November 2015)

Michael S. LaTour (ITHACA COLLEGE, USA) *and*
Kathryn A. LaTour (CORNELL UNIVERSITY, USA)

Introduction

The sheer volume and diversity of communications in the hospitality industry as well as the dynamics of new channels of social media present a timely challenge for the hotel industry. Undoubtedly, the social media component of these communication channels in the context of the hotel chain service-scape is no fad. The social media explosion reflects the longstanding desire for interpersonal connectedness, which is now enabled by mobile technology. While many companies view social media as a means to target Millennials, this phenomenon is culturally anchoring (LaTour and Roberts, 1992) multiple generations of consumers, and encouraging what is effectively an 'addiction to technology.' Hotel chains like Hilton have embraced this consumer desire by developing mobile apps where consumers can check-in from their phones, creating efficiencies both for the guest as well as for the hotel's front desk. Other companies like Four Seasons allow guests to text requests. A single staff member can interact with many guests simultaneously, and in a communication form guests are more comfortable with (than having to wait through call service frames). In their own market testing, Marriott found over 10,000 text requests were made, and the majority (80 per cent) chose the 'anything else' two-way chat option (Trejos, 2015).

Not all social media changes have been beneficial to chains, however, as use of these channels is no longer in direct control of marketers. TripAdvisor has a fraud division to monitor reviews that may be posted by companies wishing to increase their scores (or decrease their competitor's scores). This social space is also creating new competitors, facing very low barriers to entry into the traditional high cost of brick and mortar hotels (AirBnB). Hoteliers need to think differently about their customers and how to evolve to meet their needs. Viewing the customer experience as a linear journey is no longer a valid approach. Customers share opinions, discover new services and openly engage socially with brands they love. This chapter explores the dimensions of Integrated Marketing Communications (IMC), in connection with consumers' beliefs and actions, as reflected in these many communication channels in the context of hospitality.

A crucial point regarding IMC for the hospitality industry is that IMC is anchored on a key interface between consumer psychology theory and promotional strategy. For that reason, this chapter demonstrates the importance of driving such efforts with well-articulated objectives and goals, which in turn helps focus the choices of theoretically deep market research, selection of promotional vehicles and assessment of communication efforts – all the while keeping in mind that true insight into these strategic efforts lies between the ears of customers and prospective customers.

Moving from 1.0 to 2.0 marketing

Promotional strategy in the past was one-directional, where the marketer sent out a message to the consumer. The market research firm Yankelovich estimates that 30 years ago customers were exposed to roughly 2000 messages a day, and in 2007, that number jumped to 5000 messages a day. Marketers' main concern was 'breaking through' this advertising clutter so that their message was received. The prevailing wisdom was that after message reception, consumers would use that information to make their product decision. The customer journey was viewed as a funnel, where the message was sent broadly and then more targeted as the customer expressed more involvement with the brand.

Consumers today are still bombarded with thousands of messages. But with social media these messages are no longer just one directional. As highlighted in Williams, (2015), an Edison Research study on social media use noted that, in 2008 just 5 per cent of Americans checked their social network 'several times a day' by 2014 this had risen to 28 per cent or 75 million people checking their social networking site several times a day. For hospitality providers this represents an enormous opportunity to strengthen customer loyalty and impression management.

According to Holmes (2014), in 2010 Forrester Research claimed the 'funnel is dead' and rather the journey involves discovery, exploration, buying and engagement. With this new view, customers are entering and leaving the marketer's funnel, and the marketplace is becoming highly fractionalised. Social media metrics can be deceptive. A company might consider directing messages to those customers with the most followers, but research has shown that the most loyal and engaged brand fans are actually those with a more moderate following (Lee, 2014).

Further, firms might experience the most upside when the message is not driven by the company. One trend in social media has been on highlighting customer-driven content which appears to be more genuine and authentic. However the downside of 2.0 is that consumers can spread their own messages without the firm's knowledge. Consider the case where after an airline service failure resulted in Dave Carroll having his guitar destroyed by a United ground team, and United's customer service drew out his complaint for a year, Dave and his band developed a song on YouTube 'United Breaks Guitars' that had millions of views, and CNN coverage, within days of posting (Deighton and Kornfield, 2010).

Marketing managers today have a very difficult job. Not only do they need to create content, they also need to manage social media response. Research on Twitter has found that if a company fails to respond to a complaint within an hour, it is deemed a service failure. United did respond to Dave's complaint on social media, but even then could not stop the viral video. The type of response also matters; we are moving from a verbal to a visual communication world. According to Phillip Ross (2014) on Social Barkers, 87 per cent of

Facebook page interactions are driven by photos. The popularity of Instagram also highlights the importance of imagery for communications.

Hotel chains need to have a team to manage the social media universe. New sites and apps are always being introduced. As this chapter is being written, the top three sites that best drive customer traffic to brand purchase are Facebook, Twitter and Pinterest (Lee 2014). Certainly, hotel chains should focus efforts on sites that are most relevant for their area and industry. Research shows too that customer habits on these sites vary. Recent research suggests that for travel postings on Facebook Saturdays are most active, whereas overall, Facebook sees more engagement from users on Fridays. This was mentioned by Lee (2014), quoting the Social Intelligence report from Adobe which analysed over 225 billion Facebook posts. Each property and chain will experience different usage rates, and this will vary seasonally as well. The hotel chain's promotional plan needs to consider the communication goals of the company broadly and integrate social media into its promotional mix. Before the IMC promotional plan is (re)configured and executed, all involved hotel managers need to deeply understand what the achievement of a strategic objective will do for the brand. Therefore, the objectives need to be articulated with great clarity and driven by deep, insightful research so that all involved can understand when they arrive at that point, and how they are progressing towards that arrival. Consider for example using this as the basis for a hotel chain manager multi-day retreat. With the appropriately trained facilitator running rounds of re-estimation, this brings management together in a way that clarifies and articulates IMC objectives as measurable, time-based and mutually shared.

Therefore, the linchpin for managers is advancing towards a comprehensive, working, strategic communications plan. The outcome of this process will produce a reference document that will aid communications strategic planning. Beyond that, the need to revisit, refine, prioritise and (in some cases) set objectives will in turn feed ideation, enhance the management process, and help to fine tune the strategic and eventual tactical efforts.

'Dipping our toes in the pond' of IMC assessment and market analyses

The challenge begins with the multiplicity of channels, coupled with diversity of consumer beliefs. In this modern social media-laden environment, there are a huge number of options for assessing promotional outcomes. It is crucial to choose metrics that align with in-depth market research and carefully thought through goals and objectives tying into market performance (e.g. occupancy rate, market share, REVPAR, etc.). Otherwise, hospitality managers can literally drown in the confusion that ensues with so many distracting measurement options. This chapter would do the reader a disservice to initially discuss the huge array of options in IMC without directing managerial attention initially to this 'So what?' crux of IMC strategy.

To do this right, hospitality managers need to deeply understand their brand from the customer's point of view. This extends far beyond the common exhortation to be consumer centric and arrives at a more fundamental plane, in which management is so deeply enlightened as to engage in demand stimulation and customer education, that can only happen when there is true managerial understanding of what is in the minds of existing and prospective customers on a world-wide basis. So, this overview of assessment options is cast by the seeking of a differentiating 'return on deep emotion', linked to goals and objectives that accompany customers' brand experience. Obviously key to differentiating hotel changes is 'customer experience management' and making this unique and memorable (as will be addressed in a later section on deep research). All too often this is done without consideration of the level of customer engagement, which uses a metaphorical concept known as 'the funnel' and recognises the fluidity of that, posed by social media.

Understanding the funnel and moving beyond it

As mentioned earlier in the chapter, the traditional metaphor portrays the media environment in conjunction with a funnel that reflects a progressively deepening focus of consumers' awareness, albeit with fewer consumers at each level of the funnel. For strategic orientation and assessment purposes, hospitality managers need to conceive of their brand messages, no matter how delivered, as engaging this consumer 'funnel' (Belch and Belch, 2015). The top of the funnel comprises the greatest number of people, who are engaged with initial 'awareness' of the brand message. From this top level, the funnel narrows as each subsequent stage of engagement involves continuous consumer subsets, constituting greater intensity of message comprehension and eventually action. Within marketing 2.0 this funnel is no longer a one-way communication channel.

Strategically speaking, managers want to stimulate interest in their product. Clearly, the recipient would be engaged at this more intense level if the message is personally relevant. The consequence would likely be the desire to sample aspects of the service experience at a property, but might also involve a website-based virtual engagement. Ideally this interaction should encourage discovery and sharing among the consumer's social network. For example, those fully engaged in a hotel property's loyalty programme should have a robust social media presence and subscribe to a RSS feed for daily updates and promotions, while sharing recent experiences with other members.

The sea of assessment tools

A variety of texts (e.g. Belch and Belch, 2015; Barker et al., 2013) provide in depth discussions of specific IMC assessment tools and approaches, and therefore that is not the goal here. In fact, there are a confusing number of choices of metrics, unless carefully articulated goals and objectives are thoroughly understood by all managers involved with brand building and support. Twitonomy, for instance, can measure number of followers, number of re-tweets, etc.

As mentioned before, though, sometimes the numbers can appear counterintuitive. For instance, we would generally think of an opinion leader as one that has the most followers, so efforts should be directed toward that individual. However, according to Lee (2014), social monitoring website Mention analysed over 1 billion social mentions between 2013 and 2015 and found that 91 per cent of them came from people with fewer than 500 followers. These are potential brand advocates as only 6 per cent of these mentions were negative. Therefore, fewer than 1 out of 10 mentions of your brand will come from a power user with many followers. Your team might still prioritise opinion leaders, but to get the most effectiveness in social media, identifying those customers that talk about your brand will be most effective. There are tools available whereby brands can tell in real time when and who is mentioning them – as stated before, timeliness of response is important.

The good/bad news in this environment is that no single tactic or metric is enough. It is a highly fractionalised and moving marketplace. There are many metrics (and even more in development) that can assess your social media presence. But given that the end result is how your brand and experience is viewed by the customer, it is important to utilise insights from consumer psychology research that was brought to the industry primarily via the efforts of academe, as it is 'light years' ahead of the era of 'Mad Men' (which was progressive for its time). What has emerged from this intense scientific focus upon 'The Mind of the Market'

(Zaltman, 2003) is the realisation that the mind is akin to an iceberg, with so much of the consumers' emotional reactions to brands rooted 'below the water level' in the subconscious. So, while our theoretically grounded tools have advanced, so has the realisation grown that the complexity of the consumer psyche is far more robust than previously thought. This is the reason for this chapter's opening call for depth in consumer research in connection with communication strategies. Hence we are calling for a fundamental mental shift to a theoretically rich, intellectually deep mindset that fully behoves the hotel chain manager to be on a constant curious quest to gain deeper consumer insight. This is the crux of true differentiation and as such, is competitively vital in this unique service-scape. To do otherwise is to descend into a myopia of the 'lukewarm' status quo, undifferentiated and continuously eroding competitive brand position.

Key categories of assessment options

Traditionally, especially with old media, a great deal of experimentation has been done with advertising and other promotions to test how consumers would respond to a message or campaign. The notion of achieving internal validity of isolating the impact of a promotion upon consumers has a great deal of managerial appeal. If the structure of such tests is ill-designed, of course, the old adage of 'garbage in leading to garbage out' could well apply. Managers electing to sponsor experiments with promotional messages need to select representative samples of human subjects and have their research staff randomly assign subjects to 'treatment' and 'control' groups, to control for pre-existing attitudes toward the hospitality brand in question. Response to promotions can be captured via professionally validated questionnaires as well as physiological hardware devices such as Galvanic Skin Response, Eye Tracking, and Electromyography (LaTour, 1986; Noone and Robson, 2014; Belch and Belch, 2015). However, to achieve internal validity and isolate these effects in a laboratory setting, one would also need to supplement this type of analysis with a field study in the purchase environment with actual customers to probe responses to promotional efforts. One sees how complex this may become.

Obviously, sales promotions (e.g., short term 'buy now' incentives) need to be tracked, so that those responding can be profiled and contrasted with those who do not respond. Entering those observations into a customer database allows for the system to get 'smarter' over time and for managers to fine-tune future promotions. This has particular utility in the modern media environment with group incentives (e.g., Groupon). Again, the choice of particular approaches should always be clearly and inextricably tied to well-understood strategic objective outcomes. As promotions unfold, managers need to have a gut level feeling of 'hey we are making headway towards objective A'.

Evaluating promotions and experiments is sufficiently complicated, but social media choices have become even more blurry due to the supposed difficulty with measuring incremental performance and return on investment. Managers need to avoid superficial dives into this arena for fear of being left behind. Rather, navigating through this can be greatly aided by thinking strategically first about the brand's locus in relation to consumers at various points on a set time line. When considering any one of these social media choices, the value of measuring such, needs to be again tied to brand fit, that is, the particular communication objectives that have been established and the intended level of engagement. Again, without those goals, determining a course of action becomes problematic. That said, it is useful to seek a balance between quantitative and qualitative measures as part of a strategic bailiwick.

Typical quantitative measures focus on counting volume of social media activities, including page views, followers, re-tweets, website conversions, fan numbers, ratio of comments to videos, visitors' comments to posts, RSS feed activity, and traffic arriving at the website from the social media vehicles. While any and all of these metrics can be of great value, they are of dubious consequence on their own, especially if not considered on a segment by segment basis and indeed at times cross-culturally. Instead, any measurement must be associated with what have come to be called SMART goals: specific, measurable, achievable, realistic and time-based goals. SMART goals need to be articulated for each vehicle that actually tie to clearly understood objectives and which specify the impact for the brand if achieved. Follow-up analysis can also be executed with perceptual mapping tools to take competitive brand space snapshots before and after promotional campaigns.

Quantitative measures seldom reveal the whole story, however. Those metrics must be augmented by qualitative measures, which typically centre on assessing customer relationships, including customer retention and loyalty. In this context, sentiment analysis software using computer algorithms to detect affect, mood and emotions, has generated a lot of 'buzz' lately. These social media monitoring tools allow the user to 'drill down' to further explore software-driven categorisations of textual expressions posted via the 'earned' social media (Tuten and Solomon, 2012). More detailed qualitative assessment choices with descriptors are depicted in Table 46.1.

As Table 46.1 indicates, the options presented have different degrees of penetration into the consumer experience. Therefore, each choice needs to be evaluated in terms of its juxtaposition with strategic objectives. For example, Share of Voice takes a fairly shallow dive by tallying the proportion of brand mentions in earned media vis-à-vis total mentions in the industry. Measurement at that level can provide an early gauge of competitive progress in the social media, whereas the Audience Engagement and Conversation Reach measures start drilling down to record measurable actions. All those measures, however, are still fairly shallow. As we move towards Active Advocates, the engagement measured becomes deeper. Again, managers need to reflect on what they measure in line with what makes sense to capture for the sake of their objectives and goals. Deeper still is the Advocacy Impact measure, which correlates the contributions of advocacy to conversions. Collectively, what these measures should do is to 'paint a picture' of social media stimuli processing that hopefully leads to consumers' behaviours. In that regard, customer satisfaction scores assume some behavioural throughput, while sentiment ratios ascribe a valence to social media commentary and are instrumental in tracking current developments in brand sentiment in real time. Key to this is a resource commitment to monitoring these data so that response to negative sentiment can be timely. While measures are more numerous than those illustrated in Table 46.1, hotel chain managers need to seek out and agree on measures that make strategic sense for their carefully articulated strategic plans.

As one can see from examining the measurement options, there is a danger of being overwhelmed by the number of choices if one were bereft of a clear 'strategic frame'. Such a frame should include in-depth research of the service delivery environment, while the appropriate measures are concurrently pondered along with strategically formulated objectives and goals. Together, these formulate a holistic managerial strategy. To illustrate the research that drives towards that end, presented next are two highly proven approaches that have particular veracity in hospitality service environments.

Market research to solidify IMC objectives: be real, be deep

DeepResearch 1: The Zaltman Metaphor Elicitation Technique

The Zaltman Metaphor Elicitation Technique (ZMET) is a process by which pictures and metaphors are used by respondents to represent how they think and feel about a company,

Table 46.1 Key performance indicators for social media

Dialog Key Performance Indicator #1: Share of Voice

$$Share\ of\ Voice = \frac{Brand\ Mentions}{Total\ Mentions\ (Brand + Competitor\ A,\ B,\ C\ .\ .\ .\ n)}$$

Dialog Key Performance Indicator #2: Audience Engagement

$$Audience\ Engagement = \frac{Comments + Shares + Trackbacks}{Total\ Views}$$

Dialog Key Performance Indicator #3: Conversation Reach

$$Conversation\ Reach = \frac{Total\ People\ Participating}{Total\ Audience\ Exposure}$$

Advocacy Key Performance Indicator #1: Active Advocates

$$Active\ Advocates = \frac{\#\ of\ Active\ Advocates\ (with\ in\ past\ 30\ days)}{Total\ Advocates}$$

Advocacy Key Performance Indicator #2: Active Influence

$$Active\ Influence = \frac{Unique\ Adovate's\ Influence}{Total\ Adovates\ Influence}$$

Advocacy Key Performance Indicator #3: Advocacy Impact

$$Advocacy\ Impact = \frac{Number\ of\ Advocacy\ Driven\ Conversions}{Total\ Volume\ of\ Advocacy\ Traffic}$$

Support Key Performance Indicator # 1: Issue Resolution Rate

$$Issue\ Resolution\ Rate = \frac{Total\ \#\ Issues\ Resolved\ Satisfactorily}{Total\ \#\ Service\ Issues}$$

Support Key Performance Indicator # 2: Issue Resolution Time

$$Resolution\ Time = \frac{Total\ Inquiry\ Response\ Time}{Total\ \#\ Service\ Inquiries}$$

Support Key Performance Indicator # 3: Satisfaction Score

$$Satisfaction\ Score = \frac{Customer\ Feedback\ (input\ A,\ B,\ C\ .\ .\ .\ n)}{All\ Customer\ Feeback}$$

Innovation Key Performance Indicator # 1: Topic Trends

$$Topic\ Trends = \frac{\#\ of\ Specfic\ Topic\ Mentions}{All\ Topic\ Mentions}$$

Innovation Key Performance Indicator # 2: Sentiment Ratio

$$Sentiment\ Ratio = \frac{Positive : Neutral : Negative\ Brand\ Mentions}{All\ Brand\ Mentions}$$

Innovation Key Performance Indicator # 3: Idea Impact

$$Idea\ Impact = \frac{\#\ of\ Positive\ Conversations,\ Shares,\ Mentions}{Total\ Idea\ Conversations,\ Shares,\ Mentions}$$

Source: Barker, M. et al. (2013) *Social Media Marketing: A Strategic Approach*. Mason, OH: South-Western Cengage Learning, pp. 288–94.

brand or organisation. The process was developed by Jerry Zaltman, now an emeritus faculty member at the Harvard Business School. It is based on research from social and cognitive neuroscience, which found that consumers do not think in words, but rather in images. More critically, most of what influences behaviour is not readily available to conscious thought (Zaltman, 1997). Given that most traditional research assumes conscious cognition, when researchers ask consumers to verbalise what they think in a focus group or to respond to a written question on a survey, Zaltman's findings suggest that most research misses out on what actually drives consumer behaviour.

The ZMET is a multistage process beginning with the respondent's representation and ending with the researcher's interpretation. To start, respondents are asked to bring in pictures that represent their thoughts and feelings about a company, idea or organisation. They are given several days lead time to think about this and find the relevant pictures. In the interview itself, the researcher uses those images to guide respondents in uncovering thoughts or ideas that they may not have been otherwise able to articulate. The interview is then transcribed and coded for important ideas ('constructs') and themes. This is done with about ten or so participants within an important segment. In addition to finding recurring themes, the goal is to identify the deep metaphors that underlie the service and brand in the customer's experience. As Zaltman and Zaltman (2008) find 'deep metaphors play powerfully yet silent in the unconscious minds of consumers, are relatively few, and are universal' (xxiii). In their research involving over 12,000 participants in over 30 countries Zaltman and Zaltman find that the following seven deep metaphors underlie most customer service experiences: balance, journey, transformation or change, container, connection, resource and control. The ZMET interviews help the company not only identify the deep metaphor relevant for their service experience, but also how their company can align their brand toward that underlying universal.

This process can also challenge closely held management assumptions. In one study, for instance, Flavia Hendler and Kathy LaTour used ZMET interviews to analyse the beliefs and motivations of loyalty club members at a megaresort casino in Las Vegas (Hendler and LaTour 2008). The results confounded management beliefs. Management had previously conducted telephone surveys with members as a means to improve their loyalty club experience, but that research was essentially uninformative and unhelpful. That study basically found that customers wanted more for less (more free rooms with less purchase volume).

The ZMET study proved far more fruitful. It identified deep metaphors for different target groups. For instance, locals (who lived in the Las Vegas vicinity) saw the club as a means of connecting – not to the company but rather to their friends and associates. Based on that observation, the mega resort's management determined that this segment was using the club for freebies, and that the locals were not a profitable segment. The tourists, however, viewed the loyalty club and casino resort differently – they saw the resort more as part of their escape from everyday life. They put the transformative nature of the experience foremost in their thinking, and the luxurious setting was appealing in that connection. To them, though, the club itself seemed 'dead' and lacking human qualities. Based on that image, management began adding more personal connections to the service experience and improved how they connected with this important segment. The study uncovered the deep thinking of other consumer groups, and the ZMET provided the company with insights into improving the loyalty club experience that they would not have learned with traditional measures or surveys.

Because the ZMET study employs customer images that represent the brand or company, some firms have used these images to drive their communications. For example, the container concept was a prevalent deep metaphor for Michelin tyres, and one of the images used to portray the tyres' integrity involved the visual image of a baby in the tyre with Noah's ark animals. One could see how such images could be used in a variety of social media contexts such as Facebook or Twitter. Another outcome of a ZMET interview involves having consumers put together a digital summary or narrative about the brand. Such stories could be used to develop movies for Snapchat, involving key customer experiences, for instance. The important aspect, though, is that these tactics overall align with the brand meaning and how it relates to the customer as indicated in the deep metaphors elicited. Given that social media content is visual, ZMET data can also be a source for communicating information about the company.

Deep research 2. Experience assessment via Sticktion Analysis

Once the customer experience has been designed, it is important to know what aspects are 'sticky', that is, memorable to the consumer, and what elements are easily forgotten. Just as the ZMET surfaces unspoken metaphors, Sticktion analysis was developed by two former Harvard Mind of the Market Lab associates of Professor Zaltman, Cornell Associate Professor Kathy LaTour and Lou Carbone of Experience Engineering for the purpose of accomplishing a similar function for consumer memory. 'Sticktion' is a term 3M engineers used to describe a design point between abrasion and slippage that should exist when a magnetic head 'reads' information by sensing the magnetic particles on a tape. In the context of experience management, Sticktion refers to a limited number of special clues that are sufficiently remarkable to register and remain in memory for some time, without being abrasive (Carbone and Haeckel, 1994). It is important that experience clues relate to the overall deep metaphor or experience 'motif.'

Oddly, consumers cannot always predict what will be memorable. In traditional service experience assessment, the customer is asked immediately following their experience what aspects they most liked or were satisfied with (usually in a survey). The problem is that this information does not necessarily relate to what the customer retains about their experience, even a short time later. Sticktion analysis overcomes this issue, based on four principles of human memory: first, customers' memory of an experience fades quickly; second, customers' memory of an experience comprises many sub-experiences; third, customers' memories of experiences are multidimensional and hard to understand; and fourth, consumers cannot accurately predict what they will learn or remember.

Carbone and LaTour used these four principles to test the service experience of Pizza Hut UK by identifying the memorable moments (LaTour and Carbone, 2014). They did this with two studies, which, although based on a restaurant experience, are equally applicable to casinos, hotels and any service experience. In their first study they asked customers to write detailed narratives of their service experience and to answer specific details about their visit (e.g., how long they waited, what they ordered and their server's name). They were also asked to list three things that they thought were most memorable about the experience. A week later they were contacted via an email survey and asked to recall what they experienced. The researchers found that their respondents had forgotten about half of what they had experienced in the restaurant. More troublesome, the consumers had filled in negative experiences, some of which they had not mentioned before (and some of which were invented), rather than recalling positive information. Management saw this as an opportunity to revise their experience offering, so in the second study they developed and tested four scenarios in an online survey. These written narratives walked the consumer from start to finish through the restaurant experience, including numerous details. A week after being exposed to the new concept, respondents were asked what they remembered about the service encounter described in the scenario, and were tested on their memory for different experience clues. As a result, Pizza Hut embraced two conceptual designs that had resulted in both more favourable attitudes and memories from respondents, one which was a more personalised experience, and the other which involved transforming the buffet to a rodizio style of pizza delivery. These concepts were incorporated into several prototype Huts in the UK, and have been quite profitable.

The Sticktion study clearly demonstrated to the chain's managers that asking customers to sum up their experience immediately is not an accurate way to measure service effectiveness. Moving the measurement out over time is helpful, but also incorporating memory measures to account for different clues, or aspects of the service is critical for determining the effectiveness of service design elements. For IMC, thinking about how customers remember and piece together elements that they encounter over different media is essential. Sticktion can be used to assess what medium is resulting in the greatest stickiness – for instance, testing memory of communication elements delivered over Twitter versus Facebook or, more broadly, how those communications alter what the customer remembers about the company, brand or experience.

Disney is now employing real-time customer management experiences in their parks, where they have guests wear a band and their movements are tracked via GPS. Disney can direct the customer to areas of the park with fewer lines, or toward food outlets that meet the customer's pre-specified needs. The company recognises the importance of customer experience management. Hotel companies are using software programmes to manage the customer experience in real-time as well. Moving measurement of experience to dynamic longitudinal assessment makes sense for the hospitality industry.

Competitive analysis

One purpose for presenting these two in-depth marketing research methods is to return to the main topic of strategically viable competitive analysis. What these studies show is the importance of realising the multiple emotion-laden facets of brands, which can be surfaced via in-depth methods such as those presented here. The 'brand' revealed through these methods represents all the touch points the customer has experienced, from traditional to social media exposure.

Based on this deep research, management can achieve a new vantage point on their brand's SWOT (Strengths, Weaknesses, Opportunities and Threats) – providing a vision that drives decisions based on customer emotion–centric insight regarding the juxtapositioning of competitive brands. Without this orientation, hotel executives are at best on a 'Big Data merry-go-round' and simply reacting to data blips at various points in time without the benefit of deep, theory driven insight. In particular, misuse of Big Data analytics is particularly dangerous in a service environment like hotel chains. The mind of the market is simply too complex for quantitative analysis to capture all key insights about customers.

Once a unique vision is identified, the marketer needs to translate it into a story that is easily digested by consumers (which means short and to the point). Ideally a story that engages consumer participation will help build and solidify the brand's message. As example, Vine, which is a six-second video distributor, has been used by social branding experts like Gary Vaynerchuk effectively in this way. As an example, he launched a social media campaign for Virgin Mobile USA called 'Happy Accidents' encouraged users to send in videos that demonstrated what happens when you're obsessed with your mobile phone. It resulted in more than 358,000 impressions and a follower growth of 5,900 per cent. In a mobile-first world, where consumers have short attention spans and endless amounts of content to choose from, watchable micro-content is increasingly important to branding strategy.

Conclusion

This is a brave new world for brand marketers. A very positive aspect of social media is the ability to engage customers in a two-way conversation. To engage effectively, hotel executives need to understand 'the mind of their market', and use that insight to strategically execute their promotional plans.

To conclude, this consumer-focused process of deep research must be supported and facilitated at the top of the organisation. Leadership is crucial if the entire organisation is going to be sufficiently nimble so as react strategically in real time and maintain high levels of service quality that help build the brand. This deep research also provides the metaphors and memorable service elements that can be woven into integrated marketing communication strategies at every level of the consumer experience. As a closing note, all of this is still part of a grand learning process, as we advance brands internationally and take into account the many cultural nuances and segment differences contained therein. Clearly, no matter how successful a hospitality brand may be, it cannot rest on its laurels. Continuous intellectual curiosity should be a hallmark of those advancing the best hotel brands.

References

Barker, M., Barker, D., Borhman, N. and Neher, K. (2013) *Social Media Marketing: A Strategic Approach.* Boston: Cengage Learning.

Belch, G. and Belch, M. (2015) *Advertising and Promotion, an Integrated Marketing Communications Perspective.* 10th edn. New York: McGraw-Hill Education.

Carbone, L. and Haeckel, S. (1994) Engineering experiences. *Marketing Management,* 3, 1–12.

Deighton, J.A. and Kornfeld, L. (2010) United Breaks Guitars. *Harvard Business School Case* 510–057.

Hendler, F., and LaTour, K. (2008) A qualitative analysis of slot clubs as drivers of casino loyalty. *Cornell Hospitality Quarterly,* 49, 105–21.

Holmes, R. (2014, May 26) Has social media killed this one critical sales tool? Online. Available HTTP: <http://blog.hootsuite.com/has-social-media-killed-this-one-critical-sales-tool>, accessed 11 December 2015.

LaTour, K. and Carbone, L. (2014) Sticktion: assessing memory for the customer experience. *Cornell Hospitality Quarterly,* 55, 342–53.

LaTour, M. (1986) *Arousal as an Intervening Variable in a Marketing Communications Context.* Unpublished dissertation, Ann Arbor: University Microfilms.

LaTour, M.S. and Roberts, S. (1992) Cultural anchoring and product diffusion. *Journal of Consumer Marketing,* 9, 29–34.

Lee, K. (2014, June 23) 10 surprising and important social media stats you need to know. Online. Available HTTP: <https://blog.bufferapp.com/social-media-stats-you-need-to-know>, accessed 11 December 2015.

Noone, B. and Robson, S. (2014) Using eye tracking to obtain a deeper understanding of what drives online hotel choice. *Cornell Hospitality Report,* 14(18), 6–16.

Ross, P. (2014) Are photos still king on facebook? Online. Available HTTP: <http://www.socialbakers.com/blog/2149-photos-are-still-king-on-facebook>, accessed 11 December 2015.

Trejos, N. (2015, May 13) Marriott to hotel guests: we're app your service. Online. Available HTTP: <http://www.usatoday.com/story/travel/2015/05/13/marriott-hotels-mobile-requests-two-way-chat/27255025/>, accessed 11 December 2015.

Tuten, T. and Solomon, M. (2012) *Social Media Marketing.* Upper Saddle River, NJ: Prentice Hall.

Williams, S. (2015, April 25) 2 stunning finds from a recent social networking study on brand loyalty. Online. Available HTTP: <http:www.fool.com/investing/general/2015/04/25/2-stunning-finds-from-a-recent-social-networking-s.aspx>, accessed 11 December 2015.

Zaltman, G. (1997) Rethinking market research: putting people back in. *Journal of Marketing Research* 34(4), 424–37.

Zaltman, G., (2003) *How Customers Think: Essential Insights into the Mind of the Markets*. Boston: Harvard Business School Press.

Zaltman, G. and Zaltman, L.H. (2008) *Marketing Metaphoria, what Seven Deep Metaphors Reveal about the Minds of Consumers*. Boston, MA: Harvard Business Press.

Index

Information in figures and tables is denoted by page numbers in *italics*.

For Product Safety Concerns and Information please contact our EU
representative GPSR@taylorandfrancis.com Taylor & Francis Verlag GmbH,
Kaufingerstraße 24, 80331 München, Germany

Printed and bound by CPI Group (UK) Ltd, Croydon, CR0 4YY
08/05/2025
01864507-0002